CHOICE OF FORUM CLAUSES IN ASIA

This book compares and explains the approaches taken by Asian courts when choice of forum clauses in international commercial contracts are challenged in litigation.

It examines key common law jurisdictions (Singapore, Hong Kong and Malaysia), civil law jurisdictions (China, Japan, and Indonesia), and hybrid jurisdictions (the Philippines).

With Asia's ascent in cross-border trade and investment, alongside a corresponding increase in cross-border litigation, understanding how Asian courts address choice of forum clauses in international commercial contracts has never been more critical. Employing a comparative law method, the book identifies and explains the relief and remedies used by Asian courts in enforcing choice of forum clauses, analysing how their classification as either contractual or procedural in nature shapes judicial approaches. It further distinguishes choice of forum clauses from arbitration agreements and explores their interaction with other contractual provisions. Party autonomy – as the parties' freedom to determine the contents of the choice of forum clause and the freedom to control the flow of litigation – is also critically scrutinised.

Furthermore, the book investigates the factors courts consider in resolving key choice of forum clause issues (ie, enforceability; specific relief to be granted; existence, validity, interpretation of choice of forum clauses; role of mandatory rules, public policy, and international interests) and explores the prospects for future development of this area of law in Asia.

Crucially, the book highlights the unique approaches of Asian courts, while underscoring the differences and similarities among common law, civil law, and hybrid jurisdictions.

Volume 13 in the series Studies in Private International Law – Asia

Studies in Private International Law – Asia

Editor: Anselmo Reyes
Advisory Editor: Paul Beaumont
Assistant Editors: Kazuaki Nishioka and Wilson Lui

Much has been written about private international law in the EU and the US. Less is known about the conflict of laws in Asia. Thus, little attention has been paid so far to the modernisation of private international law codes and rules that has been taking place over the last decade all over Asia. That trend continues. Now is the time to take stock of those reforms that have already taken place and suggest further improvements for the future.

Published under the celebrated series *Studies in Private International Law*, this monograph sub-series provides a forum for discussion and analysis of private international law in Asia. The series is not solely a survey of jurisdictions for practitioners. Comprising both in-depth thematic and country-specific studies, each volume considers the private international law of Asian countries from a variety of perspectives. An underlying assumption is that private international law in different jurisdictions follows broadly discernible patterns. Each volume in this sub-series highlights those patterns and discusses how rules in different Asian jurisdictions are either converging with, or diverging from, the patterns identified. Such an analytical framework will assist academics, judges, lawyers and legislators to envisage ways in which laws affecting cross-border relationships can be harmonised across jurisdictions and be made more responsive to the needs of citizens in Asia and elsewhere.

Volume 1: Recognition and Enforcement of Judgments in Civil and Commercial Matters
Edited by Anselmo Reyes

Volume 2: Indonesian Private International Law
Afifah Kusumadara

Volume 3: Chinese Private International Law
Edited by Xiaohong Liu and Zhengyi Zhang

Volume 4: Direct Jurisdiction: Asian Perspectives
Edited by Anselmo Reyes and Wilson Lui

Volume 5: Japanese Private International Law
Kazuaki Nishioka and Yuko Nishitani

Volume 6: Indian Private International Law
Stellina Jolly and Saloni Khanderia

Volume 7: Treatment of Foreign Law in Asia
Edited by Kazuaki Nishioka

Volume 8: Choice of Law and Recognition in Asian Family Law
Edited by Anselmo Reyes, Wilson Lui and Kazuaki Nishioka

Volume 9: Private International Law in East Asia: From Imitation to Innovation and Exportation
Edited by Olivier Gaillard and Krista Nadakavukaren Schefer

Volume 10: Overriding Mandatory Rules in International Commercial Disputes: Korean and Comparative Law
Min Kyung KIM

Volume 11: Privacy and Personal Data Protection Law in Asia
Edited by Adrian Mak, Ching Him Ho and Anselmo Reyes

Volume 12: Hong Kong Private International Law
Wilson Lui and Anselmo Reyes

Volume 13: Choice of Forum Clauses in Asia
Lemuel D Lopez

Choice of Forum Clauses in Asia

Lemuel D Lopez

•HART•
OXFORD • LONDON • NEW YORK • NEW DELHI • SYDNEY

HART PUBLISHING

Bloomsbury Publishing Plc

Kemp House, Chawley Park, Cumnor Hill, Oxford, OX2 9PH, UK

1385 Broadway, New York, NY 10018, USA

Bloomsbury Publishing Ireland Limited, 29 Earlsfort Terrace, Dublin 2, D02 AY28, Ireland

HART PUBLISHING, the Hart/Stag logo, BLOOMSBURY and the Diana logo are trademarks of Bloomsbury Publishing Plc

First published in Great Britain 2025

A catalogue record for this book is available from the British Library.

A catalogue record for this book is available from the Library of Congress.

Library of Congress Control Number: 2025936802

ISBN: HB: 978-1-50996-751-3
ePDF: 978-1-50996-753-7
ePub: 978-1-50996-752-0

Typeset by Compuscript Ltd, Shannon

For product safety related questions contact productsafety@bloomsbury.com

To find out more about our authors and books visit www.hartpublishing.co.uk. Here you will find extracts, author information, details of forthcoming events and the option to sign up for our newsletters.

This book is lovingly dedicated to my parents,
Carlos Cahugum Lopez and Nena Didulo Lopez,
who taught me to dream big and work hard for my dreams.

SERIES EDITORS' PREFACE

Dr Lemuel D Lopez' work on *Choice of Forum Clauses in Asia* is the third volume in the monograph sub-series of Hart's *Studies in Private International Law – Asia* and the second book in that sub-series to be written from beginning to end by a single author. The book is a comparative study of the validation, enforcement and over-ruling of choice of forum clauses in seven Asian jurisdictions – three common law (Singapore, Hong Kong and Malaysia), one mixed (the Philippines), and three civil law (China, Indonesia and Japan).

The book begins with the beguilingly simple proposition that the use of choice of forum clauses (also referred to as jurisdiction clauses or choice of court agreements) reduces transaction risks, improves business efficiency, and provides commercial certainty and predictability. Dr Lopez then examines how precisely choice of forum clauses achieve such beneficial effects in two analytical chapters, focussing on the roles played by party autonomy and the characterisation of choice of court agreements as substantive or procedural in nature. Dr Lopez moves on to an analysis of the similarities and often subtle differences in how the selected jurisdictions approach the validity, construction and overriding of such agreements. A final chapter sets out Dr Lopez' conclusions. Throughout the volume, in light of his insights, Dr Lopez reflects on the utility of Asian countries acceding to the 2005 HCCH Convention on Choice of Agreements and the 2019 HCCH Convention on the Recognition and Enforcement of Foreign Judgments in Civil or Commercial Matters.

There is much that is novel from Dr Lopez' discussion. Solely as an example, a topic (which Dr Lopez himself highlights in his Conclusions) might be mentioned here. The topic is language. Asia being a continent of diverse local languages, the interpretation of choice of forum clauses poses a 'unique challenge' in the Asian context. Dr Lopez observes that Asian commercial contracts may 'not be in English or use a different writing system, making courts dependent on translators during evidentiary hearings'. Translators and expert witnesses may put forward conflicting understandings of a choice of forum clause. To make matters more difficult, when the court attempts to discern the parties' intentions from the language of the clause, it will often find that the 'parties … lack strong English skills or proper legal advice during drafting, compounded by cultural differences in commercial expectations'. The discussion of what might be done by a judge in such circumstances, drawn from a close examination of case law from various jurisdictions, will offer fascinating perspectives for practitioners, academics and interested lay readers on what Dr Lopez describes as 'the curious case of international commercial contracts in Asia'.

The Editors
Kyoto
1 January 2025

ACKNOWLEDGEMENTS

My journey with this monograph began in 2014 when I commenced my PhD at the University of Melbourne. This long and extensive undertaking has been shaped by the invaluable support of numerous individuals, without whom this project would not have come to fruition.

First and foremost, I extend my deepest gratitude to my PhD thesis supervisors, Professor Richard Garnett and Professor Andrew Mitchell. Richard is a towering figure in this field, and his expertise and insights were instrumental in refining the topics, themes, and key issues explored in my thesis, which is the foundation of this monograph. I am especially grateful to Andrew for facilitating my access to critical legal resources and expertise in Hong Kong and Singapore, particularly during my time as a visiting researcher at the National University of Singapore and the University of Hong Kong. The mentorship, advice, reassurance, and unwavering support of Richard and Andrew have been invaluable throughout my PhD. Beyond providing insightful feedback on drafts and answering my many questions, they continually reaffirmed the significance of this work and my ability to complete such a formidable task.

This monograph includes a new chapter on Asian civil law jurisdictions – China, Indonesia, and Japan. Researching these jurisdictions presented unique challenges, including language barriers, limited access to materials, and unfamiliarity with local laws and judicial approaches. I am profoundly grateful to Professor Naoshi Takasugi and Professor Koji Takahashi of Doshisha University, Japan, for facilitating access to their library during my attendance at the 2023 Asian Private International Law Academy Conference in Kyoto. I also extend my sincere appreciation to Professor Afifah Kusumadara of Brawijaya University, Indonesia, for her invaluable assistance in confirming key aspects of Indonesian court approaches to Choice-of-Forum clauses.

I am equally indebted to my colleagues at the RMIT University School of Law (formerly the Graduate School of Business and Law). My sincere thanks go to Professor Simon Pervan, Professor Lola Akin Ojelabi, and Professor Mark Leenders for supporting my applications for research funding and an increased research workload allocation – both of which were crucial in enabling me to complete this monograph. I also extend my gratitude to my colleagues at RMIT for providing opportunities to refine this project, as well as for their friendship and encouragement.

The publication of this monograph would not have been possible without the tremendous support of Hart Publishing. I am particularly grateful to Professor Anselmo Reyes, series editor of *Private International Law – Asia*, for his strong endorsement of this project. My heartfelt thanks also go to Roberta Bassi, Verity Stuart, and Joanne Choulerton, whose invaluable contributions ensured that this monograph is published promptly and to the highest standard. My sincere appreciation also extends to Kazuaki Nishioka for his efforts in monitoring the progress of this project.

My colleagues and friends in Melbourne, the Philippines and beyond have made this undertaking far from being a mostly solitary endeavour. I am incredibly fortunate for the friendship, support and encouragement that I have received from so many people. To each of you, *maraming salamat*.

Above all, my family has been my greatest source of strength. To my parents, Carlos and Nena, I am forever grateful for your unwavering love, encouragement, and support throughout my academic journey, from my PhD to this monograph. To my sisters, Lovely Grace, Lenecel, Loraine, and Charlaine, thank you for your generosity in helping care for Lucas, both in Melbourne and in the Philippines during my PhD, allowing me to focus on my research. To my parents-in-law, Sonia and Edgar, and my sister-in-law, Edessa, I deeply appreciate the rest, support, and assistance you have provided whenever we are in Naga.

To my son, Lucas Carlisle – you are my source of joy and hope. Your laughter each evening after a long day's work has been my greatest comfort. And to my wife, Julie Lucille – words cannot fully capture my gratitude. Your love, patience, and countless sacrifices have sustained me and inspired me to persevere. This monograph is as much yours as it is mine.

Finally, to God, may this work be for His greater glory.

Lemuel D Lopez
Melbourne, Australia
9 February 2025

CONTENTS

TABLE OF CASES

Asia

China

Short Title	Full Citation	
	Case on the Application of Gomi Akira (A Japanese Citizen) to Chinese Court for Recognition and Enforcement of Japanese Judicial Decision – Application for Recognition and Enforcement of Japanese Judicial Decision (日本公民五味晃申请中国法院承认和执行日本法院判决案) [1996] 1 *Gazette of the Supreme People's Court of the People's Republic of China* (Dalian City Intermediate People's Court)	214
	Daizhibai v Hangzhou Leihuo Science & Technology Ltd [2016] Case No 00129 (Lianyungang Intermediate People's Court of Jianggsu), 18 January 2016	221
	Grace Young International Ltd v Seoil Agency Co Ltd [2016] Lu 72 Min Chu No 2039 (Qingdao Maritime Court)	208
Guolei Jiang	*Guolei Jiang v Dongyang Red Star Clothing Co Ltd* [2011] Zhe Shao Xia Zhong Zi No 37 (Shaoxing Intermediate People's Court)	215
Hangzhou Liaosiankai	*Hangzhou Liaosiankai Chemical Co Ltd v Suzhou Jiecheng Dyeing Co Ltd* [2010] Hang Shang Shang Chu Zi No 434-1 (Shangcheng District People's Court)	215
Hin-Pro Logistics	*Hin-pro International Logistics Limited v Compania Sud Americana De Vapore SA* (2013) Zhe Xia Zhong Zi No 144 (Zhejiang High People's Court (CA))	216–17
Huatai Property	*Huatai Property & Casualty Insurance Co Ltd Shenzhen Branch v Clipper Chartering SA* [2017] E72XB 3 (Wuhan Maritime Court)	50, 208
Jiangsu Guanyun	*Jianping Guanyun International Economic and Trade Co Ltd v Compagnie Maritime D'Affretement and Burns Philp Agencies (HK)* [1999] GHFSZ No 41 (Guangzhou Maritime Court)	217
	Lai Jaiping v ABN AMRO Bank NV [2010] Hu Gao Min Wu (Shang) Zhong Zi No 49 (Shanghai High People's Court)	50, 221
	Liao Yandong v Tencent [2016] Case No 06646 (Foshan Intermediate People's Court of Guangdong) 24 May 2016	221

Liupanshui	*Liupanshui Hengding Industrial Co, Ltd v Chongqing Qianniu Construction Co Ltd* [2016] Zui Gao Fa Min Zhong No 415 (Supreme People's Court)	209
Shandong Jufeng	*Shandong Jufeng Network Co, Ltd v Mgame Co, Ltd of Korea and Tianjin Fengyun Network Technology Co, Ltd – A case about a challenge to jurisdiction over disputes arising from an online game distribution and license agreement* (山东聚丰网络有限公司与韩国MGAME公司、天津风云网络技术有限公司网络游戏代理及许可合同纠纷管辖权异议案) [2010] 3 *Gazette of the Supreme People's Court of the People's Republic of China*] (Supreme People's Court)	41, 215, 217
	The Bank of East Asia Shanghai Branch v Sjanghai Jisheng Real Estate Co Ltd [2001] Min Er Zhong Zi No 154 (Supreme People's Court)	216
Sumitomo Bank	*The Sumitomo Bank Co Ltd v Xinhua Real Estate Co Ltd* [1999] Jing Zhong Zi No 194 (Supreme People's Court)	216–17
	Xinhuawen International Leasing Co Ltd v Deutsche Bank Guangzhou Branch [2003] Jing Zhong Zi No 194 (Beijing High People's Court)	216

Hong Kong

Short Title	Full Citation	
	A v B [2022] HKCFI 1031	132
Achieve Goal	*Achieve Goal Holdings Ltd v Zhong Xin Ore Material Holdings Ltd* [2022] HKCFI 2638	97
Agritrade	*Agritrade Resources Ltd v Ashok Kumar Sahoo* [2021] HKCFI 3126	92
AJ Lucas	*AJ Lucas (Hong Kong) Ltd v Drilltec GUT GmbH Grossbohr- und Umwelttechnik* [2006] HKCFI 144	93, 179
Yang Fan	*Bank of China Ltd v Yang Fan* [2016] HKCFI 708	102, 170
	Bank of Credit and Commerce International (Overseas) Ltd v Bank of Credit and Commerce International (Overseas) Ltd – Macau Branch [1997] HKCA 573	184
	Beijing Renji Real Estate Development Group Co, Ltd v Zhu Min [2022] HKCFI 1027	101, 155, 170–71
Bluegold	*Bluegold Investment Holdings Ltd v Kwan Chun Fun Calvin* [2016] HKCFI 415	32
Brody	*Brody Limited v Chu Kong Shipping Enterprises (Holdings) Co Limited* [1998] HKCFI 476	93
	Bond Tak (Holdings) Ltd v King Fame Trading Ltd [2020] HKCFI 1509	33

Indonesia

Indah Kiat	*Indah Kiat International Finance Company BV v Bank America National Trust Company*, Supreme Court, Judgment No 1713K/Pdt/2007, 26 February 2008	229
	Morgan Stanley Company Inc v APP International Finance Company BV, Supreme Court, Judgment No 338PK/Pdt/2014, 7 January 2015	226
	Perusahaan Pertambangan Minyak dan Gas Bumi Negara v Karaha Bodas Company LLC, Supreme Court, Judgment No 01/BANDING/WASIT.INT/2002, 8 March 2004	230
	PT Garuda Indonesia (Persero) v Mahsin, SH, Supreme Court, Judgment No 1317 K/Pdt.Sus-BPSK/2017, 19 December 2017	234
	PT Abadi Adimulia v PT Unilever Indonesia, Tangerang District Court, Judgment No 269/Pdt.G/2018/PN.Tng, 29 May 2019	228–29
PT Indah-Bengkalis	*PT Indah Kiat Pulp & Paper Tbk v Bank America National Trust Company*, District Court of Bengkalis, Judgment No 05/PDT.G/2003/PN-BKS, 21 September 2004	228, 230
PT Indah-Riau	*PT Indah Kiat Pulp & Paper Tbk v Bank America National Trust Company*, High Court of Riau, Judgment No 40/PDT/2005/PTR, 16 June 2005	228
PT Indah-SC Appeal	*PT Indah Kiat Pulp & Paper Tbk v Bank America National Trust Company*, Supreme Court, Judgment No 381 K/Pdt/2006, 21 June 2006	228
PT Indah	*PT Indah Kiat Pulp & Paper Tbk v Bank America National Trust Company*, Supreme Court, Judgment No. 445 PK/Pdt/2007, 19 August 2008	227–28, 230
PT Pelayaran	*PT Pelayaran Manalagi v PT Asuransi Harta Aman Pratamana*, Supreme Court, Judgment No 1935 K/Pdt/2012, 14 January 2013	226
PT Rainbow	*PT Rainbow Indah Karpet v PT TNT Skypak International Express*, Supreme Court, Judgment No 1238K/Pdt/2014, 27 November 2014	227
	PT Sumi Asih v Vinmar Overseas Ltd and AAA, Central Jakarta District Court, Judgment No 271K/Pdt G/2010/PN.Jkt Pst, 31 May 2011	234
	Richard Bruce Ness v Jane Perlez, District Court of Central Jakarta, Judgment No 408/Pdt.G/2007/PN.Jkt.Pst, 25 March 2009	229
	Richard Bruce Ness v Jane Perlez and the New York Times Company, District Court of Central Jakarta, Judgment No 181/PDT.G/2007/PN.JKT.PST, 8 October 2007	228, 259

	Societe Generale v Hari Raharja, Supreme Court, Judgment No 3253K/PDT/1990, 30 November 1993	224
	Yani Haryanto v ED&F Man (Sugar) Ltd, Supreme Court, Judgment No 1205K/Pdt/1990, 4 December 1991	233

Japan

Short Title	Full Citation	
Company X	*Company X v Company Y1 and Y2*, Tokyo High Court, Case No 2017WLJPCA10256010, 25 October 2017	240, 246, 248
	Family Co Ltd v Shin Miyahara, Supreme Court, Case No HJ (1626) 74 [1998], HT (960) 102 [1998], 11 November 1997	236, 239
Hiyoki	*Hiyoki KK v Codif International SAS*, Tokyo District Court, Case No HT (1276) 332 [2008], 11 April 2008 [tr Michael Kuzma (2009) 52 *Japanese Yearbook of International Law* 688]	39, 244
	Malaysian Airlines Bhd v Michiko Goto, Supreme Court, Case No 130 (o) of 1980, 16 October 1981	236
Shimano	*Shimano Manufacturing Co Ltd v Apple Inc*, Tokyo District Court, Case No [2016WLJPCA02156001], 15 February 2016	242–43
Sogo	*Sogo Koeki Kabushiki Kaisha v Aktieselskabet Dampskibsselskabet Svenborg*, Tokyo District Court, Case No 6859 (wa), 17 October 1967	241
Chisadane	*Tokyo Kaijo Kasai Kabushi Kaisha v Koniglike Java China Daketvaat Litjein BV Amsterdam*, Supreme Court, Case (O) No 297 of 1973, 28 November 1975	50, 237, 241–42, 244, 246–48
Vulcan	*Vulcan International Services Ltd v Mukashiya Ltd*, Tokyo District Court, Case No HT (1077) 282 [2002], 24 November 2000	242, 244–45
	X KK v Y, Inc, Tokyo District Court, Case (wa) No 31124(2008), 17 November 2009	39
Nouvelle Vague	*X v Kabushiki Kaisha Nouvelle Vague Japon*, Tokyo District Court, Case No 2014WLJPCA03269011, 26 March 2014	242
MRI International	*X and Others v MRI International, Incorporated*, Tokyo High Court, Case No HJ (2243) 28 [2015], 17 November 2014	242, 246
Yugen-Gaisha	*Yugen-Gaisha AR v APF Asset Management KK*, Osaka High Court, Case No HJ (2225) 77 [2014], 20 February 2014	247

Malaysia

Short Title	Full Citation	
American Express	*American Express Bank Ltd v Mohamed Toufic Al-Ozeir* [1995] 1 MLJ 160 (SC Kuala Lumpur)	48, 105, 109–10, 130, 133
Allianz	*Allianz General Insurance Company (M) Bhd v Kapar Energy Ventures Sdn Bhd* (Unreported, HC Kuala Lumpur, Noorin Badaruddin JC, 27 October 2016)	35
B Braun	*B Braun Medical Industries Sdn Bhd v Pyramid Lines Singapore Pte Ltd* [2023] MLJU 2760 (HC Kuala Lumpur)	108–09, 118, 132, 262
Ngan	*Bank of China v Ngan Ching Wen* [2011] 2 MLJ 645 (HC Kuala Lumpur)	52, 118, 139
Bank Kerjasama	*Bank Kerjasama Rakyat Malaysia v Emcee Corporation Sdn Bhd* [2003] 2 MLJ 408	48, 104, 151
Banque Nasionale	*Banque Nasionale de Paris v Wuan Swee May* [2000] 3 MLJ 587 (HC Kuala Lumpur)	187
BSNC	*BSNC Leasing Sdn Bhd v Sabah Shipyard Sdn Bhd* [2000] 2 MLJ 70 (CA Kuala Lumpur)	110, 193
	Dato' Ho Seng v Rabobank Asia Ltd (Unreported, HC Kuala Lumpur, Vincent Ng Kim Khoay J, 8 March 2002)	108
	Elf Petroleum SE Asia Ltd v Winelf Petroleum Sdn Bhd [1986] 1 MLJ 177 (OCJ Kuala Lumpur)	58
Globus	*Globus Shipping & Trading Co (Pte) Ltd v Taiping Textiles Berhad* [1976] 2 MLJ 154 (FC Penang)	58, 105–06
	Intergraph Cadworx & Analysis Solutions, Inc v EDS Asia Sdn Bhd [2013] 8 MLJ 729 (HC Kuala Lumpur)	166
Inter Maritime	*Inter Maritime Management Sdn Bhd v Kai Tai Timber Co Ltd, Hong Kong* [1995] 1 MLJ 322 (CA Kuala Lumpur)	25, 58, 106, 117–18, 128–29, 131–32–33
Juaramedic	*Juaramedic Sdn Bhd v MRCB Engineering Sdn Bhd* [2017] 11 MLJ 427 (HC Kuala Lumpur)	32
	Jupiters Ltd v Gan Kok Beng [2007] 7 MLJ 228 (HC Kuala Lumpur)	184
KGI Securities	*KGI Securities (Singapore) Pte Ltd (previously known as Amfraser Securities Pte Ltd) v Nelson Fernandez* (Unreported, HC Kuala Lumpur, Khadijah Idris JC, 29 June 2018)	109–10, 135

Kraken	*Kraken Services Ltd (formerly known as Kraken Reinsurance Services Ltd) v Q Life Medical Insurance Company Asia Region* [2021] MLJU 2956 (HC Kuala Lumpur)	107, 143, 167
	Kyrox Sdn Bhd v International Sustainability & Carbon Certification System Gmbh [2022] MLJU 2639 (HC Klang).	179
Lembaga	*Lembaga Pelabuhan Kelang v Kuala Dimensi Bhd* [2011] 2 MLJ 606 (CA Putrajaya)	32, 178
	Maxicont Shipping Agencies Sdn Bhd v Sefair Technical Sdn Bhd [2022] MLJU 3508 (HC Malaya)	111
	Nam Fatt Corporation Berhad v Petrodar Operating Co Ltd (Unreported, HC Kuala Lumpur, Lee Swee Seng JC, 30 June 2010)	135
	Ng Lai Tien v Peregrine [1995] 4 MLJ 7 (HC Johor Bahru)	52, 58
Nutri Mills	*Nutri Mills Products Sdn Bhd v CMA CGM Malaysia Sdn Bhd* [2013] 8 MLJ 377 (HC Kuala Lumpur)	57, 106, 118, 131–32
Open Country Dairy	*Open Country Dairy Ltd v Able Food Sdn* [2021] MLJU 969 (CA)	107, 109, 133, 157, 253, 262
Pemilik	*Pemilik Kapal Atau Vesel 'Lavela' v Pemilik Kapal Atau Vesel 'Basilia'* (Unreported, HC Johor Bahru, Mohd Ivan JC, 31 October 2018)	37
	Petrodar Operating Co Ltd v Nam Fatt Corp Bhd (in liquidation) [2014] 6 MLJ 189 (FC Putra Jaya)	130
Rintis	*Rintis Malay Motors Sdn Bhd v Agasta Co Ltd* (Unreported, HC Kuala Lumpur, Faizah Jamaludin JC, 5 June 2017)	118, 132
Sabah Gas	*Sabah Gas Industries Sdn Bhd v Trans Samudera Lines (S) Sdn Bhd* [1993] 2 MLJ 396 (HC Kota Kinabalu)	110
	Sakuragawa Pump S Pte v Perkapalan Mesra Sdn Bhd [2007] 7 MLJ 555 (HC Kuching)	192
	Sealink Engineering and Slipways Sdn Bhd v Malayan Banking Bhd (Unreported, HC Miri, Stephen Chung Hian Guan JC, 21 July 2011)	106
Southern Acids	*Southern Acids (M) Bhd v Standard Chartered Bank Malaysia Bhd* (Unreported Case, HC Kuala Lumpur, Mah Weng Kwai JC, 3 March 2011)	109, 133–34

SRS Sports	*SRS Sports Centre Sdn Bhd v World Triathlon Corp* [2018] 8 MLJ 32 (HC Kuala Lumpur)	107, 118, 129, 132
Syarikat	*Syarikat Pembinaan Anggerik Sdn Bhd v Malaysia Airports Holdings Bhd* (Unreported, HC Shah Alam, See Mee Chun J, 20 November 2017)	34
Tahan Steel	*Tahan Steel Corporation Sdn Bhd v Bank Islam Malaysia Bhd* [2004] 6 MLJ 1 (HC Kuala Lumpur)	151, 189
Lung Yung	*The 'Lung Yung' & 'Thai Yung' Owners v Sadit Timber Sdn Bhd* [1984] 1 MLJ 29 (FC Kuching)	108, 118, 133
	The Sinar Mas [1982] 1 MLJ 279 (OCJ Kuala Lumpur).	171
United Overseas Bank	*United Overseas Bank Ltd v United Securities Sdn Bhd* [2021] 6 MLJ 897 (CA)	107, 109, 133, 253, 262
	Wynn Resorts (Macau) SA v Wang Yen Liang [2017] 11 MLJ 169 (HC Kuala Lumpur)	140
Yong Songhua	*Yong Songhua v Basic Venture International Ltd* [2017] 8 MLJ 681 (HC Kuala Lumpur)	106, 119

Philippines

Short Title	Full Citation	
	Allied Banking Corporation v Spouses Villaluz, GR No 202525, 12 September 2018	161
	Alfonzo v Villamor (1910) 16 Phil 315	60
	Banco Español-Filipino v Palanca (1918) 37 Phil 921	112
Bank of America	*Bank of America NT&SA v Court of Appeals* (2003) 400 SCRA 156	146–47, 190
Communication Materials	*Communication Materials and Design, Inc v Court of Appeals* (1996) 260 SCRA 673	145–48
	delos Reyes v Court of Appeals (1999) 313 SCRA 632	161
	Eusebio v Eusebio (1976) 70 SCRA 268	60
	Francisco v Herrera (2002) 392 SCRA 317	161
	Fujiki v Marinay (2013) 700 SCRA 69	185, 190
	Gabriel v Monte de Piedad (1941) 71 Phil 497	187
Hasegawa	*Hasegawa and Nippon Engineering Consultants Co Ltd v Minoru Kitamura* (2007) 538 SCRA 261	61, 112, 114–15, 145

Singapore

Short Title	Full Citation	
6DM	*6DM (S) Pte Ltd v AE Brands Korea Ltd* [2021] SGHC 257 (HC)	73, 82–83, 154, 189
Abdul Rashid	*Abdul Rashid bin Abdul Manaf v Hii Yii Ann* [2014] 4 SLR 1042 (HC)	74, 78, 121, 123, 131, 164–66, 174, 198
	Allianz Capital Partners GmbH, Singapore Branch v Goh Andress [2022] SGHC 266 (HC)	166
Amerco	*Amerco Timbers Pte Ltd v Chatsworth Timber Corp Pte Ltd* [1977–1978] SLR(R) 112 (CA)	58, 74–75, 118, 128–29, 131, 135–36
Asia-Pacific Ventures	*Asia-Pacific Ventures II Ltd v PT Intimutiara Gasindo* [2001] 2 SLR(R) 371 (HC)	77, 121, 134
	Astrata (Singapore) Pte Ltd v Portcullis Escrow Pte Ltd [2011] 3 SLR 386 (CA)	31
Baiduri	*Baiduri Bank Bhd v Dong Sui Hung* [2000] 2 SLR(R) 271 (HC)	25, 48, 76–77, 121, 175, 195
Bambang	*Bambang Sutrisno v Bali International Finance Ltd* [1999] 2 SLR(R) 632 (CA)	75–77, 109, 121, 125
Bayerische Landesbank	*Bayerische Landesbank Girozentrale v Kong Kok Keong* [2002] 1 SLR(R) 485 (HC)	121, 134
	Belbana NV v APL Co Pte Ltd [2014] SGHCR 17 (HC)	80
	Belfield International (Hong Kong) Ltd v Sheagar s/o TM Veloo [2014] 1 SLR 24 (HC)	184
BGC Partners	*BGC Partners (Singapore) Ltd v Tan Wee Hiong Kevin* [2017] SGHC 214 (HC)	73, 118, 129–30
BNP Paribas	*BNP Paribas Wealth Management v Jacob Agam* [2016] SGHC(I) 5 (SICC)	81, 141–42
Brinkerhoff	*Brinkerhoff Maritime Drilling Corp v PT Airfast Services Indonesia* [1992] 2 SLR(R) 345 (CA)	76, 128–30, 137, 182–84
	Bulthaup GMBH & Co KG v KHL Marketing Asia-Pacific Pte Ltd [2007] SGDC 64 (DC)	136
Bunge	*Bunge SA v Shrikant Bhasi* [2020] SGCA 94 (CA)	31, 119, 166, 179
	BXH v BXI [2020] SGCA 28 (CA)	32

	Chan Chin Cheung v Chan Fatt Cheung [2009] SGCA 64 (CA)	79
	Chen Yun Hian Christopher v BHNV Online Ltd [2020] SGHC 284 (HC)	138, 165–66
	China Insurance Co (Singapore) Pte Ltd v Liberty Insurance Pte Ltd [2005] 2 SLR(R) 509 (HC)	165
CIMB Bank	*CIMB Bank Bhd v Dresdner Kleinwort Ltd* [2008] 4 SLR(R) 543 (CA)	77, 130, 133, 135, 142, 153, 155–56
Citibank	*Citibank NA v Robert* [2011] 3 SLR 465 (HC)	77, 131, 136, 144, 175
Chloe V	*Credit Suisse AG v Owner of the Vessel 'Chloe V'* [2022] SGHCR 9 (HC)	71
Econ Corp	*Econ Corp International Ltd v Ballast-Nedam International BV* [2003] 2 SLR(R) 15 (HC)	31
ED&F	*ED&F Man Capital Markets Ltd v Straits (Singapore) Pte Ltd* [2019] SGHC 203 (HC)	84
	Ermgassen & Co Ltd v Sixcap Financials Pte Ltd [2018] SGHCR 8 (HC)	90
	Evergreen International SA v Volkswagen Group Singapore Pte Ltd [2004] 2 SLR(R) 457 (HC)	85
Siswanto	*Frans Bambang Siswanto v Coutts & Co AG* [1996] SGHC 250 (HC)	134
Golden Shore	*Golden Shore Transportation Pte Ltd v UCO Bank* [2004] 1 SLR(R) 6 (CA)	75, 77, 118, 137, 172
	Goldilocks Investment Co Ltd v Noble Group Ltd [2018] SGHC 108 (HC)	182
Humpuss	*Humpuss Sea Transport Pte Ltd (in compulsory liquidation) v PT Humpuss Intermoda Transportasi TBK* [2016] 5 SLR 1322 (HC)	79, 123
Banco Ambrosiano	*Industrial & Commercial Bank Limited v Banco Ambrosiano Veneto SPA*, [2000] SGHC 188 (HC)	133, 153
Ivanishvili	*Bidzina Ivanishvili v Credit Suisse AG* [2019] SGHC 6 (HC)	79, 179
	Bidzina Ivanishvili v Credit Suisse Trust Ltd [2020] SGCA 62 (CA)	178
	Las Vegas Hilton Corporation v Khoo Teng Hock [1996] 2 SLR(R) 589 (HC)	183
Lehman Brothers	*Lehman Brothers Special Financing Inc v Hartadi Angkosubroto* [1998] 3 SLR(R) 664 (HC)	128, 131, 133–34, 192

	Vibrant Group Ltd v Tong Chi Ho [2022] SGHC 256 (HC)	144
Vinmar	*Vinmar Overseas (Singapore) Pte Ltd v PTT International Trading Pte Ltd* [2018] 2 SLR 1271 (CA)	75, 78, 137–38, 154, 156, 198, 252
	VKZ v VJZ [2021] SGCA 72 (CA)	84
William Jacks	*William Jacks & Co (Singapore) Pte Ltd v Nelson Honey & Marketing (NZ) Ltd* [2015] SGHCR 21 (HC)	88, 153–54

Other Jurisdictions

Australia

Short Title	Full Citation	
	Akai Pty Ltd v People's Insurance Company Ltd [1996] HCA 39	182
	Compagnie des Messageries Maritimes v Wilson (1954) 94 CLR 577	54
	John Pfeiffer Pty Ltd v Rogerson (2000) 203 CLR 503	19
	McKain v RW Miller & Co (South Australia) Pty Ltd (1991) 174 CLR 1	19
Oceanic Sun	*Oceanic Sun Line Special Shipping Co Inc v Fay* (1988) 79 ALR 9	13, 154
	O'Driscoll v J Ray McDermott SA [2006] WASCA 25	150

Canada

Short Title	Full Citation	
	Burrard-Yarrows Corp v The 'Hoegh Merchant' [1982] 1 FC 248; [1983] 1 FC 495	13
	Nissho Iwai Corp v Paragon Grand Carriers Corp (1987) 11 FTR 134	13
	Volkswagen Canada Inc v Auto Haus Fröhlich Ltd [1986] 1 WWR 380	13

France

Short Title	Full Citation	
Rothschild	Cour de cassation, 13-27.264, *ICH v Crédit Suisse*, 25 March 2015	195
	Cour de cassation, 11-26.022, *Madame X v Banque Privée Edmond de Rothschild*, 26 September 2012	195

New Zealand

Short Title	Full Citation	
	Hyslop v Society of Lloyd's (1992) 6 PRNZ 204	79
	Society of Lloyd's and Oxford Members' Agency Ltd v Hyslop [1993] 3 NZLR 135	13

United Kingdom

Short Title	Full Citation	
Amin	*Amin Rasheed Shipping Corporation v Kuwait Insurance* Co [1984] AC 50	150–51
	A/S D/S Svendborg D/S af 1912 A/S (Bodies Corporate trading in partnership as 'Maersk Sealand') v Akar [2003] EWHC 797	16
British Aerospace	*British Aerosplace Plc v Dee Howard Co* [1993] 1 Lloyd's Rep 368	14, 120, 125, 198
	British Airways Board v Laker Airways Ltd [1985] AC 58	84
	Chopra v Bank of Singapore [2015] EWHC 1529	14
Coast Lines	*Coast Lines Ltd v Hudig & Veder Chartering NV* [1972] 2 QB 34	150–51
	Compania Sud Americana De Vapore SA v Hin-pro International Logistics Limited [2014] EWHC 3632 (Comm)	217
	Compania Sud Americana De Vapore SA v Hin-pro International Logistics Limited [2015] EWCA Civ 401	217
Donohue	*Donohue v Armco Inc* [2002] 1 Lloyd's Rep 425	14, 16, 85–86
	Dunlop Pneumatic Tyre v Selfridge and Co Ltd [1915] AC 847	36
Fiona Trust	*Fiona Trust & Holding Corporation v Privalov* [2008] 1 Lloyd's Rep 254	33
	Fry v Lane (1888) 40 Ch D 312	194
	Gienar v Meyer (1796) 2 H Bl 603; 126 ER 728	28–29
Investors Compensation	*Investors Compensation Scheme Ltd v West Bromwich Building Society* [1998] 1 WLR 896	165, 167, 170

	Konkola Copper Mines plc v Cromin Ltd (No 2) [2006] EWHC 1093	14
	Law v Garret (1878) 8 Ch D 26	28–29
MacShannon	*MacShannon v Rockware Glass Ltd* [1978] 2 WLR 362	120
	Mercury Communications Ltd v Communication Telesystems International [1999] 2 All ER 33	14
	Prenn v Simmonds [1971] 1 WLR 1381	165
	Printing and Numerical Registering Co v Sampson (1875) 19 Eq 462	46
	R v International Trustee for the Protection of Bondholders Aktiengesellschaft [1937] AC 500	151
Racecourse Betting	*Racecourse Betting Control Board v Secretary of State for Air* [1944] Ch 114	13, 29, 56
	Re United Railways of the Havana and Regla Warehouses Ltd [1960] Ch 52	150
	RTS Flexible Systems Ltd v Molkerei Alois Müller GmbH & Co KG [2010] UKSC 14	155
Berisford	*S & W Berisford plc v New Hampshire Insurance Co* [1990] 2 QB 631	75–78, 109, 120, 122, 125
	Scott v Avery (1856) 5 HL Cas 811; 10 ER 1121	54
Spiliada	*Spiliada Maritime Corp v Cansulex Ltd* [1987] AC 460	70, 76–78, 80, 91–95, 105, 107, 109, 117–29, 146, 166, 206–08, 229, 239, 252–54, 262, 265
	St Pierre v South American Stores (Garth & Chaves) Ltd [1936] 1 KB 382	120
	The Abidin Daver [1984] AC 398	120
	The Atlantic Star [1974] AC 436	120
	The Assunzione [1954] P 150	151
	The 'El Amria'. Aratra Potato Ltd v Egyptian Navigation Co [1981] 2 Lloyd's Rep 119	92

LEGISLATION AND DERIVATIVE INSTRUMENTS

China

Hong Kong

Indonesia

Japan

Malaysia

Philippines

Singapore

Other

TREATIES AND OTHER INTERNATIONAL INSTRUMENTS

Other

1

Introduction

I. Overview

Despite Asia's leadership in cross-border trade,[1] no comprehensive comparative study exists on how Asian courts address Choice-of-Forum clauses in international commercial contracts. This book fills that gap by exploring the approaches of courts in Singapore, Hong Kong, Malaysia, the Philippines, China, Japan and Indonesia when these clauses are challenged. It identifies six key factors influencing how courts resolve Choice-of-Forum clause issues: (1) courts' characterisation of these clauses, (2) party autonomy, (3) procedural rules for enforcement, (4) judicial discretion in granting relief, (5) the choice of law process and (6) the overriding effect of state and international interests. The findings emphasise the importance of well-drafted clauses, predictable and coherent judicial analysis, court discretion, and procedural reforms. They also highlight a favourable environment for Asian countries to strengthen party autonomy and consider joining the Choice-of-Court Convention[2] and even The Hague Judgments Convention.[3]

II. The Curious Case of International Commercial Contracts in Asia

The twenty-first century is often referred to as the Asian Century,[4] with Asia driving global economic growth and influencing the composition of the world economy, trade, and investments. Asia also shapes corporate transactions, business strategies, and the direction of technological innovation.[5] These economic trends are reflected in the contracts of the parties involved, although they mirror those used in Western countries, particularly Anglo-American companies.[6] These contracts are typically drafted in a style that seeks to

[1] See Roman Tomasic and Leon Wolff (eds), *Commercial Law in East Asia* (Ashgate, 2014) xiii.

[2] Convention on Choice of Court Agreements, opened for signature 30 June 2005, 44 ILM 1294 (entered into force 1 October 2015) ('Choice-of-Court Convention').

[3] Convention on the Recognition and Enforcement of Foreign Judgments in Civil or Commercial Matters, opened for signature 2 July 2019, United Nations Certificate of Registration 58036 (entered into force 1 September 2023): https://www.hcch.net/en/instruments/conventions/full-text/?cid=137 ('The Hague Judgments Convention').

[4] Tomasic and Wolff (n 1).

[5] See William Scheela, *Venture Capital in Asia: Investing in Emerging Countries* (Business Expert Press, 2014) 17; Anil Gupta and Haiyan Wang, 'Building the Next-Generation Global Enterprise' in Anil Gupta, Toshiro Wakayama, and U Srinivasa Rangan (eds), *Global Strategies for Emerging Asia* (Jossey-Bass, 2012) 3, 3; Niraj Dawar and Charan Bagga, 'Is Your Business Model Ready to Drill into the Core of the Diamond' in Anil Gupta, Toshiro Wakayama and U Srinivasa Rangan (eds), *Global Strategies for Emerging Asia* (Jossey-Bass, 2012) 29, 36.

[6] See Giuditta Cordero-Moss, *International Commercial Contracts: Applicable Sources and Enforceability* (Cambridge University Press, 2014) 8; see also Lemuel D Lopez, 'The Curious Case of International Commercial

regulate the contractual relationship exhaustively, aiming to eliminate interference from external elements, such as interpreter discretion or governing law principles.[7] This style stems from the common law models, which operate on the principle of *caveat emptor*.[8] Under common law, parties are expected to assess risks and make provisions accordingly, with the final contract reflecting this assessment.[9] However, this common law approach may not fit well in other legal traditions. For example, while civil law also respects party autonomy, contracts are evaluated based on a system of rules governing specific types of contract.[10] In the civil law tradition, judges and lawyers rely on default provisions,[11] thus making extensive provisions unnecessary.[12] Asia's diverse legal systems, including civil, common, Islamic and socialist law, along with various hybrids, present significant challenges for interpreting and enforcing international commercial contracts, especially those written in the common law style.

The common law drafting style of international commercial contracts, however, is just the tip of the iceberg. International commercial contracts in Asia often face significant challenges during negotiations. For example, provisions may lack coherence because of compromises during negotiations.[13] Other issues include unequal bargaining power,[14] language limitations,[15] differing views on the contract's significance,[16] the risk that the written agreement may not reflect the parties' true intent,[17] incomplete contracts,[18] and imperfect information during negotiations.[19] These negotiation challenges increase the risk that parties' expectations may not be realised, leading to what is known as transactions risk. As a result, legal opinions supporting cross-border transactions are often more qualified. In Indonesia, for instance, legal opinions may note that there is no reliable comprehensive database for laws and regulations.[20] Similarly, Thai legal opinions on project financing transactions may point to gaps in Thai law, such as the absence of rules on enforceability of non-exclusive jurisdiction clauses stipulating foreign courts, on waivers of venue objections,

Contracts in Asia' in Muruga Perumal Ramaswamy (ed), *Harmonising Trade Law to Enable Private Sector Regional Development* (Victoria University of Wellington, Hors Serie Volume XX, 2016) 253.

[7] Cordero-Moss (n 6) 8.

[8] ibid 11.

[9] ibid.

[10] ibid 85.

[11] ibid 11, 85.

[12] ibid 11.

[13] David Echenberg, 'Negotiating international contracts: does the process invite a review of standard contracts from the point of view of national legal requirements?' in Giuditta Cordero-Moss (ed), *Boilerplate, Clauses, International Commercial Contracts and the Applicable Law* (Cambridge University Press, 2011) 11, 18.

[14] See Robert Hillman and Jeffrey Rachlinski, 'StandardForm Contracting in the Electronic Age (2002) 77(2) *New York University Law Review* 429, 432–33.

[15] See Larry A DiMatteo, *International Contracting: Law and Practice* (Kluwer Law International, 2013) 15.

[16] See Philip McConnaughay, 'Rethinking the Role of Law and Contracts in East-West Commercial Relationships' (2001) 41(2) *Virginia Journal of International Law* 427, 446.

[17] See Andrew Godwin, 'Obligations to Negotiate in Good Faith in Cross-Border Deals' (2013) 3 *Harvard Business Law Review Online* 92, 96.

[18] Frederick Lipman and Larry Dongxiao Qiu, *International Strategic Alliances Joint Ventures Between Asian and US Companies* (World Scientific, 2nd edn, 2014) 48; see also Godwin (n 17) 96.

[19] Echenberg (n 13) 15; see also Baker & McKenzie, *Asia Pacific Guide to Mergers & Acquisitions* (Baker & McKenzie, 2013) 94–95, 182–83, 270, 358, 363–64, 665.

[20] Allens, Linklaters, Widyawan & Partners, *Legal Guide to Investment in Indonesia* (Allens, Linklaters, Widyawan & Partners, 2014) 3.

and on judgment currency indemnities.[21] These qualifications reflect the deficiency and uncertainty in the legal infrastructure of Asian countries, stemming from the lack of laws and decisions on specific issues. Credit-rating agencies may also rate Asian companies lower than their Western counterparts,[22] due to the perceived higher risk and lower quality accounting standards of emerging market firms.[23] Western governments also recognise Asia's particular sensitivity to transaction risk.[24]

Because of the various problems inherent in Asian contracts, parties require a good mechanism to manage their risks. As this book argues, risks may be managed better through the use of the Choice-of-Forum clause. The next section discusses how such clauses manage these risks.

III. Function and Purpose of Choice-of-Forum Clauses

Keyes identifies three key interests relevant to a court's exercise of jurisdiction in international litigation: the interests of parties, forum state, and foreign and international community.[25] The importance of Choice-of-Forum clauses becomes clearer when viewed through the lens of these three interests. For the parties, these clauses reduce risks, improve efficiency, and provide certainty and predictability. For the forum state, they attract investments and trade. For the international community, they promote international commerce through judicial cooperation and consistent outcomes.

A. Parties' Interests

The parties' interest in Choice-of-Forum clauses has important commercial aspects. Fentiman highlights that litigation risk is the primary threat to a transaction because risks only materialise during litigation.[26] Where litigation occurs is therefore crucial in commercial transactions;[27] thus, Choice-of-forum clauses affect how obligations are enforced and remedies are obtained.[28] Where litigation occurs also has financial implications,[29] and crystallises the parties' relative strengths and weaknesses. This provides a framework for negotiating a settlement, which parties may factor into the transaction's financial value.[30]

[21] Al Chandler, 'Thailand: Something Special', *International Financial Law Review* (1 June 2011): http://www.iflr.com/Article/2855518/Thailand-Something-special.html (accessed 28 October 2024).

[22] Giovanni Ferri and Li-Gang Liu, 'How Do Global Credit-Rating Agencies Rate Firms from Developing Countries?' (2004) 2(3) *Asian Economic Papers* 30, 35.

[23] Kee-Hong Bae, Lynette Purda and Michael Welker, 'Credit rating initiation and accounting quality for emerging-market firms' (2013) 44(3) *Journal of International Business Studies* 216, 219.

[24] Justin Gleeson, 'An Australian Perspective on International Commercial Litigation: The Challenges and Opportunities' (Conference Paper, International Litigation in the Asia Pacific, Wuhan University, China, 23–24 September 2013) 8–9.

[25] Mary Keyes, *Jurisdiction in International Litigation* (Federation Press, 2005) 178–225.

[26] Richard Fentiman, *International Commercial Litigation* (Oxford University Press, 2nd edn, 2015) 5.

[27] ibid 276.

[28] ibid 276–277.

[29] ibid 277.

[30] ibid.

Further, Choice-of-Forum clauses define a range of legal and tactical issues – both substantive and procedural. First, selecting the forum guides the parties in drafting the contract. For example, forum law influences many legal issues, which the parties can only consider by specifying the forum through the Choice-of-Forum clause.[31] The clause therefore gives parties greater predictability regarding the legal impact of their contract.

Second, the Choice-of-Forum clause influences the claimant's choices whether to claim, what to claim, and how to claim. Key considerations in deciding *whether* to litigate a claim include the location[32] and value of the defendant's assets,[33] the availability of mechanisms to seize and secure assets,[34] the costs of locating assets,[35] court costs,[36] and any immunities available to the defendant.[37] *What* to claim may depend on the forum's conflict of laws rules[38] which define the dispute's characterisation (eg, contractual, tort?),[39] the court's jurisdiction, provisional remedies available,[40] and the nature and amount of damages that can be awarded.[41] What to claim may also depend on the judicial discretion granted by the forum[42] in matters such as dismissal under *forum non conveniens*,[43] as well as the available defences,[44] and the final outcome sought (eg, declaration of title?).[45] What to claim may also rely on the chosen court's rules on determining the Choice-of-Forum clause's validity or enforceability, and interpretation. Lastly, as regards *how* to claim, the forum court governs all procedural aspects, including how to file the claim, the contents of the pleading, and the types of interlocutory relief available,[46] which can influence the other party to negotiate and gain a tactical advantage during negotiations.[47] Likewise, the chosen court determines discovery procedures, which can affect out-of-court settlements,[48] as well as the rules governing evidence and presentation of documents and witnesses.[49] The possibility of third-party proceedings also depends on the forum court's rules.[50]

Third, important aspects of the Choice-of-Law clause also depend on the rules of the chosen forum. Even before applying the chosen law, the court has broad discretion to decide whether to proceed with the case through its inherent power to define its own jurisdiction (*kompetenz-kompetenz* principle). If this is resolved, the forum court's

[31] Trevor Hartley, *Choice-of-Court Agreements under the European and International Instruments* (Oxford University Press, 2013) 4.
[32] See Fentiman (n 26) 279.
[33] ibid.
[34] ibid 283.
[35] ibid 279.
[36] ibid 279.
[37] See, eg, Reid Mortensen, Richard Garnett and Mary Keyes, *Private International Law in Australia* (LexisNexis Butterworths, 3rd edn, 2015) 80.
[38] Fentiman (n 26) 279.
[39] ibid; Peter Nygh, *Autonomy in International Contracts* (Clarendon Press, 1999) 88.
[40] Fentiman (n 26) 283.
[41] ibid.
[42] Adrian Briggs, *Agreements on Jurisdiction and Choice of Law* (Oxford University Press, 2008) 198.
[43] Ronald Brand and Scott Jablonski, *Forum Non Conveniens: History, Global Practice, and Future Under the Hague Convention on Choice of Court Agreements* (Oxford University Press, 2007) 1.
[44] Fentiman (n 26) 282.
[45] ibid 282.
[46] Richard Garnett, *Substance and Procedure in Private International Law* (Oxford University Press, 2012) 5.
[47] See Fentiman (n 26) 277.
[48] ibid 284.
[49] See Garnett (n 46) 189.
[50] Fentiman (n 26) 284.

characterisation of the dispute may determine which law applies. The forum also determines the parties' ability to designate the chosen law,[51] the clause's existence,[52] and the evidence required to prove foreign law.[53] Whether to apply *depeçage* (ie, splitting the case into issues governed by different laws)[54] or *renvoi* (ie, reference to foreign law under conflicts rules)[55] also depends on the forum court. If the Choice-of-Law clause is absent or unenforceable, the forum's rules determine the next steps.[56] Mandatory rules[57] and public policy[58] of the chosen forum can also override the chosen law. Thus, the application of the Choice-of-Law clause depends on the Choice-of-Forum clause. Fentiman even argues that success in a cross-border dispute depends on the relevant rules for choice of law, the relative scope of the domestic substantive law and the forum's rules for establishing foreign law.[59]

Fourth, the chosen court also determines important litigation issues like neutrality,[60] susceptibility to corruption,[61] predictability of outcomes,[62] technical expertise,[63] and other case management issues (eg, the number of cases in court dockets).[64]

B. State Interests

States have a strong interest in promoting Choice-of-Forum clauses. These clauses are integral to attracting investments, promoting trade, and maintaining global competitiveness, as they are now common in international commercial contracts.[65] In *The Bremen v Zapata Off-Shore Co* ('*The Bremen*'), the US Supreme Court highlighted that 'the elimination of all such uncertainties by agreeing in advance on a forum acceptable to both parties is an indispensable element in international trade, commerce, and contracting'.[66] Enforcing these clauses demonstrates a state's commitment to contract reliability, which may improve the prospects that the forum judgments' will be enforced and recognised internationally. This is especially true because such enforcement shows that the forum

[51] Nygh (n 39) 86.
[52] ibid 90.
[53] See Fentiman (n 26) 668.
[54] Nygh (n 39) 137.
[55] ibid 86.
[56] ibid 266.
[57] ibid 199.
[58] See, eg, Civil Code (Philippines) art 1306; Nygh (n 39) 233.
[59] Fentiman (n 26) 283.
[60] ibid 287.
[61] Trevor Hartley, *The Modern Approach to Private International Law: International Litigation and Transactions from a Common-Law Perspective* (Brill Nijhoff, 2006) 115.
[62] See, eg, Chandler (n 21); Fentiman (n 26) 285.
[63] See *The Bremen v Zapata Off-Shore Co*, 407 US 1, 12 (1972) ('*The Bremen*'); Hannah Buxbaum, 'Forum Selection in International Contract Litigation: The Role of Judicial Discretion' (2004) 12(2) *Willamette Journal of International and Dispute Resolution* 185, 195.
[64] See Fentiman (n 26) 460; Buxbaum (n 63) 190.
[65] Eg, Explanatory Memorandum to the Proposal for a Council Decision on the approval, on behalf of the European Union, of the Hague Convention of 30 June 2005 on Choice of Court Agreements COM/2014/046 final – 2014/0021 (NLE), 3–4; Singapore Academy of Law, 'Report of the Law Reform Committee on the Hague Convention on Choice of Court Agreements 2005' (Report, Singapore Academy of Law, March 2013) 2.
[66] *The Bremen* (n 63) 13–14.

court shares similar values with the enforcing state, thus reducing the risk of public policy objections. Moreover, for forum states and dispute resolution centres, enforcing these clauses provides opportunities to influence the development of the law as regards certain commercial issues.[67]

Furthermore, the commercial nature of the transaction provides states with strong commercial incentives. For example, the Commercial Court in London has ensured a steady flow of court fees, a flourishing practice for the expert advisers, solicitors and barristers, and business for the hotel proprietors and travel firms,[68] thus making commercial litigation an important income source for the United Kingdom.[69] In the United States, the American Bar Association's survey showed that over 98 per cent of the respondents would support a convention on choice of court agreements because it would be useful for their practice.[70]

Enforcing Choice-of-Forum clauses helps prevent forum shopping (ie, filing actions in different courts to gain procedural advantage or to harass the defendant[71]) and the problems associated with it, like unfairness, strain on local court resources, and undermining of foreign legal systems.[72]

C. Interests of the International Community

The primary reason the international community would want to promote Choice-of-Forum clauses is to advance international commerce and trade through enhanced judicial cooperation and certainty in jurisdictional outcomes.[73] The reliability of these clauses is considered essential for economic growth, particularly in facilitating global and intra-regional trade.[74] As an expression of party autonomy, promoting these clauses aligns with the liberalist philosophy of promoting freedom and contract reliability. Choice-of-Forum clauses are also viewed as instruments of wealth creation, contributing to progress, development and even global stability.

IV. Aim and Research Questions

This book aims to explore, identify, compare and explain the approaches of courts in three common law jurisdictions (Singapore, Hong Kong, Malaysia), a hybrid jurisdiction (the

[67] See Singapore Academy of Law (n 65) 2.
[68] Keyes (n 25) 25.
[69] ibid.
[70] American Bar Association, Recommendation Adopted by the House of Delegates August 7–8, 2006 (Survey, American Bar Association, 2006) 2.
[71] See *Puyat v Zabarte* (2001) 353 SCRA 738, 751.
[72] See Keyes (n 25) 28–29.
[73] eg, Convention on Choice of Court Agreements, opened for signature 30 June 2005, 44 ILM 1294 (entry into force 1 October 2015) preamble ('Choice-of-Court Convention'); American Bar Association (n 70) 5.
[74] Yeo Tiong Min, 'International Litigation in Asia: Will the Hague Choice of Court Convention Make Any Difference?' (Conference Paper, Japanese Society of International Law Annual Meeting, Shizuoka, 12–14 October 2013) 1: http://www.jsil.jp/annual_documents/2013/1012224.pdf accessed 28 October 2024.

Philippines) and three civil law countries (China, Japan and Indonesia) in Asia when Choice-of-Forum clauses in international commercial contracts are challenged, ie, cases or actions are filed in their respective courts to enforce these clauses, to ask for certain forms of relief pursuant to these clauses, or to question their existence, validity and interpretation.

Specifically, this book seeks to answer the following research questions:

1. How do courts in these Asian jurisdictions characterise Choice-of-Forum clauses?
2. What is the role of party autonomy in disputes involving Choice-of-Forum clauses?
3. What forms of relief and remedies are available to enforce Choice-of-Forum clauses in these Asian jurisdictions?
4. What factors are considered by the courts in granting relief pursuant to the Choice-of-Forum clauses?
5. How do courts determine the issues of existence, validity and interpretation of Choice-of-Forum clauses?
6. How do mandatory rules, public policy and other state and international interests affect the Choice-of-Forum clause analysis?
7. What are the implications for the progressive development of the law of Choice-of-Forum clauses in Asia?

V. Outline of the Book

To achieve the book's aim, each chapter answers a research question. Chapter two explores how courts characterise Choice-of-Forum clause issues as either contractual or procedural, and how this characterisation determines the legal tools available for analysis. Chapter three probes into party autonomy, particularly the freedom to determine the contents of the Choice-of-Forum clause and the freedom to control the flow of litigation, which allow parties to shape court approaches. Chapter four analyses enforcement in Singapore, Hong Kong and Malaysia, and the Philippines, thus showing that enforcement depends on the forum court's procedural rules. Chapter five discusses how courts in these jurisdictions consider various factors when granting relief, thus highlighting the importance of court discretion. Chapter six revisits the same jurisdictions to examine the relationship between the Choice-of-Forum clause and the law selected by the choice of law process, focusing on how the applicable law determines validity and interpretation. Chapter seven highlights how the interests of the forum state, the international community, and third-party states limit the effects of Choice-of-Forum clauses in Singapore, Hong Kong and Malaysia, and the Philippines. Chapter eight focuses on the civil law jurisdictions – China, Japan, and Indonesia – discussing the relief and remedies available, factors that courts consider in granting relief, how issues of existence, validity and interpretation are resolved, and finally, how state and international interests, and the interest in protecting weaker parties limit their enforcement. The final chapter, Chapter nine, synthesises key lessons from the previous chapters and assesses their implications for the progressive development of Choice-of-Forum law in Asia.

VI. Rationale and Relevance

This book fills a crucial gap, given the limited literature on how Asian courts enforce Choice-of-Forum clauses. Hart Publishing's 'Studies in Private International Law – Asia series' is a significant contribution to Asian scholarship, and this book builds on that by offering a comprehensive in-depth comparative study of the approaches of seven major Asian economies. Singapore, Hong Kong, Malaysia, the Philippines, China, Japan and Indonesia are key players in global trade and investment, making them critical for understanding Choice-of-Forum clauses. Singapore and Hong Kong, as global dispute resolution centres,[75] provide valuable legal and practical insights for the region and beyond. With key sectors, like energy, forestry, agriculture, mining, labour export, and Islamic banking, Malaysia and the Philippines offer lessons on the interaction between party autonomy and state interests in these sectors. Malaysia's blend of Islamic law and English common law, and the Philippines' hybrid legal system combining Spanish civil law and American common law, further offer unique perspectives. Hong Kong's integration with China also allows for observations on the intersection of common law and socialist legal systems. The civil law jurisdictions of China, Japan and Indonesia are G20 economies, making their study critical for understanding global commerce and dispute resolution.

At a theoretical level, this book addresses the need to define the scope and limitations of the principle of party autonomy, the legal and conceptual basis of Choice-of-Forum clauses, and the role of 'consent' as the foundation of cross-border litigation. This makes the book valuable to academics, researchers and legal scholars. At a practical level, this book aims to provide a comprehensive guide for litigators, legal advisers and lawyers in Asia. By articulating the scope and limitations of party autonomy and the judicial grounds for enforcing and limiting this principle, the book also aims to make international commercial litigation in Asia more manageable by offering practitioners a clear road-map to Choice-of-Forum clause litigation across jurisdictions.

The lessons from this book have significant implications for the development of the law on Choice-of-Forum clauses. By examining the approaches of seven Asian jurisdictions, the book advocates for a more coherent approach to resolving Choice-of-Forum clause issues. As this book shows, piecemeal and inconsistent approaches in resolving these issues are neither ideal nor efficient. One hope is that multilateral discussions will lead to a regional legal framework, similar to the Brussels I Recast,[76] or encourage accession to international treaties like the Choice-of-Court Convention and The Hague Judgments Convention. Singapore's accession to and China's signing of the Choice-of-Court Convention are significant regional developments. Ideally, more Asian countries will recognise that regional or international cooperation can reduce commercial risks and transaction costs for foreign investors and international traders, given that reliable, consistent, predictable and transparent enforcement of Choice-of-Forum clauses is an important pillar of global commerce.[77]

[75] Laura Philomin, 'Singapore to remake itself as Asia's legal hub with new commercial court', *Reuters* (11 February 2014): https://www.reuters.com/article/world/singapore-to-remake-itself-as-asia-s-legal-hub-with-new-commercial-court-idUSDEEA1A0JD/ accessed 28 October 2024.

[76] Regulation (EU) No 1215/2012 of the European Parliament and of the Council of 12 December 2012 on Jurisdiction and the Recognition and Enforcement of Judgments in Civil and Commercial Matters [2012] OJ L 351/1 art 25(1)(a), (b), (c) ('Brussels I Recast').

[77] See Choice-of-Court Convention (n 2) preamble.

VII. Scope and Limitations

A. Key Limitations

For Singapore, Hong Kong, Malaysia and the Philippines, the statutes, court decisions and procedural rules referred to in this book come from government websites,[78] national law reports and journals,[79] and legal databases.[80] Most legal materials from these jurisdictions are available in English, and official versions are used whenever possible. If no official copy is available, a version from the legal databases is used. For Malaysian decisions, only those written in English or with English translations were considered. Decisions of the predecessor colonial courts in these four jurisdictions are also included. All published or available decisions from the establishment of the court systems by the British or Americans until 31 December 2023 are included. In addition to cases involving Choice-of-Forum clauses, this book also considers decisions that, while not directly addressing these clauses, provide relevant guidance on how courts might deal with Choice-of-Forum clause issues.

Particularly, the decisions of the following courts in Singapore, Hong Kong, Malaysia and the Philippines are considered:

Singapore	Court of Appeal, High Court, Singapore International Commercial Court and some lower courts
Hong Kong	Court of Final Appeal, Court of Appeal, Court of First Instance, and some lower courts
Malaysia	Court of Appeal, High Court (Malaya and Sabah and Sarawak) and some lower courts
Philippines	Supreme Court of the Philippines

Conducting legal research on China, Indonesia and Japan presents unique challenges due to language barriers and the limited availability of comprehensive legal databases. When no English translation of a court decision, statute or legal material was available, translations were generated using Google Translate and ChatGPT, and subsequently cross-referenced with secondary sources to ensure accuracy. Secondary sources – such as books, journal articles, theses, online articles and law-focused websites, and databases – therefore provided valuable resources for research on these three civil law jurisdictions. Research was primarily

[78] Government of Singapore, 'Singapore Statutes Online' (website): https://sso.agc.gov.sg/; Government of Hong Kong, 'Hong Kong e-Legislation' (website): https://www.elegislation.gov.hk/ accessed 28 October 2024; Attorney General's Chambers of Malaysia, 'Federal Legislation' (website): https://lom.agc.gov.my/ accessed 28 October 2024; Government of the Republic of the Philippines, 'Official Gazette' (website): https://www.officialgazette.gov.ph/ accessed 28 October 2024.

[79] eg, Singapore Law Reports (Singapore), Hong Kong Law Reports and Digest (Hong Kong), Malayan Law Journal (Malaysia), and Supreme Court Reports Annotated (Philippines).

[80] Singapore Academy of Law, 'LawNet' (online database): https://www-lawnet-sg.eu1.proxy.openathens.net/lawnet/group/lawnet/legal-research/basic-search (subscription required); Hong Kong Legal Information Institute, 'HKLII' (online database): https://hklii.hk/ (open access); Lexis+Australia (Malayan Law Journal Reports, subscription required); Central books, 'eSCRA' (online database): https://central.com.ph/e-scra/) (Supreme Court Reports Annotated, subscription required); CDAsia, CDAsiaClassic (online database): https://cdasiaonline.com/ (Philippine legal materials, subscription required).

conducted using unofficial legal databases, government websites, and secondary sources, but official English translations or those from government agencies were used whenever available. For China, pkulaw.com (*Beida Fabao*),[81] a legal database maintained by Peking University, was the primary research source, offering materials in both Chinese and English. Due to limited access to lower court decisions and their English translations, secondary sources were used, except in cases published by the Supreme People's Court's general gazette or designated as model cases. For Indonesia, *HukumOnline*,[82] with materials in both *Bahasa Indonesia* and English, served as the primary database. Where available, decisions from the Indonesian Supreme Court website[83] were accessed and then translated into English.[84] For Japan, English translations of statutes by the Japanese Ministry of Justice on the Japanese Law Translation website[85] were used. Additionally, court decisions published in the *Japanese Yearbook of International Law* and its predecessor, the *Japanese Annual of International Law*, were utilised. The research cut-off date for materials was 31 December 2023, except for key government issuances, such as the Chinese Supreme People's Court Judicial Interpretation on the China-Hong Kong Judgments Arrangement.

How the terms 'international commercial contract' and 'Choice-of-Forum clause' are defined below also circumscribed the research conducted for this book.

B. International Commercial Contracts

This book adopts the broadest possible definition of international commercial contracts, following the approaches in the UNIDROIT Principles,[86] Choice-of-Law Principles,[87] UNCITRAL Model Law[88] and Choice-of-Court Convention.[89] Contracts are 'international' unless both parties are resident in the same state and all elements relevant to the dispute are connected only with that state, regardless of the chosen court's location.[90] Even the choice of a foreign applicable law can give a contract international character.[91] Contracts are deemed 'commercial' when each party acts in the course of its trade or profession. While employment contracts are generally excluded, cases involving them may be considered if they offer useful discussion on principles applicable to Choice-of-Forum clauses. This book also does

[81] PKU.COM: https://www-pkulaw-com/ (subscription required).

[82] HukumOnline: https://pro.hukumonline.com/ (subscription required).

[83] Makamah Agung Republik Indonesia, 'Direktori Putusan' (website): https://putusan3.mahkamahagung.go.id/ (open access).

[84] Translations were made using Google Translate and ChatGPT, and then compared to discussions of the relevant legal material found in secondary sources.

[85] Ministry of Justice, Japan, 'Japanese Law Translation' (online database): https://www.japaneselawtranslation.go.jp/en/laws (open access).

[86] International Institute for the Unification of Private Law, UNIDROIT Principles of International Commercial Contracts (UNIDROIT, 2010 and 2016).

[87] Hague Conference on Private International Law, The Draft Hague Principles on Choice of Law in International Commercial Contracts, Preliminary Document No. 6 (July 2014).

[88] United Nations Commission on International Trade Law, UNCITRAL Model Law on International Commercial Arbitration, 24 ILM 1302 (1985), art 1(3)(a) ('UNCITRAL Model Law').

[89] Choice-of-Court Convention (n 2).

[90] Choice-of-Court Convention (n 2) art 1(2).

[91] See Convention on the Law Applicable to Contractual Obligations, opened for signature 19 June 1980, 1980 OJ (L 266) (entered into force 1 April 1991), arts 1.1 and 3.3 ('Rome Convention').

not distinguish between commercial contracts and consumer contracts, as some jurisdictions do.

Since this book focuses exclusively on contracts between private parties, it excludes international commercial contracts involving a state, government agency or international organisation. As a result, the analysis does not cover the privileges and immunities typically granted to states, government agencies, and international organisations.[92]

C. Choice-of-Forum Clauses

Choice-of-Forum clauses, also known as 'jurisdiction agreements', 'jurisdiction clauses', 'Choice-of-Court clauses', 'forum selection clauses' or 'litigation agreements' are defined in this book as contractual clauses that identify in which jurisdiction(s) a party may litigate disputes arising from or connected to an international commercial contract. These clauses may refer the disputes to a domestic, foreign or international court, and generally have two aspects. The first aspect, prorogation, involves conferring jurisdiction on a certain court (or courts) by agreement, even if the court would not otherwise have jurisdiction. The second aspect, derogation, excludes the jurisdiction of one or more forums that *would* otherwise have jurisdiction.[93] While some clauses contain both aspects, others, such as non-exclusive clauses, may only have prorogation effects. Choice-of-Forum clauses can also be exclusive (mandatory), conferring jurisdiction on one forum to the exclusion of all other forums, or non-exclusive (permissive), where the agreement identifies a preferred forum or excludes specific jurisdictions.[94] This book also examines 'unilateral' and hybrid clauses, which may require one party to litigate exclusively in one jurisdiction while allowing the other party to choose from multiple fora.[95] Additionally, Choice-of-Forum clauses that combine litigation with alternative dispute resolution (ADR) methods, such as arbitration, are considered, with several permutations possible. While international treaties[96] and regional or domestic laws[97] may specify formal requirements for Choice-of-Forum clauses, this book considers all clauses regardless of their form.

VIII. Methodology and Research Design

The research questions define the methodology of this book.[98] Since the goal is to explore, identify, compare and explain how courts in Singapore, Hong Kong, Malaysia, the Philippines, China, Indonesia and Japan resolve Choice-of-Forum clause issues, this requires the use of comparative law methods. Comparison is 'a process of contrasting and

[92] See Mortensen, Garnett and Keyes (n 37) 80.
[93] Nygh (n 39) 15.
[94] ibid.
[95] Mortensen, Garnett and Keyes (n 37) 97.
[96] Choice-of-Court Convention (n 2) art 3(c).
[97] Brussels I Recast (n 76) art 25(1)(a), (b), (c).
[98] See Maurice Adams, 'Doing What Doesn't Come Naturally. On the Distinctiveness of Comparative Law' in Mark Van Hoecke (ed), *Methodologies of Legal Research Which Kind of Method for What Kind of Discipline?* (Hart Publishing, 2011) 229, 236.

comparing, juxtaposing the unknown and the known, and comprehending the phenomena around us by observing differences and similarities'.[99] The specific techniques employed depend on the research objectives,[100] which are to 'enhance understanding of legal phenomena and create legal knowledge',[101] specifically, how courts in these seven jurisdictions approach Choice-of-Forum clauses and how the law may further develop in Asia. It is therefore essential that the methodology probes the legal reasoning in court decisions, identifying the principles, values, concepts, and other factors that courts consider when resolving disputes.

Particularly, the method used closely followed Kamba's three main stages of comparison: (1) the descriptive phase, which involves describing the norms, concepts and institutions of the legal systems or examining the socio-economic problems and legal solutions they provide; (2) the identification phase, where differences and similarities between the systems are identified; and (3) the explanatory phase, where divergences and resemblances are explained.[102] These phases are not always distinct or followed in a specific order.[103] Nonetheless, the execution of these phases is influenced by three factors: (1) the comparatist's jurisprudential outlook, which may be sociological, historically-oriented or positivistic (focusing on the textual material);[104] (2) the social context of the legal systems under comparison;[105] and (3) the legal context of the specific topic or phenomenon being compared.[106]

Each chapter in this book addresses a specific research question. Research typically begins with an enquiry into the relevant legal norms and concepts, an examination of the legal community's views on the issues, and a consideration of the broader contexts (eg, procedural systems, institutional frameworks, and political and cultural factors). The choice of norms and legal concepts is usually guided by the English, American and Commonwealth decisions, as well as scholarly writings, that highlight legal principles typically involved in analysing a particular Choice-of-Forum clause issue. Relevant case decisions and rules from each jurisdiction are then identified to reveal how these legal norms or concepts are applied, how opposing views are debated or resolved, and how the analysis and decision may be contextualised within the wider legal, cultural or political contexts. The legal reasoning in each case decision is compared with other decisions on similar issues, both within the legal system and across the other jurisdictions, to identify key similarities and differences. These similarities and differences are then explained, leading to the identification of key themes and lessons.

[99] Esin Örücü, 'Methodological Aspects of Comparative Law' (2006) 8(1) *European Journal Law of Reform* 29, 29.
[100] ibid 31.
[101] ibid 32.
[102] WJ Kamba, 'Comparative Law A Theoretical Framework' (1974) 23(3) *International and Comparative Law Quarterly* 485, 511–12.
[103] ibid 512.
[104] ibid 512–13.
[105] ibid 513.
[106] ibid 516.

2

The Nature of Choice-of-Forum Clauses

I. Introduction

This chapter probes various approaches to Choice-of-Forum clauses, focusing on debates over their nature, particularly divergent characterisations, and debates among common law scholars. It introduces an analytical framework for issues arising from Choice-of-Forum clause disputes and reviews how courts in Singapore, Hong Kong, Malaysia, the Philippines, China, Indonesia and Japan characterise these clauses. The chapter also compares Choice-of-Forum clauses with arbitration agreements, how they affect non-parties, and how they relate to other contract provisions.

II. The Varying Approaches to Choice-of-Forum Clauses

A. The Debate on the Nature of Choice-of-Forum Clauses

(i) The Divergent Characterisations: Contract v Procedure

Particularly between common law and civil law jurisdictions, the debates over Choice-of-Forum clauses often revolve around whether they should be characterised as either contractual or procedural. English common law decisions typically begin with a statement that says, 'the principle [is] that a party should be bound by a jurisdiction clause to which he has agreed, unless there is strong reason to the contrary'.[1] This perspective, rooted in contract law, treats the clause as a legally enforceable promise between parties, and thus a breach will not be sanctioned by the court unless there is a 'strong cause' to do so.[2] Other common law jurisdictions follow this approach.[3] In the United States, *The Bremen*[4]

[1] *Owners of Cargo lately laden on board ship or vessel Eleftheria v The Eleftheria (Owners), The Eleftheria* [1970] P 94, 104.

[2] *Racecourse Betting Control Board v Secretary of State for Air* [1944] Ch 114 ('*Racecourse Betting*'); *The Fehmarn* [1958] 1 WLR 159.

[3] See, eg, *Burrard-Yarrows Corp v The 'Hoegh Merchant'* [1982] 1 FC 248; [1983] 1 FC 495; *Nissho Iwai Corp v Paragon Grand Carriers Corp* (1987) 11 FTR 134; *Volkswagen Canada Inc v Auto Haus Fröhlich Ltd* [1986] 1 WWR 380; JJ Fawcett, *Declining Jurisdiction in Private International Law: Reports to the XIV Congress of the International Academy of Comparative Law Athens, August 1994* (Clarendon Press, 1995) 137; *Oceanic Sun Line Special Shipping Co Inc v Fay* (1988) 79 ALR 9, 28 ('*Oceanic Sun*'); *Society of Lloyd's and Oxford Members' Agency Ltd v Hyslop* [1993] 3 NZLR 135, 142.

[4] *The Bremen v Zapata Off-Shore Co*, 407 US 1 (1972).

confirmed that a freely negotiated forum clause, 'unaffected by fraud, undue influence, or overweening bargaining power',[5] must be enforced.

Common law cases show that choosing a forum can be treated as a commodity worth bargaining for. Just as parties may waive protections, they can bargain away litigation rights in exchange for consideration.[6] Courts can then enforce these contractual obligations through stay orders and anti-suit injunctions. Since parties can enforce these clauses as a contractual right not to be sued in a different court,[7] courts can award damages to compensate parties for the costs of being sued in the wrong court or to penalise for contractual breach.[8]

The contractual characterisation applies to both exclusive and non-exclusive clauses. Of course, the effect of the two varies, but this is because of the contractual nature given to them. As a contractual term, exclusive Choice-of-Forum clauses bind parties to a specific forum to the exclusion of any other forum because parties have agreed to such exclusivity of jurisdiction to resolve their disputes. Non-exclusive clauses, on the other hand, can have varied effects, depending on the words used by the parties, the facts of the dispute, applicable choice of law rules, and procedural rules of the forum. What is common, though, is that parties are not limited to filing in just one forum. Rather, they have other options as to where to file, depending upon which jurisdictions the parties stipulated. In England, one important effect is that if an English court is named in the clause and a party chooses to file an action in that court, the other party is bound to recognise and proceed to litigate in such court.[9] This is because the parties have agreed 'to submit to the [English] jurisdiction' and recognised that '[English courts] would be an appropriate forum for the trial of the action'.[10] Similar effects have been given to non-exclusive clauses by Singapore and Hong Kong courts. In effect, the 'non-exclusive' becomes 'exclusive'. In other jurisdictions like Malaysia, a non-exclusive Choice-of-Forum clause is still treated as merely one of the factors courts consider in determining the natural forum for the dispute. England continues to apply this analysis to a non-exclusive clause that does not stipulate English courts.[11] In Singapore and Hong Kong, courts also adopt this approach, but as explained in Chapter four, this effect does not depend per se on whether Singapore or Hong Kong is the chosen forum (unlike in England when English courts are chosen), but on the effect as intended or stipulated by the parties. Hence, if the parties have intended or stipulated in the Choice-of-Forum clause that their non-exclusive clause shall have effects similar to those given to exclusive clauses when the suit is filed in certain forums, then such 'exclusive' effects shall be provided. Nonetheless, the starting point of the court's analysis is what the parties agreed – did the parties agree on just one jurisdiction to the exclusion of any other courts or did they agree to simply have a

[5] ibid 12.

[6] Henry Noyes, 'If you (Re)build It, They Will Come: Contracts to Remake the Rules of Litigation in Arbitration's Image' (2006) 30(2) *Harvard Journal of Law and Policy* 579, 618–19.

[7] Sara Sanchez Fernandez, 'Choice-of-Court Agreements: Breach and Damages Within the Brussels I Regime' [2010](12) *Yearbook of Private International Law* 377, 383.

[8] eg, *Donohue v Armco Inc* [2002] 1 Lloyd's Rep 425 ('*Donohue*').

[9] See *UBS AG v HSH Nordbank AG* [2009] 2 Lloyd's Rep 272, 287 ('*UBS*'); *British Aerospace Plc v Dee Howard Co* [1993] 1 Lloyd's Rep 368, 376 ('*British Aerospace*').

[10] *Mercury Communications Ltd v Communication Telesystems International* [1999] 2 All ER (Comm) 33, 40.

[11] See eg, *Chopra v Bank of Singapore* [2015] EWHC 1529, [140]–[154]; *Konkola Copper Mines plc v Cromin Ltd (No 2)* [2006] EWHC 1093, [31].

particular jurisdiction available for future litigation without excluding others? Clearly, this confirms the binding nature of the promises even in non-exclusive clauses.

On the other side of the debate is the procedural characterisation of Choice-of-Forum clauses, primarily supported by civil law jurisdictions and regimes like the Brussels I Recast. Takahashi noted that the European Economic and Social Committee excluded Choice-of-Forum clauses from the Rome I Regulation[12] 'based on the same reasoning as that of procedural issues. This position is inherited from its predecessor, the Rome Convention,[13] which also excluded a choice-of-court agreement on the same reasoning'.[14] The Giuliano-Lagarde Report clearly expresses this procedural viewpoint:

> There was a lively debate … on whether or not to exclude agreements on the choice of court. The majority in the end favoured exclusion for the following reasons: the matter lies within the sphere of procedure and forms part of the administration of justice (exercise of State authority) … It was also noted that rules on jurisdiction are a matter of public policy and there is only marginal scope for freedom of contract.[15]

In contrast to the contractual approach, the procedural characterisation is framed from an administration of justice perspective – giving effect to Choice-of-Forum clauses is an exercise of the court's power to regulate its own jurisdiction, which remains outside the parties' power, and over which they have no private rights.[16] Rather, Choice-of-Forum clauses are recognised as waivers of default jurisdictional rules of the forum,[17] based on the 'consent' of the parties which then allows courts to ignore default procedural rules, and not because of the parties' contractual agreement.[18]

Continental European countries have usually approached Choice-of-Forum clauses as procedural,[19] because in jurisdictions which adopted the Austrian inquisitorial procedural model, the 'mandatory character of procedural rules which are part of public law' is emphasised.[20] Because procedural rules are mandatory, and therefore public law, they cannot be the subject of agreement between parties, and thus jurisdiction agreements cannot be contractual.[21] French courts, however, have taken the view that jurisdiction involving matters with foreign elements, without exception, is a matter of purely private interest and not a matter of *ordre public*, thus emphasising the private law character of

[12] Regulation (EC) No 593/2008 of the European Parliament and of the Council of 17 June 2008 on the law applicable to contractual obligations [2008] OJ L 177/6.

[13] Convention on the Law Applicable to Contractual Obligations, open for signature 19 June 1980, 19 ILM 1492 (1980) (entered into force 1 April 1991).

[14] Koji Takahashi, 'Damages for Breach of Choice-of-Court Agreement' [2008](10) *Yearbook of Private International Law* 57, 67.

[15] Mario Giuliano and Paul Lagarde, Report on the Convention on the law applicable to contractual obligations, OJ C 1982, 21/10/1980, 11.

[16] See Edwin Peel, 'Forum Shopping in the European Judicial Area – Introductory Report' (Oxford Legal Studies Research Paper No 39/2006, University of Oxford Faculty of Law, September 2006) 2.

[17] See Joseph Perillo, 'Selected Forum Agreements in Western Europe' (1964) 13(1) *American Journal of Comparative Law* 162, 162.

[18] See ibid.

[19] Arthur Lenhoff, 'The Parties' Choice of a Forum: "Prorogation Agreements"' (1961) 15(3) *Rutgers Law Review* 414, 429, 454, 458, 466, 472–73, 481.

[20] Paul Oberhammer, 'Party Autonomy and Procedural Law: A Few Comments from an Austrian Perspective' in Mattias Dahlberg (ed), *Party Autonomy – Civil Procedural Views on Party Autonomy, Franz Klein, EU Law and More* (Iustus Förlag, 2011) 51, 60.

[21] ibid 55–56, 61.

these clauses.[22] Consequently, in France, rules of both territorial competence and exercise of jurisdiction on cases with foreign elements are construed based on the private interests involved.[23]

Nonetheless, even in common law, the effect of Choice-of-Forum clauses (ie, the issue of enforcement) is still determined by the forum's procedural rules. Whether the court should exercise its jurisdiction or not, what remedies are available to enforce the Choice-of-Forum clause, and what 'public interests' the courts should consider are all determined by forum law. Hence, 'while English courts attach a great deal of weight to party autonomy … that is always subordinate to the court's ability to police its own jurisdiction'.[24] Therefore, as Merrett would point out, this shows the common law's convergence with the procedural approach of the civil law jurisdictions.[25] However, the common law approach remains different because of the strong weight given to the parties' intention in its analysis and the unique private law consequences.[26]

(ii) The Debate Among Common Law Scholars

When English courts in *Donohue v Armco*[27] ('*Donohue*') and other cases[28] began awarding damages for breaches of exclusive English jurisdiction clauses, it sparked fresh debate among the common law scholars on the nature of Choice-of-Forum clauses. Briggs argued that damages are a natural consequence of breaching Choice-of-Forum clauses. He said that '[n]othing is more fundamental than the fact that breach of contract gives rise to a *right* to damages: that *pacta sunt servanda*, contracts are to be performed, and that damages for breach are a matter of right and entitlement'.[29] This position is also shared by Tan and Yeo, who pinpointed that the 'breach of a jurisdiction clause, like the breach of any other contractual term, ought to ground an action for damages in the ordinary fashion'.[30] Tham, however, proposed basing damages for these breaches on tort law.[31]

At the opposing end, some scholars argue that civil law jurisdictions are correct in finding damages for breaching Choice-of-Forum clauses inappropriate. Knight, for example, argued that '[w]hat Professor Briggs does not really question … is the possibility that the methodology of the civilian … has a better understanding of what jurisdiction is about than the common law does'.[32] He argued that '[e]valuating the jurisdictional competencies

[22] Lenhoff (n 19) 440.

[23] ibid 441.

[24] Louise Merrett, 'Interpreting non-exclusive jurisdiction agreements' (2018) 14(1) *Journal of Private International Law* 38, 43.

[25] ibid.

[26] ibid.

[27] *Donohue* (n 8) 443.

[28] *Union Discount Co Ltd v Zoller* [2002] 1 WLR 1517 ('*Union Discount*'); *A/S D/S Svendborg D/S af 1912 A/S (Bodies Corporate trading in partnership as 'Maersk Sealand') v Akar* [2003] EWHC 797 (Comm).

[29] Adrian Briggs, *Agreements on Jurisdiction and Choice of Law* (Oxford University Press, 2008) 10 ('*Agreements on Jurisdiction*').

[30] Daniel Tan and Nik Yeo, Breaking Promises to Litigate in a Particular Forum: Are Damages an Appropriate Remedy? [2003](4) *Lloyd's Maritime and Commercial Law Quarterly* 435, 437.

[31] Chee Ho Tham, 'Damages for breach of English jurisdiction clauses: more than meets the eye' [2004](1) *Lloyd's Maritime and Commercial Law Quarterly* 46, 71.

[32] CJS Knight, 'The Damages of Damages: Agreements on Jurisdiction and Choice of Law' (2008) 4(3) *Journal of Private International Law* 501, 505.

of a judicial body is a quintessentially public law topic'.[33] Ho similarly argued that the Choice-of-Forum clause works only 'because the basis of jurisdiction is consent'.[34] In other words, a Choice-of-Forum clause is consent to the forum court's jurisdiction, nothing more.

Tham contradicted Ho's arguments by stressing that Choice-of-Forum clauses are not just between the parties and courts but also operate as mutual promises between the parties.[35] He argued that a jurisdiction clause 'does not merely operate as consent to the jurisdiction of the selected forum. It also operates at the level of mutual promise, the content … depend[s] on the specifics of the clause itself'.[36]

While characterising Choice-of-Forum clauses as either contractual or procedural is convenient, it oversimplifies the issue. Tham's approach, recognising both contractual and procedural elements, is more accurate. Hence, a better approach is to recognise their dual character. What warrants the application of either procedural or contract law, however, would depend on the issue being resolved by the courts. Takahashi suggested that 'the issues forming part of the administration of justice which impinge directly on the resources of the State should be characterised as procedural and accordingly be determined by the law of the forum'.[37] As such, 'other issues should be characterised as substantive and accordingly be submitted to the normal choice-of-law process'.[38]

Takahashi's test is encouraging, but may be difficult to apply, as it can be hard to distinguish issues which 'impinge directly on the resources of the State' from other matters. Furthermore, his test faces the chicken-and-egg dilemma. As Knight noted, '[d]ebates are always dependent upon starting points'.[39] For instance, damages are inconceivable if Choice-of-Forum clauses are seen as procedural. However, if the regulation of jurisdiction is a matter of contract law, like in English law, there is room for private law principles of contractual party autonomy and *pacta sunt servanda*. By advocating that issues can be characterised differently, Takahashi appears to take this premise. Hence, Takahashi's approach may not work in civil law jurisdictions that view these clauses as strictly procedural.

Yeo discussed a similar unbundling, aligning with Tham's distinction. He noted that common law separates the jurisdiction agreement as a contract, which is substantive, from its effect, which is procedural.[40] This distinction allowed Yeo to categorise questions of validity and interpretation as subject to the choice of law rules governing contracts,[41] while the procedural law of the forum governs enforcement.[42] Nonetheless, while Yeo recognised the dual character of Choice-of-Forum clauses, this analysis may be limited to common law jurisdictions, not to mention that unbundling remains challenging. For instance, when a court interprets the scope of the clause, it must also determine its effects and available remedies. If the clause includes a foreign principle or uses unfamiliar terms, the court must

[33] ibid 507.
[34] Look Chan Ho, 'Anti-Suit Injunctions in Cross-Border Insolvency: A Restatement' (2003) 52(3) *International and Comparative Law Quarterly* 697, 708.
[35] Tham (n 31) 57.
[36] ibid 59.
[37] Takahashi (n 14) 67.
[38] ibid.
[39] Knight (n 32) 512.
[40] Yeo Tiong Min, 'The Contractual Basis of the Enforcement of Exclusive and Non-Exclusive Choice of Court Agreements' (2005) 17(1) *Singapore Academy of Law Journal* 306, 314.
[41] ibid.
[42] ibid 315.

decide whether a similar principle or remedy exists in the forum. Answering these issues may require references to forum law. Furthermore, the forum cannot award relief that does not exist under its own laws.[43]

Knight emphasised that even if Choice-of-Forum clauses are treated as a private law matter, they differ from other contracts, and remedies like damages may not be appropriate.[44] Damages risk antagonising foreign courts,[45] as these clauses are transnational and must account for foreign interests and comity. While the contractual approach considers these matters, it often prioritises contractual promises over comity, thus resolving disputes as purely contractual matters. This point is expounded in Chapter seven.

These discussions suggest that unbundling issues related to Choice-of-Forum clauses, as proposed by Takahashi, is an attractive approach, as it recognises that not all issues pertain to the administration of justice. The Choice-of-Court Convention and the Brussels I Recast adopt this approach. Article 6 of the Choice-of-Court Convention provides that an exclusive Choice-of-Forum clause's validity is determined by the law of the chosen court.[46] Similarly, the law of the chosen court determines validity under Article 25 of the Brussels I Recast.[47] Hence, by allowing foreign law to determine validity, both instruments recognise that Choice-of-Forum clauses are not just procedural but are also substantive in nature. Hence, forum law does not necessarily determine all aspects of Choice-of-Forum clauses, which is the case if they are regarded as fully procedural. Nonetheless, this dual treatment of Choice-of-Forum clauses is only possible because it was agreed upon in an international convention or a regional organisation instrument. Recognition of the differences in approaches and the interaction of common law and civil law allowed such development in the European Union and the Hague Conference.

One must note that between the civil law and common law traditions, the latter appears to be more open to recognising the dual character of Choice-of-Forum clauses and the possibility of unbundling the issues involved. The contractual approach in common law allows this distinctive duality of being both a contract and procedural matter. In contrast, the civil law's procedural position bars recognising the clauses' contractual character, unless, of course, there is an international treaty or domestic law which changes the approach. Matters of public law, like procedural rules, simply do not provide any space for private rights to be recognised. Choice-of-Forum clauses, which express the parties' consent to the court's jurisdiction, operate like any other jurisdictional basis. As Ho emphasised, '[t]he forum selection clause works only "because the basis of jurisdiction is consent"'.[48] Court-led reforms allowing recognition of the dual character of Choice-of-Forum clauses, including the need to unbundle the issues, may be more difficult to achieve in civil law jurisdictions.

[43] Richard Garnett, *Substance and Procedure in Private International Law* (Oxford University Press, 2012) 295 ('*Substance and Procedure*').

[44] Knight (n 32) 512.

[45] ibid.

[46] Convention on Choice of Court Agreements, opened for signature 30 June 2005, 44 ILM 1294 (entered into force 1 October 2015) art 6.

[47] Regulation (EU) No 1215/2012 of the European Parliament and of the Council of 12 December 2012 on Jurisdiction and the Recognition and Enforcement of Judgments in Civil and Commercial Matters [2012] OJ L 351/1, art 25.

[48] Ho (n 34) 708.

B. The Challenge of Classifying Choice-of-Forum Issues

(i) The Difficulty of Classifying Issues

Determining whether issues related to Choice-of-Forum clauses are procedural/public or contractual/substantive/private is contentious. How does a Choice-of-Forum clause issue acquire an administrative aspect and when does it concern substantive rights? This is challenging, even in common law jurisdictions, because '[t]he concepts of substance and procedure were … often blurred and overlapping'.[49] Furthermore, the right-remedy distinction is also unhelpful, as parties seek enforcement of Choice-of-Forum clauses as both remedy and right. Identifying procedural versus substantive matters is crucial, as substantive issues follow choice of law rules, while procedural issues are governed by forum law.

Takahashi suggested that issues affecting state resources should be characterised as procedural, echoing Balduinus, who defined procedural rules as norms which were '*ad ordinandam litem*' or the rules by which the judge conducted the proceedings.[50] Similarly, in *McKain v RW Miller & Co (South Australia) Pty Ltd*, Mason CJ suggested that 'the essence of what is procedural may be found in those rules directed to governing or regulating the mode or conduct of proceedings'.[51] Lorenzen described procedure as 'that branch of law which governs the process of litigation'.[52] These statements imply that procedure should be understood as having an administrative connotation, relating to judicial machinery or protocol.[53] While procedural rules vary across jurisdictions and are often not explicitly defined and contained in one corpus of procedural law, issues that are considered procedural typically involve the relationship between the parties and the courts. Creating a definitive list of procedural issues, however, is challenging due to the unpredictability of litigation.

An alternative approach is to define what is substantive first. In *John Pfeiffer Pty Ltd v Rogerson*, the Australian High Court held that 'matters that affect the existence, extent or enforceability of the rights or duties of the parties to an action' are substantive, with everything else (presumably) procedural.[54] This 'outcome determinative' test classifies any rule that alters a case's result as substantive.[55] However, Garnett pointed out that this test is flawed, as procedural rules can also affect the rights and duties of the parties and so alter the result.[56] He argued that many laws regulating the mode or conduct of court proceedings may also have a material effect on the outcome of a case.[57] Garnett argued that where 'a matter clearly falls within the scope of "mode or conduct of proceedings," the fact that it may also be outcome determinative should not disturb its procedural characterization'.[58]

[49] Garnett, *Substance and Procedure* (n 43) 7.
[50] ibid 6.
[51] *McKain v RW Miller & Co (South Australia) Pty Ltd* (1991) 174 CLR 1, 26.
[52] See Garnett, *Substance and Procedure* (n 43) 8.
[53] See ibid.
[54] *John Pfeiffer Pty Ltd v Rogerson* (2000) 203 CLR 503, [99]; Garnett, *Substance and Procedure* (n 43) 21.
[55] Garnett, *Substance and Procedure* (n 43) 21.
[56] ibid.
[57] ibid 22.
[58] ibid.

To determine whether issues are procedural or substantive, it is useful to outline what happens in litigation involving Choice-of-Forum clauses. In international civil litigation, the first step is establishing jurisdiction. In civil law countries, jurisdiction is typically based on the defendant's domicile, the location of his property, or the dispute's legal connection to the forum.[59] Civilian courts also acquire jurisdiction through parties' 'consent', with a Choice-of-Forum clause serving as 'consent' to override default procedural rules.[60] Moreover, the chosen court may not always have jurisdiction absent the contractual stipulation.[61] Whether the law of the stipulated forum provides for the creation of judicial authority by stipulation – a question often treated as a procedural matter – is an important question for the Choice-of-Forum clause to be given effect.[62] Furthermore, in many continental European states, parties conferring exclusive jurisdiction on a court surrender their right to litigate elsewhere and to object to that court's jurisdiction.[63]

In common law jurisdictions, jurisdiction is established by service of process.[64] According to Briggs, often the plaintiff is faced with the question of how and when he may serve process upon a defendant.[65] If the defendant is present within the court's territorial jurisdiction, the claimant has a right to serve him.[66] If the defendant is outside, with no appointed agent to accept processes on his behalf, the claimant has no right to serve him.[67] Instead, the claimant has to obtain permission from the court for service out of the jurisdiction, subject to exceptions provided by law.[68] The grounds for the granting of such leave are generally based on connections between the forum and one of the following: the defendant, the subject matter of the dispute, or the cause of action.[69] Before leave is granted, the court must be satisfied that there is a good arguable case that the situation falls within one of the provisions providing for service of process out of jurisdiction,[70] that there is a serious issue to be tried on the merits,[71] and that it is a proper case for leave to be granted, which would require establishing that the court is the most appropriate forum to hear the case.[72] Similarly, where the defendant is out of the jurisdiction, a Choice-of-Forum clause (where it stipulates the forum courts) provides a firm basis for permission to serve out of the jurisdiction.[73] Nonetheless, in both situations, an agreement on jurisdiction for the English courts does not, as a matter of common law, establish the jurisdiction of the court: only service does that.[74]

After establishing subject matter and personal jurisdiction, the court should decide whether it will exercise this jurisdiction. In most common law countries, this largely involves the consideration of the 'natural forum' doctrine, also known as *forum non conveniens* or

[59] Ernest Lorenzen, 'Huber's De Conflictu Legum' (1919) 13(2) *Illinois Law Review* 375, 390.
[60] See Perillo (n 17) 162.
[61] Lenhoff (n 19) 417.
[62] See ibid 417, 466, 473.
[63] Perillo (n 17) 162.
[64] Adrian Briggs, *Civil Jurisdiction and Judgments* (Informa Law, 6th edn, 2015) 380 ('*Civil Jurisdiction*').
[65] ibid.
[66] ibid.
[67] ibid.
[68] ibid.
[69] See, eg, Practice Direction 6B – Service out of the Jurisdiction, para 3.1. (UK).
[70] Briggs, *Civil Jurisdiction* (n 64) 461.
[71] ibid 462.
[72] ibid 461–62.
[73] ibid 431–32.
[74] ibid 431.

forum conveniens principle. Talking about the experience of Singapore courts, Yeo describes what happens at this stage:

> This question involves balancing the considerations of the interests of the parties involved (especially factors of costs and convenience), as well as wider concerns of convenience and justice to third parties involved in the litigation, wastage of resources, the risk of inconsistent judgments from different courts and justice in the broadest sense, as well as … international comity.[75]

Further, a plaintiff may seek relief such as an anti-suit injunction to prevent the defendant from commencing or continuing proceedings in another country.[76] An exclusive Choice-of-Forum clause choosing English courts (or exclusively the courts of some other common law jurisdiction) can support an anti-suit injunction or even a claim for damages for breach of contract if any loss is proved.[77] For foreign exclusive clauses, the challenge may involve a stay application.[78] While such clauses do not automatically oust jurisdiction established by service, they provide a strong basis for staying the local proceedings.[79]

Jurisdictional issues, such as whether service of process was proper, grounds for service out of jurisdiction, or the issuance of a stay or anti-suit injunction, are generally procedural. Nonetheless, before courts can deal with enforcement, they usually need to address first issues involving parties' rights, as noted by Briggs:

> Rights come before remedies; grounds come before relief. Before coming to the question of enforcement, a court will need to determine any questions of construction, validity, nature, and scope (material and personal) of the parties' agreement on choice of court on which the application will turn.[80]

Garnett called for re-examination of the enforcement of Choice-of-Forum clauses as procedural. He noted that courts generally enforce Choice-of-Forum clauses through stay orders or anti-suit injunctions, unless the claimant shows 'strong reasons' for the forum to retain or decline jurisdiction in each case.[81] While there is a connection with the forum's interest in determining access to its courts, the forum court is also being asked to enforce a contract of the parties with clear outcome-determinative effect.[82] He therefore argued that 'enforceability of jurisdiction clauses is primarily contractual rather than jurisdictional and should be treated as substantive and governed by the law applicable to the clause'.[83]

In cases requiring enforcement of a Choice-of-Forum clause, courts must also address issues beyond procedural matters, such as the construction, validity, nature, and scope (material and personal) of the parties' agreement.[84] These require applying choice of law rules, not just procedural rules. Similarly, Garnett identified three issues requiring the application of choice of law rules: the interpretation and meaning of the clause, formal and essential validity of the clause, and enforceability of the clause.[85] The choice of law rules

[75] Yeo (n 40) 311.
[76] Briggs, *Civil Jurisdiction* (n 64) 469.
[77] ibid 432.
[78] ibid 431–32.
[79] ibid 432.
[80] ibid.
[81] Garnett, *Substance and Procedure* (n 43) 108.
[82] ibid.
[83] ibid.
[84] Briggs, *Civil Jurisdiction* (n 64) 432.
[85] Garnett, *Substance and Procedure* (n 43) 105.

used by courts in the examined Asian jurisdictions to answer these issues are discussed in Chapters six and eight, but it is clear that some issues are substantive and require the application of choice of law rules.

Focusing on the interpretation of Choice-of-Forum clauses, Garnett noted that it has two aspects. One deals with whether the clause is 'exclusive' or 'non-exclusive', which is always determined by forum law.[86] Another is whether the clause, as a matter of scope, applies to the claims pleaded by the claimant against the defendant, which is an issue determined by the law governing the clause.[87] Hence, interpretation of a Choice-of-Forum clause may involve the application of both the forum law and the choice of law rule, which may point towards the application of a foreign law. Furthermore, courts may refer to procedural rules when terms used in the clause differ from available remedies or principles. As noted earlier, the forum has no power to award relief existing under foreign law which has no counterpart under the law of the forum.[88] Garnett also noted that even if the enforcement of Choice-of-Forum clauses is treated as procedural, common law courts have referred to foreign law in answering the question of whether the foreign court would itself have jurisdiction over the dispute.[89] Hence, even if enforcement is procedural, it may not be wholly subject to forum law (thus, his argument for a substantive treatment of the enforceability issue to avoid this situation).[90]

(ii) The Conceptual Framework of Classifying Issues

Based on these discussions, the issues related to the Choice-of-Forum litigation may be illustrated by three concentric circles:

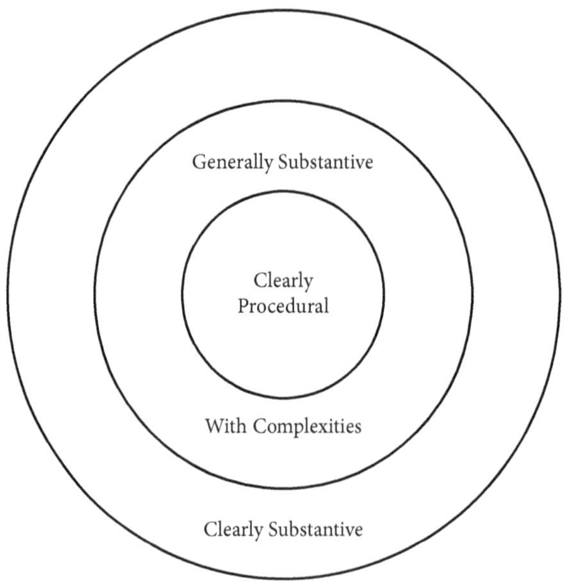

[86] ibid.
[87] ibid 106.
[88] ibid 295.
[89] ibid 108.
[90] ibid.

This conceptual framework addresses Knight and Ho's concern that Choice-of-Forum clauses have a strong procedural or public law character – at its core, these clauses involve the regulation of adjudicatory jurisdiction. Hence, the core issues are those which are exclusively between the parties and the court, or those which deal with the court governing or regulating 'the mode or conduct of proceedings', like whether service was properly made (the questions of how and when the claimant may serve process upon a defendant), whether there are grounds for service out of the jurisdiction, and whether a stay order or anti-suit injunction should be issued.

As cases become more complex, courts may address substantive issues that allocate rights between the parties. Hence, courts must move from the core to the outer circles. Represented by the two outer circles, these areas show the second relationship recognised by Tham, ie, Choice-of-Forum clauses also represent mutual promises between the parties. These areas also reflect the approach in the Choice-of-Court Convention and the Brussels I Recast. Issues in the outermost circle are those substantive issues which clearly concern the relationship of the parties. A good example would be issues concerning the essential validity of the Choice-of-Forum clause.

In the middle would be the area for issues which are characterised by their substantive dimension plus a close connection with the procedural or forum law, or vice versa. These issues require the application of forum law and/or choice of law rules, or foreign law. Within this middle circle are issues which have several aspects to them, ie, there is a further need to divide the issue and apply either the forum law or choice of law rules, depending on the aspect being resolved. Also, within this area are issues which became problematic because the Choice-of-Forum clause uses terms which are alien or different from those available in the forum (eg, an application for an anti-suit injunction is named as among the actions a chosen court has jurisdiction to decide on when in fact its procedural rules do not provide for such remedy). Likewise included are issues which are traditionally classified as procedural, but their resolution requires reference to foreign law (eg, whether the foreign court chosen actually has jurisdiction over the dispute).

The following arguments can therefore be made:

(1) Categorising issues solely as procedural/public or contractual/substantive/private is unhelpful in understanding the nature of Choice-of-Forum clauses;
(2) These issues can be procedural or substantive, depending on whether they involve the court's regulation of proceedings;
(3) Determining parties' private rights may involve procedural and substantive issues; and
(4) Some issues are complex due to the interaction between characterisation, forum procedure, and forum's choice of law process.

Further, the resolution of these issues is circumscribed by three main areas of limitation – party interests, which are reflected in their exercise of party autonomy; forum state interests, which are reflected in its mandatory rules and public policy; and international community interests, which are usually reflected in the principle of 'comity' and other international treaties and norms. These limitations are discuessed in detail in Chapters seven and eight.

III. What is the Nature of Choice-of-Forum Clauses?

The examined Asian jurisdictions recognise the dual nature of Choice-of-Forum clauses as both contractual and procedural, albeit to varying degrees. In common law jurisdictions, courts balance contractual rights with procedural rules and public interest, particularly in administering justice. Singapore and Hong Kong tend to prioritise the contractual aspect before exercising their discretion to apply procedural or public law principles. In contrast, Malaysia and to a much greater extent, the Philippines, emphasise court discretion in enforcing public interests.

The differing approaches stem partly from the legal history of these jurisdictions. Singapore, Hong Kong and Malaysia, as former British colonies, base their legal systems on English common law and refer to decisions from English and Commonwealth courts. Malaysia's contract law, rooted in common law, is codified in the Contracts Act 1950.[91] Key differences, however, arise due to subsequent historical developments, socio-cultural, political institutions and economic factors, which will be discussed in later chapters.

The Philippines, as a former Spanish and American colony, is a hybrid civil and common law jurisdiction. Much of its private law, codified in the Civil Code of 1949 (Republic Act No 386), is influenced by the Spanish Civil Code of 1889, and by Latin American and European civil codes.[92] Due to American colonial rule and extensive reference to American case law, Philippine contract law also draws on US federal court and State court doctrines.[93] This has largely been achieved through the doctrine of precedent, another legacy of the American colonial rule.[94] Hence, judicial decisions form part of Philippine law.[95] Civil procedure, on the other hand, is largely American in origin, incorporating its adversarial approach and common law rules of civil procedure.[96] Notable common law remedies, such as stay of proceedings and anti-suit injunctions, are, however, absent. The Philippines, likewise, does not have jury trials.

China, Indonesia and Japan are civil law countries. China and Japan adopted the civil law system, including the Civil Code and Code of Civil Procedure, during their efforts to modernise in the late nineteenth to early twentieth century, to align their legal systems with Europe.[97] Indonesia inherited the civil law system from the Dutch colonial period. In these countries, continental European approaches were adopted, including the recognition that parties can agree on the court for their dispute, albeit acting as a waiver of default jurisdictional rules of the forum.

[91] Contracts Act 1950 (Malaysia).

[92] See Arturo Tolentino, *Commentaries and Jurisprudence on the Civil Code of the Philippines* (Central Professional Books, Inc, 1990) vol 1, 6–10.

[93] See Pacifico Agabin, *Mestizo: The Story of the Philippine Legal System* (University of the Philippines College of Law, 2011) 203–16.

[94] See ibid 201–2.

[95] Civil Code (Philippines), art 8.

[96] Agabin (n 93) 190–91.

[97] See Xin Cai, 'History of Private International Law' in Xiaohong Liu and Zhengyi Zhang, *Chinese Private International Law* (Hart Publishing, 2021) 15, 16; Jun Yokoyama, *Private International Law* (Kluwer Law International BV, 2nd edn, 2019) 15.

A. Singapore, Hong Kong and Malaysia

The Singaporean approach is illustrated in *Baiduri Bank Bhd v Dong Sui Hung*,[98] ('*Baiduri*') where the Singapore High Court examined the parties' Choice-of-Forum clause, recognising that non-exclusive clauses cannot just be grouped into one category but several, and that they are differently worded, and thus can have different effects.[99] In this sense, the Singaporea High Court recognised Choice-of-Forum clauses as contracts with various effects depending on what is stated in the clause. Furthermore, the Court also recognised the public or procedural law side of the analysis:

> [W]hen deciding the question whether to decline jurisdiction in favour of a foreign jurisdiction because of the exclusive foreign jurisdiction clause, the pure contractual principle must necessarily be balanced against the plaintiff's right to have the matter heard and tried in Singapore, which he has established under the law here.[100]

This recognition of the dual nature of Choice-of-Forum clauses is also evident in the decision of the Hong Kong Court of First Instance ('Hong Kong CFI') in *Noble Power Investments Ltd v Nissei Stomach Tokyo Co Ltd* ('*Noble Power*'):

> [W]hen dealing with questions of jurisdiction and forum, as a matter of public policy, it is for the courts ultimately to determine where the interests of justice lie, and the courts may, in exceptional circumstances, ignore the contractual bargain between the parties.[101]

By contrast, the Malaysia Court of Appeal in *Inter Maritime Management Sdn Bhd v Kai Tai Timber Co Ltd, Hong Kong*[102] ('*Inter Maritime*') has strongly rejected an approach which undermines court discretion and would reduce the Choice-of-Forum clause analysis to a mere application of contractual principles.[103] In short, the Court rejected a purely contractual type of analysis, thus again recognising the dual nature of Choice-of-Forum clauses. The Court rejected the United States decision *The Bremen*, by refusing enforcement of Choice-of-Forum clauses based only on grounds that effectively negate consent:

> It follows that on a realistic application of the test … in [*The Bremen v*] *Zapata*, a judge hearing an application for a stay mounted on a forum selection clause would have no discretion at all in the matter. He may only refuse a stay on grounds sufficient to avoid a contract, that is to say, grounds that effectively negate consent … An adoption of the Zapata test by this court would … put at risk … authority … that recognize a wide discretion in a judge hearing an application for a stay.[104]

What issues are considered contractual or procedural in Singapore, Hong Kong and Malaysia is discussed in Chapters four, six and seven. In brief, those issues concerning the enforcement of Choice-of-Forum clauses – like requirements to allow service out of jurisdiction, granting of relief such as stay orders and anti-suit injunctions, and enforcement and

[98] *Baiduri Bank Bhd v Dong Sui Hung* [2000] 2 SLR(R) 271 (HC).
[99] ibid 276–77, 281–82.
[100] ibid 279 [17].
[101] *Noble Power Investments Ltd v Nissei Stomach Tokyo Co Ltd* [2008] HKCA 255, [27].
[102] *Inter Maritime Management Sdn Bhd v Kai Tai Timber Co Ltd, Hong Kong* [1995] 1 MLJ 322 (CA Kuala Lumpur).
[103] ibid 336.
[104] ibid.

recognition of foreign judgments – are resolved by applying domestic procedural rules, thus implying their procedural character. On the other hand, those issues concerning existence, validity and interpretation are resolved according to the law applicable to the contract or the forum's contract law, thus implying the substantive or contractual character of these issues. Lastly, certain issues discussed in Chapter seven have a distinctly public law dimension, thus requiring the application of mandatory rules and public policy.

B. The Philippines

The Philippines has been ambiguous in its treatment of Choice-of-Forum clauses. The Philippine Supreme Court has not definitively stated their nature under Philippine law, though it recognises these clauses as valid and enforceable, without explicitly clarifying the basis for such treatment. There are two possible sources for recognising Choice-of-Forum clauses in the Philippines. One arises from contract and the other, from the Philippine procedural rules. Article 1306 of the Civil Code states that:

> The contracting parties may establish such stipulations, clauses, terms and conditions as they may deem convenient, provided they are not contrary to law, morals, good customs, public order, or public policy.

Scholarly writings and legal opinions have cited this provision as the authority behind a whole range of contractual stipulations, including Choice-of-Law and Choice-of-Forum clauses.[105]

Meanwhile, rule 4, section 4(b) of the Philippine Rules of Court exempts parties from the mandatory application of the rules on venue: '[w]here the parties have validly agreed in writing before the filing of the action on the exclusive venue thereof'. While this rule does not deal with jurisdiction but venue issues (ie, in which court having jurisdiction should the dispute be brought), Philippine decisions have treated Choice-of-Forum clauses as falling within the ambit of this rule; thus, the rule on exclusivity of the choice as provided in rule 4 has been strongly emphasised. In *Hong Kong and Shanghai Banking Corporation v Sherman* ('*HSBC*'), the Philippine Supreme Court applied rule 4, section 4(b) to determine whether, not being the forum named in the parties' Choice-of-Forum clause, it should dismiss the case for lack of jurisdiction. Highlighting the technical requirements of rule 4, section 4(b), the Court pinpointed that because the parties did not use words implying exclusivity in their choice of the courts of Singapore as the jurisdiction which could resolve their disputes, the parties, in effect, did not exclude other courts, including the Philippine courts.[106] The Court, therefore, did not dismiss the case in favour of the Singapore courts.[107] In *Philippine Banking Corporation v Tensuan* ('*Tensuan*'), the Supreme Court stated that the approach in *HSBC* is consistent with the other cases involving domestic Choice-of-Forum

[105] See, eg, Elizabeth Aguiling-Pangalangan, 'Philippines' in Alejandro Carballo Leyda (ed) *Asian Conflict of Laws* (Kluwer Law International, 2015) 157, 161; Herminio Ozaeta and Marie Camille Bautista, 'Security over Collateral Philippines', *Lex Mundi* (Web Page) <http://www.lexmundi.com/images/lexmundi/practicegroups/bankfinance/socsurvey/philippines.pdf> accessed 28 October 2024.

[106] *Hong Kong and Shanghai Banking Corporation v Sherman* (1989) 176 SCRA 331, 337–38 ('*HSBC*').

[107] ibid 338.

clauses, which all applied rule 4, section 4(b).[108] The Supreme Court, in effect, confirmed that Choice-of-Forum clauses are venue stipulations.[109]

In *Philippine International Trading Corporation v MV Zileena*[110] ('*MV Zileena*'), the Philippine Supreme Court emphasised that since parties cannot stipulate jurisdiction but only venue, then a Choice-of-Forum clause can only be a venue stipulation.[111] Hence, in that case, the Choice-of-Forum clause, on its own terms, clearly conferred exclusive jurisdiction on the Singapore High Court.[112] Nonetheless, the Court said that such a clause could not be a '*competencia*' or an agreement on court jurisdiction, and thus 'the parties must have intended to fix the venue only, for jurisdiction over an action is conferred by law, and may not be changed by mere agreement of the parties'.[113]

Hence, the Philippines recognises Choice-of-Forum clauses as venue stipulations, not as contracts conferring jurisdiction, under rule 4, section 4(b) of the Rules of Court. Notably, the Supreme Court allows parties to select both domestic and foreign courts as venues, provided the choice is exclusive and meets the other formal requirements of rule 4, section 4(b).[114]

Moreover, in *Saudi Arabian Airlines (Saudia) v Rebesencio*,[115] ('*Saudia*') the Philippine Supreme Court emphasised that, beyond technical compliance, the choice of forum is subject to considerations such as the 'the availability and adequacy of recourse to a foreign tribunal … and … the question of where, as between the forum court and a foreign court, the balance of interests inhering in a dispute weighs more heavily'.[116] This introduces public law into the analysis of Choice-of-Forum clauses in Philippines.

Hence, the Philippine approach differs from Singapore, Hong Kong, and Malaysia in several ways. First, these clauses are not seen as contracts granting private rights, so remedies like damages, rescission or specific performance are unavailable. Second, they do not affect the grant of leave for extraterritorial service, which is based solely on meeting the procedural requirements under the Rules of Court.[117] Third, while Choice-of-Forum clauses stipulating foreign courts inform the exercise of discretion to grant a dismissal based on the affirmative defences which may be raised by the defendant in its answer under rule 6, they are not considered by way of the grounds associated with jurisdiction (eg, non-existent subject-matter or personal jurisdiction),[118] but rather upon other grounds, as argued in Chapter three, such as improper venue,[119] *lis pendens*,[120] *res judicata*[121] or non-compliance with a condition precedent.[122] Fourth, as discussed in Chapter four, their role in the *forum non conveniens* test, which may be argued at the merits stage, is subordinate

[108] *Philippine Banking Corporation v Tensuan* (1994) 230 SCRA 413, 420.
[109] ibid.
[110] *Philippine International Trading Corporation v MV Zileena* (1992) 215 SCRA 309.
[111] ibid 312–13.
[112] ibid 310.
[113] ibid 312–13.
[114] See *HSBC* (n 106) 337–38.
[115] *Saudi Arabian Airlines (Saudia) v Rebesencio* (2015) 746 SCRA 140, 169.
[116] ibid.
[117] *The Dial Corp v Soriano* (1988) 161 SCRA 737, 742.
[118] Rules of Court (Philippines) r 16, s 1(a)–(b).
[119] ibid s 1(c).
[120] ibid s 1(e).
[121] ibid s 1(f).
[122] ibid s 1(j).

to administration of justice and public interest factors. Lastly, as discussed in Chapter five, because Choice-of-Forum clauses are venue stipulations, issues of validity and interpretation are determined not by the law chosen by the choice of law process but by forum law. Furthermore, unlike in common law, even the parties' intention does not generally play a role in the interpretation of these clauses.

C. China, Indonesia and Japan

China, Indonesia and Japan generally regard Choice-of-Forum clauses as procedural, operating as basis for the local courts to assume jurisdiction and to a certain extent, as special waivers of default jurisdictional rules of the forum. However, their treatment has evolved to include contractual elements. For example, Indonesian courts refer to the freedom to contract, contained in the *Burgerlijk Wetboek* (Civil Code or BW), as the basis for Choice-of-Forum clauses.[123] In Japan, substantive validity is determined by the law applicable to the contract, pursuant to the choice of law process as provided under the Act on General Rules for Application of Laws (Act No 78 of 2006) ('JAGRAL').[124] Chinese courts follow a similar approach; thus, validity is determined by Chinese contract law. This dual character of Choice-of-Forum clauses is discussed in detail in Chapter eight.

IV. Differentiating Choice-of-Forum Clauses from Arbitration Agreements

A. Similar Yet Different

As early as 1796, beginning with *Gienar v Meyer*, English courts held that parties may designate a forum to resolve their disputes.[125] However, the acceptance of Choice-of-Forum clauses in English law was largely influenced by arbitration agreements. The Common Law Procedure Act 1854 allowed stays of proceedings where a contract contained arbitration clauses. In *Law v Garret*[126] ('*Garret*'), the English court treated a Choice-of-Forum clause like an arbitration agreement, thus establishing that English courts could stay proceedings. Particularly, *Garret* established: (1) the power of English courts to stay proceedings in breach of a Choice-of-Forum clause, (2) the power of parties to select courts for their disputes, and (3) the readiness of courts to provide a legal remedy. It was not clear, however, why English courts had to rely on the arbitration statutes and not on cases like

[123] See Afifah Kusumadara, *Indonesian Private International Law* (Hart Publishing, 2021) 51–52; Alvansa Vickya and Tiurma M Pitta Allagan, 'Implications of Non-exclusive Choice of Forum Clauses in Determining the Competent Dispute Resolution Forum in Indonesia' (2022) 12(1) *Indonesia Law Review* 70, 71–72.

[124] Eg Jun Yokoyama, *Private International Law* (Kluwer Law International, 2nd edn, 2019) 154–55; Takahashi (n 14) 69; Kazuaki Nishioka and Yuko Nishitani, *Japanese Private International Law* (Hart Publishing, 2021) 46.

[125] *Gienar v Meyer* (1796) 2 H Bl 603; 126 ER 728, 729.

[126] *Law v Garret* (1878) 8 Ch D 26.

Gienar v Meyer.[127] Nonetheless, *Garret* became the authority and its reasoning was followed in later English, Canadian and Australian cases.[128] Curiously, the earliest recorded case in Hong Kong which involved Choice-of-Forum clauses, the 1905 case of *Schwer and Others v Von Uffel*[129] ('*Schwer*'), mentioned *Garret*,[130] but questioned its application to Choice-of-Forum clause cases.[131] In that case, the Hong Kong Supreme Court Chief Justice correctly noted that an arbitral award is different from a foreign judgment, and thus, pointed out that the applicable procedure may be different.[132]

In *Racecourse Betting*,[133] English courts began grounding decisions on contract law rather than arbitration laws. Lord Greene lamented:

> [i]t is … rather unfortunate that the power and duty of the court to stay the action was said to be under s. 4 of the *Arbitration Act*, 1889. In truth, that power and duty arose under a wider general principle namely, that the court makes people abide by their contracts.[134]

Hence, in *The Fehmarn*,[135] Lord Denning clarified that a Choice-of-Forum clause is not equivalent to an arbitration clause.[136] Despite this shift, some confusion persisted.

The confusion arises from the similarities between Choice-of-Forum clauses and arbitration agreements. Both are dispute resolution clauses which identify the jurisdiction, venue or institution which will resolve the dispute. They reflect procedural party autonomy and are treated as separate and independent of the validity of the main contract. Both are supposed to facilitate international trade and enhanced judicial cooperation. Furthermore, both require independent non-partisan judge(s) whose decisions are binding on the parties (subject to appeal in the case of litigation). Due to these parallels, courts and scholars often draw analogies between the two, concluding that certain effects should be similar.[137]

A major difference between the two, however, is the dual character of Choice-of-Forum clauses as both public and private, contractual and procedural, while arbitration agreements are purely contractual. Furthermore, the court's authority to enforce Choice-of-Forum clauses is not only derived from consent but fundamentally from the state itself.[138] Moreover, because of the fully contractual nature of arbitration, parties to arbitration agreements can entirely choose the procedural and even substantive rules of law which will govern

[127] Zelman Cowen and Derek Mendes Da Costa, 'The Contractual Forum: Situation in England and the British Commonwealth' (1964) 13(1) *American Journal of Comparative Law* 179, 182.
[128] ibid.
[129] *Schwer and Others v Von Uffel* (Unreported, SC Hong Kong, CJ, 11 September 1905).
[130] ibid 8.
[131] ibid 9.
[132] ibid.
[133] *Racecourse Betting* (n 2) 126.
[134] ibid.
[135] *The Fehmarn* (n 2).
[136] ibid 162.
[137] See *Scherk v Alberto-Culver Co*, 417 US 506, 519 (1974); David Taylor, 'The Forum Selection Clause: A Tale of Two Concepts' (1993) 66(3) *Temple Law Review* 785, 787; Ingrid Farquharson, 'Choice of Forum Clauses – A Brief Survey of Anglo-American Law' (1974) 8(1) *International Lawyer* 83, 95; Patrick Borchers, 'Forum Selection Agreements in the Federal Courts after Carnival Cruise: A Proposal for Congressional Reform' (1992) 67(1) *Washington Law Review* 55, 61, 67; Linda Mullenix, 'Another Choice of Forum, Another Choice of Law: Consensual Adjudicatory Procedure in Federal Court' (1988) 57(3) *Fordham Law Review* 291, 315–19.
[138] Tham (n 31) 55.

proceedings and resolution of a dispute by the arbitral tribunal.[139] In contrast, except to the extent allowed by forum law, parties cannot provide in their Choice-of-Forum clauses that rules of procedure other than those of the forum shall apply, or vary the contents of the applicable law which will govern a dispute. Hence while parties can displace default jurisdiction through their Choice-of-Forum clause, they cannot override, in general, procedural, substantive and institutional arrangements designed by the state to ensure the integrity of the dispute resolution process and protect public interests. Moreover, as regards Choice-of-Forum clauses, a national law always determines their validity and scope.[140] In contrast, and although this is not the case in common law jurisdictions, the validity and scope of arbitration agreements will not necessarily be determined by a national law.[141]

Another major difference is the lack of a truly global system for enforcing Choice-of-Forum clauses. The Choice-of-Court Convention is far less comprehensive than the New York Convention,[142] partly because of such clauses' impact on state sovereignty, making it harder for states to agree.[143] Furthermore, there is no model law for harmonising standards, unlike the UNCITRAL Arbitration Model Law.[144] Notably, unlike arbitration where the New York Convention has laid down the maximum formal requirements regarding arbitration agreements which national laws cannot override, Choice-of-Forum clauses have been subjected domestically to unduly stringent formal requirements largely because of the absence of an international treaty regulating these clauses internationally (until recently) and a model law.[145] Even the Brussels I Regulation proved to be inadequate in bridging the wide difference in approaches between the common law and civil law traditions (eg, use of anti-suit injunction and the approach of *lis pendens*), thus prompting the Brussels I Recast.

Because of their more advanced enforcement mechanisms, arbitration agreements are often mistakenly considered superior to Choice-of-Forum clauses. There is no theoretical basis, however, for such treatment especially since both are built on the same foundation – party autonomy.[146] Hence, unless the parties intended that one should be preferred over the other, both should be treated equally. Furthermore, the New York Convention, the UNCITRAL Model Law and the associated national statutes are silent on situations where there are both arbitration and Choice-of-Forum clauses.[147] Hence, in situations where both arbitration and Choice-of-Forum clauses coexist, Garnett emphasised that the 'conundrum must be resolved by courts using principles of contractual interpretation rather than contemporary notions of amiability towards arbitration'.[148]

[139] See Arthur Taylor von Mehren, *Adjudicatory Authority in Private International Law: A Comparative Study* (Brill Academic Publishers, 2006) 229.

[140] Stavros Brekoulakis, 'The Notion of the Superiority of Arbitration Agreements over Jurisdiction Agreements: Time to Abandon it?' (2007) 24(4) *Journal of International Arbitration* 341, 352.

[141] ibid.

[142] Convention on the Recognition and Enforcement of Foreign Arbitral Awards, opened for signature 10 June 1958, 330 UNTS 38 (entered into force 7 June 1959) ('New York Convention').

[143] See William Woodward Jr, 'Saving the Hague Choice of Court Convention' (2008) 29(3) *University of Pennsylvania Journal of International Law* 657, 660–61; Gabriel Sanchez, 'The Future of the Hague Convention on Choice of Court Agreements' (2008) 17(2) *International Law Students Association Quarterly* 12, 15.

[144] See Brekoulakis (n 140) 345.

[145] ibid 353.

[146] See ibid 356.

[147] Richard Garnett, 'Coexisting and Conflicting Jurisdiction and Arbitration Clauses' (2013) 9(3) *Journal of Private International Law* 361, 362.

[148] ibid.

B. Singapore, Hong Kong and Malaysia

(i) Different Set of Rules Apply

Courts in Singapore, Hong Kong and Malaysia recognise the differences between Choice-of-Forum and arbitration clauses. In *Well Hoped Ltd v Nippon Yusen Kaisha*,[149] the Hong Kong High Court emphasised that arbitration-related decisions are not precedents for Choice-of-Forum cases.[150] Similarly, in *The 'Dai Yun Shan'*,[151] the Singapore High Court emphasised that, since the clause is not strictly an arbitration clause because there is an option to either go to the courts or proceed with arbitration in China, the arbitration law does not automatically apply.[152] Interestingly, the Court used *forum non conveniens* to conclude that the proceedings, either by arbitration or litigation, should be in China.[153]

(ii) Inconsistencies in Interrelated Contracts

Confusion may arise in disputes involving interrelated contracts which inconsistently refer to either arbitration or litigation. Courts have inconsistent approaches for such cases. The first approach is to identify the contract directly involved in the dispute and then proceed with the mode stated in the dispute resolution clause of such contract. In *Econ Corp International Ltd v Ballast-Nedam International BV*,[154] the Singapore High Court clarified that that when the interrelated agreements provide for different modes of dispute resolution, the provision in the relevant contract prevails.[155] Since the subject matter of the dispute arose from the bond and guarantee agreements, the Choice-of-Forum clauses in those agreements in favour of Singapore courts would prevail.[156] Similarly, in *China Medical Ltd v Autoscale Resources Ltd*,[157] the Hong Kong CFI found that since the cause of action was based on the guarantee agreement which contained a Choice-of-Forum clause stipulating Hong Kong courts, no stay may be issued,[158] even if the related subscription agreement provided for arbitration.[159] And, in *CPC Construction Hong Kong, Ltd v Harvest Engineering (HK) Ltd*[160] ('*CPC Construction*'), the Hong Kong CFI emphasised that the choice to litigate in Hong Kong, as stated in the Choice-of-Forum clauses in the loan agreement and guarantee, and supplemental agreement and supplemental guarantee, clearly expressed the desire not to resort to arbitration, which was the mode found in the subcontract.[161] The Court agreed with CPC that the payments advanced under the loan

[149] *Well Hoped Ltd v Nippon Yusen Kaisha* [1982] 1 HKC 155, 159 (HC).
[150] ibid; See also *Joseph Ghossoub v Team Y & R Holdings Hong Kong Ltd* [2016] HKCFI 1793.
[151] *The 'Dai Yun Shan'* [1992] 1 SLR(R) 461, [1992] 2 SLR 508 (HC).
[152] ibid 466.
[153] ibid.
[154] *Econ Corp International Ltd v Ballast-Nedam International BV* [2003] 2 SLR (R) 15 (HC), [2002] SGHC 293 ('*Econ Corp*').
[155] ibid 20–22; see also *Astrata (Singapore) Pte Ltd v Portcullis Escrow Pte Ltd* [2011] 3 SLR 386, 394–95 (CA) ('*Astrata*'); *Bunge SA v Shrikant Bhasi* [2020] SGCA 94, [42].
[156] *Econ Corp* (n 154) 21–22.
[157] *China Medical Ltd v Autoscale Resources Ltd* [2009] HKCFI 425.
[158] ibid [9].
[159] ibid.
[160] *CPC Construction Hong Kong, Ltd v Harvest Engineering (HK) Ltd* [2015] HKCFI 1173 ('*CPC Construction*').
[161] ibid [58], [60]–[61].

agreement and the supplemental loan agreement were stand alone and independent transactions, even though they may have been used for the expenses under the subcontract.[162] However, when a dispute is intrinsically related to the main agreement providing for arbitration, and the procurement agreement, which contained the exclusive Choice-of-Forum clause, is but an extension of the main agreement, the court may stay proceedings in favour of arbitration.[163]

The second approach aims to reconcile conflicting clauses between interrelated contracts and provisions. '[A] generous and harmonious interpretation should be given to the purposedly conflicting clauses such as to give effect to the parties' true intention'.[164] In *Bluegold Investment Holdings Ltd v Kwan Chun Fun Calvin*,[165] the Hong Kong CFI decided that because of the references to the arbitration clause found in the subscription agreement, which is phrased widely, parties should resort to arbitration even if a related agreement – the guarantee agreement – contained a non-exclusive Choice-of-Forum clause.[166] The Hong Kong CFI pinpointed that the plaintiff's claims arguably arose from the subscription agreement.[167] The Court also noted that a non-exclusive Choice-of-Forum clause can co-exist with arbitration provisions in other contracts.[168]

In *The Yaoki*,[169] confusion arose from two charterparties, with the time charterparty referring to the voyage charterparty.[170] The voyage charterparty contained a Choice-of-Forum clause, while the time charterparty contained an arbitration clause.[171] The Hong Kong CFI ruled that the bill of lading, which was directly the subject matter of dispute, was issued pursuant to the time charterparty, and not the voyage charterparty.[172] The general reference alone, in the time charterparty to the voyage charterparty, could not oust the clearly-stated arbitration clause in the time charter.[173] Hence, the parties should proceed with arbitration.[174]

Similarly, in *Lembaga Pelabuhan Kelang v Kuala Dimensi Bhd*,[175] the Malaysia Court of Appeal held that the Choice-of-Forum clauses in the subsequent supplemental agreements effectively express the parties' 'predominant agreement to submit to the court's jurisdiction' and abandonment of arbitration.[176] The Court noted that the arbitration clause and Choice-of-Forum clauses contradict and could not 'function harmoniously … It is either arbitration or litigation'.[177] The Court observed that the use of the permissive 'may' allowed

[162] ibid [84].
[163] *Juaramedic Sdn Bhd v MRCB Engineering Sdn Bhd* [2017] 11 MLJ 427, 436, 440 (HC Kuala Lumpur).
[164] *BXH v BXI* [2020] SGCA 28, [60] (CA).
[165] *Bluegold Investment Holdings Ltd v Kwan Chun Fun Calvin* [2016] HKCFI 415.
[166] ibid [20].
[167] ibid [17].
[168] ibid [23]; see also *Neo Intelligence Holdings Ltd v Giant Crown Industries Ltd* [2017] HKCFI 2088, [29].
[169] *The Owners of and/or Other Persons Entitled to Sue in Respect of Cargo Lately Laden on Board the Ship or Vessel Yaoki v The Owners of and/or Demise Charterers of the Ship or Vessel Yaoki & the Ships or Vessels Listed in Schedule Hereto* [2006] HKCFI 479.
[170] ibid [3].
[171] ibid.
[172] ibid [9].
[173] ibid [16].
[174] ibid [19].
[175] *Lembaga Pelabuhan Kelang v Kuala Dimensi Bhd* [2011] 2 MLJ 606 (CA Putrajaya).
[176] ibid 629.
[177] ibid.

parties to abandon arbitration.[178] The Court concluded that parties had subsequently abandoned arbitration when they expressly submitted to the court's jurisdiction.[179]

Another way to reconcile conflicting dispute resolution clauses is to interpret one as a carve-out from the other. In *Silverlink Resorts Ltd v MS First Capital Insurance Ltd*, the general conditions of the policy provided for mediation, arbitration and litigation in Singapore courts.[180] Clause 11, which was the arbitration clause, expressly applied to disputes arising out of or in connection with the policy not settled by Clause 10 (the mediation clause).[181] Meanwhile, the Choice-of-Forum clause applies to 'any dispute … regarding the [policy's] interpretation or … application'.[182] The Singapore High Court held that the parties intended the jurisdiction clause to carve out disputes regarding the policy's interpretation or application from the scope of the arbitration clause.[183]

Another approach is to determine whether one mode of dispute resolution has superseded the other. In *Bond Tak (Holdings) Ltd v King Fame Trading Ltd*, the Hong Kong CFI found that the Choice-of-Forum clause had superseded the arbitration agreement.[184] The Court emphasised that the party seeking to stay proceedings under a non-exclusive Choice-of-Forum clause choosing Hong Kong courts (ie, the defendant) must prove that the arbitration agreement remains valid and binding.[185] In this case, the defendant failed to do so, especially given the clear language of the Choice-of-Forum clause.[186]

A third approach, mentioned in *CPC Construction*[187] and citing *Fiona Trust & Holding Corporation v Privalov*,[188] ('*Fiona Trust*') emphasises unifying all dispute resolution in one jurisdiction.[189] The Hong Kong CFI said: 'commercially minded parties are likely to want all disputes arising from their relationship to be decided by the same tribunal and will want to avoid different disputes being resolved by different tribunal or courts'.[190] While *CPC Construction* did not reject this approach, the Court did, however, decide to proceed based on the clear terms agreed by the parties.[191]

In *Oei Hong Leong v Goldman Sachs International*, the Singapore High Court, though not citing *Fiona Trust*, emphasised that 'fragmentation [of related proceedings] … in multiple jurisdictions is undesirable and could not have been reasonably intended by the parties'.[192] Favouring arbitration, the Court reconciled conflicting Choice-of-Forum and arbitration clauses in the ISDA Agreement and the Account Agreement Pack respectively, stating that a stay should only be refused if it is clear that the 'whole or part of the dispute … should

[178] ibid.
[179] ibid.
[180] *Silverlink Resorts Ltd v MS First Capital Insurance Ltd* [2021] 3 SGHC 251, [16].
[181] ibid [18].
[182] ibid.
[183] ibid [55].
[184] *Bond Tak (Holdings) Ltd v King Fame Trading Ltd* [2020] HKCFI 1509, [24].
[185] ibid [26].
[186] ibid [25].
[187] *CPC Construction* (n 160).
[188] *Fiona Trust & Holding Corporation v Privalov* [2008] 1 Lloyd's Rep 254, [12]–[13], [31].
[189] *CPC Construction* (n 160) [55]; see also *Gurkhas Construction Ltd v Craft Façade Tech (Hong Kong) Co Ltd (Formerly known as Eft-Craft Co Ltd)* [2021] HKDC 1166, [34]–[36].
[190] *CPC Construction* (n 160) [55].
[191] ibid [61].
[192] *Oei Hong Leong v Goldman Sachs International* [2014] SGHCR 2, [28].

not be subject to the arbitration agreement'.[193] Since the parties did not clearly intend for the English non-exclusive Choice-of-Forum clause in the ISDA Agreement to apply over the arbitration agreement in the Account Agreement Pack, a stay was granted in favour of arbitration.[194]

The presumption in *Fiona Trust* that disputes should be resolved in one venue may not apply if the disputes involve multiple contracts containing different dispute resolution clauses, or 'when certain disputes have explicitly been excluded', or when 'the parties did not intend to have all their disputes resolved by one tribunal, but to have them determined separately'.[195]

(iii) Which Prevails: Choice-of-Forum Clauses v Arbitration Agreements?

When a contract stipulates both arbitration and litigation, courts must decide which prevails and whether such a clause is void for uncertainty. In *William Co v Chu Kong Agency Ltd*[196] ('*William Co*'), the Hong Kong High Court rejected the idea that such clauses are void, emphasising the need to interpret the contract and give effect to the clause.[197] If both litigation and arbitration are provided, parties can choose either, but once a choice is made, it becomes binding.[198] In this case, the Court treated the application for stay under the Arbitration Model Law as an election for arbitration in China,[199] staying the Hong Kong proceedings accordingly.[200]

In *Lee Cheong Construction & Building Materials Ltd v The Incorporated Owners of the Arcadia*,[201] the Hong Kong CFI ruled that a Choice-of-Forum clause does not create an obligation to resolve disputes exclusively in Hong Kong,[202] noting that both Choice-of-Forum and arbitration clauses 'have different purposes and run in parallel in the context of the whole contract'.[203] Similarly, in *PT Tri-MG Intra Asia Airlines v Norse Air Charter Limited*, the Singapore High Court found that the contract did not allow parties to choose between arbitration and litigation.[204] Rather, the arbitration clause referred 'all disputes' to arbitration, while the litigation clause pertained only to the supervisory jurisdiction of the Singapore courts over arbitration.[205]

In *R Kathiravelu a/l Ramasamy v American Home Assurance Co Malaysia*, the Malaysia Court of Appeal emphasised that both arbitration and litigation clauses in the insurance contract could be harmonised.[206] Clause 10 required any 'dispute, difference or question' to

[193] ibid [21].
[194] ibid [27]–[29].
[195] *H v G* [2022] HKCFI 1327, [18], [21].
[196] *William Co v Chu Kong Agency Ltd* [1993] 2 HKC 377 (HC) ('*William Co*').
[197] ibid 380–81.
[198] ibid 381; see also *Syarikat Pembinaan Anggerik Sdn Bhd v Malaysia Airports Holdings Bhd* (Unreported, HC Shah Alam, See Mee Chun J, 20 November 2017) [13].
[199] *William Co* (n 196) 381.
[200] ibid.
[201] *Lee Cheong Construction & Building Materials Ltd v The Incorporated Owners of the Arcadia* [2012] HKCFI 473.
[202] ibid [13].
[203] ibid [21].
[204] *PT Tri-MG Intra Asia Airlines v Norse Air Charter Limited* [2009] SGHC 13, [47].
[205] ibid [47], [67].
[206] *R Kathiravelu a/l Ramasamy v American Home Assurance Co Malaysia* [2009] 1 MLJ 572, 578 (CA Putra Jaya).

be resolved through arbitration, and 'since the respondent had rejected the claim followed by the disagreement by the appellant', such conditions 'were fulfilled [and] then arbitration should proceed'.[207] Clause 17 gave the Malaysian courts jurisdiction only for contract interpretation.[208] Similarly, in *Allianz General Insurance Company (M) Bhd v Kapar Energy Ventures Sdn Bhd*, the Malaysia High Court emphasised that only disputes over the amount payable under the insurance policy should be resolved by arbitration, while non-monetary disputes should go to litigation.[209]

This discussion on Choice-of-Forum and arbitration clauses highlights the unique contractual nature of Choice-of-Forum clauses in Singapore, Hong Kong and Malaysia. Unlike other contracts, including arbitration agreements, Choice-of-Forum clauses are not fully governed by contract law. Questions about how parties can control dispute resolution, how contract law determine the interpretation of conflicting provisions, and which issues are contractual, may also be determined by procedural law and other areas of law.

C. The Philippines

Philippine law distinguishes between arbitration agreements and Choice-of-Forum clauses, with both governed under separate legal regimes. The Alternative Dispute Resolution Act of 2004 (Republic Act No 9285) applies to arbitration clauses and recognises their contractual character.[210] Being procedural in nature, Choice-of-Forum clauses are governed by the Rules of Court. Philippine courts have yet to address how contracts containing both arbitration and Choice-of-Forum clauses, or dispute resolution clauses referring disputes to both, would be resolved or interpreted.

D. China, Indonesia and Japan

In China, arbitration agreements are governed by the Arbitration Law of the People's Republic of China ('PRC Arbitration Law') while the Chinese Civil Procedure Law ('CCPL') applies to Choice-of-Forum clauses. Article 5 of the PRC Arbitration Law prevents courts from accepting the case if an arbitration agreement exists unless it is null and void. Similarly, article 288 of the CCPL precludes parties from commencing litigation if there is an arbitration agreement.[211] In contrast, article 277 of the CCPL uses the permissive 'may have jurisdiction'. Hence, the non-exercise of jurisdiction is mandatory when there is a valid arbitration agreement, while the people's court may still exercise its discretion in assuming jurisdiction pursuant to a Choice-of-Forum clause. Hence, it appears that arbitration agreements may take precedence over Choice-of-Forum clauses.

[207] ibid 578–79.
[208] ibid 578.
[209] *Allianz General Insurance Company (M) Bhd v Kapar Energy Ventures Sdn Bhd* (Unreported, HC Kuala Lumpur, Noorin Badaruddin JC, 27 October 2016) [129], [176].
[210] Alternative Dispute Resolution Act (Philippines), s 7(1); see also See *Korea Technologies Co, Ltd v Lerma* (2008) 542 SCRA 1, 21–22.
[211] Civil Procedure Law of the People's Republic of China (中华人民共和国民事诉讼法) 2011 (adopted 19 April 1991, amended 2023) National People's Congress Order No 44 of the President art 288.

In Indonesia, arbitration agreements are governed by the Arbitration Act 1999, while Choice-of-Forum clauses are subject to procedural rules from the Dutch colonial-era codes of civil procedure. Article 3 of the Arbitration Act 1999 states that district courts lack jurisdiction over disputes involving parties bound by an arbitration agreement. Given that the principle of *actor sequitur forum rei* ('the plaintiff must sue in the proper forum') can supersede Choice-of-Forum clauses, which is discussed in detail in Chapter eight, the effect of article 3 of the Arbitration Act 1999 is to establish a preference towards arbitration agreements whenever the contract contains provision for both arbitration and local litigation.

In Japan, arbitration is governed by the Arbitration Act[212] ('JAA'), while Choice-of-Forum clauses in both domestic[213] and international[214] matters are governed by the Japanese Code of Civil Procedure ('JCCP'). Under the JAA, an arbitral tribunal has exclusive competence in disputes where an arbitration agreement exists,[215] and courts can only intervene if arbitration cannot proceed.[216] For a Choice-of-Forum clause choosing the Japanese courts in 'international' disputes, Japanese courts apply the 'special circumstances test' under article 3-9 JCCP, unless the choice is exclusive. Hence, when a contract contains both an arbitration clause and an exclusive Choice-of-Forum clause in favour of Japanese courts, which one prevails is not clear. Arguably, the arbitration agreement prevails due to the JAA's presumption of tribunals' exclusive competency and Japan's obligations under the New York Convention. For non-exclusive clauses, the Japanese court may dismiss the case in favour of arbitration using the 'special circumstances test'.

V. Third Parties and Choice-of-Forum Clauses

Privity, the principle that contracts bind only their parties,[217] is key in Choice-of-Forum clause analysis in Hong Kong and the Philippines. This should also apply in Singapore and Malaysia, where such clauses are recognised as contracts. In civil law countries, though procedural, Choice-of-Forum clauses are enforced based on consent, binding only the parties unless administration-of-justice-related reasons justify their application to non-parties.

A. The General Rule

In *The Griesheim*,[218] the Hong Kong High Court ruled that a non-party to the bill of lading could not benefit from the Choice-of-Forum clause.[219] Likewise, in *The Mahkutai*,[220] the Hong Kong Court of Appeal held that only parties to the contract can validly invoke

[212] Arbitration Act (仲裁法 平成十五年八月一日法律第百三十八号) Act No 138 of 2003 (Japan) [tr Ministry of Justice: https://www.japaneselawtranslation.go.jp/en/laws/view/4440].
[213] Code of Civil Procedure (民事訴訟法 平成八年六月二十六日法律第百九号) Act No 109 of 1996 (Japan) [tr Ministry of Justice: https://www.japaneselawtranslation.go.jp/en/laws/view/2053].
[214] ibid art 3-7.
[215] JAA (n 212) art 14(1).
[216] ibid.
[217] *Dunlop Pneumatic Tyre v Selfridge and Co Ltd* [1915] AC 847.
[218] *The Griesheim* [1983] 1 HKC 251 (HC).
[219] ibid 273.
[220] *The Mahkutai* [1993] 2 HKC 71 (CA).

its Choice-of-Forum clause.[221] Since the bill of lading which provided for Jakarta in the Choice-of-Forum Clause did not include the shipowners as parties, but only the time charterers, the shipowners could not benefit from the clause and ask for a stay of the Hong Kong proceedings filed by the cargo owners.[222] Notably, the Privy Council upheld this decision,[223] emphasising that non-parties must prove their right to benefit under the law applicable to the contract.[224] Hence, in *Joseph Ghossoub v Team Y&R Holdings Hong Kong Ltd* ('*Ghossoub*'), the Hong Kong Court of Appeal precluded a defendant from invoking the exclusive clause after failing to prove that under Indian law, the contract to which he was a party and another contract in which the exclusive clause was found but to which he was a non-party, constituted one agreement.[225]

Similarly, the Philippine Supreme Court in *KK Shell Sekiyu Osaka Hatsubaisho v Court of Appeals*[226] decided that a third party to the Choice-of-Forum clauses cannot be bound, including sub-agents unless expressly stated.[227] This rule has also been confirmed in the related case *Keihin Narasaki Corporation v Crystal Navigation.*[228]

Consequently, a Choice-of-Forum clause does not prevent a party from suing non-parties in a different jurisdiction. In *Ghossoub*,[229] the Hong Kong CFI ruled that since the respondents were not parties to the share purchase agreement specifying England as the forum, the plaintiffs could sue them in Hong Kong.[230] When third parties are joined and a stay is reversed, these third parties may be compensated for expenses and inconvenience.[231]

B. Exceptions

Courts may extend the effect of Choice-of-Forum clauses through principles such as agency, incorporation by reference, assignment, novation, estoppel, waiver, succession, subrogation, alter ego, veil piercing, trust and equity.[232] Hence, in *Pemilik Kapal Atau Vesel 'Lavela' v Pemilik Kapal Atau Vesel 'Basilia'*, since the 'Letter of Understanding' ('LOU') which contained the exclusive Choice-of-Forum clause stipulating the English courts was signed by the parties' agents, the defendant, while not a party to the LOU, should be entitled to stay the Malaysian proceedings.[233] Moreover, a beneficiary who wishes to take advantage of a trust can be expected to accept that he is bound by the terms of the trust, including its Choice-of-Forum clause. However, since the plaintiffs in *China Shanshui Investment Co*

[221] ibid 83–85.
[222] ibid.
[223] *The Mahkutai* [1996] AC 650, 666–68.
[224] See *Joseph Ghossoub v Team Y&R Holdings Hong Kong Ltd* [2017] HKCA 603, [22].
[225] ibid [34].
[226] *KK Shell Sekiyu Osaka Hatsubaisho v Court of Appeals* (1990) 188 SCRA 145 ('*KK Shell*').
[227] ibid 151–52.
[228] *Keihin Narasaki Corporation v Crystal Navigation, Kumagai Kaiun Kaisha, Ltd v Atlantic Venus Co* (1990) 193 SCRA 484, 492.
[229] *Ghossoub* [2016] HKCFI 1019.
[230] ibid [46]–[47], [51], [63]–[67].
[231] *Ghossoub* [2016] HKCFI 1793, [27].
[232] Vaughan Black and Stephen Pitel, 'Forum-selection clauses: beyond the contracting parties' (2016) 12(1) *Journal of Private International Law* 26, 29.
[233] *Pemilik Kapal Atau Vesel 'Lavela' v Pemilik Kapal Atau Vesel 'Basilia'* (Unreported, HC Johor Bahru, Mohd Ivan JC, 31 October 2018) [19]–[41].

Ltd as entrusted by Zhang Caikui v Zhang Caikui,[234] were not seeking to enforce any rights or obligations under the trusts,[235] they could not be forced to litigate in the British Virgin Islands ('BVI') pursuant to the BVI trusts' Choice-of-Forum clauses.[236]

Singapore's accession to the Choice-of-Court Convention and the establishment of the Singapore International Commercial Court ('SICC') provide additional exceptions for joining third parties in Choice-of-Forum clause litigation. Under the Choice-of-Court Convention, third parties may have standing to bring proceedings if they assume the rights and obligations of the original parties.[237] In addition, the SICC can join third parties if the joinder rules under the SICC Rules of Court are satisfied and if the claims are suitable for the SICC to hear.[238]

Significantly, Hong Kong and Singapore have enacted legislation[239] similar to the UK's Contracts (Rights of Third Parties) Act 1999,[240] thus creating additional exceptions to the privity rule. In Hong Kong, when expressly stated, third parties can invoke exclusive Choice-of-Forum clauses[241] provided that (1) the clause is exclusive, (2) the clause expressly states that third parties can benefit, (3) the third party is identified or part of an identified class of persons, and (4) the dispute involves a contract term.[242] While the Singaporean statute does not explicitly deal with Choice-of-Forum clauses,[243] it may apply similarly to exclusive Choice-of-Forum clauses, as assumed under English law.[244]

In the Philippines, *KK Shell Sekiyu Osaka Hatsubaisho v Court of Appeals*[245] confirmed that third parties may benefit from Choice-of-Forum clauses if expressly stated.[246] Notably, the Philippine Civil Code also allows contractual stipulations in favour of a non-party.[247]

A court's interpretation of a Choice-of-Forum clause in litigation involving some of the contracting parties but not all may also bind the other contracting parties and even third parties who are not part of the litigation.[248] Moreover, in the United States and Canada, courts have introduced other exceptions allowing Choice-of-Forum clauses to apply beyond the contracting parties,[249] such as third-party beneficiaries, parties to a 'global transaction', and 'closely related' non-parties 'so that enforcement of the clause is foreseeable by virtue of the relationship between them'.[250] While these exceptions have not been adopted in the Asian jurisdictions examined, they demonstrate that privity is weaker in Choice-of-Forum clauses; as Black and Pitel argued, 'public concerns, such as efficient use of court resources and the legitimate exercise of adjudicatory jurisdictions, are stronger'.[251]

[234] *China Shanshui Investment Co Ltd as entrusted by Zhang Caikui v Zhang Caikui* [2015] HKCFI 780.
[235] ibid [104].
[236] ibid [110].
[237] Trevor Hartley and Masato Dogauchi, *Explanatory Report on the Convention of 30 June 2005 on Choice of Courts Agreements*, ed Permanent Bureau (Hague Conference on Private International Law, 2013) 51.
[238] Singapore International Commercial Court Rules of Court 2021 (Singapore, 2021) ord 10, r 10.
[239] Contracts (Rights of Third Parties) Ordinance (Hong Kong) cap 623; Contracts (Rights of Third Parties) Act 2001 (Singapore, cap 53B, 2020 rev edn).
[240] Contracts (Rights of Third Parties) Act 1999 (UK).
[241] Contracts (Rights of Third Parties) Ordinance (Hong Kong) cap 623, s 13(2).
[242] ibid ss 13(3), (4).
[243] Contracts (Rights of Third Parties) Act 1999 (Singapore, cap 53B, 2020 rev edn).
[244] Explanatory Notes to Contracts (Rights of Third Parties) Act 1999, [32].
[245] *KK Shell* (n 226).
[246] ibid 151–52.
[247] Civil Code (Philippines), art 1311.
[248] Black and Pitel (n 232) 29.
[249] ibid 26.
[250] *Freeford Ltd v Pendleton*, 53 AD 3d 32, 38–39 (NY App Div, 2008).
[251] ibid 52.

In litigation involving third parties, courts may apply different tests – applying the 'strong cause' test to the contracting parties to an exclusive Choice-of-Forum clause, and *forum non conveniens* for the non-contracting parties. This can lead to odd results, especially if the Choice-of-Forum clause is the only connection to the forum. Hence, including third parties adds procedural complexity and may introduce public interest concerns, extending the analysis beyond contract law.

C. China, Indonesia and Japan

In civil law jurisdictions, the Choice-of-Forum clause's procedural nature and its purpose as an administration of justice tool may lead to a more liberal approach to joining third parties in disputes. Courts may allow joinder when necessary to fully resolve the case, but if third parties use a foreign Choice-of-Forum clause to avoid the local jurisdiction, this defence may be dismissed due to lack of consent to submit to the foreign forum. Similarly, a plaintiff who has no other basis for invoking the local court's jurisdiction but a Choice-of-Forum clause to which he is not a party, may not be allowed to proceed with his claim. Like in common law jurisdictions, consent is a foundational requirement for enforcing Choice-of-Forum clauses in civil law jurisdictions.

In Japan, the effects of the Choice-of-Forum clause generally apply only to signatories. In *X KK v Y, Inc*,[252] the Tokyo District Court ruled that a Choice-of-Forum clause in the memorandum of understanding (MOU) signed by the subsidiary did not bind the Californian mother company,[253] as there was no evidence that the subsidiary acted as an agent. In contrast, in *Hiyoki KK v Codif International SAS*,[254] ('*Hiyoki*') the Tokyo District Court dismissed the proceedings based on the Choice-of-Forum clauses in favour of Saint-Malo Commercial Court in France, even though two joined defendants were not contracting parties, as the joint tort claims against them in the Japanese proceedings appear to be unmeritorious.

VI. Choice-of-Forum Clauses and Other Contractual Provisions

A. Singapore, Hong Kong, Malaysia and the Philippines

Choice-of-Forum clauses often function within a larger contract or group of interrelated agreements, and other contractual provisions can affect their operation. Conditions precedent, interpretation clause, limitations on liability, waivers, and other procedural clauses may impact their operation. In *Rich Village Ltd v Grand Pride Holdings Ltd*[255] ('*Rich Village*'),

[252] *X KK v Y, Inc*, Tokyo District Court, Case (wa) No 31124(2008), 17 November 2009 [tr John Ribeiro (2011) 54 *Japanese Yearbook of International Law* 536].

[253] ibid 537.

[254] *Hiyoki KK v Codif International SAS*, Tokyo District Court, Judgment No HT (1276) 332 [2008], 11 April 2008 [tr Michael Kuzma (2009) 52 *Japanese Yearbook of International Law* 688].

[255] *Rich Village Ltd v Grand Pride Holdings Ltd* [2013] HKCA 33.

the Hong Kong Court of Appeal emphasised that the 'true meaning [of a Choice-of-Forum clause] has to be discovered by looking at the agreement as a whole in the light of the relevant factual matrix'.[256] Hence, while the separability principle applies to Choice-of-Forum clauses, they must be read in connection with other contract provisions.

An important provision affecting Choice-of-Forum clauses is the Choice-of-Law clause, as explored in Chapter seven. In *Rich Village*, the Hong Kong CFI emphasised that Choice-of-Forum and Choice-of-Law clauses go hand-in-hand,[257] meaning issues like validity, interpretation and even the existence of the forum clause are often determined by the law stated in a Choice-of-Law clause.

A Choice-of-Law clause does not imply that the jurisdiction identified is also the chosen forum for disputes. In short, a choice of law is not a choice of forum. In *Raytheon International Inc v Rouzie*, the Philippine Supreme Court clarified that jurisdiction and choice of law are distinct concepts.[258] Similarly, Hook also criticised some common law courts for assuming jurisdiction based on the law chosen,[259] arguing that this practice undermines conflict of laws principles,[260] and the parties' freedom to choose their forum.[261]

Choice-of-Forum clauses may include conditions precedent, requiring certain steps before litigation can proceed. In *PT Selecta Bestama v Sin Huat Huat Marine Transportation Pte Ltd*[262] ('*PT Selecta*'), the Singapore High Court ruled that a party cannot avoid a Choice-of-Forum clause by breaching the conditions precedent.[263] The Court held that a plaintiff's failure to attempt mandatory negotiation did not prevent the defendant from relying on the Choice-of-Forum clause,[264] emphasising that a party cannot benefit from its own breach.[265]

A unique feature of Choice-of-Forum clauses is the principle of separability, meaning that challenging the validity of the contract does not automatically invalidate the Choice-of-Forum clause.[266] This principle, discussed in detail in Chapter six, ensures that the Choice-of-Forum clause remains unaffected even if the underlying contract's validity is disputed.[267]

B. China, Indonesia and Japan

In civil law jurisdictions like China, Indonesia and Japan, the Choice-of-Forum clause is also seen as necessarily closely related to the main contract. For example, the contents of the main contract determine whether parties can enforce their Choice-of-Forum clause.

[256] ibid [16].
[257] ibid.
[258] *Raytheon International Inc v Rouzie* (2008) 546 SCRA 555, 563.
[259] Maria Hook, 'The Choice of Law Agreement as a Reason for Exercising Jurisdiction' (2014) 63(4) *International and Comparative Law Quarterly* 963, 964.
[260] ibid.
[261] ibid.
[262] *PT Selecta Bestama v Sin Huat Huat Marine Transportation Pte Ltd* [2016] 1 SLR 729 (HC).
[263] ibid 740–41.
[264] ibid 741.
[265] ibid.
[266] ibid 743.
[267] ibid.

In Japan, courts may alter the effects of the Choice-of-Forum clause in contracts classified as consumer or employment contracts. In China, exclusive jurisdiction rules may depend on the main contract's contents. Similarly, in Indonesia, if the main contract is governed by the Sharia Banking Act, religious courts may exercise jurisdiction despite the Choice-of-Forum clause.

Further, because Choice-of-Forum clauses are generally treated as procedural in nature, the forum law may apply even if the main contract is governed by a different law (ie, the law applicable to the contract). However, the applicable forum law is not limited to procedural laws. In China, for example, the Chinese Civil Code may be used to interpret Choice-of-Forum clauses.

The separability principle is also recognised. In China, Choice-of-Forum clauses are generally considered separate from the main contract,[268] and thus their validity is independently determined from the rest of the contract.[269]

[268] Civil Code of the People's Republic of China (中华人民共和国民法典) 2020 (adopted 28 May 2020) National People's Congress Order No 45 of the President art 507; also Contract Law of the People's Republic of China (中华人民共和国合同法) 1999 (adopted 15 March 1999) National People's Congress Order No 15 of the President art 57.

[269] *Shandong Jufeng Network Co, Ltd v Mgame Co, Ltd of Korea and Tianjin Fengyun Network Technology Co, Ltd – A case about a challenge to jurisdiction over disputes arising from an online game distribution and licence agreement* (山东聚丰网络有限公司与韩国MGAME公司、天津风云网络技术有限公司网络游戏代理及许可合同纠纷管辖权异议案) [2010] 3 *Gazette of the Supreme People's Court of the People's Republic of China*.

3

Party Autonomy and Choice-of-Forum Clauses

I. Introduction

In cross-border disputes, the absence of an international sovereign enforcing rules and imposing sanctions emphasises the reliance on consensual relationships.[1] 'Indeed, consent to jurisdiction is and must be the keystone of international dispute resolution'.[2] Litigation involving Choice-of-Forum clauses usually involves two forms of consent: first, the bilateral exercise of party autonomy to select a forum in advance;[3] and second, consent expressed through participation in litigation.[4] These forms of consent reflect the relationships between the courts and the parties, and between the parties themselves.

This chapter explores party autonomy through the two forms of consent mentioned. First, it provides an overview of party autonomy in civil procedure, then examines the freedom of parties to determine the contents of their Choice-of-Forum clause. It then probes the second form of consent, which is the parties' freedom to control litigation. The chapter also considers the ouster rule, as an illustration of the struggle between party autonomy and other interests which may play a role in court analysis. Finally, the chapter analyses how the Choice-of-Court Convention enshrines party autonomy globally, before summarising key lessons.

II. The Principle of Party Autonomy in Civil Litigation

A. Developments in Civil Law and Common Law Procedures

Party consent as a basis of jurisdiction precedes the concept of state itself. In ancient Roman law, where a cause fell outside the court's territorial or subject-matter jurisdiction, the court could assume jurisdiction if the parties consented.[5] This consent was deemed to exist when,

[1] See Linda Mullenix, 'Another Choice of Forum, Another Choice of Law: Consensual Adjudicatory Procedure in Federal Court' (1988) 57(3) *Fordham Law Review* 291, 314.

[2] ibid.

[3] Arthur von Mehren, *Adjudicatory Authority in Private International Law: A Comparative Study* (Brill Academic Publishers, 2006)176.

[4] See ibid.

[5] Arthur Engelmann, *A History of Continental Civil Procedure* (tr Robert Wyness Millar, Little Brown & Co, 1927) 334.

with the parties being aware of the lack of jurisdiction, *litiscontestation* (ie, matters in dispute were prepared for the investigation of the *judex* or the judiciary) had occurred without their objection.[6] These early Roman law concepts laid the foundations for the modern principle of party autonomy in civil procedure.

The concept of *prorogatio fori* or *forum prorogatum* (stipulation of a forum) originated in canon law.[7] This canonical procedural rule explicitly allowed parties to choose a forum for their dispute.[8] Secular courts would later adopt this rule as part of their attempt to increase revenues related to court litigation.[9] Significantly, during this period, the principles prevailing in the civil procedures following the Romano-Canonical framework were described as supporting procedural party autonomy in a broader sense.[10] These procedures 'stayed loyal to the principle that the scope and content of the judicial controversy was to be defined by the parties or, conversely that the court was restricted to a consideration of what the parties had put before it'.[11] Moreover, parties had 'full control over [their] substantive and procedural rights and … [enjoy] the power of free choice in the exercise of these rights'.[12]

When Europe's procedural codes were drafted, they preserved the parties' freedom in controlling their litigation,[13] including the freedom to choose a forum.[14] This ensured that party autonomy remained central to continental civil procedures.[15] Even after reforms were implemented, brought about by the ideas of Frank Klein who advocated for stronger roles for judges, party autonomy remained a fundamental principle.[16]

Unlike continental procedures, English civil procedure evolved through 'silent development of traditional practice and conventions',[17] rather than through codified rules. Its adversarial system exemplifies party autonomy, especially since the 'English civil litigation has always been regarded as a predominantly voluntary system'.[18] Hence, parties can freely formulate and develop the demand for a remedy, present factual and legal issues for

[6] ibid 334.

[7] Arthur Lenhoff, 'The Parties' Choice of a Forum: "Prorogation Agreements"' (1961) 15(3) *Rutgers Law Review* 414, 415–16.

[8] ibid 416.

[9] See CH van Rhee, 'Harmonisation of Civil Procedure: An Historic and Comparative Perspective' in XE Kramer and CH van Rhee (eds), *Civil Litigation in a Globalising World* (Asser Press, 2012) 39, 47.

[10] RC van Caenegem, 'History of European Civil Procedure' in Mauro Cappelletti (ed), *Civil Procedure, International Encyclopedia of Comparative law Vol XVI* (Mohr Siebeck & Martinus Nijhoff Publishers, 2014) 14.

[11] ibid 14.

[12] ibid.

[13] See ibid.

[14] See Sienho Yee, *Towards an International Law of Co-progressiveness* (Martinus Nijhoff Publishers, 2004) 88; Shabtai Rosenne, ed Malcolm Shaw, *Rosenne's Law and Practice of the International Court: 1920–2015* (Brill Nijhoff, 5th edn, 2016) vol 2, [181]; Sienho Yee, 'Article 40' in Andreas Zimmermann, Christian Tomuschat, Karin Oellers-Frahm and Christian Tams (eds), *The Statute of the International Court of Justice: A Commentary* (Oxford University Press, 2nd edn, 2012) 920, 985; Shabtai Rosenne, 'The Forum Prorogatum in the International Court of Justice' (1953) 6(1) *Revue Hellenique de Droit International* 1, 1–2.

[15] See CH van Rhee, 'Introduction' in CH van Rhee (ed), *European Traditions in Civil Procedure* (Intersentia, 2005) 3, 6.

[16] See Paul Oberhammer and T Domej, 'Germany, Switzerland, Austria (circa 1800–2005)' in CH van Rhee (ed), *European Traditions in Civil Procedure* (Intersentia, 2005) 103, 121; Paul Oberhammer, 'Party Autonomy and Procedural Law: A Few Comments from an Austrian Perspective' in Mattias Dahlberg (ed), *Party Autonomy – Civil Procedural Views on Party Autonomy, Franz Klein, EU Law and more* (Iustus Förlag, 2011) 51, 52–55.

[17] CH van Rhee, 'English Civil Procedure until the Civil Procedure Rules (1998)' in CH van Rhee (ed), *European Traditions in Civil Procedure* (Intersentia, 2005) 129, 132.

[18] Cyril Glasser, 'Civil Procedure and the Lawyers: The Adversary System and the Decline of the Orality Principle' (1993) 56(3) *The Modern Law Review* 307, 307.

determination by the court, bargain for settlement and withdraw the case at any stage prior to judgment.[19] Furthermore, the defendant's consent is key to jurisdiction, as jurisdiction depends, as Briggs succinctly states, upon the service of process.[20] A defendant who submits to the jurisdiction of the court confirms the court's jurisdiction over him.[21]

In the United States, Brand notes that party autonomy in forum selection was recognised early in the First Restatement on Conflict of Laws,[22] which allowed courts to acquire jurisdiction over individuals and foreign corporations by consent.[23] Initially, this applied only to prorogation. The acceptance of Choice-of-Forum clauses as having derogation effects came later, following *The Bremen*.

Despite a system promoting party autonomy, common law courts were long reluctant to accept Choice-of-Forum clauses with derogatory effects. English and American courts maintained that parties cannot 'oust' their jurisdiction, although admiralty courts, with their unique concerns (eg, high mobility of parties with high possibility of evasion of suit), were an exception.[24] Furthermore, English courts were slower to accept such clauses, because English procedure was not fashioned after the Romano-Canonical procedure. Particularly, the rule on *prorogatio fori* is not an expressly incorporated mechanism in the common law rules as England developed a modern, centralised and professional judicature at a very early date, and worked much with native elements even before the Romano-Canonical procedure had taken a definite shape.[25] Moreover, English courts would normally consider Choice-of-Forum clauses in the context of proceedings to stay actions brought in contravention of the provisions of such agreements,[26] applications for leave to serve process out of jurisdiction,[27] and anti-suit injunctions. Since these forms of relief are granted in the exercise of the court's discretion,[28] the English recognition of Choice-of-Forum clauses was also discretionary and, thus, their acceptability took a longer time to develop. Notably, without a clear statutory or common law basis, judges could not rely on a procedural rule like that in continental Europe.

B. The Content and Scope of Party Autonomy

The modern principle of procedural party autonomy gives parties significant control over their litigation, including the choice of forum. In civil law countries, this autonomy is defined by public law and procedural law. The French model is an exception, as the freedom

[19] ibid.

[20] Adrian Briggs, *Civil Jurisdiction and Judgments* (Informa Law, 6th edn, 2015) 380.

[21] ibid.

[22] Ronald Brand, *Transaction Planning Using Rules on Jurisdiction and the Recognition and Enforcement of Judgments* (Hague Academy of International Law, 2014) 195–96.

[23] American Law Institute, Restatement (First) of Conflict of Laws (1933) §§ 81, 88.

[24] David Marcus, 'The Perils of Contractual Procedure: A Revised History of Forum Selection Clauses in the Federal Courts' (2008) 82(3) *Tulane Law Review* 973, 997.

[25] RC van Caenegem, 'History of European Civil Procedure' in Mauro Cappeloleti (ed), *Civil Procedure, International Encyclopedia of Comparative law Vol XVI* (Mohr Siebeck & Martinus Nijhoff Publishers, 2014) 14, 15.

[26] Zelman Cowen and Derek Mendes Da Costa, 'The Contractual Forum: Situation in England and the British Commonwealth' (1964) 13(1) *American Journal of Comparative Law* 179, 180.

[27] ibid.

[28] ibid.

to designate a forum, when exercised in the international sense, is considered a private law matter.[29] In contrast, common law countries view important aspects of party autonomy in Choice-of-Forum clauses as matters of 'private law of contractual promises'.[30]

The scope and content of party autonomy in civil procedure mirror the changing preferences between state regulation (state planning) and party autonomy. Von Mehren noted that since the industrial revolution, 'blends or mixtures of central planning and private autonomy have dominated the theory and practice of social and economic ordering'.[31] In state-controlled societies, like the former Soviet Union, parties had little control over the identity of and the procedures used by the adjudicating authority,[32] as plaintiffs were not free to withdraw suits, defendants could not concede, and the parties could not settle if to do so would, in the court's opinion, violate the law or any person's rights or legally protected interest.[33] In Western countries, private parties remain largely free to dispose by agreement of contested substantive rights; albeit less free to control the manner in which the proceedings will unfold.[34] This balance between state regulation or planning and party autonomy, nonetheless, has continually shifted over the years.

Recent developments in civil procedure for commercial disputes show the growing influence of party autonomy. Procedural flexibility is being promoted especially in commercial courts[35] like the Commercial Court in London[36] which introduced flexible procedures (eg, the UK's Flexible Trial Procedure[37]) to make business litigation cheaper and simpler,[38] improve competitiveness and attract more investments and disputes to those courts.[39] Moreover, countries like Ireland[40] and Singapore[41] now allow litigants to choose alternative procedural rules as regards certain aspects of their case, while Sweden permits modifications to judicial relief to suit the parties' business interests.[42]

The evolution of party autonomy in contracts also reflects the shifting balance between state regulation and party autonomy. While laissez-faire initially dominated, the late twentieth century saw states narrowing party autonomy to protect weaker parties, such as consumers and employees, and expanding state regulations like anti-trust legislation.[43]

[29] Lenhoff (n 7) 440.

[30] See Louise Merrett, 'Interpreting non-exclusive jurisdiction agreements' (2018) 14(1) *Journal of Private International Law* 38, 39.

[31] von Mehren (n 3) 207.

[32] ibid 209.

[33] ibid.

[34] ibid 210.

[35] See Shelby Gribbs and Peter North, *International Civil Procedure* (Kluwer Law, 2003) 183; Man Yip, 'The Resolution of Disputes Before the Singapore International Commercial Court' (2016) 65(2) *International and Comparative Law Quarterly* 439,445.

[36] UK Government, 'Commercial Court' (webpage): https://www.gov.uk/courts-tribunals/commercial-court#:~:text=Who%20we%20are,in%20the%20City%20of%20London. (accessed 28 October 2024).

[37] See Judiciary of the United Kingdom, 'Shorter and Flexible Trial Procedures Pilot Schemes' (Web Page, October 2015): https://www.judiciary.gov.uk/wp-content/uploads/2015/09/Shorter-and-Flexible-Trial-Schemes-Announcement.pdf (accessed 28 October 2024).

[38] ibid.

[39] Man Yip (n 35) 444–45.

[40] Cassandra Byrne and Jareth Heneghan, 'New Horizons? Trends Influencing Effective Projects and Construction Dispute Resolution in Ireland' (2011) 6(2) *Construction Law International* 9, 10.

[41] Man Yip (n 35) 439, 445.

[42] Laura Ervo and Anna Nylund (eds) *Current Trends in Preparatory Proceedings: A Comparative Study of Nordic and Former Communist Parties* (Springer, 2016) 53.

[43] See von Mehren (n 3) 211–12.

Nonetheless, party autonomy remains the primary principle in business-to-business contracts.

The debates on classifying Choice-of-Forum clauses therefore highlight the tension between state regulation and party autonomy. Classifying them as public or procedural law subjects them to greater state control. On the other hand, classifying them as contractual strengthens party autonomy. However, as earlier discussed, the preferred approach now is not to classify them simply as contractual or procedural but to address Choice-of-Forum clauses on a per issue basis.

While Western liberal philosophies generally support party autonomy, Eastern religions and philosophies do not explicitly endorse it, except in Islam, which recognises the freedom of contract (*hurriyyat al-taaqud*).[44] However, there is no inherent opposition to party autonomy either in Asia's value systems. Confucianism emphasises honouring promises – 'a promise, once made shall worth thousand ounces of gold'[45] and '[t]herefore, a violation of agreement would be deemed as a violation of virtue and moral standard, for which a punishment shall be imposed'.[46] Buddhism, which values personal freedom,[47] may also support party autonomy.

III. The Freedom to Determine the Contents of Choice-of-Forum Clauses

A. The Common Law Freedom of Contract

In common law, Choice-of-Forum clauses are treated as legally enforceable contractual promises which give rise to private law rights.[48] This approach is rooted in the principle of freedom of contract, which allows parties to freely negotiate and agree to any lawful terms to serve their own interests.[49] This means that parties can include in their Choice-of-Forum clauses a wide range of promises, limited only by law. However, this freedom of contract is not absolute, as the extent of this right – what parties can promise to each other which can be legally enforced – is circumscribed by forum law,[50] choice of law rules, mandatory rules and public policy.

What the parties promised each other should be the starting point of the Choice-of-Forum clause analysis. As earlier pointed out, what parties can validly promise depends on the forum's choice of law rules. In common law, the freedom of contract is limited by the law applicable to the contract, the forum's mandatory rules and public policy. The applicable law

[44] See Atikullah Abdullah, 'The Doctrine of the Freedom of Contract *(Hurriyyat al-Taaqud)* in Islamic *Mu'amalat*: An exposition on the concepts and rules of the contract of *muqaqalah* in the construction industry' (2011) 50 *Islamic Studies* 365, 366.

[45] Mo Zhang, *Chinese Contract Law: Theory and Practice* (Martinus Nijhoff Publishers, 2006) 28.

[46] ibid.

[47] See Ian Mabbett, 'Buddhism and Freedom' in David Kelly and Anthony Reid (eds), *Asian Freedoms: The Idea of Freedom in East and Southeast Asia* (Cambridge University Press, 1998) 19.

[48] Merrett (n 30) 39.

[49] See, eg, *Printing and Numerical Registering Co v Sampson* (1875) 19 Eq 462, 465.

[50] Nygh, Peter, *Autonomy in International Contracts* (Clarendon Press, 1999) 37.

also determines interpretation rules, which are crucial in determining the content of the contractual promises contained in the Choice-of-Forum clause.

Merrett explains what promises may be included in Choice-of-Forum clauses. She notes that Choice-of-Forum clauses usually have positive and negative effects.[51] The positive effect (prorogation) is when parties confer jurisdiction on a particular court(s).[52] The negative effect (derogation) is when parties obligate each other not to sue in any other or certain jurisdiction.[53] However, in common law, the enforceability of these promises is a matter determined by the forum's procedural law and not by the parties themselves.[54] Merrett further notes that the difference between exclusive and non-exclusive Choice-of-Forum clauses lies in the interplay between these positive and negative effects.[55] She emphasises, however, that the difference between the two is not as 'clear-cut nor straightforward as a simple binary classification might imply'.[56] She further develops this point:

> Both the positive and negative aspects may confer a measure of discretion or choice. For example, a clause could positively confer jurisdiction on 2 named courts, say France and Germany, and only those courts. Such an agreement is exclusively non-exclusive, conferring a choice but in relation to a limited pool of courts. The obligations may also be different for each party (as in an asymmetric clause). And a party may have promised different things, expressly or impliedly, in different contexts: for example, never to sue anywhere other than England; not to object to English jurisdiction; conceding that England is the appropriate forum; or promising not to start proceedings elsewhere once proceedings have been commenced in England. Furthermore, apparently non-exclusive agreements may also contain express or implied obligations of a negative nature, for example, not to seek an anti-suit injunction from another court.[57]

In short, classifying Choice-of-Forum clauses into either exclusive or non-exclusive oversimplifies the diverse promises parties may have provided. Nonetheless, courts often focus and develop tests in relation to the remedies provided to enforce Choice-of-Forum clauses based on this binary classification rather than interpreting the specific promises made, thus potentially disregarding the principle of freedom of contract. As Merrett points out, this approach risks ignoring the parties' intentions, such as allowing parallel proceedings, which may be disallowed if the court insists on litigation in only one forum.

B. Singapore, Hong Kong and Malaysia

Court decisions from Singapore, Hong Kong and Malaysia rarely address the freedom to determine the contents of Choice-of-Forum clauses directly, probably because it is assumed to be part of the inherent right of freedom of contract. Most cases focus on enforcement where the dispute involves circumstances which can avoid the effects of the Choice-of-Forum

[51] Merrett (n 30) 43.
[52] ibid 43.
[53] ibid 44.
[54] ibid 43.
[55] ibid 44.
[56] ibid.
[57] ibid.

clause, rather than questioning contractual freedom. Although courts do not mention the freedom of contract, they often emphasise that parties should abide by their own agreement or bargain, thus implying its foundational role.

Several decisions in Singapore, Hong Kong and Malaysia confirm the freedom to include diverse promises in Choice-of-Forum clauses, thus reinforcing the freedom of contract principle. In *TMT Co Ltd v The Royal Bank of Scotland plc (trading as RBS Greenwich Futures)* ('*TMT*'), the Singapore High Court upheld freely-negotiated asymmetrical exclusive Choice-of-Forum clauses, stating that such clauses are enforceable even if such a clause operates to benefit only one of the parties.[58] In *Baiduri*, the Singapore High Court recognised the various categories of Choice-of-Forum clauses – exclusive, non-exclusive and 'semi-exclusive' or those Choice-of-Forum clauses where a few countries are specified in the clause.[59] Furthermore, the Singapore High Court also confirmed that other promises may be included, such as a stipulation not to object to the chosen court's jurisdiction in the parties' Choice-of-Forum clause.[60] The Hong Kong Court of Appeal has similarly confirmed the parties' freedom to vary the 'positive' and 'negative' effects of their Choice-of-Forum clauses depending on the court named therein.[61] In *HBZ Finance Ltd v Nippon Yusen Kaisha* ('*HBZ Finance*'), the Hong Kong Court of Appeal allowed a 'floating' Choice-of-Forum clause, which is a clause that allows parties to firm up their choice only at a later stage.[62] The Hong Kong CFI also confirmed in *William Co* that parties can also indicate in their clauses that they can 'choose' between litigation or arbitration.[63] In *American Express Bank Ltd v Mohamed Toufic Al-Ozeir* ('*American Express*'), the Malaysia Supreme Court recognised unilateral asymmetric Choice-of-Forum clauses, which are common in financial contracts.[64]

The law governing the contract, subject to the mandatory rules and public policy of the forum, circumscribes what promises parties can include in Choice-of-Forum clauses (discussed in Chapter seven). Further, in common law, the enforceability of these promises (ie, the actual effects given to promises contained in the Choice-of-Forum clauses) is determined by the forum's procedural laws (discussed in Chapter four).

Considering the significance of Islamic banking and finance in Malaysia, it is important to note that Islamic law, also referred to as *Shariah*, applies to these contracts along with the applicable substantive law.[65] Party autonomy is notably compatible with Islamic law principles; thus, in contracts where Islamic law applies, parties should be free to choose the court which may hear their dispute. Nonetheless, as discussed in Chapter six, Islamic law principles may determine whether the parties' choice may be upheld, as well as any other promises which they may have included in their Choice-of-Forum clause. However, there is no central authority or singular interpretation of Islamic law, and as such, the

[58] *TMT Co Ltd v The Royal Bank of Scotland plc (trading as RBS Greenwich Futures)* [2018] 3 SLR 70, 92 (HC).
[59] *Baiduri Bank Bhd v Dong Sui Hung* [2000] 2 SLR(R) 271 (HC) 276–85.
[60] *OCBC Capital Investment Asia Ltd v Wong Hua Choon* [2010] 4 SLR 904, 908–9 (HC).
[61] *Noble Power Investments Ltd v Nissei Stomach Tokyo Co Ltd* [2008] HKCA 255, [33].
[62] *HBZ Finance Ltd v Nippon Yusen Kaisha* [2002] HKCA 377, [32].
[63] *William Co v Chu Kong Agency Ltd* [1993] 2 HKC 377, 381 (HC).
[64] *American Express Bank Ltd v Mohamed Toufic Al-Ozeir* [1995] 1 MLJ 160, 165–66 (SC Kuala Lumpur).
[65] See *Bank Kerjasama Rakyat Malaysia Bhd v Emcee Corporation Sdn Bhd* [2003] 2 MLJ 408, 408 (CA); Ahmad Hidayat Buang, 'Islamic Contracts in a Secular Court Setting? Lessons from Malaysia' (2007) 21(4) *Arab Law Quarterly* 317, 324.

differences in the understanding and interpretation of Islamic law (expressed through *fatwa* – an authoritative interpretation of Islamic law rules and principles by certain bodies and Islamic law scholars) across countries provide incentives for parties to choose jurisdictions which may be more favourable to them should a dispute arise.[66] In fact, '*fatwa*-shopping' is a real occurrence in Islamic banking and finance transactions;[67] thus parties may choose the jurisdiction most favourable to their transaction, and this may be reflected in their choice of court.

C. The Philippines

In the Philippines, Choice-of-Forum clauses are treated as venue stipulations, and therefore, as procedural in nature and not containing promises which may give rise to private law rights. Hence, in this sense, the Philippine approach is closer to the civil law approach than the common law. To be given effect, Choice-of-Forum clauses need to comply with the specific requirements under the rule 4, section 4(b) of the Rules of Court, namely: (1) be in writing, (2) be agreed before the action is filed, and (3) contain an exclusive choice of venue.[68] Courts have strictly enforced these requirements, particularly the requirement that the choice should be exclusive.[69] As a result, party autonomy is limited, allowing parties to choose a court, but only if the choice is exclusive (ie, to the exclusion of any other court), with little room to include other promises that could alter Philippine procedural rules.

D. China, Indonesia and Japan

Though civil law jurisdictions do not treat Choice-of-Forum clauses as private law rights, they allow certain freedoms in drafting them. An ancient feature of civil law procedures, *prorogatio fori* permits parties to select a forum and include positive and negative effects. Specifically, they can provide for one or several courts which can hear their disputes and deny jurisdiction to one, some, or all other courts. However, the extent to which parties can provide, vary or mix the positive and negative effects of their Choice-of-Forum clauses would depend on forum law, particularly its procedural rules.[70] In some jurisdictions, only prorogation is allowed,[71] while others restrict variations of jurisdictional rules, unless no specific rules apply.[72] Some countries impose additional requirements

[66] Umar Oseni, 'The Legal Implications of "*Fatwa* Shopping" in the Islamic Finance Industry: Problems, Perceptions and Prospects' (2016) 30(2) *Arab Law Quarterly* 107, 113.

[67] ibid 121.

[68] Rules of Court (Philippines), r 4 s 4(b).

[69] See *Philippine Banking Corporation v Tensuan* (1994) 230 SCRA 413, 420–21.

[70] See Emilio Gonzalez, 'The Hague Convention on Choice of Court Agreements of June 30, 2005: A Mexican View' (2006) 13(1) *Southwestern Journal of Law and Trade in the Americas* 37, 44, 46.

[71] eg, in Chinnawat Thongpackdee & Vanina Sucharitkul, 'Thailand' in Alejandro Carballo Leyda (ed), *Asian Conflict of Laws* (Kluwer Law International, 2015) 233, 236, stipulations derogating from jurisdiction of Thai courts are void.

[72] eg, in Naoki Iguchi and Naoko Kamimura, 'Japan' in Alejandro Carballo Leyda (ed) *Asian Conflict of Laws* (Kluwer Law International, 2015) 67, 71, parties are free to choose a foreign court except when the Japanese courts

such as a reasonable connection to the chosen forum.[73] And yet in other civil law jurisdictions, parties are given the freedom to choose one or more courts and at the same time, derogate from the jurisdiction of one, some or all other courts.[74] Furthermore, whether a Choice-of-Law clause may allow parties to vary or provide other promises in their Choice-of-Forum clause would also depend on the forum's choice of law rules, as discussed in Chapter six.

In China, Indonesia and Japan, what parties can include in their Choice-of-Forum clauses varies but all allow prorogation in favour of local courts. China and Japan, except for matters which are defined as falling within their exclusive jurisdiction,[75] allow derogation, thus allowing parties to choose foreign courts. Notably, this capacity to prorogate and derogate extend to adopting asymmetric Choice-of-Forum clauses,[76] where one party is given the right to bring litigation in only one jurisdiction, while the other party is given the freedom to bring litigation in any jurisdiction or a limited number of jurisdictions. In Indonesia, however, choices must align with *actor sequitur forum rei* (eg, the chosen forum is also where the defendant has their domicile),[77] for them to have derogative effects.

Beyond prorogation and derogation, the procedural rules in China, Indonesia and Japan do not specify what parties can include in Choice-of-Forum clauses. Courts in these countries limit the effect of choice of law rules, in the sense that validity and interpretation can be determined by the forum law and not by the applicable law. Hence, an a priori waiver of certain defences (eg, the appropriateness of the chosen forum), which are recognised in common law jurisdictions, may have limited or no effect. Private law rights, such as claims for damages, are not recognised, although China allows remedies similar to anti-suit injunctions.[78]

have exclusive jurisdiction; also in Munkhselenge Purevdorjiin, 'Mongolia' in Alejandro Carballo Leyda (ed), *Asian Conflict of Laws* (Kluwer Law International, 2015) 145, 148, where parties are free to choose any foreign jurisdiction except for matters referred especially to Mongolian jurisdiction.

[73] eg, in Young Seok Lee, Sae Youn Kin and Sy Nae Kim, 'Republic of Korea' in Alejandro Carballo Leyda (ed), *Asian Conflict of Laws* (Kluwer Law International, 2015) 85, 89–90, there should be a reasonable connection between the dispute and the Korean forum under Korean law; also in Yongpiung Xiao and Wenwen Liang, 'Mainland China' in Alejandro Carballo Leyda (ed), *Asian Conflict of Laws* (Kluwer Law International, 2015) 1, 8, parties may choose in writing, under Chinese law, a foreign court with real connections with the dispute.

[74] See Gonzalez (n 70) 51–52.

[75] Civil Procedure Law of the People's Republic of China (中华人民共和国民事诉讼法) 2011 (adopted 19 April 1991, amended 2023) National People's Congress Order No 44 of the President, art 279 ('CCPL'); Code of Civil Procedure (民事訴訟法 平成八年六月二十六日法律第百九号) Act No 109 of 1996 (Japan) [tr Ministry of Justice: https://www.japaneselawtranslation.go.jp/en/laws/view/2053], art 3–5.

[76] See eg, *Lai Jianping v ABN AMRO Bank NV* [2010] Hu Gao Min Wu (Shang) Zhong Zi No 49 (Shanghai High People's Court); *Tokyo Kaijo Kasai Kabushi Kaisha v Koniglike Java China Daketvaat Litjein BV Amsterdam*, Supreme Court, Case (O) No 297 of 1973, 28 November 1975 [English version (1976) 20 *Japanese Annual of International Law* 106, 110].

[77] eg, *Bali Energi Ltd v Mitomo Shoji KK*, District Court of Central Jakarta, Judgment No 359/Pdt.G/2011/PN. Jkt Past, 31 July 2012; see Afifah Kusumadara, 'Jurisdiction of courts chosen in the parties' choice of court agreements: an unsettled issue in Indonesian private international law and the way out' (2022) 18(3) *Journal of Private International Law* 424, 427–28.

[78] eg, *Huatai Property & Casualty Insurance Co Ltd Shenzhen Branch v Clipper Chartering SA* [2017] E72XB 3 (Wuhan Maritime Court); see also Peter Yu, Jorge Contreras and Yu Yang, 'Transplanting Anti-Suit Injunctions' (2022) 71(4) *American Law Review* 1537, 1594.

IV. The Freedom to Control Choice-of-Forum Clause Litigation

A. The Freedom to Control Litigation

Parties are also free to determine, within the procedural framework, the course of their litigation. They are free, for instance, to determine their cause of action or the subject matter of the action filed in court. In civil law systems, the freedom rests in the principle of party disposition. Von Mehren cogently discussed the consequences of this autonomy given to the parties:

> [Party disposition] contains several subsidiary propositions: (a) generally speaking, a court cannot institute a proceeding *ex officio*; (b) claims, defences, and counterclaims are to be asserted by the parties; (c) the court's judgment does not address issues that the parties have not raised nor accord relief that they have not requested; (d) in principle, only the parties can settle a case; and (e) only a party can challenge a judgment.[79]

Common law's adversarial system emphasises litigants' control over their litigation. Parties can choose their claim, cause of action (eg, contracts, torts, etc), forum, legal theory to substantiate their claim, the contents of their pleadings, what evidence to present, procedural tactics to expedite or delay proceedings, remedies to seek, etc.[80] Both the plaintiff and the defendant have choices on the foregoing matters except that the defendant can also decide the extent of his participation in the proceedings, which may affect his rights under the Choice-of-Forum clause.

Procedural rules shape how party autonomy is exercised in both civil law and common law systems. 'Accordingly, in every legal system, the outer limits of "cause of action" and functionally comparable concepts are closely connected with the system's procedural rules governing pleadings and discovery'.[81] The procedural framework that shapes the parties' exercise and the content of their consent, is moulded, in turn, by the philosophy, values, or policies of the state. For example, in the United States, because of emphasis on economy and efficiency, multiple actions arising from the same transaction are discouraged and therefore, the grounds for allowing splitting causes of action are limited.[82] In contrast, splitting causes of action is problematic, under German rules, 'only if it results in a situation that is egregiously unfair to the other party'.[83] Therefore, while parties need not seek the fullest measure of relief arguably due to them, their failure to do so may result to their ineligibility to seek further relief in the future.

B. Singapore, Hong Kong and Malaysia

As common law jurisdictions, Singapore, Hong Kong and Malaysia adopt an adversarial system that grants parties broad control over their litigation, including actions involving

[79] von Mehren (n 3) 209.
[80] See Fentiman, Richard, *International Commercial Litigation* (Oxford University Press, 2nd edn, 2015) 275–76.
[81] von Mehren (n 3) 178.
[82] ibid 180.
[83] ibid 181.

Choice-of-Forum clauses. Cases show how party strategy can influence not only litigation outcomes but also how Choice-of-Forum clause issues are resolved. For example, how the parties exercise this freedom may allow them to totally avoid the Choice-of-Forum clause (eg, by choosing their cause of action from a legal category other than contracts),[84] vary its interpretation (eg, by not providing evidence of the foreign applicable law),[85] or even extinguish their rights under the Choice-of-Forum clause (eg, by waiving the Choice-of-Forum clause through their actions).[86]

How parties control their litigation can affect their rights under the Choice-of-Forum clause, as seen in cases of implied waiver. In *The Thorscan*, the defendants were considered to have impliedly waived their rights when they brought an action in the wrong jurisdiction in breach of the Choice-of-Forum clause,[87] which required parties to sue at the carrier's principal place of business.[88] Despite knowing that the plaintiff's place of business was in the Netherlands Antilles, the defendants commenced an action in Amsterdam.[89] Hence, the Hong Kong court refused to stay the proceedings because 'the right [to ask for a stay in favour of the Antilles] had been waived'.[90] Similarly, the defendant's failure to object in a timely manner to the court's jurisdiction and his filing of counterclaims against the plaintiff may prevent the defendant from alleging that there exists an exclusive jurisdiction clause in favour of the foreign courts.[91]

In *Bank of China v Ngan Ching Wen* ('*Ngan*'), the Malaysia High Court found that the defendant's multiple applications and appeals amounted to voluntary submission to the Malaysian jurisdiction, notwithstanding the existence of a Choice-of-Forum clause choosing Singapore.[92] The Malaysia High Court also found in *Ng Lai Tien v Peregrine* that the defendant waived his right to sue in Hong Kong, the chosen forum, by appearing unconditionally and filing a defence in Malaysia.[93]

C. The Philippines

The adversarial system in the Philippines allows parties significant freedom in litigation. However, parties may be deemed to have waived their rights under the Choice-of-Forum clause because they have failed to raise the clause or because of the strategies they have employed. In *MV Zileena*,[94] the Philippine Supreme Court found that the respondents had lost their right to question the venue because they had voluntarily submitted to the Philippine

[84] eg, *Rickshaw Investments Ltd v Nicolai Baron von Uexkull* [2007] 1 SLR(R) 377, 396 (CA) ('*Rickshaw*'); *Rem Assets Ltd v MIR Investments Ltd* [2008] HKCFI 589, [18].

[85] *Yu Lap Man v Good First Investment Ltd* [1998] 1 HKC 726, 731.

[86] *Trafalgar House Construction (Asia) Ltd v Owners and/or Demise Charterers of MV 'Thorscan'* (*The Thorscan*) [1998] 4 HKC 536, 542 (Court of Appeal); *Bank of China v Ngan Ching Wen* [2011] 2 MLJ 645, 656 (HC Kuala Lumpur); *Ng Lai Tien v Peregrine* [1995] 4 MLJ 7, 14 (HC Johor Bahru).

[87] *The Thorscan* (n 86) 542.

[88] ibid 539.

[89] ibid 540.

[90] ibid 542.

[91] *Lam Yuk Cheung T/A Corbieres Wine Company v Maison Riviere Fils* [2014] HKDC 668, [31].

[92] *Ngan* (n 86) 656.

[93] *Ng Lai Tien* (n 86) 14.

[94] *Philippine International Trading Corporation v MV Zileena* (1992) 215 SCRA 309 ('*MV Zileena*').

court's jurisdiction despite their exclusive jurisdiction clause choosing Singapore. Hence, filing various motions to lift the writ of attachment, posting a counterbond to dissolve the writ of attachment, filing a demurrer on the additional ground that the petitioner had no cause of action, and filing a reply to the petitioner's opposition to their motion to dismiss amounted to voluntary submission.[95] The Court highlighted that 'verily, venue involves no more and no less than a personal privilege which may be lost by failure to assert it seasonably, by formal submission in a cause, or by submission through conduct'.[96] Similarly, in *International Harvester Company in Russia v Hamburg-American Line* ('*International Harvester*'), the Philippine Supreme Court ruled that the defendant had waived its right to sue in the chosen forum, the Hamburg courts, through its unconditional appearance and failure to object to Philippine jurisdiction.[97]

D. China, Indonesia and Japan

In China, Indonesia and Japan, the plaintiff usually determines the cause of action,[98] but the inquisitorial system allows judges to play a more active role in the determination of the proceedings. For example, in China, a judge can require plaintiffs to revise or change the cause of action or *moto propio* change it at his discretion.[99] Similarly, in Japan, the judge may order the plaintiff to correct the defect in its complaint.[100] The cause of action chosen or as determined by the judge is important as it may determine whether the mandatory jurisdictional rules apply or whether there are limitations to the enforcement of the Choice-of-Forum clause. For example, construction contract cases in China must be tried where the property is located.[101] Hence, whether the dispute will be characterised as a construction contract dispute, or financing dispute, or supply agreement dispute, or an action in tort would have a direct effect on whether the chosen court will be recognised by the forum court.

In civil law jurisdictions, judges have more extensive fact-finding powers. Notably, in China, direct exchanges between counsel rarely occur, since service of documents and witness examination occur through the court.[102] Significantly, there are also no specific provisions on cross-examination.[103] Nonetheless, China has started to allow a 'discovery'

[95] ibid 315.

[96] ibid 314 (quoting Vicente J Francisco, *Revised Rules of Court in the Philippines* (2nd edn, 1973) 366.

[97] *International Harvester Company in Russia v Hamburg-American Line* (1918) 42 Phil 845, 855 ('*International Harvester*').

[98] See eg, Chenyang Zhang, *Win in Chinese Courts: practice guide to civil litigation in China* (Springer, 2023) 14; Supreme Court of Japan, 'Questions and Answers on Civil Procedure' (website): https://www.courts.go.jp/english/judicial_sys/qa_on_Civil_Procedure/index.html (accessed 28 October 2024); Herziene Indonesisch Reglement 1941 [Revised Indonesian Regulations 1941] (Indonesia) art 118(1) ('HIR').

[99] Chenyang Zhang (n 98) 14.

[100] Supreme Court of Japan (n 98).

[101] Interpretation of the Supreme People's Court on the Application of the Civil Procedure Law of the People's Republic of China (最高人民法院关于适用《中华人民共和国民事诉讼法》的解释) 2015 (adopted 30 January 2015, amended 2022) Supreme People's Court Interpretation No 5, art 28 ('CCPL Judicial Interpretation').

[102] eg, Chenyang Zhang (n 98) 88; see also Jason Yue Wang and Li Dong, 'China: Litigation & Dispute Resolution Laws and Regulations 2023' in Justin Michaelson (ed), *Global Legal Insights: Litigation & Dispute Resolution* (Global Legal Group Ltd, 12th edn, 2023) 32.

[103] eg, Chenyang Zhang (n 98) 88.

procedure through the evidence presentation order mechanism,[104] which remains limited, however, in terms of scope.[105] In Japan, judges can directly ask parties for explanations when evidence is unclear.[106] This active judicial role in managing evidence can influence how tests like 'special circumstances' test or *forum non conveniens* or even *lis pendens* are applied, thus necessarily affecting the enforcement of Choice-of-Forum clause.

The absence of a doctrine of precedent in civil law jurisdictions means that courts are not bound by earlier decisions, although courts still aim for consistency. Without clear rules in statutes, procedure or judicial interpretations, judges have to exercise sound discretion in their rulings and may rely on principles of natural justice, like Japan's *jori* (*naturalis ratio*) and Indonesia's *rechvinding* to fill in gaps. This judicial authority, without the constraint of precedent, can impact party autonomy in litigation, as seen with the application of the *actor sequitur forum rei* principle in Indonesia.[107]

V. The Ouster Rule as an Illustration of Party Autonomy and Court Interaction

A. The Ouster Rule and its Demise

The view that Choice-of-Forum clauses 'oust' courts' jurisdiction long prevented common law courts from accepting them. The resistance stemmed from the 'derogation' effect, which refers matters to courts or bodies other than the default court or jurisdiction. Hence, this ouster rule was also applied to arbitration agreements. Fullagar J in the High Court of Australia in *Compagnie Des Messageries Maritimes v Wilson* explained:

> But, so far as such a clause purported to place beyond [the English courts'] reach disputes otherwise within their competence, they refused to give effect to it, and would entertain an action or suit in disregard of such a clause.[108]

In *Schwer* (1905),[109] the Hong Kong Supreme Court confirmed the ouster rule, citing the English case of *Scott v Avery*, where Lord Campbell explained that the rule likely originated from historical disputes over jurisdiction, with courts opposing 'anything that would altogether deprive every one of them of jurisdiction'.[110] Hence, '[w]here an action is indispensable', parties 'cannot oust the Court of its jurisdiction over the subject, because justice cannot be done without the exercise of that jurisdiction' which is the foundation of the

[104] CCPL Judicial Interpretation (n 101) arts 112, 113.
[105] Chenyang Zhang (n 98) 114.
[106] Supreme Court of Japan (n 98).
[107] HIR (n 98) art 118(4); Regulations on Civil Procedure 1857 (Reglement op de Burgerlijke Rechsvordering 1857) (Indonesia) art 99 ('Rv'); see also Afifah Kusumadara, *Indonesian Private International Law* (Hart Publishing, 2021) 51–52; Alvansa Vickya and Tiurma M Pitta Allagan, 'Implications of Non-exclusive Choice of Forum Clauses in Determining the Competent Dispute Resolution Forum in Indonesia' (2022) 12(1) *Indonesia Law Review* 70, 71–72.
[108] *Compagnie des Messageries Maritimes v Wilson* (1954) 94 CLR 577, 587 (citations omitted).
[109] *Schwer v Von Uffel* (Unreported, SC Hong Kong, CJ, 11 September 1905).
[110] *Scott v Avery* (1856) 5 HL Cas 811, 853; 10 ER 1121.

ouster rule.[111] It therefore appears that the English ouster rule is rooted on access to justice grounds.

American courts similarly considered stipulations which prevent parties from suing in forums as 'the most obvious example of an attempt to oust'.[112] Likewise, if parties intend 'to confine litigation to certain specified forums', this also amounted to 'ouster of other available fora'.[113] The courts would further widen the range of what amounted to 'ouster' and in the process, courts employed 'whatever definition of the ouster rule'.[114] Notably, the ouster rule was justified on various public law grounds – public policy,[115] contravention of the basic right to access State courts,[116] unlawful waiver of the right to sue initially in a particular court,[117] arguments concerning convenience,[118] prevention of upsetting the very 'symmetry of the law',[119] and protection of the weaker parties.[120] The most reasonable justification, however, would be that 'the law, not the contracting parties, was expected to provide the remedy',[121] as '[m]atters of redress should not be disposed of by the fiat of the contracting parties'.[122]

Eventually in the United States, the ouster rule gave way to the 'prima facie valid' test in *Mitthenthal v Mascagni*, where the Massachusetts Supreme Court considered Choice-of-Forum clauses prima facie valid.[123] Courts, however, still considered factors like the convenience of the parties and the witnesses.[124] Notably, the validity of a Choice-of-Forum clause, in the early 'prima facie valid' analysis, depended upon its reasonableness.[125]

This general hostility to Choice-of-Forum clauses took a radical turn in *The Bremen*.[126] The United States Supreme Court ruled that a Choice-of-Forum clause was prima facie valid, unless its enforcement was 'unreasonable under the circumstances',[127] such as depriving a party of his day in court[128] or violating public policy.[129] The Supreme Court also confirmed that the clause could be set aside based on the traditional contractual grounds for invalidity – 'fraud, undue influence, or overweening bargaining power'.[130] According to the Court, this approach was consistent with the 'present-day commercial realities and expanding international trade'.[131] In sum, the Court introduced a two-pronged approach: Choice-of-Forum clauses shall be enforced unless the resisting party

[111] ibid 853.
[112] Patrick J Barrett, 'Choice of Forum Provisions and the Intrastate Dilemma: Is Ouster Ousted? (1980) 48(4) *Fordham Law Review* 568, 569.
[113] eg, *Prince Steam-Shipping Co v Lehman*, 39 F 704 (SDNY 1889); see Barrett (n 112) 570 fn 9.
[114] Barrett (n 112) 569.
[115] ibid 570.
[116] *Slaughter-House Cases*, 83 US 36 (1872); see Barrett (n 112) 570.
[117] *Insurance Co v Morse*, 87 US 445, 451–52, 458 (1874); see Barret (n 112) 571.
[118] Barrett (n 112) 572.
[119] ibid.
[120] ibid.
[121] see ibid.
[122] ibid.
[123] ibid 573; *Mittenthal v Mascagni*, 183 Mass 19 (1903); 68 NE 425.
[124] ibid 575.
[125] ibid 574.
[126] *The Bremen v Zapata Off-Shore Co*, 407 US 1 (1972) ('*The Bremen*').
[127] ibid 11.
[128] ibid 19.
[129] ibid 16.
[130] ibid 12.
[131] ibid 16.

'could clearly show' (1) that 'enforcement would be unreasonable and unjust' ('unreasonable and unjust' test), or (2) 'that the clause was invalid for such reasons as fraud or overreaching' ('invalidity' test).[132]

In England, the acceptance of Choice-of-Forum clauses, as discussed earlier, evolved through arbitration agreements until *Racecourse Betting*[133] in 1944, which shifted the analysis to contract law. The ouster rule, however, persisted. Lord Denning emphasised the ouster rule in his opinion in *The Fehmarn* in 1958:

> [i]t is a matter to which the courts of this country will pay much regard and to which they will normally give effect, but it is subject to the overriding principle that no one by his private stipulation can oust the courts of their jurisdiction.[134]

The Eleftheria[135] in 1970 continued this approach but placed a very high burden on plaintiffs asking for the continuance of proceedings which are contrary to the Choice-of-Forum clause. As a result, *The Eleftheria* made the English approach closer to the prima facie valid test used in the United States. Brandon J opined:

> I think … the court should give full weight to the prima facie desirability of holding the parties … [and] not just to pay lip service … and then fail to give effect to it because of a mere balance of convenience.[136]

The Eleftheria forms the basis of approaches in common law courts including those of Singapore, Hong Kong and Malaysia, as regards exclusive Choice-of-Forum clauses. The decision is particularly notable because of the test it developed in determining whether there is a strong cause not to stay the proceedings, to wit:

> The principles established by the authorities can … be summarised as follows:
>
> (1) Where plaintiffs sue in England in breach of an agreement to refer disputes to a foreign court, and the defendants apply for a stay, the English court, assuming the claim to be otherwise within its jurisdiction, is not bound to grant a stay but has a discretion whether to do so or not.
> (2) The discretion should be exercised by granting a stay unless strong cause for not doing so is shown.
> (3) The burden of proving such strong cause is on the plaintiffs.
> (4) In exercising its discretion the court should take into account all the circumstances of the particular case.
> (5) In particular, but without prejudice to (4), the following matters, where they arise, may properly be regarded: —
>   (a) In what country the evidence on the issues of fact is situated, or more readily available, and the effect of that on the relative convenience and expense of trial as between the English and foreign courts.
>   (b) Whether the law of the foreign court applies and, if so, whether it differs from English law in any material respects.
>   (c) With what country either party is connected, and how closely.

[132] ibid 15.
[133] *Racecourse Betting Control Board v Secretary of State for Air* [1944] Ch 114, 126.
[134] *The Fehmarn* [1958] 1 WLR 159, 162.
[135] *The Eleftheria* [1970] P 94.
[136] ibid 103.

(d) Whether the defendants genuinely desire trial in the foreign country, or are only seeking procedural advantages.
(e) Whether the plaintiffs would be prejudiced by having to sue in the foreign court because they would: (i) be deprived of security for their claim; (ii) be unable to enforce any judgment obtained; (iii) be faced with a time-bar not applicable in England; or (iv) for political, racial, religious or other reasons be unlikely to get a fair trial.[137]

In theory, the ouster rule still exists in Anglo-American common law as the official view.[138] However, English courts routinely enforce Choice-of-Forum clauses, with exceptions being rare.[139] In the United States, the rule against ouster has been described as being totally emasculated.[140] In *The Bremen*, the United States Supreme Court called the idea that such clauses 'oust' courts' jurisdiction a 'vestigial legal fiction'.[141]

Hence, the common law now aligns with civil law in recognising and enforcing Choice-of-Forum clauses. However, while civil law has hundreds of years of history behind its institution of *prorogatio fori*, the common law struggled in coming up with an approach towards Choice-of-Forum clauses. The use of 'vague and metaphormic'[142] arguments behind the ouster rule meant that the common law was ill-equipped to analyse them if the approach was through the language of procedural or public law. Only when it used the language of contract law did common law find better tools and clarity in its legal reasoning.

B. The Ouster Rule in Singapore, Hong Kong and Malaysia

In common law, Choice-of-Forum clauses, even those in favour of foreign courts, do not 'oust' per se the jurisdiction of forum courts. The Malaysia High Court in Kuala Lumpur in *Nutri Mills Products Sdn Bhd v CMA CGM Malaysia Sdn Bhd* ('*Nutri Mills*') explained:

> In essence where there is a forum selection clause that in itself does not oust the jurisdiction of the court. The jurisdiction of the court exists, subject to the court's power to stay the matter in order to give effect to the forum selection clause.[143]

In short, the Malaysian court asserted that its jurisdiction continues to exist even if the Choice-of-Forum clause has a derogatory effect, as jurisdiction is defined by legislation. When courts enforce these clauses, they do so through a specific procedural mechanism, which is usually a stay application, thus allowing them to exercise discretion. This conscientious exercise of discretion allows the court to weigh several factors, but their starting point is still the need to enforce the Choice-of-Forum clause, subject to the plaintiff discharging the heavy burden of establishing strong cause that effect ought not to be given to the clause.

[137] ibid 99–100.
[138] Trevor Hartley, *International Commercial Litigation: Text, Cases and Materials on Private International Law* (Cambridge University Press, 2009) 181.
[139] ibid 189.
[140] Barrett (n 112) 582.
[141] *The Bremen* (n 126) 12.
[142] Barrett (n 112) 570.
[143] *Nutri Mills Products Sdn Bhd v CMA CGM Malaysia Sdn Bhd* [2013] 8 MLJ 377, 386 (HC Kuala Lumpur).

Hence, enforcing a Choice-of-Forum clause does not oust the court's jurisdiction. Rather, the Choice-of-Forum clause goes into the propriety of exercising that jurisdiction. 'It is asking the court to exercise its discretion not to assume jurisdiction over the case but to let the case be heard in another more appropriate forum, in this instance, a contractual forum'.[144]

Nonetheless, because the analytic process is discretionary, the watering down of the ouster rule does not automatically result in a mechanical enforcement of Choice-of-Forum clauses. At least that has been the case in jurisdictions adhering to the English common law approach. In *Inter Maritime*,[145] the Malaysian court rejected the allegedly mechanistic purely contractual approach of *The Bremen*.[146] This reading of *The Bremen* may have been wrong but nonetheless, the court emphasised discretion and its ability to consider other elements in its Choice-of-Forum clause analysis.[147] As such, since the Choice-of-Forum clause in favour of a foreign court does not 'oust' the local courts' jurisdiction, they can still proceed to exercise jurisdiction over the case,[148] as jurisdiction is vested by law.[149]

The Eleftheria's approach was first followed in Singapore in *Amerco Timbers Pte Ltd v Chatsworth Timber Corp Pte Ltd*[150] ('*Amerco*'), where the court considered similar factors for granting a stay, albeit without explicitly citing *The Eleftheria*. In Hong Kong, it was first adopted by the Hong Kong High Court in *Fine Furs Ltd v Louis Levine*.[151] In Malaysia, *The Eleftheria* was first adopted by the Penang Federal Court in *Globus Shipping & Trading Co (Pte) Ltd v Taiping Textiles Berhad*[152] ('*Globus*'). By following the 'strong cause' test developed in *The Eleftheria*, Singapore, Hong Kong and Malaysia have aligned themselves with the English approach.

C. The Ouster Rule in the Philippines

The 1906 case of *Molina v de la Riva*[153] ('*Molina*') sets the Philippine approach to Choice-of-Forum clauses. Although the case involved a domestic Choice-of-Forum clause, the case has been cited as the authority in cases involving Choice-of-Forum clauses in favour of foreign courts. The case established the following: (1) the jurisdiction of a court is fixed by law and not by the will of the parties;[154] (2) as a matter of public policy, parties can only stipulate in regard to that which is expressly authorised by law;[155] (3) agreements made contrary to the jurisdictional rules under the law are null and void.[156] The Philippines

[144] *The 'Jian He'* [1999] 3 SLR (R) 432, 447 (CA).

[145] *Inter Maritime Management Sdn Bhd v Kai Tai Timber Co Ltd, Hong Kong* [1995] 1 MLJ 322 (CA Kuala Lumpur).

[146] ibid 334–37.

[147] ibid 336.

[148] ibid 337.

[149] *Ng Lai Tien v Peregrine* (n 98) 13; see also *Elf Petroleum SE Asia Ltd v Winelf Petroleum Sdn Bhd* [1986] 1 MLJ 177, 179 (OCJ Kuala Lumpur).

[150] *Amerco Timbers Pte Ltd v Chatsworth Timber Corp Pte Ltd* [1977–1978] SLR(R) 112, [1977] 2 MLJ 181 (CA).

[151] *Fine Furs Ltd v Louis Levine* [1976] HKLR 544 (HC).

[152] *Globus Shipping & Trading Co (Pte) Ltd v Taiping Textiles Berhad* [1976] 2 MLJ 154 (FC Penang) ('*Globus*').

[153] *Molina v de la Riva* (1906) 6 Phil 12.

[154] ibid 15.

[155] ibid.

[156] ibid.

Supreme Court cited these rules in *International Harvester*,[157] and reiterated that '[a]n express agreement tending to deprive a court of jurisdiction conferred on it by law is of no effect'.[158] In *International Harvester*, the bill of lading contained a clause which stated that all disputes arising under the contract were, at the option of the Hamburg-American Line, to be decided according to German law and exclusively by the Hamburg courts.[159] The Court said that 'it cannot be admitted that a provision of this character has the effect of ousting the jurisdiction of the courts of the Philippine Islands in the matter now before it'.[160]

The Supreme Court would stress that '[p]rimarily, jurisdiction is conferred by law and not subject to stipulation of the parties'.[161] The approach of the Philippine Supreme Court in *MV Zileena*,[162] is illustrative, where the court read Choice-of-Forum clauses as not synonymous to a '*competencia*' or an agreement on jurisdiction, to wit:

> [I]t must be impressed upon petitioner that paragraph 10 of the Agreement may not be equated with *competencia* and neither does it suggest that Philippine courts are divested of authority by reason of the parties' express preference to vest jurisdiction in the High Court of Singapore.[163]

It is unfortunate though that the Supreme Court in that case, after recognising the Choice-of-Forum clause in favour of Singapore as valid,[164] did not develop a test on when a venue stipulation stipulating a foreign jurisdiction may be given effect and the Philippine case be dismissed. Instead, the Supreme Court resolved the case by concluding that the venue had been waived.[165]

Similarly, in *Ligner & Fisher GmbH v Intermediate Appellate Court*, the Supreme Court characterised the exclusive Choice-of-Forum clause as a 'covenant on venue'.[166] This means, therefore, that Choice-of-Forum clauses should only be read as venue stipulations, and that the jurisdiction of the local courts in the Philippines, can not in any way be affected or diminished by any agreement on where disputes may be heard. The corollary effect of this is that no one can argue that Philippine courts are without jurisdiction because of the Choice-of-Forum clause stipulating foreign courts. Choice-of-Forum clauses, in short, have no derogation effects. The court will just dismiss this argument because 'an agreement to deprive a court of jurisdiction conferred on it by law is void and of no legal effect'.[167] Notably, the Philippine approach also did not adopt the American 'prima facie valid' test or an *Eleftheria*-type test which gives the plaintiff, the one preventing the enforcement of a foreign Choice-of-Forum clause, the high burden of establishing 'strong cause'. Further, the starting point is not necessarily the need to enforce the Choice-of-Forum clause.

[157] *International Harvester* (n 97).
[158] ibid 855.
[159] ibid 854–55.
[160] ibid 855.
[161] *Radiowealth Finance Co, Inc v Nolasco* (2016) 808 SCRA 639.
[162] *MV Zileena* (n 94).
[163] ibid 312–13.
[164] ibid.
[165] ibid 320.
[166] *Ligner & Fisher GmbH v Intermediate Appellate Court* (1983) 125 SCRA 522.
[167] *Principe v Philippine-Singapore Transport Services Inc* (1989) 176 SCRA 515, 522.

Significantly, the Philippine approach mirrors a sizable number of cases in the United States which characterise Choice-of-Forum clauses as 'venue selection clauses'.[168] In *Stewart Organization, Inc v Ricoh Corp*, for instance, the United States Supreme Court characterised the parties' Choice-of-Forum clause as a venue stipulation – 'Rather, the first question for consideration should have been whether § 1404(a) itself controls respondent's request to give effect to the *parties' contractual choice of venue* and transfer this case to a Manhattan court' (emphasis added).[169]

Is there a difference if Choice-of-Forum clauses are treated as venue stipulations and not as agreements on jurisdiction? The Philippine approach raises this important question. Jurisdiction, specifically subject-matter jurisdiction, and venue are distinct in procedural law.

> Subject matter jurisdiction refers to the institutional power of a court to adjudicate a case; venue dictates which among several courts having jurisdiction is appropriate as most convenient. A court must be seized of both jurisdiction and venue if properly to hear a case.[170]

Notably, subject-matter jurisdiction can only be conferred by law while venue has long been held as subject to parties' agreement. Furthermore, since a venue stipulation is subject to the rules on venue (eg, the formal and language requirements, defences), this means that the chosen venue has to be exclusive because that is what the rules require. As a result, the Choice-of-Forum clause analysis tends to be limited to the compliance with the exclusivity requirement. Moreover, because venue is considered a procedural technicality, unlike a jurisdictional defect, an objection to venue may be waived.[171] Likewise, because it may be considered a procedural technicality, the court may be more liberal[172] and may not strictly enforce the Choice-of-Forum clause for a number of reasons.

Furthermore, when the Supreme Court refers to jurisdiction as not being a subject of party stipulation,[173] it appears that its understanding covers both subject-matter jurisdiction and personal jurisdiction. From the Philippine courts' perspective, there is not much about jurisdiction, in its two aspects, which can be subject to stipulation. Philippine law determines whether a court has subject-matter jurisdiction while proper service of summons determines personal jurisdiction. Notably, court decisions and the Rules of Court have not yet articulated or included Choice-of-Forum clauses as another way of submitting to the court's jurisdiction. Under the Rules of Court, voluntary appearance is the only exception to proper service of summons where the court acquires personal jurisdiction over

[168] See, eg, *Boyd v Grand Trunk Western Railroad Co*, 338 US 263, 264 (1949); *Sun World Lines Ltd v March Shipping Corp*, 801 F 2d 1066, 1069 (8th Cir 1986); *Snyder v Smith*, 736 F 2d 409, 419 (7th Cir), 469 US 1037 (1984); *In re Fireman's Fund Insurance Cos*, 588 F 2d 93, 95 (5th Cir 1979); *Richardson Engineering Co v International Business Machines Corp*, 554 F Supp 467, 469 (D Vt 1981), 697 F 2d 296 (2d Cir 1982); *Anastasi Bros Corp v St Paul Fire & Marine Ins Co*, 519 F Supp 862, 863–64 (ED Pa 1981); *St Paul Fire & Marine Insurance Co v Travelers Indemnity Co*, 401 F Supp 927, 929–30 (D Mass 1975); *Davis v Pro Basketball, Inc*, 381 F Supp 1, 3 (SDNY 1974); *Brown v Gingiss International, Inc*, 360 F Supp 1042, 1044 (ED Wis 1973); *National Equip Rental v Sanders*, 271 F Supp 756, 761 (EDNY 1967); See Mullenix (n 1) 325.

[169] *Stewart Organization, Inc v Ricoh Corp*, 487 US 22, 29 (1988).

[170] *Stewart Organization, Inc v Ricoh Corp*, 779 F 2d 643, 647 fn 7 (11th Cir 1986).

[171] See *Eusebio v Eusebio* (1976) 70 SCRA 268, 270.

[172] See *Alfonzo v Villamor* (1910) 16 Phil 315; *Ledesma Overseas Shipping Corporation v Avelino* (1978) 82 SCRA 396, 403–4.

[173] See *MV Zileena* (n 94) 312–13.

the defendant.[174] Furthermore, prorogation in favour of Philippine courts and the court's capacity to exercise such jurisdiction are uncontroversial, as long as both subject-matter and personal jurisdiction exist. In contrast, the derogation favouring *foreign* jurisdictions, especially in exclusive clauses, remains controversial. Hence, if the court has to give effect to derogation clauses, it appears that the best approach would be to treat them as venue stipulations.

Is the Philippine approach practically different from Singapore, Hong Kong and Malaysia, where Choice-of-Forum clauses are also seen as not capable of taking away the court's power to adjudicate as conferred by law but instead 'only encourag[ing] a court to exercise its discretion, which it has independent of the clause, to give effect to the parties' wishes'?[175] Notably, like the Philippines, these three jurisdictions also confirm that Choice-of-Forum clauses cannot affect subject-matter jurisdiction, and in that sense an agreement on 'jurisdiction' can be read as an agreement on 'venue'. Nonetheless, the Philippine approach is still different because, while in Singapore, Hong Kong and Malaysia, a local Choice-of-Forum clause can deal with personal jurisdiction as it provides the basis for the court to serve summons for defendants outside jurisdiction or grant a stay of proceedings, such clauses in the Philippines have no role at all even at the level of the court's acquisition of personal jurisdiction over the parties. Rule 14 of the Rules of Court on the service of summons[176] does not mention the role of a Choice-of-Forum clause. Only compliance with the specific requirements of rule 14 does that. The Choice-of-Forum clause only matters after jurisdiction is acquired, particularly when courts consider the affirmative defences under rule 8 section 12, and a dismissal based on the principle of *forum non conveniens* during the merits stage of the proceedings.[177] When considered as an affirmative defence, only compliance with the technical requirements of the Rules of Court matters, rather than a whole array of factors which may amount to 'strong cause'. Even the clauses' role in the *forum non conveniens* test is different because they are subordinate to administration of justice and public interest factors.

VI. The Choice-of-Court Convention and Party Autonomy

A. An Affirmation of Party Autonomy

The desire to promote international trade and investments through enhanced judicial cooperation on a global scale has encouraged states and international organisations like the Hague Conference on Private International Law to promote treaties which institutionalise the recognition of Choice-of-Forum clauses. The earliest attempts were made in the Hague Convention of 15 April 1958 on the Jurisdiction of the Selected Forum in the Case

[174] Rules of Court (Philippines), r 14, s 23.

[175] See David Marcus, 'The Perils of Contractual Procedure: A Revised History of Forum Selection Clauses in the Federal Courts' (2008) 82(3) *Tulane Law Review* 973,1026.

[176] Rules of Court (Philippines), r 14.

[177] See *Hasegawa v Minoru Kitamura* (2007) 538 SCRA 261, 277–78 ('*Hasegawa*').

of the International Sale of Goods,[178] and the Hague Convention of 25 November 1965 on the Choice of Court.[179] Both, however, did not enter into force due to lack of support among states. Outside Europe, there were also several regional attempts. In Latin America, the 1940 Montevideo Treaty on International Civil Law[180] and the Bustamante Code on Private International Law[181] were successful and became the template for laws in several countries in the Spanish-speaking world. Another recent regional treaty dealing with Choice-of-Forum clauses is the 2008 Trans-Tasman Court Proceedings and Regulatory Enforcement Agreement[182] between Australia and New Zealand, which also recognises, in article 8(1)(c), that parties may agree about the court or place where proceedings may be heard, and a breach of such agreement is a ground for the forum court to declining jurisdiction. While these attempts were unsuccessful or limited, as in the case of regional treaties, they provide lessons for drafting a truly global instrument involving Choice-of-Forum clauses. Nonetheless, it was the European experience with the Brussels Convention, Brussels I Regulation and Brussels I Recast which finally breathed life into the global agenda to institutionalise recognition of Choice-of-Forum clauses.

While the original goal was to conclude a much grander Hague Convention on Jurisdiction and Judgments, the Choice-of-Court Convention[183] successfully institutionalised the recognition of Choice-of-Forum clauses into a global treaty, thus confirming on a global-scale party autonomy in litigation. The Choice-of-Court Convention was adopted on 30 June 2005 and came into effect on 1 October 2015. As of 19 September 2024, there are 36 party-states and regional economic integration organisations (REIOs). On 25 March 2015, Singapore signed the Choice-of-Court Convention and ratified it on 2 June 2016. It entered into force for Singapore on 1 October 2016.

The Choice-of-Court Convention has three basic rules. First, the chosen court must hear the case,[184] unless the agreement is void under its own law.[185] Under article 5, the chosen court may not decline jurisdiction even if allowed by its own law, including under *forum non conveniens*.[186] Article 5, though, does not affect rules on subject-matter jurisdiction and allows courts to transfer the case to another court if its internal law allows such discretionary transfer, although due consideration should still be given to the parties'

[178] Hague Convention of 15 April 1958 on the Jurisdiction of the Selected Forum in the Case of International Sale of Goods, opened for signature 15 April 1958 (not yet in force): https://www.hcch.net/en/instruments/conventions/full-text/?cid=34.

[179] Hague Convention of 25 November 1965 on the Choice of Court, opened for signature 25 November 1965 (not yet in force): https://www.hcch.net/en/instruments/conventions/full-text/?cid=77.

[180] Treaty on International Procedural Law, opened for signature 19 March 1940, 7 Lecciones y ensayos 80 (entered into force 19 March 1940): https://web.archive.org/web/20150902082940/http://www.parlamento.gub.uy/htmlstat/pl/tratados/trat10272-7.htm.

[181] Convention on Private International Law, opened for signature 20 February 1928, (entered into force 20 April 1928): http://www.oas.org/juridico/spanish/tratados/a-31.html.

[182] Agreement between the Government of Australia and the Government of New Zealand on Trans-Tasman Court Proceedings and Regulatory Enforcement, Australia-New Zealand, opened for signature 24 July 2008, [2013] ATS 32 (entered into force 10 November 2013).

[183] Convention on Choice of Court Agreements, opened for signature 30 June 2005, 44 ILM 1294 (entered into force 1 October 2015) preamble ('Choice-of-Court Convention').

[184] ibid art 5.

[185] ibid art 5(1).

[186] Andrea Schulz, 'The Hague Convention of 30 June 2005 on Choice of Court Agreements' [2005](7) *Yearbook of Private International Law* 1, 9; also Trevor Hartley, *Choice-of-Court Agreements Under the European and International Instruments* (Oxford University Press, 2013) 177.

choice.[187] Second, under article 6, any non-chosen court must decline to hear the case.[188] This complements the first rule and removes the discretion from the non-chosen court to hear the action. The exceptions to this rule are when the agreement is void under the law of the chosen court,[189] when a party lacked the capacity under the law of the court seised,[190] when giving effect to the agreement would be manifestly contrary to local public policy,[191] when the agreement cannot be reasonably performed for reasons beyond the parties' control,[192] or when the chosen court has decided not to hear the case.[193] These exceptions echo the grounds under the New York Convention: the agreement does not have to be respected where it is 'null and void, inoperative or incapable of being performed'.[194] Nonetheless, the Choice-of-Court Convention is an improvement because article 6(a) specifies the test to determine validity (ie, the law of the state of the chosen court), unlike the New York Convention, which is silent on the applicable test. Third, any judgment rendered by the chosen court must be recognised and enforced in other contracting states, except where a ground for refusal applies.[195] Grounds for refusal include the nullity of the Choice-of-Forum clause under the law of the chosen court, a party's lack of legal capacity, failure to properly notify the other party, procedural fraud,contravention of public policy and *res judicata*.[196] The judgment may also be refused recognition or enforcement if it awards exemplary or punitive damages that do not compensate a party for actual loss or harm suffered.[197]

Significantly, under article 5 of the Choice-of-Court Convention, the test for substantive validity of the Choice-of-Forum clause is determined by the law of the chosen court.[198] While considered an improvement, there is doubt whether article 5 is truly effective. For example, the application of the chosen court's law by the court seised does not always lead to the same material result, especially given that the application of foreign law in the forum may be difficult.[199] Likewise, the chosen court's law does not govern all the situations of substantial validity.[200] The determination of whether consent really exists, for instance, is a factual question which requires the application of the forum law.[201] Similarly, when the parties' capacity is challenged, the question shall be resolved using forum law, pursuant to article 6(b).[202] In addition, the Choice-of-Court Convention does

[187] ibid 9.
[188] Choice-of-Court Convention (n 183) art 6.
[189] ibid art 6(a).
[190] ibid art 6(b).
[191] ibid art 6(c).
[192] ibid art 6(d).
[193] ibid art 6(e).
[194] Convention on the Recognition and Enforcement of Foreign Arbitral Awards, opened for signature 10 June 1958, 330 UNTS 3 (entered into force 7 June 1959), art 2(3); Schulz (n 186) 9.
[195] Choice-of-Court Convention (n 183) arts 8, 9.
[196] ibid art 9.
[197] ibid art 11.
[198] ibid art 5(1).
[199] Diana Sancho Villa, 'Jurisdiction over Jurisdiction and Choice of Court Agreements: Views on the Hague Convention of 2005 and Implications for the European Regime' [2010] (12) *Yearbook of Private International Law* 399, 411.
[200] ibid.
[201] ibid.
[202] ibid.

not contain explicit rules on transmission of rights to third parties,[203] although in the Hartley-Dogauchi Report, the Choice-of-Court Convention is said to allow a third party to benefit if they have taken over the rights and obligations of one of the original parties as provided under the relevant national law.[204]

The Choice-of-Court Convention also has a much more limited scope compared to the Brussels I Recast. It only applies 'in international cases to exclusive choice of court agreements concluded in civil or commercial matters',[205] albeit with an optional extension to non-exclusive choice of court agreements through reciprocal declarations by contracting states.[206] While it presumes exclusivity, article 2 lists several subject-matter exclusions, and does not affect interim protective measures. Its interaction with treaties and legal regimes like the Brussels I Recast in Europe, adds further complexity.[207]

In any case, the Choice-of-Court Convention has already sparked important developments in the law of Choice-of-Forum clauses in Asia. This has been seen in Singapore, Hong Kong and China. However, due to its limited scope, and the variety of non-exclusive clauses and transactions, countries may face a complex legal regime. This added complexity may deter some countries from adopting the Choice-of-Court Convention.

B. Freedom to Determine Contents of the Choice-of-Forum Clause

The distinct obligations of the chosen court and non-chosen court under articles 5 and 6 respectively also show that the Choice-of-Court Convention recognises that parties can provide for 'positive' (prorogation) and 'negative' (derogation) effects in their Choice-of-Forum clauses. However, if parties would like the Choice-of-Court Convention to apply, they need to promise that they would submit their dispute only to the courts or specific courts of a party-state.[208] Likewise, they also need to promise not to sue in any other courts except the chosen court.[209] Hence, the positive effect recognised by the Choice-of-Court Convention is prorogation in favour of only one party-state while the negative effect is total derogation of all courts except for the courts in the chosen jurisdiction. If parties vary the positive and negative effects, such as when they provide that the courts of two Choice-of-Court Convention parties may hear their disputes, their dispute may fall outside the scope of the Choice-of-Court Convention. Notably, asymmetrical agreements or agreements which may be exclusive for one party but non-exclusive for the other are not considered exclusive under the Choice-of-Court Convention.[210]

Other than prorogation and derogation, the Choice-of-Court Convention does not specify what other promises parties can include in their Choice-of-Forum clauses. Provided that

[203] ibid.

[204] Trevor Hartley and Masato Dogauchi, *Explanatory Report on the Convention of 30 June 2005 on Choice of Courts Agreements*, Permanent Bureau (ed) (Hague Conference on Private International Law, 2013) 51 ('Hartley-Dogauchi Report').

[205] Choice-of-Court Convention (n 183) art 1(1).

[206] ibid art 22.

[207] See Sancho Villa (n 199).

[208] Choice-of-Court Convention (n 183) art 3(a).

[209] ibid art 3(a).

[210] Brooke Adelle Marshall and Mary Keyes, 'Australia's Accession to the Hague Convention on Choice of Court Agreements' (2017) 41(1) *Melbourne University Law Review* 246, 277–78.

the promises do not involve matters specifically excluded under article 2, the Choice-of-Court Convention may allow them. Furthermore, the Choice-of-Court Convention is silent as to whether the promises may give rise to contractual rights, as it only ensures that chosen courts will assume jurisdiction over the dispute, while non-chosen courts decline it. Hence, the validity,[211] enforceability of other promises in the Choice-of-Forum clause and the remedies available under them (which are not specifically regulated by the Choice-of-Court Convention) would depend on the law of the chosen forum. Therefore, if allowed under the relevant national law, parties may provide that breach of the exclusive Choice-of-Forum clause would entail damages.

The exclusion of consumer and employment contracts under article 3 reflects concerns about the 'authenticity' of party autonomy in these agreements, given potential bargaining inequalities.[212] These 'limits' of party autonomy, recognised by the Choice-of-Court Convention, are further explored in Chapter seven.

C. Freedom to Control Litigation

The Choice-of-Court Convention does not limit the parties' freedom to control litigation. A party can file a claim under a different cause of action, say under certain torts which are excluded under article 2.[213] Of course, whether or not the court enforces the exclusive Choice-of-Forum clause would depend on the court's interpretation and the provisions of the Choice-of-Court Convention. Moreover, the parties' choice of relief to enforce or avoid the Choice-of-Forum clause, like a stay, injunction or dismissal, remains with the party applicant, subject to the requirements under local procedural rules. Notably, article 7 preserves a party's right to seek interim relief including an anti-suit injunction,[214] but the Convention's rules may affect how relief is granted. For instance, the obligations of the chosen and non-chosen courts and the limited grounds which may be cited to avoid an exclusive Choice-of-Forum clause under articles 5 and 6 may be inconsistent with the inherently discretionary nature of granting anti-suit injunctions.

Because of articles 5 to 9, arguments to enforce or avoid an exclusive Choice-of-Forum clause, or to recognise or enforce a foreign judgment, may be limited. However, national law still governs grounds like validity, public policy, fraud, and breaches of procedural fairness, thus potentially offering more grounds than the Choice-of-Court Convention. Likewise, while factors under *forum non conveniens*, like convenience or location of evidence are excluded, 'the width of the exceptions in article 6 may allow scope for arguments based on differences in applicable law'.[215]

Furthermore, during the enforcement and recognition of foreign judgments, parties must comply with both the Choice-of-Court Convention's procedural requirements

[211] Choice-of-Court Convention (n 183) art 6(a).

[212] See, eg, Alex Mills, *Party Autonomy in Private International Law* (Cambridge University Press, 2018) 85–86.

[213] Choice-of-Court Convention (n 183) art 2(2)(k).

[214] Alex Mills, 'The Hague Choice of Court Convention and Cross-Border Commercial Dispute Resolution in Australia and the Asia-Pacific' (2017) 18(1) *Melbourne Journal of International Law* 1, 9.

[215] Richard Garnett, 'The Hague Choice of Court Convention: Magnum Opus or Much Ado about Nothing' (2009) 5(1) *Journal of Private International Law* 161, 165.

and the law of the requested court.[216] Article 13 outlines the necessary documents,[217] including the form for such an application.[218] While the Choice-of-Court Convention limits parties' freedom to choose the manner in which they can enforce a foreign judgment, should a party fail to produce the required documents, '[t]he law of the requested State determines the consequences of failure to produce the required documents'.[219] Hence, whether or not the court is liberal or strict in response to the parties' failure to closely follow the requirements depends on the law of the requested court. The Hartley-Dogauchi Report, however, emphasises that courts should avoid excessive formalism.[220] The availability of alternative enforcement methods, like registration or common law proceedings, is debatable.

[216] Choice-of-Court Convention (n 183) arts 13–14.
[217] ibid art 13(1).
[218] ibid art 13(3).
[219] Hartley-Dogauchi Report (n 204) 211; see Choice-of-Court Convention (n 183) art 14.
[220] Hartley-Dogauchi Report (n 204) 211.

4

The Enforcement of Choice-of-Forum Clauses: Singapore, Hong Kong, Malaysia, Philippines

I. Introduction

This chapter examines the relief and remedies available in Singapore, Hong Kong, Malaysia and the Philippines for enforcing Choice-of-Forum clauses. Each jurisdiction enforces these clauses with distinct approaches, reflecting the complexity of Choice-of-Forum clause analysis even among jurisdictions with shared legal heritage. New elements introduced because of economic ambitions have added to the diversity and complexity. Notably, each jurisdiction balances party autonomy against court discretion or state regulation to varying degrees. Singapore is the most contract-driven and party autonomy-oriented jurisdiction, while the Philippines, constrained by the ouster rule, offers limited recognition of Choice-of-Forum clauses. Singapore's establishment of the Singapore International Commercial Court ('SICC') and accession to the Choice-of-Court Convention further signal its move towards less court discretion in enforcing these clauses. Hong Kong takes a more cautious, common law-oriented approach, while Malaysia still emphasises court discretion. Overall, these approaches highlight that Choice-of-Forum clauses are analysed from the vantage points of contracts, procedure and private international law.

II. Singapore

A. Singapore's Approach to Jurisdiction

(i) The Court System

Singapore's Constitution vests judicial power in the Supreme Court and subordinate courts created by law.[1] The Supreme Court of Judicature Act ('SCJA') defines the jurisdiction of the Supreme Court of Singapore, which includes the High Court and the Court of Appeal.[2] The High Court can transfer cases between itself and subordinate courts.[3] Unless otherwise

[1] Constitution of the Republic of Singapore (Singapore, 1999 reprint), s 93.
[2] Supreme Court of Judicature Act (Singapore, cap 322, 2020 rev edn) pt 2 s 3 ('SCJA').
[3] ibid sch 1, s 10.

specified by statute or the Rules of Court, the High Court generally follows common law principles. Below the Supreme Court are the District Courts, Magistrates' Courts and Small Claims Tribunal, with jurisdiction depending on the claim amounts.[4] Cross-border cases involving Choice-of-Forum clauses may be heard in any of these courts and the High Court in its exercise of civil jurisdiction.

The current Rules of Court, issued on 1 December 2021, took effect on 1 April 2022.[5] All references to the Singapore Rules of Court refer to the 2021 version unless otherwise stated.

(ii) Singapore International Commercial Court

The Supreme Court of Judicature (Amendment) Act 2014 ('SICC Law') established the SICC as a division of the High Court.[6] Effective 1 January 2015, the SICC Law and the accompanying amendments[7] to the Rules of Court introduced new tests for the grant of a stay,[8] allowed the SICC to transfer cases and join third parties,[9] created a presumption of exclusivity for Choice-of-Forum clauses stipulating the SICC,[10] and removed the need for leave or permission to serve process out of Singapore.[11] In 2021, the SICC Rules of Court ('SICC Rules') were introduced as a standalone procedural framework, replacing order 110 in the Rules of Court 2014, thus highlighting the SICC's independence and flexibility, distinct from the High Court's general division.[12]

As a specialist court, the SICC's jurisdiction is limited and does not cover all cases involving a Choice-of-Forum clause. The SICC can hear cases which are (1) international and commercial nature;[13] (2) submitted to the SICC's jurisdiction under a Choice-of-Forum agreement[14] or transferred from the High Court;[15] and (3) not seeking prerogative orders (including any mandatory order, prohibiting order, quashing order, or order for review of detention).[16] Recent amendments to the SCJA expanded the SICC jurisdiction to include cases related to 'international commercial arbitration',[17] and corporate insolvency.[18] While similar to the Choice-of-Court Convention's jurisdiction, the SICC covers a broader range of transactions.[19]

[4] 'Singapore Judicial System', Supreme Court Singapore (Web Page, 3 September 2018): https://www.supremecourt.gov.sg/about-us/the-supreme-court/singapore-judicial-system.

[5] Rules of Court (Singapore, 2021) ('Rules of Court').

[6] SCJA (n 2) pt 3 ss 18A–18M.

[7] Rules of Court (Singapore, 2014) ord 110 ('Rules 2014').

[8] ibid r 8.

[9] SCJA (n 2) pt 3 s 18J(1).

[10] SCJA (n 2) pt 3 s 18F(a).

[11] Rules 2014 (n 7) ord 110, r 6(2).

[12] Adeline Chong and Man Yip, *Singapore Private International Law* (Oxford University Press, 2023) 116.

[13] SCJA (n 2) pt 3 s 18D(a); Singapore International Commercial Court Rules of Court 2021 (Singapore, 2021) ord 2, r 1(1)(a) ('SICC Rules').

[14] ibid ord 2, r 1(1)(b).

[15] ibid ord 2, r 1(2)(a).

[16] ibid ord 2, r 1(1)(c).

[17] SCJA (n 2) s 18D(2); SICC Rules (n 13) ord 2, r 1(2)(d).

[18] SCJA (n 2) s 18D(2); SICC Rules (n 13) ord 2, r 1(2)(da).

[19] *cf* Convention on Choice of Court Agreements, opened for signature 30 June 2005, 44 ILM 1294 (entered into force 1 October 2015), art 2(a) ('Choice-of-Court Convention').

The SICC Rules provide a list of circumstances or transactions which make a claim international (eg, when the parties' places of business are in different states)[20] and commercial (ie, the subject matter of the action arises from a commercial relationship, or relates to an *in personam* intellectual property dispute).[21] Significantly, parties can agree that the subject matter of the claim is both international (involving more than one state)[22] and commercial.[23] When a Choice-of-Forum clause in favour of the SICC exists at the time of filing, there is a presumption that the action is international and commercial.[24]

Under the SICC Rules, agreeing to the jurisdiction of the High Court or general division also implies submission to the SICC,[25] unless the agreement pre-dates 1 October 2016.[26] However, submission to the SICC does not extend to the High Court's general division.[27] Notably, stating submission to the SICC's jurisdiction is satisfied even if parties have only stated 'Courts of Singapore' without specifying the SICC.[28]

The SICC cannot decline jurisdiction solely because the dispute is linked to another jurisdiction if there is a written Choice-of-Forum clause stipulating the SICC.[29] A Choice-of-Forum agreement can be by any other means of communication, including orally or by conduct, as long as the information is accessible for future reference.[30] Unless stated otherwise, the SICC Law presumes exclusivity[31] when the law applicable is Singapore law.[32] This presumption also holds when the Choice-of-Court Convention applies, regardless of the applicable law. However, it is unclear whether the presumption applies when foreign law governs the clause and the Choice-of-Court Convention does not apply.[33] In contrast, in common law, no presumption exists. Nonetheless, the SICC still maintains the dichotomy of exclusive and non-exclusive clauses,[34] although the SICC Rules remove, in both instances, the need for permission to serve process out of Singapore.[35] Furthermore, the SICC only declines jurisdiction 'if exercising jurisdiction would be contrary to the Court's international and commercial character or would be an abuse of the process of the Court',[36] which is narrower than the previous test – 'if it is not appropriate for the action to be heard in the Court' – in order 110, rule 8 Rules of Court 2014.

The SICC can hear cases transferred from the High Court, if it is 'more appropriate'[37] and can join third or subsequent parties,[38] even in instances where there are Choice-of-Forum clauses. Part of a liberal approach towards contractual privity, these two innovations differ from traditional common law and raise difficult jurisdictional issues. For instance, when

[20] SICC Rules (n 13) ord 2, r 1(3)(a).
[21] ibid ord 2, r 1(3)(b).
[22] ibid ord 2, r 1(3)(a)(ii).
[23] ibid ord 2, r 1(3)(b)(iii).
[24] ibid ord 2, r 1(8).
[25] ibid ord 2, r 2(1).
[26] ibid ord 2, r 2(2).
[27] ibid ord 2, r 2(3).
[28] *Roll SG Pte Ltd v Cong Ty Co Phan Van Tai Lien Hiep Huy Hoang* [2023] SGHC(I) 5, [42].
[29] SICC Rules (n 13) ord 2, r 3(3).
[30] ibid ord 2, r 1(7)(b).
[31] SCJA (n 2) pt 3 s 18F(1)(a), (2).
[32] Chong and Yip (n 12) 121.
[33] ibid.
[34] SICC Rules (n 13) ord 2, r 1(7).
[35] ibid ord 5, r 6(2).
[36] ibid ord 2, r 3(2).
[37] ibid ord 2, r 4(1).
[38] ibid ord 10, r 5(1); ord 10, r 6.

jurisdiction is contested in the High Court prior to transfer, what test should the SICC apply given the differences in the tests applied under the SICC Law and common law?[39] Similarly, when the SICC declines jurisdiction and transfers the case to the High Court without consent from the parties,[40] should the test under the common law be applied? The inclusion of third parties also complicates matters, as they are not bound by the Choice-of-Forum clause; thus leave is required and the SICC will necessarily use the 'natural forum' test in *Spiliada Maritime Corp v Cansulex Ltd*[41] ('*Spiliada*') if the clause is non-exclusive, or the 'strong cause' test under *The Eleftheria* if the clause is exclusive.[42] However, the SICC uses a different test – 'if exercising jurisdiction would be contrary to the Court's international and commercial character or would be an abuse of the process of the Court'[43] – which raises the question of whether the SICC should harmonise this test with the 'natural forum' and 'strong cause' tests usually used in applications for leave and for stay of proceedings.[44] Furthermore, there are difficult enforcement and recognition of judgments issues involved when the judgments are against third parties.[45]

For disputes involving exclusive clauses governed by the Choice-of-Court Convention, its rules apply rather than the SICC Rules. However, for matters not covered by the convention, such as service, transfer and joinder, the SICC Rules apply. The Choice-of-Court Convention aims to enforce exclusive Choice-of-Forum clauses, so if the clause designates only the High Court or general division, all parties must consent to the transfer to the SICC.[46] If the clause specifies only the SICC, a transfer to the High Court or the general division is made conditionally 'upon the consent of every party to that agreement to vary it so as to designate the General Division as a chosen court for the case',[47] to ensure that the resulting judgment could be recognised and enforced.[48] Where the clause does not mention the SICC, the rule designating the High Court or the general division as including an agreement to submit to the SICC applies; thus 'each party to the agreement is treated as having consented to the transfer of the case to that court'.[49] Chong and Yip, however, are unsure whether this technique of implying consent satisfies the Choice-of-Court Convention's requirements.[50]

(iii) Choice of Court Agreements Act 2016

On 14 April 2016, Singapore enacted the Choice of Court Agreements Act 2016 ('CCAA'), incorporating the Choice-of-Court Convention into Singaporean law. This added complexity to the treatment of Choice-of-Forum clauses, but since the Choice-of-Court Convention

[39] Yeo Tiong Min, 'Staying Relevant: Exercise of Jurisdiction in the Age of SICC' (Yong Pung How Professorship of Law Lecture, Singapore Management University, 13 May 2015) 17.
[40] See ibid.
[41] *Spiliada Maritime Corp v Cansulex Ltd* [1987] AC 460.
[42] See Yeo (n 39) 18.
[43] SICC Rules (n 13) ord 2, r 3(2).
[44] See Yeo (n 39) 19–20.
[45] See ibid 20.
[46] SICC Rules (n 13) ord 2, r 4(4).
[47] ibid ord 2, r 5(2).
[48] Chong and Yip (n 12) 125.
[49] SICC Rules (n 13) ord 2, r 4(7).
[50] Chong and Yip (n 12) 126.

only covers exclusive clauses;[51] non-exclusive Choice-of-Forum clauses remain governed by existing law, although there is now a presumption of exclusivity of choice.[52] Significantly, unilateral exclusive Choice-of-Forum clauses in common law are not regarded as exclusive, for lack of mutuality.[53] In *Credit Suisse AG v Owner of the Vessel 'Chloe V'*, the Singapore High Court confirmed that asymmetric or unilateral clauses are excluded from the scope of the CCAA.[54] Referring to the Hartley-Dogauchi Report, the Court stressed that 'the agreement must be exclusive irrespective of the party bringing the proceedings'.[55] Nonetheless, the Choice-of-Court Convention presumes the exclusivity of a clause 'which designates the courts of one Contracting State or one or more specific courts of one Contracting State … unless the parties have expressly provided otherwise'.[56] Notably, an exclusive designation of the Singapore High Court even when there is only a reference to its general division should be construed to include the SICC, unless otherwise indicated.[57]

The Choice-of-Court Convention applies only to exclusive Choice-of-Forum clauses in 'civil and commercial matters',[58] a term which has an autonomous meaning;[59] it thus does not entail reference to Singaporean law and is intended to exclude public law and criminal law.[60] Furthermore, certain matters which may ordinarily be considered civil or commercial are excluded under article 2.[61] Moreover, the Choice-of-Court Convention regime applies only to disputes arising after the treaty's implementation on 1 October 2016. Because Singapore has not made any of the optional declarations,[62] matters and cases which are excluded continue to be covered by common law, Singapore statutes, or other relevant treaty regimes to which Singapore is a party.

Based on these discussions, Singapore today has several prevailing legal regimes which are applicable to exclusive and non-exclusive Choice-of-Forum clauses, thus making Singapore a very complex jurisdiction, as Yeo noted:

> There used to be only two tests for international jurisdiction in the common law. Once the [Hague Choice of Court] Convention comes into force in Singapore, depending on the context, the exercise of international jurisdiction could be subjected to four different tests for exclusive choice of court clauses, two different tests for non-exclusive choice of court cases, and five different tests for joining third parties.[63]

Singapore therefore presents a window where one can observe the complex interactions of the Choice-of-Court Convention and domestic law. Hence, the vision of promoting harmony and uniformity of rules may not be easy to achieve given this Gordian interaction.

[51] Choice-of-Court Convention (n 19) art 1; Choice of Court Agreements Act 2016 (Singapore, cap 39A, 2020 rev edn), s 8 ('CCAA').

[52] Choice-of-Court Convention (n 19) art 3(b).

[53] ibid art 3(a); *cf* Brooke Adelle Marshall and Mary Keyes, 'Australia's Accession to the Hague Convention on Choice of Court Agreements' (2017) 41(1) *Melbourne University Law Review* 246, 277–78.

[54] *Credit Suisse AG v Owner of the Vessel 'Chloe V'*, [2022] SGHCR 9, [19].

[55] ibid [17].

[56] Choice-of-Court Convention (n 19) art 3(b); CCAA (n 51) s3(2).

[57] CCAA, s 2(2)–(3).

[58] ibid art 1; CCAA (n 51), s 8.

[59] Trevor Hartley and Masato Dogauchi, *Explanatory Report on the Convention of 30 June 2005 on Choice of Courts Agreements*, Permanent Bureau (ed) (Hague Conference on Private International Law, 2013) 41.

[60] ibid.

[61] Choice-of-Court Convention (n 19) art 2; CCAA (n 51) s 9.

[62] Choice-of-Court Convention (n 19) art 22.

[63] Yeo (n 39) 28.

B. Service of Process

'*In personam*' jurisdiction is the aspect of jurisdiction which is relevant to the Choice-of-Forum clause in common law jurisdictions. Under section 16 SCJA, '*in personam*' jurisdiction of the High Court may be established by proper service of a writ of summons within Singapore, and outside Singapore 'in the circumstances authorised by and in the manner prescribed by Rules of Court',[64] or when the defendant submits to the jurisdiction of the High Court, or as vested by Singaporean law.[65]

Service within Singapore is a matter of right[66] while service outside Singapore is a matter of court discretion.[67] This means that any person can commence a civil action by serving the defendant the writ or other originating process in accordance with the Rules of Court if the defendant or his representative is within Singapore.[68] Neither the High Court, nor any Singaporean court, can deny this right to serve process within Singapore. And once service within Singapore has properly been made, in accordance with order 7 of the Rules of Court, the court acquires jurisdiction over the defendant. In actions involving Choice-of-Forum clauses, once jurisdiction has been established as of right, the defendant may apply for a stay of the proceedings based on grounds depending on whether the Choice-of-Forum clause is exclusive or non-exclusive.

Service out of Singapore is governed by the SCJA, section 16(1)(a)(ii). A defendant may be served with process overseas provided 'leave of court' or 'permission of court' is obtained in accordance with order 8, which spells out the grounds and conditions for permission to be granted.[69] However, the consideration of these grounds is left to the court's discretion.[70] For the court to permit service, the applicant must show that the court: (a) has jurisdiction, or (b) is appropriate to hear the action.[71] However, the court's permission is not required if extra-territorial service is allowed under the contract.[72] Arguably, when the Choice-of-Court clause only designates Singapore but there is no agreement on extra-territorial service, the applicant must satisfy the conditions for grant of 'permission of court'.[73] Significantly, extra-territorial service may also be effected pursuant to bilateral civil procedure conventions to which Singapore is a party[74] (eg, the Hague Convention on the Service Abroad and Extra-Judicial Documents 1965[75]). The plaintiff has the onus of establishing the basis for extra-territorial service.[76] Hence, both exclusive and non-exclusive Choice-of-Forum clauses (either because Singapore has jurisdiction or is an appropriate

[64] SCJA (n 2) pt 3 s 16(1)(a).
[65] ibid pt 3 s 16(1)(b).
[66] ibid pt 3 s 16(1)(a)(i).
[67] ibid pt 3 s 16(1)(a)(ii).
[68] ibid pt 3 s 16(1)(a)(i).
[69] Rules of Court (n 5) ord 8, r 1(2).
[70] ibid ord 8, r 1(1).
[71] ibid.
[72] ibid ord 8, r 1(3).
[73] Chong and Yip (n 12) 55.
[74] LexisNexis Singapore, *Halsbury's Laws of Singapore*, vol 6(2) (at 1 November 2009) 75 Conflict of Laws, '1 Jurisdiction' [75.030].
[75] Hague Convention on the Service Abroad and Extra-Judicial Documents 1965, opened for signature 15 November 1965, 658 UNTS 163 (entered into force 10 November 1969).
[76] ibid.

forum to hear the case) stipulating Singapore provide a basis for granting permission. Notably, the 'strong cause' test now applies to set aside service of process pursuant to both exclusive and non-exclusive clauses in favour of Singapore courts which are not covered by the Choice-of-Court Convention.[77]

Unless there is 'strong cause', permission to serve out of jurisdiction will be denied when the exclusive Choice-of-Forum clause not covered by the Choice-of-Court Convention stipulates for a foreign forum. In *BGC Partners (Singapore) Ltd v Tan Wee Hiong Kevin* ('*BGC Partners*'), the High Court granted leave even though the partnership agreement's exclusive Choice-of-Forum clause stipulated the Delaware courts because the main issues in dispute were intimately related to the defendant's employment termination in BGC Singapore, and 'it would be in the interests of justice' that the defendant's counterclaim in relation to his termination as a partner would also be resolved in Singapore.[78]

Where an applicant seeks to set aside the order for service of an originating process, and alternatively also asks for a stay, the usual procedure is for the Singapore court to deal with the setting-aside prayer before addressing the issue of stay of proceedings.[79] 'This is because a prayer seeking the setting-aside … disputes the existence of … jurisdiction; whereas a … stay … [challenges] the exercise … of that jurisdiction rather than … [its] existence'.[80]

Cases under the SICC are commenced through similar procedures. The SICC Rules of Court, however, forego the need for permission when there is a written Choice-of-Forum clause stipulating the SICC or if service out of Singapore is allowed under an agreement.[81] This radical procedural change applies to both exclusive and non-exclusive clauses, thus making the service of process in and out of Singapore a matter of right.[82] Notably, the defendant, in both instances, has the burden of convincing the court not to exercise its jurisdiction.[83] However, when a third party is joined, service out of Singapore has to be with the SICC's permission after showing that the court has jurisdiction and it is appropriate for the case to be heard at the SICC.[84]

The Choice-of-Court Convention and the CCAA do not address service of process for commencing proceedings involving Choice-of-Forum clauses. However, the test for service out of Singapore is modified for matters under the convention. If Singapore is chosen, leave to serve process outside Singapore appears to be no longer discretionary, as such step is necessary for the court to exercise jurisdiction. If Singapore is not chosen, the court must dismiss the application under these circumstances. Permission can be granted (ie, when Singapore court is not chosen) or refused (ie, when Singapore court is chosen), as the case may be, on the grounds stated in article 5(1) (ie, the agreement is null and void under Singapore law)[85] and article 6 (ie, the agreement is null and void under the law of the chosen court; a party lacks the capacity to conclude the agreement under Singapore law; giving

[77] See eg, *U Myo Nyunt (alias Michael Nyunt) v First Property Holdings Pte Ltd* [2021] 2 SGCA 73, [34].
[78] *BGC Partners (Singapore) Ltd v Tan Wee Hiong Kevin* [2017] SGHC 214, [6].
[79] *6DM (S) Pte Ltd v AE Brands Korea Ltd* [2021] SGHC 257, [4] ('*6DM*').
[80] ibid.
[81] SICC Rules (n 13) ord 5, r 6(2).
[82] Yeo (n 39) 10.
[83] ibid 11.
[84] SICC Rules (n 13) ord 5, r 6(1).
[85] Choice-of-Court Convention (n 19) art 5(1).

effect to the agreement would lead to a manifest injustice or would be manifestly contrary to Singapore's public policy; the agreement cannot reasonably be performed because of exceptional reasons beyond the control of the parties; or the chosen court has decided not to hear the case).[86] CCAA cases under the SICC do not encounter these issues, as permission is not required when there are exclusive Choice-of-Forum clauses.[87]

C. Stay of Proceedings

(i) Common Law

In proceedings commenced by service within Singapore, the SCJA authorises the High Court to stay proceedings where there is multiplicity of proceedings or when the natural forum test demands it.[88] This applies whether the Choice-of-Forum clause is exclusive or non-exclusive. The same test is used in granting leave for service outside Singapore, thus highlighting the court's discretion regardless of the nature of the Choice-of-Forum clause. As stays are procedural, Singapore law applies.[89]

When an exclusive Choice-of-Forum clause is not covered by the CCAA, the court applies the more stringent 'strong cause' test, while the 'natural forum' test traditionally applies when the clause is non-exclusive. For the exclusive clauses, the applicant must establish a strong cause, amounting to exceptional circumstances, why he should not be held to that agreement.[90] In exercising its discretion, the court considers all the circumstances of the particular case.[91] Although the factors may be similar in both the 'natural forum' and 'strong cause' tests, the starting points of these tests are different. The 'strong cause' test begins by giving effect to the exclusive Choice-of-Forum clause as a matter of contract, and the plaintiff has the heavy burden of establishing strong cause.[92] In the 'natural forum' test, on the other hand, because the plaintiff has invoked the court's jurisdiction as a matter of right, the defendant bears the legal burden of proving that there is an available and clearly more appropriate forum elsewhere.[93] If the defendant cannot discharge this burden, then ordinarily a stay will be denied.[94] If the defendant *can* demonstrate this, then a stay will be granted unless the plaintiff can show that there are circumstances by reason of which justice requires that the court should nonetheless refuse the stay.[95] The 'natural forum' test, therefore, involves two stages where the burden shifts from the defendant to the plaintiff. Singapore courts have also used the 'natural forum' test in mixed clauses, where parties can choose between arbitration or litigation in a certain jurisdiction.[96] Nonetheless, in instances when parties have intended the non-exclusive clause to have a greater weight vis-à-vis the

[86] ibid art 6.
[87] SICC Rules (n 13) ord 5, r 6(2)(a).
[88] SCJA (n 2) sch 1 s 9.
[89] *Abdul Rashid bin Abdul Manaf v Hii Yii Ann* [2014] 4 SLR 1042, 1047 (HC) ('*Abdul Rashid*').
[90] *Amerco Timbers Pte Ltd v Chatsworth Timber Corp Pte Ltd* [1977–1978] SLR(R) 112, 115 (CA) ('*Amerco*').
[91] ibid.
[92] ibid.
[93] *UBS AG v Telesto Investments Ltd* [2011] 4 SLR 503, 520 (HC) ('*UBS*').
[94] ibid.
[95] ibid.
[96] See *The 'Dai Yun Shan'* [1992] 1 SLR(R) 461, 469 (HC).

other factors, the applicable test for non-exclusive Choice-of-Forum clauses can be closer to the 'strong cause' test.[97]

Although exclusive and non-exclusive Choice-of-Forum clauses are treated differently, courts may not explicitly classify them before applying the 'strong cause' or 'natural forum' test. This probably stems from *Amerco*,[98] where Singapore's Court of Appeal introduced a test for granting a stay but did not clarify whether it applied solely to exclusive Choice-of-Forum clauses. The Court said:

> Where a plaintiff sues in Singapore in breach of an agreement to submit their disputes to a foreign court, and the defendant applies to a stay, the Singapore court, assuming the claim to be otherwise within its jurisdiction, is not bound to grant a stay but has a discretion to do so or not. The court in exercising its discretion should grant the stay and give effect to the agreement between the parties unless strong cause is shown by the plaintiff for not doing so.[99]

Because of this approach, later Singaporean decisions appear to have followed this language, with courts not seeing the need to qualify the clause first as either exclusive or non-exclusive.[100]

In *Vishva Apurva*,[101] the Court of Appeal introduced new factors to those in *The Eleftheria*. The Court said that it 'should accord full recognition to exclusive jurisdiction clauses which are freely negotiated between the parties and which are unaffected by "fraud, undue influence or overwhelming bargaining power"'.[102] Notably, this shift, plus a significant change in the list of factors which should be included in the 'strong cause' test (not those in *The Eleftheria* but the factors mentioned in *The Bremen*), show that the 'strong cause' test is flexible. Moreover, factors considered in the 'strong cause' test carry less weight if they were foreseeable when the parties contracted.[103]

Following the English case *S & W Berisford plc v New Hampshire Insurance Co*[104] ('*Berisford*'), the 'strong cause' test was also applied to non-exclusive clauses. In *Bambang Sutrisno v Bali International Finance Ltd*,[105] ('*Bambang*'), despite the non-exclusive clause designating Indonesian courts,[106] the Court of Appeal used the 'strong cause' test to stay Singapore proceedings,[107] finding exceptional circumstances amounting to strong cause to allow a stay and that the 'Indonesian court is clearly and distinctly more appropriate than the Singapore forum for the trial of the matter in dispute'.[108] Notably, a waiver of 'any objections

[97] *Orchard Capital I Ltd v Ravindra Kumar Jhunjhunwala*, [2012] 2 SLR 519, 532–33 (CA) ('*Orchard Capital*'); *Shanghai Turbo Enterprises Ltd v Liu Ming* [2019] 1 SLR 779, 816 (CA) ('*Shanghai Turbo*').

[98] *Amerco* (n 90).

[99] ibid 114–15.

[100] eg, *The 'Asian Plutus'* [1990] 1 SLR(R) 504, 512 (HC); *The 'Eastern Trust'* [1994] 2 SLR(R) 511, 515, 519–20 (HC); *The 'Botic'* [1999] 2 SLR(R) 494 (HC); *The 'Jian He'* [1999] 3 SLR(R) 432 (CA); *The 'Hung Vuong-2'* [2000] 2 SLR(R) 11 (CA); *The Hyundai Fortune* [2004] 2 SLR(R) 213 (HC).

[101] *The 'Vishva Apurva'* [1992] 1 SLR(R) 912 (CA).

[102] ibid 927.

[103] *Golden Shore Transportation Pte Ltd v UCO Bank* [2004] 1 SLR(R) 6, [38] (CA) ('*Golden Shore*'); *The Hyundai Fortune* (n 100) [30]; *Vinmar Overseas (Singapore) Pte Ltd v PTT International Trading Pte Ltd* [2018] 2 SLR 1271, 1292 (CA) ('*Vinmar*').

[104] *S & W Berisford plc v New Hampshire Insurance Co* [1990] 2 QB 631.

[105] *Bambang Sutrisno v Bali International Finance Ltd* [1999] 2 SLR(R) 632 (CA) ('*Bambang*').

[106] ibid 635.

[107] ibid 637.

[108] ibid 640.

on the ground of venue or *forum non conveniens* or any similar grounds',[109] in the clause may have affected the Court's analysis, possibly signalling a shift in Singapore's approach to non-exclusive clauses. The Court cited *PT Jaya Putra Kundur Indah v Guthrie Overseas Investments Pte Ltd*[110] ('*PT Jaya*'), which in turn referred to *Berisford*, which extended the strong cause test to situations where English courts are named in the non-exclusive clause and the action is filed in an English court. In *Bambang*, however, the situation was different because the non-exclusive clause stipulated for Indonesian courts and not for Singapore courts.[111] Notably, in *PT Jaya*,[112] the Singapore High Court first classified the clause non-exclusive[113] and still applied the usual *Spiliada* test[114] (not the 'strong cause' test), albeit the court considered the non-exclusive Choice-of-Forum clause as a 'strong' factor[115] after citing *Berisford*.[116]

Classifying clauses as either exclusive or non-exclusive became more explicit after *Baiduri*.[117] The High Court in *Baiduri* identified three types of Choice-of-Forum clause and the corresponding test which should be applied.[118] First are non-exclusive Choice-of-Forum clauses, which the court held must be evaluated following the principles of *Spiliada*, adopted in Singapore in *Brinkerhoff Maritime Drilling Corp v PT Airfast Services Indonesia*[119] ('*Brinkerhoff*'). The relevant test involves a 'balancing exercise … necessary to ascertain the *forum conveniens*'.[120] The second type is the exclusive Choice-of-Forum clause, which must be given effect unless vitiating factors such as fraud, undue influence, or overwhelming bargaining power are present.[121] This formula appears to follow *Vishva Apurva*, which introduced *The Bremen* factors to the 'strong cause' test in Singapore. The third type are 'semi-exclusive' clauses, otherwise known as hybrid clauses in other jurisdictions, whereby the 'jurisdiction clause limits the jurisdiction to a few countries, but no special or specific right of election or option is given to either party to select which of those countries to proceed in'.[122] These clauses require the application of the *forum non conveniens* principle. However, when the plaintiff has the right to select any one of these specified countries in which to institute his action,[123] and Singapore is one of the specified jurisdictions, the plaintiff, by filing a case in Singapore, is acting on his contractual right; thus the defendant has the burden of showing 'exceptional circumstances' amounting to 'strong cause' why the action brought by the plaintiff in Singapore should be stayed.[124]

[109] ibid 635.
[110] *PT Jaya Putra Kundur Indah v Guthrie Overseas Investments Pte Ltd* [1996] SGHC 285 ('*PT Jaya*').
[111] *Bambang* (n 105) 640.
[112] *PT Jaya* (n 110).
[113] ibid [62]–[63].
[114] ibid [66]–[67].
[115] ibid [65].
[116] ibid [64].
[117] *Baiduri Bank Bhd v Dong Sui Hung* [2000] 2 SLR(R) 271 (HC).
[118] ibid 276–82.
[119] ibid 276; *Brinkerhoff Maritime Drilling Corp v PT Airfast Services Indonesia Brinkerhoff Maritime Drilling Corp v PT Airfast Services Indonesia* [1992] 2 SLR(R) 345.
[120] *Baidurai* (n 117) 276.
[121] ibid 277.
[122] ibid 281.
[123] ibid 282.
[124] ibid.

Baiduri established a framework for future cases. Hence, courts would first categorise the Choice-of-Forum clause involved as either exclusive, non-exclusive or semi-exclusive, before applying the relevant test.[125] Citing *Bambang*,[126] *Societe Generale v Tai Kee Sing @ Tai Hean Sing*[127] ('*Societe Generale*') moved the Singaporean approach for non-exclusive clauses closer to *Berisford* by applying the 'strong cause' test to non-exclusive clauses stipulating Singapore courts.[128] However, as seen later, Singapore will develop a test that differs from *Berisford*.

Baiduri's recognition of 'semi-exclusive' clauses highlights that non-exclusive clauses cannot be categorised under one category and one applicable test – the 'natural forum' test. In *Orchard Capital I Ltd v Ravindra Kumar Jhunjhunwala*[129] ('*Orchard Capital*'), the Court of Appeal, relying on Yeo's article mentioned in section II.A above, proposed two approaches to non-exclusive clauses.[130] First, the contract's language and the parties' intention[131] must be examined, as a non-exclusive clause could function like an exclusive clause (or at least have a similar effect) depending 'on the precise intention of the parties themselves which is to be gathered from the language utilised by the parties as well as the surrounding factual matrix'.[132] The Court cautioned, nonetheless, against the contractual approach as it may lead to uncertainty and difficulties at the interlocutory level.[133] Second, non-exclusive Choice-of-Forum clauses should be treated as 'a factor – in all cases – in ascertaining whether or not the action concerned ought to be stayed … although … its qualitative strength … will differ, depending on the precise circumstances before the court'.[134] It appears, then, based on *Orchard Capital*, that to ascertain whether or not a stay may be granted, one must look first into the intention of the parties (as may be discerned in the language of the Choice-of-Forum clause) to determine the relative weight of the non-exclusive clause vis-à-vis the other factors in *Spiliada*'s 'natural forum' test. If the parties have intended an effect akin to an exclusive Choice-of-Forum clause or the parties' intended to give the clause a greater weight other than its being a factor in the *Spiliada* analysis, 'it may be a breach of the non-exclusive jurisdiction clause to object to the exercise of jurisdiction by the selected forum'.[135] In such case, 'strong cause would be required to be demonstrated by the party seeking to sue in a jurisdiction other than that stated in the relevant clause itself'.[136] Otherwise, if no such effect is intended, a grant of a stay would depend on the classical *Spiliada* analysis.[137] Citing the Hong Kong decision in *Noble Power*,[138] the Court in

[125] *Asia-Pacific Ventures II Ltd v PT Intimutiara Gasindo* [2001] 2 SLR(R) 371 (HC); *Golden Shore* (n 103); Rickshaw *Investments Ltd v Nicolai Baron von Uexkull* [2007] 1 SLR(R) 377 (CA); *CIMB Bank Bhd v Dresdner Kleinwort Ltd* [2008] 4 SLR(R) 543 (CA); *OCBC Capital Investment Asia Ltd v Wong Hua Choon* [2010] 4 SLR 904 (HC); *Citibank NA v Robert* [2011] 3 SLR 465 (HC).

[126] *Bambang* (n 105).

[127] *Societe Generale v Tai Kee Sing @ Tai Hean Sing* [2003] SGHC 139.

[128] ibid [7].

[129] *Orchard Capital* (n 97).

[130] ibid 530.

[131] ibid 530–31.

[132] ibid 532.

[133] ibid.

[134] ibid.

[135] ibid 530.

[136] ibid 530.

[137] ibid 532.

[138] *Noble Power Investments Ltd v Nissei Stomach Tokyo Co Ltd* [2008] HKCA 255 ('*Noble Power*').

Orchard Capital recognised that the defendant's burden may be less heavy where the action was commenced in a jurisdiction which was not the forum named in the non-exclusive Choice-of-Forum clause.[139] As explained in Chapter five, this test developed in *Orchard Capital* is notably different from that in *Berisford* and the other relevant English cases.

Nonetheless, in *Abdul Rashid bin Abdul Manaf v Hii Yii Ann*[140] ('*Abdul Rashid*'), the High Court rejected the attempt to move the test further. In *Abdul Rashid*, the Court dismissed the argument that a non-exclusive Choice-of-Forum clause always means that 'parties agreed that the contractual jurisdiction is the [most appropriate jurisdiction] to hear their dispute'.[141] Whether the non-exclusive clause designates the named forum as the most appropriate jurisdiction will depend on 'the context and the rest of the terms'.[142] If such was the parties' intention, 'this will bring the negotiated [non-exclusive jurisdiction] clause very close to an [exclusive jurisdiction] clause'.[143] In such cases, 'the evidential burden shifts to a plaintiff suing in the non-contractual jurisdiction to show strong cause as to why he should be permitted to do so'.[144]

The 2019 decision *Shanghai Turbo Enterprises Ltd v Liu Ming* ('*Shanghai Turbo*') reaffirmed *Abdul Rashid* on this point – '[a] non-exclusive jurisdiction clause only indicates that the parties thought that the forum named therein was an appropriate one'.[145] Hence, even if a non-exclusive clause is intended to carry more weight, as in *Orchard Capital*, parties can present evidence to establish 'strong cause', to sue elsewhere. The Court of Appeal emphasised that the factors relevant to the strong cause test for exclusive clauses also apply.[146] Further, if *The Eleftheria* factors (a) and (c) (eg, location of evidence and parties) were foreseeable at the time of contract formation, they hold little weight.[147] As noted in *Vinmar Overseas (Singapore) Pte Ltd v PTT International Trading Pte Ltd* ('*Vinmar*'),[148] factor (d) of *The Eleftheria* (ie, whether the defendants genuinely desire trial in the contractual forum) is only relevant if the applicant is acting abusively in seeking a stay.[149] *Shanghai Turbo* therefore represents the modified *Spiliada* as it currently stands in Singapore.

Shanghai Turbo noted that in a freely negotiated non-exclusive Choice-of-Forum clause, parties who 'submit' to the named forum waived their right to object to forum's appropriateness.[150] However, the Court did not decide whether this applies to standard contracts.[151] Hence, in a freely-negotiated non-exclusive agreement, either party is precluded from contesting the jurisdiction of the named forum, either through an application to set aside service or for a stay of proceedings.[152]

[139] *Orchard Capital* (n 97) 528–29, citing *Nobel Power* (n 138) [31]–[33].
[140] *Abdul Rashid* (n 89).
[141] ibid 1053.
[142] ibid 1054.
[143] ibid.
[144] ibid 1054.
[145] *Shanghai Turbo* (n 97) 817.
[146] ibid 823.
[147] ibid 824.
[148] *Vinmar* (n 103).
[149] *Shanghai Turbo* (n 97) 824.
[150] ibid 820.
[151] ibid.
[152] ibid 820–21.

Aside from traditional stays, Singaporean courts can grant a 'partial' stay of proceedings. In *Humpuss Sea Transport Pte Ltd (in compulsory liquidation) v PT Humpuss Intermoda Transportasi TBK*,[153] ('*Humpuss*') the High Court explained that a partial stay, which can involve staying one of the claims against a defendant but not the rest,[154] is possible when claims against multiple defendants are not closely related and there is no possibility of inconsistent decisions across jurisdictions.[155] A partial stay can also be granted when the forum is the natural forum for deciding on one claim but not others.[156] The Court referred to *Hyslop v Society of Lloyd's*,[157] where the New Zealand High Court declined to stay all the claims despite an exclusive clause for English courts because of various New Zealand statutes containing mandatory rules and reflecting public policy.[158] In *Bidzina Ivanishvili v Credit Suisse AG*[159] ('*Ivanishvili*'), however, the Singapore High Court refused a partial stay,[160] as Geneva was central to all claims,[161] and the trust deed's non-exclusive clause did not bind all five plaintiffs in this case.[162]

Singaporean courts can also grant a temporary or limited stay. In *RBS Coutts Bank Ltd v Brunner Hans-Peter*,[163] the High Court distinguished this from a permanent stay, which is typically granted in Choice-of-Forum clause cases. The Court said that granting a 'limited stay order pending conclusion of foreign proceedings did not require the application of *forum non conveniens* principles … [because] the court has the full discretion'.[164] Granting a temporary stay, even with an exclusive Choice-of-Forum clause stipulating Singapore courts, 'would not amount to the court assisting in a breach of a contractual arrangement'.[165] This is because '[a]fter the resolution of the Zurich action, the plaintiff could still continue with the present action in Singapore to determine its rights under the loan agreement'.[166] The key considerations include international comity, case management and fairness to the parties.[167] In this case, the Court granted a temporary stay because of the prior commencement and more advanced stage of the Zurich proceedings, and to avoid both courts from ruling on the same issue.[168]

Before proceeding, it is worth commenting on partial, temporary or limited stays. While these forms of relief offer flexibility in managing complex litigation, they may undermine the effects of Choice-of-Forum clauses and even lead to fragmented proceedings, which probably could be the reason why the parties stipulated a Choice-of-Forum clause. For

[153] *Humpuss Sea Transport Pte Ltd (in compulsory liquidation) v PT Humpuss Intermoda Transportasi TBK* [2016] 5 SLR 1322 (HC) ('*Humpuss*').
[154] ibid 1349.
[155] ibid.
[156] ibid.
[157] *Hyslop v Society of Lloyd's* (1992) 6 PRNZ 204.
[158] *Humpuss* (n 153) 1349, citing *Hyslop* (n 157).
[159] *Bidzina Ivanishvili v Credit Suisse AG* [2019] SGHC 6.
[160] ibid [78].
[161] ibid [79].
[162] ibid [28].
[163] *RBS Coutts Bank Ltd v Brunner Hans-Peter* [2010] SGHC 342 ('*RBS*').
[164] ibid [13] citing *Chan Chin Cheung v Chan Fatt Cheung* [2009] SGCA 64, [47]; see also *UD Trading Group Holdings Pte Ltd v TA Private Capital Security Agent Ltd* [2022] SGHC(A) 3, [29].
[165] *RBS* (n 163) [30].
[166] ibid.
[167] ibid [28].
[168] ibid [29].

example, granting a partial stay in disputes involving exclusive clauses can allow a plaintiff to escape the requirement to prove 'strong cause', by simply arguing that certain claims may be more appropriately heard in the present forum, while others, in the chosen forum. In non-exclusive clauses, these stays can result in fragmented proceedings, inconsistent decisions, and increased litigation complexities and costs, which disproportionately affect lesser-resourced parties who may be discouraged from pursuing claims in various forums. Such stays also incentivise forum shopping, potentially leading to abuse of the judicial process and undermining the enforcement of Choice-of-Forum clauses.

If a foreign court declines jurisdiction after a Singapore court grants a stay, the Singapore court remains seised of the proceedings and may lift the stay later.[169] This is because, in the first stage of the *Spiliada* framework, 'the court is engaged in only a prima facie determination of whether there is some other available forum that is more appropriate for the trial of the case'.[170] If

> the premise on which it decides to grant a stay should turn out to be mistaken or unduly optimistic, we see no reason why the stay cannot, in such 'exceptional circumstances which strike at the very basis on which the stay was granted', be revisited.[171]

Given this reasoning, this should also arguably apply to cases involving exclusive Choice-of-Forum clauses.

Hence, in *Belbana NV v APL Co Pte Ltd*,[172] the High Court ruled that, despite the plaintiff breaching the exclusive Choice-of-Forum clause by filing in Belgium instead of Singapore, a stay rather than discontinuance, was appropriate. The clause stipulated the Singapore courts, and challenging jurisdiction in Belgium (eg, where jurisdiction is determined after the merits) could leave the plaintiff without recourse if the challenge to jurisdiction in the foreign court succeeded.[173] However, if the Belgian court rules against the plaintiff on the merits, he cannot re-litigate in Singapore, as he would be deemed to have elected the Belgium proceedings.[174]

(ii) Singapore International Commercial Court

The SICC introduced a new test for stays that does not distinguish between exclusive and non-exclusive clauses, although the factors and their relative weights may vary. Under the old rules (order 110, rule 8(1)), a court may decline jurisdiction 'if it is not appropriate for the action to be heard in the Court'.[175] The new SICC Rules of Court modified this test to 'if exercising jurisdiction would be contrary to the Court's international and commercial character or would be an abuse of the process of the Court'.[176] This test clarifies the SICC's jurisdiction, which is limited to international and commercial cases. When the SICC lacks jurisdiction: (1) it must transfer the case to the general division, if it considers the general

[169] *Rappo, Tania v Accent Delight International Ltd* [2017] 2 SLR 265, 300 (CA) ('*Rappo*').
[170] ibid.
[171] ibid.
[172] *Belbana NV v APL Co Pte Ltd* [2014] SGHCR 17.
[173] ibid [33].
[174] ibid [40].
[175] Rules of Court (n 5) ord 110, r 8(1).
[176] SICC Rules (n 13) ord 2, r 3(2).

division to have jurisdiction and all parties consent to such transfer;[177] (2) it may dismiss or stay the case or claim;[178] or (3) it may make any order.[179]

The second ground requires abuse of process; the court is no longer required to consider any other 'more appropriate forum', but rather only to consider whether the actions of the parties amount to abuse of the process of the court. Neither the SICC Rules of Court nor the SICC Practice Directions, however, elaborate further on what may be considered abuse of the 'process of the court', so the common law definition likely applies.

In *Rappo, Tania v Accent Delight International Ltd*[180] ('*Rappo*') the Court of Appeal stressed that the High Court, when determining whether to exercise international jurisdiction, should consider transferring the case to the SICC. 'This is because in determining whether a particular forum is *forum non conveniens*, the court is required to take *all factors into consideration*, and this must include the possibility of a transfer to SICC'.[181] Nonetheless, the plaintiff must demonstrate why the SICC is the more appropriate forum and show that 'the dispute was of a nature that lent itself to the SICC's capabilities'.[182]

In *BNP Paribas Wealth Management v Jacob Agam*,[183] the SICC confirmed it could grant a limited or temporary stay of proceedings based on case management considerations, 'to avoid the risk of conflicting judgments on account of multiplicity of proceedings'.[184] The court must assess the circumstances behind the multiplicity of proceedings, including who is responsible and whether the parallel foreign proceedings are bona fide or contrived.[185] In this case, the Court refused the temporary stay, as the French proceedings were intended to delay the Singapore action.[186] Notably, the French counter-action was the mirror image of the Singapore action.[187] Although a temporary stay is usually issued to avoid the risk of conflicting judgments, such 'is not by itself sufficient reason for the grant of limited stay of proceedings'.[188] The court must ensure efficient and fair resolution of the entire dispute.[189]

(iii) Choice of Court Agreements Act

The CCAA removes discretion in declining jurisdiction when Singapore is chosen in an exclusive Choice-of-Forum clause.[190] The only ground for refusing exercise of jurisdiction is when the Choice-of-Forum clause is null and void under Singaporean law,[191] because of fraud, mistake, duress, parties' lack of capacity to contract, lack of subject-matter jurisdiction of the chosen court, etc.[192] Since the test for nullity is based on Singaporean law,

[177] ibid ord 2, r 3(5)(a).
[178] ibid ord 2, r 3(5)(b).
[179] ibid.
[180] *Rappo* (n 169).
[181] ibid 305.
[182] ibid 306.
[183] *BNP Paribas Wealth Management v Jacob Agam* [2016] SGHC(I) 5 (SICC).
[184] ibid [4].
[185] ibid.
[186] ibid [5].
[187] ibid.
[188] ibid [46].
[189] ibid.
[190] CCAA (n 51) pt 2 s 11(1).
[191] ibid pt 2 s 11(1).
[192] See Hartley-Dogauchi Report (n 59) 55.

the grounds may differ from the other Choice-of-Court Convention states. Furthermore, a Singapore court with jurisdiction may transfer the case to another Singapore court.[193]

Applications for stay or dismissal under section 12(1) CCCA follow two stages. First, the court must determine if a non-Singapore exclusive clause exists, using the 'good arguable case' test under common law (ie, that the exclusive clause exists and governs the dispute).[194] Here, the burden of showing a 'good arguable case', which imposes 'a higher threshold than a mere prima facie case but is different from the standard of a balance of probabilities',[195] lies with the applicant.[196] If the applicant denies the contractual relationship, 'there is no factual basis on which it can allege the existence of an exclusive jurisdiction agreement, much less demonstrate a "good arguable case"'.[197] If the applicant has demonstrated a 'good arguable case', the Singapore court is required to stay or dismiss the proceedings (unless any of the five exceptions in section 12(1) is established at the second stage) even if it has jurisdiction under its national law.[198]

At the second stage, the court determines whether any of the five exceptions under section 12(1) exists,[199] with the burden on the party resisting the stay. The exceptions are: (a) the agreement is null and void under the law of the chosen court; (b) a party to the agreement lacked the contractual capacity under Singapore law; (c) enforcing the agreement would result in manifest injustice or violate Singapore's public policy; (d) exceptional reasons beyond the control of the parties make the agreement unperformable; or (e) the chosen court has declined to hear the case.[200] Note that Singapore law governs grounds (b), (c) and likely (d), while ground (a) is determined by the law of the chosen court. Moreover, the CCAA also allows courts to dismiss or stay the case or proceeding on other grounds.[201] However, given that the CCAA implements the Choice-of-Court Convention, it cannot be the case that the CCAA expands the grounds stated in article 6. Paragraph 12(2) of the CCAA may be referring only to the procedural grounds under the Rules of Court for stay or dismissal of an action or proceeding (eg, abuse of process).

The 'strong cause' test under common law is therefore insufficient to dismiss an application under section 12(1) of the CCAA.[202] Once the Singapore court, which is seised but not chosen, stays or dismisses the proceedings, 'the chosen court's determination of its jurisdiction cannot be appealed by way of recourse to the court seised'.[203] However, if the Singapore court does not stay proceedings due to an exception under article 6 of the Choice-of-Court Convention,[204] Singapore law determines whether it has jurisdiction.[205]

Section 11(2) of the CCAA precludes a chosen Singapore court from declining to exercise its jurisdiction based on the reason that the dispute should be decided in another country.

[193] CCAA (n 51) pt 2 s 11(5).
[194] *Qompass Voyage Ltd v APACPAY Pte Ltd* [2023] SGHCR 20, [13] ('*Qompass*'); *6DM* (n 79) [34].
[195] *Qompass* (n 194) [20].
[196] ibid [13].
[197] ibid [23]; *6DM* (n 79) [39].
[198] *6DM* (n 79) [39].
[199] *Qompass* (n 194) [13].
[200] CCAA (n 51) pt 2 s 12(1).
[201] ibid pt 2 s 12(2).
[202] *Qompass* (n 194) [13]; *6DM* (n 79) [36], [38].
[203] *6DM* (n 79) [31].
[204] CCAA (n 51), pt 2 s 12(1).
[205] *6DM* (n 79) [38].

It also prevents Singapore courts from ignoring any exclusive Choice-of-Forum clauses covered by the Choice-of-Court Convention.[206] Because section 11(2) is never intended to apply in situations covered by section 12(1),[207] if the exclusive clauses in other contracts attract the operation of section 12(1), the court may still dismiss or stay the proceedings. In *6DM (S) Pte Ltd v AE Brands Korea Ltd* ('*6DM*'), the High Court confirmed, after referring to the Hartley-Dogauchi Report, that section 11(2) contemplates two applicable doctrines – *forum non conveniens* and *lis pendens* – which can no longer be the basis for dismissing the case 'on the ground that the dispute should be decided in a court of another State'.[208]

In *6DM*, the High Court also confirmed that Singapore courts can either stay or dismiss the proceedings under the CCAA.[209] If part of the dispute between the parties falls outside the scope of the exclusive clause,[210] that part is stayed while the rest proceeds.[211] However, if the entire dispute falls within the exclusive clause, the case should be dismissed.[212]

Applications for a stay in CCAA cases at the SICC follow the CCAA grounds. For cases outside the CCAA (eg, non-exclusive clauses and exclusive clauses in transactions outside its scope), the test is whether 'exercising jurisdiction would be contrary to the court's international and commercial character or would be an abuse of the process of the court'. The SICC's ability to join third parties complicates matters, as they too can seek a stay, likely subject to the same test under the SICC Rules of Court. Although generally the Choice-of-Court Convention is envisioned to affect only parties, the Hartley-Dogauchi Report has actually considered third parties being involved[213] if they have taken over the rights and obligations of one of the original parties[214] under Singapore laws. Hence, in actions under the CCAA where the third party seeks a stay, the SICC will apply the tests under the CCAA. However, in instances when CCAA applies and yet the third party involved does not meet the Hartley-Dogauchi Report criteria, the test under the SICC Rules of Court applies.

Applications for a stay in CCAA cases at the High Court or other courts of Singapore follow CCAA rules, including where the exclusive choice is the High Court or another court, and parties refuse to transfer to the SICC, or where claims are below S$250,000 which means that second-tier courts should assume jurisdiction, especially when the choice does not state any particular Singaporean court.[215] In non-CCAA cases (eg, non-exclusive Choice-of-Court cases and exclusive Choice-of-Court cases in transactions not covered by the CCAA and where the choice is not the SICC), the High Court and other courts apply common law tests (ie, the 'strong cause' test and 'natural forum' test or its modified version, for exclusive and non-exclusive and non-exclusive Choice-of-Forum clause respectively). For third parties, cases under the Choice-of-Court Convention apply CCAA rules, while others follow the common law rules and the Rules of Court.

[206] ibid [95].
[207] ibid.
[208] ibid [96]; See also Hartley-Dogauchi Report (n 59) [134].
[209] *6DM* (n 79) [91].
[210] ibid.
[211] ibid.
[212] ibid.
[213] Hartley-Dogauchi Report (n 59) 51.
[214] ibid.
[215] Supreme Court Singapore, 'Role and structure of the Supreme Court' (Web Page, 22 June 2024): https://www.judiciary.gov.sg/who-we-are/role-structure-supreme-court (accessed 28 October 2024).

The situation becomes complex when a case typically falls under the CCAA but involves interconnected legal issues in areas excluded from the CCAA (eg, a shareholders' agreement dispute where the court needs to look into the rules of succession). Given that the CCAA explicitly excludes certain matters like succession,[216] if these matters are material and primary issues to the case, the case should not be subjected to the CCAA even if there is an international and commercial contract with an exclusive Choice-of-Forum clause. In these circumstances, the High Court and the other courts should apply common law rules for a stay.

D. Anti-suit Injunctions and Other Relief

An anti-suit injunction may be sought to compel a party to a Choice-of-Forum clause to stop or refrain from pursuing foreign proceedings. This discretionary remedy, rooted in equity, is granted 'when the ends of justice require it'.[217] Notably, the power to issue an anti-suit injunction is considered included in the court's powers under a Choice-of-Forum clause.[218] However, the Court of Appeal in *VKZ v VJZ* referred to this as a 'contractual basis for an anti-suit injunction',[219] limiting its benefit to contracting parties.[220] Third parties cannot seek an anti-suit injunction, as the silence in the Contracts (Rights of Third Parties) Act 2001 can only mean that the Singapore Parliament has made a conscious determination to exclude Choice-of-Forum clauses from the statute's application.[221]

An anti-suit injunction operates *in personam*, but its indirect effect on foreign legal proceedings has long been recognised.[222] Judicial caution is exercised in the interest of international comity, which is understood in Singapore as respecting another nation's legislative, executive or judicial acts, while considering international duty, convenience, and the rights of Singaporean citizens.[223] Comity also requires avoiding unnecessary judicial time and costs, meaning that 'the longer the delay [in seeking an anti-suit injunction] and the more advanced the foreign court proceedings become, the stronger the considerations of comity'.[224]

Singapore courts' jurisdiction to issue an anti-suit injunction is to be found in section 4(10) of the Civil Law Act.[225] Common law recognises various types of anti-suit injunction, including to protect the jurisdiction of the forum from interference, to protect legal rights – particularly the right not to be sued in a foreign jurisdiction – and to prevent equitable wrongs.[226] These injunctions can extend beyond substantive foreign proceedings since they may be granted to prevent a party from proceeding with an anti-suit injunction in

[216] CCAA (n 51) pt 1 s 9(2)(c).

[217] *Morgan Stanley Asia (Singapore) Pte (formerly known as Morgan Stanley Dean Witter Asia (Singapore) Pte) v Hong Leong Finance Ltd* [2013] 3 SLR 409, 418 (HC) ('*Morgan Stanley*').

[218] See *Teo Choon Mong Frank v Wilh Schulz GmbH* [1998] 2 SLR(R) 312, 318–19 (CA); *Qompas* (n 211) [27].

[219] *VKZ v VJZ* [2021] SGCA 72, [16] (CA).

[220] ibid [54].

[221] ibid [59].

[222] See eg, *British Airways Board v Laker Airways Ltd* [1985] AC 58, 95.

[223] *Morgan Stanley* (n 217) 422, citing *The 'Reecon Wolf'* [2012] SGHC 22, [23].

[224] *ED&F Man Capital Markets Ltd v Straits (Singapore) Pte Ltd* [2019] SGHC 203, [47].

[225] Civil Law Act (Singapore, cap 43, 2020 rev edn), s 4(10); also SCJA (n 2) sch 1, s 18(2) para 14.

[226] LexisNexis Singapore (n 74) [75.125].

a foreign court (an anti-anti-suit injunction).[227] Similarly, an anti-anti-anti-suit injunction may be granted to prevent an application for an anti-anti-suit injunction in a foreign court.[228] Furthermore, to grant an anti-suit injunction, a court must have *in personam* jurisdiction over the respondent, either by service within the jurisdiction or service outside the jurisdiction.[229]

An anti-suit injunction may be issued based on the following factors: (a) whether the defendants are subject to the Singapore court's jurisdiction; (b) the natural forum for resolving the dispute; (c) potential vexation or oppression to the plaintiffs if the foreign proceedings continue; (d) potential injustice to the defendants if an injunction deprives them of advantages in the foreign proceedings; and (e) whether the foreign proceedings breach any agreement between the parties.[230] Notably, factors (a) to (e) are considered cumulatively when issuing an anti-suit injunction.[231] The court usually follows a two-stage analysis: (1) determining if Singapore is the 'natural forum', and (2) determining whether the foreign proceedings involve any unconscionable conduct or unconscientious exercise of legal rights (the vexatious and oppressive test).[232] The 'natural forum' test is the same as in applying for leave for service out of Singapore or stay applications involving non-exclusive Choice-of-Forum clauses.[233] The applicant must prove that Singapore is clearly and distinctly the more appropriate forum, but this alone does not justify restraining foreign proceedings.[234] Similarly, it does not follow that whenever a stay is refused, an anti-suit injunction may be granted as well,[235] as an injunction is only granted and justified when the second step is also satisfied – 'in the clearest of circumstances that the foreign proceedings are vexatious or oppressive'.[236]

When foreign proceedings breach an exclusive Choice-of-Forum clause the court may grant an anti-suit injunction without considering comity or the vexatiousness or oppressiveness of the foreign conduct, unless 'there are strong reasons not to do so'.[237] The anti-suit injunction enforces the contractual right not to be sued elsewhere.[238] In any case, the 'strong reasons' referred to are akin to the 'strong cause' test used in stay applications. On the other hand, in non-exclusive Choice-of-Forum clauses, 'the law requires the applicant to demonstrate that the conduct of the foreign proceedings is vexatious and/or oppressive to warrant the court's intervention in granting an injunction'.[239] As noted in *UBS AG v Telesto Investments Ltd*,[240] ('*UBS*') a party to a non-exclusive clause pursuing proceedings in an

[227] ibid.
[228] ibid.
[229] ibid [75.126].
[230] *John Reginald Stott Kirkham v Trane US Inc* [2009] 4 SLR(R) 428, 445–46 (CA) citing *Evergreen International SA v Volkswagen Group Singapore Pte Ltd* [2004] 2 SLR(R) 457, [16] (HC) ('*Kirkham*'); see also *Qompass* (n 194) [27].
[231] *Morgan Stanley* (n 217) 418.
[232] See ibid 425.
[233] See *UBS* (n 93) 540.
[234] *Morgan Stanley* (n 217) 418.
[235] *UBS* (n 93) 540.
[236] *Kirkham* (n 230) 454.
[237] *Morgan Stanley* (n 217) 419; *Donohue v Armco Inc* [2002] 1 Lloyd's Rep 425.
[238] *Morgan Stanley* (n 217) 425.
[239] *UBS* (n 93) 541.
[240] *UBS* (n 93).

alternative jurisdiction', is not usually in breach,[241] unless the clause's wording indicates otherwise or the forum court treats non-exclusive clauses like exclusive ones. Because there is no presumption that multiplicity of proceedings is *ipso facto* vexatious, 'the burden is on the applicant to show that foreign proceedings are "vexatious or oppressive for some reason independent of the mere presence of the non-exclusive [jurisdiction] clause"'.[242] '[T]he possibility of parallel proceedings and risks of conflicting judgments do not, by themselves, warrant the grant of an anti-suit injunction'.[243] Significantly, the existence of strong reasons in favour of proceeding in the foreign jurisdiction would negate the claim that the action therein is vexatious and oppressive.[244]

Except for the recognition and enforcement of judgments stage under article 14, the Choice-of-Court Convention does not affect the party states' internal procedural, including interim measures.[245] Hence, the CCAA does not impact rules on anti-suit injunctions or other remedies for enforcing exclusive Choice-of-Forum clauses. An anti-suit injunction may therefore be issued to enforce an exclusive clause stipulating Singapore courts. However, if Singapore is a non-chosen court and the injunction seeks to restrain proceedings in another non-chosen Choice-of-Court Convention court, arguably, its issuance strengthens the effect of the exclusive Choice-of-Forum clause.[246] However, if the non-chosen court exercises jurisdiction under the exceptions to the Choice-of-Court Convention, then the anti-suit injunction from Singapore may undermine the convention's framework.[247] Please note, however, that if the anti-suit injunction is directed against a non-Choice-of-Court Convention state, this concern will not arise.[248]

The SICC, as a division of the High Court, retains the power to grant anti-suit injunctions. However, the SICC Rules of Court do not specify guidelines for such orders. The SICC's distinct *in personam* jurisdiction framework, which is different from the High Court general division, raises questions about how this affects traditional rules on anti-suit injunctions, especially in cases transferred from the High Court.[249] In short, common law principles continue to govern anti-suit injunctions in the SICC and cases under the CCAA, although the differences in the *in personam* jurisdiction framework may require some adjustments.

Controversially, English courts have awarded damages for expenses incurred in defending foreign proceedings commenced in breach of an English Choice-of-Forum clause.[250] In *Tradewaves Ltd v Standard Chartered Bank*[251] ('*Tradewaves*') the High Court cited *Union Discount Co Ltd v Zoller*[252] and outlined the exceptional circumstances under which Singapore courts may also award damages: (1) the claimant seeks to recover costs incurred as a defendant in foreign proceedings brought by the defendant in the English proceedings; (2) the foreign proceedings were brought in breach of the exclusive jurisdiction clause,

[241] ibid 544.
[242] ibid.
[243] ibid 550.
[244] See *Morgan Stanley* (n 217) 429.
[245] See Choice-of-Court Convention (n 19) art 7 which preserves the national law on interim measures.
[246] Chong and Yip (n 12) 147.
[247] ibid.
[248] ibid 148.
[249] ibid 136.
[250] See *Union Discount Co Ltd v Zoller* [2002] 1 WLR 1517; *Donohue* (n 237).
[251] *Tradewaves Ltd v Standard Chartered Bank* [2017] SGHC 93 ('*Tradewaves*').
[252] *Union Discount* (n 269).

which is assumed 'has the effect of entitling the English claimant to damages for its breach'; (3) the foreign forum only allows costs recovery in exceptional circumstances; and (4) the foreign court made no ruling on costs.[253] In *Tradewaves* the High Court refused to award damages because none of these exceptional features were present and proven.[254]

E. Recognition and Enforcement of Judgments

(i) *Common Law and Statutes*

In Singapore, foreign judgments may be enforced under common law or statutes allowing registration.[255] Under common law, foreign judgments obtained in breach of Choice-of-Forum clauses are not automatically denied recognition. Even with exclusive clauses, foreign judgments may be enforced if a rigorous test similar to the 'strong cause' test was applied before allowing the foreign court to hear the case. 'It is a question of balancing the upholding of the parties' agreement on one hand, and the international comity underlying the recognition and enforcement of foreign judgments on the other'.[256] The relevant statutes also do not deal with this scenario.

In *Merck Sharp & Dohne Corp (formerly known as Merck & Co, Inc) v Merck KGaA (formerly known as E Merck)* ('*Merck*'), the Court of Appeal emphasised the need for convergence between common law and statutes such as the CCAA and Reciprocal Enforcement of Foreign Judgments Act (REFJA).[257] The common law should be developed in a manner 'that is compatible and consistent with legislation which covers a broadly similar area'.[258] This requires the recognising Singapore court consider legislative developments when striking a balance 'between comity, international relations and the need to aid in the development of a transnational system of justice, while also safeguarding the rule of law within [Singapore's] jurisdiction'.[259] In *Merck*, the Court considered pre-emptive litigation to prevent the recognition of an impending foreign judgment, noting that all circumstances, including 'how the foreign judgment came to be issued … and whether there was undue haste or any action by a party that is suggestive of deliberate attempt to pre-empt the recognition of the foreign judgment in Singapore', should be assessed, although no specific rule was established.[260] Further, the Court noted that the absence of reciprocity is rarely an obstacle to the recognition of a foreign judgment in Singapore.[261] Additionally, it refrained from ruling on whether foreign judgments applying Singapore law incorrectly would raise public policy concerns or limit transnational issue estoppel, but nonetheless suggested that a distinction should be made between cases where the foreign court clearly erred in its application of Singaporean

[253] *Tradewaves* (n 251) [292] citing *Union Discount* (n 269).
[254] ibid [293].
[255] Reciprocal Enforcement of Commonwealth Judgments Act (Singapore, cap 98, 2020 rev edn); Reciprocal Enforcement of Foreign Judgments Act (Singapore, cap 265, 2020 rev edn).
[256] LexisNexis Singapore (n 74) [75.236].
[257] *Merck Sharp & Dohne Corp (formerly known as Merck & Co, Inc) v Merck KGaA (formerly known as E Merck)* [2021] SGCA 14, [37] (CA) ('*Merck Sharp*').
[258] ibid.
[259] ibid.
[260] ibid [38].
[261] ibid [39].

law and cases where Singapore law is uncertain and the foreign court simply adopted a position, after taking expert evidence, which was eventually proved to be incorrect by a subsequent Singapore decision.[262]

In *William Jacks & Co (Singapore) Pte Ltd v Nelson Honey & Marketing (NZ) Ltd* ('*William Jacks*'), the High Court held that a foreign court's decision on the appropriateness of a forum can never give rise to an issue estoppel in Singapore.[263] Hence, 'any explicit pronouncement by a foreign court on the appropriateness of Singapore would not be binding on a Singapore court'.[264] Furthermore, if a foreign judgment conflicts with Singapore's public policy, issue estoppel invoked in Singapore may be denied to the judgment.[265]

(ii) Choice of Court Agreements Act

Singapore's accession to the Choice-of-Court Convention prevents the enforcement of foreign judgments from another party-state that breach an exclusive Choice-of-Forum clause.[266] Only judgments from the forum designated in the exclusive clause can be recognised and enforced in Singapore under article 8(1).[267] Under the Choice-of-Court Convention, judgments from non-chosen courts cannot be enforced.[268] Applications for recognition and enforcement of foreign judgments under the Choice-of-Court Convention are filed with the Singapore High Court.[269]

Under order 37 of the Rules of Court, an application for recognition and enforcement of a foreign judgment under the CCAA must first include an affidavit stating that the judgment is a foreign judgment under the CCAA, that it has the same effect in the state of origin, and that it is enforceable in the state of origin, etc.[270] The affidavit must provide: (1) a complete and certified copy of the foreign judgment, (2) the exclusive choice-of-Forum agreement, (3) for default judgments, proof that the defaulting party was notified, and (4) any other document proving the judgment's enforceability in the state of origin, and other matters like establishing that the Choice-of-Forum clause was concluded in a civil or commercial matter, etc.[271] The application may also include a document from the originating court, per article 13(3) of the Choice-of-Court Convention as published by The Hague Conference on Private International Law.[272]

The CCAA allows limited grounds for refusing recognition and enforcement of foreign judgments under the Choice-of-Court Convention.[273] It explicitly prohibits review on expanded grounds, including the merits of the foreign judgments.[274] Except for

[262] ibid [61].
[263] *William Jacks & Co (Singapore) Pte Ltd v Nelson Honey & Marketing (NZ) Ltd* [2015] SGHCR 21, [60].
[264] ibid [61].
[265] *Merck Sharp* (n 257) [58].
[266] Choice-of-Court Convention (n 19) art 8.
[267] ibid art 8(1).
[268] ibid.
[269] CCAA (n 51) pt 3 s 13(1).
[270] Rules of Court (n 5) ord 37, r 2(2).
[271] ibid ord 37, r 2(3).
[272] ibid ord 37, r 4.
[273] CCAA (n 51) pt 3 ss 14, 15.
[274] Choice-of-Court Convention (n 19) art 8(2); CCAA (n 51) pt 3 s 13(3)(a).

default judgments, Singapore courts are bound by the factual findings underpinning the originating court's jurisdiction.[275] A judgment is recognisable and enforceable in Singapore if it is enforceable in the originating state.[276] Likewise, recognition and enforcement may be suspended or refused if the judgment is under review or the review period has not elapsed.[277] Nonetheless, courts may still enforce foreign judgments obtained after a valid transfer has been made to another court under the Choice-of-Court Convention.[278]

The CCAA provides compulsory and discretionary grounds for refusing recognition and enforcement. The High Court must refuse if proper notice to the defendant was absent, or if the judgment was obtained by fraud or manifestly violates Singapore's public policy, including its fundamental principles on procedural fairness.[279] The High Court may also refuse where the non-chosen court proceeded with the proceedings (eg, where the exclusive Choice-of-Forum clause is null and void, or the parties lacked legal capacity),[280] where *res judicata* applies,[281] or service of the originating process was made in a manner incompatible with Singapore's fundamental principles of giving notice to the defendant.[282] Notably, while these grounds are the same grounds stated in article 9 of the Choice-of-Court Convention, they are only discretionary grounds for refusal under the CCAA.

Under the CCAA, rulings on excluded matters (eg, family law matters) under section 9(2) or 9(4)(a) which arose as preliminary questions in a foreign judgment should be refused recognition and enforcement.[283] Foreign judgments based on rulings on matters under section 9(4)(a) (ie, specific matters excluded by the minister under his power to issue regulations under the CCAA) may be refused to the extent that they rely on such rulings.[284] However, for rulings on the intellectual property right's validity (excluding copyright or a related right), the High Court may refuse recognition and enforcement only if the ruling contradicts a decision made under the law of the state where the intellectual property right originated, or if proceedings concerning its validity are still pending there.[285]

Judicial settlements can also be enforced and recognised under the Choice-of-Court Convention.[286] The CCAA allows the High Court to enforce a settlement approved by or concluded before the chosen court, if it is enforceable in the same way as a judgment in the state of origin.[287] Refusal of enforcement follows the same rules, prescribing compulsory and discretionary grounds, as those for foreign judgments under the CCAA.[288]

[275] CCAA (n 51) pt 3 s 13(3)(b).
[276] ibid pt 3 s 13(2)(b).
[277] ibid pt 3 s 15(2).
[278] ibid pt 3 s 15(3), (4).
[279] ibid pt 3 s 14.
[280] ibid pt 3 s 15(a)–(b).
[281] ibid pt 3 s 15(1)(d)–(e).
[282] ibid pt 3 s 15(c).
[283] ibid pt 3 s 17(1).
[284] ibid pt 3 s 17(4).
[285] ibid pt 3 s 17(3).
[286] Choice-of-Court Convention (n 19) art 12.
[287] CCAA (n 51) pt 3 s 20(2).
[288] ibid pt 3 s 20(3).

In *Ermgassen & Co Ltd v Sixcap Financials Pte Ltd*,[289] the High Court enforced a summary judgment from the High Court of Justice of England and Wales. The court noted that the judgment came from a contracting state (UK), involved an international case with an exclusive Choice-of-Forum clause in a 'civil or commercial matter', and no interim measure of protection was sought.[290] Although the plaintiff failed to provide a complete and certified copy of the foreign judgment as required by order 111, rule 2(3)(a) of the Rules of Court, the Court held that this omission was not fatal,[291] as other documents could establish the necessary requirements,[292] thus confirming the Hartley-Dogauchi Report's caution against excessive formalism.[293]

III. Hong Kong

A. Hong Kong's Approach to Jurisdiction

The Court of Final Appeal is Hong Kong's highest court.[294] Below it is the High Court, which is composed of the Court of Appeal and the Court of First Instance (CFI),[295] and further below, the district courts.[296] Cases involving Choice-of-Forum clauses may be filed in the district courts or the CFI, depending on the amount claimed or remedy sought.

Statutes are the primary sources of Hong Kong's civil procedure. Procedural rules, issued by the Rules Committee of the various courts, including the Hong Kong Court of Final Appeal Rules,[297] Rules of the High Court,[298] and District Court Rules[299] supplement statutory law and have the same effect. As these rules are similarly worded, the Rules of the High Court will be used for illustration, with any material differences being noted. Judicial decisions also significantly shape the development and interpretation of Hong Kong's civil procedure.

The Basic Law of the Hong Kong Special Administrative Region ('Basic Law') and the Hong Kong Reunification Ordinance, which came into effect in Hong Kong upon its reunification with the People's Republic of China on 1 July 1997, state that the laws previously in force in Hong Kong, including the common law, will be maintained, unless they contravene the Basic Law, subject to subsequent amendment by the legislature of the Hong Kong SAR.[300] As a result, Choice-of-Forum clauses remain largely governed by English common law, except in the enforcement of foreign judgments where local ordinances and regional arrangements have modified the rules.

[289] *Ermgassen & Co Ltd v Sixcap Financials Pte Ltd* [2018] SGHCR 8.
[290] ibid [17].
[291] ibid [24].
[292] ibid.
[293] ibid.
[294] Hong Kong Court of Final Appeal Ordinance (Hong Kong) cap 484, s 3.
[295] High Court Ordinance (Hong Kong) cap 4, pt 2 s 3(1).
[296] District Court Ordinance (Hong Kong) cap 336, pt 2 s 3.
[297] Hong Kong Court of Final Appeal Rules (Hong Kong) cap 484A.
[298] Rules of the High Court (Hong Kong) cap 4A.
[299] District Court Rules (Hong Kong) cap 336H.
[300] Basic Law of the Hong Kong Special Administrative Region of the People's Republic of China, art 8 ('Basic Law'); Hong Kong Reunification Ordinance 1997 (Hong Kong), s 5.

B. Service of Process

Service within Hong Kong, which is a matter of right for process originating from the High Court, is governed by order 10 of the Rules of the High Court. Service out of Hong Kong, governed by order 11, requires leave unless a statute or the Rules of the High Court provide otherwise.[301] Because parties are contractually bound to their chosen forum, exclusive Choice-of-Forum clauses stipulating Hong Kong courts provide sufficient basis for leave to serve out of Hong Kong, as order 11 rule 1(d)(iv) states that service is permissible with the court's leave if the claim concerns: 'a contract which … contains a term to the effect that the Court of First Instance shall have jurisdiction to hear and determine [the] action'. Also, the court need not engage in a *forum non conveniens* or *Spiliada*-type analysis.[302] '[When] a party agrees to the jurisdiction of a particular forum, particularly if it is on an exclusive basis, there is far less room for it to suggest general *forum non conveniens* points'.[303] The plaintiff bears the burden of proof to establish the existence of the exclusive clause.[304] Conversely, an exclusive clause stipulating foreign courts provides a ground to deny leave (assuming there is no other ground available for overseas service under order 11). Since commencing an action in Hong Kong constitutes a breach of the clause, only 'strong cause', amounting to exceptional circumstances why the plaintiff should not be held to that agreement, can overthrow such presumption in favour of denying leave. Factors like national security issues and public policy of another country may constitute strong cause.[305]

In *Lammas Global Corporation v Barclays Bank (Suisse) SA*,[306] the CFI stated that factors establishing strong cause must be unforeseeable at the time of entering into the contract containing the exclusive Choice-of-Forum clause.[307] This unforeseeability requirement, however, appears to be new. In *Chinachem Financial Services Ltd v Century Venture Holdings Ltd*[308] ('*Chinachem*'), the Hong Kong CFI clarified, in the context of stay of proceedings, that 'there may be circumstances that were foreseeable, but may still amount to strong causes, overwhelming reasons and/or exceptional circumstances to displace the named/chosen forum'.[309] Nonetheless, in a later case, *Deltatre SPA v Hong Kong Sports Industrial Development Ltd* ('*Deltatre*'), the CFI emphasised that 'strong cause' can either be 'something unforeseeable at the time of contract' or 'something so exceptional that goes to the interests of justice'.[310] Although *Deltatre* appears to counter *Chinachem*, they may be reconciled by considering that *Chinachem*'s foreseeable factors are *Deltatre*'s 'exceptional' ones. Hence, as regards non-'exceptional' factors, unforeseeability is required in Hong Kong.

For cases with non-exclusive Choice-of-Forum clauses stipulating Hong Kong courts, leave is traditionally granted based on order 11 grounds and based on *Spiliada* principles.

[301] Rules of the High Court (n 298) ord 11, r 1(1).
[302] See *Lammas Global Corporation v Barclays Bank (Suisse) SA* [2011] HKCFI 247 ('*Lammas*').
[303] *Pacific Aerosupplies Limited v Dakota Air Parts, Intl Inc* [2011] HKCFI 438 ('*Pacific Aerosupplies*').
[304] See *Continental Mark Ltd v Verkerhrs-Club de Schweiz* [2002] 2 HKC 513 (CA) ('*Continental Mark*').
[305] See *Pacific Aerosupplies* (n 303).
[306] *Lammas* (n 302).
[307] ibid [33].
[308] *Chinachem Financial Services Ltd v Century Venture Holdings Ltd* [2015] HKCFI 20 ('*Chinachem*').
[309] ibid [90].
[310] *Deltatre SPA v Hong Kong Sports Industrial Development Ltd* [2018] HKCFI 1942, [46] ('*Deltatre*'); see also *Li Lian International Ltd v Herport Hong Kong Ltd* [2019] HKCFI 826, [30].

When proceedings were commenced in the named forum, the plaintiff may show that the named forum was clearly the appropriate one by referring to the non-exclusive clause. A party choosing to contest the jurisdiction had an overwhelming burden to discharge; in effect, making a non-exclusive clause in practice the same as an exclusive jurisdiction clause. However, when Hong Kong is not the named forum, the court grants leave based on other order 11 grounds and the usual *forum non conveniens* test. This approach of using the *Spiliada* test at the service out of Hong Kong stage, however, has been modified by *Noble Power*, which is discussed in the next sub-section. Hence, where the court has jurisdiction to hear a case because of a non-exclusive clause in favour of Hong Kong, the plaintiff can seek any relief, including service out of jurisdiction.[311]

C. Stay of Proceedings

(i) General Approaches

A defendant disputing the High Court's jurisdiction may seek various forms of relief, including a stay under order 12, rule 8 of the Rules of the High Court. A stay can be granted if the court lacks jurisdiction[312] or if the defendant asks the court to refrain from exercising it.[313] Grounds for granting a stay include: (a) the parties and witnesses' best interests and convenience favour another court; (b) the defendant can rely on an agreement excluding the jurisdiction of the Court; and (c) in respect of the same cause of action, there are other proceedings pending between the parties in another court.[314] These grounds are drawn from common law. Ground (a) looks into the factors considered in the *forum non conveniens* test. Ground (b), on the other hand, gives effect to derogation clauses or exclusive Choice-of-Forum clauses which have the effect of excluding Hong Kong as a forum for their disputes. The burden of establishing exclusivity or the derogatory effect of a Choice-of-Forum clause lies with the person invoking it, who is usually the defendant.[315] Common law, through *The Eleftheria*, would elaborate that a stay shall be granted unless the plaintiff establishes 'strong cause' amounting to exceptional circumstances why he should not be held to his agreement. Notably, *The Eleftheria* was first cited in Hong Kong in the 1981 case *The Nedlloyd Seine*.[316] Hong Kong courts would also cite *The 'El Amria'*,[317] as their authority for the 'strong cause' test, as adopted in the 1998 case *The Thorscan*.[318] Lastly, ground (c) deals with parallel proceedings or *lis alibi pendens* (literally, a suit pending somewhere), which is usually resolved through the *forum non conveniens* test, with the fact that litigation is already under way in another jurisdiction as an important factor.

[311] *Agritrade Resources Ltd v Ashok Kumar Sahoo* [2021] HKCFI 3126, [22].
[312] Rules of the High Court (n 298) ord 12, r 8(1)(ga).
[313] ibid ord 12, r 8(1)(b).
[314] ibid ord 12, r 8(2A).
[315] See *Lucky Days Industrial Co Ltd v Translink Shipping (Hong Kong) Ltd* [2007] HKDC 163.
[316] *Owners of the Ship or Vessel 'Nedlloyd Seine' v Owners of Cargo Lately Laden on Board the Ship or Vessel 'Nedlloyd Seine'* [1981] HKC 72, 74 (CA).
[317] *Aratra Potato Ltd v Egyptian Navigation Co (The 'El Amria')* [1981] 2 Lloyd's Rep 119.
[318] *Trafalgar House Construction (Asia) Ltd v Owners and/or Demise Charterers of the MV Thorscan* [1998] 4 HKC 536, 542–43 (CA) ('*The Thorscan*'); See also *Zhoushan Xinhong Aquatic Co Ltd v Sino Trans Ltd* [2006] HKDC 251, [17].

(ii) Exclusive Choice-of-Forum Clauses

Granting a stay when an exclusive Choice-of-Forum clause exists, as developed in *The Eleftheria*, depends on whether there is a 'strong cause',[319] a requirement of which 'is no more than a function of the bargain'.[320] In exercising its discretion, the court considers all the circumstances of the case[321] and evidence.[322] One must note that the 'strong cause' test, although the factors considered in the test may be the same, is different from the *forum non conveniens* principle. The goal is not just to show Hong Kong to be more convenient but to establish exceptional circumstances amounting to 'strong cause' that justify breaching the agreement.[323] Notably, stays are rarely refused when there is a foreign exclusive Choice-of-Forum clause.

(iii) Non-exclusive Choice-of-Forum Clauses

In cases involving non-exclusive Choice-of-Forum clauses, the *forum non conveniens* (also known as 'natural forum' or *forum conveniens*) principle developed in *Spiliada* was traditionally applied. The same test has also been called the 'centre of gravity' test (ie, whether Hong Kong is the forum to which the factors gravitate in light of all the circumstances and the evidence before the court).[324] Nonetheless, when the Hong Kong court's jurisdiction is founded as of right, the burden is on the defendant to show that Hong Kong is *not* the natural forum for the trial of the action.[325] Notably, the non-exclusive Choice-of-Forum clause is 'simply an element within the factual matrix upon which the court is asked to take a view in each case'.[326] While treated as just an element, the non-exclusive Choice-of-Forum clause 'is not something [with] little weight' but rather representative of the contractual agreement to recognise the named forum as an appropriate forum.[327] Nonetheless, unlike exclusive clauses, the defendant must establish the appropriateness of the foreign court(s) named in the non-exclusive clause, for the purpose of *forum non conveniens*.[328]

Hong Kong eventually developed a more nuanced test in *Noble Power*.[329] Although the approach was developed in the context of setting aside leave granted to serve the writ of summons out of Hong Kong, the discussions are applicable to stay applications.[330] *Noble Power* held that when proceedings are filed in the jurisdiction named in the clause, the effect of the non-exclusive Choice-of-Forum clause is no different from an exclusive clause. 'I see no difference in principle between an exclusive jurisdiction clause and a non-exclusive jurisdiction clause to the extent that in both situations, the parties agreed, if they are sued

[319] *Well Hoped Ltd v Nippon Yusen Kaisha* [1982] 1 HKC 155, 157 (HC) ('*Well Hoped*').
[320] *Mashreq Asia Ltd v Furness Logistics (HK) Ltd* [1999] 4 HKC 317, 326 (CFI) ('*Mashreq*').
[321] *The Thorscan* (n 318) 543.
[322] *Mashreq* (n 320) 326.
[323] *AJ Lucas (Hong Kong) Ltd v Drilltec GUT GmbH Grossbohr- und Umwelttechnik* [2006] HKCFI 144, [20].
[324] See *Brody Limited v Chu Kong Shipping Enterprises (Holdings) Co Limited* [1998] HKCFI 476, [5].
[325] *Sichuan Shunli Changlong Technology Co, Ltd v Sze Ming Yee* [2021] HKCFI 2289, [33].
[326] *Peregrine Fixed Income Ltd v JP Morgan Chase Bank* [2005] 2 HKC 374, 383 (CFI).
[327] ibid.
[328] ibid 378.
[329] *Noble Power* (n 138).
[330] See *Chinachem* (n 308).

in the named forum, to submit'.[331] Where proceedings were commenced in a non-chosen forum, the effect of a non-exclusive clause would depend on the precise wording of the clause in question. The court said that '[i]f the other forum is one to which the parties have also agreed to submit in the event of their being sued, it may be that there is little difference between the two situations'.[332] However, where the suit was commenced in a forum 'in which proceedings can be instituted without any obligation on the party sued actually to submit to that forum', the party contesting the forum may be 'in a better position so to do … simply because he would not be seeking to avoid a forum to which he has contractually agreed to submit'.[333] The decision illustrates these three scenarios:

> (1) A sues B in Hong Kong. Hong Kong is named as a non-exclusive jurisdiction to which the parties have agreed to submit in the event of their being sued. The burden on B, if he contests the appropriateness of the Hong Kong courts, is a heavy one.
> (2) A sues B in Hong Kong. Hong Kong is on this occasion not named as a jurisdiction but the courts of, say, Japan are named as the non-exclusive jurisdiction. However, on a true construction of the relevant clause, the parties have nevertheless agreed to submit to the jurisdiction of the courts of any other forum (which would include Hong Kong) in the event of their being sued there. Again, in view of the agreement actually to submit, the burden on B is also a heavy one.
> (3) A sues B in Hong Kong. Again, Hong Kong is not named as the non-exclusive jurisdiction but the courts of Japan are. However, this time the parties have not agreed to submit to any jurisdiction other than the Japanese courts. In other words … no positive obligation exists for a party to submit to any jurisdiction other than Japan. Here, the burden on B is less heavy.[334]

Noble Power, as a result, modified the test applied when there is a non-exclusive Choice-of-Forum clause, moving from a straight-forward *forum non conveniens* analysis, to being mindful of (1) what is actually written in the clause so as to properly determine its effect; and (2) where the proceedings have been brought. If Hong Kong is named in the clause, the effect of the non-exclusive clause is the same as the exclusive clause. It will then be for the defendant to demonstrate the existence of 'strong cause'. If Hong Kong is not named, but the clause provides that the parties 'agreed to submit to the jurisdiction of the courts of any other forum (which would include Hong Kong) in the event of them being sued there', the clause would be given the same effect as an exclusive clause; thus, the 'strong cause' test applies. Notably, a waiver of the *forum non conveniens* challenge would also have the same effect and could defeat a case management stay.[335]

However, if Hong Kong is not named and there is no positive obligation to submit to the forum eventually chosen, then the clause does not carry a heavier weight vis-à-vis the other factors considered in the *forum non conveniens* inquiry.[336] In cases involving multiple contracts, where not all include a non-exclusive Choice-of-Forum clause covering the specific contract in issue, the court may use a *Spiliada*-type analysis, treating the clause as one

[331] *Noble Power* (n 138) [29].
[332] ibid [32].
[333] ibid.
[334] ibid [33].
[335] *Universal Entertainment Corporation v GLAS Trust Company LLC* [2022] HKCFI 3454, [55].
[336] See *MGM Grand Paradise Limited v Chiu Tak Wah* [2012] HKCFI 1529; *Marmor Hotavlje D.o.o. v Peter Silling & Associates Hotel Interior Design Ltd* [2015] HKCFI 979.

factor among others.[337] When the chosen court in the non-exclusive clause determines that it has no jurisdiction to hear the case, the Hong Kong court will also resort to a *Spiliada*-type analysis, and if the defendant fails to establish that there is another available forum, a stay will be refused.[338] If no other forum is available, or no natural forum is found, a stay will be refused when the Hong Kong court's jurisdiction is established as of right.[339]

These principles from *Noble Power* were applied in *Chinachem Financial Services Ltd v Century Venture Holdings Ltd*[340] ('*Chinachem*'), where the plaintiff and defendant agreed to a non-exclusive clause stipulating Hong Kong. After the defendant commenced proceedings in Beijing ('the PRC Litigation'),[341] the plaintiff sued in Hong Kong ('the HK Action'),[342] arguing that Hong Kong was the appropriate forum given (a) the clause mentioning Hong Kong, (b) the absence of identity in parties or issues, and (c) other factors of convenience in favour of Hong Kong.[343] Following *Noble Power*, the CFI regarded the non-exclusive Choice-of-Forum clause as similar to an exclusive clause given that the action was filed in Hong Kong, which was the named forum.[344] Furthermore, the Court rejected a *Spiliada*-type analysis[345] and concluded that the defendant had failed to establish strong grounds to stay the Hong Kong proceedings because '[a]ll the "convenience" connecting factors, eg witnesses, language, enforcement, PRC-related background etc', were foreseeable at the time of the agreement, and no public policy or interests of justice were involved in either Hong Kong or China litigation.[346]

Like Singapore, Hong Kong courts can grant case management stays, which the Court of Appeal in *Ghossoub* distinguished from *forum non conveniens* stays.[347] Case management stays 'operate where both courts are equally appropriate … or neither is an appropriate forum'.[348] Nonetheless, they are exceptional: 'to be made only in "rare and compelling circumstances", where the arguments for a stay clearly outweigh any resulting disadvantage to the claimant'.[349] In this case, the Court of Appeal refused a case management stay, citing the absence of rare and compelling circumstances, despite the plaintiff's reliance on an exclusive Choice-of-Forum clause or *forum non conveniens* grounds.[350]

(iv) Some Confused Approaches

In early Hong Kong cases (1980s), similarly to Singapore, courts did not begin by qualifying the relevant Choice-of-Forum clause as either exclusive or non-exclusive, before applying

[337] *High Hope Zhongding Corporation v Xiamen Dunfeng Import and Export Co, Ltd* [2017] HKCFI 56.
[338] *Vasileva Elena Nikolaevna, Liquidator of Agricultural Productive Cooperative v Dragon Seafoods Ltd* [2019] HKCFI 1287, [10], [22].
[339] *Patrick James Joseph O'Mara v Chin Shau Tong* [2022] HKCFI 768 [12].
[340] *Chinachem* (n 308).
[341] ibid [6].
[342] ibid.
[343] ibid [9].
[344] ibid [87].
[345] ibid [93].
[346] ibid [146].
[347] *Joseph Ghossoub v Team Y&R Holdings Hong Kong Ltd* [2017] HKCA 298, [50] (CA).
[348] ibid.
[349] ibid [52].
[350] ibid [51]–[52].

the relevant test. Rather, after citing the Choice-of-Forum clause, the strong cause test was applied.[351] Since the 1990s, however, courts have adopted a more structured approach by first classifying the clause as either exclusive or non-exclusive, before applying the corresponding test. Despite this, there have been instances of where courts would mix up their analysis. In *Canavan v Battenfeld*[352] (2010), the CFI classified the Choice-of-Forum clause as exclusive in favour of the Thai court and yet, the Court proceeded to perform both the 'strong cause' test[353] and a *forum non conveniens* analysis.[354] A similar error occurred in *Hyundai Engineering & Construction Co Ltd v UBAF (Hong Kong) Ltd*[355] ('*Hyundai Engineering*'), where the Court incorrectly reduced an exclusive Choice-of-Forum clause to a mere factor in the *forum non conveniens* analysis, despite acknowledging that the strong cause test applied (albeit citing *Noble Power*, a case involving a non-exclusive clause).[356] While these cases show some inconsistency, most recent decisions are coherent and consistent with common law.

D. Anti-suit Injunctions and Other Relief

Under the Rules of the High Court, order 12, rule 8(1), a defendant contesting jurisdiction may also apply for an anti-suit injunction to restrain another party from pursuing proceedings on the same matters elsewhere. Hong Kong's approach to anti-suit injunctions remains aligned with the English approach, ignoring Australian and Canadian approaches as alternatives.[357] These injunctions are directed '*in personam*' and must be issued with restraint due to potential breaches of comity, thus 'the threshold for the applicant to meet is the enhanced high degree of probability'.[358] Without a formal concept of *lis alibi pendens*, Hong Kong courts may tolerate concurrent proceedings in both jurisdictions,[359] and will grant anti-suit injunctions in only two situations: (1) where an exclusive Choice-of-Forum clause stipulates Hong Kong;[360] and (2) where there is unconscionability and the anti-suit injunction is required to support the 'ends of justice'.[361] The court may decline an injunction if parallel proceedings risk inconsistent decisions, especially if 'the foreign proceedings not bound by the … [exclusive jurisdiction clause] are involved or grounds of claim not the subject of the clause are part of the relevant dispute'.[362] Furthermore, the Hong Kong court

[351] See *The Nedlloyd Seine* (n 316); *Well Hoped* (n 319); *Confecciones del Atlantico v Lamont Shipping Incorporated*, [1982] HKCFI 130; *Palace Hotel Ltd v Owners of the Ship or Vessel Happy Pioneer* [1982] HKC 640 (HC).
[352] *Samuel Hutchison Canavan v Brenton George Battenfeld* [2010] HKCFI 691.
[353] ibid [16]–[37].
[354] ibid [38]–[44].
[355] *Hyundai Engineering & Construction Co Ltd v UBAF (Hong Kong) Ltd* [2013] HKCFI 1579.
[356] ibid.
[357] Graeme Johnston and Paul Harris, *The Conflict of Laws in Hong Kong* (Thomson Reuters, 3rd edn, 2017) 125.
[358] *Capital Wealth Holdings Ltd v Nantong Jiahe Technology Investment and Development Co, Ltd* [2021] HKCFI 272, [33].
[359] *Chinachem* (n 308) [106].
[360] See *XL Insurance Company SE v Manley Toys Ltd* [2015] HKCFI 1033, [23]–[24] ('*XL Insurance*').
[361] *Liaoyang Shunfeng Iron and Steel Company Limited v Yeung Tsz Wang* [2011] HKCFI 453, [31]–[33] ('*Liaoyang*').
[362] *Giorgio Armani SPA v Elan Clothes Co Ltd (formerly known as Dalian Les Copious Clothes Co Ltd)* [2019] HKCFI 530, [32] ('*Armani*').

need not wait for the jurisdictional challenge to be resolved by the foreign court before it can grant an anti-suit injunction.[363]

An exclusive Choice-of-Forum clause stipulating Hong Kong courts is a ground for the issuance of an anti-suit injunction,[364] as the applicant has a contractual right not to be sued in the foreign country.[365] In such cases, comity plays a minimal role,[366] but the issuance of an anti-suit injunction remains discretionary.[367] For instance, delay and other timing considerations are important; thus, an application for an anti-suit injunction to be issued has to be made promptly and before foreign proceedings are too far advanced.[368] An injunction can still be denied for strong reasons,[369] and proof of grounds for an anti-suit injunction would usually be sufficient to establish strong reasons for a stay.[370]

In other cases, like where the relevant Choice-of-Forum clause is not exclusive, the applicable principles are summarised in *Liaoyang Shunfeng Iron and Steel Company Limited v Yeung Tsz Wang*:[371]

> (1) … [The] wrongful or unconscionable conduct … amounts to vexation and oppression.
>
> (2) … the applicant's … legitimate interest should be the existence of proceedings in Hong Kong and the defendant has in bad faith commenced proceedings in another jurisdiction for the purpose of frustrating and obstructing the Hong Kong proceedings.
>
> For these purposes: (a) The applicant must be a party to the existing local litigation … (b) The applicant also has to show a 'clear need to protect [local] proceedings'.[372]

Unconscionability includes conduct which is 'vexatious or oppressive or interferes with the due process of this court'.[373] Moreover, Hong Kong must be the natural forum,[374] and 'justice does not require that the action should nevertheless proceed in the foreign court'.[375]

When the clause is asymmetric, and the defendant in the Hong Kong proceedings has been given the option to commence litigation in other fora, including where the foreign action is pending, the defendant cannot be prevented by an anti-suit injunction from continuing foreign proceedings.[376]

In Hong Kong, damages may be awarded for breaching an exclusive Choice-of-Forum clause,[377] based on any loss the plaintiff suffers, such as additional litigation expenses.[378] While the plaintiff can fully recover proven additional expenses as damages, the costs of

[363] *Achieve Goal Holdings Ltd v Zhong Xin Ore Material Holdings Ltd* [2022] HKCFI 2638, [60] ('*Achieve Goal*').
[364] See *XL Insurance* (n 360) [23]–[24].
[365] *Worth Achieve Associates Ltd v Huang Sheng Yi* [2007] 3 HKC 7, 22 (CFI), citing *Turner v Grovit* [2002] 1 WLR 107, [27].
[366] ibid.
[367] *Sea Powerful II Special Maritime Enterprises (ENE) v Bank of China Ltd* [2017] 1 HKCA 153, 166.
[368] See ibid 161.
[369] *Armani* (n 362) [27].
[370] *Chen Hongqing v The Persons whose names are set out in the second column of the schedule hereto* [2018] HKCFI 1170, [42].
[371] *Liaoyang* (n 361).
[372] ibid [33].
[373] Johnston and Harris (n 357) 127.
[374] *Liaoyang* (n 361) [34].
[375] ibid.
[376] *Suen Kwai Kam v Central China Dragon Select Growth Fund* [2020] HKCFI 69, [31].
[377] *Dickson Valora Group (Holdings) Co Ltd v Fan ji Qian* [2019] HKCFI 2953, [4] ('*Dickson*').
[378] *Quaestus Capital Pte Ltd v Everton Associates Ltd* [2021] HKCFI 1367, [61].

the action for damages will be awarded on a party-party basis,[379] especially when the clause is non-exclusive.[380] In *XL Insurance Company SE v Manley Toys Ltd*,[381] however, the CFI awarded costs on an indemnity basis due to the defendant's refusal to comply with the exclusive clause, stating that the plaintiff should not bear any costs when the defendant's conduct was a misuse of judicial resources.[382] However, indemnity costs should not be a substitute for damages, as damages must still be pleaded and proven.[383]

In *Shanghai Gopher Asset Management Co Ltd v China Base Group Ltd*, the CFI noted that there are English and Hong Kong authorities[384] to the effect that upon grant of a stay based on an exclusive Choice-of-Forum clause, costs should be awarded on an indemnity basis.[385] On appeal, the Court of Appeal, while upholding the CFI's discretion on costs, left the question of awarding costs on an indemnity basis open.[386] Notably, the court noted that the Hong Kong CFI judge had carefully analysed the specific conduct of parties in this case,[387] thus the award of costs appears to be dependent on the parties' conduct. Finally, in *Re: Guy Kwok-Hung Lam v Ex Parte: TOR Asia Credit Master Fund LP Creditor*, the Court of Appeal clarified that costs for breaching a non-exclusive clause are generally awarded on a party-party basis and only on an indemnity basis when the conduct of the parties warrants it.[388]

E. Choice-of-Forum Clauses and Insolvency

In *Guy Kwok-Hung Lam*, the Court of Appeal addressed the role of Choice-of-Forum clauses in insolvency proceedings, noting that while winding up is a class remedy which depends on the insolvency of the company and the views of unsecured creditors, the preliminary question of whether the petitioner is a member of that class[389] may be resolved in the agreed forum in the Choice-of-Forum clause.[390] Hence, even if the winding-up order is available only in Hong Kong, it does not follow that the preliminary question about the debt relied on for the petition may not be resolved through the agreed dispute resolution mechanism.[391] This includes enforcing the Choice-of-Forum clause as in any ordinary action.[392] This approach affirms the strong policy of enforcing contracts, prevents parties from by-passing Choice-of-Forum clauses through a winding-up or bankruptcy petition, and avoids uncertainty and conflicting approaches, especially in the enforcement of exclusive

[379] *Dickson* (n 377) [4].
[380] *Re: Guy Kwok-Hung Lam v Ex Parte: TOR Asia Credit Master Fund LP* [2023] HKCA 1099, [24] ('*Guy Kwok-CA* (Costs)').
[381] *XL Insurance* (n 360) [24]; see also *Shanghai Gopher Asset Management Co Ltd v China Base Group Ltd* [2022] HKCA 1724, [35].
[382] *XL Insurance* (n 360) [24].
[383] *Guy Kwok-CA* (Costs) (n 380) [30].
[384] eg, *A v B* (Costs) [2007] 1 Lloyds Rep 358, [15]; *Deltatre* (n 310) [125].
[385] *Shanghai Gopher Asset Management Co Ltd v China Base Group Ltd* [2022] HKCFI 114, [21].
[386] ibid [35].
[387] ibid.
[388] *Guy Kwok-CA* (Costs) (n 380) [24], [30].
[389] *Re: Guy Kwok-Hung Lam v Ex parte: TOR Asia Credit Master Fund LP* [2022] HKCA 1297, [78].
[390] ibid [65].
[391] ibid [81].
[392] ibid [82].

Choice-of-Forum clauses.[393] Nonetheless, the presence of an exclusive Choice-of-Forum clause in favour of the foreign forum does not mean that the court is *bound* to dismiss or suspend the winding-up or insolvency petition,[394] especially when there is strong cause.[395] Given that the matters related to indebtedness in *Guy Kwok-Hung Lam* fell within the exclusive Choice-of-Forum clause in favour of New York courts, and New York proceedings were still on-going, the Court of Appeal ruled that the petitioner should be held to its agreement and the Hong Kong bankruptcy petition be dismissed or stayed unless there were strong reasons to the contrary.[396]

The Court of Final Appeal upheld the ruling, emphasising that the public policy concerns behind the collective scheme in bankruptcy proceedings are diminished where the petition is brought by one creditor against another and there is no evidence of a creditor community at risk.[397] Furthermore, the established approach in bankruptcy – where the petitioner is entitled to a bankruptcy order if the petition debt is not subject to dispute on substantial grounds – would not apply where an exclusive Choice-of-Forum clause was involved.[398] '[A]bsent countervailing factors such as the risk of insolvency affecting third parties and a dispute that borders on the frivolous or abuse of process, the petitioner and debtor ought to be held to their contract'.[399]

F. Recognition and Enforcement of Judgments

(i) Common Law and Statutes

Two regimes govern the recognition and enforcement of foreign judgments in Hong Kong: (1) common law; and (2) statutes allowing registration of foreign judgments.[400] Under both, Hong Kong courts may refuse recognition and enforcement if the foreign judgment was issued by an incompetent court, involved unfair proceedings and fraud, or contravenes the *res judicata* principle or Hong Kong public policy.[401] Since Hong Kong is not party to the Choice-of-Court Convention, contravention of Choice-of-Forum clauses, even those which are exclusive, is not a direct ground for refusal of recognition and enforcement of a foreign judgment. However, Hong Kong's mandatory rules and public policy may prevent the recognition and enforcement of foreign judgments involving Choice-of-Forum clauses if they are 'contrary to the fundamental conceptions of morality and justice' of Hong Kong.[402] Interestingly, Hong Kong courts may enforce Taiwan judgments without contravening public policy.[403]

[393] ibid [83]–[85].
[394] ibid [86].
[395] ibid.
[396] ibid [87].
[397] *Re Guy Kwok-Hung Lam v Ex Parte: TOR Asia Credit Master Fund LP* [2023] HKCFA 9, [102] (*Guy Kwok-CFA*).
[398] ibid [105].
[399] ibid.
[400] Foreign Judgments (Reciprocal Enforcement) Ordinance (Hong Kong) cap 319; Foreign Judgments (Restriction on Recognition and Enforcement) Ordinance (Hong Kong) cap 46.
[401] Johnston and Harris (n 357) 595, 597.
[402] *ML v YJ* [2008] 3 HKC 362, 374 (CFI).
[403] *Chen Li Hung v Ting Lei Miao* [2000] 1 HKC 461 (CFA).

In *Compania Sud America de Vapores SA v Hin-Pro International Logistics Ltd*[404] ('*Compania Sud*'), the Court of Final Appeal assisted the English court in enforcing damages for breach of an exclusive Choice-of-Forum clause. The Court noted that if the action of the English court in awarding such damages involved a breach of comity towards Chinese courts, then enforcing those damages in Hong Kong would also involve a breach of comity.[405] However, there can be no breach of comity because the award of damages was in respect of a contractual breach (ie, breach of the English exclusive jurisdiction clause).[406] Since the action of the English court did not involve a breach of comity, the court likewise found no breach of Hong Kong public policy which could prevent the enforcement.[407]

(ii) China-Hong Kong Judicial Arrangements

After Hong Kong's return to China under the 'one country, two systems' policy,[408] there was controversy over how to treat judgments from Mainland China, Macau and Taiwan. While one possibility is to treat them as municipal judicial awards,[409] the dominant approach has been to treat them as foreign judgments.[410] This lack of clarity led to issues like controversial interpretation of Choice-of-Forum clauses, parallel proceedings resulting in conflicting judgments, forum shopping, and using home court advantage for a declaratory ruling as a defensive tactic against any possible Mainland China proceedings.[411] Eventually in 2006, China concluded arrangements with Hong Kong and Macau on the recognition and enforcement of judgments in their courts.[412]

The Arrangement on Reciprocal Recognition and Enforcement of Judgments in Civil and Commercial Matters by Courts of the Mainland and of the Hong Kong Special Administrative Region Pursuant to Choice of Court Agreements between Parties Concerned[413] ('Choice-of-Court Arrangement') allows certain types of judgments (ie, judgments arising from Choice-of-Forum agreements involving civil and commercial matters) to be recognised and enforced in both regions. Inspired by the Choice-of-Court Convention,[414] the Choice-of-Court Arrangement has notable differences: (1) only judgments involving exclusive Choice-of-Forum clauses are addressed; (2) only money judgments are dealt with;[415] (3) it was drafted with finality of Chinese judgments in mind, and

[404] *Compania Sud America de Vapores SA v Hin-Pro International Logistics Ltd* [2016] HKCFA 79.
[405] ibid [59].
[406] ibid.
[407] ibid.
[408] See, eg, *Basic Law* (n 320) arts 2, 5, 8.
[409] Xianchu Zhang and Philip Smart, 'Development of Regional Conflict of Laws: On the Arrangement of Mutual Recognition and Enforcement of Judgments in Civil and Commercial Matters between Mainland China and Hong Kong SAR' (2006) 36(3) *Hong Kong Law Journal* 553, 560.
[410] ibid 561.
[411] ibid.
[412] ibid 563.
[413] Arrangement on Reciprocal Recognition and Enforcement of Judgments in Civil and Commercial Matters by the Courts of the Mainland and of the Hong Kong Special Administrative Region, signed by the Supreme People's Court (China) and Department of Justice (Hong Kong SAR), 14 July 2006: https://www.doj.gov.hk/en/mainland_and_macao/pdf/mainlandrej20060719e.pdf ('Choice-of-Court Arrangement').
[414] See Zhang and Smart (n 409) 570; Guangjian Tu, 'Recognition and enforcement of mainland China's civil and commercial judgments in Hong Kong – an update' (2017) 25(2) *Asia Pacific Law Review* 190, 194.
[415] Choice-of-Court Arrangement (n 413) art 1.

as such, is very specific as to the originating Chinese courts;[416] (4) by not enumerating the types of civil and commercial disputes, it appears to have a wider scope;[417] (5) the enforcement and recognition has to be made within two years, presumably, from judgment.[418] Notably, recognised judgments have the same legal effect as local judgments.[419] Only judgments from the Supreme People's Court, Higher People's Court at the provincial level, Intermediate People's Courts at the city level and 47 Basic People's Courts in 15 provinces and municipalities directly under the central government are covered,[420] and failure to designate the specific mainland Chinese court in the clause may make the judgment non-registrable.[421] In Hong Kong, it covers any legally effective judgment of the Court of Final Appeal, Court of Appeal, CFI, and the district courts.[422] The Mainland Judgments (Reciprocal Enforcement) Ordinance[423] and Rules of the High Court, order 71A implement the Choice-of-Court Arrangement in Hong Kong.[424]

To enforce a judgment under the Choice-of-Court Arrangement, the following conditions must be met: (1) a valid written Choice-of-Forum clause exclusively choosing a Hong Kong or Chinese court;[425] (2) an 'enforceable and final' judgment;[426] (3) a money judgment;[427] (4) a subject matter that is 'civil and commercial';[428] (5) an application made within the limitation period;[429] and (6) a judgment not involving any of the excluded categories.[430] Employment contracts, consumer contracts concluded by natural persons, and contracts on family matters or other non-commercial purposes are excluded.[431] Notably, the Choice-of-Court Arrangement is not restricted to judgments involving interregional elements, as parties may both come from China, and the judgment or dispute may arise from transactions outside Hong Kong and China, provided that the Choice-of-Forum clause stipulates Hong Kong or China.

In *Wang Qian Wei v Guo Wenyu*, the CFI ruled that a Chinese judgment could be enforced in Hong Kong even if the judgment creditor was not a party to the exclusive Choice-of-Forum clause, as his rights were vested through assignment.[432] Furthermore, the Court considered the judgment final because no appeal was lodged within the appeal period and a certificate of effectiveness was issued.[433] Although an application for retrial was filed at the higher court, it was dismissed and no appeal was made against the dismissal.[434]

The Choice-of-Court Arrangement does not define what makes Choice-of-Forum clauses exclusive, leaving this to the enforcing court's domestic law, which may lead to uncertainty,

[416] ibid annex.
[417] ibid art 3.
[418] ibid art 8.
[419] ibid art 11.
[420] ibid art 2(1), annex.
[421] *Beijing Renji Real Estate Development Group Co, Ltd v Zhu Min* [2022] HKCFI 1027,[43].
[422] ibid art 2(2).
[423] Mainland Judgments (Reciprocal Enforcement) Ordinance (Hong Kong) cap 597.
[424] Rules of the High Court (n 298) ord 71A.
[425] Choice-of-Court Arrangement (n 413) arts 1, 3.
[426] ibid art 1.
[427] ibid.
[428] ibid.
[429] ibid art 8.
[430] ibid art 3.
[431] ibid art 3.
[432] *Wang Qian Wei v Guo Wenyu* [2018] HKCFI 2253, [23].
[433] ibid [45].
[434] ibid [46].

as it may depend on the approach adopted by the enforcing court to the nature of these clauses (eg, whether it considers the Choice-of-Forum clause procedural or substantive) as well as the law applicable to specific issues (eg, is the issue substantive or procedural?). This could result in unintended outcomes and varying interpretations across courts. Furthermore, the applicable law to an issue (eg, how to interpret the Choice-of-Forum clause) may be substantive law, and therefore, would require a court to engage in the choice of law process, as discussed in Chapter six. This would raise additional complexities. Nonetheless, Hong Kong courts have been liberal in determining whether the clause involved in a case under the Choice-of-Court Arrangement is exclusive.[435] A Hong Kong court may even just *assume* that the clause involved is exclusive.[436] In *Bank of China v Yang Fan*, the CFI noted that party intention ultimately determines exclusivity, although certain words used in the clause may not generally be construed to be imperative.[437] In *The Export-Import Bank of China v Taifeng Textile Group Co Ltd*, the CFI emphasised that the parties need not use the word 'exclusive but [it is enough if the agreement is] exclusive in substance and effect on a proper construction according to the relevant governing law'.[438] Likewise, the Chinese judgment may be proven other than by the production of the original court certificate, provided that the Hong Kong court is satisfied that the judgment is enforceable in China.[439] Notably, judgments involving asymmetric clauses are outside the scope of the Choice-of-Court Arrangement.[440]

On 18 January 2019, the Chinese Supreme People's Court and Hong Kong SAR government signed the Arrangement on Reciprocal Recognition and Enforcement of Judgments in Civil and Commercial Matters by the Courts of the Mainland and of the Hong Kong Special Administrative Region,[441] ('Judgments Arrangement'), which replaced the Choice-of-Court Arrangement on 29 January 2024.[442] The Mainland Judgments in Civil and Commercial Matters (Reciprocal Enforcement) Ordinance[443] ('Judgments Arrangement Ordinance') and the Mainland Judgments in Civil and Commercial Matters (Reciprocal Enforcement) Rules[444] ('Judgments Arrangement Rules') implement the Judgments Arrangement into Hong Kong law. However, the Choice-of-Court Arrangement remains applicable to a written Choice-of-Forum clause signed before the Judgments Arrangement's commencement.[445] The corresponding implementing instruments in China are discussed in Chapter eight.

[435] See, eg, *Bank of China Ltd v Yang Fan* [2016] HKCFI 708, [31] ('*Yang Fan*').

[436] See, eg, *Wu Zuocheng v Leung Lai-ching* [2016] HKCFI 261.

[437] *Yang Fan* (n 435) [31].

[438] *The Export-Import Bank of China v Taifeng Textile Group Co Ltd* [2018] HKCFI 1840, [65].

[439] ibid [86].

[440] *Industrial and Commercial Bank of China (Asia) Ltd v Wisdom Top International Ltd* [2020] HKCFI 322, [52].

[441] The Arrangement on Reciprocal Recognition and Enforcement of Judgments in Civil and Commercial Matters by Courts of the Mainland and of the Hong Kong Special Administrative Region, signed by the Supreme People's Court (China) and Hong Kong SAR, 18 January 2019: https://www.doj.gov.hk/en/mainland_and_macao/pdf/Doc3_477379e.pdf ('Judgments Arrangement').

[442] Department of Justice Government of the Hong Kong Special Administrative Region, *Enforcement of civil and commercial judgments between Hong Kong and the Mainland* (Website, 11 February 2019): https://www.doj.gov.hk/eng/public/enforcement.html (accessed 28 October 2024).

[443] Mainland Judgments in Civil and Commercial Matters (Reciprocal Enforcement) Ordinance (Hong Kong) cap 646 ('Judgments Arrangement Ordinance').

[444] Mainland Judgments in Civil and Commercial Matters (Reciprocal Enforcement) Rules (Hong Kong) LN 152 of 2023.

[445] Judgments Arrangement (n 441) art 30.

The Judgments Arrangement applies to the reciprocal recognition of 'legally effective' civil and commercial judgments between Chinese and Hong Kong courts,[446] provided that the laws of both jurisdictions recognise the matter as 'civil and commercial'.[447] Article 3 lists matters which are excluded, such as maritime claims,[448] bankruptcy,[449] tortious infringements of patents and some intellectual property rights disputes.[450] Excluded judgments include rulings concerning preservation matters, anti-suit injunctions and interim-relief orders.[451] However, unlike the Choice-of-Court Arrangement, judgments containing both monetary and non-monetary rulings are covered.[452] Partial recognition is also allowed.[453] Moreover, the Judgments Arrangement applies only to judgments from Chinese courts of the second instance, or of the first instance if no appeal is allowed or filed.[454] Hence, the Judgments Arrangement no longer limits its application to a number of Chinese courts. On the other hand, the list of Hong Kong courts was expanded to include the Labour Tribunal, Small Claims Tribunal and the Competition Tribunal.[455] Applications for recognition and enforcement under the Judgments Arrangement are still filed with the Hong Kong High Court,[456] with local procedural rules and prescriptive periods being applicable.[457]

Particularly, the judgment creditor should apply for registration of the Chinese judgment at the Hong Kong CFI,[458] which then issues an order of registration if the jurisdictional and other requirements are satisfied. Such issuance requires a certification from the Chinese court that the Chinese judgment in a civil or commercial matter is effective under Chinese laws.[459] After registration, the Chinese judgment has the same effect as a Hong Kong judgment given on the day of registration.[460] Hence, if the same matter is litigated in Hong Kong, those proceedings will be stayed[461] until the court finally determines whether the proceedings should be resumed or terminated.[462] Consequently, the registration also bars any proceedings on the same cause(s) of action in Hong Kong.[463]

Notably, the Judgments Arrangement contains several indirect jurisdictional rules.[464] First, the originating court is considered to have jurisdiction if the parties have entered a written Choice-of-Forum agreement, which can either be exclusive or non-exclusive.[465] However, where all parties reside in the requested place (say, China), the requesting place (ie, Hong Kong) should be the place of contractual performance or formation or where the

[446] ibid art 1.
[447] ibid art 2.
[448] ibid art 3(4).
[449] ibid art 3(5).
[450] ibid arts 3(3), 5.
[451] ibid art 4.
[452] ibid art 16.
[453] ibid art 19.
[454] ibid art 4(1).
[455] ibid art 4(2).
[456] ibid art 7(2).
[457] ibid art 10.
[458] Judgments Arrangement Ordinance (n 443) s 10(1).
[459] ibid s 13(2).
[460] ibid s 26(1)(a), (b).
[461] ibid s 29(3).
[462] ibid s 29(4).
[463] ibid s 30(2).
[464] Judgments Arrangement (n 441) art 11.
[465] ibid art 11.

subject matter was situated, which is needed to satisfy the actual connection requirement.[466] This 'actual connection' requirement follows the approach under the Chinese Civil Procedure Law prior to the 2023 Amendment (see Chapter eight) and the requirement for domestic Choice-of-Forum clauses in China. If Hong Kong lacks any of the required 'actual connection', the Hong Kong court, even if chosen by the parties, may be considered by the Chinese court to lack jurisdiction. Furthermore, a judgment issued in breach of a valid Choice-of-Forum clause may be refused recognition and enforcement.[467] These grounds for refusal may be raised during an application to set aside the registration of the Chinese judgment.[468]

Article 11 of the Judgments Arrangement allows the Hong Kong CFI to determine, according to its own laws, whether Hong Kong courts have exclusive jurisdiction over the dispute, thus recognising that certain matters fall within the exclusive jurisdiction of the requested court (ie, mandatory jurisdiction). Hence, if a local rule requires that a matter should be heard exclusively by a Hong Kong court, then the requested Hong Kong court may declare that the originating Chinese court lacks jurisdiction. Furthermore, article 11 requires that the originating court's exercise of jurisdiction should be consistent with the law of the requested place, except when such jurisdiction is based on the defendant's residence, or the case involves a contractual dispute and the place of performance is the requesting state. As such, Hong Kong courts should determine, pursuant to section 22 of the Judgments Arrangements Ordinance, whether the defendant was properly served with summons, whether the judgment was obtained by fraud, whether *res judicata* applies, whether enforcement is barred by an existing arbitral award, or whether the Chinese judgment is incompatible with Hong Kong public policy. Section 23 of the Judgments Arrangements Ordinance, nonetheless, qualifies section 22 for specific areas such as competition and intellectual property law.

IV. Malaysia

A. Malaysia's Approach to Jurisdiction

Malaysia's court system consists of the High Courts,[469] Court of Appeal,[470] Federal Court,[471] Special Court,[472] and various inferior courts. Because Islamic law forms part of Malaysian law,[473] *Shariah* courts have jurisdiction on Islamic family law matters among Muslims.[474] However, disputes involving Islamic banking and other commercial contracts, even if governed by Islamic law, fall within the jurisdiction of Malaysia's civil courts.[475]

[466] ibid art 11(5).
[467] ibid art 13.
[468] Judgments Arrangement Ordinance (n 443) s 22(1).
[469] Federal Constitution (Malaysia), pt 9, art 121(1)(a), (b).
[470] ibid pt 9, art 121(1B).
[471] ibid pt 9, art 121(2).
[472] ibid pt 15, art 182.
[473] ibid art 76(2).
[474] ibid sch 9; see ibid, art 121(1A); see Farid Schuaib, 'The Islamic Legal System in Malaysia' (2012) 21(1) *Pacific Rim Law & Policy Journal* 85, 94.
[475] *Bank Kerjasama Rakyat Malaysia v Emcee Corporation Sdn Bhd* [2003] 2 MLJ 408, 408; Ahmad Hidayat Buang, 'Islamic Contracts in a Secular Court Setting? Lessons from Malaysia' (2007) 21(4) *Arab Law Quarterly* 317, 321–22.

The Rules of Court 2012 govern procedures in the High Court, Sessions Court and Magistrates' Court.[476] In line with common law jurisdictions, jurisdiction *in personam* depends on proper service of originating process – whether within or out of jurisdiction.[477] Even if a Malaysian court has jurisdiction, it can choose not to exercise such jurisdiction,[478] based on the *forum non conveniens* principle, also known in Malaysia as the natural forum test or *forum conveniens* principle. This principle determines whether to grant leave for service out of the jurisdiction or a stay of proceedings, when there is a non-exclusive Choice-of-Forum clause. Malaysia adopted this test from *Spiliada* in the 1994 case of *American Express.*[479] On the other hand, the 'strong cause' test from *The Eleftheria* applies to exclusive clauses and was first adopted in the 1976 case of *Globus.*[480] Both the *forum non conveniens* and 'strong cause' tests involve the court's discretion in determining whether to exercise jurisdiction.

B. Service of Process

In Malaysia, civil actions are usually commenced by writ or originating summons,[481] with writ of summons being the most common.[482] If the defendant is within the jurisdiction, he is liable to be served with the writ *in personam.*[483] Service of the originating process must be made personally, by registered mail or electronic communication, unless the court authorises some alternative method.[484]

Order 11, Rules of Court 2012 outlines the circumstances, requirements, modes and effects of service out of the jurisdiction, which is treated as the exercise of judicial power over a foreigner who owes no allegiance to Malaysia or over a person who is resident or domiciled out of the jurisdiction but is nevertheless called upon to answer claims in Malaysia.[485] This assumption of jurisdiction over the defendant who is not present within the jurisdiction is implicit when a Malaysian court grants leave.[486] Significantly, extra-territorial service is permitted in cases involving a contract which 'contains a term to the effect that the Court shall have jurisdiction to hear and determine any action in respect of the contract'.[487] Hence, for exclusive Choice-of-Forum clauses stipulating Malaysian courts, extra-territorial service is allowed unless there is strong cause, following *The Eleftheria.*[488] For non-exclusive Choice-of-Forum clauses, the *forum non conveniens* test developed in *Spiliada* applies,[489] in which case, the non-exclusive clause is 'a very glaring factor'.[490]

[476] Rules of Court 2012 (Malaysia), ord 1, r 2(2)(1).
[477] *American Express Bank Ltd v Mohamed Toufic Al-Ozeir* [1995] 1 MLJ 160, 166 (SC Kuala Lumpur) ('*American Express*').
[478] ibid.
[479] *American Express* (n 477).
[480] *Globus Shipping & Trading Co (Pte) Ltd v Taiping Textiles Berhad* [1976] 2 MLJ 154 (FC Penang) ('*Globus*').
[481] Rules of Court (n 476) ord 5, r 1.
[482] ibid ord 5, r 2.
[483] ibid ord 10, r 1(1).
[484] ibid ord 10, r 1(1).
[485] LexisNexis, *Halsbury's Laws of Malaysia* (online at 29 March 2019) 190 Civil Procedure, '2 Commencement of Proceedings' [190.2-063].
[486] *American Express* (n 477) 166.
[487] Rules of Court 2012 (n 476) ord 11, r 2.
[488] *Globus* (n 480).
[489] *American Express* (n 477) 167.
[490] ibid 168.

C. Stay of Proceedings

A Malaysian court may stay proceedings filed in breach of an exclusive Choice-of-Forum clause stipulating a foreign forum,[491] with the defendant bearing the burden of establishing its existence. Once its existence is established, the court exercises its discretion to stay in favour of the defendant and the plaintiff has the burden of establishing a 'strong cause' why he should be allowed to breach his contract.[492] In exercising this discretion, the court considers all circumstances of the case including: (1) location of evidence, (2) governing law, (3) to which country the parties are closely connected, (4) the genuineness of the defendant's desire to try the case abroad, (5) prejudicial factors against the plaintiff (eg, inability to enforce any judgment obtained, time bar not applicable in Malaysia, lack of fair trial).[493] In establishing strong cause, the plaintiff has the burden of establishing the existence of a relevant factor.[494] Notably, these factors are similar to those considered in the *forum non conveniens* test, but the 'strong cause' test is considered distinct in Malaysia.[495] Furthermore, Malaysia rejected the allegedly mechanistic purely contractual approach of *The Bremen*.[496] The Malaysian court emphasised that the grant of a stay is discretionary even if the Choice-of-Forum clause involved is exclusive.[497]

While Malaysian courts generally apply *The Eleftheria* principles, thus favouring a stay when an exclusive choice-of-Forum clause stipulates foreign courts,[498] they adopt a more flexible approach by treating the factors constituting 'strong cause' in the same way as the factors in *forum non conveniens* – a balancing act which would ultimately point to a forum which is more convenient.[499] In *Inter Maritime*, the Court of Appeal, after citing *The Eleftheria*, said that the plaintiff had established 'strong grounds' – 'the vessel and the appellant are … Malaysian … cargo was loaded at a Malaysian port … evidence is admittedly both here and in Manila … [and] trial in [Malaysia] … will be less expensive and more convenient'.[500] Hence, the stay should be refused despite an exclusive Choice-of-Forum clause stipulating Tokyo courts.[501] A similar approach was applied in *Nutri Mills Products Sdn Bhd v CMA CGM Malaysia Sdn Bhd*,[502] where the court deemed that the plaintiff had established 'strong cause' because 'the witnesses to the formation of the contract, the role of the parties, the admission of wrongdoing and the quantum of the loss are all in Malaysia'.[503] Hence, because the 'evidence on the issues of fact are largely situated or more

[491] Rules of Court 2012 (n 476) ord 12, r 10(2).
[492] *Inter Maritime Management Sdn Bhd v Kai Tai Timber Co Ltd, Hong Kong* [1995] 1 MLJ 322, 337–38 (CA Kuala Lumpur) ('*Inter Maritime*').
[493] ibid 331–32.
[494] *Yong Songhua v Basic Venture International Ltd* [2017] 8 MLJ 681, 691 (HC Kuala Lumpur).
[495] *Inter Maritime* (n 492) 337–38.
[496] ibid 336.
[497] ibid.
[498] *Globus* (n 480); *Sealink Engineering And Slipways Sdn Bhd v Malayan Banking Bhd* (Unreported, HC Miri, Stephen Chung Hian Guan JC, 21 July 2011).
[499] *Inter Maritime* (n 492) 338.
[500] ibid.
[501] ibid.
[502] *Nutri Mills Products Sdn Bhd v CMA CGM Malaysia Sdn Bhd* [2013] 8 MLJ 377 (HC Kuala Lumpur).
[503] ibid 387.

readily available in Malaysia (or Gambia) rather than in France … I accept that it will cause the plaintiff substantial inconvenience and expense to take all these witnesses to France'.[504] Therefore,

> as such the relative convenience and expense of trial as between Malaysia and France weighs in favour of Malaysia in the present factual matrix and serves as a strong factor to rebut the prima facie case in favour of a stay.[505]

In *SRS Sports Centre Sdn Bhd v World Triathlon Corp* ('*SRS Sports*'), because the evidence on issues of fact was situated or more readily available in Malaysia, the High Court said that there was strong cause to refuse a stay in favour of the exclusive forum: the Florida courts.[506]

Recent cases have affirmed the 'strong cause' test and may signal the Malaysian courts' readiness to adopt an approach closer to those in Singapore and Hong Kong. In *United Overseas Bank Ltd v United Securities Sdn Bhad (in liquidation)* ('*United Overseas Bank*'), the Court of Appeal highlighted that when there is an exclusive Choice-of-Forum clause in favour of Singapore courts, the plaintiff 'bears the burden to show strong reasons why it [should] be allowed to continue with the USSB suit [in Malaysia]'.[507] The Court then emphasised that it is not necessary 'to go to the route of *Spiliada* on *forum conveniens*'.[508] Further, 'the factors in *Spiliada* do not amount to strong reasons in the face of an exclusive jurisdiction clause'.[509] Notably, the Court said that the exclusive jurisdiction clause and waiver of objection to Singapore as a proper forum 'make it clear that as a matter of contractual obligation, the submission to the jurisdiction of the Singapore courts should not be challenged'.[510] This approach was reaffirmed in *Open Country Dairy Ltd v Able Food Sdn*[511] ('*Open Country Dairy*'), where the exclusive Choice-of-Forum clause in favour of New Zealand courts – incorporated by reference via the weblink as provided in each sales contract that was signed by the respondent Malaysian company[512] – was upheld. The Court said, 'the respondent must be held to their bargain and a Malaysian court is obliged to give effect to the exclusive jurisdiction clause, unless … there are exceptional circumstances'.[513]

Subsequent lower court decisions have followed the same approach. In *Kraken Services Ltd (formerly known as Kraken Reinsurance Services Ltd) v Q Life Medical Insurance Company Asia Region*, the High Court (Kuala Lumpur) used the term 'exceptional circumstances' rather than 'strong reasons' or 'strong cause',[514] and confirmed that the party challenging the exclusive Choice-of-Forum clause stipulating Qatari courts must 'show exceptional circumstances to warrant a refusal to stay'.[515] Notably, 'exceptional circumstances' should not refer to 'difficulties that [the plaintiff] may encounter if the matter is tried in Qatar'.[516] 'No matter

[504] ibid.
[505] ibid 388.
[506] *SRS Sports Centre Sdn Bhd v World Triathlon Corp* [2018] 8 MLJ 32, 40 (HC Kuala Lumpur).
[507] *United Overseas Bank Ltd v United Securities Sdn Bhad* [2021] 6 MLJ 897, [32] (CA).
[508] ibid.
[509] ibid [38].
[510] ibid [39].
[511] *Open Country Dairy Ltd v Able Food Sdn* [2021] MLJU 969 (CA).
[512] ibid [73].
[513] ibid [79].
[514] *Kraken Services Ltd (formerly known as Kraken Reinsurance Services Ltd) v Q Life Medical Insurance Company Asia Region* [2021] MLJU 2956, [31] (HC Kuala Lumpur).
[515] ibid [34].
[516] ibid [31].

how unpalatable the terms of the Agreements are, it is not open for one party to abandon its original position simply because the practical effect of the agreement does not favour the objecting party'.[517] In *B Braun Medical Industries Sdn Bhd v Pyramid Lines Singapore Pte Ltd* ('*B Braun*'), the High Court (Kuala Lumpur) summarised the applicable test, and noted that the test is not the same for exclusive and non-exclusive Choice-of-Forum clauses:

> (I) Where plaintiffs sue in [Malaysia] in breach of an agreement to refer disputes to a foreign court, and the defendants apply for a stay, the [Malaysian] court, assuming the claim to be otherwise within its jurisdiction, is not bound to grant a stay but has a discretion whether to do so or not;
> (II) The discretion should be exercised by granting a stay unless strong cause for not doing so is shown;
> (III) *The burden of proving such strong cause is on the plaintiffs*;
> (IV) In exercising its discretion, the court should take into account *all the circumstances* of the particular case;
> (V) In particular, but without prejudice to (IV), the following matters, where they arise, may properly be regarded:
>
> (a) *In what country the evidence on the issues of fact is situated, or more readily available*, and the effect of that on the relative convenience and expense of trial as between the [Malaysian] and foreign courts;
> (b) Whether the law of the foreign court applies and, if so, whether *it differs* from [Malaysia] law in any material respects;
> (c) *With what country either party is connected, and how closely*
> (d) *Whether the defendants genuinely desire trial in the foreign country, or are only seeking procedural advantages*
> (e) Whether the plaintiffs would be prejudiced by having to sue in the foreign court because they would—
>
> (i) be deprived of security for that claim;
> (ii) be unable to enforce any judgment obtained;
> (iii) be *faced with a time-bar not applicable in [Malaysia]* or
> (iv) for political, racial, religious or other reasons be unlikely to get a fair trial.[518]

Previously, Malaysian courts have also used estoppel to prevent plaintiffs from invoking Malaysian jurisdiction when there is an exclusive foreign forum clause. In *Dato' Ho Seng Chuan v Rabobank Asia Ltd*,[519] the court declined jurisdiction because the plaintiff is estopped after choosing Singapore as the exclusive forum.[520]

Nonetheless, Malaysian courts may still consider the 'strong cause' threshold to be not so high to overcome. In the 1983 case, *The 'Lung Yung' & 'Thai Yung' Owners v Sadit Timber Sdn Bhd*[521] ('*The Lung Yung*') the Kuching Court used the balance of convenience test to justify its refusal to stay proceedings in Sarawak despite an exclusive Choice-of-Forum clause

[517] ibid [19].
[518] *B Braun Medical Industries Sdn Bhd v Pyramid Lines Singapore Pte Ltd* [2023] MLJU 2760, [22] (HC Kuala Lumpur) ('*B Braun*').
[519] *Dato' Ho Seng Chuan v Rabobank Asia Ltd* [2002] MLJU 216 (Unreported, HC Kuala Lumpur, Vincent Ng Kim Khoay J, 8 March 2002).
[520] ibid 17.
[521] *The 'Lung Yung' & 'Thai Yung' Owners v Sadit Timber Sdn Bhd* [1984] 1 MLJ 29 (FC Kuching) ('*Lung Yung*').

in favour of China.[522] Even in *B Braun*, the Kuala Lumpur High Court cited convenience factors in concluding that there is 'strong cause', such as the cost-effectiveness of litigation in Malaysia, defendants and witnesses located in Malaysia, and the defendant (Pyramid Lines) being 'well-versed in navigating diverse legal systems'.[523] In Singapore and Hong Kong, courts do not consider convenience factors as 'strong cause' sufficient not to enforce exclusive forum clauses. However, *B Braun*, as a lower court decision, may not prevail over the more 'contractual approach' in *United Overseas Bank* and *Open Country Dairy* cases.

In Malaysia, non-exclusive clauses are treated as a factor in the *forum non conveniens* test, without stronger effect.[524] The *forum non conveniens* principles developed in *Spiliada* apply to stay applications involving non-exclusive clauses, as confirmed in *American Express*, where the Supreme Court said that a stay requires the defendant to satisfy the court that 'some other forum is more appropriate'.[525] The 2018 case of *KGI Securities (Singapore) Pte Ltd (previously known as Amfraser Securities Pte Ltd) v Nelson Fernandez* ('*KGI Securities*') confirmed this by citing *American Express* as establishing the applicable test for non-exclusive Choice-of-Forum clauses in Malaysia.[526]

In *Southern Acids (M) Bhd v Standard Chartered Bank Malaysia Bhd*,[527] ('*Southern Acids*') the Malaysian High Court characterised the non-exclusive clause stipulating English courts as a clause which has the purpose of identifying the 'primary place of jurisdiction'.[528] The Court ruled that by filing in Malaysia, the plaintiff had 'wantonly disregarded the non-exclusive jurisdiction clause'.[529] The Court then said:

> [t]he burden is on the plaintiff to show why the suit should proceed in Malaysia since the parties had agreed to submit to the jurisdiction of the English courts. The agreement creates a strong *prima facie* case that the English jurisdiction is the appropriate forum.[530]

The Court emphasised that the waiver: 'waives any objection … that such Proceedings have been brought in an inconvenient forum … [and] such court does not have any jurisdiction over such party'[531] should mean that the plaintiff 'has waived any objection that England is an inconvenient forum'.[532] While the Court considered the clause as a weightier factor in the *Spiliada* analysis, it did not apply the strong cause test, despite citing the English and Singaporean decisions of *Berisford*[533] and *Bambang*[534] respectively. Probably, the reason for this was that while the waiver made the analysis different, the Court was not prepared to give non-exclusive clauses the same effect as exclusive clauses. *Southern Acids*' approach

[522] ibid 43.
[523] *B Braun* (n 518) [36]–[37].
[524] See *American Express* (n 477).
[525] *American Express* (n 477) 167.
[526] *KGI Securities (Singapore) Pte Ltd (previously known as Amfraser Securities Pte Ltd) v Nelson Fernandez* (Unreported, HC Kuala Lumpur, Khadijah Idris JC, 29 June 2018) [64] ('*KGI Securities*').
[527] *Southern Acids (M) Bhd v Standard Chartered Bank Malaysia Bhd* (Unreported Case, HC Kuala Lumpur, Mah Weng Kwai JC, 3 March 2011) ('*Southern Acids*').
[528] ibid [14].
[529] ibid.
[530] ibid.
[531] ibid.
[532] ibid.
[533] *Berisford* (n 104).
[534] *Bambang* (n 105).

has not been adopted in later cases, with Malaysian courts continuing to favour the broader discretion of the *American Express* approach.[535]

In *KGI Securities*, a summary judgment case, the Malaysian High Court reaffirmed that non-exclusive Choice-of-Forum clause are just one factor in the *forum non conveniens* analysis, without carrying extra weight. Although the Court acknowledged that the non-exclusive clause stipulating Singapore courts weakened the plaintiff's argument for Malaysian jurisdiction,[536] it did not give the clause greater significance. Instead, the Court found the defendant's jurisdictional challenge untenable, noting that the defendant's Malaysian citizenship and residence and the location of witnesses in Malaysia outweighed the plaintiff bank's location in Singapore.[537]

D. Anti-suit Injunctions and Other Relief

Malaysian courts may issue an anti-suit injunction to prevent a person from pursuing foreign proceedings[538] if it would breach a legal or equitable right not to be sued abroad.[539] This injunction is directed at the respondent, not to the foreign court,[540] but is exercised cautiously in consideration of international comity.[541] Anti-suit injunctions can be granted when there is an exclusive Choice-of-Forum clause, pursuant to section 52(1) to (2) of the Specific Relief Act 1950, which provides courts with jurisdiction to grant an anti-suit injunction to prevent breach of contract.[542] In *Sabah Gas Industries Sdn Bhd v Trans Samudera Lines (S) Sdn Bhd*[543] ('*Sabah Gas*'), the High Court in Kota Kinabalu stated that such discretion is only exercised exceptionally where the foreign proceedings breach an exclusive jurisdiction clause in favour of local courts.[544] Hence, the order will be granted unless strong cause or strong reasons are established that it should not. Nonetheless, the court may refuse to issue an anti-suit injunction where the plaintiff has submitted to the foreign jurisdiction instead of relying on the exclusive clause.

An anti-suit injunction can also be issued for non-exclusive clauses stipulating Malaysian courts, but since no breach of contract is involved, it falls under common law rather than the Specific Relief Act.[545] The injunction requires that the Malaysian court be the 'natural forum' and that the foreign proceedings are oppressive and vexatious.

[535] See *KGI Securities* (n 526) [64].
[536] ibid [64]–[66].
[537] ibid [66].
[538] LexisNexis, *Halsbury's Laws of Malaysia* (online at 29 March 2019) 90 Conflict of Laws, '3 Jurisdiction' [90.090].
[539] *BSNC Leasing Sdn Bhd v Sabah Shipyard Sdn Bhd* [2000] 2 MLJ 70, 87–88 (CA Kuala Lumpur).
[540] LexisNexis (n 538) [90.090].
[541] See Arunachalam Kasi, 'Anti-suit Injunction in Enforcement of Arbitration Agreement and Exclusive Jurisdiction Agreement' [2013](6) *Malayan Law Journal* i, viii.
[542] Specific Relief Act 1950 (Malaysia) s 52(1)-(2); See Kasi (n 541) iii.
[543] *Sabah Gas Industries Sdn Bhd v Trans Samudera Lines (S) Sdn Bhd* [1993] 2 MLJ 396 (HC Kota Kinabalu).
[544] ibid 405.
[545] See Kasi (n 541) iii.

E. Recognition and Enforcement of Judgments

Foreign judgments can be recognised and enforced through common law and statute.[546] The Reciprocal Enforcement of Judgments Act 1958 reflects common law rules, particularly regarding the foreign court's jurisdiction in issuing the judgment and the grounds for setting aside registration.[547] Significantly, the Act deems a court to lack jurisdiction if proceedings were initiated in breach of an exclusive Choice-of-Forum clause.[548]

In *Maxicont Shipping Agencies Sdn Bhd v Sefair Technical Sdn Bhd*, the High Court in Shah Alam enforced the stay order issued by the Singapore High Court as a judgment of the High Court of Malaya, pursuant to the Reciprocal Enforcement of Judgments Act 1958.[549] The Court dismissed the application to set aside the registration, after noting that the Singaporean orders were issued to enforce the exclusive clause stipulating Cayman Islands courts, and not recognising them would violate international comity and reciprocity.[550] Despite the stay being 'suspensory in nature', it was enforced, recognising that it may only be lifted in exceptional circumstances.[551]

V. Philippines

A. The Philippine Approach to Jurisdiction

The Philippine court system includes the Supreme Court,[552] Court of Appeals,[553] regional trial courts (RTC),[554] metropolitan trial courts (MeTC), municipal trial courts (MTC) and municipal circuit trial courts (MCTC).[555] Depending on the claim amount involved and the remedy sought, original actions involving Choice-of-Forum clauses may be filed with the RTC, MeTC, MTC or MCTC. Civil procedure follows the rules of procedure issued by the Supreme Court, which is vested with the power to promulgate such rules under the Philippine Constitution.[556] Rules 1 to 71 of the Rules of Court compose the 1997 Rules of Civil Procedure, which Administrative Matter No 19-10-20-SC amended in 2019 (2019 Amendments), thus modifying several procedures, including dismissal of actions.[557] Supreme Court decisions, including those on civil procedure, form part of Philippine law.[558]

[546] Reciprocal Enforcement of Judgments Act 1958 (Malaysia).
[547] See ibid pt 2, s 5.
[548] ibid pt 2, s 5(3)(a).
[549] *Maxicont Shipping Agencies Sdn Bhd v Sefair Technical Sdn Bhd* [2022] MLJU 3508, [22] (HC Malaya).
[550] ibid [38], [45].
[551] ibid [38].
[552] Constitution (Philippines) art 8, s 1.
[553] Batas Pambansa Blg 129 ('The Judiciary Reorganization Act of 1980') (Philippines) ch 1, ss 3-12 ('BP 129').
[554] ibid ch 2, ss 13–24.
[555] ibid ch 3, ss 25–38.
[556] Constitution (n 552) art 8, s 5(2).
[557] Proposed Amendments to the 1997 Rules of Civil Procedure, AM No 19-10-20-SC (Philippines) approved through Supreme Court Resolution dated 15 October 2019 effective 1 May 2020: https://sc.judiciary.gov.ph/2019-proposed-amendments-to-the-1997-rules-of-civil-procedure/ ('2019 Amendments').
[558] Civil Code (Philippines) art 8.

Jurisdiction in the Philippines has two aspects: subject-matter jurisdiction and personal jurisdiction. Defined by law, subject-matter jurisdiction determines the nature and type of cases a court may hear and try,[559] and as regards lower courts, is specified in Batas Pambansa 129 or 'The Judiciary Reorganization Act of 1980'[560] and as regards the Supreme Court, in the Constitution.[561] Personal jurisdiction is acquired either through a party's voluntary appearance or the court's service of process,[562] which is usually through summons. Both aspects of jurisdiction must coincide. Additionally, jurisdiction is also determined by the allegations in the complaint, which reflect procedural party autonomy.[563]

As earlier mentioned, section 4(b), rule 4 of the Rules of Court allows parties to predetermine the venue of their action through written agreement; otherwise the default venue rules apply. While primarily intended for domestic litigation, this rule has been applied to foreign 'venues'.[564] A Choice-of-Forum clause is treated as a venue stipulation, with the analysis often focusing on whether the technical requirements, such as the clause being in writing and exclusive, are met. As a result, Philippine courts tend to apply case law on venue stipulations in general, without distinguishing whether the named forum is domestic or foreign.

Unlike in Singapore, Hong Kong and Malaysia, the *forum non conveniens* principle is applied not at the jurisdictional stage but during the merits stage.[565] However, Choice-of-Forum clauses, including non-exclusive clauses, can significantly influence the application of this principle, as they are generally considered when determining the forum's appropriateness.

B. Service of Process

Proper service of summons is crucial for procedural due process in the Philippines, and improper service may lead to dismissal of an action. Rule 14 of the Rules of Court outlines service within and outside the Philippines. Personal service on the defendant is preferred,[566] with access to other modes of service available only as alternatives.[567] Extraterritorial service is allowed to a non-resident defendant but only in actions *in rem* or *quasi in rem*, such as actions affecting the property or personal status of the plaintiff or where the defendant's property has been attached in the Philippines.[568] Often, in actions *in personam*, a strategy by plaintiffs to avail themselves of extraterritorial service, is to also ask for an attachment of the defendant's property in the Philippines, which then transforms the action into a *quasi in rem*. Moreover, extraterritorial service is also allowed when the defendant who is a

[559] *Hasegawa and Nippon Engineering Consultants Co Ltd v Minoru Kitamura* (2007) 538 SCRA 261, 274 ('*Hasegawa*').

[560] BP 129 (n 553) ss 9, 19–23, 32–37.

[561] Constitution (n 552), art 8, s 5.

[562] *Banco Español-Filipino v Palanca* (1918) 37 Phil 921, 927.

[563] *Hasegawa* (n 559) 274.

[564] Eg, *Philippine International Trading Corporation v MV Zileena* (1992) 215 SCRA 309 ('*MV Zileena*').

[565] *Hasegawa* (n 559) 277–78.

[566] Rules of Court (Philippines), r 14, s 6.

[567] ibid r 14, s 6.

[568] ibid r 14, s 17.

Philippine resident is temporarily outside the Philippines.[569] In both instances of extraterritorial service, leave of court is required.[570] Unlike in Singapore, Hong Kong or Malaysia, Choice-of-Forum clauses do not play any role in the granting of leave for service outside the Philippines.

C. Stay of Proceedings

(i) Affirmative Defences and Motion to Dismiss

The Philippines lacks rules on the staying of proceedings. Instead, actions may be dismissed through a motion to dismiss or by raising affirmative defences through the defendant's answer, where Choice-of-Forum clauses may play a role. The 2019 Amendments significantly altered the grounds for dismissal. Prior to the amendments, rule 16, section 1 of the Rules of Court listed several grounds for a motion to dismiss, including improper venue and lack of jurisdiction over the person or subject matter of the claim. After the 2019 Amendments, rule 16 has totally been deleted and only three grounds (lack of jurisdiction over the person or subject matter, *lis pendens* and *res judicata*) were retained as grounds for a Motion to Dismiss, now under rule 15.[571] Filing a motion to dismiss under other grounds is considered a prohibited motion.[572] Instead, the other grounds previously provided under the former rule 16, including improper venue and non-compliance with a condition precedent, are now considered affirmative defences to be raised in the defendant's answer.[573] The court may resolve these defences on its own[574] or through a summary hearing, leading to a possible dismissal within 30 days.[575]

Choice-of-Forum clauses do not affect subject-matter or personal jurisdiction, so they cannot be invoked as a basis for a motion to dismiss or as affirmative defences which can also lead to a dismissal. Unlike Singapore, Hong Kong or Malaysia, there is no presumption in favour of a stay of proceedings for breaching an exclusive Choice-of-Forum clause. Philippine courts will not dismiss an action solely due to breach of such a clause.

Since Philippine courts treat Choice-of-Forum clauses as venue stipulations, a breach of one of these clauses may amount to improper venue, which is among the affirmative defences under rule 6, section 5,[576] and can lead to a dismissal. However, a breach in itself does not mean that the venue is improper, as other factors, like the convenience of the parties to the dispute,[577] will also be considered. In effect, '[s]ince convenience is the *raison d'etre* of the rules of venue … venue stipulations should be deemed permissive … and that interpretation should be adopted which most serves the parties' convenience'.[578] Additionally, when

[569] ibid r 14, s 18.
[570] ibid r 14, ss 17–18.
[571] ibid r 15, s 12(a).
[572] ibid.
[573] ibid r 6, s 5.
[574] ibid r 8, s 12(c).
[575] ibid r 8, s 12(d).
[576] See also ibid r 8, s 12(2).
[577] *Radiowealth Finance Co, Inc v Nolasco* (2016) 808 SCRA 639, 645.
[578] ibid 767–68.

substantial justice demands it, venue rules may be relaxed: 'Time and again, this [Supreme] Court has consistently held that rules [of procedure] must not be applied rigidly so as not to override substantial justice'.[579] Nonetheless, any objection based on improper venue must be raised early, ie, upon the filing of the answer, or risk being waived, especially when the defendant has applied for interlocutory relief which is 'tantamount to voluntary submission to the jurisdiction of the lower court'.[580] Arguably, the procedural reasons for not enforcing an exclusive Choice-of-Forum clause may be wide.

When a case has already been filed in the chosen foreign forum, a motion to dismiss or an affirmative defence based on *lis pendens* (*litis pendentia*) may be available, with the Choice-of-Forum clause serving as evidence that a parallel action involving the same parties and the same cause of action exists.[581] The defendant must, however, prove the identity of the parties, cause of action and the likelihood that the foreign action will result to *res judicata*.[582] Similarly, if the foreign forum has already rendered judgment, the Choice-of-Forum clause may be presented as proof that the judgment rendered was between the same parties, on the same cause of action and that the foreign judgment bars any further litigation based on the principle of *res judicata*.[583] Lastly, the Choice-of-Forum clause can arguably also be considered an unfulfilled condition precedent, which bars the defendant from filing an action in the Philippines.[584] However, unlike *lis pendens* and *res judicata*, which can be raised both in a motion to dismiss[585] and as an affirmative defence,[586] the non-fulfilment of a condition precedent can only be raised as an affirmative defence,[587] although all can lead to a dismissal of action.

(ii) Forum Non Conveniens

The Rules of Court do not expressly list *forum non conveniens* as a ground for dismissal; nor is it mentioned among the affirmative defences under rule 6, section 5(b). Philippine case law, however, has established it as a ground for dismissal in cases with foreign elements.[588] The application of *forum non conveniens* assumes that the Philippine court has jurisdiction but chooses not to exercise it because another forum is deemed more appropriate. The aim is not only to address 'parallel litigation and undermine a litigant's capacity to vex and secure undue advantages by engaging in forum shopping on an international scale' but to also consider 'principles of comity and judicial efficiency'.[589] Peculiarly, however, *forum non conveniens* cannot be invoked directly as a ground in a motion to dismiss. In *Hasegawa v*

[579] *Sanchez v Court of Appeals* (2003) 404 SCRA 540.
[580] *MV Zileena* (n 564) 313.
[581] Rules of Court (Philippines) r 6, s 5(b) and r 15, s 12.
[582] See *Villarica Pawnshop, Inc v Gernale* (2009) 582 SCRA 67, 78–79.
[583] See *Saudi Arabian Airlines (Saudia) v Rebesencio* (2015) 746 SCRA 140, 164 ('*Saudia*').
[584] Rules of Court (Philippines) r 6, s 5(b).
[585] ibid r 15, s 12(a).
[586] ibid r 6, s 5(b).
[587] ibid r 6, r 5(b) and r 8, s 12.
[588] See *Hong Kong and Shanghai Banking Corporation v Sherman* (1989) 176 SCRA 331, 338–39 ('*HSBC*').
[589] *Saudia* (n 583) 164.

Kitamura,[590] the Supreme Court emphasised that the principle is better raised as a matter of defence during the trial stage (merits),[591] in short as an affirmative defence.

The *forum non conveniens* principle has been applied in cases involving Choice-of-Forum clauses.[592] In *HSBC*, the Supreme Court interpreted the Choice-of-Forum clause stipulating Singaporean courts as non-exclusive because it lacked the exclusivity required under rule 4, section 2(b).[593] Because the clause was non-exclusive, it could not justify a dismissal under the former rule 16. Since the Court found jurisdiction and proper venue, the Court then applied the principle of *forum non conveniens* to determine whether it should proceed to exercise its jurisdiction.[594] The Court found it puzzling that the Philippine residents themselves, and not the Singaporean parties, were the ones avoiding litigation in the Philippines and were seeking to enforce the Choice-of-Forum clause stipulating Singaporean courts.[595] The Court suggested that the defendants might be attempting to delay or avoid their obligations.[596] Despite acknowledging that HSBC should not be allowed to take a stand contrary to the contractual stipulations, a 'substantial basis exist[ed]' for its choice of Philippine forum. Arguably, the Supreme Court considered the defendants' lack of genuine desire for trial in Singapore and the convenience of trying the case in the Philippines as reasons why the Philippine court should proceed to exercise its jurisdiction.

D. Anti-suit Injunctions and Other Relief

Philippine courts do not issue anti-suit injunctions. Nonetheless, an injunction under rule 58 of the Rules of Court may be available to prevent certain acts, and may produce the same effects as an anti-suit injunction.[597] Under section 3 of rule 58, a preliminary injunction may be granted by the court when (1) the applicant is entitled to the relief demanded, (2) the act complained of would probably cause injustice to the applicant, or (3) certain acts are probably in violation of the rights of the applicant respecting the subject of the action or proceeding, and tend to render the judgment ineffectual.[598]

It may be argued that preventing a party from filing or pursuing an action in breach of an exclusive Choice-of-Forum clause is a form of relief which the plaintiff is entitled to. Furthermore, the additional costs, inconvenience and the prejudice that the filing or continuance of a foreign action would 'probably work injustice to the applicant'. Significantly, a foreign judgment issued in breach of an exclusive Choice-of-Forum clause is not prevented from becoming *res judicata*; thus, in that sense, the judgment to be rendered by the Philippine court may become ineffectual. However, the Supreme Court has not yet ruled that a preliminary injunction is available for breach or imminent breach of a Choice-of-Forum clause.

[590] *Hasegawa* (n 559).
[591] ibid 278.
[592] See *HSBC* (n 588) 339.
[593] ibid 337.
[594] ibid 338–39.
[595] ibid 336.
[596] ibid.
[597] See Rules of Court (Philippines), r 58, s 1.
[598] ibid r 58, s 3.

E. Recognition and Enforcement of Judgments

As a matter of international comity, Philippine courts recognise and enforce foreign judgments pursuant to rule 39, section 48 of the Rules of Court. A foreign judgment on a specific thing (*in rem*) is conclusive concerning the title to the thing,[599] while a foreign judgment against a person (*in personam*) is presumptive evidence of a right between the parties and their successors in interest.[600] A foreign judgment may be refused 'by evidence of a want of jurisdiction, want of notice to the party, collusion, fraud, or clear mistake of law or fact'.[601]

Foreign judgments obtained in breach of Choice-of-Forum clauses are not automatically invalid for execution and recognition in the Philippines unless such breach constitutes a 'want of jurisdiction' by the foreign court. This would require evidence of the foreign court's basis for jurisdiction and how this was not met.[602] Furthermore, because the Philippines considers that 'a State does not have jurisdiction in the absence of some reasonable basis for exercising it',[603] 'to be reasonable, the jurisdiction must be based on some minimum contacts that will not offend traditional notions of fair play and substantial justice'.[604] Hence, a breach of a Choice-of-Forum clause may not necessarily mean absence of jurisdiction if other elements (eg, domicile) link the parties to the foreign forum. Significantly, even if the Choice-of-Forum clause stipulated Philippine courts, the foreign judgment may bar future litigation because of *res judicata*. If the breach resulted from 'collusion, fraud or clear mistake of law or fact', this can also prevent recognition and enforcement, provided a preponderance of evidence is established.[605]

[599] ibid r 39, s 48(a).
[600] ibid r 39, s 48(b).
[601] ibid r 39, s 48.
[602] See *William Borthwick v Castro-Bartolome* (1987) 152 SCRA 229, 235.
[603] *HSBC* (n 588) 338.
[604] ibid.
[605] Rules of Court (Philippines), r 133, s 1.

5

The Factors Considered in Granting Relief: Singapore, Hong Kong, Malaysia, Philippines

I. The Antecedents: *The Eleftheria* and *Spiliada*

In enforcing Choice-of-Forum clauses, Singapore, Hong Kong and Malaysia have identified similar factors as relevant in the analysis. Two English cases are considered normative in determining what factors are relevant: *The Eleftheria*[1] (1969), for exclusive clauses, and *Spiliada*[2] (1986), for non-exclusive clauses. As these factors are treated as factual issues, they are 'pre-eminently within the province of the trial judge',[3] with each factor's weight dependent on the facts and circumstances of the case. Courts take a cumulative approach, weighing each factor, as no single one can 'by itself be sufficient to justify refusing a stay'.[4] Notably, the evaluation of these 'connecting factors' remains discretionary.[5]

A. Exclusive Choice-of-Forum Clauses and the Dominance of *The Eleftheria* Approach

Singapore, Hong Kong and Malaysian courts have followed *The Eleftheria*, albeit inconsistently in the earlier years. *The Eleftheria* factors include: (1) the location of evidence and relative convenience and expense of trial between the forum and foreign courts; (2) whether the foreign court's law applies to the merits; (3) the strength of each party's connection to a country; (4) whether the defendant genuinely seeks trial in the foreign forum; (5) potential prejudice to the plaintiff in the foreign court, such as (i) lack of security for its claim, (ii) unenforceable foreign judgments, (iii) time-bar issues, or (iv) a potentially unfair trial due to political, racial, religious or other reasons; (6) the risk of multiple proceedings; and (7) other relevant factors.[6]

In Singapore and Hong Kong, 'strong cause' requires that it be shown that the defendant lacks genuine desire for trial and that prejudice to the plaintiff would result if the trial proceeded in the chosen forum. While convenience factors initially sufficed to establish

[1] *The Eleftheria* [1970] P 94.
[2] *Spiliada Maritime Corp v Cansulex Ltd* [1987] AC 460.
[3] See *Inter Maritime Management Sdn Bhd v Kai Tai Timber Co Ltd, Hong Kong* [1995] 1 MLJ 322 (CA Kuala Lumpur) 323 ('*Inter Maritime*').
[4] *The 'Eastern Trust'* [1994] 2 SLR(R) 511, 519 (HC).
[5] See *Siemens AG v Holdrich Investment Ltd* [2010] 3 SLR 1007, 1010 (CA) ('*Siemens*').
[6] *The Eleftheria* (n 1) 99–100.

'strong cause', their significance has since diminished over the years. In contrast, Malaysia still considers convenience and multiplicity of proceedings as sufficient to establish 'strong cause'. The following table summarises factors recognised by courts in Singapore, Hong Kong and Malaysia as constituting 'strong cause':

Jurisdiction	**Factors Amounting to 'Strong Cause'**
Singapore	• Location of material elements (1 case)[7] • Location of evidence, relative convenience and economy (3 cases)[8] • Applicable law (1 case)[9] • Lack of genuine desire for trial (5 cases)[10] • Prejudicial factors (1 case)[11]
Hong Kong	• Location of evidence, relative convenience and economy (4 cases)[12] • Multiplicity of proceedings (2 case)[13] • Lack of genuine desire for trial (3 cases)[14] • Prejudicial factors (3 cases)[15]
Malaysia	• Location of material elements (2 cases)[16] • Location of evidence, relative convenience and economy (6 cases)[17] • Prejudicial factors (1 case)[18]

In stay applications, *The Eleftheria* analysis requires the defendant to first prove that an exclusive Choice-of-Forum clause stipulating the foreign forum exists. Once this is proven, the burden shifts to the plaintiff to establish 'strong cause' why the court should override the agreed forum selection clause.[19] However, if the defendant cannot prove

[7] *BGC Partners (Singapore) Ltd v Tan Wee Hiong Kevin* [2017] SGHC 214 ('*BGC Partners*').

[8] *Amerco Timbers Pte Ltd v Chatsworth Timber Corp Pte Ltd* [1977–1978] SLR(R) 112 (CA) ('*Amerco*'); *The 'Eastern Trust'* (n 4); *The 'Hyundai Fortune'* [2004] 2 SLR(R) 213 (HC).

[9] *The 'Asian Plutus'* [1990] 1 SLR(R) 504, 514 (HC).

[10] *The 'Hyundai Fortune'* (n 8); *Golden Shore Transportation Pte Ltd v UCO Bank* [2004] 1 SLR(R) 6 (CA) ('*Golden Shore*'); *The 'Jian He'* [1999] 3 SLR(R) 432 (CA); *The 'Hung Vuong-2'* [2000] 2 SLR(R) 11 (CA); *Societe Generale v Tai Kee Sing @ Tai Hean Sing* [2003] SGHC 139, [12] ('*Societe Generale*').

[11] *The 'Hyundai Fortune'* (n 8); *Trisuryo Garuda Nusa Pte Ltd v SKP Pradiksi (North) Sdn Bhd* [2017] 2 SLR 814 (CA).

[12] *Trafalgar House Construction (Asia) Ltd v Owners and/or Demise Charterers of the MV Thorscan* ('*The Thorscan*') [1998] 4 HKC 536, 543 (CA); *Star Cruises (HK) Ltd v Tung Ho Wah* [2006] HKDC 61 ('*Star Cruises*'); *Superstrong Industries Limited t/a M & T International v Furness Logistics (HK) Ltd* [1999] HKCFI 314, [23] ('*Superstrong*'); *Royal Skarkia Life Insurance Ltd v Sparkle Consultants (HK) Ltd* [2006] HKDC 118 ('*Royal Skarkia*').

[13] *Konsumex Foreign Trade Co v Sun Luen Transportation Co* [1990] 1 HKC 247 (HC) ('*Konsumex*'); *Quaestus Capital Pte Ltd v Everton Associates Ltd* [2021] HKCFI 1367, [61]–[62] ('*Quaestus*').

[14] *The Thorscan* (n 12); *Madison Communications Private Ltd v Le Ecosystem Technology India Private Ltd* [2017] HKCFI 1567 ('*Madison*'); *Superstrong* (n 12) [24]–[25].

[15] *Confecciones del Atlantico v Lamont Shipping Incorporated* [1982] 1 HKC 327 (HC) ('*Confecciones*'); *Joseph Ghossoub v Team Y&R Holdings Hong Kong Ltd* [2016] HKCFI 1019 ('*Ghossoub-CFI(1)*'); *The Griesheim* [1984] HKC 416 (CA).

[16] *Inter Maritime* (n 3); *SRS Sports Centre Sdn Bhd v World Triathlon Corp* [2018] 8 MLJ 32 (HC Kuala Lumpur).

[17] *Inter Maritime* (n 3); *Nutri Mills Products Sdn Bhd v CMA CGM Malaysia Sdn Bhd* [2013] 8 MLJ 377 (HC Kuala Lumpur) ('*Nutri Mills*'); *The 'Lung Yung' & 'Thai Yung' Owners v Sadit Timber Sdn Bhd* [1984] 1 MLJ 29 (FC Kuching); *SRS Sports* (n 16); *Rintis Malay Motors Sdn Bhd v Agasta Co Ltd* (Unreported, HC Kuala Lumpur, Faizah Jamaludin JC, 5 June 2017) ('*Rintis*'); *B Braun Medical Industries Sdn Bhd v Pyramid Lines Singapore Pte Ltd* [2023] MLJU 2760, [25], [36], [37], [40] (HC Kuala Lumpur) ('*B Braun*').

[18] *Bank of China v Ngan Ching Wen* [2011] 2 MLJ 645, 657 (HC Kuala Lumpur) ('*Ngan*').

[19] *SRS Sports* (n 16) 39.

the clause's existence and the court's jurisdiction was established of right, the court will hear the case unless there are grounds for stay on the basis of *forum non conveniens*.[20] In *Bunge SA v Shrikant Bhasi*, the Singapore Court of Appeal considered the contractual waiver of *forum non conveniens* as complementing the exclusive Choice-of-Forum clause.[21]

B. *Forum Non Conveniens* and Non-Exclusive Choice-of-Forum Clauses

(i) Spiliada's *Quest for the Natural Forum*

Given the explicitly balancing nature of the *forum non conveniens* test, identifying which factors are relevant is more complicated than the 'strong cause' test. Courts often need to identify multiple factors to determine the more appropriate forum, as under the classic *Spiliada* test, when the plaintiff has instituted the action as of right, the proceedings are not easily stayed unless the defendant shows that there is a more appropriate forum.[22] Hence, 'it is wrong to say that Singapore is *forum non conveniens* … because the connecting factors which point to Singapore are outweighed by all the connecting factors which point away from Singapore'.[23] Significantly, a 'real and genuine tension' between one jurisdiction and at least one other jurisdiction where a case may be tried more suitably should be demonstrated for a court to apply *forum non conveniens*.[24]

Furthermore, 'the court is [also] required to focus on the appropriateness … from the point of view of the trial of the action'.[25] Hence, '[d]etermination of the identity of the natural forum … must depend upon the nature of the disputed issues in any particular case'.[26] Likewise, the *forum non conveniens* analysis may change over time, as the *Spiliada* factors may change.[27] For instance, witnesses may relocate or die, and parties may concede certain legal or factual issues.[28]

Nonetheless, which factors are relevant and why (ie, a possible theoretical justification for their inclusion) are important questions which often elude the makers of many court decisions, prompting commentators to describe the English *forum non conveniens* analysis as arbitrary.[29] In *Spiliada*, Lord Templeman observed: '[t]he factors which the court is entitled to take into account … are legion. The authorities do not, perhaps cannot, give

[20] See *Yong Songhua v Basic Venture International Ltd* [2017] 8 MLJ 681, 690–91 (HC Kuala Lumpur).
[21] *Bunge SA v Shrikant Bhasi* [2020] SGCA 94, [40] (CA).
[22] *Spiliada* (n 2) 476.
[23] *Siemens* (n 5) 1010.
[24] *TA Private Capital Security Agent Ltd v UD Trading Group Holdings Pte Ltd* [2021] SGHCR 10, [22]–[23].
[25] *Rambas Marketing Co LLC v Chow Kam Fai David* [2001] 3 HKC 250, 255 (CFI).
[26] ibid 255.
[27] *China North Industries Investment Ltd v Ronald RC Chum* [2006] HKCFI 407, [118].
[28] ibid.
[29] See Wendy Kennett, '*Forum Non Conveniens* in Europe' (1995) 54(3) *Cambridge Law Journal* 552, 555; JJ Fawcett, 'General Report' in JJ Fawcett (ed), *Declining Jurisdiction in Private International Law: Reports to the XIVth Congress of the International Academy of Comparative Law Athens, August 1994* (Clarendon Press, 1995) 1, 23; *cf* in Simona Grossi, '*Forum Non Conveniens* as a Jurisdictional Doctrine' (2013) 75(1) *University of Pittsburgh Law Review* 31, the American *forum non conveniens* test was also criticised as arbitrary.

any clear guidance as to how these factors are to be weighed'.[30] Nonetheless, the history of stay of proceedings may explain why certain factors have been included. Traditionally, a stay is granted based on factors showing that the local action is 'oppressive and vexatious' to the defendant.[31] Over time, these factors became irrelevant.[32] Rather, the factors established by the Scottish doctrine of *forum non conveniens*, which English courts adopted, have become central to the analysis.[33] Hence, parties need to refer to factors showing legitimate advantages to the plaintiff juxtaposed with disadvantages which the defendant may suffer.[34] Furthermore, the *forum non conveniens* principle has also adopted elements associated with the concept of 'natural forum' in other legal contexts,[35] like determining the 'natural forum' for divorce proceedings under the Matrimonial Causes Act 1950, which requires establishing factors showing 'substantial connection',[36] the requirement of a substantial connection for establishing discretionary jurisdiction,[37] and the approach employed in contract choice of law cases which also requires a substantial connection with a legal system.[38] Hence, under the *forum non conveniens* principle nowadays, the applicable law becomes a significant factor.[39] The overall effect, then, is an English *forum non conveniens* analysis which includes connecting and convenience factors, applicable law, prejudicial factors, genuine desire for trial, and multiplicity of proceedings. Singapore, Hong Kong and Malaysia follow this approach.

(ii) The Modified Spiliada *Analysis in Singapore and Hong Kong*

In the classic *Spiliada* analysis, a non-exclusive Choice-of-Forum clause (as a connecting factor) is one of several factors used to identify the more appropriate forum. However, the 1990s saw modifications to this approach. *Berisford* established that a non-exclusive clause stipulating English courts creates a strong prima facie case for England as the appropriate forum.[40] In *British Aerospace*, the parties were barred from raising foreseeable convenience factors during contract negotiations.[41] Together, these cases gave non-exclusive clauses an effect akin to exclusive ones when the English forum is named by the parties, thus altering how these clauses factor into the *forum non conveniens* analysis.

[30] *Spiliada* (n 2) 465; *The Atlantic Star* [1974] AC 436, 454; *MacShannon v Rockware Glass Ltd* [1978] 2 WLR 362, 367 ('*MacShannon*').

[31] *MacShannon* (n 30) 813; *The Abidin Daver* [1984] AC 398, 401.

[32] See *St Pierre v South American Stores (Garth & Chaves) Ltd* [1936] 1 KB 382, 398.

[33] *The Abidin Daver* (n 31), 411; *Spiliada* (n 2) 475.

[34] *Spiliada* (n 2) 477–78.

[35] See ibid.

[36] See JJ Fawcett, 'Forum Shopping – Some Questions Answered' (1984) 35(2) *Northern Ireland Legal Quarterly* 141, 146.

[37] See Alexander Reus, 'Judicial Discretion: A Comparative View of the Doctrine of Forum Non Conveniens in the United States, the United Kingdom, and Germany' (1994) 16(2) *Loyala of Los Angeles International and Comparative Law Journal* 455, 478–79; Fawcett (n 36) 151; David Robertson, 'Forum non conveniens in America and England: 'a rather fantastic fiction' (1987) 103(3) *Law Quarterly Review* 398, 411.

[38] See Fawcett (n 36) 149–50.

[39] See Guan Siew Teo, 'Choice of Law in Forum Non Conveniens Analysis' (2010) 22(2) *Singapore Academy of Law Journal* 440, 449–50.

[40] *S & W Berisford plc v New Hampshire Insurance Co* [1990] 2 QB 631, 646 ('*Berisford*').

[41] *British Aerosplace Plc v Dee Howard Co* [1993] 1 Lloyd's Rep 368, 376 ('*British Aerospace*').

The Rothnie[42] went further by extending the effect of prima facie appropriateness to non-exclusive Choice-of-Forum clauses stipulating foreign courts. Cresswell J reasoned that a non-exclusive clause stipulating foreign courts (ie, the Gibraltar courts) and an applicable foreign law created a strong prima facie case for that jurisdiction.[43] He added that, even if he erred in shifting the burden of proof, Gibraltar was the appropriate forum due to its having the most real and substantial connections. He emphasised that the non-exclusive Choice-of-Forum clause stipulating Gibraltar courts was a 'very strong factor'.[44] *The Rothnie's* reasoning, however, appears not to have been followed in later English cases. Furthermore, in *Abdul Rashid*, the Singapore High Court noted, 'it was not clear to me whether *The Rothnie* represented English law or was not considered to be good law'.[45] Therefore, it appears that English courts are not ready to extend further the modified *Spiliada* logic to recognise named foreign courts as appropriate, and shift the burden to the plaintiff, who established the English court's jurisdiction as of right.

The impact of modified *Spiliada* principles on the *forum non conveniens* analysis in Singapore, Hong Kong and Malaysia remained unclear until the 2000s. For example, Lee observed that in Singapore three approaches were adopted:[46] (1) some decisions followed *Spiliada* without modifications (eg, *PT Jaya*[47]), (2) some decisions applied the *Spiliada* approach, but excluded foreseeable factors (eg, *Asia-Pacific Ventures II Ltd v PT Intimutiara Gasindo*,[48] *Bayerische Landesbank Girozentrale v Kong Kok Keong*,[49] and possibly *Baiduri*[50]), (3) some decisions applied the 'strong cause' test to non-exclusive clauses (eg, *Bambang*).[51] In *Bambang*,[52] where the Singapore Court of Appeal applied the 'strong cause' test to a non-exclusive clause stipulating Jakarta courts, the application of the 'strong cause' test resulted from the joint effect of a non-exclusive Choice-of-Forum clause with the defendant's waiver of objections based on *forum non conveniens*.[53] Hence, the modified *Spiliada* analysis in Singapore appears different, as the distinction was not necessarily drawn based on whether Singapore is chosen in the non-exclusive clause. Unlike *The Rothnie*, *Bambang* also cited neither the chosen foreign forum's prima facie appropriateness nor the status of the non-exclusive clause as a very strong factor.

Hong Kong's shift was clearer. In *Noble Power*,[54] the Hong Kong Court of Appeal declared that where the parties have submitted to the named forum, such obligation should be treated as no different from cases where the clause is exclusive.[55] Given that the

[42] *ED & F Man Ship Ltd v Kvaerner Gibraltar Ltd ('The Rothnie')* [1996] 2 Lloyd's Rep 206.
[43] ibid 211.
[44] ibid.
[45] *Abdul Rashid bin Abdul Manaf v Hii Yii Ann* [2014] 4 SLR 1042, 1051 (HC) ('*Abdul Rashid*').
[46] See Joel Lee, 'Non-exclusive Jurisdiction Clauses-Changing Approaches?' (2003) (2) *Singapore Journal of Legal Studies* 593.
[47] *PT Jaya Putra Kundur Indah v Guthrie Overseas Investments Pte Ltd* [1996] SGHC 285 ('*PT Jaya*').
[48] *Asia-Pacific Ventures II Ltd v PT Intimutiara Gasindo* [2001] 2 SLR(R) 371, 383 (HC) ('*Asia-Pacific Ventures*').
[49] *Bayerische Landesbank Girozentrale v Kong Kok Keong* [2002] 1 SLR(R) 485, 490 (HC) ('*Bayerische Landesbank*').
[50] *Baiduri Bank Bhd v Dong Sui Hung* [2000] 2 SLR(R) 271, 281 (HC) ('*Baiduri*').
[51] Lee (n 46) 594.
[52] *Bambang Sutrisno v Bali International Finance Ltd* [1999] 2 SLR(R) 632 (CA) ('*Bambang*').
[53] Lee (n 46) 594.
[54] *Noble Power Investments Ltd v Nissei Stomach Tokyo Co Ltd* [2008] HKCA 255 ('*Noble Power*').
[55] ibid [29].

non-exclusive clause required the parties to submit to the jurisdiction of the Hong Kong courts, and that proceedings were commenced in Hong Kong, the plaintiffs were considered to have demonstrated the appropriateness of Hong Kong as a forum in the context of an Order 11 application (ie, asking the court to exercise its discretionary jurisdiction and allow service out of Hong Kong).[56] Hence, the *Noble Power* case was a situation 'where proceedings are instituted in the named forum (to which the parties have agreed to submit)'; thus, 'the party who seeks a stay or otherwise to contest the jurisdiction or appropriateness … has a very heavy burden to discharge, since that party has by definition agreed contractually to submit to the jurisdiction'.[57] Absent strong reasons, the defendant would not be allowed to escape the effects of his contract.[58] Likewise, the same heavy burden applies when the parties have not named Hong Kong as a forum but have nonetheless agreed to submit to the jurisdiction of the courts of any other forum (including Hong Kong) in the event of their being sued there.[59] The Court emphasised that the traditional *Spiliada* approach only applies when Hong Kong is not the named forum and the parties have not agreed to submit to its courts when sued there.[60] In paragraph 40, however, the Court discussed the possibility that 'proceedings were instituted in *the very forum* to which the parties had agreed to submit'.[61] In that situation, parties still need to show 'strong reasons … as to why the agreement should not be enforced'.[62] This reasoning appear to move further away from the approach in *Berisford* and has the same effect as in *The Rothnie*. Nonetheless, as will be explained later, *The Rothnie* could not be the basis of the Court's decision. Significantly, *Noble Power* is confirmed in several Hong Kong decisions.[63]

The approach in *Noble Power* was eventually adopted by the Singapore Court of Appeal in *Orchard Capital*,[64] a case involving a non-exclusive Choice-of-Forum clause stipulating Hong Kong courts.[65] Nonetheless, because *Noble Power* was an application to set aside leave allowing extraterritorial service and not a stay of proceedings like *Orchard Capital*, the Singapore court did not expressly endorse its principles.[66] Instead, the Court referred to Yeo's article which advocated for a contractual approach to non-exclusive clauses.[67] Yeo argued that a non-exclusive Choice-of-Forum clause can be given the same effect as an exclusive clause, thus requiring the application of the 'strong cause' test.[68] Nonetheless, the Court emphasised that the non-exclusive clause is not the only factor; nor it should be a strong indicator.[69] Whether the non-exclusive clause has a similar effect to an exclusive clause depends 'on the precise intention of the parties themselves which is to be gathered

[56] ibid [63].
[57] ibid [31].
[58] ibid [35].
[59] ibid [33].
[60] ibid [33].
[61] ibid [40].
[62] ibid.
[63] eg, *Chinachem Financial Services Ltd v Century Venture Holdings Ltd* [2015] HKCFI 20, [78] ('*Chinachem*'); *High Hope Zhongding Corporation v Xiamen Dunfeng Import and Export Co, Ltd* [2017] HKCFI 56, [48]–[49]; *China Agri-Products Exchange Ltd v Wang Xiu Qun* [2013] HKCFI 1819, [129].
[64] *Orchard Capital I Ltd v Ravindra Kumar Jhunjhunwala* [2012] 2 SLR 519 (CA) ('*Orchard Capital*').
[65] ibid 528–29.
[66] *Shanghai Turbo Enterprises Ltd v Liu Ming* [2019] 1 SLR 779, 813 (CA) ('*Shanghai Turbo*').
[67] *Orchard Capital* (n 64) 530.
[68] ibid.
[69] ibid 532.

from the language utilised by the parties as well as the surrounding factual matrix'.[70] Here, because there was no evidence of such parties' intention, the non-exclusive clause stipulating Hong Kong courts was not considered a strong indicator that Hong Kong was clearly more appropriate.[71] Likewise, the Court ruled that other factors like the respondent's residence and the similarity between Hong Kong and Singapore laws did not make Hong Kong clearly or distinctly more appropriate.[72] *Orchard Capital* has since been cited in several Singapore High Court decisions.[73]

In Singapore, the contractual approach was expressly adopted in *Shanghai Turbo*,[74] which, like *Noble Power*, was also an application to set aside leave to serve out of jurisdiction.[75] *Shanghai Turbo* confirmed that the effect of a non-exclusive clause depends on its precise construction.[76] When parties 'submit to the non-exclusive jurisdiction', the meaning of the word 'submit' is that the 'parties consent to the exercise of jurisdiction by the courts of that forum and waive any objection'.[77] In short, to 'submit' means to 'waive any objection'.[78] Therefore, this prohibition from contesting the jurisdiction of the named forum applies 'with equal force to each of the jurisdictions to which the parties agreed to submit',[79] including instances where the named forum is a foreign court. In these circumstances, 'strong cause' would be required to allow a party not to proceed in the named forum. In sum, this contractual approach in *Shanghai Turbo* confirms the primacy of the parties' intention in determining the effect of a non-exclusive Choice-of-Forum clause. Hence, in *Chang Chee Kheo v Fatfish Investment Partners Pte Ltd* ('*Chang*'), the High Court said that 'a particular jurisdiction comes to be regarded as an appropriate forum … only because the parties intended it to be so'.[80] Further, the weight given to such choice in the *forum non conveniens* test depends on the contractual intention of the parties.[81]

Although Hong Kong and Singapore courts have taken approaches similar to that in *The Rothnie*, courts have not cited it – probably due its earlier rejection in Hong Kong[82] and doubts raised by Singapore courts.[83] Hence, in Hong Kong and Singapore, a non-exclusive Choice-of-Forum clause stipulating a foreign court does not automatically serve as a 'very strong factor' or establish the foreign court's prima facie appropriateness, which could shift the burden to the plaintiff even if the forum court's jurisdiction was established as of right. Instead, both the *Noble Power* and *Orchard Capital* cases treat a non-exclusive clause for a foreign court as a very strong factor only when the parties have stipulated or intended it as such.

[70] ibid.
[71] ibid 535.
[72] ibid 536.
[73] eg, *Morgan Stanley Asia (Singapore) Pte (formerly known as Morgan Stanley Dean Witter Asia (Singapore) Pte) v Hong Leong Finance Ltd* [2013] 3 SLR 409 (HC) ('*Morgan Stanley*'); *Abdul Rashid* (n 45); *Humpuss Sea Transport Pte Ltd (in compulsory liquidation) v PT Humpuss Intermoda Transportasi TBK* [2016] 5 SLR 1322 (HC); *Mann Holdings Pte Ltd v Ung Yoke Hong* [2016] SGHC 112 ('*Mann Holdings*').
[74] *Shanghai Turbo* (n 66) 814.
[75] ibid 788.
[76] ibid 814.
[77] ibid 815.
[78] ibid.
[79] ibid 820–21.
[80] *Chang Chee Kheo v Fatfish Investment Partners Pte Ltd* [2023] SGHR 12, [51].
[81] ibid.
[82] *T&K Electronics Ltd v Tai Ping Insurance Co Ltd* [1997] 3 HKC 330, 336–337 (CFI) ('*T&K Electronics*').
[83] See *Abdul Rashid* (n 45) 1051.

(iii) The Theoretical Justification for the Modified Spiliada *Analysis*

When parties expressly state that they will submit to the named forum (eg, by using the word 'submit' or other words with the same effect), they are obligated to submit to such forum as a matter of contract.[84] The effect of this submission, in the context of non-exclusive clauses, is no different from 'submission' in exclusive clauses.[85] In both, there is a contractual obligation to submit to the named forum.[86] Hence, the effects provided in *Noble Power* result from this contractual approach.

While contract law supports the modified *Spiliada* analysis, it also justifies not treating all non-exclusive clauses equally, as giving them a heavier weight or 'burden' would depend on the particular language of the clause. In *Noble Power*, this will depend on whether the parties have submitted to the jurisdiction of the named forum (ie, situations A and B).[87] In *Orchard Capital*, it depends on the precise intention of the parties.[88] *Orchard Capital* appears to provide a wider basis for allowing the effects of exclusive clauses to apply to non-exclusive ones, since 'intention' can cover situations other than a submission (eg, waiver of objections to *forum non conveniens*), plus the fact that the test in *Orchard Capital* allows courts to consider the factual matrix when determining the parties' intent.[89] In both *Noble Power* and *Orchard Capital*, the key is the interpretation of the non-exclusive clause – a very contractual approach to Choice-of-Forum clauses.

This contractual basis also allows courts to infer certain obligations from the parties' agreement, primarily the right to sue in the named forum. This right is important, as some scholars equate it with submission to jurisdiction under common law.[90] Consequently, the burden falls on the party seeking another forum to justify the denial of this right to sue in the forum.[91] Such submission also provides the contractual ground to allow service out of jurisdiction[92] and even an anti-suit injunction absent 'strong reasons'.[93] It also allows the application of the 'strong cause' test for non-exclusive clauses.[94]

A contractual basis implies that a breach may occur if a party opposes a suit in the named forum through a stay application or attempts to set-aside service, as refusal to accept a writ from the chosen forum is typically a breach of an agreement to submit to the jurisdiction.[95] Likewise, seeking an anti-suit injunction to defeat the action in the named forum could also constitute a breach.[96] However, controversy arises over whether an objection or questioning the forum's appropriateness is itself a breach, especially in the absence of an explicit contractual waiver of objection to the court's appropriateness. To answer this, one must

[84] Tan Seow Hon, 'A New-Found Significance for Non-Exclusive Jurisdiction Agreements' [2000] (1) *Singapore Journal of Legal Studies* 298, 299.

[85] *Noble Power* (n 54) [29].

[86] ibid.

[87] ibid [33].

[88] *Orchard Capital* (n 64) 532.

[89] ibid.

[90] Tan (n 84) 299.

[91] Yeo Tiong Min, 'The Contractual Basis of the Enforcement of Exclusive and Non-Exclusive Choice of Court Agreements' (2005) 17(1) *Singapore Academy of Law Journal* 306, 337.

[92] *Noble Power* (n 54) [15].

[93] *Morgan Stanley* (n 73) [30]–[31].

[94] *Noble Power* (n 54) [37].

[95] Yeo (n 91) 339.

[96] ibid.

go back to the tripartite framework discussed in Chapter two. A distinction must be made on matters which are between parties (ie, matters agreed upon by the parties, contained in their contract and to be resolved as a matter of contract) and matters which are between the parties and the courts (ie, the enforcement portion and matters of public law or those outside the realm of contract). If parties have not explicitly provided in their contract that they have an obligation not to object to the forum court's appropriateness, then a subsequent objection by one party cannot be considered a breach of contract. Hence, if an objection is still considered by the court to be a breach, it follows that the theoretical justification cannot be under contract law but lies somewhere else.

What basis, then, allowed the English courts to say in *Berisford*[97] and *The Rothnie*[98] that a non-exclusive clause creates a strong prima facie case that that jurisdiction is an appropriate one, or in *British Aerospace*,[99] to preclude objections based on foreseeable convenience factors? In England, the view is that the waiver of objection – an agreement not to object to the named forum exercising its jurisdiction on the principles of natural forum – is necessarily implied into every non-exclusive Choice-of-Forum clause, at least where English law is the applicable law.[100] This turns all non-exclusive clauses into exclusive clauses when proceedings are commenced in the named forum, but not when commenced in another jurisdiction.[101] Nonetheless, the limited support for *The Rothnie* suggests reluctance by English courts to extend this presumption of appropriateness to foreign courts, especially when English jurisdiction is founded as of right.

Although *Noble Power* and *Orchard Capital* apply a form of modified *Spiliada* analysis, they reject reading implied waivers of objections into non-exclusive clauses, unlike in *The Rothnie*. Hong Kong and Singapore courts permit defendants to challenge the named forum's appropriateness unless there is an express waiver, as in *Bambang*, where the combination of the waiver of objection and non-exclusive clause amount to an exclusive clause when the proceedings are commenced in the named forum. *Noble Power*, for instance, continues to acknowledge the right of the defendant to challenge the appropriateness of the named forum or the forum coupled with an agreement to submit to its jurisdiction; albeit such objection carries with it a very heavy burden.[102] *Orchard Capital* is more explicit as it refuses to abandon the more general approach laid down in *Spiliada*, thus allowing objections to the court's exercise of jurisdiction.[103] The Singapore Court of Appeal, however, noted that

> to the extent that the more general [*Spiliada*] approach … entails a consideration of the circumstances surrounding the making of the non-exclusive jurisdiction clause, there is – on a practical level – at least some possible blurring of the lines [with the contractual approach].[104]

Even the reading of the waiver of objection in *Shanghai Turbo* was only a consequence of the use of the word 'submit' in the clause.[105] Hence, arguably, a more general waiver of objection

[97] *Berisford* (n 40).
[98] *The Rothnie* (n 42).
[99] *British Aerospace* (n 41).
[100] Yeo (n 91) 343.
[101] ibid 344.
[102] *Noble Power* (n 54) [33].
[103] *Orchard Capital* (n 64) 532, 534.
[104] ibid 534.
[105] *Shanghai Turbo* (n 66) 815.

applicable to *all* non-exclusive clauses has not been established by *Shanghai Turbo*. Thus, in Singapore, the non-exclusive clause remains just one of the many factors, albeit an important one when parties have intended it to be so.

In Hong Kong and Singapore, therefore, neither contract law nor implied waivers fully explain their modified versions of *Spiliada*. The weight of non-exclusive clauses is not solely determined by contract, and implied waivers cannot be read into the non-exclusive clauses when proceedings are commenced in the named forum. Hence, the *Spiliada* approach – and the theoretical justifications behind its adoption – continues to provide the very backbone of the analysis of courts, and the much-valued discretion to 'determine where the interests of justice lie' provides the justification of giving greater weight to non-exclusive clauses if warranted. It means that the contractual aspect of the non-exclusive clause is still just one of the many factors being weighed by the court in its *forum non conveniens* analysis. Nonetheless, what is different in *Noble Power* and *Orchard Capital* from the traditional *Spiliada* approach is that the contractual aspect of the non-exclusive clause becomes an important factor relative to the other factors; thus, its practical effect is similar to English decisions.

However, in instances when the intention to provide a stronger effect to their non-exclusive clauses is not clear or explicit, are there other circumstances that warrant a stronger weight being given to non-exclusive clauses? In Singapore, this may be possible when the intention to give stronger weight can be concluded from the factual milieu. A possible example is when there is already an independent basis for jurisdiction (eg, the foreign court already has jurisdiction because a party is domiciled in that country), and therefore 'it makes no sense for the parties to enter into the agreement unless they intend something more'.[106] Nonetheless, parties may not be acquainted with the intricacies of the jurisdictional requirements of the named forum;[107] thus, whether a stronger effect was actually intended may be doubtful. Another possibility is when the parties have deliberately stated in their contract that their choice of forum was due to the foreign court's neutrality[108] or expertise. In these circumstances, the factual matrix may show that the parties intended a stronger effect to be granted to their non-exclusive clause. An implied grant of stronger weight, however, may be more difficult to establish in Hong Kong, as the words or language of the non-exclusive clause form the limits of determining whether the strong cause test may be applied. Nonetheless, this is a matter of interpretation and as such, Hong Kong courts may go beyond the express words of the clause, as warranted by the relevant interpretation rules.

Noble Power and *Orchard Capital* appear to escape the English courts' issues (ie, to imply waivers by parties, which may not be theoretically justified by contract law) by basing the 'stronger' effect of non-exclusive clauses on the parties' contractual intention, though challenges remain. What happens if the parties' intention to give stronger effect to their non-exclusive clauses is not clear or explicit? There may not be a problem when the named forum is the forum court. In both *Noble Power* and *Orchard Capital*, the course of action is clear – the non-exclusive clause is treated as exclusive and the party questioning the clause needs to establish 'strong reasons'. This happens even when the parties have not clearly

[106] See Tan (n 84) 307.
[107] See *Shanghai Turbo* (n 66) 816.
[108] See Tan (n 84) 311–12.

provided for stronger effect to be given to their non-exclusive Choice-of-Forum clause naming the forum court. However, when the parties have named a foreign court, how does the forum court determine that the parties must have intended a stronger effect? As seen in Chapter six, the process of determining the parties' contractual intention, as part of contract interpretation, is determined by the law applicable to the contract. There was no mention of this in *Noble Power* and *Orchard Capital*. Rather, the courts appear to base their reasoning solely on common law, ie, forum law. Hence, for failing to take into account the choice of law process, including the need to prove in evidence the foreign interpretation rules relevant in determining party intention, private international law may raise issues with the approach in *Noble Power* and *Orchard Capital* when a foreign court is chosen.[109] Furthermore, there is danger of 'unnecessary extrapolation of the parties' intention' when justifying giving stronger effect to such a clause.[110]

Given these problems, Singapore and Hong Kong courts may need to reconsider whether the modified *Spiliada* approach should be extended to foreign non-exclusive Choice-of-Forum clauses. Courts may be better off by applying the classic *Spiliada* test in those situations.[111] Rather than using the factors which may be considered to establish the parties' intention, why not consider those same factors directly as connecting factors (as in the classic *Spiliada* approach) to assess the appropriateness of the foreign court? In this way, the court may avoid the problem of adopting an approach that is inconsistent with private international law and prone to court error, or worse, abuse.

The following sections discuss the other factors considered in *forum non conveniens* cases. Although some cases involving non-exclusive Choice-of-Forum clauses predate the modified *Spiliada* formula in Hong Kong and Singapore, their reasoning remains relevant under the classic *Spiliada* analysis, which still applies when the forum court is not chosen, or when the parties intended not to give the non-exclusive clause greater weight than the other factors, or when the case is in Malaysia.

II. Factors Considered by Common Law Jurisdictions

A. Location of Material Elements

(i) Characterising the Dispute

What elements are considered material depends on the plaintiff's choice of legal category or classification for his cause of action. If he chooses to bring his case under a contract, then contract law will dictate the elements he needs to establish to get proper relief. Moreover, the contentious issues specifically raised under that legal category will further identify which elements are material. Hence, this choice of legal category is strategic, as it influences the applicable choice of law and is usually carefully chosen to influence the outcome of the case.

[109] See also ibid 321.
[110] See also ibid.
[111] See also ibid.

As such, even if the suit involves a contract, but if the plaintiff chooses a claim in, say, tort or equity, he is bound to proceed and prove his case based on the law of torts or equity.[112]

Nonetheless, the court may still disregard the plaintiff's choice and resolve the dispute under another category, especially if the choice was made in order to escape the effects of the Choice-of-Forum clause. 'A plaintiff cannot avoid a foreign exclusive jurisdiction clause by simply framing his action in tort'.[113] Alternatively, the court may allow the tort claim (or any non-contract cause of action) to stand but still apply the Choice-of-Forum clause because it is broadly phrased to cover disputes 'arising out of or in connection with' the contract.[114] In other words, a Choice-of-Forum clause may 'bite' even if the plaintiff's cause of action is not in contract. Similarly, the defendant's counterclaim based on a different legal category like tort cannot displace the natural forum of a dispute based on contracts (the cause of action in the main action).[115]

In *Rickshaw*,[116] since the claim was based in tort, Singapore's conflicts rules dictated that the place of the tort (ie, Singapore), along with other connecting factors, would be the most important factor in determining whether the Singapore court should exercise its jurisdiction,[117] thus diminishing the importance of the Choice-of-Law and non-exclusive Choice-of-Forum clauses stipulating German law and courts respectively.[118] Hence, Singapore was recognised as 'the most natural and appropriate forum to hear the claims in tort' because of the general connecting factors,[119] and Germany was deemed not necessarily more appropriate, following the classic *Spiliada* analysis.[120]

(ii) Location of the Party

The party's location is an important element in the analysis, as nationality, domicile or place of incorporation may determine issues like contractual capacity, and practical considerations such as the location of assets for satisfaction of judgments,[121] the location of security, or as a connecting factor in the choice of law analysis.[122]

(a) Exclusive Clauses

The parties' location is considered sufficient to establish strong cause, although generally not a decisive factor. In *Amerco*, the Singapore Court of Appeal emphasised that the fact that Amerco is a Singaporean company: 'merits some consideration … though

[112] See *John Reginald Stott Kirkham v Trane US Inc* [2009] 4 SLR(R) 428, 452 (CA) ('*Kirkham*').
[113] *The 'Jian He'* (n 10) 439, citing *The 'Eastern Trust'* (n 4) [36].
[114] See, eg, *Ghossoub* [2017] HKCA 296, [8]–[18].
[115] *UBS AG v Telesto Investments Ltd* [2011] 4 SLR 503, 531 (HC) ('*UBS*').
[116] *Rickshaw Investments Ltd v Nicolai Baron von Uexkull* [2007] 1 SLR(R) 377 (CA).
[117] ibid 392.
[118] ibid 396, 409–10.
[119] ibid 409–10.
[120] ibid 409.
[121] eg, *Lehman Brothers Special Financing Inc v Hartadi Angkosubroto* [1998] 3 SLR(R) 664, 677 (HC) ('*Lehman Brothers*').
[122] See *Brinkerhoff Maritime Drilling Corp v PT Airfast Services Indonesia* [1992] 2 SLR(R) 345, 355 (CA) ('*Brinkerhoff*'); *Yu Lap Man v Good First Investment Ltd* [1998] 1 HKC 726, 732 (CFI) ('*Yu Lap Man-CFI*'); *Inter Maritime* (n 3) 338.

the weight … would be slight'.[123] Similarly, in *Inter Maritime*, since both the vessel and appellant were Malaysian, the Malaysia Court of Appeal considered both to be 'strong grounds' that can displace the exclusive Choice-of-Forum clause stipulating Tokyo courts.[124] This factor, however, was considered along with other factors – namely, that the cargo was loaded at a Malaysian port, that trial in Malaysia would be less expensive and more convenient, and that evidence was available both in Manila and Malaysia.[125] In *SRS Sports*, the Malaysia High Court considered the plaintiff's incorporation and business location in Malaysia sufficient to establish 'strong cause'.[126]

(b) Non-exclusive Clauses

In *Orchard Capital*, despite the non-exclusive clause choosing Hong Kong courts, the Singapore Court of Appeal considered Singapore more appropriate based on the plaintiff's residence in Singapore and the broad similarity between the laws of Singapore and Hong Kong.[127] Likewise, in *MGM Grand Paradise Limited v Chiu Tak Wah*[128] ('*MGM*'), the Hong Kong CFI disregarded a non-exclusive clause stipulating Macau due to the defendant's Hong Kong domicile,[129] the case's minimal connections with Macau,[130] and the plaintiff's failed attempt to serve process in Macau.[131] Temporary presence in the forum, however, is generally less relevant,[132] but if the plaintiff's absence in the forum appears intended to evade litigation, such absence may be disregarded.[133]

When parties intend a 'stronger effect' for the named forum in a non-exclusive clause, the parties' location in other jurisdictions is less relevant for establishing 'strong cause' under the modified *Spiliada* formula. In Singapore and Hong Kong, such factors as a party's location are foreseeable, and thus carry little weight.[134] This also applies to the place of contracting, and to location of the breach and of witnesses.[135]

(iii) Location of Subject Matter of the Dispute

(a) Exclusive Clauses

The location of the dispute's subject matter (eg, the place of performance is in a jurisdiction other than the forum court) is generally not considered 'strong cause'. Possibly, this is because *The Eleftheria* did not explicitly refer to this factor, or because the location of the dispute's subject matter is considered in other *Eleftheria* factors, like the law applicable to the dispute or with what country either party is connected. In *BGC Partners*, however, the

[123] *Amerco* (n 8) 118.
[124] *Inter Maritime* (n 3) 338.
[125] ibid.
[126] *SRS Sports* (n 16) 39.
[127] *Orchard Capital* (n 64) 536.
[128] *MGM Grand Paradise Limited v Chiu Tak Wah* [2012] HKCFI 1529 ('*MGM*').
[129] ibid [41].
[130] ibid [44].
[131] ibid [42].
[132] See *Brinkerhoff* (n 122) 356.
[133] *Venetian Macau Ltd v Chen Mei Huan* [2014] HKCFI 128, [43]–[44] ('*Venetian Macau*').
[134] *Shanghai Turbo* (n 66) 824; *Deltatre SPA v Hong Kong Sports Industrial Development Ltd* [2018] HKCFI 1942, [46] ('*Deltatre*').
[135] See, eg, *Shanghai Turbo* (n 66) 825.

Singapore High Court ruled that, due to the dispute's close ties to Kevin's employment in Singapore, resolving his counterclaim in Singapore served the 'interests of justice',[136] despite an exclusive clause stipulating Delaware courts.[137]

(b) Non-exclusive Clauses

The location of the dispute's subject matter is significant in the *forum non conveniens* analysis. In *Hwoo Huang Linda v Fu Being San* ('*Hwoo Huang*'), because the action concerned ownership of a Hong Kong bank account pursuant to a deed signed in Hong Kong, the court decided that trial in Hong Kong should proceed despite the non-exclusive clause stipulating US courts.[138] Similarly, the location of the events forming the elements of the claim is a significant consideration.[139] In *CIMB Bank Bhd v Dresdner Kleinwort Ltd*[140] ('*CIMB Bank*'), since the matters which were considered significant by the applicable law occurred in Singapore,[141] Singapore had the most and closest connection to the claim compared to England, the named forum.[142] In *PT Jaya*, since the relevant contracts with non-exclusive Choice-of-Forum clauses stipulating Jakarta courts were performed in Indonesia, the Singapore High Court stayed the proceedings in favour of Indonesia.[143] In *Brinkerhoff*, although the non-exclusive clause stipulating 'the courts where the agreement [was] made' (ie, Jakarta) was voided for being contrary to the Warsaw Convention,[144] the Singapore Court of Appeal nevertheless considered Indonesia to be the natural forum because the relevant accident had occurred there.[145] In *Multi-Top Limited v BKE-Media (HK) (A Firm)* ('*Multi-Top*'), since all relevant matters had occurred in Hong Kong – the marketing of equipment and alleged tortious acts – then, despite the non-exclusive clause stipulating German courts,[146] Hong Kong was deemed the natural forum.[147] Likewise, in *Petrodar Operating Co Ltd v Nam Fatt Corp Bhd (in liquidation)*, since the performance guarantee was issued in Malaysia by a Malaysian bank and the money sought to be preserved by an injunction was at all material times in Malaysia, the court ruled in Malaysia's favour despite the non-exclusive clause stipulating Sudanese courts.[148] In *American Express*, where the non-exclusive Choice-of-Forum clause stipulated Singapore courts, the Malaysia Supreme Court set aside the leave to serve outside jurisdiction (namely in Malaysia) after finding that all the foreign exchange transactions happened outside Malaysia, and the securities of the customers were deposited elsewhere.[149]

[136] *BGC Partners* (n 7) [8].
[137] ibid [6].
[138] *Hwoo Huang Linda v Fu Being San* [2002] HKCFI 34, [77] ('*Hwoo Huang*').
[139] ibid [78].
[140] *CIMB Bank Bhd v Dresdner Kleinwort Ltd* [2008] 4 SLR(R) 543 (CA) ('*CIMB Bank*').
[141] ibid 566.
[142] ibid 574.
[143] *PT Jaya* (n 47) [66].
[144] Convention for the Unification of Certain Rules Relating to International Carriage by Air, open for signature 12 October 1929, 137 LNTS 11 (entered into force 13 February 1933).
[145] *Brinkerhoff* (n 122) 355.
[146] *Multi-Top Limited v BKE-Media (HK) (A Firm)* [1999] HKCFI 551, [36].
[147] ibid [42].
[148] *Petrodar Operating Co Ltd v Nam Fatt Corp Bhd (in liquidation)* [2014] 6 MLJ 189, 204 (FC Putra Jaya).
[149] *American Express Bank Ltd v Mohamed Toufic Al-Ozeir* [1995] 1 MLJ 160, 168 (SC Kuala Lumpur) ('*American Express*').

When the company's assets are the only connection to the foreign forum, this generally carries limited weight. The Singapore High Court stated in *Lehman Brothers Special Financing Inc v Hartadi Angkosubroto* that '[t]he important considerations in *forum non conveniens* cases relate more to the trial process than to the post-trial remedies (like execution of judgments and appeals)'.[150] In other words, '[t]hat one party may eventually seek to enforce a judgment there', is not a sufficiently 'strong reason' to assume jurisdiction.[151] Similarly, if the presence of assets in the named forum was its primary connection with the dispute,[152] this may not be sufficient to establish the named forum's appropriateness, especially when the defendant also has assets, aside from the connection established by other elements of the dispute, in the jurisdiction of the court hearing the dispute.[153] However, if the assets' location is the reason why the forum was named, their location becomes important. In *Citibank NA v Robert* ('*Citibank*'), since the 'semi-exclusive' Choice-of-Forum clause (hybrid clause) was purposely drafted to facilitate the plaintiff's recovery,[154] Singapore was considered more appropriate, despite not being chosen, since the defendant had assets in Singapore.[155]

(iv) 'All Circumstances'

The evaluation of material elements is usually combined with other elements and factors. When no single element or factor decisively determines the more appropriate jurisdiction, courts often enumerate various relevant factors.[156]

B. Location of Evidence, Relative Convenience and Economy

(i) Exclusive Clauses

While the location of evidence (ie, witnesses, documents, etc) can establish 'strong cause',[157] its importance has diminished over the years, except in Malaysia.[158] Furthermore, when no evidence at all relating to the relevant issues is before the forum court, its importance is also dramatically diluted.[159] Hence, the contractual choice may no longer be disturbed easily, and issues of convenience like the location of witnesses and other forms of evidence do not weigh heavily.[160] In *The 'Vishva Apurva'*, because the plaintiffs had commenced an action in Singapore and in the chosen forum court, Bombay, India,[161] the court said: '[b]y a parity of reasoning, it could be said that the [plaintiffs] had also regarded India as an acceptable forum'.[162] Likewise, in admiralty cases, where evidence can be located in places

[150] *Lehman Brothers* (n 121) 678.
[151] *People's Insurance Co Ltd v Akai Pty Ltd* [1997] 2 SLR(R) 291, 295 (HC).
[152] eg, *Abdul Rashid* (n 45) 1051–52.
[153] See ibid 1056–57.
[154] *Citibank NA v Robert* [2011] 3 SLR 465, 472 (HC) ('*Citibank*').
[155] ibid.
[156] See eg, *T&K Electronics* (n 82) 334.
[157] eg, *Amerco* (n 8) 120; *The 'Eastern Trust'* (n 4) 523; *The 'Hyundai Fortune'* (n 8) 217; *The Thorscan* (n 12) 543; *Inter Maritime* (n 3) 338.
[158] eg, *Nutri Mills* (n 17) 387–88.
[159] See *The 'Carl Offersen'* [1977–1978] SLR(R) 589, 594 (HC).
[160] See *The 'Vishva Apurva'* [1992] 1 SLR(R) 912, 924 (CA); *The 'Botic'* [1999] 2 SLR(R) 494, 502 (HC).
[161] *The 'Vishva Apurva'* (n 160) 924–26.
[162] ibid 924.

quite distant from one another, if there is no evidence that the witnesses and other pieces of evidence cannot be brought to the chosen forum, this factor cannot be given any weight.[163] In *Hyundai Engineering*, the Hong Kong CFI stressed that if the parties foresaw 'some inconvenience resulting from the application of the exclusive jurisdiction clause … then such inconvenience is generally irrelevant'.[164] In *Longlife International (Hong Kong) Co Ltd v May Delight Ltd*, the Hong Kong CFI even stressed that defendants are precluded from raising issues relating to inconvenience of witnesses.[165] Even during the COVID-19 pandemic, courts did not treat the location of evidence as 'strong cause'.[166]

Nonetheless, there are cases in which exclusive clauses have been disregarded for reasons of convenience and location of evidence. In *Star Cruises (HK) Ltd v Tung Ho Wah*, the Hong Kong District Court considered that because most witnesses were in Hong Kong, this became the most compelling factor in disregarding the choice of either Singapore or Malaysia (at the sole option of Star Cruises) as alternative exclusive fora,[167] not to mention the small amount of the claim involved. In *Superstrong Industries Limited t/a M & T International v Furness Logistics (HK) Ltd*, the Hong Kong CFI refused a stay in favour of Rotterdam, Netherlands because the claim had been revised to be under tort law, and also because the claimed amount was 'so relatively little'.[168] Similarly, in *Royal Skarkia Life Insurance Ltd v Sparkle Consultants (HK) Ltd*, the Hong Kong District Court disregarded the exclusive clause stipulating the Isle of Man 'in view of the size of the claim',[169] which the Court considered to be insufficient to justify the travelling expenses.[170] In sum, in cases where the amount involved is little, there is a greater chance that convenience and location of evidence will be given greater weight.

Malaysian courts still consider convenience factors sufficient to oust foreign exclusive Choice-of-Forum clauses. In *Inter Maritime*, the Malaysia Court of Appeal considered that there were 'strong grounds' to refuse a stay because trial in Malaysia would 'be less expensive and more convenient'.[171] In *Nutri Mills*, because 'the evidence on the issues of fact [is] … largely situated or more readily available in Malaysia (or Gambia) rather than in France', 'it will cause the plaintiff substantial inconvenience and expense to take all these witnesses to France',[172] thus, this was found to 'rebut the prima facie case in favour of the defendants under the forum selection clause'.[173] A similar reasoning was used in *SRS Sports*,[174] *Rintis Malay Motors Sdn Bhd v Agasta Co Ltd*,[175] and, recently, in *B Braun*.[176] Interestingly, even

[163] See *Chan Chi Keung v Delmas Hong Kong Ltd* [2004] 4 HKC 28, 39 (CFI).
[164] *Hyundai Engineering & Construction Co Ltd v UBAF (Hong Kong) Ltd* [2013] HKCFI 1579, [43] ('*Hyundai Engineering*').
[165] *Longlife International (Hong Kong) Co Ltd v May Delight Ltd* [2017] HKCFI 1381, [34].
[166] eg, *A v B* [2022] HKCFI 1031, [56]–[57]; *Lo Ka Lee Kelly t/a Leader Packing (HK) Co v Spiriant Asia Pacific Ltd* [2021] HKDC 787, [27], [31] ('*Lo Ka Lee*'); *China Industrial Securities International Brokerage Ltd v Li Hailong* [2022] HKCFI 2694, [9], [10].
[167] *Star Cruises* (n 12) [73].
[168] *Superstrong* (n 12) [23].
[169] *Royal Skarkia* (n 12) [7].
[170] ibid.
[171] *Inter Maritime* (n 3) 338.
[172] *Nutri Mills* (n 17) 387.
[173] ibid 384.
[174] *SRS Sports* (n 16) 39–40.
[175] *Rintis* (n 17) [24].
[176] *B Braun* (n 17) [36]–[37], [40].

when the convenience factors tend to point to the chosen foreign forum, a Malaysian court may still require a 'preponderance of (in)convenience' to justify a stay of proceedings.[177]

Because of this approach, some argue that in Malaysia, *The Eleftheria* only shifts to the plaintiff the burden of proof in a stay application, and nothing more.[178] Hence, the Malaysian approach arguably still does not elevate the parties' intention even in the case of exclusive clauses in the same way as in Singapore and Hong Kong.[179] The parties' contract to settle their dispute exclusively in their chosen foreign court is still weighed along with convenience factors, and what results from this analysis remains subject to the court's discretion, although the plaintiff bears the heavy burden of a refusal to stay. If Malaysian courts fully enforce *The Eleftheria*, considerations of convenience should arguably be given less weight. Nonetheless, two recent Court of Appeal decisions, *United Overseas Bank*[180] and *Open Country Dairy*,[181] signal a possible shift towards an apparently strong 'contractual approach' like in Singapore and Hong Kong.

(ii) Non-exclusive Clauses

In contrast, factors such as the location of evidence, relative convenience and economy are important because *forum non conveniens* is, after all, about convenience. When witnesses and other pieces of evidence are not found in the forum (not chosen) but elsewhere, convenience factors matter more.[182] In *Lehman Brothers*, the Singapore High Court was prompted to conclude that 'if the forum is Singapore, practically everyone involved would have to travel. Clearly then, New York and Indonesia are more convenient and appropriate when compared to Singapore'.[183] The reverse applies when the witnesses or evidence *are* mostly within the jurisdiction of the forum court (not a named forum).[184] When the witnesses or evidence, however, are located somewhere near the forum court (but outside its jurisdiction), like Hong Kong, Macau and the neighbouring regions of China with respect to each other, or as may be the case with Malaysia and Singapore, and there is no evidence that the witnesses cannot travel or that the other pieces of evidences could not be brought to the forum, then this factor is less important.[185] Furthermore, because of proximity, the cost of bringing the witnesses and other evidence would be considered to be roughly the same.[186] Moreover, technological advancements have also made documentary evidence portable,[187] and witnesses considered capable of giving testimony through video conferencing.[188] Notably, only the location of material witnesses and other evidence is significant.[189]

[177] *Lung Yung* (n 17) 43.

[178] See, eg, Tan (n 84) 299.

[179] See also *Inter Maritime* (n 3) 336.

[180] *United Overseas Bank Ltd v United Securities Sdn Bhd (in liquidation)* [2021] 6 MLJ 897, [36], [38], [39] (CA).

[181] *Open Country Dairy Ltd v Able Food Sdn Bhd* [2021] MLJU 969, [79] (CA).

[182] eg, *The 'Dai Yun Shan'* [1992] 1 SLR(R) 461, 469 (HC).

[183] *Lehman Brothers* (n 121) 677; See also *Southern Acids (M) Bhd v Standard Chartered Bank Malaysia Bhd* (Unreported Case, HC Kuala Lumpur, Mah Weng Kwai JC, 3 March 2011) [16] ('*Southern Acids*'); *Industrial & Commercial Bank Limited v Banco Ambrosiano Veneto SPA* [2000] SGHC 188, [18] ('*Banco Ambrosiano*').

[184] See *DFS Trading Ltd v Swiss Air Transport Co Ltd* [1997] 1 HKC 547, 551 (HC).

[185] See *Yu Lap Man-CFI* (n 122) 734; *Medisell Medical Instrument Co Ltd v Sanyou International (Group) Co Ltd* [2007] HKDC 467,[12]; *American Express* (n 149) 165; *MGM* (n 128) [61].

[186] See *American Express* (n 149) 165.

[187] See *Kirkham* (n 112) 450.

[188] See *Banco Ambrosiano* (n 183) [19].

[189] *CIMB Bank* (n 140) 569; *Venetian Macau* (n 133) [48]; *Mann Holdings* (n 73) [56].

Nonetheless, the plaintiff may be precluded from complaining about the litigation costs in the foreign court when the Choice-of-Forum clause chooses such foreign forum.[190]

C. Applicable Law

(i) Exclusive Clauses

The applicable law can be the law explicitly or implicitly chosen by the parties or, in the absence of a choice, that determined by the forum's conflicts rules. In cases involving exclusive clauses stipulating foreign courts, stays are usually granted based on the contractual obligation to bring disputes to the chosen forum and not on this factor. Hence, concerns about the law or procedure applicable in the chosen forum are not usually considered.[191] Nonetheless, when the applicable law is the law of the chosen foreign forum, courts often say that when the applicable law is foreign law, its contents, application and interpretation are best decided by the chosen court.[192] Moreover, the same reasoning applies when the applicable law is the law of the forum (but not the chosen forum). Stays are still granted and the fact that the applicable law is the forum law does not amount to 'strong cause' sufficient to disregard the exclusive Choice-of-Forum clause stipulating the foreign court. Nonetheless, foreign law may exceptionally be a 'strong cause' factor if the foreign procedure has serious defects.[193] It appears that this objection is also anchored in public policy.

(ii) Non-exclusive Clauses

When the clause is non-exclusive, foreign law as the applicable law becomes an important factor in deciding a stay.[194] Hence, courts declare that it is desirable that the foreign law be interpreted by the courts whence that foreign law came.[195] If the applicable foreign law is also the law of the chosen forum, then the two constitute significant connecting factors in favour of the chosen jurisdiction.[196] The reverse is also true. If forum law is applicable, this becomes an important factor for the forum court to determine itself as the more appropriate forum,[197] even when another court is chosen.[198] Furthermore, if the choice of forum law is the reason for entering into the contract, the forum court may see its refusal to exercise jurisdiction as assisting one of the parties to frustrate the contract.[199]

However, even if the applicable law is that of the chosen court, it does not follow that the case should be heard there.[200] The Choice-of-Law clause's significance 'depends on the issues

[190] See *Southern Acids* (n 183) [16].

[191] See *The 'Vishva Apurva'* (n 160) 925.

[192] See *Frans Bambang Siswanto v Coutts & Co AG* [1996] SGHC 250, [19].

[193] See *The 'Asian Plutus'* (n 9) 514.

[194] See *PT Jaya* (n 47) [66]; *Praptono Honggopati Tjitrohupojo v His Royal Highness Tunku Ibrahim Ismail Ibni Sultan Iskandar Al-Haj* [2001] 3 SLR(R) 872, 885–86 (HC) ('*Praptono*'); *The 'Dai Yun Shan'* (n 182) 469; *Kirkham* (n 112) 452.

[195] eg, *Lehman Brothers* (n 121) 676.

[196] See *Peregrine Fixed Income Ltd v JP Morgan Chase Bank* [2005] 2 HKC 374, 384 (CFI) ('*Peregrine*').

[197] See *Asia-Pacific Ventures* (n 45) 380; *UBS* (n 115) 531; *Bayerische Landesbank* (n 49) 490; *Perfect Direct Ltd v Dejin Resources Group Co Ltd* [2015] HKCFI 1087, [58].

[198] *Shanghai Turbo* (n 66) 826.

[199] *Yantai Wanhua Polyurethanes Co Ltd v Pur Products Ltd* [2012] HKCFI 1992, [37] ('*Yantai*').

[200] *Venetian Macau* (n 133) [50].

which are likely to arise at trial and other questions relating to the appropriate forum'.[201] If the applicable law is a neutral third country's law, 'it must have been the [parties'] deliberate and conscious decision to choose a neutral system of law',[202] and courts must note this deliberate choice in their *forum non conveniens* analysis. An attempt by the defendant to apply another law could be seen as undermining the parties' common intention.[203]

(iii) Qualifying the Applicable Law Factor

When the foreign applicable law is unidentifiable[204] or is similar to forum law,[205] its role as the applicable law holds little weight in the analysis.[206] In *Hwoo Huang*, the Hong Kong CFI found ambiguity in a clause referring only to US law, when there are 50 State jurisdictions and one federal jurisdiction of the United States.[207] In *CIMB Bank*, Singapore law's similarity to English law on unjust enrichment gave English law no advantage.[208] The same reasoning applies when the applicable law is Malaysian law with Singapore as the forum.[209] In *Nam Fatt Corporation Bhd v Petrodar Operating Co Ltd*, the Malaysian High Court noted that Sudanese law, including the applicable *Shariah* principles in Sudan, mirrored Malaysia's *Shariah* principles applicable to Islamic loans and facilities;[210] thus Malaysian courts can assume jurisdiction even when the non-exclusive clause chose Sudanese courts.[211] Likewise, when the applicable foreign law's contents are 'very much part of the universal law' (eg, mercantile law) which is 'very similar in all countries', and which the forum court has often applied in the past, the foreign law's significance in *forum non conveniens* diminishes.[212] Similarly, even when the foreign applicable law was arguably complex, but the defendant failed to identify the relevant provisions requiring expert opinion, the need for such an expert witness is downplayed and could not be considered a significant factor.[213]

Furthermore, the forum court may not see the need for referring the foreign law's interpretation and application only to the chosen courts. In *Amerco*, the Singapore Court of Appeal ruled that a Singapore court would not have difficulty in applying Indonesian law,[214] considering Singapore's experience with admiralty cases, and the fact that the relevant contract incorporated The Hague Rules,[215] which are part of Singapore law. Similarly, in *Wynn Las Vegas LLC v Lam Kwok Hung*, the Hong Kong CFI refused a stay because 'the

[201] *Yantai* (n 199) [26].
[202] ibid [30].
[203] ibid.
[204] See *Hwoo Huang* (n 138) [60].
[205] *CIMB Bank* (n 140) 567.
[206] See *Orchard Capital* (n 64) 536.
[207] *Hwoo Huang* (n 138) [60].
[208] *CIMB Bank* (n 140) 536.
[209] *OCBC Capital Investment Asia Ltd v Wong Hua Choon* [2010] 4 SLR 904, 912 (HC).
[210] *Nam Fatt Corporation Berhad v Petrodar Operating Co Ltd* (Unreported, HC Kuala Lumpur, Lee Swee Seng JC, 30 June 2010).
[211] ibid.
[212] *Harain Lai Navalani v Tokai Bank Ltd* [1994] 3 HKC 203, 207–8 (CA).
[213] *KGI Securities (Singapore) Pte Ltd (previously known as Amfraser Securities Pte Ltd) v Nelson Fernandez* (Unreported, HC Kuala Lumpur, Khadijah Idris JC, 29 June 2018) [69].
[214] *Amerco* (n 8) 120.
[215] International Convention for the Unification of Certain Rules of Law relating to Bills of Lading, opened for signature 25 August 1924, 120 LNTS 187 (entered into force 2 June 1931).

courts in Hong Kong are well able to deal with aspects of Nevada law relating to gaming'.[216] In *Ko Lai Kuen v Li Tak Ming*, the Hong Kong CFI exercised jurisdiction even when Indonesian law was the governing law because 'it is possible for expert evidence as to what the Indonesian law is on the issue of implied terms to be adduced by the parties and for the Hong Kong courts then to apply that law',[217] not to mention that a number of factors (eg, Hong Kong as the place of contract formation) pointed to Hong Kong.[218]

Under English common law, foreign law is treated as a factual issue.[219] If the foreign law's contents have not been proven sufficiently, the forum court may assume that the foreign law has the same content as forum law.[220] In *The 'Hyundai Fortune'*, a case involving an exclusive Choice-of-Forum clause stipulating Korean courts, the Singapore High Court dismissed the need to consider Korean law (which would give Korean courts the key advantage) because no evidence was provided.[221] An affidavit is usually insufficient evidence of a foreign law's contents.[222] Similarly, unless the plaintiff raises legal issues under foreign law, and in effect establishes that trial in the foreign court is more convenient, the court may not consider foreign law as a factor.[223] Hence, the court may not apply foreign law if its role is unclear or immaterial to the issues being tried.[224] Likewise, the ease of bringing in legal experts to testify about foreign law diminishes the weight of foreign law.[225]

D. Lack of Genuine Desire for Trial

(i) Exclusive Clauses

Lack of genuine desire for trial can justify denying a stay in both exclusive and non-exclusive Choice-of-Forum clause cases.[226] Genuine desire is usually established by extensive filings and various points of disagreement between parties,[227] thus demonstrating that a genuine defence or disagreement on points of law exists. Conversely, the lack of a genuine defence, or worse, failure to state any defence at all,[228] may indicate that there is no genuine desire for trial. Hence, courts may review alleged defences to assess their substance;[229] although a high threshold is not imposed – 'so long as there are issues for a defence which can be identified' – and the court need not consider, in every case, the merits of the defence raised.[230] When the law applicable is

[216] *Wynn Las Vegas LLC v Lam Kwok Hung* [2008] HKCFI 434, [27]; *MGM* (n 128) [57].
[217] *Ko Lai Kuen v Li Tak Ming* [2011] HKCFI 304, [51].
[218] ibid [58].
[219] eg, *The 'Hung Vuong-2'* (n 10) 17.
[220] eg, *Amerco* (n 8) 120.
[221] *The 'Hyundai Fortune'* (n 8) 220.
[222] *The 'Hung Vuong-2'* (n 10) 17.
[223] *The 'Jin Hui 588'* [2016] HKCFI 480, [54].
[224] See *S-Net Freight (HK) Ltd v Namsung Shipping Company Ltd* [2011] HKCFI 519, [41].
[225] *The 'Jin Hui 588'* (n 223) [54].
[226] See *The 'Hung Vuong-2'* (n 10) 15; *The 'Jian He'* (n 10) 453; *Xu Ziming v Ruifeng Petroleum Chemical Holdings Ltd* [2014] HKCFI 1552, [14]–[15] ('*Xu Ziming*'); *Madison* (n 14) [50].
[227] *Citibank* (n 154) 473; *Mashreq Asia Ltd v Furness Logistics (HK) Ltd* [1999] 4 HKC 317, 328–29 (CFI) ('*Mashreq*').
[228] *Royal Skarkia* (n 12) [10].
[229] See *The 'Hung Vuong-2'* (n 10) 19; *Lo Ka Lee* (n 166) [39]; *Treasure Ascend Investments Ltd v Lai Kui Shing* [2021] HKCFI 1446, [41].
[230] *China Construction Bank (Asia) Corp Ltd v Shanghai Pudong Development Bank Co Ltd* [2015] HKCFI 2251, [15]; see also *Madison* (n 14) [65]; *Bulthaup GmbH & Co KG v KHL Marketing Asia-Pacific Pte Ltd* [2007] SGDC 64, [28].

foreign law, 'it is up to the party applying for a stay to adduce evidence to state what the plausible defences under a different legal system are'.[231] 'But once it is shown that there is no defence to the claim, and thus no dispute … then there is really nothing to go for trial at the contractual forum'.[232] In *The 'Hyundai Fortune'*, because the defendants' liability was indefensible, as the charts clearly showed that the 'reefer container was not able to maintain the requisite refrigerating temperature throughout the transit', the Singapore High Court declared that the defendants had no arguable defence.[233] Hence, their desire to be sued in Seoul lacked credibility.[234]

Delay in asserting claims or failing to seek timely remedies can indicate a lack of genuine desire for trial. Nonetheless, evidence establishing delay should be adduced,[235] including the absence of any legal justification or defence.[236] In *Societe Generale*, the Singapore High Court viewed the six-month delay in filing in the named forum, Malaysia, as an attempt to thwart the Singapore proceedings.[237] Similarly, in *The Thorscan*, the defendant's filing in Amsterdam, instead of the Netherlands Antilles (the chosen forum), indicated both a waiver of rights and lack of genuine desire to pursue an action in the chosen forum.[238]

Failure to establish a credible defence, through evidence, may indicate lack of genuine desire for trial. In *Golden Shore Transportation Pte Ltd v UCO Bank* ('*Golden Shore*') the Singapore Court of Appeal agreed with the plaintiff, UCO Bank, that the defendant, Golden Shore's desire for trial in India (the chosen forum) was not genuine because its defences were unmeritorious or highly speculative.[239] Similarly, in *Madison Communications Private Ltd v Le Ecosystem Technology India Private Ltd* ('*Madison*'), the Hong Kong CFI disregarded the exclusive Choice-of-Forum clause stipulating Bangalore courts because one of the defendants lacked any credible defence.[240] In contrast, in *Deltatre*, the Hong Kong CFI disagreed with *Madison* and emphasised that absence of a meritorious defence per se does not amount to 'strong cause'.[241] Further, only matters which are unforeseeable during contract formation or something so exceptional that it goes to the interests of justice can amount to 'strong cause'.[242] Since a party, especially in commercial contexts, could have foreseen where one party would have no defence to a straightforward claim, lack of a credible defence per se is not an 'unforeseeable, overwhelming or exceptional matter', and thus, cannot constitute a 'strong cause'.[243] This is also consistent with the 'strong policy in favour of upholding contractual bargain'.[244] Singapore would eventually follow *Deltatre* in *Vinmar* by emphasising that the lack of, or failure to establish, a genuine defence should not be a 'strong cause' factor.[245] Not only is this approach consistent with party autonomy,[246] it also promotes certainty in

[231] *Madison* (n 14) [64].
[232] *The 'Hung Vuong-2'* (n 10) 19.
[233] *The 'Hyundai Fortune'* (n 8) 216.
[234] ibid.
[235] *The 'Vishva Apurva'* (n 160) 925–26.
[236] See *Brinkerhoff* (n 122) 357.
[237] *Societe Generale* (n 10) [12].
[238] *The Thorscan* (n 12) 547.
[239] *Golden Shore* (n 10) 18–19.
[240] *Madison* (n 14) [52]; see also *Xu Ziming* (n 226) [14]–[15].
[241] *Deltatre* (n 134) [84].
[242] ibid [46].
[243] ibid [84].
[244] ibid [86].
[245] *Vinmar Overseas (Singapore) Pte Ltd v PTT International Trading Pte Ltd* [2018] 2 SLR 1271, 1301 (CA).
[246] ibid 1302.

international trade,[247] and aligns with the approaches in *forum non conveniens* where the merits of the defence are irrelevant to the grant of a stay,[248] and in applications for anti-suit injunctions where 'no defence to the claim' is likewise irrelevant.[249] Hence, *Vinmar* modified factor (d) of *The Eleftheria* formula by narrowing it to situations where there is an abuse of process or denial of justice.[250] Emphasising that the threshold for abusive conduct is high, the court gave an example where the applicant had started a media campaign in the agreed forum to malign the plaintiff, thus undermining the prospects of a fair trial.[251] In contrast, a 'denial of justice' situation may arise where, for example, the agreed court has been dissolved or is not realistically available to determine the dispute because of war.[252]

When a case is straightforward or the claim is relatively small, the insistence to only sue in the chosen forum may be considered a tactical move for procedural advantage, suggesting that the defendant lacks genuine desire for trial in the chosen forum.[253]

(ii) Non-exclusive Clauses

It appears that this factor has yet to be considered in cases involving non-exclusive Choice-of-Forum clauses, likely due to the optional nature of such clauses, which may render irrelevant whether the defendant has genuine desire to sue in the named forum. Genuine desire to sue in the named forum does not, in itself, establish the named forum as more appropriate, nor does it eliminate the need for the court to assess other factors to determine the more appropriate forum.

E. Prejudicial Factors

(i) Time-bar

(a) Exclusive Clauses

A time-bar may be considered prejudicial, thus prompting a court to refuse a stay despite a foreign exclusive Choice-of-Forum clause. However, a time-bar alone does not justify a stay, as defendants may waive it if allowed under the law of the court where the stay is sought.[254] 'It is really a neutral point', as plaintiffs may provide justification and evidence that they did not act unreasonably in not commencing proceedings within time in the contractual forum.[255] In *The 'Botic'*, the Singapore High Court found the plaintiffs' near-year delay unjustified, as they did little or nothing for almost a whole year between the time the goods landed in Croatia (the chosen forum) and the date when they took out the writ in this action.[256]

[247] ibid.
[248] ibid 1303.
[249] ibid.
[250] ibid 1305–6.
[251] ibid 1306.
[252] ibid.
[253] *Superstrong* (n 12) [24]–[25].
[254] See *Peregrine* (n 196) 383–84.
[255] *The 'Jian He'* (n 10) 444; See also *Mashreq* (n 227) 331–32.
[256] *The 'Botic'* (n 160) 501; see also *Chen Yun Hian Christopher v BHNV Online Ltd* [2020] SGHC 284, [69].

'It suggests that the failure to take protective action could be due as much to the lack of effort on the part of the plaintiffs or their advisors'.[257] Oddly, in *The 'Hyundai Fortune'*, the Singapore High Court considered the time-bar factor not because the delay was justified but because the defendants were unwilling to waive the time-bar defence in the chosen forum.[258] According to the court, without the waiver, the cargo damage 'could not realistically be determined in Korea'.[259] This erroneously puts the burden on the defendant rather than on the plaintiff to justify the delay in the exclusive forum. Nonetheless, the plaintiff may not be blamed for failing to seek timely relief in the chosen forum before the time-bar sets in when he merely relied on expert advice,[260] when confirming the expert advice's veracity is difficult in the chosen forum,[261] or when the plaintiff's counsel had advised not to file the action in the chosen forum because of the relatively small amount involved.[262] However, when the plaintiff has consciously decided not to take action in the chosen forum, the action consequently becoming time-barred could not be 'strong cause'.[263]

(b) Non-exclusive Clauses

In cases involving non-exclusive clauses, a time-bar in the chosen forum may carry more weight, since parties are not contractually bound to seek relief there. In *Ngan*, Malaysia was considered the *forum conveniens* when the Malaysian court was shown to have validly acquired jurisdiction over the defendant and it would have been prejudicial to force the plaintiff to sue in Singapore (the chosen forum), where the statute of limitations had already set in.[264]

(ii) Loss of Juridical Advantage

The loss of juridical advantage can vary from absence of a remedy available in the foreign court,[265] a lower limit of recoverable liability,[266] inability to recover legal fees,[267] enforcement-related issues,[268] or lower legal interest imposed on damages, to higher court fees and other legal costs.[269]

(a) Exclusive Clauses

In *The Humulesti*, the Singapore High Court cautioned against assuming lost juridical advantage or 'inferring that any foreign system is inferior … without attempting a comprehensive

[257] ibid.
[258] *The 'Hyundai Fortune'* (n 8) 219.
[259] ibid.
[260] See *The Griesheim* (n 15) 427; see also *The Nedlloyd Seine* [1981] HKC 72, 75 (CA).
[261] See *The Griesheim* (n 15) 427.
[262] See *The Nedlloyd Seine* (n 260) 74.
[263] *Hong Ziyun v Chan Kwan Ming* [2019] HKCFI 2125, [38]–[39].
[264] *Ngan* (n 18) 657.
[265] See *Ghossoub-CFI(1)* (n 15) [85].
[266] See *The 'Botic'* (n 160) 500.
[267] *Peregrine* (n 196) 387.
[268] *MGM* (n 128) [61].
[269] See *The 'Humulesti'* [1991] SGHC 161.

or balanced comparison'.[270] In *Li Lian International Ltd v Herport Hong Kong Ltd*, the Hong Kong CFI enforced the exclusive Choice-of-Forum clause stipulating Tokyo courts after finding the plaintiff's arguments – that Japanese proceedings would not result in a judgment enforceable in foreign courts, or a monetary judgment under Japanese procedural law – were not 'strong reasons'.[271]

If there are litigants whose status as contractual parties is contentious, courts may refuse a stay to avoid prejudicing the other parties. In *Confecciones del Atlantico v Lamont Shipping Inc*, the Hong Kong High Court refused a stay, noting that if the first defendant was not a party to the exclusive Choice-of-Forum clause stipulating Caracas, Venezuela, the plaintiff could be left without any remedy, especially in a 'straightforward action for a legitimate claim'.[272]

(b) Non-exclusive Clauses

In *William Co*, the Hong Kong High Court recognised the restrictions in the bill of lading which could be implemented under Chinese law (but not under the Hong Kong version of the Hague-Visby Rules) as juridical disadvantages to refuse a stay. Nonetheless, the Court stayed the proceedings because the non-exclusive clause also stipulated for arbitration in China, which the defendants chose after applying for a stay under Hong Kong's arbitration law.[273] In *Peregrine*, the Hong Kong CFI ruled that non-recovery of legal fees was not a sufficient juridical disadvantage, given the significantly higher amount of the claim involved.[274] In *MGM*, the court found that forcing the plaintiff to sue in Macau, absent a reciprocal enforcement arrangement with Hong Kong, could deprive them of juridical advantages.[275] Similarly, in *Wynn Resorts (Macau) SA v Wang Yen Liang*, the Malaysia High Court refused a stay because Macau was not covered by its Reciprocal Enforcement of Judgments Act 1958,[276] despite the non-exclusive clause stipulating Macau.[277]

The court may stay the local proceedings and not regard the lower limits of recoverable liability in the chosen foreign forum as prejudicial if the contract includes a provision setting a higher limit (presumably, this higher limit will be applied by the chosen forum).[278]

(iii) Competence of Foreign Courts

(a) Exclusive Clauses

Explored further in Chapter seven, comity prevents courts from drawing conclusions about the foreign court's competence, independence, or speed of resolution, or whether their law was sufficiently developed.[279] Without 'positive and cogent evidence' that 'justice is

[270] ibid.
[271] *Li Lian International Ltd v Herport Hong Kong Ltd* [2019] HKCFI 826, [25]–[27] ('*Li Lian*').
[272] *Confecciones* (n 15) 331–32.
[273] *William Co v Chu Kong Agency Ltd* [1993] 2 HKC 377, 392 (HC).
[274] *Peregrine* (n 196) 387.
[275] *MGM* (n 128) [61]–[62].
[276] *Wynn Resorts (Macau) SA v Wang Yen Liang* [2017] 11 MLJ 169, 186 (HC Kuala Lumpur).
[277] ibid 183.
[278] *The 'Botic'* (n 160) 500.
[279] See *The 'Hung Vuong-2'* (n 10) 20; *PT Bali Hospitality Utama v Mathias Echene* [2010] HKCFI 115, [19] ('*PT Bali*').

unattainable in the natural forum because of inexperience or deficiencies of courts', the court must start with a working assumption that 'courts in other judicial systems will endeavour to do justice according to the law and will be free from improper interference or constraints'.[280] Hence, in *The 'Hung Vuong-2'* the Singapore Court of Appeal commented: 'it is not for this court to say whether the maritime law of Vietnam is sufficiently developed ... when the parties themselves had agreed that Vietnam law would apply'.[281] Likewise, concerns about the chosen court's procedure should not be prejudicial because 'inevitably there will always be procedural differences and disadvantages between competing jurisdictions'.[282] Hence, the forum court's ability to call additional witnesses *motu proprio* should not be prejudicial,[283] and similarly the absence of particular remedies in the foreign court.[284] In fact, the very choice of a forum may be regarded as a choice of the procedure of the court.[285] Hence, 'it is difficult to see how either party can ... complain of the procedure of that court ... by choosing the court, they have chosen the procedure'.[286]

Absence of diplomatic relations also does not necessarily imply that parties would be discriminated against before each other's courts.[287] Proof of actual bias, discrimination or impartiality of the courts should be presented.[288]

(b) Non-exclusive Clause

In *PT Jaya*, the Singapore High Court pointed out that the plaintiffs could not justifiably complain about delays in Indonesian proceedings, as such factors 'would have been known to the parties at the time of contracting'.[289] As with exclusive clauses, the competence of foreign courts may be considered in non-exclusive Choice-of-Forum clause cases, but courts are generally reluctant to base decisions on it.

F. Multiplicity of Proceedings

(i) Exclusive Clauses

Multiplicity of proceedings occurs when claims from the same set of operative facts are pursued in multiple jurisdictions – often a primary reason why an exclusive Choice-of-Forum clauses is stipulated. Hence, multiplicity of proceedings is a factor often considered in the context of non-exclusive choices, as courts determine the natural forum or the *forum conveniens*. Nonetheless, in *Konsumex Foreign Trade Co v Sun Luen Transportation Co*,[290] the Hong Kong High Court did not enforce the exclusive Choice-of-Forum clause

[280] *Samuel Hutchison Canavan v Brenton George Battenfeld* [2010] HKCFI 691, [30].
[281] *The 'Hung Vuong-2'* (n 10) 20.
[282] *Mashreq* (n 227) 329; see also *Palace Hotel Ltd v Owners of the Ship or Vessel Happy Pioneer* [1982] 1 HKC 640, 649 (HC) ('*Palace Hotel*'); *Hyundai Engineering* (n 164) [38]; *PT Bali* (n 279) [21].
[283] *The 'New Hailong'* [1994] HKCFI 321, [25].
[284] *BNP Paribas Wealth Management v Jacob Agam* [2016] SGHC(I) 5, [109]–[110] (SICC) ('*BNP Paribas*').
[285] *The 'Asian Plutus'* (n 9) 514.
[286] ibid; see also *Mashreq* (n 227) 329.
[287] *Palace Hotel* (n 282) 649.
[288] ibid.
[289] *PT Jaya* (n 47) [74].
[290] *Konsumex* (n 13).

designating Chinese courts because of the need to try in one forum the various interrelated disputes and determine who is responsible for what happened.[291] The court recognised that multiple proceedings in China and Hong Kong would be potentially disastrous and inconvenient.[292] Similarly, in *Quaestus Capital Pte Ltd v Everton Associates Ltd* ('*Quaestus*'), the exclusive Choice-of-Forum clause stipulating London courts contained in Axis' brokerage agreement was not enforced, as Axis (the second defendant) was already involved in several Hong Kong proceedings, and thus, was 'not being required to litigate in a completely unfamiliar environment'.[293] Besides, the Hong Kong CFI added that it could 'see no reason why Axis could not claim damages for any loss it has suffered' for the breach of the exclusive clause;[294] thus, refusing to set aside the service of writ.[295]

(ii) Non-exclusive Clauses

In cases involving non-exclusive clauses, parties are deemed to accept the possibility of multiple proceedings and the risk of inconsistent outcomes, and thus, such risks are not strong factors to be considered by courts.[296] Nonetheless, in assessing the weight of this factor, 'the degree of overlap of issues and parties is a relevant consideration'.[297]

In *Morgan Stanley*, the Singapore High Court denied an anti-suit injunction, as the Singapore action arose from the same operative facts as claims already pending in New York, which was considered the more appropriate forum. 'This is one case where this court could, in accordance with the ends of justice, help to ensure that all claims concerning the plaintiffs in relation to the Pinnacle Notes are heard in one jurisdiction'.[298]

Because multiple actions may also arise from third-party claims, albeit undesirable,[299] 'whether a third party action should be heard together with the main action is not that of connection alone but whether they are inextricably linked and … integral and inseparable part of the main action'.[300] In *CIMB Bank*, since the Singapore Court of Appeal noted that the third-party claim was not integral to the main action, it thus cannot be considered a significant factor.[301]

When multiple proceedings have been consolidated, staying the action is undesirable as '[t]his will result in increased legal costs and time costs for the Plaintiffs and a danger of conflicting results'.[302] However, if the parties clearly envisioned parallel proceedings by stipulating it in their contract (eg, different chosen forums for various contracts) and actually providing for different national laws to be applied, then the argument against multiple proceedings fails.[303] By choosing different forums, the parties have accepted

[291] ibid 251.
[292] ibid.
[293] *Quaestus* (n 13) [61].
[294] ibid.
[295] ibid [62].
[296] *Chinachem* (n 63) [133]; *BNP Paribas* (n 284) [46].
[297] *Shanghai Turbo* (n 66) 826.
[298] *Morgan Stanley* (n 73) 431.
[299] *CIMB Bank* (n 140) 569.
[300] ibid 574.
[301] ibid 575.
[302] *The 'Jin Hui 588'* (n 223) [33].
[303] See *Hyundai Engineering* (n 164) [32]–[33].

the risk of conflicting judgments, and courts should not 'disturb the parties' allocation of risk'.[304]

Multiple actions may also happen when the chosen court assumes jurisdiction under a non-exclusive clause, but the relevant facts have exclusively arisen in another jurisdiction, where another case is pending. The foreign forum is not necessarily the natural forum because of its connection to the material facts, especially if the chosen court has experience with similar disputes from that foreign jurisdiction. In *Chinachem*, the Hong Kong CFI refused a stay, citing Hong Kong's extensive experience with 'PRC related disputes given Hong Kong's role as a major financial centre … [and its experience with] disputes with PRC elements and documents in simplified Chinese'.[305]

The further foreign proceedings have progressed, the more weight they carry as a factor in an application to stay the proceedings in the named forum. However, if they are still in their early stages, this should not be held against the plaintiffs.[306] Further, commencing foreign proceedings does not determine 'whether the foreign court is in fact a natural and appropriate forum'.[307] '[T]he precise characteristics of the particular foreign litigation (including the parties and subject matter) will have to be weighed'.[308] Moreover, if irreconcilable decisions between the different forums are unlikely, this becomes a strong factor for the named forum to proceed, even if the foreign proceedings are more advanced.[309]

G. Others

(i) Exclusive Clauses

Language can be a factor in granting a stay, especially if the evidence (witness testimony, documents, etc) or applicable foreign law is in a language not used by the forum court. However, the need for translation may carry little weight in a multi-lingual society where courts can easily use the relevant language.[310] Language difficulties alone cannot constitute strong cause.[311]

The Eleftheria did not mentioned factors like fraud, undue influence or overweening bargaining power, but these were recognised in *The Bremen*.[312] In *The Vishva Apurva*, the Singapore Court of Appeal recognised them as relevant,[313] but since they were absent in that case, the exclusive clause was enforced.[314] One must note, however, that it is more appropriate to consider fraud, undue influence or overweening bargaining power as going to the court's determination of the Choice-of-Forum clause's validity rather than the court's

[304] ibid [40].
[305] *Chinachem* (n 63) [145].
[306] See *PT Jaya* (n 47) [75].
[307] *Chinachem* (n 63) [102].
[308] ibid [106].
[309] *China REIT Ltd v Su Ping* [2007] HKCFI 282, [49].
[310] See *The 'Eastern Trust'* (n 4) 524.
[311] eg, *Kraken Services Ltd (formerly known as Kraken Reinsurance Services Ltd) v Q Life Medical Insurance Company Asia Region* [2021] MLJU 2956, [32] (HC Kuala Lumpur).
[312] *The Bremen v Zapata Off-Shore Co*, 407 US 1, 12–13 (1972).
[313] *The 'Vishva Apurva'* (n 160) 927.
[314] ibid 928.

exercise of discretion in determining 'strong cause'. This is discussed further in Chapters six and seven. Abuse of process was also considered in *Tsudakoma Corp v Global Trade Well Pte Ltd* but was eventually dismissed because it was insufficiently proven.[315]

In *Re Guy Kwok-Hung*, the Hong Kong Court of Appeal ruled that an exclusive Choice-of-Forum clauses can be avoided (ie, without the need of resolving first the question of debt at the agreed exclusive forum) and thus, proceed with the winding up or bankruptcy petition in Hong Kong, if the debtor is 'incontestably and massively insolvent quite apart from the disputed petition debt', where there can be a 'menace to commercial society if allowed to continue to trade', or 'there are creditors seeking a winding up which are not subject to any jurisdiction agreement', or the dismissal or stay of the petition would 'deprive the petitioner of real remedy or would otherwise amount to injustice'.[316]

(ii) Non-exclusive Clauses

In cases involving non-exclusive clauses, the use of foreign language can be considered a convenience factor. In *Citibank*, the Singapore High Court refused a stay[317] because the guaranty's applicable law – New York law – was in English, and thus, a suit in Indonesia would be inconvenient given that the proceedings would not be conducted in English but Indonesian.[318]

The '*Cambridgeshire* factor', or the efficiency and skill generated by the accumulated experience of counsel and solicitors derived from their participation in highly complex and sophisticated disputes, has been recognised as a relevant factor by Singapore courts.[319]

The chosen forum in interrelated contracts, even if not the subject-matter of dispute, can be considered a factor. In *Praptono Honggopati Tjitrohupojo v His Royal Highness Tunku Ibrahim Ismail Ibni Sultan Iskandar Al-Haj*, the choice of Malaysian courts in the four loan agreements providing the project's working capital was considered, although the action involved the draft master agreement.[320] Similarly, in *Vibrant Group Ltd v Tong Chi Ho*,[321] the Singapore High Court deemed Australia the proper forum due to several related contracts containing exclusive choice of the Australian courts.

III. Factors Considered in the Philippine Approach

A. Choice-of-Forum Clause as a *Forum Non Conveniens* Factor

The Philippine approach to Choice-of-Forum clauses is different. First, no special distinction exists between exclusive and non-exclusive clauses. Further, because venue stipulations require exclusivity of choice,[322] only exclusive clauses are recognised. Both exclusive and

[315] *Tsudakoma Corp v Global Trade Well Pte Ltd* [2023] SGHC 26, [15]–[16].
[316] *Re: Guy Kwok-Hung v Ex Parte: Tor Asia Credit Master Fund LP* [2022] HKCA 1297, [86].
[317] *Citibank* (n 154) 474.
[318] ibid 472.
[319] See *Morgan Stanley* (n 73) 427–28.
[320] *Praptono* (n 194) 885–86.
[321] *Vibrant Group Ltd v Tong Chi Ho* [2022] SGHC 256, [80]–[81].
[322] Rules of Court (Philippines), rule 4, s 2(b).

non-exclusive Choice-of-Forum clauses, however, are relevant when courts consider dismissals under *forum non conveniens*, albeit only during trial or at the merits stage.[323] However, as regards exclusive clauses, unlike in *The Eleftheria*, they do not carry greater weight but are only similarly considered along with other factors.

Salonga discussed the doctrine of *forum non conveniens* in American case law[324] in his widely used private international law textbook. Citing this work, the Philippine Supreme Court mentioned the doctrine in *HSBC*,[325] a case involving a non-exclusive clause stipulating Singapore courts.[326] The Supreme Court described *forum non conveniens* as a test which 'depends largely upon the facts of the particular case and is addressed to the sound discretion of the trial court',[327] albeit without enumerating the relevant factors. The Court instead emphasised the exclusivity required by the venue rules. Since the choice of Singapore courts was non-exclusive, the Philippine courts were able to assume jurisdiction.

The *forum non conveniens* factors were first articulated in *Communication Materials and Design, Inc v Court of Appeals* ('*Communication Materials*').[328] Again citing Salonga, the Supreme Court said that Philippine courts may not dismiss an action and assume jurisdiction themselves if: (1) the parties can conveniently access them, (2) they can make 'an intelligent decision as to the law and the facts', and (3) their decisions can be enforced.[329] In effect, the Supreme Court listed factors which Philippine courts may cite to justify their exercise of jurisdiction. Conversely, in *Puyat v Zabarte* ('*Puyat*'), the Supreme Court again cited Salonga to identify factors for declining jurisdiction:

> 1) … the main aspects of the case transpired in a foreign jurisdiction or the material witnesses have their residence there; 2) The belief that the non-resident plaintiff sought the forum[,] a practice known as forum shopping[,] merely to secure procedural advantages or to convey [*sic*] or harass the defendant; 3) The unwillingness to extend local judicial facilities to non-residents or aliens when the docket may already be overcrowded; 4) The inadequacy of the local judicial machinery … and [t]he difficulty of ascertaining foreign law.[330]

Communication Materials and *Puyat* did not expressly mention Choice-of-Forum clauses as a factor, but regarding them as such should be uncontroversial. First, the right to choose a forum, including foreign forums, is recognised under the Rules of Court and Philippine case law. Second, in *HSBC*, the Supreme Court suggested that foreign Choice-of-Forum clauses meeting the exclusivity requirement[331] should be enforceable. Third, since both *Communication Materials*[332] and *Puyat*[333] indicate that the list of *forum non conveniens* factors is non-exhaustive, a sound exercise of court discretion should be able to recognise the importance of the very forum chosen by parties. Fourth, courts may note that neither *Communication Materials* nor *Puyat* involved a Choice-of-Forum clause, thus explaining

[323] *Hasegawa and Nippon Engineering Consultants Co Ltd v Minoru Kitamura* (2007) 538 SCRA 261, 278.
[324] Jovito Salonga, *Private International Law* (Regina Publishing Co, 1995).
[325] *Hong Kong and Shanghai Banking Corporation v Sherman* (1989) 176 SCRA 331, 339 ('*HSBC*').
[326] ibid 339.
[327] ibid.
[328] *Communication Materials and Design, Inc v Court of Appeals* (1996) 260 SCRA 673 ('*Communication Materials*').
[329] ibid 695.
[330] *Puyat v Zabarte* (2001) 353 SCRA 738, 751 ('*Puyat*'). Jovito Salonga, *Private International Law,* (Central Lawbook Publishing Co, 1979), 47.
[331] *HSBC* (n 325) 337–38.
[332] *Communication Materials* (n 328) 695.
[333] *Puyat* (n 330) 751.

why these cases were unable to expressly mention them in the *forum non conveniens* test. Fifth, given that in the Philippines, *forum non conveniens* is considered during the merits or trial stage, this increases the probability that courts will be able to consider these clauses, as during trial, evidence on their existence and validity would have been established, thus allowing the courts to weigh them together with the other factors.

B. Choice-of-Forum Clauses vis-à-vis the Other Factors

How the Choice-of-Forum clause relates to the other factors can be implied from *Bank of America NT&SA v Court of Appeals* ('*Bank of America*'):

> *[F]orum non-conveniens* … deter[s] the practice of global forum shopping, that is to prevent non-resident litigants from choosing the forum or place wherein to bring their suit for malicious reasons, such as to secure procedural advantages, to annoy and harass the defendant, to avoid overcrowded dockets, or to select a more friendly venue. Under this doctrine, a court … may refuse impositions on its jurisdiction where it is not the most convenient or available forum and the parties are not precluded from seeking remedies elsewhere.[334]

This definition highlights the connection between *forum non conveniens* and global forum shopping, particularly as a safeguard against non-resident litigants exploiting local remedies to the prejudice of the defendant. It also emphasises the two main functions of the Philippine version: (1) administration of justice, and (2) finding the most convenient and available forum.

Hence, the Philippine approach mirrors that of the United States, and differs from the *Spiliada* approach. In *Gulf Oil Corp v Gilbert*[335] (1947), the United States Supreme Court recognised the public and private interests involved in *forum non conveniens*, ie, the court's caseload and other administrative difficulties, the burden on local juries, and the local interest in having localised controversies decided at home,[336] as well as the relative ease of accessing evidence, availability of compulsory processes and the cost related to witness attendance, the need for examining premises when relevant, and other practicalities that make trial easy, expeditious, and inexpensive.[337] Salonga would later discuss this American approach by emphasising *forum non conveniens*' dual functions.[338] Hence, when Salonga was referred to in *Communication Materials* and *Puyat*, both the public and private functions were recognised. In *Saudia*, the Supreme Court elaborated:

> Two (2) factors weigh into a court's appraisal … first, the vinculum which the parties and their relation have to a given jurisdiction; and second, the public interest that must animate a tribunal, in its capacity as an agent of the sovereign, in choosing to assume or decline jurisdiction. The first is more concerned with the parties, their personal circumstances, and private interests; the second concerns itself with the state and the greater social order.[339]

[334] *Bank of America NT&SA v Court of Appeals* (2003) 400 SCRA 156, 169 ('*Bank of America*').
[335] *Gulf Oil Corp v Gilbert*, 330 US 501 (1947).
[336] ibid 508–9.
[337] ibid 508.
[338] See Salonga (n 324) 58.
[339] *Saudi Arabian Airlines (Saudia) v Rebesencio* (2015) 746 SCRA 140, 169 ('*Saudia*').

(i) The Administration of Justice Function of Forum Non Conveniens

Communication Materials identified these administration of justice factors as including the capacity of the Philippine court to make an intelligent decision as to the law and the facts,[340] and the power and ability of the Philippine court to enforce its own decision.[341] *Puyat* identified factors like the overcrowded court dockets, the inadequacy of the local judicial machinery for effectuating the right sought to be maintained,[342] and the difficulty of ascertaining foreign law.[343] Further, in *Bank of America*, the ability of *forum non conveniens* to stop forum shopping was noted.[344] Most Philippine cases involving *forum non conveniens* follow this approach.[345] In *Saudia*, the Supreme Court emphasised that: 'Should [the court] find that public interest weighs more heavily in favor of its assumption of jurisdiction, it should proceed in adjudicating the dispute … [notwithstanding] the preponderance of linkages'.[346] In other words, public interests trump private interests in the Philippine version of *forum non conveniens*.

With *forum non conveniens* focusing on administration of justice, the key factors, then, would be the local court's effective capacity to manage the case, make intelligent decisions as to the law and facts, and enforce its decision. Hence, to dismiss a Philippine action under *forum non conveniens*, parties invoking a foreign forum must establish the local court's deficiencies in delivering justice.

(ii) Choice-of-Forum Clauses and Abuse of Court Process

Deterring abuse of court process is an important aspect of the administration of justice function of *forum non conveniens*.[347] Since Philippine law grants litigants the right to choose a forum, including foreign courts, litigating at the chosen forum should not be considered malicious and meant to 'annoy and harass' the other party, and thus, not viewed as an abuse of process. Furthermore, when the parties mutually chose the forum, this choice reflects their consideration of procedural advantages, the friendliness of the chosen court, rules on evidence, costs, and other convenience factors. Hence, arguments from one party that a forum was chosen by the other 'to secure procedural advantages', or 'to select a more friendly venue' should carry minimal weight. In that sense, stipulating a Choice-of-Forum clause and commencing an action at the chosen court aligns with the *forum non conveniens* goal of stopping scheming non-residents from taking advantage of the local forum to the defendant's prejudice, as highlighted in *Bank of America*.[348] Nonetheless, the argument above holds only when there is mutuality of choice between parties. If mutuality is absent – such as when the Choice-of-Forum clause was not freely negotiated or was affected by fraud, undue influence or overweening bargaining power – the filing of an action in the

[340] *Communication Materials* (n 328) 695.
[341] ibid 695.
[342] *Puyat* (n 330) 751.
[343] ibid.
[344] *Bank of America* (n 334) 169.
[345] *Puyat* (n 330) 751; *Bank of America* (n 334); *Pacific Consultants International Asia Inc v Schonfeld* (2007) 516 SCRA 209; *Raytheon International Inc v Rouzie* (2008) 546 SCRA 555, 564; *Saudia* (n 339) 170.
[346] *Saudia* (n 339) 170.
[347] *Bank of America* (n 334) 169.
[348] ibid.

named forum may be considered an abuse of court process. In other words, evidence of these factors, which were considered relevant in *The Bremen*, can establish abuse of process.

(iii) Choice-of-Forum Clauses and Convenience Factors

Convenience factors (eg, location of evidence and material witnesses, costs) are considered relevant factors under *Communication Materials*[349] and *Puyat*.[350] Hence, courts consider them regardless of the Choice-of-Forum clause involved. They may only be outweighed by factors related to the court's administration of justice and abuse of court process.[351]

[349] *Communication Materials* (n 328) 695.
[350] *Puyat* (n 330) 751.
[351] *Saudia* (n 339) 170.

6

Existence, Validity and Interpretation: Singapore, Hong Kong, Malaysia, Philippines

I. Choice-of-Forum Clauses and the Choice of Law Process

A. A Contentious Relationship

The applicable law plays a crucial role in determining the nature and effects of Choice-of-Forum clauses. However, defining the content, scope and consequences of this relationship can be contentious. First, identifying which legal system governs a dispute depends on several factors: where the action was filed; the plaintiff's cause of action; how the court characterises Choice-of-Forum clauses; procedural rules, including the extent parties exercised their party autonomy; rules of evidence used to prove the applicable law's contents; and the court's approach to legal reasoning. For example, if the plaintiff sues in a jurisdiction which does not recognise Choice-of-Forum and Choice-of-Law clauses, the forum court may apply its own law, disregarding the intended dispute resolution mechanism. Furthermore, if the plaintiff characterises his action as non-contractual (eg, in tort), it could fall outside the scope of the Choice-of-Forum clause, allowing different legal rules to apply. Sometimes, the failure to follow forum rules of evidence or the lawyers' omission to plead the applicable law may all lead to another law being applied to the dispute.

Even in jurisdictions that enforce Choice-of-Forum clauses, choosing the applicable law remains contentious due to differing characterisations. Some treat these clauses as procedural, thus leading to the forum law's application based on the conflicts rule that forum law governs procedure. Others consider them contracts with private law consequences, thus leading to the application of forum or foreign substantive law based on the choice of law rule applicable to contracts. Party autonomy complicates this further because while parties are given the power to choose the applicable law through their Choice-of-Law clause, how courts should use this chosen law in resolving issues (eg, to determine a Choice-of-Forum clause's existence) may be controversial.[1] For instance, why should courts allow a contractual provision to determine at the outset the contract's existence? Isn't this equivalent to putting the cart before the horse? Instead, should the forum law determine these issues, given that enforcement is primarily a procedural issue?

[1] See Kevin Bufford, 'Threshold or Procedural Issue: The Order of Interpretation Required by Contractual Choice-of-Law Provisions Versus the Law of the Forum Where the Suit is Commenced' (2016) 40(1) *American Journal of Trial Advocacy* 131, 131–32.

As discussed in Chapters two and four, even in jurisdictions with the same legal tradition, courts may apply similar rules and yet arrive at different results. Furthermore, they may approach legal problems differently because of different approaches to legal reasoning. For example, the sequencing – what step follows which – may be result-determinative, and thus, may controversially shape the litigation's flow. For example, the failure to classify a clause as either exclusive or non-exclusive when the same is crucial in choosing the applicable test may lead to incorrect or unintended results. Ultimately, as discussed in the next chapter, state interests may overrule party autonomy, thus also leading to unintended results.

This chapter articulates the content, scope and consequences of this intimate relationship between Choice-of-Forum clauses and the choice of law process by focusing on how issues involving the existence, validity and interpretation of Choice-of-Forum clauses are resolved. In these jurisdictions, the applicable law, ie, the law applicable to the underlying contract, determines the bulk of issues related to the clause's existence, validity and interpretation. In jurisdictions following English common law, however, the law which determines the contract's existence remains uncertain, as court decisions appear to either refer to the 'putative' applicable law or forum law. Furthermore, the doctrine of separability is examined in this chapter to determine its impact on the applicable law.

B. The Law Applicable to the Choice-of-Forum Clause

(i) Key Attributes

Party autonomy ensures that the law governing existence, validity and interpretation of contracts is the one chosen by the parties through the Choice-of-Law clause. In its absence, courts usually consider three options: (1) the forum law, (2) the law of the chosen court (if the chosen court is not the forum court), and (3) the applicable or 'proper' law of the underlying contract. This could be the law of the place of contract formation *(lex loci contractus)*, of the place of performance *(lex loci solutionis)*, the law intended by the parties, the law of closest connection, or the forum law. Notably, the applicable law has to be determinate, and not a law which 'floats',[2] and can be changed if the parties agree. Multiple legal systems may govern different aspects of a contract or Choice-of-Forum clause,[3] but traditionally *renvoi* does not apply to contracts in common law,[4] meaning that the proper law refers to domestic law, excluding its private international law rules.

(ii) Common Law

In the English common law, unless stated otherwise, the law applicable to the Choice-of-Forum clause is the law applicable to the underlying contract.[5] Known also as the proper law of the contract, it is the law the parties intended.[6] This law can be designated expressly through a

[2] *Chan Chi Keung v Delmas Hong Kong Ltd* [2004] 4 HKC 28, 36 (CFI).

[3] *Re United Railways of the Havana and Regla Warehouse* [1960] Ch 52, 92.

[4] See *Amin Rasheed Shipping Corporation v Kuwait Insurance* Co [1984] AC 50, 61–62 ('*Amin*'); cf *O'Driscoll v J Ray McDermott SA* [2006] WASCA 25, [12], [59]–[60].

[5] See *Amin* (n 4) 60.

[6] See *Coast Lines Ltd v Hudig & Veder Chartering NV* [1972] 2 QB 34, 50 ('*Coast Lines*').

Choice-of-Law clause or a similar provision,[7] and may appear in a separate document from the Choice-of-Forum clause executed several years apart.[8] Nonetheless, both Choice-of-Law and Choice-of-Forum clauses should be construed as a whole.[9] If no express choice was made, the court examines the facts to determine whether the parties made an implied choice of law.[10] If no choice was made, express or implied, the court ceases to consider the parties' intention and proceeds to determine the legal system with which the transaction has the closest and most real connection.[11] This law is determined by weighing connecting factors such as the place of contracting, residence or business of the parties, nature and subject matter of the contract, and place of contractual performance.[12] Nonetheless, distinguishing implied choice from absence of choice can be difficult.[13] In any case, there must be an applicable law and it is not possible to have a contract which was not governed by some legal system.[14] Courts in Singapore, Hong Kong and Malaysia follow this approach.

In the United States, courts do not always apply the law applicable to the contract if no Choice-of-Law clause exists. Because some States characterise Choice-of-Forum clauses as procedural, courts skip the conflicts process.[15] In *The Bremen*, for instance, the US Supreme Court barely mentioned the choice of English law and how the conflicts process may affect the analysis. Clermont notes that the absence of 'looking to the place whose law will cover the contract, [is] perhaps because of the common distaste for the conflicts process's difficulty and uncertainty'.[16]

In Malaysia, Islamic law applies to Islamic banking and finance contracts along with the applicable substantive law.[17] *Shariah* can be chosen explicitly or may apply due to the nature of the transaction or the involvement of an Islamic bank or financial institution.[18] Unlike other applicable laws, which are the product of the choice of law process and identify the law of a certain state or jurisdiction, Islamic law, being based on the *Quran*, is a-national law. Moreover, the absence of a central Islamic law authority means that its content and interpretation (as maybe articulated in an opinion or *fatwa*) may vary across countries, institutions and scholars.[19] In Malaysia, these variations have not made Islamic law uncertain, as courts may refer the matter to the National *Shariah* Advisory Council, which is Malaysia's ultimate authority for any questions on *Shariah* by financial institutions and civil courts.[20] Notably, any ruling made by it shall be binding on Islamic financial institutions, courts and arbitral tribunals.[21]

[7] See *Amin* (n 4) 61.

[8] *China Railway (Hong Kong) Holdings Ltd also known as China Railway Services (Hong Kong) Ltd v Chung Kin Holdings Company Ltd* [2023] HKCFI 132, [35] ('*China Railway*').

[9] ibid.

[10] See *The Assunzione* [1954] P 150, 185–86.

[11] See *Coast Lines* (n 6) 44.

[12] See ibid 50.

[13] See *R v International Trustee for the Protection of Bondholders Aktiengesellschaft* [1937] AC 500, 529.

[14] See *Amin* (n 4) 65.

[15] Kevin Clermont, 'Governing Law on Forum-Selection Agreements' (2015) 66(3) *Hastings Law Journal* 643, 649.

[16] ibid.

[17] *Bank Kerjasama Rakyat Malaysia v Emcee Corporation Sdn Bhd* [2003] 2 MLJ 408, 408.

[18] See *Tahan Steel Corp Sdn Bhd v Bank Islam Malaysia Bhd* [2004] 6 MLJ 1, 30 ('*Tahan Steel*').

[19] See Umar Oseni, 'The Legal Implications of "*Fatwā* Shopping" in the Islamic Finance Industry: Problems, Perceptions and Prospects' (2016) 30(2) *Arab Law Quarterly* 107, 113.

[20] Central Bank of Malaysia Act 2009 (Malaysia), s 51(1).

[21] ibid s 57.

(iii) Choice-of-Court Convention

Under the Choice-of-Court Convention, the law of the chosen court determines whether the Choice-of-Forum clause is null and void.[22] In Singapore, cases under the Choice-of-Court Convention follow this approach[23] rather than using the law applicable to the contract or even the law chosen by the parties. The Hartley-Dogauchi Report clarifies that the 'null and void' refers to substantive (not formal) grounds of invalidity under the chosen court's law (eg, fraud, mistake, misrepresentation, duress and lack of capacity).[24] While the non-chosen court, under article 6, may also decline jurisdiction because the Choice-of-Forum clause is 'null and void', the difference with the chosen court applying the same ground under article 5 is that the non-chosen court would be applying foreign law.[25] Notably, because the law of the state of the chosen court referred to in articles 5(1) and 6(1) includes its choice of law rules,[26] this means that proof of the foreign law may be required not just under the non-chosen court's procedural rules but even when the suit is filed in the chosen court, ie, in situations when the chosen court's conflict of laws rules point to a foreign law, thus requiring proof of its contents under the chosen court's procedural rules. Hence, proof of foreign law may be required either where the Singapore court is chosen (eg, when no law is expressly or impliedly chosen, and a foreign jurisdiction has the closest connection) or non-chosen.

Under article 6 of the Choice-of-Court Convention, forum law applies, as the law applicable to the other grounds for suspension and dismissal of actions, to issues like lack of contractual capacity,[27] and in determining whether enforcement will result in manifest injustice or 'manifestly' contradict public policy.[28] The convention is silent, however, on the two other grounds under article 6 (ie, whether there are 'exceptional reasons beyond the control of the parties' which lead to the contract not being reasonably performed, and whether the chosen court has decided not to hear the case). Arguably, forum law also applies because enforcing Choice-of-Forum clauses is a procedural matter.

(iv) The Philippines

Philippine law recognises and gives effect to the law expressly or impliedly chosen by parties.[29] In the absence of such express or implied choice, the law which has the closest and most real connection governs the contract.[30] In the Philippines, this law is determined after considering various 'test factors' or 'points of contact' or 'connecting factors' like the parties' nationality or domicile, the location of the property, the place of performance, etc.[31]

[22] Convention on Choice of Court Agreements, opened for signature 30 June 2005, 44 ILM 1294 (entered into force 1 October 2015), arts 5(1), 6(a) ('Choice-of-Court Convention').

[23] Choice of Court Agreements Act (Singapore, cap 39A, 2020 rev edn), pt 2, ss 11(1), 12 ('CCAA').

[24] Trevor Hartley and Masato Dogauchi, *Explanatory Report on the Convention of 30 June 2005 on Choice of Courts Agreements*, Permanent Bureau (ed) (Hague Conference on Private International Law, 2013) 55 ('Hartley-Dogauchi Report').

[25] ibid 61.

[26] ibid 55.

[27] Choice-of-Court Convention (n 22) art 6(b).

[28] ibid art 6(c).

[29] *Philippine Export and Foreign Loan Guarantee Corp v VP Eusebio Construction Inc* (2004) 434 SCRA 202, 215 ('*Philippine Export*').

[30] ibid.

[31] *Saudi Arabian Airlines v Court of Appeals* (1998) 297 SCRA 469, 491.

However, this presumes that Philippine courts can recognise Choice-of-Forum clauses as contracts. Currently, Philippine courts view these clauses as venue stipulations, governed by forum law (Philippine law) without the need to apply the choice of law process. In *HSBC*, a Choice-of-Forum clause stipulating Singapore courts was analysed using Philippine law, without determining the chosen Singapore law's relevance.[32]

II. Issues of Existence and Validity

A. Singapore, Hong Kong and Malaysia

(i) Existence

(a) Law of the Forum v Putative 'Applicable Law'

In Singapore, Hong Kong and Malaysia, the law applicable to the contract, as the putative 'applicable law', generally determines whether a contract exists. However, some Singaporean decisions show that courts may also apply forum law; thus, what law applies to the issue of existence may remain unsettled for some time.[33] Furthermore, how courts frame issues influences how existence is approached, not to mention the need to establish facts, which relies on the forum's rules of evidence. To illustrate, each jurisdiction may have different ways of understanding when a contract is formed. While courts may refer to the applicable law to determine this issue, they are limited by their own rules of evidence, which may limit presentation of certain pieces of evidence, particularly those pertaining to the parties' state of mind, or which may alter the contents of the contract. Furthermore, the judges' experience with pleadings, like how parties state their arguments and make admissions, influences their preference on where to look for clues in determining whether the contract exists.

If factual and legal requirements for contract formation are missing, the contract never came into existence, and thus none of its clauses apply, as there was 'no meeting of the minds … *eg*, where the defence of *non est factum* is applicable'.[34] As mentioned, most cases resolve existence issues using the putative applicable law, as seen in Singapore's *CIMB Bank*[35] and Hong Kong's *Star Cruises*.[36]

There are logical difficulties, however, with this approach. How can a non-existent contract guide courts as to what law should apply to its very own existence? But again, the doctrine of putative 'applicable' law is favoured because it provides a practical solution.[37] Chong, however, warns about the dangers of this approach, especially since the doctrine has not been applied in practice on a principled basis.[38] 'Any alleged express or implied

[32] *Hong Kong and Shanghai Banking Corporation v Sherman* (1989) 176 SCRA 331, 336–39 ('*HSBC*').
[33] See *William Jacks & Co (Singapore) Pte Ltd v Nelson Honey & Marketing (NZ) Ltd* [2015] SGHCR 21, [68] ('*William Jacks*').
[34] *CIMB Bank Bhd v Dresdner Kleinwort Ltd* [2008] 4 SLR(R) 543 (CA) ('*CIMB Bank*').
[35] ibid 555; see also *Industrial & Commercial Bank Limited v Banco Ambrosiano Veneto SPA* [2000] SGHC 188, [16].
[36] *Star Cruises (HK) Ltd v Tung Ho Wah* [2006] HKDC 61, [21] ('*Star Cruises*').
[37] *CIMB Bank* (n 34) 555–56.
[38] Adeline Chong, 'Choice of Law for Void Contracts and Their Restitutionary Aftermath: The Putative Governing Law of the Contract' in Paula Giliker (ed), *Re-examining Contract and Unjust Enrichment* (Koninklijke Brill, NV, 2007) 155, 159.

choice, or law of closest connection derived from alleged terms, will straightforwardly be identified as the putative law of the contract'.[39] Furthermore, '[t]he lack of thought that goes into identifying the putative governing law of the contract favours the party who alleges validity'.[40] In addition, the doctrine encounters problematic application when there are conflicting contractual terms.[41] In short, while pragmatically desirable, the approach is severely challenged by its logical weakness and the inconsistent and unprincipled application by courts.

Probably because of these difficulties, some common law decisions have referred to forum law to determine whether a contract exists.[42] In *William Jacks & Co (Singapore) Pte Ltd v Nelson Honey & Marketing (NZ) Ltd*, the Singapore High Court acknowledged this possibility,[43] but did not resolve the issue, as Singapore law was both the forum and putative proper law of the contract.[44]

The recent Singaporean cases *Qompass*[45] and *6DM*,[46] however, have referred to the 'good arguable case' test referred to in *Vinmar* as the first part of the two-step process in applications for stay of proceedings in cases under both the common law and CCAA. Notably, the 'good arguable case' test involves first determining the clause's existence and scope. In *Qompass*, the Singapore High Court explained that the Choice-of-Forum clause's existence necessitates the existence of a contractual relationship.[47] Hence, when the applicant completely denies any contractual relationship, the 'good arguable case' test is not satisfied.[48] The standard of proof is that 'the applicant must, on the evidence before the court, have the better of the argument that the agreement *exists* and that it *applies* to the dispute'.[49] Further, the Court explained that '[t]his is a higher threshold than a mere prima facie case but is different from the standard of a balance of probabilities'.[50] At no stage did the court in *Qompass* refer to the law applicable to the contract or mention its relevance to the 'good arguable case' test. However, *Qompass* and the earlier *6DM* were decided under the CCAA, which means that the law applicable to the contract had limited application. Nonetheless, because both cases highlighted that the 'good arguable case' test applies to all cases under both the common law and CCAA, it now appears that issues of existence should be resolved under Singaporean law. In *Reputation Administration Service v Spamhaus Technology Ltd*, the Singapore High Court, while citing *PT Selecta*, noted that issues concerning existence may be resolved using the Choice-of-Forum clause as a general rule as if the contract is valid, except when the parties are *ad idem* that there was no contract, or where there was fraud giving rise to *non est factum*.[51]

[39] ibid.
[40] ibid.
[41] ibid 160.
[42] eg, *Oceanic Sun Line Special Shipping Co Inc v Fay* (1988) 79 ALR 9, 29.
[43] *William Jacks* (n 33) [68].
[44] ibid.
[45] *Qompass Voyage Ltd v APACPAY Pte Ltd* [2023] SGHCR 20 ('*Qompass*').
[46] *6DM (S) Pte Ltd v AE Brands Korea Ltd* [2021] SGHC 257 ('*6DM*').
[47] *Qompass* (n 45) [23].
[48] ibid [31].
[49] ibid [20].
[50] ibid [20].
[51] *Reputation Administration Service v Spamhaus Technology Ltd* [2020] SGHC 240, [9] ('*Reputation*').

In Hong Kong, the law applicable to the contract determines whether the Choice-of-Forum clause was incorporated into the contract. In *Beijing Renji Real Estate Development Group Co Ltd v Zhu Min*, the Hong Kong CFI applied Chinese law, which was the law applicable to the guarantee agreement, to determine whether the Choice-of-Forum clause 'exists' by incorporation.[52] Since a Chinese decision and judicial interpretation of the Chinese Guarantee Law were presented as evidence on how Choice-of-Forum clauses are deemed to be incorporated, the Hong Kong court concluded that the alleged Choice-of-Forum clause applied to the guarantee agreement.[53] Hence, it was not necessary to apply Hong Kong law.[54]

In *China National Geological & Mining (HK) Ltd v Tianjin Hopetone Co Ltd*, the Hong Kong CFI noted that issues of contract existence (eg, whether the main contract was rescinded, avoided, frustrated or terminated), which ultimately determine whether a Choice-of-Clause applies, should be resolved during trial and not by summary judgment.[55]

(b) Specific Issues Concerning Existence

In common law, the contract's existence, understood as contract formation, refers to the minimum acts required to give rise to a contract: the parties must have come to an agreement; they must have intended to contract; their agreement must be supported by valuable consideration; and any formalities (eg, a written agreement) must be satisfied.[56] The guiding principle is based on the objective theory of contract which requires courts not to depend on the parties' subjective state of mind, 'but upon a consideration of what was communicated between them by words or conduct, and whether that leads objectively to a conclusion that they intended to create legal relations'.[57] What has been said or done by the parties, which led to the agreement, is determined from the perspective of a reasonable person in the position of the parties.[58] Often, this has been a purely objective quest based on evidence.[59]

Consequently, the question of contract formation is a factual issue, proven by evidence from conduct prior, during and after the contract formation process. In *CIMB Bank*, the Singapore Court of Appeal said that '[t]here is a need to examine the factual circumstances of each case to see the cause for the contract being void'.[60] Determining whether the parties have reached an agreement requires evidence that they have agreed on the terms of bargain, that those terms are certain and complete, and that the bargain is informed by an intention to contract and immediately assume legal obligations.[61] The traditional test is that of offer and acceptance.[62]

[52] *Beijing Renji Real Estate Development Group Co Ltd v Zhu Min* [2022] HKCFI 1027, [34] ('*Beijing Renji*').
[53] ibid [37].
[54] ibid [38].
[55] *China National Geological & Mining (HK) Ltd v Tianjin Hopetone Co Ltd* [2020] HKCFI 1338, [26], [39].
[56] Michael Furmston, GJ Tolhurst and Eliza Mik, 'Formation and the Concept of Agreement' in Michael Formston and GJ Tolhurst (eds), *Contract Formation: Law and Practice* (Oxford University Press, 2nd edn, 2015) 1, 1.
[57] *RTS Flexible Systems Ltd v Molkerei Alois Müller GmbH & Co KG* [2010] UKSC 14.
[58] See *Toll (FGCT) Pty Ltd v Alphapharm Pty Ltd* (2004) 219 CLR 165, 179.
[59] See ibid.
[60] *CIMB Bank* (n 34) 563.
[61] Furmston, Tolhurst and Mik (n 56) 6.
[62] ibid.

A careful analysis involving contract formation is needed when the Choice-of-Forum clause is found elsewhere but argued to be incorporated by reference into the main agreement. In *Star Cruises*, the Hong Kong District Court emphasised that the query as to offer and acceptance in such instances relies on the contemporaneous or subsequent acts of parties.[63] In this case, the plaintiff disputed the inclusion of the confirmation slip containing the Choice-of-Forum clause, but the court rejected this argument because the defendant had failed to reject the confirmation slip when he boarded the vessel,[64] not to mention that it had also been faxed with the other documents, the existence of which the plaintiff was not contesting.[65] By contrast, in *Continental Mark Ltd v Verkerhrs-Club de Schweiz*, the Hong Kong Court of Appeal found that the export conditions which included the alleged Choice-of-Forum clause were not accepted because the only evidence was that they were faxed to the defendant the day following the signing of the alleged contract,[66] and there were no contemporaneous or subsequent circumstances of acceptance.

Nonetheless, the parties' intention to enter into an agreement may be read from the very arguments they raise during litigation. For instance, in *CIMB Bank*, the Singapore Court of Appeal pointed out that both parties argued that their contract was ineffective, implying they had intended to enter into a contract, but this later 'had become void or ineffective or a contractual failure had arisen'.[67]

In *Vinmar*, the Singapore Court of Appeal applied this test to determine whether the exclusive Choice-of-Forum clause was incorporated into the contract:

> [W]hether, at the time of contracting, each party as a reasonable person was *entitled to infer from the past dealings and the actions and the words of the other in the instant case*, that the [term] [was] to be a part of the contract.[68]

The Court added that a high threshold should be met for a party to be 'entitled to infer' that a term sought to be incorporated is part of the contract.[69] In this case, the exclusive Choice-of-Forum clause was deemed incorporated, as the previous contracts included the same exclusive Choice-of-Forum clause,[70] involved the purchase of chemical commodities,[71] were concluded in the same manner (oral negotiations followed by correspondence setting out the key terms),[72] and the exclusive clause was not onerous or unusual and could reasonably be expected in similar contracts.[73] Notably, in *Tsudakoma Corp v Global Trade Well Pte Ltd*, the Singapore High Court confirmed that a Choice-of-Forum clause can be incorporated by course of dealing, but reiterated the much higher threshold required, after applying the 'good arguable case' test.[74]

[63] *Star Cruises* (n 36) [33].
[64] ibid.
[65] ibid [32].
[66] *Continental Mark Ltd v Verkerhrs-Club de Schweiz* [2002] 2 HKC 513, 515 (CA).
[67] *CIMB Bank* (n 34) 559.
[68] *Vinmar Overseas (Singapore) Pte Ltd v PTT International Trading Pte Ltd* [2018] 2 SLR 1271, 1287, citing Michael Furmston (ed) *The Law of Contract* (LexisNexis, 6th edn, 2017) [3.18].
[69] ibid.
[70] ibid 1289.
[71] ibid.
[72] ibid.
[73] ibid.
[74] *Tsudakoma Corp v Global Trade Well Pte Ltd* [2023] SGHC 26, [14].

In *Open Country Dairy*, the Malaysia Court of Appeal considered the exclusive Choice-of-Forum clause in favour of New Zealand binding on the respondent Malaysian company because it was properly incorporated by reference via the weblink provided in each sales contract, which the respondent signed.[75] Notably, the appellant had taken reasonable steps to bring the terms and conditions containing the exclusive clause to the respondent's attention by making them accessible via the weblink provided.[76] The Court also noted that the respondent's choice to ignore the weblink after having noticed the endorsement and the word 'attached' was necessarily at his own peril,[77] and there was no need to furnish him with a copy of the terms and conditions as it was just a 'click away'.[78]

Issues concerning the existence of a contract can also be a matter of interpretation, especially when the contractual terms and conditions are brief, thus making it difficult to determine the parties' intention.[79] For example, the parties may have erroneously referred to a court in a certain jurisdiction in their Choice-of-Forum clause when, in fact, no such court exists or the court they intended is known under another name. Did the parties agree to some court, or does the error indicate an absence in the meeting of the minds? Likewise, because a Choice-of-Forum clause exists only between parties, interpretation may also be needed to determine whether a non-party should be bound as well.[80]

(ii) Validity

The validity of a contract may be an issue of form or substance, affecting either the whole contract or just some provisions. Formal or extrinsic validity refers to compliance with formal requirements (eg, the requirement of writing), without which the contract or provisions may be illegal or unenforceable. Substantive validity, also known as intrinsic or essential validity, is broader, with each legal system defining its scope and content differently. Drawing from the Vienna Convention on Contracts for the International Sale of Goods of 1980 ('CISG'),[81] Drobnig categorises the causes of substantive invalidity into four types: (1) those which compete with remedies of non-performance (eg, mistakes about goods' quality or the seller's title); (2) those which do not compete with remedies of non-performance (eg, defective consent, fraudulent misrepresentation, threat); (3) those located in civil law but outside contract law (eg, invalidity, incapacity, lack of authority, immorality and illegality); (4) those founded in public law (eg, public policy, mandatory rules, states interests).[82] All but the first category can affect the validity of Choice-of-Forum clauses.

As seen in the four groups, the law determining causes of substantive invalidity may come from different areas of the applicable law and not just from contract law. While the first two groups are determined by contract law, civil law (private law) determines the third group, like the law on persons (eg, legal capacity), while public law determines the fourth group.

[75] *Open Country Dairy Ltd v Able Food Sdn* [2021] MLJU 969, [73].
[76] ibid [78].
[77] ibid [71].
[78] ibid.
[79] See Furmston, Thurlston and Mik (n 56) 7.
[80] See, eg, *The Mahkutai* [1993] 2 HKC 71, 77–81 (CA).
[81] Vienna Convention on Contracts for the International Sale of Goods, opened for signature 11 April 1980, 1489 UNTS 3 (entered into force 1 January 1988) ('CISG').
[82] Ulrich Drobnig, 'Substantive Validity' (1992) 40(3) *American Journal of Comparative Law* 635, 637–43.

Nonetheless, contract law still determines the consequences, such as whether the contract is void, voidable, or unenforceable, which varies by legal system. Since Choice-of-Forum clauses are 'severable' or separate, invalidity affecting the rest of the contract does not necessarily render the Choice-of-Forum clause void or unenforceable.[83]

In common law, the applicable law or proper law of the contract determines its validity and most contractual issues.[84] This is primarily the law intended by the parties, either expressly or impliedly, or in the absence thereof, the law which has the closest connection to the transaction.[85] Common law has assigned the law chosen by the parties to decide on matters concerning validity such as formalities, the effect of mistake, defective consent, fraud, and legal capacity. Nonetheless, the forum court may still apply its own law to enforce mandatory rules, or issues of public policy or state interest that affect the contract's validity.

Although a legal question, validity relies on facts established before the court. When the applicable law is foreign, the question of validity also becomes a matter of evidence. Notably, forum law determines how foreign law is proven. In *Venetian Macau Ltd v Chen Mei Huan* ('*Venetian Macau*'), the Hong Kong CFI had to interpret under Macau law a Choice-of-Forum clause with apparently contradictory parts, and determine its validity.[86] An expert witnesses testified that the Choice-of-Forum clause contradicted Macau law and thus, the clause was invalid and ineffective,[87] while another argued the opposite.[88] Although the Court referred to expert evidence in interpreting the Macau statute and contract,[89] its approach was informed by how common law would approach such situations by preferring an interpretation which upholds the validity of the entire clause.[90] Rather than reading the second part of the clause as invalidating the first, and therefore rendering the entire clause invalid for being contrary to Macau law, the second part should be read as a qualification to the first.[91] When the forum law is the applicable law, the court may simply proceed to construe the Choice-of-Forum clause using the forum's interpretation rules. Hence, in *Industrial and Commercial Bank of China (Asia) Ltd v Wisdom Top International Ltd*, the Hong Kong CFI concluded, after using common law's purposive approach to interpretation, that asymmetric clauses fall outside the Choice-of-Court Arrangement Ordinance's scope.[92]

Hence, validity, as an essentially legal question, highlights the key role of contractual interpretation in the analysis. As seen in *Venetian Macau*,[93] however, interpretation is often informed by the forum court's approaches regardless of the applicable law. In *HBZ Finance*, five different bills of lading referred the disputes to Tokyo courts under Japanese law.[94] However, subsequently stamped clauses on each bill submitted disputes to Valparaiso courts, with an agreement not to submit disputes to arbitration unless agreed otherwise.[95]

[83] *Hong Ziyun v Chan Kwan Ming* [2019] HKCFI 2125, [33].
[84] JG Collier, *Conflict of Laws* (Cambridge University Press, 2nd edn, 1994) 185.
[85] Adrian Briggs, *Private International Law* (Oxford University Press, 2014) 503.
[86] *Venetian Macau Ltd v Chen Mei Huan* [2014] HKCFI 128, [21]–[30] ('*Venetian Macau*').
[87] ibid [23].
[88] ibid.
[89] ibid [24].
[90] ibid [30].
[91] ibid.
[92] *Industrial and Commercial Bank of China (Asia) Ltd v Wisdom Top International Ltd* [2020] HKCFI 322, [52].
[93] *Venetian Macau* (n 86).
[94] *HBZ Finance Ltd v Nippon Yusen Kaisha* [2002] HKCA 377, [5].
[95] ibid [6].

Chilean law experts confirmed that the stamped clauses allowed opting out of Chilean law's requirement to refer disputes to arbitration,[96] and noted that Chilean law does not recognise the choice of foreign court and law.[97] The Hong Kong Court of Appeal, rather than invalidating the exclusive Choice-of-Forum clause, used the quintessentially common law approach of reconciling the various parts of the contract.[98] The Court said that the stamped clause would only apply if the action were commenced in Chile.[99] Hence, the effect was that the stamped clauses and exclusive Choice-of-Forum clause could stand together.[100] Because the exclusive Choice-of-Forum clause still applied and because no 'strong cause' was established, the Hong Kong action was stayed.[101] Notably, the Court did not mention how Japanese or Chilean law would affect the interpretation.

In Malaysia, the validity of Choice-of-Forum clauses in Islamic banking and finance contracts, is generally governed by common law. A possible exception, however, is where a Choice-of-Forum clause is argued to be uncertain under Islamic law, such as to implicate the application of *gharar*, a principle of Islamic law that nullifies provisions which are uncertain. Rasyid, for example, argues that settlement of future disputes through arbitration is contrary to Islamic principles because '[a] dispute may or may not arise' and that a very long gap may occur between the point of contracting and the actual dispute, and during this period, 'either party may lose its zeal and yet would still be legally forced into it with counterproductive consequences'.[102] While Rasyid has applied this analysis only to arbitration clauses, because Choice-of-Forum clauses are similar, they may also be invalidated under the principle of *gharar*, although no decision has addressed this issue so far.

(iii) Some Practical Considerations

A key practical consideration for the plaintiff is that his cause of action must arise during the contract's existence.[103] A challenge to the Choice-of-Forum clause's existence can be waived if the defendant fails to contest its existence and instead argues on the merits.[104] Similarly, a challenge may be lost if a party takes contradictory positions, such as relying on a contractual clause while simultaneously arguing that the contract is not binding.[105]

These practical considerations show how forum law affects litigation even if the law applicable is foreign. Rules on causes of action, how arguments are pleaded and whether the court is limited to considering the arguments raised by the parties, and the failure to raise certain issues (eg, not questioning the Choice-of-Forum clause's existence) as amounting to waivers have been analysed through the lens of forum law, without referring to the contract's proper law. This is largely because courts continue to characterise these issues as procedural, even though

[96] ibid [19].
[97] ibid [28].
[98] ibid [30].
[99] ibid [28].
[100] ibid [33].
[101] ibid [36].
[102] Abdul Rasyid, 'Relevance of Islamic Dispute Resolution Processes in Islamic Banking and Finance' (2013) 27(4) *Arab Law Quarterly* 343, 358–59.
[103] *The 'Kapitan Mezentsev'* [1995] 1 SLR(R) 652, 665 (HC).
[104] *Dene Hunt v Gordon William Fisher* (Unreported, SC Hong Kong High Court, D Yam J, 4 October 1994).
[105] ibid.

these issues may be fundamentally related to substantive issues involving existence, validity and interpretation. Furthermore, the role of the applicable law in the resolution of issues like waivers, for example, has hardly been addressed in commentaries.[106] Keyes notes that if the rights which have been waived are founded in the parties' agreements, then the role of forum law in determining whether those rights have been lost becomes less obvious.[107] She further argues that if waiver of rights under an arbitration agreement is determined by the governing law, by parity of reasoning, the same should also apply to Choice-of-Forum agreements.[108]

(iv) Choice-of-Court Convention

The law of the chosen court determines whether the Choice-of-Forum clause is null and void.[109] Hence in Singapore, cases under the Choice-of-Court Convention follow this approach.[110] Moreover, Choice-of-Forum clauses are required to be in writing, or by any other means of communication which renders information accessible so as to be usable for subsequent reference.[111] The Hartley-Dogauchi report emphasises that states should not impose any additional other formal requirements under their national law.[112] In any case, non-compliance with these formal requirements does not per se make the Choice-of-Forum clauses invalid but it removes them from the Choice-of-Court Convention's application.

B. The Philippines

(i) Existence and Validity of Contracts

Philippine contract law is heavily influenced by the Spanish Civil Code of 1889, which was the law applicable up until 1949. Hence, in the Philippines, the perfection or birth of a contract – the moment when the contract is deemed to exist – is understood as the moment when the parties come to agree on the terms of the contract.[113] While no specific form is required on how minds should meet to create a contract (hence, it need not be in the form of an offer and acceptance), article 1318 of the Civil Code requires three elements for a contract to exist: (a) consent of the contracting parties, (b) 'object certain which is the subject matter of the contract', and (c) cause (*causa*).[114] There is perfection of a contract when there is meeting of the minds of the parties on each of these requisites.[115] In *Moreno, Jr v Private Management Office*, the Supreme Court emphasised that

[106] See Mary Keyes, 'Party Autonomy in Dispute Resolution: Implied Choices and Waiver in the Context of Jurisdiction' [2015] (58) *Japanese Yearbook of International Law* 223, 242.
[107] ibid.
[108] ibid 245.
[109] Choice-of-Court Convention (n 22) arts 5(1), 6(a).
[110] CCAA (n 23) pt 2, ss 11(1), 12.
[111] Choice-of-Court Convention (n 22) art 3(c).
[112] Hartley-Dogauchi Report (n 24) 53.
[113] Arturo Tolentino, *Commentaries and Jurisprudence on the Civil Code of the Philippines* (Central Lawbook Publishing, Inc, 1991) vol 4, 410.
[114] This is similar to common law's 'consideration' but unlike in common law, even mere 'liberality' in contracts of pure beneficence, is sufficient *causa*; see, eg, *Liguez v Court of Appeals* (1957) 102 Phil 577, 580.
[115] *Spouses Pen v Spouses Julian* (2016) 778 SCRA 56, 67.

to reach 'perfection' or 'existence', the parties must agree on the same thing with no terms left open for negotiation.[116] If any of the three essential requisites is absent, the contract is non-existent. Examples include simulated or fictitious contracts where no real consent occurred, contracts with an illegal object or outside the 'commerce of man', or those lacking cause or consideration.[117] A non-existent contract produces no legal effects and may not be cured, even by ratification.

Furthermore, while foreign law may become the law applicable to a contract, the Civil Code may still inform the way Philippine courts approach the issue of existence of any contract. The essentiality of the three requirements under article 1318 has been emphasised in numerous Supreme Court decisions,[118] and no exceptions are mentioned. This suggests that the rule is mandatory, regardless of the applicable law.

Under Philippine law, issues of validity are usually assessed based on defects in the three essential elements. A void contract has a cause, object or purpose which is contrary to law, morals, good customs, public order or public policy.[119] A voidable contract arises when parties lack contractual capacity or when the consent was vitiated by mistake, violence, intimidation, undue influence or fraud.[120] Notably, the legal capacity of Filipino contracting parties is always determined by Philippine law.[121] Meanwhile, unenforceable contracts lack the required formalities, such as those under the statute of frauds in the Civil Code.[122] Except for void contracts, this classification of defective contracts applies only when Philippine law governs the contract.

Article 17 of the Civil Code states that 'the forms and solemnities of contracts, wills, and other public instruments shall be governed by the laws of the country in which they are executed'. Hence, as regards formal validity, *lex loci contractus* applies except when the contract is executed before Philippine diplomatic or consular officers in a foreign country.[123] Further, the formal validity of contracts is subject to Philippine mandatory laws[124] or those '[p]rohibitive laws concerning persons, their acts or property, and those which have, for their object, public order, public policy and good customs'.[125]

In *Philippine Export and Foreign Loan Guarantee Corp v VP Eusebio Construction Inc*[126] ('*Philippine Export*'), the Supreme Court confirmed that 'parties [are allowed] to select the law applicable to their contract'.[127] In the absence of choice, the applicable law is the law which 'bear[s] substantial connection to the transaction',[128] or the law which 'has the most significant relationship to the transaction and the parties'.[129] The Supreme Court also

[116] *Moreno, Jr v Private Management Office* (2006) 507 SCRA 63, 72.
[117] Tolentino (n 113) 629–30.
[118] eg, *Francisco v Herrera* (2002) 392 SCRA 317, 323; *Manzano v Garcia* (2011) 661 SCRA 350, 362; *delos Reyes v Court of Appeals* (1999) 313 SCRA 632, 642; *Allied Banking Corporation v Spouses Villaluz*, GR No 202525, 12 September 2018 (Supreme Court).
[119] Civil Code (Philippines), art 1409.
[120] ibid art 1390.
[121] ibid art 15.
[122] ibid art 1403.
[123] ibid art 17.
[124] See *Industrial Personnel & Management Services, Inc (IPAMS) v de Vera* (2016) 785 SCRA 562, 582–83; *Pakistan International Airlines Corp v Ople* (1990) 190 SCRA 90, 99 ('*Pakistan Airlines*').
[125] Civil Code (Philippines), art 17.
[126] *Philippine Export* (n 29).
[127] ibid 215.
[128] ibid.
[129] ibid.

emphasised that the chosen law and the applicable law derived through the choice of law process are circumscribed by the 'law, morals, or public policy of the forum and that the chosen law must bear a substantive relationship to the transaction';[130] thus, like in common law, the applicable law determines substantive validity.

A foreign applicable law should be proven as a matter of fact.[131] Absent such evidence, the foreign law's contents shall be presumed to be the same as Philippine law.[132] Furthermore, courts may encounter difficulty in applying foreign law or may chose not to go through the choice of law process. Hence, in a number of cases, the contract may be analysed from the perspective of Philippine law despite the applicable foreign law.[133]

The foregoing analysis assumes that Philippine courts may recognise Choice-of-Forum clauses as contracts. However, if viewed as venue stipulations, the court may resort to a completely procedural approach. In this case, existence and validity are determined by the clause's compliance with the Rules of Court rule on venues – 'parties have validly agreed in writing before the filing of the action on the exclusive venue thereof'.[134] As a result, the need to comply with the black letter of this rule makes the usual distinction between existence and validity irrelevant.

(ii) Choice-of-Forum Clauses as Contracts?

In the Philippines, Choice-of-Law clauses are recognised as an 'offshoot of the fundamental principle of autonomy of contracts'.[135] Choice-of-Forum clauses, on the other hand, struggle to be recognised as flowing from the same contractual principle. The most that they have been recognised by Philippine courts so far is that they are venue stipulations under the Rules of Court, and thus, are considered procedural in nature. This characterisation, however, does not necessarily preclude the possibility that Choice-of-Forum clauses, when governed by a foreign applicable law, can be recognised as having contractual characteristics, if not as contracts in themselves. Since Choice-of-Law clauses are recognised as long as they are 'not contrary to law, morals, good customs, public order or public policy' of the Philippines and have a 'substantive relationship to the transaction',[136] it may be argued that if the validly chosen foreign applicable law characterises the Choice-of-Forum clauses as contracts, these clauses may therefore be regarded as contracts too. Since the foreign law stated in the Choice-of-Law clause determines the validity of a Choice-of-Forum clause, Philippine law should not apply. However, this contractual treatment is just a possibility, and no Philippine decision has confirmed this at this point. On the contrary, Philippine case law would seem to show that enforcement of Choice-of-Forum clauses may be refused even if the chosen foreign law recognises Choice-of-Forum clauses as contracts.[137]

[130] ibid.
[131] Rules of Court (Philippines), rule 132, s 24.
[132] See *Northwest Orient Airlines, Inc v Court of Appeals* (1995) 241 SCRA 192, 200.
[133] See, eg, *HSBC* (n 32) 335–37; *International Harvester Company in Russia v Hamburg-American Line* (1918) 42 Phil 845, 855 ('*International Harvester*').
[134] Rules of Court (Philippines), rule 4, s 4(b).
[135] *Saudi Arabian Airlines (Saudia) v Rebesencio* (2015) 746 SCRA 140, 157 ('*Saudia*').
[136] *Philippine Export* (n 126) 215; *Saudia* (n 135) 157.
[137] *HSBC* (n 32) 334.

C. The Doctrine of Separability

(i) Singapore, Hong Kong and Malaysia

The doctrine of separability, which applies to both Choice-of-Law and Choice-of-Forum clauses,[138] shields these two clauses from the invalidity of the underlying contract. Hence, the Choice-of-Forum clause can survive even when the underlying contract is found to be invalid. In *Quaestus*, the Hong Kong CFI emphasised that the doctrine of separability precludes the finding that the Choice-of-Forum clause is also vitiated simply because the main contract is alleged to be 'a sham and an instrument of fraud'.[139] Furthermore, when both the Choice-of-Law and the Choice-of-Forum clauses are contained in the same clause, and the former has been found invalid, this invalidity does not also invalidate the Choice-of-Forum clause.[140] Nevertheless, when the Choice-of-Forum clause is so 'intimately linked' as to 'convey … interdependence or contingency' with the invalid Choice-of-Law in the same clause, it may also be rendered invalid.[141]

Furthermore, the doctrine of separability only applies when the Choice-of-Forum clause actually exists.[142] When there is no meeting of the minds between parties in the first place, and thus the entire contract, including the Choice-of-Forum clause, has evidently never come into existence, even the doctrine of separability finds no application. Furthermore, an allegation of forgery of the main contract may present a 'fundamental challenge' because this means that the defendant never agreed to the jurisdiction clauses.[143]

(ii) Choice-of-Court Convention

The doctrine of separability has found expression in article 3(d) of the Choice-of-Court Convention:

> an exclusive choice of court agreement that forms part of a contract shall be treated as an agreement independent of the other terms of the contract. The validity of the exclusive choice of court agreement cannot be contested solely on the ground that the contract is not valid.

(iii) The Philippines

The Philippines has a similar concept of separability applicable to arbitration clauses.[144] The doctrine has not been extended, however, to Choice-of-Forum clauses given their status as procedural venue stipulations.

[138] *PT Selecta Bestama v Sin Huat Huat Marine Transportation Pte Ltd* [2016] 1 SLR 729, 743 (HC) ('*PT Selecta*'); *Hiromi Okada v Tomohiro Okada* [2019] HKCFI 2310, [38]–[43], [46] ('*Okada*'); *China Baoli Technologies Holdings Ltd v Orient Equal International Group Ltd* [2017] HKCFI 1047, [100].
[139] *Quaestus Capital Pte Ltd v Everton Associates Ltd* [2021] HKCFI 1367, [43] ('*Quaestus*').
[140] See eg, *Shanghai Turbo Enterprises Ltd v Liu Ming* [2019] 1 SLR 779, 808 ('*Shanghai Turbo*').
[141] ibid.
[142] See *PT Selecta* (n 138) 743.
[143] *China Construction Bank (Asia) Corporation Ltd v Zhang Kangyang* [2022] HKCFI 2135, [21].
[144] Alternative Dispute Resolution Act (Philippines), app A, art 16(1).

III. Issues of Interpretation

A. The Challenge of Interpreting International Commercial Contracts in Asia

Interpreting Choice-of-Forum clauses in international commercial contracts usually involves not just legal issues but also factual and other evidentiary issues. In Asia, contracts may not be in English or may use a different writing system, making courts dependent on translators during evidentiary hearings. Notably, translators and expert witnesses on foreign law may offer conflicting interpretations of the Choice-of-Forum clause. As will be discussed, in such situations, courts generally follow the principle that contracts should be interpreted according to the parties' intention.

In Asia, this task of determining the parties' intention is more complex. Despite commercial sophistication, parties may lack strong English skills or proper legal advice during drafting, compounded by cultural differences in commercial expectations.[145] Even local lawyers may be unfamiliar with common law concepts and legal jargon. As a result, a strict textual and objective approach may not reflect the parties' true intention and could lead to unreasonable results.

In most legal systems, courts interpret Choice-of-Forum clauses according to the parties' intention, which is objectively ascertained.[146] Courts would consider what was written and the surrounding factual matrix.[147] Hence, if the language shows the parties wanted flexibility or the clause was drafted to benefit a party, the interpretation of the Choice-of-Forum clause should give effect to such intention.[148] Consequently, the parties' understanding of their terms and conditions is crucial, and unless otherwise provided, parties are deemed to have carefully chosen their words and as such, the ordinary meaning of the words used is to be preferred.[149]

When the Choice-of-Forum clauses are simple or generic, ascertaining the party's intention is harder. Often treated like other boiler-plate provisions, these clauses are drafted by lawyers and parties with little attention to their meaning and effect.[150] Briggs observes that '[i]t sometimes appears that by the time they reached the jurisdiction agreement, the drafters were out of time, energy, fresh coffee and clean shirts; and quality of work suffered accordingly'.[151] Thus, based on the language alone, there is unlikely to be any meaningful evidence as to the actual intent of the parties, making the surrounding factual matrix crucial. In *PT Bali Hospitality Utama v Mathias Echene*, clause 13 stated that 'parties submit to the jurisdiction of the courts of Denpasar, Bali' without including any word or phrase

[145] See Philip McConnaughay, 'Rethinking the Role of Law and Contracts in East-West Commercial Relationships' (2001) 41(2) *Virginia Journal of International Law* 427, 446.

[146] *Silverlink Resorts Ltd v MS First Capital Insurance Ltd* [2020] SGHC 251, [55].

[147] See *Orchard Capital I Ltd v Ravindra Kumar Jhunjhunwala* [2012] 2 SLR 519, 532 (CA) ('*Orchard Capital*'); *PT Bali Hospitality Utama v Mathias Echene* [2010] HKCFI 115, [12] ('*PT Bali*'); *Taiao Aluminium (Taishan) Co Ltd v Maze Aluminium Engineering Co Ltd* [2006] HKCFI 220, [26].

[148] See *Orchard Capital* (n 147) 532–33.

[149] *Abdul Rashid bin Abdul Manaf v Hii Yii Ann* [2014] 4 SLR 1042, 1054 (HC) ('*Abdul Rashid*').

[150] See Briggs, Adrian, *Agreements on Jurisdiction and Choice of Law* (Oxford University Press, 2008) 112.

[151] ibid.

indicating exclusivity of choice.[152] Nonetheless, the Hong Kong CFI ruled that clause 13 exclusively conferred jurisdiction on Balinese courts because everything about the dispute pointed to Bali – the legal relationship arising from a management agreement of villas in Bali; the plaintiff's incorporation in Indonesia and legal domicile in Bali; and the choice of Indonesian law.[153] 'That exclusiveness is so obvious in all of these circumstances that it did not require the parties to go any further than they did in Clause 13'.[154] In *Chen Yun Hian Christopher v BHNV Online Ltd*, the Singapore High Court, after agreeing with Briggs' expert opinion, regarded the careless and inconsistent references to the UK courts – when the rest of the Choice-of-Forum clause mentioned Belize courts – as 'slips of the pen', thus making the clause exclusive.[155] 'Despite these errors, the meaning of [the Choice-of-Forum clause] would be apparent to any reasonable person – that parties agreed to litigate any Contract-related disputes in Belize and in Belize only'.[156] Hence, 'mentions of the UK courts … were failures of omissions rather than deliberate inclusions'.[157] Rectification rather than 'voiding the clause altogether' would be 'the more appropriate and less draconian response'.[158]

Because parties' intention matters, courts should refrain from giving words and phrases any special meaning beyond what is stated in the contract. Hence, the meaning of words in a negotiated contract should be no different than the meaning of the same words in standardised contracts. In *Abdul Rashid*, the Singapore High Court emphasised that a non-exclusive Choice-of-Forum clause does not morph into a 'most appropriate' Choice-of-Forum clause (which has an effect akin to exclusive clauses) simply because the contract is negotiated.[159]

Pre-contractual discussions or negotiations are irrelevant and should be ignored in interpreting the clause,[160] as only the contract's written terms matter once it is concluded. The rules of evidence echo this prohibition. In the Philippines, the parol evidence rule prohibits parties from presenting evidence which will vary the contract's written terms, except when there is intrinsic ambiguity, failure to express the parties' true intention, the contract's validity is questioned, or other terms were agreed after executing the contract.[161] Being procedural in nature, the rule may be applied regardless of the applicable law. Notably, the parol evidence rule is founded in the English common law[162] and has been adopted in Singapore,[163] Hong Kong[164] and Malaysia.[165] Nonetheless, in Singapore, the rule does not apply to contracts under the CISG.[166]

[152] *PT Bali* (n 147) [3].
[153] ibid [12].
[154] ibid.
[155] *Chen Yun Hian Christopher v BHNV Online Ltd* [2020] SGHC 284, [50] ('*Chen Yun*').
[156] ibid [52].
[157] ibid [51].
[158] ibid [52].
[159] *Abdul Rashid* (n 149) 1054.
[160] See *Ko Lai Kuen v Li Tak Ming* [2011] HKCFI 304, [20] ('*Ko Lai*').
[161] Rules of Court (Philippines) rule 130, s 9.
[162] eg, *Investors Compensation Scheme Ltd v West Bromwich Building Society* [1998] 1 WLR 896, 913 ('*Investors Compensation*'); *Prenn v Simmonds* [1971] 1 WLR 1381, 1383, 1385.
[163] See *China Insurance Co (Singapore) Pte Ltd v Liberty Insurance Pte Ltd* [2005] 2 SLR(R) 509, 518 (HC).
[164] See *Nanyang Commercial Bank Ltd v Fung Piu* [1999] HKCFI 420, [8].
[165] See Evidence Act 1950 (Malaysia), ss 91–92.
[166] Vienna Convention on Contracts for the International Sale of Goods, opened for signature 11 April 1980, 1489 UNTS 3 (entered into force 1 January 1988), art 11.

The law applicable to the contract dictates the canons of interpretation. In *The 'Jian He'*, the Singapore Court of Appeal acknowledged that the governing Chinese law determines the interpretation of the Choice-of-Forum clause,[167] but due to lack of evidence, the Court applied Singaporean interpretation rules.[168] This recourse to forum law for interpretation is notably common. As noted in *Orchard Capital*, the Singapore Court of Appeal states that 'the *lex fori* would apply to questions of interpretation by default in most cases because of the presumption of similarity'.[169] This situation also arises when the foreign law is not pleaded.

Notably, the forum court's determination of the contents of the applicable law (eg, whether it also includes the procedural law of the chosen law or just its substantive or internal law) has important implications for the interpretation of the Choice-of-Forum clause. In *Abdul Rashid*, the defendant argued that since the Choice-of-Law clause stipulated English law, the *onus* lay with the plaintiff to establish strong cause why a stay should not be granted in favour of Queensland, the jurisdiction named in the non-exclusive Choice-of-Forum clause.[170] In contrast, the plaintiff argued that while the Choice-of-Law clause stipulated English law, the applicable test should be *Spiliada*, as applied in Singapore.[171] The Singapore High Court agreed, stating that a stay based on *forum non conveniens* is a matter of procedure; thus, Singaporean law applies.[172] In effect, the Court excluded the procedural law of the chosen applicable law. Therefore, English law governed the clause's interpretation, while Singaporean law determined the effects of such interpretation.[173]

The commercial nature of the relationship between parties should guide courts' interpretation.[174] Since parties contract in order to give life to their business transactions, courts unsurprisingly prefer interpretations which uphold the contract's validity, provided no clear ground for invalidating the contract is present.[175] Courts also declare that unless otherwise provided, commercially minded parties would want all disputes arising from their relationship to be decided by the same tribunal or court, and avoid disputes being resolved by different tribunals or courts.[176] This is especially useful in determining whether certain pre-contractual matters and non-contractual matters could also be covered by the Choice-of-Forum clause.[177] In Singapore, however, disputes arising from another contract, even where the agreements are interrelated, may not be covered by this principle.[178] Nonetheless, the particular business or industry also provides insight into the parties' intention and informs the interpretation of the Choice-of-Forum clause.[179]

[167] *The 'Jian He'* [1999] 3 SLR(R) 432, 437 (CA) ('*The Jian He*').
[168] ibid; see also *Intergraph Cadworx & Analysis Solutions, Inc v EDS Asia Sdn Bhd* [2013] 8 MLJ 729, 735–36 (HC Kuala Lumpur).
[169] *Orchard Capital* (n 147) 532.
[170] *Abdul Rashid* (n 149) 1045.
[171] ibid.
[172] ibid 1047.
[173] ibid.
[174] See *Wynn Las Vegas, LLC v Mong Henry* [2009] HKCFI 501, [17] ('*Wynn-Mong*').
[175] See eg, *William Co v Chu Kong Agency Ltd* [1993] 2 HKC 377, 381–82 (HC); *Palace Hotel Ltd v Owners of the Ship or Vessel 'Happy Pioneer'* [1982] 1 HKC 640, 644 (HC); *Shanghai Turbo* (n 140) 809.
[176] *CPC Construction Hong Kong Ltd v Harvest Engineering (HK) Ltd* [2015] HKCFI 1173, [55]; *Bunge SA v Shrikant Bhasi* [2020] SGCA 94, [37] ('*Bunge*'), citing *Fiona Trust & Holding Corporation v Privalov* [2007] 4 All ER 951 ('*Fiona Trust*').
[177] ibid; *Chen Yun* (n 155) [60].
[178] *Allianz Capital Partners GmbH, Singapore Branch v Goh Andress* [2022] SGHC 266, [33], [35].
[179] See *Wynn-Mong* (n 174) [17]; *Star Cruises* (n 36) [53].

The interpretation adopted by the court can bind those who are not parties to the litigation.[180] It can also bind third-party beneficiaries and successors-in-interest. The same interpretation can also bind parties to similar agreements, especially where standardised agreements are used, such as for cruise ships or bank loans. Once a court interprets standardised terms in one case, the same meaning may apply in future cases involving similarly-worded contracts.

B. Singapore, Hong Kong and Malaysia

English common law adopts an objective approach to interpretation, with emphasis on the ordinary meaning of the text. However, this strict objective approach has slowly evolved to consider the objective meaning of the words in light of relevant surrounding circumstances:

> Interpretation is the ascertainment of the meaning which the document would convey to a reasonable person having all the background knowledge which would reasonably have been available to the parties in the situation in which they were at the time of the contract.[181]

However, 'there is no duty on this Court to read clauses differently when the terms are clear'.[182]

(i) Interpretation and Procedural Law

In Singapore, Hong Kong and Malaysia, the interpretation rules under the applicable foreign law must be proven; otherwise, the forum court will assume that they are no different from the forum rules.[183] When the issue requires a specific question of construction, like whether the applicable law would interpret the clause as either exclusive or non-exclusive, and the same has not been proven sufficiently in evidence, the court may regard the specific foreign rule to have the same contents as that in the forum.[184] To prove the foreign law's contents, evidence which may be presented can range from testimony or affidavits of expert witnesses,[185] to written legal opinions,[186] an agreement among all parties' foreign law experts on the contents of the foreign law,[187] and letters from foreign lawyers.[188] Nonetheless, when parties provide expert evidence on how the Choice-of-Forum clause would be interpreted under the foreign law, such interpretation does not necessarily bind

[180] Vaughan Black and Stephen Pitel, 'Forum-selection clauses: beyond the contracting parties' (2016) 12(1) *Journal of Private International Law* 26, 29.

[181] *Investors Compensation* (n 162) 912.

[182] *Kraken Services Ltd (formerly known as Kraken Reinsurance Services Ltd) v Q Life Medical Insurance Company Asia Region* [2021] MLJU 2956, [20] ('*Kraken*').

[183] *The 'Jian He'* (n 167) 437; *Yu Lap Man v Good First Investment Ltd* [1998] 1 HKC 726, 730–31 ('*Yu Lap Man*'); *Winnitex Investment Co Ltd v Oxford Products (International) Ltd* [2004] 4 HKC 660, 678 (DC); *Vander Limited v P&O Nedlloyd BV* [1998] HKCFI 473, [15] ('*Vander*'); *Re: Guy Kwok-Hung Lam v Ex Parte: TOR Asia Credit Master Fund LP* [2022] HKCA 1297, [62].

[184] *PT Jaya Putra Kundur Indah v Guthrie Overseas Investments Pte Ltd* [1996] SGHC 285, [62]–[63] ('*PT Jaya*'); *Star Cruises* (n 36) [23]–[24]; *Wang Qian Wei v Guo Wenyu* [2018] HKCFI 2253, [33] ('*Wang*').

[185] *Venetian Macau* (n 86) [24].

[186] *PT Jaya* (n 184) [37].

[187] *Lammas Global Corporation v Barclays Bank (Suisse) SA* [2011] HKCFI 247, [37] ('*Lammas*').

[188] *Yu Lap Man* (n 183) 731.

the forum court.[189] The court, however, would still interpret the clause with reference to the expert evidence.[190]

Whenever there are differences in the parties' expert evidence, the judge has to resolve them if he can.[191] Otherwise, if there is so much inconsistency or lack of clarity per evidence presented, the court may declare that the foreign law has not been proven sufficiently, and therefore consider the foreign rules to be the same as the forum rules. Nevertheless, in resolving conflicting expert evidence, the court would consider each expert's independence,[192] their years of practice in the foreign jurisdiction,[193] their particular expertise in the relevant area of foreign law, and the cogency of the delivered legal opinion.[194] Furthermore, accepting the opposition's translation as accurate precludes the other party from objecting and proposing contrary translations of the Choice-of-Forum clause written in a foreign language or a different writing system.[195] In assessing the evidence on foreign law, 'the judge is obliged to use his legal training where it has a bearing on determining such facts, especially where the concepts are not very different from [forum] law'.[196]

Parties may need to present evidence, so the court can fully interpret the Choice-of-Forum clause. In *The 'Botic'*, the parties chose to have their dispute settled in the carrier's 'principal place of business'.[197] Since there was uncertainty as to who the carrier was,[198] the court needed to know the carrier's identity before interpreting the phrase, 'principal place of business'.[199] In this case, the bill of lading did not include the carrier's name or its place of business,[200] thus prompting the court, after noting the plaintiff's reasonable efforts to locate the defendant, to allow service through a law firm.[201] Eventually, the defendants applied for a stay, alleging that the carrier's principal place of business was Split, Croatia.[202] Their allegation was supported by affidavits and documents showing that a certain entity, 'Santa Fe Shipping Co of Liberia' was the owner of the vessel; that Santa Fe was a Liberian company but was not doing business there; that its principal place of business was a certain address in Split, Croatia; and that all its officers were nationals and residents of Croatia.[203] Hence, the defendants argued that the phrase 'principal place of business' in the Choice-of-Forum clause should be interpreted to mean Split, Croatia.[204] The High Court did not comment on whether the plaintiffs contested the evidence presented by the defendants. Nonetheless, the Court accepted the proposed interpretation and stayed the Singapore proceedings.[205]

[189] *Venetian Macau* (n 86) [24].
[190] *Mashreq Asia Ltd v Furness Logistics (HK) Ltd* [1999] 4 HKC 317, [26] ('*Mashreq*').
[191] *Lammas* (n 187) [16].
[192] ibid [17].
[193] See *Wynn-Mong* (n 174) [16].
[194] See ibid.
[195] See *Rickshaw Investments Ltd v Nicolai Baron von Uexkull* [2006] 2 SLR(R) 850, 855 (HC).
[196] *Huang Shu Jian v Dai Wei* [2019] HKCFI 1386, [34].
[197] *The 'Botic'* [1999] 2 SLR(R) 494, 496 (HC).
[198] ibid 496–97.
[199] ibid 496.
[200] ibid.
[201] ibid 496–97.
[202] ibid 497.
[203] ibid.
[204] ibid.
[205] ibid 502.

In *Mashreq Asia Ltd v Furness Logistics (HK) Ltd*, the Hong Kong CFI also needed to identify the carrier in order to interpret the Choice-of-Forum clause.[206] Although the defendant had made an admission in a parallel case in the Netherlands, the Court refused to recognise it, as Hong Kong courts are barred from recognising admissions made in foreign courts.[207] Instead, the Court considered the defendant a carrier because it had 'established a good arguable case that the conditions of the carriage that undoubtedly was effected were governed by the conditions upon the reverse of the bill of lading'.[208] The Court also confirmed that the exclusive foreign jurisdiction clause bites in terms of the legal relationship between parties, and the defendant should be able to enforce the exclusive clause stipulating Dutch courts.[209]

Necessarily, the evidence to be presented should coincide with the issues raised. Hence, even when the dispute involves a transaction composed of several contracts, parties may be barred from presenting evidence on other related contracts when only issues of specific contracts are brought before the court.[210]

(ii) Lost in Translation

Translation issues are expected when parties communicate and contract in different local languages and write their contracts using a different writing system. In Hong Kong, translation issues have become a common feature of Choice-of-Forum clause disputes when one party is from Mainland China, and the contract is in Chinese or has a Chinese-language counterpart.

In *Yu Lap Man v Good First Investment Ltd*, the dispute involved identical Choice-of-Forum clauses found in two agreements, both written in Chinese.[211] The parties obtained two different English translations.[212] One read 'All disputes arising hereunder shall be subject to the jurisdiction of the Courts in the People's Republic of China', while the other said 'all disputes are subject to the jurisdiction of the Courts in the [PRC]'.[213] The court translator confirmed that both translations were possible,[214] but clarified that the Chinese character does not connote the more assertive 'shall be'.[215] Hence, the clause should be translated as 'all disputes are subject',[216] and therefore, non-exclusive.[217] The judge, who was a bilingual speaker, adopted this translation.[218] In effect, the personal knowledge of the local language by the judge resolved the differences in translation.[219]

[206] *Mashreq* (n 190) 325–6; also see *The Griesheim* [1983] 1 HKC 251 (HC).
[207] *Mashreq* (n 190) 326.
[208] ibid.
[209] ibid.
[210] *Xu Ziming v Ruifeng Petroleum Chemical Holdings Ltd* [2014] HKCFI 2315, [10].
[211] *Yu Lap Man* (n 183) 729.
[212] ibid.
[213] ibid.
[214] ibid.
[215] ibid 730.
[216] ibid.
[217] ibid 732–33.
[218] ibid 730.
[219] See also *Tianjin Yufenglong Asset Management Co, Ltd v Ho Kin Wa* [2019] HKCFI 556, [21] ('*Tianjin*').

When the case was appealed to the Court of Appeal, the defendant argued that since the parties were not given proper legal advice when the clause was being drafted, the lower court should have adopted a common sense understanding and interpreted the clause an exclusive submission to Chinese courts.[220] The Court, however, disagreed and stressed that lack of proper legal advice during the drafting of the clause is not a significant consideration.[221] The Court instead noted that both parties had strong Hong Kong connections and 'if a dispute arose on any other matter than one specifically relating to the parcel of land in Xiamen, it would make obvious sense for the litigation to be conducted in Hong Kong'.[222]

In *Bank of China Ltd v Yang Fan*, the Hong Kong CFI had to interpret two similarly-worded Choice-of-Forum clauses in two contracts written in Chinese as either exclusive or non-exclusive.[223] While there were two inconsistent translations,[224] the Court observed that the ordinary meaning of the relevant clauses in Chinese would generally be non-exclusive rather than exclusive.[225] It declared, nevertheless, that this observation was only prima facie, since parties can give the phrase a special meaning, and that ultimately, the parties' intention should govern the interpretation.[226] To resolve the dispute, the Court referred to the interpretation principles in the English case *Investors Compensation Scheme Ltd v West Bromwich Building Society*,[227] which it declared pertinent to the case.[228] The application of these English common law principles appears misplaced, however, considering that the Court had already noted that Chinese law applied.[229] Nonetheless, using the English rules, the Court found that since different dispute resolution procedures were envisioned in the clause – resolution first, through mediation or negotiation, and only then, by litigation[230] – the parties appeared to only allow legal proceedings in China if mediation were to fail.[231] Hence, the Chinese phrase should be interpreted as having the imperative meaning 'shall', thus making the clauses exclusive.[232]

In *Rich Village*, the recorder translated the opening line of the Chinese-language Choice-of-Forum clause as 'matters not covered in the Agreement', and opined that these words made the clause assertive, not permissive.[233] He admitted, however, that this interpretation was unreasonable since orders from a Ningbo court (the chosen court) are unenforceable in Hong Kong.[234] To avoid this unreasonable result, the Hong Kong Court of Appeal considered the contract in its totality, together with relevant surrounding facts.[235] The Court noted that, given the exclusive clause's importance,[236] the absence of phrases

[220] *Yu Lap Man* [1999] 1 HKC 622, 625 (CA).
[221] ibid.
[222] ibid.
[223] *Bank of China Ltd v Yang Fan* [2016] HKCFI 708, [28]–[31] ('*Yang Fan*').
[224] ibid [28].
[225] ibid [31].
[226] ibid [31].
[227] *Investors Compensation* (n 162).
[228] Yang Fan (n 223) [32].
[229] ibid [28].
[230] ibid [34].
[231] ibid.
[232] ibid.
[233] *Rich Village Ltd v Grand Pride Holdings Ltd* [2013] HKCA 33, [12].
[234] ibid.
[235] ibid [16].
[236] ibid [17]; see also *Beijing Renji* (n 52) [56].

in Chinese that would mean 'should, shall, must, etc' but were found in other parts of the contract, was conspicuous.[237] Accordingly, this anomaly could only be resolved if the clause was considered non-exclusive – 'in relation to those provided for in the agreement, there is no jurisdiction clause at all; in relation to those not provided for in the agreement, they are covered by a non-exclusive clause'.[238] Moreover, this interpretation also made sense as 'the most natural and convenient forum for an action to enforce obligations for the transfer and buy back of the Rich City shares must be Hong Kong, these being shares of a Hong Kong company'.[239] Hence, the Court held the Choice-of-Forum clause to be non-exclusive.[240] Similarly, in *Tianjin Yufenglong Asset Management Co, Ltd v Ho Kin Wa*, the Hong Kong CFI considered the Choice-of-Forum clause exclusive because it contained Chinese characters which were also used in other parts of the contract to express mandatory obligations.[241]

In *Beijing Renji Real Estate Development Group Co, Ltd v Zhu Min*, the Hong Kong CFI applied the law applicable to the contract (Chinese law) in concluding that the Chinese-language Choice-of-Forum clause was exclusive,[242] by referring to the Chinese Civil Procedure Law, relevant judicial interpretations and decisions by Chinese courts, and expert evidence.[243] Nonetheless, because the guarantee agreement, which was the contract relevant to the dispute, lacked any direct reference to the partnership contract which contained the relevant Choice-of-Forum clause (interpreted as exclusive under Chinese law), the Court ruled that the Chinese judgment could not be registered under the Choice-of-Court Arrangement.[244]

(iii) Meaning of Words and Phrases

(a) Identifying Choice-of-Forum Clauses

When a clause lacks the words usually associated with a Choice-of-Forum clause such as 'disputes' and only includes 'claims', its nature as a Choice-of-Forum clause may be doubtful. In *The Sinar Mas*, the defendant asked for a stay pursuant to clause 17, which stated: 'Claims. Any claims that may arise hereunder must be made at the port of delivery for determination and settlement at that port only'.[245] Referring to the *Shorter Oxford Dictionary* to determine the ordinary meaning of the word 'claims', the Malaysian court concluded that the word 'claims', does not amount to litigation.[246] 'It is confined to "claims" pure and simple as, for example, where a consignee wishes to claim for the goods under the Bill of Lading, then it must be done only in Kuching, which is the port of delivery'.[247] Hence, clause 17 was not a jurisdiction clause.[248]

[237] ibid.
[238] ibid [19].
[239] ibid [23].
[240] ibid [26].
[241] *Tianjin* (n 219) [23].
[242] *Beijing Renji* (n 52) [48].
[243] ibid.
[244] ibid [42].
[245] *The Sinar Mas* [1982] 1 MLJ 279, 279 (OCJ Kuala Lumpur).
[246] ibid.
[247] ibid.
[248] ibid.

In *Oriental Insurance Co Ltd v Bhavani Stores Pte Ltd*, the clause – 'In the event of loss or damages which may involve a claim under this insurance, immediate notice thereof and application for survey should be given to: Survey Settling Agents … Tuticorin' – was held to refer only to the initial stages in processing a claim and not to filing a claim or commencing litigation in the courts in India.[249] The Singapore Court of Appeal ruled that this clause was a payment clause which only indicated a place of payment, and was thus incapable of limiting the processing of a claim to India or Singapore, and determining the proper forum for the dispute.[250]

In *Golden Shore*, the defendant argued that the sentence – 'Any claims that may arise hereunder must be made at the port of delivery for determination and settlement at that port only' – was not an exclusive Choice-of-Forum clause but rather just a provision for the place of notification and making of a claim.[251] The court disagreed after construing 'claims' and 'determination' as referring to suits and disputes.[252] According to the court, '[a] claim which is not met becomes a dispute which would require determination'.[253] Hence, the clause was an exclusive Choice-of-Forum clause.[254]

(b) Exclusive and Non-Exclusive

Whether a Choice-of-Forum clause is exclusive would usually depend on the words indicating exclusivity. Words and phrases like 'only', 'exclusive', 'to the exclusion of', etc may indicate that the clause is exclusive. Courts have consistently emphasised, however, that using the word 'exclusive' is not necessary to establish exclusivity.[255] Ultimately, the 'the true question is whether on its proper construction the clause obliges the parties to resort to the relevant jurisdiction'.[256] The onus lies with the party asserting the clause's exclusivity.[257]

In *Yu Lap Man*, the Choice-of-Forum clause, which was discussed in the previous subsection, did not contain the word 'exclusive', but the defendant argued that the clause was exclusive because the phrases 'subject to', and '[b]oth parties agree' were included, and that it referred to Chinese mainland law as the governing law.[258] The court disagreed because 'subject to' does not necessarily connote exclusivity.[259] Furthermore, '[b]oth parties agree' only meant agreement by both parties like in every contractual term.[260] Moreover, the reference to Chinese law only meant that the parties agreed to Chinese law, but being governed by Chinese Law did not make the Choice-of-Forum clause exclusive.[261] The Court of Appeal confirmed this interpretation on appeal.[262]

[249] *Oriental Insurance Co Ltd v Bhavani Stores Pte Ltd* [1997] 3 SLR(R) 363, 371–72 (CA).
[250] ibid 372.
[251] *Golden Shore Transportation Pte Ltd v UCO Bank* [2004] 1 SLR(R) 6 (CA).
[252] ibid.
[253] ibid 15.
[254] ibid 16.
[255] See *Yu Lap Man* (n 183) 732.
[256] *Wang* (n 184) [29]; see also *T&K Electronics Ltd v Tai Ping Insurance Co Ltd* [1997] 3 HKC 330 (CFI); *Vander* (n 183) [10].
[257] See *Multi-Top Limited v BKE-Media (HK) (A Firm)* [1999] HKCFI 551, [37] ('*Multi-Top*').
[258] *Yu Lap Man* (n 183) 731.
[259] ibid 732.
[260] ibid.
[261] ibid 732–33.
[262] *Yu Lap Man* (n 183) 628.

In *Luso International Banking Ltd v Summi (Group) Holdings Ltd* ('*Luso*'), the Hong Kong CFI observed that the Choice-of-Forum clause was 'neutral on the exclusivity of jurisdiction'; thus, it referred to the applicable Macau law, particularly the Macau Civil Procedure Code.[263] It considered the expert evidence on the proper construction of article 29(2) of the Macau Civil Procedure Code, and concluded that the Choice-of-Forum clause was non-exclusive.[264]

In *Vander Limited v P&O Nedlloyd BV*, the Hong Kong CFI ruled that the clause was exclusive because the words 'all claims' and 'shall' were found together,[265] as well as the phrase 'no other court shall have jurisdiction … unless the Carrier appeals'.[266] The Court interpreted the clause to mean that no other court except those in the Netherlands should have jurisdiction over the disputes between the parties.[267] In *Tianjin*, since the same Chinese character would appear in other parts of the contract to express mandatory obligations, the court ruled that the same mandatory meaning must have been intended for the same Chinese character in the Choice-of-Forum clause.[268]

In *Multi-Top*, the Hong Kong CFI found the relatively simple clause – 'This contract is settled under German (law). Legal domicile is Goettingen Germany' – to be non-exclusive because '[t]he wordings used is non-assertive of exclusive jurisdiction'.[269] Similarly, the Singapore High Court in *PT Bank Bali v Santosa Widjaja* interpreted the choice of domicile provision in the Indonesian language – 'That in respect of this agreement and all its consequences … the guarantor elects as the general and permanent legal domicile at the Registry of District Court at West Jakarta' – as non-exclusive because while the Jakarta court was identified, it did not say that courts outside Indonesia would not have jurisdiction.[270] Similarly, the use of the Chinese character which means 'absolute' to qualify 'jurisdiction' does not necessarily make the clause exclusive.[271] 'The word "absolute" refers to the extent or scope of the jurisdiction rather than its exclusivity'.[272]

Determining whether a Choice-of-Forum clause is exclusive becomes more difficult when parties have stipulated for different parallel processes or sets of rules in resolving disputes. In *Chan Chi Keung v Delmas Hong Kong Ltd* ('*Chan*'), the Hong Kong CFI needed to interpret a relatively complex clause, which stated:

> Any claim or dispute against the Carrier … shall be governed, for the maritime part of the carriage either by … and, for the nonmaritime part of the carriage either by the provisions contained in any International Convention or National Law compulsorily applicable, or by the French Law applicable to the means of transport utilized and shall be determined in France by the 'Tribunal de Commerce du Havre'.[273]

[263] *Luso International Banking Ltd v Summi (Group) Holdings Ltd* [2021] HKCFI 906, [32].
[264] ibid [33].
[265] *Vander* (n 183) [11].
[266] ibid.
[267] ibid [15].
[268] *Tianjin* (n 219) [23].
[269] *Multi-Top* (n 257) [36]–[37].
[270] *PT Bank Bali v Santosa Widjaja* [1997] SGHC 142, [12].
[271] *Chen Hongqing v The Persons whose names are set out in the second column of the schedule hereto* [2018] HKCFI 1170, [39].
[272] ibid.
[273] *Chan Chi Keung v Delmas Hong Kong Ltd* [2004] 4 HKC 28, 33 (CFI).

The Hong Kong CFI regarded as exclusive the clause 'whereby the parties have agreed that any claim or dispute against the defendant as carrier shall be determined in France by the "Tribunal de Commerce du Havre"'.[274] To reach this conclusion, the Court had to ask: '(1) what is it that "shall be governed"? and (2) what is it that "shall be determined"?'.[275] Based on the plain reading of the clause, the Court said that the answer to both questions must be 'any claim or dispute against the Carrier arising under this Bill of Lading'.[276] Hence, the clause was exclusive.[277]

At the other end are non-exclusive Choice-of-Forum clauses, which are usually identifiable with the use of words and phrases like 'non-exclusive', 'proceedings in any other jurisdictions', 'without limiting the right to file in other courts', to convey that the filing of actions in the named forum is optional or permissive. In *Ko Lai Kuen v Li Tak Ming*, the defendant asked the Hong Kong CFI to interpret as exclusive the following Choice-of-Forum clause:

> 11.3 The Customer irrevocably and unconditionally submits to the jurisdiction of the courts of Indonesia to settle any dispute arising out of or in connection with this Agreement, and hereby agrees that any legal action or proceedings arising out of or in connection with this Agreement may be brought in those courts. Nothing in the foregoing shall however limit the Company [ie 3rd defendant].[278]

The defendant argued that 'irrevocably and unconditionally submits to the jurisdiction of the courts of Indonesia' meant exclusivity. The Hong Kong CFI disagreed because the inclusion of the phrase 'may be brought in those courts' found in other parts of the clause, and the limitation in the last sentence which meant that the company could litigate in jurisdictions other than Indonesia, made the clause non-exclusive.

Because non-exclusive clauses may have different effects, the words and phrases used are also helpful in determining their specific effects. In *Abdul Rashid*, the Singapore High Court examined whether the phrase 'irrevocably submit' altered the meaning of 'non-exclusive' in the clause.[279] The Court found that 'irrevocably' qualifies 'submit' but does not change the meaning of 'non-exclusive.'[280] Hence, no special meaning can be given,[281] and the clause was not transformed into a 'most appropriate jurisdiction' clause.[282]

In *Ho Siu Pui v Yue Sheng Finance Ltd*, the Hong Kong Court of Appeal was required to interpret a curiously worded Choice-of-Forum clause in a guarantee agreement:

> The laws of Hong Kong or the laws of the People's Republic of China are applicable to the formation … interpretation and the resolution of dispute … these matters are protected by the laws of both places. In the event of a dispute, Party A [ie Yue Sheng] has the right to choose to resolve the dispute via legal channel under the laws of Hong Kong or … People's Republic of China.[283]

Yue Sheng, the defendant, first argued that the clause was not a Choice-of-Forum clause but rather a Choice-of-Law clause.[284] The Court dismissed this argument because the second

[274] ibid 34.
[275] ibid.
[276] ibid.
[277] ibid.
[278] *Ko Lai* (n 160) [16].
[279] *Abdul Rashid* (n 149) 1055–56.
[280] ibid 1056.
[281] ibid 1055–56.
[282] ibid 1056.
[283] *Ho Siu Pui v Yue Sheng Finance Ltd* [2003] 1 HKC 621, 629 (CA).
[284] ibid 630.

sentence specifically referred to a 'legal channel' under either Hong Kong or Chinese law, which according to the Court implied resort to either Hong Kong or China's courts.[285] Second, Yue argued that under the clause, he had the option to choose the forum but not so Ho, the plaintiff in the Hong Kong action.[286] The Court again disagreed, as the clause clearly provided that 'these matters' (ie, disputes arising from the guarantee agreement) were protected by the laws of both places.[287] 'It would be idle to suggest that Hong Kong law and the jurisdiction of the Hong Kong courts can be excluded from the other party … at the whim of Yue Sheng.'[288] Likewise, the Court emphasised that since Ho was not a party to the Chinese action previously filed by Yue, the latter's right to choose the forum had not arisen against the former; therefore he could still exercise his right to choose the forum.[289]

In *Citibank*, the asymmetric Choice-of-Forum clause stated that the parties irrevocably submit to the non-exclusive jurisdiction of New York State and federal courts but the plaintiff Citibank had the right 'to commence any legal action or proceeding in any appropriate jurisdiction including without limitation … Indonesia'.[290] Furthermore, the clause stated

> [w]ithout limiting the foregoing, the [defendant] agrees that [Citibank] may at its option submit any dispute to any other District Court or to District Court where the [defendant]'s Deed of Establishment is registered or any court in Indonesia or elsewhere having jurisdiction over the [defendant's] assets.[291]

The Singapore High Court interpreted the clause as conferring on Citibank a right to sue based on the location of the defendant's assets.[292] Since the defendant had assets in Singapore, Citibank could file an action in Singapore.[293] The Court found that the clause reduced the significance of other factors, like convenience factors, the defendant's Indonesian nationality, and the tenuous connection of the dispute with Singapore.[294] Applying *Baiduri*,[295] the Court ruled that the defendant had failed to establish strong cause for a stay.[296]

(c) Ordinary and Special Meaning

Courts emphasise that words and phrases be given their ordinary meaning unless otherwise intended by the parties. The ordinary or 'plain' meaning is the meaning attributed by an ordinary reasonable person. In *The 'Jin Hui 588'*, the Hong Kong CFI interpreted the Choice-of-Forum clause – 'All disputes arising under and in connection with this Bill of Lading shall be determined by the Court in the Mainland of People's Republic of China.'[297] – as non-exclusive.[298] The Court found no clear indication of 'exclusivity' and questioned the logic of a Hong Kong company requiring a Hong Kong shipper to bring litigation in the

[285] ibid.
[286] ibid.
[287] ibid.
[288] ibid.
[289] ibid.
[290] *Citibank NA v Robert* [2011] 3 SLR 465, 471–72 (HC) ('*Citibank*').
[291] ibid 471–72.
[292] ibid 472.
[293] ibid.
[294] ibid.
[295] *Baiduri Bank Bhd v Dong Sui Hung* [2000] 2 SLR(R) 271 (HC).
[296] *Citibank* (n 290) 474.
[297] *The 'Jin Hui 588'* [2016] HKCFI 480, [6].
[298] ibid [22].

Chinese courts, regardless of relevance or convenience.[299] Hence, it stated: 'this court is not satisfied it is so obvious that it goes without saying [the Choice-of-Forum clause] is an exclusive jurisdiction clause'.[300]

When a contract confers special meaning on a provision, it may do so by explicitly defining certain words or phrases. Nonetheless, parties may also implicitly confer such special meaning based on the overall effect of the words and phrases they have used. In *Sun-Line (Management) Ltd v Canpotex Shipping Services Ltd*, Canpotex argued that the phrase 'this agreement may be made a rule of the court'[301] implied submission of the judgment debtors to English courts.[302] The Singapore High Court disagreed because the dispute resolution clause clearly stated arbitration in London, and nothing more.[303] Specifically, the phrase 'rule of the court' did not mean 'rules of the English courts' but 'rules of the arbitration proceedings'.[304] The Court, in short, deviated from the ordinary meaning of the word 'court' and conferred a different meaning – arbitration proceedings. This approach may have resulted from the overwhelming references to arbitration and its elements (eg, arbitrators, award) in the clause.[305] Furthermore, other than the phrase 'rule of the court', there were no explicit references to courts, or any presence of words associated with litigation. Hence, reading 'rule of the court' as conferring jurisdiction on the English courts would have deviated from the general nature of the dispute resolution clause, which was an arbitration clause.

Courts may look for alternative words which parties may use if they intended a different meaning. For example, in *OCBC Capital Investment Asia Ltd v Wong Hua Choon*, the non-exclusive Choice-of-Forum clause included a waiver of objections based on *forum non conveniens*.[306] The two-part clause was governed by Malaysian law and conferred non-exclusive jurisdiction on Malaysian courts.[307] The issue was whether this waiver extended to actions outside Malaysia. The Singapore High Court construed the waiver's scope narrowly by interpreting, '[p]roceedings in any court' to mean proceedings in any court in Malaysia only.[308] The Court said that if the parties had intended to extend the waiver to actions outside Malaysia, they should have used the word, 'jurisdiction' instead of court,[309] as appeared in the second paragraph of the same Choice-of-Forum clause where the plaintiff was given the right to file '[p]roceedings in any other jurisdictions'.[310] Accordingly, by using different words, the parties intended different meanings for 'court' and 'jurisdiction'.[311] Hence, the defendant could still validly raise objections based on *forum non conveniens* in the Singaporean action.[312]

[299] ibid [20].
[300] ibid.
[301] *Sun-Line (Management) Ltd v Canpotex Shipping Services Ltd* [1985–1986] SLR(R) 695, 697 (HC).
[302] ibid 699.
[303] ibid 703.
[304] ibid.
[305] See ibid 697.
[306] *OCBC Capital Investment Asia Ltd v Wong Hua Choon* [2010] 4 SLR 904, 908 (HC).
[307] ibid.
[308] ibid 909–10.
[309] ibid 909.
[310] ibid 909–10.
[311] ibid.
[312] ibid 910.

(d) To Harmonise and Clarify the Various Parts

Interpretation is an important tool to harmonise and clarify contradictory or ambiguous portions of the underlying contract or the Choice-of-Forum clause.[313] In *Shanghai Turbo*, the Singapore Court of Appeal interpreted the word 'submit' to clarify the relationship of the two named non-exclusive forums[314] mentioned in the phrase 'and each of the parties hereto submits to the non-exclusive jurisdiction of the Courts of Singapore/or People's Republic of China'.[315] The Court found the clause not 'too ambiguous to be enforceable',[316] stating that the parties must have meant submitting to the non-exclusive jurisdiction of *both* Singapore and China, 'and not that they *would* submit to the non-exclusive jurisdiction of the forum where a claim was subsequently brought'.[317] This is because the parties 'could not have known in advance where the claim will be brought [thus,] this could only mean that the parties submitted to the jurisdiction of *whichever* forum the claim was brought in, whether China or Singapore'.[318] Hence, the parties 'probably intended their *submission* to extend to the non-exclusive jurisdiction of *both* fora'.[319]

In *The Yaoki*, the bill of lading incorporated a 'charter party' agreement by reference but failed to identify whether it was the voyage or time charter party.[320] This situation raised problems because while the time charter party provided for a London arbitration, the voyage charter party contained an exclusive Choice-of-Forum clause stipulating the English High Court.[321] To add to the confusion, the bill of lading itself had its own arbitration clause.[322] Nonetheless, the Hong Kong CFI noted that both parties preponderantly never intended litigation,[323] and that the time charter party required certain provisions to be included in the bill of lading, which were.[324] Hence, the Court concluded that the bill of lading referred to the time charter party, ruling that disputes should go to arbitration,[325] and a stay was granted.[326]

A contract's headings should guide interpretation but should not control the meaning of its provisions, especially when the wording contradicts them. In *Mayar (HK) Ltd v Sayal*, the Hong Kong CFI considered whether the clause – '[Any] dispute or difference arising between the parties out of this agreement shall be governed by the Laws of Hong Kong'[327] – which had 'jurisdiction' as its heading, was a Choice-of-Forum or arbitration clause.[328] The Court ruled it was only a Choice-of-Law clause based on the wording of the clause (there

[313] See *Venetian Macau* (n 86) [24]; *HBZ Finance* (n 94) [30]; *Habib Finance International Limited v APL Co Pte Ltd* [2001] HKCFI 51, [8].
[314] *Shanghai Turbo* (n 140) 809.
[315] ibid 788.
[316] ibid 809.
[317] ibid 809–10.
[318] ibid.
[319] ibid 810.
[320] *The 'Yaoki'* [2006] HKCFI 479, [3].
[321] ibid.
[322] ibid [2].
[323] ibid [8]–[9].
[324] ibid [9]–[10].
[325] ibid [13]–[15].
[326] ibid [19].
[327] *Mayar (HK) Ltd v Sayal* [2005] 2 HKC 389, 392.
[328] ibid.

was no mention of a court).[329] Similarly, clauses labelled as 'forum of administration clauses' referring to Singapore courts as the forum for the administration of the Mandalay Trust, were interpreted to denote the supervisory and authorising court 'for actions the trustee may need to take' and were 'not intended to function as exclusive jurisdiction clauses for the settlement of disputes between trustees and beneficiaries'.[330]

When contracts are amended or supplemented, harmonising provisions may be necessary. In *Lembaga Pelabuhan Kelang v Kuala Dimensi Bhd*, the Malaysia Court of Appeal observed that the Choice-of-Forum clauses in the supplemental agreements effectively expressed the parties' 'predominant agreement to submit to the court's jurisdiction', and abandoning of the arbitration mentioned in the earlier versions.[331] In contrast, in *Gurkhas Construction Ltd v Craft Façade Tech (Hong Kong) Co Ltd*, the Hong Kong District Court required a 'clear intention of parties', such as phrases like 'unless otherwise agreed', to override an earlier arbitration clause with a later exclusive Choice-of-Forum clause.[332] Absent such intention, both clauses can operate in parallel.[333] Nonetheless, when multiple agreements exist, with each dealing with different aspects of their relationship, the proper test to ascertain the parties' intention 'is to identify the nature of the claim, and the agreement which has the closest connection with such claim and dispute'.[334] Hence, if the claim has the closest connection to a certain agreement, the dispute resolution mechanism contained in that agreement applies.[335]

(iv) Questions of Scope

Choice-of-Forum clauses should specify where an action may be filed. In Singapore, the 'good arguable case' test requires that the applicant for a stay establish that the matter in dispute falls within the clause's scope.[336] In *TMT*, the Singapore High Court emphasised that 'it would be natural to assume … that any jurisdiction clause would be intended to be given wide import, with all disputes being heard in the same court'.[337] This presumption, derived from the English case *Fiona Trust*,[338] – that rational parties likely intended all disputes from their relationship to be resolved in the same forum – has been applied to Choice-of-Forum clauses,[339] though originally applied to arbitration clauses. Nonetheless, this presumption can be overridden by a clear intent for separate dispute resolution mechanisms, or when certain matters are excluded,[340] and does not apply when multiple distinct contracts are involved.[341] However, it may potentially apply where the multiple agreements were 'part of a package of agreements which contained no competing jurisdiction clauses'.[342]

[329] ibid 394.
[330] *Ivanishvili v Credit Suisse Trust Ltd* [2020] SGCA 62, [76].
[331] *Lembaga Pelabuhan Kelang v Kuala Dimensi Bhd* [2011] 2 MLJ 606, 629; see also *Longlife International (Hong Kong) Co Ltd v May Delight Ltd* [2017] HKCFI 1381, [25].
[332] *Gurkhas Construction Ltd v Craft Façade Tech (Hong Kong) Co* Ltd [2021] HKDC 116, [87].
[333] ibid.
[334] *X v Y* [2020] HKCFI 2782, [46].
[335] See ibid.
[336] *Qompass* (n 45) [10].
[337] *TMT Co Ltd v The Royal Bank of Scotland plc (trading as RBS Greenwich Futures)* [2018] 3 SLR 70, 88.
[338] *Fiona Trust* (n 176).
[339] eg, *H v G* [2022] HKCFI 1327, [18].
[340] ibid [21].
[341] ibid [17]–[19].
[342] *Magnus Leonard Roth v Vitaly Petrovich Orlov* [2020] HKCFI 525, [37], citing *Etihad Airways v Lucas Flother* [2019] EWHC 3017 (Comm).

Choice-of-Forum clauses should also specify the types of disputes covered, though parties rarely list every possible type of case, action, proceedings or dispute. In *PT Selecta*, the Choice-of-Forum clause covered 'all disputes arising in connection with the contract including but not limited to the validity',[343] which the court found broad enough to include disputes involving existence[344] and validity.[345] In *Bunge SA v Shrikant Hasi*, it was decided that the phrase 'arising out of or in connection with' should also cover any disputes arising from pre-contractual conduct.[346] In *AJ Lucas (Hong Kong) Ltd v Drilltec GUT GmbH Grossbohr- und Umwelttechnik*,[347] the Hong Kong CFI interpreted 'any dispute whatsoever' to include both contractual and tort claims.[348] In *Hong Ziyun v Chan Kwan Ming*, the Hong Kong CFI concluded that disputes connected with another separate but interrelated contract (ie, second loan agreement), 'by its plain language', also fell within the scope of the exclusive Choice-of-Forum clause.[349] However, in *Ivanishvili*, the Singapore High Court ruled that the 'forum of administration clause' in the trust deed stating – 'the Courts of the Republic of Singapore shall be the forum of administration [of the trust deed]' – did not cover all types of trust-related litigation because there were certain aspects of the trust which could not be or were not intended to be covered by such clause.[350] In *Kyrox Sdn Bhd v International Sustainability & Carbon Certification System GmbH*, the Malaysia High Court found that when read with related contracts,[351] the exclusive Choice-of-Forum clause found in one document only applied to 'admissible disputes', which excluded the type of dispute being heard before the Malaysian court as expressly provided in another document.[352]

Interpretation should also aid courts with the relevant relief. In *Teo Choon Mong Frank v Wilh Schulz GmbH*, the Singapore Court of Appeal interpreted the Choice-of-Forum clause – which vested jurisdiction in the Singapore High Court to settle any dispute and differences touching on the interpretation or application of the shareholder agreement[353] – to include the power to issue interim injunctions.[354] Hence, the Court could issue relief which it may order in the usual exercise of its jurisdiction.

(v) *Choice-of-Court Convention*

The Choice-of-Court Convention presumes Choice-of-Forum clauses to be exclusive unless proven otherwise.[355] However, the Convention does not specify other interpretation rules, leaving it to forum law, specifically its choice of law rules, to guide the forum court. In Singapore, the interpretation rules under the applicable law therefore should determine

[343] ibid 738.
[344] ibid; see also *Okada* (n 138) [37].
[345] *PT Selecta* (n 138) 738.
[346] *Bunge* (n 176) [38].
[347] *AJ Lucas (Hong Kong) Ltd v Drilltec GUT GmbH Grossbohr- und Umwelttechnik* [2006] HKCFI 144.
[348] ibid [18].
[349] *Hong Ziyun v Chan Kwan Ming* [2019] HKCFI 2125, [30].
[350] *Ivanishvili, Bidzina v Credit Suisse AG* [2019] SGHC 6, [44].
[351] *Kyrox Sdn Bhd v International Sustainability & Carbon Certification System GmbH* [2022] MLJU 2639, [13]–[14] (HC Klang).
[352] ibid.
[353] *Teo Choon Mong Frank v Wilh Schulz GmbH* [1998] 2 SLR(R) 312, 314 (CA).
[354] ibid 318–19.
[355] Choice-of-Court Convention (n 22) art 3(b).

how courts interpret these clauses. If the applicable law is foreign law, its interpretation rules should be proven; otherwise Singapore courts will apply common law principles of contractual interpretation.

(vi) Singapore International Commercial Court

If the Choice-of-Forum clause designates the SICC, the parties are presumed to accept its exclusive jurisdiction, comply with its judgments or orders without delay, and waive recourse to courts or tribunals outside Singapore against any SICC judgment or order, as far as such recourse can be waived.[356] Under the SICC Rules, the Court must consider the international and commercial character of the transaction in deciding whether to stay or decline the action,[357] which necessarily should also apply in interpreting Choice-of-Forum clauses. For exclusive clauses under the Choice-of-Court Convention, its rules apply subject to supplementary application of the SICC Rules when not expressly provided.

C. The Philippines

Since Choice-of-Forum clauses are venue stipulations, their interpretation follows the principles applied in interpreting procedural matters. Without the required restrictive words, these clauses are to be viewed as 'agreement[s] on additional forum, not as limiting venue to the specified place',[358] thus warranting a liberal interpretation.[359] Notably, there is no presumption of exclusivity. Nonetheless, even when restrictive words are present, courts may liberally construe these clauses if needed to assist parties in obtaining just, speedy and inexpensive proceedings.[360]

Philippine courts may nonetheless interpret these clauses like any contractual term. In *KK Shell*, the Philippine Supreme Court needed to determine whether a sub-agent was bound by the Choice-of-Forum clause stipulating Japanese district courts.[361] In resolving the issue, the Court referred to the other provisions of the agreement,[362] and noted that neither the Choice-of-Forum clause nor the other provisions of the agency agreement made express reference to sub-agents.[363] Hence, pending further evidence to the contrary, the plaintiff sub-agent could proceed with its action in the Philippines.[364]

[356] Supreme Court of Judicature Act (Singapore) s 18F(1).
[357] Singapore International Commercial Court Rules of Court 2021 (Singapore, 2021) ord 1, r 3(1)(d).
[358] *Unimasters Conglomeration Inc v Court of Appeals* (1997) 267 SCRA 759, 769.
[359] ibid 773.
[360] See *HSBC* (n 32) 337.
[361] *KK Shell Sekiyu Osaka Hatsubaisho and Fu Hing Oil, Co Ltd v Court of Appeals* (1990) 188 SCRA 145, 151–52.
[362] ibid.
[363] ibid.
[364] ibid 152.

7

Mandatory Rules, Public Policy and International Interests: Singapore, Hong Kong, Malaysia, Philippines

I. The State and International Community in the Choice-of-Forum Clause Analysis

The forum state or another state, as well as the international community, have interests in the way Choice-of-Forum clause-related disputes are resolved. The use of the 'ouster principle' to prevent the enforcement of these clauses demonstrates the involvement of state interests in the Choice-of-Forum analysis. Eventually, support for the 'ouster principle' diminished and attitudes shifted towards enforcing Choice-of-Forum clauses because of growing acceptance of them as necessary features of international commerce and increasing support for party autonomy.[1] Nevertheless, state and international community interests remain important considerations in the Choice-of-Forum clause analysis, albeit articulated in a different manner.

This chapter discusses the role of forum state and international community interests in Choice-of-Forum clause disputes. It investigates the contentious and uneasy interface between public and private law by probing into how the various contemporary manifestations of state and international community interests, like mandatory rules, public policy, comity and other analogous concepts affect the resolution of substantive issues (eg, existence, validity and interpretation of clauses), applications for relief (ie, as factors considered during enforcement), and recognition and enforcement of foreign judgments. Special attention is given to the protection of weaker parties, particularly in the context of asymmetric agreements, standard-form contracts, and instances where vulnerable groups, like consumers, are involved.

II. Mandatory Rules

Mandatory rules embody important state interests and are applied 'regardless of whether a choice-of-law rule authorizes their application, and even if a choice-of-law rule calls for the application of another law'.[2] Their application by the forum is compulsory, even if a foreign

[1] See *The Bremen v Zapata Off-Shore Co*, 407 US 1, 12 (1972) ('*The Bremen*').

[2] Symeon Symeonides, *Private International Law: Idealism, Pragmatism, Eclecticism. General Course on Private International Law* (Brill Nijhoff, 2017) 164–65.

law characterises the legal relationship differently.[3] A breach of these rules, given the public interests involved, can also be considered breach of public policy, thus potentially voiding or rendering a contract unenforceable.[4]

While some statutes expressly declare a rule mandatory, its mandatory nature is often a matter of construction, only established conclusively after a court decision. Courts assess whether the rule protects some fundamental value or interest of the forum, or if 'the statutory objective was not intended to be circumvented by the existence of foreign elements in the dispute'.[5] Moreover, unlike in continental European jurisdictions where the concept of mandatory rules is well established,[6] common law courts may apply a provision akin to mandatory rules to render a contract illegal, void or unenforceable, without specifically labelling it as a 'mandatory' rule.[7]

The application of mandatory rules can impact Choice-of-Forum clauses in two ways: first, when the rule requires a different forum, and the court applies the mandatory rule regardless of the forum chosen, this renders the clause invalid or unenforceable because of 'strong cause';[8] second, when the mandatory rule overrides the applicable law, it can affect the validity or interpretation of the Choice-of-Forum clause.[9] Violation of mandatory laws can also prevent the recognition and enforcement of foreign judgments, although courts need to balance them with comity and other interests of the international community.[10]

A. Singapore, Hong Kong and Malaysia

In Singapore, examples of statutes with mandatory provisions include sections of the Unfair Contract Terms Act,[11] Carriage by Air Act,[12] Carriage by Air (Montreal Convention 1999) Act,[13] Carriage of Goods by Sea Act,[14] Securities and Futures Act,[15] Consumer Protection (Fair Trading) Act,[16] Pawnbrokers Act 2015,[17] and section 5 of the Civil Law Act which

[3] *Star City Pty Ltd v Tan Hong Woon* [2002] 1 SLR(R) 306, 322 (CA) ('*Star City*'); Yeo Tiong Min, 'Statute and Public Policy in Private International Law: Gambling Contracts and Foreign Judgments' [2005](9) *Singapore Year Book of International Law* 133, 135.

[4] *Star City* (n 3) 322; *Star Cruise Services Ltd v Overseas Union Bank Ltd* [1999] 2 SLR(R) 183, 222 (HC) ('*Star Services*').

[5] Yeo Tiong Min, *Articles on Singapore Law (2005)* (Singapore Academy of Law, 2005) para 6.3.2.

[6] See JJ Fawcett, 'Evasion of Law and Mandatory Rules in Private International Law' (1990) 49(1) *Cambridge Law Journal* 44, 57.

[7] See Trevor Hartley, 'Mandatory rules in international contracts: the common law approach' in Hague Academy of International Law (ed), *Collected Courses of the Hague Academy of International Law* (Brill Nijhoff, 1997) vol 266, 385.

[8] See *The 'Epar'* [1983–1984] SLR(R) 545, 552 (HC); *Brinkerhoff Maritime Drilling Corp v PT Airfast Services Indonesia* [1992] 2 SLR(R) 345, 357 (CA) ('*Brinkerhoff*'); *DFS Trading Ltd v Swiss Air Transport Co Ltd* [1997] 1 HKC 547, 551 (HC) ('*DFS*'); see also *Akai Pty Ltd v People's Insurance Company Ltd* [1996] HCA 39, [16].

[9] See *Brinkerhoff* (n 8) 357.

[10] See *Liao Eng Kiat v Burswood Nominees Ltd* [2004] 4 SLR(R) 690, 700, 703 (CA) ('*Liao*').

[11] Unfair Contract Terms Act 1997 (Singapore, cap 396, 2020 rev edn) s 27(2).

[12] Carriage by Air Act 1988 (Singapore, cap 32A, 2020 rev edn) sch 1, art 23.

[13] Carriage by Air (Montreal Convention, 1999) Act 2007 (Singapore, cap 32B, 2020 rev edn) sch 1, art 34.

[14] Carriage of Goods by Sea Act 1972 (Singapore, cap 33, 2020 rev edn) sch 1, art 3(8).

[15] Securities and Futures Act 2001 (Singapore, cap 289, 2020 rev edn) s 81SJ; *Goldilocks Investment Co Ltd v Noble Group Ltd* [2018] SGHC 108, [10].

[16] Consumer Protection (Fair Trading) Act 2003 (Singapore, cap 52A, 2020 rev edn) s 35.

[17] Pawnbrokers Act 2015 (Singapore) s 69.

prevents recovery of gambling debts.[18] In *The 'Epar'*, the Singapore High Court refused a stay after voiding the Choice-of-Forum clause stipulating Jakarta courts for contravening the Hague-Visby Rules.[19] In *Brinkerhoff*, the Singapore Court of Appeal interpreted the Warsaw Convention as mandatory,[20] thus voiding the clause containing both the chosen jurisdiction and law, and staying the proceedings in favour of Indonesia.[21]

In Hong Kong, ordinances which contain mandatory rules include the Carriage by Air Ordinance[22] which implements the Warsaw Convention, the Merchant Shipping (Limitation of Shipowner's Liability) Ordinance[23] which implements the 1974 Athens Convention, the Employment Ordinance,[24] the discrimination at work ordinances (the Sex Discrimination Ordinance,[25] the Family Status Discrimination Ordinance,[26] the Disability Discrimination Ordinance,[27] and the Race Discrimination Ordinance[28]) which contain express choice of law provisions, and the Labour Tribunal Ordinance which provides for the mandatory non-exclusion of the exclusive jurisdiction of Hong Kong's Labour Tribunal for employment-related cases.[29] While Hong Kong has no ordinance which expressly limits the choice of jurisdiction for consumer-related disputes, the Unconscionable Contracts Ordinance[30] has been argued to be capable of rendering a Choice-of-Forum clause unenforceable when relevant Hong Kong links are present.[31] Hence, the choice of (say) Swiss law and courts would not prevent a Hong Kong court from applying the mandatory jurisdictional provisions of the Warsaw Convention.[32]

The court need not fully override a Choice-of-Forum clause to enforce the mandatory law. In *Ghossoub*, the Hong Kong CFI ruled the exclusive English forum clause inoperative only to the extent that it deprived the plaintiff, a minority shareholder, of the right to file an unfair prejudice petition under Hong Kong's Companies Ordinance.[33] The Court of Appeal upheld this decision,[34] citing public policy considerations,[35] although this interpretation confirms the mandatory nature of section 724 of the Companies Ordinance.

In Malaysia, examples of statutes with mandatory provisions include the Carriage By Air Act 1974,[36] the Consumer Protection Act 1999,[37] and the Carriage of Goods by Sea

[18] Civil Law Act 1909 (Singapore, cap 43, 2020 rev edn) s 5; *Star Services* (n 4) 194; *cf Liao* (n 10) 695; *Las Vegas Hilton Corporation v Khoo Teng Hock* [1996] 2 SLR(R) 589, 601 (HC).

[19] *The 'Epar'* (n 8) 552.

[20] *Brinkerhoff* (n 8) 356.

[21] ibid.

[22] Carriage by Air Ordinance (Hong Kong) cap, 500 sch 1 art 32.

[23] Merchant Shipping (Limitation of Shipowners Liability) Ordinance (Hong Kong) cap 434, sch 1, art18.

[24] Employment Ordinance (Hong Kong) cap 57, s 70.

[25] Sex Discrimination Ordinance (Hong Kong) cap 480, s 87.

[26] Family Status Discrimination Ordinance (Hong Kong) cap 527, s 65.

[27] Disability Discrimination Ordinance (Hong Kong) cap 487, s 83.

[28] Race Discrimination Ordinance (Hong Kong) cap 602, s 81.

[29] Labour Tribunal Ordinance (Hong Kong) cap 25, s 7(2).

[30] Unconscionable Contracts Ordinance (Hong Kong) cap 458, s 5.

[31] Graeme Johnston and Paul Harris, *The Conflict of Laws in Hong Kong* (Thomson Reuters, 3rd edn, 2017) 135.

[32] *DFS* (n 8) 551.

[33] *Joseph Ghossoub v Team Y&R Holdings Hong Kong Ltd* [2016] HKCFI 1019, [111] ('*Ghossoub-CFI(1)*').

[34] ibid [31].

[35] ibid [43].

[36] Carriage By Air Act 1974 (Malaysia) sch 1, art 32.

[37] Consumer Protection Act 1999 (Malaysia) ss 4, 6.

Act 1950.[38] Also considered a possible mandatory rule is the rule against gambling contained in section 26 of the Civil Law Act 1956 and section 31 of the Contracts Act 1950.[39]

In Hong Kong, courts do not generally consider the mandatory rules of another jurisdiction.[40] Illegality in the place of performance appears to be the sole exception.[41] Nonetheless, in *Chen Er Hu v Wei Wen*, the Hong Kong CFI recognised the Chinese mandatory rules found in then articles 35(2) and 34(1) of the Chinese Civil Procedure Law precluding parties respectively from adopting Choice-of-Forum clauses which violate the hierarchy of Chinese courts or choosing a court that violates the *lex situs* rule for real property-related disputes.[42] While the repayment dispute involved a mortgaged property, the chosen court was not where the property was located.[43] The approach adopted by the Hong Kong court is probably because Hong Kong is now part of China, and thus recognising Chinese public policy is not recognising the public policy of another country. Likewise, the mandatory jurisdiction of Chinese courts aligns with the *lex situs* rule under common law.

In Singapore, the contravention of a foreign law is relevant only when the law is referred to by a choice of law rule, forum mandatory rule or fundamental policy of the forum.[44] Hence, in these circumstances, the foreign rule is not really 'mandatory' in the sense that its enforcement is compulsory in all circumstances.

Notably, a court may hesitate to use mandatory rules for issuing relief at the jurisdictional stage, unless the mandatory rule itself specifies the forum.[45] Hence, when a forum mandatory rule designates a foreign court as the mandatory jurisdiction for the dispute, such as in *Brinkerhoff*, the forum court shall issue a stay.[46] Furthermore, because in Singapore choice of law issues are not addressed at the jurisdictional stage, mandatory rules which have effects at the choice of law level may have limited impact. This applies similarly to non-exclusive Choice-of-Forum clauses.

When a forum mandatory rule provides that the dispute must be heard in the forum, an anti-suit injunction may be issued to prevent litigation in other venues. If the rule mandates a foreign forum and litigation is already in that forum, the application will be denied, unless litigation is taking place in another foreign forum. For example, when a party seeks an anti-suit injunction in a court located in a Warsaw Convention state and the forum is not among those enumerated under article 28(1) of the treaty, the court should deny the application, even if it is chosen in their Choice-of-Forum clause.

Those forum mandatory rules which designate a certain forum or affect the choice of law rule can also prevent the enforcement and recognition of foreign judgments in the forum court. Nonetheless, because of comity and international community interests involved in the enforcement of foreign judgments, the court may engage in a balancing of interests,

[38] Carriage of Goods by Sea Act 1950 (Malaysia) sch 1, art 3(8).

[39] *Jupiters Ltd v Gan Kok Beng* [2007] 7 MLJ 228, 240 (HC Kuala Lumpur); see Chen Chieng Ning, 'Recovery of Gambling Debts in Malaysia and Singapore' [2001] 1 *Malayan Law Journal* i.

[40] Johnston and Harris (n 31) 135.

[41] See eg, *Dow MBF Ltd v Detrick Ltd* [1987] 2 HKC 495 (CFI); *Bank of Credit and Commerce International (Overseas) Ltd v Bank of Credit and Commerce International (Overseas) Ltd – Macau Branch* [1997] HKCA 573.

[42] *Chen Er Hu v Wei Wen* [2023] HKCFI 2762, [20]–[21], [29].

[43] ibid [20].

[44] *Belfield International (Hong Kong) Ltd v Sheagar s/o T M Veloo* [2014] 1 SLR 24, 44 [61] (HC).

[45] *William Co v Chu Kong Agency Ltd* [1993] 2 HKC 377, 390 (HC).

[46] *Brinkerhoff* (n 8) 356.

rather than a straightforward denial.[47] However, when international interests and forum interests protected by the mandatory rule are aligned, there is a greater chance that the foreign judgment will be refused enforcement. Hence, when the foreign judgment violates the mandatory provisions of the Warsaw Convention and the originating and forum states are parties, its enforcement and recognition may be denied. Similarly, Singaporean courts may refuse enforcement and recognition under the Choice-of-Court Convention where the grounds under article 9 are present.[48] Under article 9(e), Singaporean courts may refuse recognition or enforcement when the foreign judgment is manifestly incompatible with Singapore's public policy and fundamental principles of procedural fairness,[49] which may arguably include contravention of its mandatory rules. The Choice-of-Court Convention, however, requires a high standard;[50] thus, such contraventions may only relate to constitutionally mandated principles of procedural fairness.[51]

B. The Philippines

The Philippines lacks an express doctrine of mandatory rules, although the Philippine Supreme Court has mentioned 'mandatory laws', along with domestic public policy, as standards which courts can use in deciding whether to recognise and enforce foreign judgments.[52] Article 17 of the Civil Code also mentions 'prohibitive laws' which 'shall not be rendered ineffective by laws or judgments promulgated, or by determinations or conventions agreed upon in a foreign country'.[53] However, whether 'mandatory laws' or 'prohibitive laws' are the same or similar to mandatory rules has not been articulated in Philippine case law. Furthermore, article 1306 of the Civil Code provides that contractual stipulations shall not be contrary to law. Tolentino, echoing the opinions of Spanish civilists, stresses that 'law' under article 1306 refers to laws which 'expressly declare their obligatory character … are prohibitive … express fundamental principles of justice … or which impose essential requisites without which the contract cannot exist'.[54] From this perspective, rules of a fundamental character, like the nationality restrictions and other limitations contained in article XII ('National Economy and Patrimony') of the Philippine Constitution, and laws enacted pursuant to these Constitutional provisions, can be considered mandatory rules.[55] Significantly, section 22 of article XII of the Philippine Constitution states that 'acts which circumvent or negate any of the provisions of this Article shall be considered inimical to

[47] See *Liao* (n 10) 703.

[48] Convention on Choice of Court Agreements, opened for signature 30 June 2005, 44 ILM 1294 (entered into force 1 October 2015) art 9 ('Choice-of-Court Convention'); Choice of Court Agreements Act (Singapore, cap 39A, 2020 rev edn) ss 14–15 ('CCAA').

[49] CCAA (n 48) s 14(c).

[50] Trevor Hartley and Masato Dogauchi, *Explanatory Report on the Convention of 30 June 2005 on Choice of Courts Agreements*, Permanent Bureau (ed) (Hague Conference on Private International Law, 2013) 71 ('Hartley-Dogauchi Report').

[51] ibid.

[52] *Fujiki v Marinay* (2013) 700 SCRA 69, 91 ('*Fujiki*').

[53] Civil Code (Philippines), art 17.

[54] Arturo Tolentino, *Commentaries and Jurisprudence on the Civil Code of the Philippines* (Central Professional Books, Inc, 1990) vol 4, 416.

[55] Constitution (Philippines), art 12, ss 1–22.

the national interest'.[56] Hence, when a contract operates within the scope of the article XII provisions (eg, mining operations, energy contracts, contracts on the operation of public utilities, etc), Philippine law shall be applied regardless of the applicable law.

Notably, there are other laws which contain provisions which may be characterised as 'mandatory', 'obligatory' or 'prohibitive'. These include the Carriage of Goods by Sea Act,[57] the Philippine Competition Act,[58] and the Consumer Act of the Philippines.[59] Although these laws do not directly provide for a forum which may override the stipulated forum in a Choice-of-Forum clause, they can arguably affect its validity, scope and interpretation.

In the Philippines, 'mandatory rules' can also be understood as rights that cannot be waived through contract, even if foreign law applies. Article 6 of the Civil Code states that waivers should not be contrary to law.[60] Thus, Choice-of-Forum clauses may be viewed as attempts to waive a right to invoke any of the venues provided in the Philippine Rules of Court. Certainly, not all rules on venue or jurisdiction are mandatory. There may be forums, however, like the Construction Industry Arbitration Commission where construction-related disputes must be settled, to which parties cannot waive access.[61]

Furthermore, 'mandatory' laws related to Choice-of-Forum clauses can impact substantive issues (ie, validity and interpretation) and the enforcement and recognition of foreign judgments. They may also affect the *forum non conveniens* analysis, in the sense that they represent important state interests and therefore may be considered by courts in justifying proceedings in the Philippines, regardless of the chosen forum.[62] They do not affect the grant of a motion to dismiss, as mandatory rules or similar concepts are not among the grounds for granting a dismissal of action.[63] They may be considered in the granting of preliminary injunctions if contravening a mandatory rule will amount to injustice for the applicant,[64] though applying this to Choice-of-Forum clauses is challenging, as 'mandatory rules' is an unfamiliar legal concept in the Philippines.

III. Public Policy

Since the early stages of development of private international law, public policy (or *ordre public*) has already been considered a limitation to conflict of laws rules' application. Notably, the ideas of Friedrich von Savigny,[65] Joseph Story,[66] and Pasquale Stanislao Mancini,[67] continue to shape understanding of public policy: (1) its compulsory character (2) its capacity to limit recognition of foreign acts and its intrinsic link with comity, and

[56] ibid art 12, s 22.
[57] Carriage of Goods by Sea Act (Philippines), s 3(8).
[58] Philippine Competition Act (Philippines), ss 14, 15, 20.
[59] Consumer Act of the Philippines (Philippines), art 106.
[60] Civil Code (Philippines), art 6.
[61] *National Irrigation Administration v Court of Appeals* (1999) 318 SCRA 255, 268.
[62] See *Saudi Arabian Airlines (Saudia) v Rebesencio* (2015) 746 SCRA 140, 169–70 ('*Saudia*').
[63] Rules of Court (Philippines), rule 16, s 1.
[64] ibid rule 58, s 3.
[65] Edgar Bodenheimer, 'The Public Policy Exception in Private International Law: A Reappraisal in the Light of Legal Philosophy' (1954) 12 *Seminar (Jurist)* 51, 53–54.
[66] ibid 56.
[67] ibid 57.

(3) its being territorial in scope and application. Each jurisdiction defines public policy differently, and it can vary depending on the context, nature or elements of the dispute. For example, the public policy in purely domestic disputes may be different in content and scope than that applicable in disputes with foreign elements. Moreover, public policy may be relevant to both substantive and procedural aspects of litigation and can apply at any stage. As with mandatory rules, the forum court can refer to its own public policy and, when the chosen law is foreign law, to the public policy of another state if allowed under forum rules. In the case of foreign public policy, it should be pleaded and proven according to the rules of evidence of the forum. Nonetheless, illegality under foreign public policy is generally considered during the merits stage, not at the jurisdictional stage.[68]

Public policy is drawn from a state's fundamental policies found in its constitution, statutes, court decisions and administrative issuances. It can stem from customs, practices, and public morals. Hence, concepts like public order, natural justice, customs, public morals and public interests are subsumed under, or interchangeably discussed with, public policy.[69] Furthermore, the content of public policy reflects ever-changing state interests and policies, and thus, it is expected to remain fluid in content and application.[70]

Public policy affects Choice-of-Forum clauses at different levels. First, it can render a Choice-of-Forum clause illegal, void or unenforceable by impacting its validity or existence, or can affect the clause through the contract's applicable law, thus, possibly varying its interpretation.[71] Second, public policy may be a factor in granting relief, such as in determining 'strong cause' for departing from exclusive clauses, or in applying the *forum non conveniens* test for non-exclusive clauses.[72] Third, it can prevent the recognition and enforcement of judgments or orders involving Choice-of-Forum clauses.[73] Although public policy can affect Choice-of-Forum clauses on many fronts, it is rarely invoked successfully in Singapore, Hong Kong or Malaysia.[74] In fact, the enforcement of these clauses is also a matter of public policy due to the emphasis on party autonomy.[75]

A. Singapore, Hong Kong and Malaysia

There are few cases in Singapore and Hong Kong, and apparently none in Malaysia, involving the application of public policy to Choice-of-Forum clauses. In *Ghossoub*, the Hong Kong CFI found the exclusive Choice-of-Forum clause 'inoperative' on public policy grounds, as it restricted the plaintiff's right as a minority shareholder to file an unfair prejudice petition

[68] *Trisuryo Garuda Nusa Pte Ltd v SKP Pradiksi (North) Sdn Bhd* [2017] 2 SLR 814, 836 (CA) ('*Trisuryo*').

[69] See eg, *Gabriel v Monte de Piedad* (1941) 71 Phil 497, 500–01; *Banque Nasionale de Paris v Wuan Swee May* [2000] 3 MLJ 587, 597 (HC Kuala Lumpur) ('*Banque Nasionale*').

[70] See *Banque Nasionale* (n 69) 597.

[71] See *Ghossoub-CFI(1)* (n 33) [111].

[72] eg, *Pacific Aerosupplies Limited v Dakota Air Parts, Intl Inc* [2011] HKCFI 438, [109] (CFI) ('*Pacific Aerosupplies*'); *Trisuryo* (n 68) 834.

[73] See *Compania Sud America de Vapores SA v Hin-Pro International Logistics Ltd* [2016] HKCFA 79, [59] ('*Compania Sud*'); *Wynn Las Vegas, LLC v Mong Henry* [2009] HKCFI 653, [33] ('*Wynn-Mong*'); *China North Industries Investment Ltd v Ronald RC Chum* [2006] HKCFI 407, [85] ('*China North*').

[74] See Johnston and Harris (n 31) 170.

[75] *Chinachem Financial Services Ltd v Century Venture Holdings Ltd* [2015] HKCFI 20, [88].

under Hong Kong's Companies Ordinance.[76] However, allegations of illegality should be established with evidence and cannot generally be summarily dismissed at the jurisdictional stage.[77]

Public policy can be considered as a 'strong cause' factor. In *Pacific Aerosupplies Limited v Dakota Air Parts, International Inc*, the Hong Kong CFI found strong cause not to enforce an exclusive Choice-of-Forum clause stipulating Hong Kong courts[78] due to United States national security concerns in the dispute.[79] The dispute involved breaches of a military-related contract,[80] which is probably what prompted the Court to say that 'matters of US public policy [are better] decided by the US Court'.[81] Hence, the Court refused to grant leave to serve outside Hong Kong.

In *Trisuryo Garuda Nusa Pte Ltd v SKP Pradiksi (North) Sdn Bhd*, the Singapore Court of Appeal stressed that merely invoking foreign public policy is not enough to displace Singapore courts' jurisdiction.[82] Nonetheless, the Court noted that foreign public policy could be considered in granting a stay, depending on the facts and circumstances of the case, including the nature of the foreign policy involved,[83] which must be proven in evidence.[84] In this case, the Court rejected the Indonesian public policy argument[85] that prohibited the holding of shares in a foreign company on trust,[86] but found 'strong cause' not to stay proceedings due to inadequate relief in Indonesia, despite the exclusive Choice-of-Forum clause stipulating Indonesian courts.[87]

Public policy may also be invoked to prevent the enforcement and recognition of foreign judgments, though it has rarely succeeded. In *Compania Sud*, the English judgment which awarded damages for breach of an exclusive Choice-of-Forum clause was enforced in Hong Kong because it did not conflict with the latter's public policy and comity towards Mainland Chinese courts,[88] and the award of damages related to contractual breach.[89] In *Wynn Las Vegas, LLC v Mong Henry*, the Nevada judgment arising from a gambling debt (which had an exclusive jurisdiction clause stipulating Nevada courts) was enforced in Hong Kong, as public policy against encouraging excessive gambling could not deny the creditor's right to repayment.[90] In *China North Industries Investment Ltd v Ronald RC Chum*, the Hong Kong CFI recognised the Bermuda judgment, preventing the plaintiffs from relitigating,[91] even though the foreign judgment allegedly resulted from 'badly managed litigation', which would still not amount to contravention of Hong Kong's public policy.[92]

[76] *Ghossoub-CFI(1)* (n 33) [111]; see *Ghossoub* [2017] HKCA 298, [31].
[77] *Suen Kwai Kam v Central China Dragon Select Growth Fund* [2020] HKCFI 69, [22]–[23].
[78] *Pacific Aerosupplies* (n 72) [22].
[79] ibid [109].
[80] ibid [4].
[81] ibid [109].
[82] *Trisuryo* (n 68) 834.
[83] ibid.
[84] ibid.
[85] ibid 846.
[86] ibid 832.
[87] ibid 848.
[88] *Compania Sud* (n 73) [59].
[89] See ibid [57]–[59].
[90] *Wynn-Mong* (n 73) [31]–[33].
[91] *China North* (n 73) [58], [86], [90].
[92] ibid [85].

In Malaysia, Islamic notions of morality, such as the prohibition against penalty interest (*riba*), play a significant role in Islamic banking and finance contracts. In *Tahan Steel Corporation Sdn Bhd v Bank Islam Malaysia Bhd*,[93] the court denied an injunction, noting that because Islamic law forbids penalty interest, Islamic banks may not be compensated for losses arising from delayed payments because of an injunction. Notably, the court framed this effect on Islamic banks as a public policy issue. While the case did not involve Choice-of-Forum clauses, it establishes that Islamic rules and principles are relevant to international commercial contracts related to Islamic banking and finance when *Shariah* law is chosen as the governing law, in the context of applications for anti-suit injunctions, and during the interpretation and determination of scope of Choice-of-Forum clauses.

B. Choice-of-Court Convention

Under article 6 of the Choice-of-Court Convention, non-chosen courts must suspend or dismiss proceedings unless 'giving effect to the agreement would lead to a manifest injustice or would be manifestly contrary to the public policy of the State of the court seised'. Nonetheless, since the phrase 'manifestly contrary' qualifies this ground for refusal, the standard imposed for breaches of public policy is high.[94] Singapore's CCAA has retained the same threshold and Singapore courts have interpreted 'manifestly contrary' as 'definitely recognisable as such' and not 'mere violations of a mandatory rule'.[95] Hence, these breaches cannot be a 'speculative possibility',[96] and instead must be 'clear and extremely serious.'[97]

The Hartley-Dogauchi Report clarifies that 'public policy' includes 'basic norms or principles of that State',[98] excluding cases where the chosen court might technically violate a mandatory rule of the court seised,[99] or where '[the Choice-of-Forum clause] is not binding under the [forum court's] domestic law'.[100] However, the report is unclear as to 'what' mandatory rule these exclusions are referring to here and 'how' the mandatory rule might be violated 'in some technical way'. Probably, the report is referring to technical violations of procedural rules, which in certain countries may be characterised as 'violations of mandatory rules'[101] or even, 'procedural injustice'.[102] But not all technical procedural violations would be 'manifestly contrary to the public policy of the court seised'. Hence, unless these 'technical violations' reach that level, they should not prevent enforcing an exclusive Choice-of-Forum clause.

[93] *Tahan Steel Corporation Sdn Bhd v Bank Islam Malaysia Bhd* [2004] 6 MLJ 1 (HC Kuala Lumpur).
[94] Hartley-Dogauchi Report (n 50) 61.
[95] *Re Thresh (British Steamship Protection and Indemnity Association Ltd)* [2023] SGHC 337, [39].
[96] *6DM (S) Pte Ltd v AE Brands Korea Ltd* [2021] SGHC 257, [67].
[97] *Qompas Voyage Ltd v APACPAY Pte Ltd* [2023] SGHCR 20, [35].
[98] ibid.
[99] ibid.
[100] ibid.
[101] See, eg, Paul Oberhammer, 'Party Autonomy and Procedural Law: A Few Comments from an Austrian Perspective' in Mattias Dahlberg (ed), *Party Autonomy – Civil Procedural Views on Party Autonomy, Franz Klein, EU Law and more* (Iustus Förlag, 2011) 51, 61.
[102] See, eg, Ronald Brand and Paul Herrup, *The 2005 Hague Convention on Choice of Court Agreements: Commentary and Documents* (Cambridge University Press, 2009) 93.

Public policy is also a ground for refusing recognition and enforcement of foreign judgments under article 9 of the Choice-of-Court Convention. Article 9(e) allows a state's public policy to prevent enforcement, especially where the proceedings violated 'fundamental principles of procedural fairness of that State'. As with article 6, the threshold imposed is high, with emphasis on procedural fairness because 'in some countries fundamental principles of procedural fairness (also known as due process of law, natural justice or right to fair trial) are constitutionally mandated'.[103] Hence, it might be unconstitutional to recognise a foreign judgment obtained under such circumstances.[104] Furthermore, substantive public policy objections arise when recognition and enforcement conflicts with the forum court's fundamental principles and rules.[105] However, 'it is the effect of the foreign judgment in the legal system which has to be contrary to the substantive public policy, not the judgment itself'.[106] Hence, this may prevent transnational issue estoppel from being allowed when the foreign judgment is perverse or reflects a sufficiently serious and material error.[107]

C. The Philippines

Parties are free to stipulate whatever contractual terms are convenient to them, but these must not violate public policy, morals, good customs or public order;[108] otherwise they are void.[109] Furthermore, Philippine courts, like those in common law jurisdictions, are prohibited from recognising or enforcing any foreign law, judgment, contract or claim that is offensive to the forum's public policy.[110]

In *Saudia*,[111] the Supreme Court emphasised that public policy is one of the *forum non conveniens* factors that courts should consider when enforcing the parties' choice of foreign forum.[112] When public interest weighs more heavily, courts 'should proceed in adjudicating the dispute, any doubt or contrary view arising from the preponderance of linkages notwithstanding'.[113] Furthermore, 'public interest' factors like clogged dockets or lack of expertise are considered independent of the parties' interests, and arguably, even when not raised by the parties. Moreover, the scope of public policy in conflicts cases is as wide as in purely domestic cases. When deciding whether to recognise and enforce foreign judgments, courts may apply 'domestic public policy',[114] 'local standards',[115] and 'constitutional values',[116] in their review.[117]

[103] Hartley-Dogauchi Report (n 50) 71.
[104] ibid.
[105] *Merck Sharp & Dohme Corp (formerly known as Merk & Co, Inc) v Merck KGaA (formerly known as E Merck)* [2021] SGCA 14, [58].
[106] ibid.
[107] ibid.
[108] Civil Code (Philippines) art 1306.
[109] ibid art 1409.
[110] *Bank of America NT&SA v Court of Appeals* (2003) 400 SCRA 156, 762.
[111] *Saudia* (n 62).
[112] ibid 168–70.
[113] ibid 170.
[114] *Fujiki* (n 52) 91.
[115] *Mijares v Ranada* (2005) 455 SCRA 397, 420.
[116] ibid 421.
[117] ibid.

Saudia also seems to allow the recognition of foreign public policy in the Philippines. '[The court] must, thus, determine if the interests of the sovereign (which acts through it) are outweighed by those of the alternative jurisdiction'.[118] Hence, if foreign public policy outweighs local public policy, the Philippine court may consider itself *forum non conveniens*. Foreign public policy, however, must be pleaded by parties and proven as a fact according to the rules of evidence.[119]

Employment contracts involving overseas Filipino workers are considered imbued with public interest; thus 'otherwise applicable Philippine laws and regulations cannot be rendered illusory by the parties agreeing upon some other law to govern their relationship'.[120] This stems from section 3, article III of the Constitution which provides: 'The State shall afford full protection to labor, local and overseas, organized and unorganized, and promote full employment and equality of employment opportunities for all'. Likewise, article 1700 of the Civil Code states: 'The relations between capital and labor are not merely contractual. They are so impressed with public interest that labor contracts must yield to the common good'. In *Pakistan International Airlines v Ople*, the exclusive choice of Karachi courts in the Choice-of-Forum clause contained in a Filipino flight attendant's employment agreement with Pakistan International Airlines was not enforced because 'the multiple and substantive contacts [of the dispute with] Philippine law and Philippine courts … point to the Philippine courts and administrative agencies as a proper forum for the resolution of contractual disputes between the parties',[121] thus the Choice-of-Forum clause cannot 'oust Philippine agencies and courts of the jurisdiction vested upon them by Philippine law'.[122] In *Saudia*, the flight attendant's illegal termination of employment due to her pregnancy made this case 'immutably a matter of public interest and public policy'.[123] Hence, 'the immense public policy considerations attendant … behove Philippine tribunals to not shy away from their duty to rule'.[124] However, when an overseas Filipino contracted in a foreign country to work in another foreign country, and all the facts relevant to the dispute occurred in the latter, with the Philippines having no connection except the plaintiff's Filipino nationality, the Philippine court or administrative tribunal may consider itself *forum non conveniens*.[125]

IV. Comity and International Interests

Comity, according to Huber, allows the recognition of foreign acts beyond the territorial boundaries of states.[126] The principle is largely based on the formulation in *Hilton v Guyot*,[127]

[118] *Saudia* (n 62) 170.
[119] Rules of Court (Philippines), rule 132, s 24.
[120] *Pakistan International Airlines Corp v Ople* (1990) 190 SCRA 90, 103.
[121] ibid.
[122] ibid.
[123] *Saudia* (n 62) 174.
[124] ibid 144–45.
[125] See, eg, *Manila Hotel Corporation v National Labor Relations Commission* (2000) 343 SCRA 1, 12–14.
[126] See Irina Getman-Pavlova, 'The Concept of "Comity" in Ulrich Huber's Conflict Doctrine' (*Working Paper No BRP 13/Law/2013*, National Research University Higher School of Economics, 2013) 8; see also Hessel Yntema, 'The Historic Bases of Private International Law' (1953) 2(3) *American Journal of Comparative Law* 297, 306.
[127] *Hilton v Guyot*, 159 US 113, 163–64 (1895).

which has been cited by courts in several jurisdictions including Singapore,[128] Malaysia[129] and the Philippines.[130] Nonetheless, its application and operation in conflicts litigation are still largely misunderstood.[131] Briggs notes that comity operates positively (eg, assisting foreign courts in obtaining evidence, cooperation in insolvency proceedings, giving effect to judicial orders)[132] and negatively (eg, not asserting jurisdiction over an absentee defendant, not adjudicating because of *forum non conveniens*, not questioning the conclusiveness of foreign judgments or lawfulness of foreign state acts, not applying local law).[133] Notably, comity is important during the jurisdiction, choice of law, and recognition and enforcement of judgment stages, and has a complex relationship with the other factors in the choice of law analysis.

A. Singapore, Hong Kong and Malaysia

(i) Comity and Choice of Law

Comity is relevant at the choice of law stage as it helps courts to avoid unnecessarily extending the scope of local law,[134] while providing justification for applying foreign law.[135] It also prevents courts from passing judgment on another state's law and legal system.[136] In the context of Choice-of-Forum clauses, comity means courts should not arbitrarily apply local law to determine their existence, validity and interpretation. Limitations or problems of the foreign legal system are only recognised in exceptional cases when argued as a factor during the enforcement of Choice-of-Forum clauses.

(ii) Comity and the Enforcement of Choice-of-Forum Clauses

When exclusive Choice-of-Forum clauses are involved, granting leave to serve out of jurisdiction or a stay to enforce the Choice-of Forum clause is consistent with contract enforcement and comity.[137] For non-exclusive clauses, comity is a factor considered under the *forum non conveniens* principle.[138] Since *forum non conveniens* is rooted in comity,[139] if a case is already pending in the chosen court, comity supports granting a stay. However, if no case is pending in the foreign court, comity may play a lesser role in the decision.

[128] eg, *The 'Reecon Wolf'* [2012] 2 SLR 289, 297–98 ('*The Reecon Wolf*').
[129] eg, *Sakuragawa Pump S Pte v Perkapalan Mesra Sdn Bhd* [2007] 7 MLJ 555, 560 (HC Kuching).
[130] eg, *JA Sison v The Board of Accountancy* (1949) 85 Phil 276, 282.
[131] eg, Adrian Briggs, *The Principle of Comity in Private International Law* (Brill Nijhoff, 2012) 77–78, 87–88.
[132] ibid 85.
[133] ibid.
[134] ibid 108–9; see *Rickshaw Investments Ltd v Nicolai Baron von Uexkull* [2007] 1 SLR(R) 377, 397 (CA); *Q & M Enterprises Sdn Bhd v Poh Kiat* [2005] SGHC 155, [25].
[135] See *Trisuryo* (n 68) 834.
[136] See *The 'Hung Vuong-2'* [2000] 2 SLR(R) 11, 20 (CA); *The 'Asian Plutus'* [1990] 1 SLR(R) 504, 514 (HC); *Oriental Insurance Co Ltd v Bhavani Stores Pte Ltd* [1997] 3 SLR(R) 363, 371 (CA); *Sea Powerful* [2016] 2 HKC 566, 583 (CFI); *Lehman Brothers Special Financing Inc v Hartadi Angkosubroto* [1998] 3 SLR(R) 664, 678 (HC); *The 'Rainbow Joy'* [2005] 3 SLR(R) 719, 725 (CA); see also Briggs (n 131) 109.
[137] *Yantai Wanhua Polyurethanes Co Ltd v Pur Products Ltd* [2012] HKCFI 1992, [29].
[138] See *The 'Reecon Wolf'* (n 128) 297.
[139] *The 'Rainbow Joy'* [2005] 3 SLR(R) 719, 725 (CA).

(iii) Comity and Anti-Suit Injunctions

When an injunction enforces an exclusive Choice-of-Forum clause, it is viewed as contractual enforcement and 'the question of international comity is not as relevant'.[140] In contrast, when an anti-suit injunction is issued following the application of the *forum non conveniens* principle, like in cases involving non-exclusive Choice-of-Forum clauses, '[c]onsiderations of comity are necessary given the impact a grant of an anti-suit injunction would have on foreign proceedings'.[141] In *Sea Powerful*, the Hong Kong Court of Appeal characterised an anti-suit injunction as 'an intrusion or obstruction of the judicial sovereignty of the Chinese courts';[142] thus, to order the plaintiff to halt existing foreign proceedings may be regarded as offensive to comity.[143]

Comity can also factor into decisions on anti-suit injunctions, especially in determining whether the instituted or threatened foreign proceedings are vexatious or oppressive, particularly when the Choice-of-Forum clause is non-exclusive. In *BSNC*, the Malaysia Court of Appeal emphasised the proper approach – 'a court must have regard to all the circumstances of the case including such matters as comity … and the need to exercise caution when restraining foreign proceedings'.[144]

(iv) Comity and the Recognition and Enforcement of Foreign Judgments

Comity prevents courts from reviewing foreign judgments unless there is a breach of fundamental principles of law. According to Briggs, comity requires that foreign adjudications be respected without questioning them, and 'explains that the compulsion in a foreign judicial order is confined to the foreign state and has no effect, as compulsion or as entitlement in England (the forum court)'.[145] Nonetheless, when the enforcement of a foreign judgment is the subject of private agreements between parties,[146] Briggs notes that comity is not offended because 'comity would not require the non-recognition of the judgments in the first place'.[147] In *Compania Sud*, the enforcement of English-court awarded damages in Hong Kong did not offend comity[148] because the damages can be considered a necessary consequence of the parties' contract.

B. The Philippines

In the Philippines, comity justifies non-exercise of jurisdiction under the *forum non conveniens* principle.[149] However, when the Philippines has the strongest connection to the

[140] *John Reginald Stott Kirkham v Trane US Inc* [2009] 4 SLR(R) 428, 446 (CA); *UBS AG v Telesto Investments Ltd* [2011] 4 SLR 503, 541 (HC); *Compania Sud* (n 73) [56]–[58].

[141] *Morgan Stanley Asia (Singapore) Pte (formerly known as Morgan Stanley Dean Witter Asia (Singapore) Pte) v Hong Leong Finance Ltd* [2013] 3 SLR 409, 422 (HC).

[142] *Sea Powerful II Special Maritime Enterprises (ENE) v Bank of China Ltd* [2016] 1 HKCA 205, [23].

[143] *Indian Corridor Sdn Bhd v China Idea Development Ltd* [2008] HKCFI 88, [16].

[144] *BSNC Leasing Sdn Bhd v Sabah Shipyard Sdn Bhd* [2000] 2 MLJ 70, 91 (CA Kuala Lumpur).

[145] Briggs (n 131) 150.

[146] ibid 152.

[147] ibid 153.

[148] See *Compania Sud* (n 73) [57]–[59].

[149] eg, *Saudia* (n 62) 164.

dispute, comity plays little or no role,[150] with legal reasoning usually shifting to protecting local sovereignty.[151] Moreover, Philippine courts may assess the fitness of the foreign forum based on 'the availability and adequacy of recourse to a foreign tribunal'.[152] In *Saudia*, the Philippine Supreme Court characterised this requirement as a matter of practical 'viability'.[153] Hence, it may review: 'exigencies, like the statute of limitations, capacity to enforce orders and judgments, access to records, requirements for the acquisition of jurisdiction, and even questions relating to the integrity of foreign courts'.[154] However, whether this evaluation aligns with comity, even under the guise of evaluating practical 'viability', was not addressed by the Supreme Court. Nonetheless, the recognition and enforcement of foreign judgments in the Philippines is grounded in comity.[155]

V. The Choice-of-Forum Clause and Protecting Weaker Parties

The rationale for protecting weaker parties is their vulnerability to abuse due to unequal bargaining power, leading to contracts containing terms which are asymmetrically in favour of the much stronger party, to the prejudice of the weaker party.[156] Hence, such asymmetric contracts are seen problematic, unfavourable or undesirable. In *The 'Eastern Trust'*, the Singapore High Court recognised that courts may intervene to help another party in instances where there is an 'overwhelming [discrepancy in] bargaining power', albeit only exceptionally.[157] In Asian jurisdictions, this issue is compounded by difficulties in understanding English language contracts and other translation issues.

Unequal bargaining power also affects Choice-of-Forum clauses, as these clauses may deprive weaker parties of court access and their procedural rights. Hence, contractual remedies to address unequal bargaining power have been applied to cases involving 'problematic' Choice-of-Forum clauses. In addition, international and regional legal instruments, such as the Brussels Convention[158] and the subsequent Brussels I Regulation[159] and Brussels I Recast,[160] have provided specific remedies and approaches, including modifying the effect of Choice-of-Forum clauses. In Singapore, Hong Kong, Malaysia and the Philippines, the problem of unequal bargaining power in Choice-of-Forum clauses is addressed through the contract law principles of unconscionability, undue influence, public policy and mandatory rules, and through special statutes.[161]

[150] See *Philippine National Construction Corp v Asiavest Merchant Bankers (M) Berhad* (2015) 767 SCRA 458, 483.
[151] See *Hong Kong and Shanghai Banking Corporation v Sherman* (1989) 176 SCRA 331, 338 ('*HSBC*').
[152] *Saudia* (n 62) 169.
[153] ibid.
[154] ibid.
[155] *Ingenohl v Walter E Olsen & Company, Inc* (1925) 47 Phil 189, 239.
[156] See, eg, *Fry v Lane* (1888) 40 Ch D 312, 322.
[157] *The 'Eastern Trust'* [1994] 2 SLR(R) 511, 518–19 (HC); also *The 'Vishva Apurva'* [1992] 1 SLR(R) 912, 927 (CA) citing *The Bremen* (n 1) 12.
[158] Convention on Jurisdiction and the Enforcement of Judgments in Civil and Commercial Matters, opened for signature 27 September 1968, 1262 UNTS 153 (entered into force 1 February 1973), arts 5, 7–12a, 13–15, 17.
[159] Council Regulation (EC) No 44/2001 of 22 December 2000 on jurisdiction and the recognition of judgments in civil and commercial matters [2001] OJ L 012/1, arts 8–13, 15–17, 18–21.
[160] Regulation (EU) No 1215/2012 of the European Parliament and of the Council of 12 December 2012 on Jurisdiction and the Recognition and Enforcement of Judgments in Civil and Commercial Matters [2012] OJ L 351/1, arts 10–16, 17–19, 20–21, 26(2), 31, 45 ('Brussels I Recast').
[161] Unfair Contract Terms Act (Singapore) (n 11); Misrepresentation Act (Singapore, cap 390, 1994 rev edn) s 3; Consumer Protection (Fair Trading) Act (Singapore) (n 16); Unconscionable Contracts Ordinance 1994 (Hong

The analysis of unequal bargaining power in the context of Choice-of-Forum clauses necessarily involves balancing party autonomy (ie, the intention of the parties) and the state's interest in protecting weaker parties. To proceed with such an analysis, however, one needs to first characterise the situation as a case involving inequality of bargaining power. This threshold question is difficult to answer, and often treated as a given, without much articulation.[162] Current literature has highlighted the difficulty of ascertaining what constitutes 'unequal' bargaining power, what constitutes 'weaker parties', the required 'threshold' of inequality which can trigger the provision of remedies, and other details like evidence, burden of proof, etc.[163] Furthermore, there has also been difficulty reconciling this need to protect weaker parties with the existing legal doctrines and approaches under contract law. In common law, there is historical allegiance to contractual freedom. As such, there is no doctrinal constraint on stronger parties from exercising their relatively stronger bargaining power during contractual negotiations, or any obligation to negotiate in good faith. Instead, the *caveat emptor* principle prevails. Parties are viewed as assuming contractual obligations to fulfil their needs or wants; hence, it is for them to determine the terms of their contract.

A. Asymmetric Choice-of-Forum Clauses

Asymmetric Choice-of-Forum clauses can be considered a manifestation of unequal bargaining power. In France, the *Cour de Cassation* has invalidated clauses allowing only one party to choose where to litigate.[164] Also known as 'unilateral optional jurisdiction clauses', they are commonly found in international financial agreements[165] and are often justified as a risk-management strategy to lower borrowing costs.[166] In the *Rothschild* case, however, the French *Cour de Cassation* did not consider these risk-management benefits but focused instead on the asymmetry, finding that the clause gave the bank an unreciprocated advantage over the borrower by giving it complete discretion where to commence litigation. Hence, the clause had a 'potestative' character (ie, conditioned completely on the will of the promisor), which is void under French law.[167]

Common law courts have taken a more benign approach to asymmetric clauses even if they reflect unequal bargaining power. Upholding contractual freedom, English courts have held unilateral optional agreements to be legitimate and enforceable. In *Baiduri*, clause 18 of the guarantee agreement stated that while both parties submit to the jurisdiction of the Brunei courts, the bank can enforce the guarantee in any court.[168] The Singapore High Court interpreted the clause as non-exclusive from the bank's perspective, while the

Kong) (n 30); Consumer Protection Act 1999 (Malaysia) (n 37), Consumer Protection (Amendment) Act 2010 (Malaysia); Consumer Act of the Philippines (Philippines).

[162] Max Helveston and Michael Jacobs, 'The Incoherent Role of Bargaining Power in Contract Law' (2014) 49(4) *Wake Forest Law Review* 1017, 1021.

[163] See ibid 1021–32.

[164] See Cour de cassation [French Court of Cassation], 11-26.022, *Madame X v Banque Privée Edmond de Rothschild*, 26 September 2012 ('*Rothschild*'); Cour de cassation [French Court of Cassation], 13-27.264, *ICH v Crédit Suisse*, 25 March 2015.

[165] Mary Keyes and Brooke Adele Marshall, 'Jurisdiction agreements: exclusive, optional and asymmetrical' (2015) 11(3) *Journal of Private International Law* 345, 346.

[166] ibid.

[167] ibid 370, citing *Rothschild* (n 164); see Civil Code (France) art 1304-2.

[168] *Baiduri Bank Bhd v Dong Sui Hung* [2000] 2 SLR(R) 271, 282 (HC).

defendants could only sue in Brunei.[169] Referring to a Brunei decision that the jurisdiction of Brunei courts under clause 18 was non-exclusive,[170] the Singapore court denied the stay application.[171] In *Industrial and Commercial Bank of China (Asia) Ltd v Wisdom Top International Ltd*, the Hong Kong CFI recognised the validity of asymmetric clauses in financial contracts, but refused to regard them as exclusive under the Choice-of-Court Arrangement.[172] They are only exclusive if the borrower commences the action, but non-exclusive if it is the lender.[173]

Like the French Civil Code, the Philippine Civil Code also prohibits 'potestative' obligations in article 1182 – '[w]hen the fulfillment of the condition depends upon the sole will of the debtor, the conditional obligation shall be void'.[174] Hence, if the choosing the venue relies solely on the will of one party, article 1182 may be invoked to void such Choice-of-Forum clause. However, because of their procedural nature, asymmetric clauses would nevertheless be considered unenforceable as venue stipulations for lacking the exclusivity required by the Rules of Court. Furthermore, the unequal bargaining power is a compelling reason to simply ignore the asymmetric clause especially 'with the view of promoting substantial justice'.[175] Hence, under Philippine law, an asymmetric clause may be difficult to enforce.

B. Consumers, Franchisees, Insured and Small Businesses as Weaker Parties

Another approach to protecting weaker parties relies on stereotypes and characteristics, categorising certain parties as the 'weaker party' according to the type of transaction involved. Hence, consumers in consumer transactions, franchisees in franchise contracts, the insured in insurance contracts, and small businesses in business-to-business transactions are considered the 'weaker party'. Their very status in the transaction is the justification for their protection.

Consumers receive the most protection, and all four jurisdictions have consumer protection laws which may be extended to render void or unenforceable Choice-of-Forum clauses. The consumer laws of Singapore,[176] Hong Kong,[177] and Malaysia,[178] however, do not specifically deal with such clauses but may nonetheless void, limit, sever or alter them

[169] ibid 285.
[170] ibid 283.
[171] ibid 285.
[172] *Industrial and Commercial Bank of China (Asia) Ltd v Wisdom Top International Ltd* [2020] HKCFI 322, [52]; see also *Union Bank of India v Glory Universal Group Inc* [2020] HKCFI 3057, [31]; *China Construction Bank (Asia) Corporation Ltd v Zhang Kangyang* [2022] HKCFI 2135, [34]; *Transasia Private Capital Ltd v Cheng Yu* [2022] HKCFI 1295, [21]; *China Merchants Heavy Industry Co Ltd v JGC Corporation* [2000] HKCFI 544.
[173] ibid [58].
[174] Civil Code (Philippines) art 1182.
[175] See *Santos v Court of Appeals* (1979) 90 SCRA 223, 226.
[176] Consumer Protection (Fair Trading) Act 2003 (Singapore) (n 16).
[177] Unconscionable Contracts Ordinance (Hong Kong) (n 30).
[178] Consumer Protection Act 1999 (Malaysia) (n 37); see also Adnan Trakic, 'Statutory protection of Malaysian consumers against unfair contract terms: Has enough been done?' (2015) 44(3) *Common Law World Review* 203, 212–13.

because these terms may be considered unconscionable, unfair or illegal under their relevant consumer statutes.[179] Notably, these consumer laws mandatorily apply regardless of the chosen law[180] and cannot be waived.[181]

In contrast, the Consumer Act of the Philippines[182] does not specifically deal with unfair, unreasonable, oppressive or unconscionable contract terms. Nonetheless, the Civil Code may void unconscionable contract terms, as the obligation to observe fair dealing flows from article 19, which requires every person, in the exercise of his rights and in the performance of his duties, act with justice, give everyone his due, and observe honesty and good faith.[183] Hence, unlike in common law, the Philippines provides for a good faith obligation between contracting parties during the negotiation, birth and performance of the contract. Furthermore, unconscionable contract terms have also been considered contrary to morals and public policy.[184] The Supreme Court, however, has yet to apply the doctrine of contractual unconscionability to Choice-of-Forum clauses.

Insurance policyholders are specially protected under insurance legislation,[185] thus deviating from the *caveat emptor* principle which prevails in contract law,[186] because insurers have the obligation of utmost good faith.[187] Similarly, specific rules affecting Choice-of-Forum clauses are not found in insurance legislation. Nonetheless, Choice-of-Forum clauses in insurance contracts which are unconscionable, unfair or unreasonable may be voided under general contract law or consumer law.

In contrast, franchisees and small businesses do not receive specific legislative protection as weaker parties. Rather, these 'weaker parties' are protected through general contract law. The only exception is Malaysia, which has special legislation on franchising.[188]

As a party to the Choice-of-Court Convention, Singapore excludes consumer transactions from the Convention's scope.[189] A consumer is understood as a 'natural person acting primarily for personal, family or household purposes'.[190] Hence, Choice-of-Forum clauses in consumer contracts are governed by Singapore's Consumer Protection (Fair Trading) Act 2003 and any other applicable law validly chosen by the parties and consistent with the consumer protection law.

[179] Consumer Protection (Fair Trading) Act 2003 (Singapore) (n 16) sch 2, pt 1(13); Unconscionable Contracts Ordinance (Hong Kong) (n 30) cap 458, ss 5, 6(1); Consumer Protection Act 1999 (Malaysia) (n 37) ss 24C(1), 24D(1), 24G(1)–(2), 24g(2); see also Adnan Trakic, 'Statutory protection of Malaysian consumers against unfair contract terms: Has enough been done?' (2015) 44(3) *Common Law World Review* 203, 212–13.

[180] Consumer Protection (Fair Trading) Act 2003 (Singapore) (n 16) pt 2 s 3, pt 4 s 35; Unconscionable Contracts Ordinance (Hong Kong) (n 30) cap 458, s 7(2); Consumer Protection Act 1999 (Malaysia) (n 37) s 4.

[181] Consumer Protection (Fair Trading) Act 2003 (Singapore) (n 16) ibid pt 4, s 35.

[182] Consumer Act of the Philippines (Philippines).

[183] Civil Code (Philippines), art 19.

[184] *Malinao v National Labor Relations Commission* (1999) 319 SCRA 65, 74–75; *Imperial v Jaucian* (2004) 427 SCRA 517, 525 ('*Imperial*') 525; *State Investment House Inc v Court of Appeals* (2001) 361 SCRA 201, 208.

[185] Insurance Act 1966 (Singapore, cap 142, 2020 rev edn); Insurance Ordinance (Hong Kong) cap 41; Insurance Act 1996 (Malaysia); Insurance Code 2013 (Philippines).

[186] See, eg, Simon Goh, 'Insurance Law' in Singapore Academy of Law, *Laws of Singapore* (webpage, 25 January 2019) para 24.4.1: https://www.singaporelawwatch.sg/Results/ch-24-insurance-law.

[187] See eg, ibid.

[188] See Franchise Act 1998 (Malaysia).

[189] Choice-of-Court Convention (n 48) art 2(1)(a).

[190] ibid art 2(1)(a).

C. Contracts-of-Adhesion

'Contracts of adhesion', a term popularised by Friedrich Kessler,[191] refers to contracts where the terms have not been negotiated or have been included as standardised terms or boilerplate provisions, or contracts made on a take-it-or-leave-it basis. Reflecting unequal bargaining power, being a 'contract-of-adhesion' can be considered an important factor in determining issues of validity, interpretation and the effect to be given to a Choice-of-Forum clause. Despite this, contractual freedom prevails; thus 'contracts-of-adhesion' are generally upheld as valid and enforceable, and seen as mechanisms which minimise costs and risks, and thus reduce prices.[192] The challenge, then, for the courts is to determine when to strike and aid 'weaker parties' without necessarily weakening the fundamental principle of contractual freedom.

In Singapore, Hong Kong and Malaysia, courts generally uphold contractual freedom by enforcing validly concluded contractual terms, including Choice-of-Forum clauses which are contracts-of-adhesion.[193] The non-negotiated nature of these clauses does not necessarily affect their validity, which is instead assessed based on general contract principles of unconscionability or undue influence, consumer laws, public policy, mandatory rules and other equitable doctrines. Notably, whether the contract is in standard form is a factor in determining whether a term is reasonable or unconscionable.[194] The Singapore High Court has rejected the approach in *British Aerospace*[195] – which argued that certain convenience factors may not be raised because the contract was not negotiated – because '[i]t is not possible to draw a bright-line between freely negotiated jurisdiction agreements and jurisdiction agreements found in contracts of adhesion'.[196]

Although standard-term Choice-of-Forum clauses are generally upheld, Philippine courts are willing to void them if they impose undue burden on weaker parties. Article 24 of the Civil Code requires vigilance in protecting a disadvantaged party 'on account of his moral dependence, ignorance, indigence, mental weakness, tender age or other handicap, the courts must be vigilant for his protection'.[197] Furthermore, in *Sweet Lines Inc v Teves*,[198] the Supreme Court refused to enforce a standard domestic Choice-of-Forum clause in a passenger ticket which provided for litigation only in the city where the headquarters of the shipping company were located and far from the passenger's habitual residence.[199] The Court justified this by noting the crowded conditions at the ports,[200] the lack of proper opportunity to examine the terms and conditions of the ticket,[201] the fact that the clause was

[191] Friedrich Kessler, 'Contracts of Adhesion – Some Thoughts about Freedom of Contract' (1943) 43(5) *Columbia Law Review* 629.
[192] ibid 631–32.
[193] See Lee Mason, 'Inadequacy and Ineffectuality: Hong Kong's Consumer Protection Regime Against Unfair Terms in Standard Form Contracts' (2014) 44 *Hong Kong Law Journal* 83, 84; see eg, *Lo Ka Lee Kelly t/a Leader Packing (HK) Co v Spiriant Asia Pacific Ltd* [2021] HKDC 1311, [68].
[194] eg, Consumer Protection Act 1999 (n 37) s 24D(2)(c).
[195] *British Aerosplace Plc v Dee Howard Co* [1993] 1 Lloyd's Rep 368, 376.
[196] *Abdul Rashid bin Abdul Manaf v Hii Yii Ann* [2014] 4 SLR 1042, 1053–54 (HC); *cf Deltatre SPA v Hong Kong Sports Industrial Development Ltd* [2018] HKCFI 1942, [46]; see *Vinmar Overseas (Singapore) Pte Ltd v PTT International Trading Pte Ltd* [2018] 2 SLR 1271, 1307 (CA).
[197] Civil Code (Philippines), art 24.
[198] *Sweet Lines Inc v Teves* (1978) 83 SCRA 361.
[199] ibid 371–72.
[200] ibid 371.
[201] ibid.

drafted solely for the benefit of the shipping line,[202] and that the nature of inter-island shipping in the Philippines virtually granted the shipping company a monopoly.[203] Significantly, the Court said that 'the bulk of those who board these inter-island vessels come from the low-income groups and are less literate, and who have little or no choice but to avail of petitioner's vessels'.[204] Given these 'peculiar circumstances', the Choice-of-Forum clause was declared void and unenforceable for being contrary to public policy.[205] Furthermore, Philippine courts construe contracts-of-adhesion against the drafter.[206]

VI. Refining the Framework

Keyes identifies three key interests influencing a court's exercise of jurisdiction: the interests of the parties, the interests of the forum state, and foreign and international community interests.[207] Chapter three discussed party interests while this chapter discusses state and international community interests. These three interests also shape how courts analyse Choice-of-Forum clause issues. Hence, the framework for addressing such issues may be refined to consider party interests, state interests, and the interests of the international community as further limiting the way courts resolve these issues. The illustration below demonstrates this:

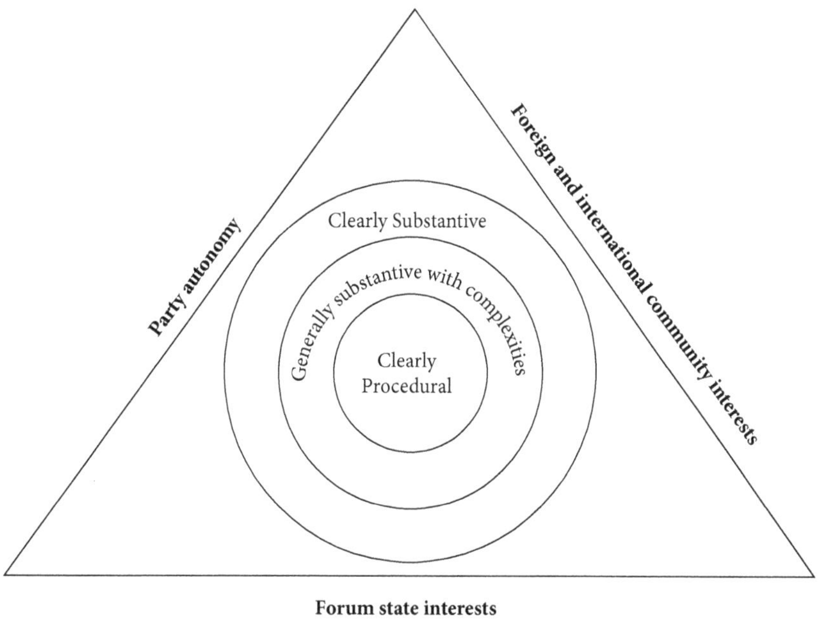

[202] ibid.
[203] ibid.
[204] ibid.
[205] ibid 370–72.
[206] *HSBC* (n 151) 339.
[207] Mary Keyes, *Jurisdiction in International Litigation* (Federation Press, 2005) 178–225.

8

Choice-of-Forum Clauses in Asian Civil Law Countries: China, Indonesia, Japan

I. The Civil Law Approach to Choice-of-Forum Clauses

The debate on the characterisation of Choice-of-Forum clauses, discussed in Chapter two, highlights differences between the common law and civil law approaches. Common law emphasises the private law nature of these clauses, focusing on *pacta sunt servanda.* In contrast, civil law views these clauses as procedural, treating them as 'expressions of consent' to the chosen jurisdiction (prorogation) or 'waivers' of jurisdiction of the court(s) which would otherwise have had jurisdiction over the dispute (derogation).[1] This approach underscores their public law character and role in the administration of justice, with no privately enforceable promises.[2] Instead, they function within a hierarchical framework of jurisdictional rules, which give preference to these clauses and operate as waivers to derogated jurisdictions.[3]

This chapter discusses three major civil law jurisdictions in Asia – China, Indonesia, and Japan – to identify, explore and explain similarities and differences between civil law and common law approaches in Asian jurisdictions, even among Asian civil law countries. Following the structure of the previous chapters, it discusses the remedies for enforcing Choice-of-Forum clauses, approaches to issues like existence, validity and interpretation of clauses, and the impact of mandatory rules, public policy and international interests. It also considers the relationship between Choice-of-Forum clauses and weaker parties.

II. China

A. Enforcement of Choice-of-Forum Clauses

(i) China's Approach to Jurisdiction

The National People's Congress ('NPC') is China's highest state organ,[4] with its Standing Committee as the permanent body.[5] Both exercise legislative power, while judicial power

[1] See eg, Mukkarrum Ahmed, *The Nature and Enforcement of Choice of Court Agreements* (Hart Publishing, 2017) 4; Adrian Briggs, *Agreements on Jurisdiction and Choice of Law* (Oxford University Press, 2008) 297–98.

[2] ibid 4.

[3] ibid; Briggs (n 1) 297–98.

[4] Constitution of the People's Republic of China (中华人民共和国宪法, Zhonghua Renmin Gongheguo Xianfa) 1982 (adopted 4 December 1982, revised 2018) *Gazette of the National People's Congress*, art 57 ('PRC Constitution').

[5] ibid art 57.

is exercised by the people's courts,[6] which are created, supervised and held accountable by the people's congresses.[7] The Supreme People's Court ('SPC'), the highest court and court of final appeal,[8] is responsible to the NPC and its Standing Committee. Other local courts are accountable to the state organs which created them.[9] The SPC supervises lower courts and specialist courts,[10] issues judicial interpretations on various questions of Chinese legislation to guide lower courts and clarify legislation,[11] and publishes model or 'typical' cases to harmonise and standardise trial practices.[12]

Below the SPC are the High People's Courts,[13] Intermediate People's Courts,[14] and the Basic People's Courts,[15] with tribunals at the township level as branches.[16] Special people's courts also exist for specific sectors or specialist areas of law (eg, military, maritime, railway, forestry, intellectual property, etc).[17] The SPC has nationwide jurisdiction.[18]

Two key factors determine a people's court's jurisdiction – (1) the court level which has jurisdiction over the matter (hierarchical jurisdiction), and (2) the court's territorial jurisdiction.[19] Hierarchical jurisdiction depends on the case type and disputed amount. High People's Courts hear civil cases only when the amount exceeds RMB 5 billion, so most cases are tried at the Basic and Intermediate People's Courts. Notably, parties cannot generally choose a court that alters the court hierarchy and required disputed amount.[20]

Territorial jurisdiction is based on the nature of the case, which determines the relevant connecting factor needed. Parties, nonetheless, can agree on a particular court, thus granting jurisdiction despite the absence of any connecting factor.[21] Without an agreement, jurisdiction lies with the court where the defendant is located[22] or where certain factors (eg, the place of performance for contractual disputes, the place where the tort happened for torts) are connected.[23] Except in matters where Chinese law confers 'exclusive jurisdiction',[24]

[6] ibid art 123.

[7] ibid art 3.

[8] Organic Law of the People's Courts of the People's Republic of China (中华人民共和国人民法院组织法) 1979 (adopted 5 July 1979) National People's Congress Order No 3 of the Chairman of the Standing Committee, art 32(1) ('People's Courts Law').

[9] PRC Constitution (n 4) art 128.

[10] ibid art 127.

[11] Legislation Law of the People's Republic of China (中华人民共和国立法法) 2000 (adopted 15 March 2000) Order No 13 of the President, art 104; People's Courts Law (n 8) art 33.

[12] Susan Finder, 'More on People's Court Typical and Major Cases, or How Typical Cases are Tempered', *Supreme People's Court Monitor* (webpage, 1 April 2022): https://supremepeoplescourtmonitor.com/2022/04/01/more-on-supreme-peoples-court-typical-and-major-cases-or-how-typical-cases-are-tempered/ (accessed 28 October 2024).

[13] People's Courts Law (n 8) art 26.

[14] ibid art 23.

[15] ibid art 18.

[16] ibid art 20.

[17] See ibid art 29; National People's Congress, 'State Structure of the People's Republic of China – The Supreme People's Court' (The National People's Congress of the People's Republic of China (webpage)): http://www.npc.gov.cn/zgrdw/englishnpc/stateStructure/2007-12/06/content_1382076.htm (accessed 28 October 2024).

[18] People's Courts Law (n 8) art 30.

[19] See Chenyang Zhang, *Win in Chinese Courts* (Springer, 2023) 25.

[20] Civil Procedure Law of the People's Republic of China (中华人民共和国民事诉讼法) 1991 (adopted 19 April 1991, amended 2023) National People's Congress Order No 44 of the President, art 130 ('CCPL').

[21] ibid arts 35, 277.

[22] ibid arts 22, 23, 24, 25, 26, 27, 28, 29.

[23] eg ibid arts 24, 29.

[24] ibid art 34.

an otherwise incompetent court may acquire jurisdiction if a party files a reply or defence.[25] China also grants certain courts cross-region jurisdiction,[26] and foreign defendants with no Chinese domicile can be sued in courts[27] connected to (1) contract execution and performance, (2) the location of the subject matter of the dispute, (3) the place where the restrained defendant's property is located, (4) where the tort occurred, or (5) the location of the defendant's representative's office.[28]

In 2019, the China International Commercial Court ('CICC') was established in Shenzhen and Xi'an as part of the Belt and Road Initiative's dispute resolution system.[29] As a division of the SPC, the CICC shares its territorial jurisdiction, and has jurisdiction over first-instance international commercial cases dealing with disputes over RMB 300 million.[30] Notably, parties may also confer jurisdiction on the CICC through their Choice-of-Forum clause.[31]

On 1 September 2023, the Standing Committee amended the Civil Procedure Law ('CCPL'), effective from 1 January 2024 ('2023 Amendment').[32] The 2023 Amendment expands the people's courts' jurisdiction over cross-border disputes, clarifies the rules on Choice-of-Forum clauses, broadens the 'exclusive jurisdiction' list, and confirms the people's courts' jurisdiction over matters involving foreign sovereignty. Unless otherwise stated, all discussions concerning the CCPL in this chapter already consider the 2023 Amendment.

Lastly, special courts, including their jurisdiction and procedures, are generally governed by the specific laws that established them. For example, the maritime courts' jurisdiction is defined under article 7 of the Special Maritime Procedure Law ('CSMPL').[33] When specific rules are absent, the CCPL applies.

(ii) Prorogation and Derogation

(a) Ordinary People's Courts and CICC

The 2023 Amendment introduced article 277, thus confirming parties' ability to prorogate jurisdiction to the people's courts in foreign-related disputes. While article 277 requires a written agreement, it no longer mentions that an 'actual connection to the dispute' be present, unlike article 35, which still applies to domestic disputes and *does* require such a

[25] ibid art 130.

[26] ibid arts 37–39.

[27] ibid art 272.

[28] ibid art 272.

[29] See China International Commercial Court, 'Opinions on Establishing the Belt and Road Dispute Settlement Mechanisms and Institutions' (webpage, 27 June 2018): https://cicc.court.gov.cn/html/1/219/208/210/819.html#:~:text=The%20Opinion%20requires%20that%20the,People's%20Court%20should%20lead%20and (accessed 28 October 2024).

[30] Provisions of the Supreme People's Court on Several Issues Regarding the Establishment of the International Commercial Court (最高人民法院关于设立国际商事法庭若干问题的规定) 2018 (adopted 27 June 2018) Supreme People's Court Interpretation No 11, art 2(1) ('CICC Interpretation').

[31] ibid.

[32] Decision of the Standing Committee of the National People's Congress to Amend the Civil Procedure Law of the People's Republic of China (全国人民代表大会常务委员会关于修改《中华人民共和国民事诉讼法》的决定) 2023 (adopted 1 September 2023) Order No 11 of the President ('2023 Amendment').

[33] Special Maritime Procedure Law of the People's Republic of China (中华人民共和国海事诉讼特别程序法) 1999 (adopted 25 December 1999) No 26 of the Ministry of Finance, art 7 ('CSMPL').

connection. With the 2023 Amendment, articles 277 and 35 are now distinguished, with the former specially applying to foreign-related disputes and the latter, to those disputes which are not. Scholars note that removing the 'connection requirement' could lead to China ratifying the Choice-of-Court Convention, which it signed in 2017,[34] and thus boost the Chinese courts' capacity to hear cases and provide judicial support for the Belt and Road Initiative.[35]

Because of the distinction introduced by the 2023 Amendment, defining foreign-related disputes is crucial. While the CCPL does not define this, article 282, which introduces a *forum non conveniens* test, may offer guidance; thus, a foreign-related dispute involves cases where key facts did not occur in China, and it is obviously inconvenient for the people's court to hear the case, and more convenient for the foreign court to hear the case. Alternatively, the court may continue to refer to the judicial interpretation on the CCPL, which was last amended on 22 March 2022 ('CCPL Interpretation').[36] Article 255 of the CCPL Interpretation defines 'foreign-related disputes' as those where: (1) one or both parties concerned are foreigners, stateless persons, foreign enterprises or organisations; (2) the habitual residence of one or both parties concerned is outside China; (3) the subject matter is outside China; (4) legal facts incurring, modifying or eliminating the civil relationship occurred outside China; or (5) other situations exist that can be recognised as a civil case involving foreigners or foreign affairs.[37] Notably, the enumeration implies that foreign-related disputes include cases where both Chinese and foreign elements are present and also where only foreign elements are involved.[38] In any case, the CCPL Interpretation should be amended because of the 2023 Amendment.

Following the 2023 Amendment, the SPC amended the judicial interpretation on the CICC ('CICC Interpretation').[39] Hence, the CICC can now hear disputes where parties have chosen the CICC through an article 277 agreement and when the amount exceeds RMB 300 million.[40] Notably, article 3 of the CICC Interpretation enumerates the same factors mentioned in the CCPL Interpretation to define international commercial cases.[41]

How about Hong Kong, Macau, and Taiwan cases? Under the 'one state, two systems' principle, Hong Kong and Macau (as well as Taiwan) are all considered separate legal systems from China. Consequently, the CCPL is unsurprisingly silent on whether these

[34] See eg, Jie Huang, 'Developing Chinese Private International Law for Transnational Civil and Commercial Litigation: The 2024 New Chinese Civil Procedure Law' (2023) 70 *Netherlands International Law Review* 205. ('Developing Chinese PIL'); Nie Yuxin, 'Overview of the 2023 Amendments to Chinese Procedure Law' in Conflict of Laws (22 September 2023): https://conflictoflaws.net/2023/overview-of-the-2023-amendments-to-chinese-civil-procedure-law/ (accessed 28 October 2024).

[35] See Nie Yuxin (n 34).

[36] Interpretation of the Supreme People's Court on the Application of the Civil Procedure Law of the People's Republic of China (最高人民法院关于适用《中华人民共和国民事诉讼法》的解释) 2015 (adopted 30 January 2015, amended 2022) Supreme People's Court, Interpretation No 11, art 255 ('CCPL Interpretation').

[37] ibid art 522.

[38] Liang Zhao, 'Party autonomy in choice of court and jurisdiction over foreign-related commercial and maritime disputes in China' (2019) 15(3) *Journal of Private International Law* 541, 544.

[39] Decision of the Supreme People's Court to Amend the Provisions of the Supreme People's Court on Several Issues Concerning the Establishment of International Commercial Courts 2023 [最高人民法院关于修改《最高人民法院关于设立国际商事法庭若干问题的规定》的决定] 2023 (adopted 18 December 2023) Supreme People's Court Interpretation No 14.

[40] CICC Interpretation (n 36) art 2(1).

[41] ibid art 3.

regions form part of the territory of China for its purposes. It seems that disputes connected to Hong Kong, Macau, and Taiwan (and not with China) are treated as 'foreign-related disputes' under the CCPL, making article 277 applicable.

Notably, article 277 does not explicitly require exclusivity. In fact, when article 277 is considered together with articles 281 (*lis pendens*) and 282 (*forum non conveniens*), they ensure that Choice-of-Forum clauses stipulating Chinese courts will always be enforced, whether exclusive or non-exclusive. The *lis pendens* test in article 281 prevents Chinese courts from suspending cases in China even if an action has already been filed abroad, as long as there is a jurisdiction agreement stipulating Chinese courts. Similarly, under article 282's *forum non conveniens* test, the absence of an agreement choosing Chinese courts is a factor, but there is no qualification as regards the clause's exclusivity.

In contrast, article 280 allows parties to choose foreign courts, but such choice should be exclusive: 'Where the parties reach an exclusive jurisdiction agreement to choose the jurisdiction of a foreign court … the people's court may rule that [the] case is not accepted [ie, dismissed]'.[42] If the choice is non-exclusive, Chinese courts need not dismiss or suspend the action, as neither article 281 nor 282 mandates it. Nonetheless, in cases involving the mandatory exclusive jurisdiction under article 279[43] or issues of China's sovereignty, security, or public interests,[44] Choice-of-Forum clauses stipulating foreign courts, whether exclusive or non-exclusive, are not enforced.

Article 280 does not specify whether the chosen foreign court must have an 'actual connection'. If the silence in article 280 is treated like article 277, this suggests the 'actual connection' requirement from article 35 no longer applies also.[45] However, some scholars argue that the connection requirement still holds,[46] despite the 2023 Amendment. This view seems inconsistent with article 280, which only precludes enforcement of Choice-of-Forum clauses choosing foreign courts if they violate rules on exclusive jurisdiction or in cases involving China's sovereignty, security or public interests.

While there is a strong case that exclusive clauses choosing foreign courts do not require an actual connection, it is unclear if the same applies to non-exclusive clauses. It seems that the lack of a connection requirement should also extend to non-exclusive clauses, to ensure that Choice-of-Forum clauses are enforced more broadly and to align the Chinese procedure with global practices. Chinese courts should instead apply the *forum non conveniens* test under article 282 to decide whether to enforce non-exclusive Choice-of-Forum clauses.

(b) Maritime Courts

Article 8 of the CSMPL allows foreign nationals, stateless persons, or foreign entities to choose a Chinese maritime court through a written agreement, even without an 'actual connection' to China.[47] This approach predates the 2023 Amendment and served as a model

[42] CCPL (n 20) art 280.
[43] ibid art 279; see below, section II.C.(i).
[44] ibid art 280.
[45] ibid art 35.
[46] See, eg, Zheng Sophia Tang, 'Choice of Court Convention and the People's Republic of China' (Presented at HCCH 2005 *Choice of Court Convention: Fostering Access to Justice for Cross-Border Commerce in the Asia Pacific Region*, 22 March 2024).
[47] CSMPL (n 33) art 8.

for procedural reform. However, Chinese citizens and entities are still subject to article 35 of the CCPL; thus, the 'actual connection' requirement applies when prorogating jurisdiction to Chinese maritime courts. Nonetheless, when parties choose foreign courts for maritime disputes, Chinese maritime courts still require an 'actual connection'[48] because the CSMPL does not explicitly exempt foreign courts from the requirement. Nonetheless, with the reforms brought by the 2023 Amendment, this practice may change.

(iii) Service of Process

Service of process is important but not required to establish jurisdiction.[49] Service is allowed, within or outside China, when Chinese courts exercise jurisdiction over the dispute. In the context of Choice-of-Forum clauses, this happens when (1) Chinese courts are chosen,[50] (2) when enforcement of an exclusive clause stipulating foreign courts is denied because it contravenes exclusive jurisdiction under article 279,[51] or due to involvement of China's sovereignty, security or public interest,[52] or (3) when Chinese courts choose to exercise jurisdiction despite the non-exclusive Choice-of-Forum clause stipulating foreign courts, after applying the *lis pendens*[53] or *forum non conveniens* test.[54] Service to a defendant without a domicile within China may follow article 283 (previously article 274) using domestic methods,[55] or procedures under international treaties.[56] China is a party to the 1965 Hague Service Convention[57] and has bilateral judicial assistance treaties with 39 countries, including France, Italy, Spain, Russia, South Korea, and Singapore.[58]

(iv) Dismissal and Stay of Proceedings

Chinese courts may dismiss or suspend proceedings when Choice-of-Forum clauses stipulating foreign courts are enforced. Article 280 requires enforcement of an exclusive clause stipulating foreign courts, provided the dispute does not fall under article 278 (exclusive jurisdiction) or involve China's sovereignty, security and public interests. Furthermore, article 280 applies to parallel proceedings (ie, a *lis pendens* rule), such as when (1) one party sues in the foreign court and the other sues in a people's court, or (2) where one party sues in both the foreign court and a people's court. The court can either rule that the case is not accepted (ie, dismissal), or if the proceedings have begun, the litigation is rejected (ie, dismissal). Notably, dismissal under article 280 applies regardless of which court accepted the case first,[59] provided that the exclusive Choice-of-Forum clause is proven.

[48] See Liang Zhao (n 38) 556–57.
[49] See eg, Jie Huang, 'Developing Chinese PIL' (n 34) 220–22.
[50] CCPL (n 20) art 277.
[51] ibid art 279; see below section II.C.(i).
[52] ibid art 280.
[53] ibid art 280.
[54] ibid art 282.
[55] For changes brought by the 2023 Amendment, see Jie Huang, 'Developing Chinese PIL' (n 34) 220–22.
[56] CCPL (n 20) art 283(1).
[57] Convention on the service abroad of judicial and extrajudicial documents in civil or commercial matters, opened for signature 15 November 1965, 658 UNTS 163 (entered into force 10 February 1969) ('The Hague Service Convention').
[58] Chenyang Zhang (n 19) 60.
[59] See Jie Huang, 'Developing Chinese PIL' (n 34) 216–18.

Outside the context of parallel proceedings, where no foreign action or concurrent litigation exists, article 280 is silent on how to enforce an exclusive Choice-of-Forum clause choosing foreign courts. In such cases, the Chinese court should still dismiss the action under article 277. Before the 2023 Amendment, Chinese courts recognised Choice-of-Forum clauses choosing foreign courts under article 35 (or article 34 before the 2021 CCPL amendment), even though it only mentions prorogation to Chinese courts. This approach should continue under article 277 for consistent enforcement of Choice-of-Forum clauses. Additionally, article 282 on *forum non conveniens* also allows such dismissal.

Article 281 allows a Chinese court to suspend proceedings if a party applies in writing and a foreign court has accepted the case first. This likely contemplates non-exclusive clauses, which are not covered by article 280. Hence, even if the Choice-of-Forum clause is non-exclusive, the Chinese court may suspend proceedings if a foreign court has already accepted jurisdiction, even if that court was not chosen in the clause. The only requirement is that the foreign court must have accepted the case before the Chinese court did.

Article 281 outlines exceptions where the Chinese court may not suspend proceedings, namely when: (1) the Choice-of-Forum clause stipulates Chinese courts, (2) exclusive jurisdiction applies, or (3) it is obviously more convenient for the people's court to hear the case. The first exception reinforces article 277 and should apply to both exclusive and non-exclusive clauses stipulating Chinese courts. The second follows article 279 but may include other Chinese legislation requiring exclusive jurisdiction, though article 279 only covers 'civil cases' while article 281 refers to 'disputes'. The third exception involves relative convenience, which is discretionary, though it must be obvious. Huang suggests that the SPC issue a judicial interpretation, with factors like access to evidence, applicable law, and state interests.[60]

Article 281 also addresses cases where the foreign court which first accepted jurisdiction, either (1) fails to take necessary measures to hear the case, or (2) does not conclude it within a reasonable time. In such cases, upon written application of both parties, the people's court may resume proceedings. This applies only if the *same* dispute is being heard abroad, and the joint application seems to have novated the Choice-of-Forum clause in relation to the same dispute. However, if a *different* dispute arises, parties can still rely on their Choice-of-Forum clause, as can those contractual parties who are not involved in the Chinese litigation. Please note that for exclusive clauses, article 280 applies and the Chinese court should dismiss, even if there is failure or unreasonable delay in the foreign proceedings.

(v) Forum Non Conveniens *with Chinese Characteristics*

Article 282 introduces the *forum non conveniens* principle into the CCPL, although Chinese courts have applied a version of it since the 1990s.[61] Before the 2023 Amendment, dismissals under this principle were made under article 530 of the CCPL Interpretation.[62] Unlike the English *Spiliada* test, China's version was originally focused on procedural efficiency rather

[60] ibid.

[61] See Zheng Sophia Tang, 'Declining Jurisdiction by *Forum Non Conveniens* in Chinese Courts' (2015) 45(1) *Hong Kong Law Journal* 351, 353–55 ('Declining Jurisdiction').

[62] 2015 CCPL Interpretation (n 36) art 530.

than comparing foreign judicial practices to ensure substantive justice for the parties.[63] The 2023 Amendment, however, arguably brings the Chinese version closer to the *Spiliada* test by considering convenience factors.

For a Chinese court to apply *forum non conveniens*, article 282 requires that: (1) the dispute is foreign-related, (2) the defendant objects to jurisdiction, and (3) the factors ('conditions') are met concurrently. If these requirements are satisfied, the court may dismiss the case and advise the plaintiff to sue in a more convenient foreign court. However, if the foreign court (1) refuses jurisdiction, (2) fails to take action, or (3) does not conclude the case in a reasonable time, the Chinese court may accept the case; thus the effect is similar to 'suspension' under article 281. Furthermore, previous court practice would show that the court may *motu proprio* dismiss the case after considering the *forum non conveniens* factors.[64] Nonetheless, the defendant bears the burden of establishing the conditions under article 282.

Under article 282, the following factors ('conditions') should be met concurrently: (1) the basic facts in dispute did not occur in China, making it obviously inconvenient for the people's court to hear the case and for parties to participate, (2) the Choice-of-Forum clause does not choose Chinese courts, (3) the case is not under the exclusive jurisdiction of the people's courts, (4) it does not involve China's sovereignty, security or public interest, and (5) it is more convenient for the foreign court to hear the case. Factors like location of evidence and witnesses, costs, language, difficulty establishing and proving foreign law emphasise procedural efficiency. Huang argues, however, that because article 282 now also considers the parties' convenience, factors establishing parties' difficulties like accessing legal aid in the foreign country and obtaining a visa may now be considered by the court.[65] Therefore, the parties' interests in achieving just results at the foreign court may now be considered; thus the Chinese *forum non conveniens* now considers, to a certain extent, justice-related factors specific to the litigating parties. Nonetheless, the impact of this change has yet to be seen. In any case, by requiring a factual connection, the test also guards against an expansive exercise of Chinese jurisdiction.

Article 282 reinforces article 277 (albeit superfluously) by ensuring that cases filed pursuant to Choice-of-Forum clauses stipulating Chinese courts, whether exclusive or non-exclusive, will not be dismissed. Dismissal under article 282 includes situations where no foreign litigation is pending and an exclusive clause stipulating foreign courts is involved. Chinese courts may find it 'more convenient for the foreign court to hear the case', as the foreign court has been expressly chosen by the parties. The same reason applies to non-exclusive clauses. However, if there are factual connections to China or the inconvenience for the people's court is not obvious, the Chinese court may not dismiss under article 282. If foreign proceedings are pending under an exclusive clause stipulating foreign courts, article 280 requires the dismissal of Chinese proceedings. Hence, only when there is no foreign pending case will Chinese courts apply article 282 in relation to exclusive Choice-of-Forum clauses. This possible application of article 282 to exclusive Choice-of-Forum clauses is another key difference between the Chinese approach and *Spiliada* or even modified *Spiliada*.

[63] Zheng Sophia Tang, 'Declining Jurisdiction' (n 61) 366.
[64] See ibid 355.
[65] Jie Huang, 'Developing Chinese PIL' (n 34) 218–19.

The *forum non conveniens* principle with Chinese characteristics, with its discretionary nature and focus on procedural efficiency, has faced criticism from Chinese scholars. Some argue that giving judges discretion in considering convenience factors conflicts with the civil law tradition's preference for a clear, almost mechanical decision-making approach.[66] Likewise, Chinese judges have been inconsistent in applying laws, and giving them more discretion may worsen the issue.[67] Tang correctly argues that the solution is to provide clear criteria and guidance for judges.[68] Furthermore, the current version still lacks an explicit focus on justice, unlike the *Spiliada* test and similar versions found in the United States and the Philippines that highlight administration of justice. Although parties' convenience is now considered, the Chinese version of *forum non conveniens* is still framed in terms of efficiency rather than justice. Moreover, because it considers the factual details of the dispute and even convenience factors, it undermines the effect of exclusive Choice-of-Forum clauses choosing foreign courts. In that sense, the effect required by the Choice-of-Court Convention is still not met by the Chinese legislation.

Because the CSMPL lacks a *forum non conveniens* rule, article 282 of the CCPL should also apply to maritime cases. In fact, maritime courts have used the *forum non conveniens* test under the CCPL Interpretation to dismiss cases.[69]

(vi) Anti-suit Injunctions and Other Relief

Maritime courts have, under article 51 of the CSMPL, issued injunctions functioning as anti-suit injunctions. Maritime injunctions under article 51 can be issued to compel or prevent a person from doing or not doing certain things 'so as to prevent the lawful rights and interest of the claimant from being infringed upon'.[70] Article 56 requires the applicant to prove (1) a specific maritime claim, (2) a necessity to correct the respondent's breach, and (3) urgency, where delay would worsen the damage already sustained.[71] Ordinary courts, meanwhile, refer to article 103 of the CCPL[72] for interim measures resembling anti-suit injunctions. Article 103 allows courts to preserve property, order specific acts, or prohibit performance of certain acts. Notably, article 103 also allows the court to grant such preservation measures *motu proprio*.

Scholars argue that CCPL's article 103 and even CSMPL's article 51 are not appropriate for the issuance of anti-suit injunctions, which differ from asset and evidence preservation.[73] However, since Chinese courts have issued anti-suit injunctions for arbitration agreements,[74] they could do the same for Choice-of-Forum clauses. Hence, provided the application meets

[66] Zheng Sophia Tang, 'Declining Jurisdiction' (n 61) 368–69.
[67] See eg ibid 370–71.
[68] ibid 371.
[69] See eg, *Grace Young International Ltd v Seoil Agency Co Ltd* [2016] Lu 72 Min Chu No 2039 (Qingdao Maritime Court) discussed in Guodong Du and Meng Yu, 'Forum Non Conveniens in China: The Most Stringent Standards Ever?' (webpage, 13 February 2019): https://www.chinajusticeobserver.com/a/forum-non-conveniens-in-china-the-most-stringent-standards-ever (accessed 18 December 2024).
[70] CSMPL (n 33) art 51.
[71] ibid art 56.
[72] See Liang Zhao (n 38) 565.
[73] See eg, ibid 566.
[74] eg, *Huatai Property & Casualty Insurance Co Ltd Shenzhen Branch v Clipper Chartering SA* [2017] E72XB 3 (Wuhan Maritime Court); see Liang Zhao (n 38) 66.

the requirements in either articles 51 and 56, CSMPL or article 103, CCPL, as applicable, an anti-suit injunction may be granted based on a Choice-of-Forum clause choosing Chinese courts.

Chinese courts have not yet awarded damages for breach of a Choice-of-Forum clause.[75] Some scholars, like Hu, argue that awarding damages is possible and could be an alternative to anti-suit injunctions. Hu suggests that since Choice-of-Forum clauses are akin to 'contracts of civil litigation rights', and damages have been awarded in disputes involving these types of contracts, damages for breach are legally feasible under Chinese law.[76] In *Liupanshui Hengding Industrial Co, Ltd v Chongqing Qianniu Construction Co Ltd*, the SPC upheld a clause restricting the period in which to sue,[77] because the clause did not deny the right to sue completely. Hence, the SPC supported the defendant's counterclaim and awarded attorney's fees, preservation costs, enforcement costs, travel expenses, etc.[78] Hu also cites intellectual property-related malicious litigation cases, where courts have awarded costs, arguing that breach of Choice-of-Forum clauses could also be characterised as 'abuse of litigation rights in a broader sense'.[79]

(vii) Recognition and Enforcement of Judgments

Foreign and regional judgments may be recognised and enforced in China either through (1) bilateral treaties, (2) regional arrangements, or (3) domestic law. Notably, Choice-of-Forum clauses are explicitly dealt with by these three regimes.

(a) Bilateral Treaties

China has 39 bilateral judicial assistance treaties, each reflecting its unique relationship with the partner country.[80] Not all treaties address the recognition and enforcement of foreign judgments or Choice-of-Forum clauses. However, treaties with Italy,[81] Ethiopia,[82] Kuwait,[83] and United Arab Emirates[84] state that the issuing court has jurisdiction if the

[75] Hu Hailong, 'Damages for Breach of Choice of Court Agreements: Foreign Experience and Domestic Approach' (2022) 3(3) *Foundation for Law and International Affairs Review* 97, 114.

[76] ibid 114–15.

[77] *Liupanshui Hengding Industrial Co, Ltd v Chongqing Qianniu Construction Co Ltd* [2016] Zui Gao Fa Min Zhong No 415 (Supreme People's Court), discussed in Hu Hailong (n 75) 116 ('*Liupanshui*').

[78] ibid; see Hu Hailong (n 75) 116.

[79] Hu Hailong (n 75) 117.

[80] See King Fung Tsang, 'Chinese Bilateral Judgment Enforcement Treaties' (2017) 40(1) *Loyola of Los Angeles International and Comparative Law Review* 1, 4–10; Weixia Guo, 'China' in Anselmo Reyes (ed), *Recognition and Enforcement of Judgments in Civil and Commercial Matters* (Hart Publishing, 2019) 31, 38.

[81] Treaty between the People's Republic of China and the Italian Republic on Judicial Assistance in Civil Matter, China-Italy, signed 20 May 1991 (entered into force 1 January 1995) art 22(1)(a): http://treaty.mfa.gov.cn/Treaty/web/detail1.jsp?objid=1531876660241 ('China-Italy Treaty').

[82] Treaty between the People's Republic of China and the Federal Democratic Republic of Ethiopia on Mutual Legal Assistance in Civil and Commercial Matters, China-Ethiopia, signed 4 May 2014 (entered into force 3 January 2018) art 25(1)(c): http://treaty.mfa.gov.cn/Treaty/web/detail1.jsp?objid=1535420588872 ('China-Ethiopia Treaty').

[83] Treaty Between the People's Republic of China and the State of Kuwait on Judicial Assistance in Civil and Commercial Matters, China-Kuwait, signed 18 June 2007 (entered into force 6 June 2013) art 19(1)(e): http://treaty.mfa.gov.cn/Treaty/web/detail1.jsp?objid=1535420269814 ('China-Kuwait Treaty').

[84] Treaty Between the People's Republic of China and the United Arab Emirates on Judicial Assistance in Civil and Commercial Matters, signed 12 April 2005 (entered into force 21 April 2004), art 19(e): http://treaty.mfa.gov.cn/Treaty/web/detail1.jsp?objid=1531876863419 ('China-UAE Treaty').

defendant has expressly submitted to the jurisdiction of the court. While not expressly stated, these treaties cover situations where the foreign court acquires jurisdiction through the Choice-of-Forum clause under forum law. When treaties do not explicitly mention Choice-of-Forum clauses, the traditional requirement that foreign judgments should be issued by courts with jurisdiction applies. As such, jurisdictional requirements under each treaty are important, but their interpretation may require reference to an applicable law, which is often not provided under the treaty.[85] Hence, the law which should be used to determine whether the jurisdictional requirement is satisfied may be uncertain. It may be argued, nonetheless, that since the questions of jurisdiction and giving effect to Choice-of-Forum clauses are procedural, they should be determined under forum law. If, under the forum law of the issuing court, Choice-of-Forum clauses can vest jurisdiction, then the foreign judgment issued pursuant to such a clause is valid and could be recognised and enforced in China.

Scholars note that bilateral treaties are often in-effective in securing recognition and enforcement of foreign judgments in China.[86] Tsang observes that courts rarely cite relevant treaties and may reject applications without explanation.[87] When reasons are given, they often rely on grounds not found in treaties, particularly public policy.[88] Tsang argues that the low success rate stems from judges' lack of understanding of the treaties and the over-reliance on public policy grounds.[89]

(b) Regional Arrangements

Under the 'one country, two systems' framework, judgments from Hong Kong, Macau and Taiwan are treated similarly to foreign judgments. To promote certainty and coherence, China has entered into regional arrangements. The Choice-of-Court Arrangement and the Arrangement between the Mainland and the Macao Special Administrative Region on the Mutual Recognition and Enforcement of Civil and Commercial Judgments ('Macau Arrangement'), both concluded in 2006, are important steps in promoting a more coherent approach towards regional judgments. In 2015, the SPC passed the 'Provisions of the Supreme People's Court on the Recognition and Enforcement of Civil Judgments Rendered by Courts in the Taiwan Region' ('Taiwan Arrangement'), thus completing the legal framework for the Greater China region. In 2019, the Judgments Arrangement was signed, thus expanding further the scope of civil and commercial judgments covered by regional arrangements between China and Hong Kong. While the details of the Choice-of-Court Arrangement and Judgments Arrangements are discussed in Chapter four, the relevant SPC judicial interpretation as well as the judicial practices of the Chinese courts are examined in this section.

[85] See Tsang (n 80) 19.
[86] See eg, ibid 31.
[87] ibid 31–33.
[88] ibid 33.
[89] ibid 40.

Hong Kong

The Choice-of-Court Interpretation implements the Choice-of-Court Arrangement in China.[90] Notably, it mirrors the regional arrangement, unlike Hong Kong's Choice-of-Court Ordinance which is worded slightly differently to suit the local context. The Choice-of-Court Interpretation allows enforcement of monetary judgments[91] involving a valid exclusive 'choice of court agreement in writing', designating Hong Kong courts.[92] Applications for recognition or enforcement are made at the Intermediate People's Court where the judgment debtor resides or owns property,[93] in accordance with Chinese procedural law.[94] Hong Kong judgments may be refused if the exclusive clauses are invalid under Hong Kong law,[95] unless the Hong Kong court had already ruled on the clause's validity.[96] Note that this is a Chinese court applying Hong Kong law to determine the clause's validity; thus, this step is dependent on Chinese rules of evidence and procedure. Refusal may also occur if the judgment has already been satisfied, falls under the Chinese court's exclusive jurisdiction, was obtained without proper notice under Hong Kong law, involves fraud, is barred by *res judicata* because of a prior Chinese or foreign judgment, or violates China's social and public interests.[97] An appeal in Hong Kong may suspend the recognition and enforcement proceedings in China.[98] If recognition is refused under article 9 of the Choice-of-Court Arrangement, a party may be allowed to commence new litigation in China on the same facts in accordance with Chinese law.[99]

Due to significant differences in the legal traditions, procedure, evidence rules, treatment of foreign law, and public policy between Hong Kong and China, gaps and indeterminacy in the applicable law have led to controversial interpretations and results. In *Japan Pipe Center Co Ltd v Beijing Zhuangsheng Real Estate Development Co Ltd*,[100] a Japanese plaintiff obtained a favourable judgment in Hong Kong under an exclusive Hong Kong Choice-of-Forum clause. However, because the judgment predated the Choice-of-Court Agreement, the plaintiff commenced new proceedings in China. The lower court dismissed the case due to the exclusive clause stipulating Hong Kong, but the Beijing High People's Court reversed this, allowing the case to proceed under the CCPL, thus disregarding the exclusive clause, and the principles of *res judicata* or *lis pendens* in its ruling.

The more comprehensive Judgments Arrangement, effective in both China and Hong Kong from 29 January 2024, aims to close existing legal gaps. In China, it is implemented

[90] Arrangement of the Supreme People's Court between the Mainland and the HKSAR on Reciprocal Recognition and Enforcement of the Decisions of Civil and Commercial Cases under Consensual Jurisdiction (最高人民法院关于内地与香港特别行政区法院相互认可和执行当事人协议管辖的民商事案件判决的安排) 2008 (adopted 4 July 2008) Supreme People's Court Interpretation No 9 ('Choice-of-Court Interpretation').

[91] ibid art 1.

[92] ibid art 3.

[93] ibid art 4.

[94] ibid art 8.

[95] ibid art 9(1).

[96] ibid.

[97] ibid art 9.

[98] ibid art 10.

[99] ibid art 13.

[100] *Japan Pipe Center Co Ltd v Beijing Zhuangsheng Real Estate Development Co Ltd* [2009] Case No 919 (Beijing High People's Court).

by an SPC judicial interpretation issued on 25 January 2024.[101] Unlike the earlier Choice-of-Court Arrangement, the Judgments Arrangement covers legally effective Hong Kong civil and commercial judgments,[102] under both Chinese and Hong Kong law,[103] and regardless of whether a Choice-of-Forum clause is involved. However, the Choice-of-Court Arrangement remains relevant for clauses signed before the Judgments Arrangement's coming into force.[104] The Judgment Arrangement excludes Hong Kong rulings on preservation measures, anti-suit injunctions and interim relief.[105] Chinese law governs the time limits, procedures and applications for recognition and enforcement of Hong Kong judgments,[106] with applications required to be filed at the Intermediate People's Court where the applicant or respondent resides or where the respondent's property is located.[107]

Hong Kong judgments involving written Choice-of-Forum clauses designating Hong Kong courts may be enforced and recognised under the Judgments Arrangement.[108] 'Written' means that its contents should be displayed in visible form.[109] Furthermore, the exclusivity requirement has been removed, allowing judgments from non-exclusive clauses to be recognisable and enforceable in China. Nonetheless, when all parties reside in China, an actual connection to Hong Kong is still required, such as being the place where the contract was signed or performed, or where the subject matter is located.[110] Despite the 2023 Amendment, this connection requirement remains.

Macau

The Macau Arrangement, signed on 28 February 2006 and effective from 1 April 2006, was China's first regional arrangement to take effect. Unlike in the Choice-of-Court Arrangement, both China and Macau directly copied the Macau Arrangement into their local laws. Its scope is broader, covering judgments beyond exclusive Choice-of-Forum clauses,[111] and including civil, commercial, marital and family matters, succession,[112] labour disputes, and civil damages in criminal proceedings.[113] Jurisdiction is based on all bases under either China or Macau law, with the only limitation being exclusive jurisdiction matters of either region.[114] Instead of listing specific heads of jurisdiction, article 11 outlines grounds for

[101] Arrangement on Reciprocal Recognition and Enforcement of Judgments in Civil and Commercial Matters by the Courts of the Mainland and of the Hong Kong Special Administrative Region (最高人民法院关于内地与香港特别行政区法院相互认可和执行民商事案件判决的安排) 2024 (adopted 25 January 2024) Supreme People's Court Interpretation No 2 ('JA Interpretation').

[102] ibid art 1.

[103] ibid art 2.

[104] ibid art 30.

[105] ibid art 4.

[106] ibid art 10.

[107] ibid art 7(1).

[108] ibid art 11(5).

[109] ibid art 11.

[110] ibid art 11(5).

[111] Arrangement between the Mainland and the Macao Special Administrative Region on the Mutual Recognition and Enforcement of Civil and Commercial Judgments (最高人民法院关于内地与澳门特别行政区相互认可和执行民商事判决的安排) 2006 (adopted 21 March 2006) Supreme People's Court Interpretation No 2, art 1.

[112] ibid art 1.

[113] ibid.

[114] ibid arts 1, 11(1).

refusing recognition.[115] Notably, Macau Arrangement's has been more successful,[116] due to the shared civil law traditions and the verbatim domestic adoption which have led to fewer disparities in interpretation and implementation.[117] However, China's negative treatment of gambling-related judgments, considered to be against Chinese public policy, remains a concern.[118]

Judgments involving Choice-of-Forum clauses are not explicitly addressed under the Macau Arrangement. Hence, the approach is to first check whether the judgment lies within article 1's scope and if any refusal grounds exist under article 11. If none exist, the Macau judgment involving Choice-of-Forum clauses can be recognised and enforced in China, provided the procedure and other requirements of the Macau Arrangement are met.

Taiwan

The Taiwan Arrangement, unlike the regional arrangements with Hong Kong and Macau, was unilaterally issued as an SPC judicial interpretation in 2015.[119] Meanwhile, Taiwan has enacted the Taiwan-Mainland Relations Act,[120] first passed in 1992, allowing recognition of Chinese judgments unless they violate Taiwan's public policy or moral traditions.[121] Improved relations led to multiple amendments, with the latest made in 2022.[122] Hence, the Taiwan Arrangement and the Taiwan-Mainland Relations Act create a liberal framework for recognising and enforcing civil and commercial judgments across the Taiwan Strait.

Judgments involving Choice-of-Forum clauses are not specifically mentioned in the Taiwan Arrangement. Hence, the approach in enforcing Taiwan judgments involving Choice-of-Forum clauses is to first check the grounds for refusing these judgments under Article 11 and other provisions of the Taiwan Arrangement. If none exists, the Taiwan judgment can be recognised and enforced in China.

(c) Domestic Law

Outside the treaty framework, foreign judgments in China are recognised and enforced based on reciprocity.[123] Article 298 of the CCPL allows either a party or a foreign court to

[115] ibid art 11.

[116] See Huang Zeyu, *Party Autonomy in Choice of Court under Chinese Inter-Regional Conflict of Laws* (Doctoral Dissertation, University of Macau, 2022) 272–73.

[117] See ibid 273–74; Jie Huang, *Interregional Recognition and Enforcement of Civil and Commercial Judgments: Lessons for China from US and EU Law* (Bloomsbury Publishing Plc, 2014) 112–13 ('*Interregional Judgments*').

[118] Guangjian Tu, 'Arrangement on Mutual Recognition and Enforcement of Judgments in Civil and Commercial Matters between China and Macau: Inherent Problems, Six Years' Experience and the Way Forward' (2013) 43(1) *Hong Kong Law Journal* 349, 363.

[119] Provisions of the Supreme People's Court on Recognition and Enforcement of the Civil Judgments of Courts of the Taiwan Region (最高人民法院关于认可和执行台湾地区法院民事判决的规定) 2019 (adopted 29 June 2019) Supreme People's Court Interpretation No 13 ('Taiwan Arrangement').

[120] Act Governing Relations between Peoples of the Taiwan Area and the Mainland Area 2022 (Taiwan) ('Taiwan-Mainland Relations Act').

[121] ibid art 74.

[122] See Ministry of Justice, 'Legislative History, Act Governing Relations between the People of the Taiwan Area and the Mainland Area in Laws & Regulations Database of The Republic of China (Taiwan)' (webpage): https://law.moj.gov.tw/ENG/LawClass/LawHistory.aspx?pcode=Q0010001 (accessed 28 October 2024).

[123] CCPL (n 20) art 297.

apply for recognition and enforcement at the relevant Chinese court.[124] Applications are filed at the Intermediate People's Court where the judgment debtor resides or where their assets are located.[125]

The meaning of reciprocity has been contentious, as it can either refer to de facto or de jure reciprocity. For a long time, judicial practice has preferred de facto reciprocity, whereby courts would require that the originating jurisdiction must be a jurisdiction that has previously recognised Chinese judgments.[126] On the other hand, de jure reciprocity does not require 'actual precedents'. Instead, reciprocity may be established (1) according to foreign law, (2) through mutually beneficial understanding or consensus between China and the originating jurisdiction, (3) where there are reciprocal diplomatic commitments and there is no evidence to suggest that the foreign country has refused to recognise and enforce a Chinese judgment due to lack of reciprocity.[127] Eventually, the Minutes of the National Court's Symposium on Foreign-related Commercial and Maritime Trials formally allowed the recognition and enforcement of foreign judgments based on de jure reciprocity.[128]

The absence of reciprocity is the main reason Chinese courts reject foreign judgments.[129] Furthermore, courts may refuse if the application violates China's basic legal principles or harms national sovereignty, security or public interest.[130] Other grounds for refusal include: (1) the foreign court lacks jurisdiction according to article 301, (2) improper service, or lack of a reasonable opportunity to respond or of proper legal representation, (3) the judgment was obtained through fraud, or (4) *res judicata* applies.[131] Furthermore, only legally effective foreign judgments – those that are final and no longer appealable – are recognised and enforceable in China.[132]

A Chinese court determines the originating foreign court jurisdiction based on the test provided under article 301, which states that jurisdiction is lacking if: (1) the foreign court has no jurisdiction under its own laws, or although it has jurisdiction, it lacks a proper connection with the dispute, (2) the foreign court violates the CCPL's exclusive jurisdiction provisions, or (3) the foreign court violates the parties' exclusive Choice-of-Forum clause.[133] The third ground reinforces the view that Chinese courts should enforce Choice-of-Forum clauses which either exclusively stipulate Chinese courts or foreign courts. While non-exclusive Choice-of-Forum clauses are not mentioned, Chinese courts can still enforce the foreign judgment if the originating court has jurisdiction and a proper connection to the dispute.

[124] ibid art 298.
[125] ibid arts 298, 304.
[126] *Case on the Application of Gomi Akira (A Japanese Citizen) to Chinese Court for Recognition and Enforcement of Japanese Judicial Decision – Application for Recognition and Enforcement of Japanese Judicial Decision* [1996] 1 最高人民法院公报 [*Gazette of the Supreme People's Court of the People's Republic of China*] (Dalian City Intermediate People's Court), discussed in Jie Huang, 'Developing Chinese PIL' (n 34) 226.
[127] Jie Huang, 'Developing Chinese PIL' (n 34) 228–29.
[128] ibid 226.
[129] CCPL (n 20) art 299.
[130] ibid arts 299–300.
[131] ibid art 300.
[132] ibid art 299.
[133] ibid art 301.

B. Existence, Validity, and Interpretation

(i) Issues of Existence and Validity

Arguably, the rule on formal validity in article 277 of the CCPL also serves as a test for determining the existence of a Choice-of-Forum clause. The requirement that the clause be in writing extends to evidence of consent, which can usually be a seal or signature.[134] This approach should apply equally to clauses selecting foreign and Chinese courts.

Article 277 sets the formal validity requirement for Choice-of-Forum clauses stipulating Chinese courts – the clause must be in writing.[135] 'Written form' includes written contracts, letters, telegrams, telex, facsimile, or any medium that tangibly expresses its contents.[136] This requirement applies to both exclusive and non-exclusive clauses if the chosen court is a Chinese court. Judicial practice has extended this written requirement to Choice-of-Forum clauses stipulating foreign courts, whether exclusive or non-exclusive.[137]

Article 277 does not specify additional requirements for validity; nor does the CCPL clarify which legal system determines it. However, based on the CCPL and judicial practice, both formal and substantive validity are determined by Chinese law.[138] However, this approach largely stems from the now-removed 'connection requirement' for foreign-related disputes, although arguably, this remains the rule for both formal and substantive validity of Choice-of-Forum clauses. First, although foreign law may govern the main contract, it is unclear if it also applies to the clause itself,[139] as such clauses are considered separate from the main contract.[140] The validity of these clauses is determined independently from the rest of the contract.[141] Furthermore, Chinese courts, including the SPC, view jurisdiction as a procedural issue, thus should be decided under forum law, ie Chinese law.[142] Moreover, article 279 and public policy considerations reinforce the preference for applying Chinese law to procedural matters, including Choice-of-Forum clauses.

[134] *Hangzhou Liaosiankai Chemical Co Ltd v Suzhou Jiecheng Dyeing Co Ltd* [2010] Hang Shang Shang Chu Zi No 434-1 (Shangcheng District People's Court) ('*Hangzhou Liaosiankai*'); *Guolei Jiang v Dongyang Red Star Clothing Co Ltd* [2011] Zhe Shao Xia Zhong Zi No 37 (Shaoxing Intermediate People's Court) ('*Guolei Jiang*'); *Hangzhou Liaosiankai* and *Guolei Jiang* are discussed in Long Jiao, *Choice of court agreements in international civil and commercial law: a comparative study of Chinese law, the 2005 Hague Choice of Court Convention and the Brussels I Recast Regulation* (LLM Thesis, University of Glasgow, 2020) 40.

[135] See also Contract Law of the People's Republic of China (中华人民共和国合同法) 1999 (adopted 15 March 1999) National People's Congress Order No 15 of the President, art 11 ('Contract Law').

[136] Civil Code of the People's Republic of China (中华人民共和国民法典) 2020 (adopted 28 May 2020) National People's Congress Order No 45 of the President, art 459 ('Chinese Civil Code').

[137] See eg, *Hangzhou Liaosiankai* (n 134) discussed in Long Jiao (n 134) 40.

[138] *Shandong Jufeng Network Co, Ltd v Mgame Co, Ltd of Korea and Tianjin Fengyun Network Technology Co, Ltd – A case about a challenge to jurisdiction over disputes arising from an online game distribution and licence agreement* [山东聚丰网络有限公司与韩国MGAME公司、天津风云网络技术有限公司网络游戏代理及许可合同纠纷管辖权异议案] [2010] 3 最高人民法院公报 [*Gazette of the Supreme People's Court of the People's Republic of China*] (Supreme People's Court) discussed in Liang Zhao (n 38) 542 ('*Shandong Jufeng 2010*'); Huang Zhang, 'International Jurisdiction under the 2005 Hague Convention on Choice of Court Agreements: Implications for China' (2017) 47(2) *Hong Kong Law Journal* 555, 560.

[139] See Law of the People's Republic of China on Choice of Law for Foreign-related Civil Relationships (中华人民共和国涉外民事关系法律适用法) 2010 (adopted 28 October 2010) National People's Congress Standing Committee Order No 36 of the President, art 3 ('Choice-of-Law Law').

[140] Chinese Civil Code (n 136) art 507; also Contract Law (n 135) art 57.

[141] *Shandong Jufeng 2010* (n 138).

[142] ibid; see also Liang Zhao (n 38) 545.

Nonetheless, Chinese courts in a small number of cases have ignored the principle that Choice-of-Forum clauses are separate from the main contract, and therefore applied the law applicable to the main contract in determining their substantive validity.[143] However, this approach is rarely applied.

Chinese scholars have also referred to the then Chinese Contract Law (now, the Chinese Civil Code) in determining whether mistake, fraud, duress, etc,[144] could invalidate the Choice-of-Forum clause. This approach is interesting, as such clauses are generally considered procedural, thus reflecting their dual nature in China as having both procedural and contractual features. Chao's survey of Chinese cases involving civil litigation and dispute settlement contracts shows that courts have frequently applied Chinese Contract Law to issues of existence, validity, and interpretation.[145] Civil litigation contracts include more than just Choice-of-Forum clauses, covering mediation agreements and waivers of right to sue, appeal, and other rights of action. Chao argues that these contracts are important procedural rights, yet subject to substantive contract law.[146] Thus, issues related to Choice-of-Forum clauses like existence, validity, and interpretation can be addressed using both procedural rules and Chinese substantive law, including the Chinese Civil Code. For example, a Choice-of-Forum clause which also waives the right to raise certain defences like the statute of limitations could be invalid under Chinese mandatory rules prohibiting advance waivers of prescriptive periods.[147]

When a Chinese court is chosen, the clause must comply with the hierarchical jurisdictional rules and the exclusive jurisdiction of ordinary and special courts.[148] Hence, real estate disputes must be filed where the property is located,[149] and disputes involving harbour operations must be brought in the court where the port is located.[150] A Choice-of-Forum clause that violates these exclusive jurisdiction or hierarchy rules could be considered invalid.

(ii) Issues of Interpretation

In China, interpretation of Choice-of-Forum clauses is generally determined by domestic law, as these clauses are seen as procedural and separate from the main contract. In *Xinhuawen International Leasing Co, Ltd v Deutsche Bank Guangzhou Branch*,[151] the Beijing High People's Court applied Chinese law in interpreting the Choice-of-Forum clause, ignoring the applicable Hong Kong law. This approach is common in Chinese decisions.[152]

[143] See eg, *The Sumitomo Bank Co Ltd v Xinhua Real Estate Co Ltd* [1999] Jing Zhong Zi No 194 (Supreme People's Court) ('*Sumitomo Bank*') discussed in Long Jiao (n 134) 35.

[144] Contract Law (n 135) arts 52, 54; Chinese Civil Code (n 136) arts 143–157.

[145] Chao Zhixiong, 'Research on the Contract of Civil Right of Action: The Influences of Judicial Experience on the Development of Legal Theory' [2017] (1) *The Jurist* 32, 33.

[146] ibid 33–34.

[147] Chinese Civil Code (n 136) art 197.

[148] See eg, Liang Zhao (n 38) 550.

[149] CCPL (n 20) art 34(1).

[150] ibid art 34(2).

[151] *Xinhuawen International Leasing Co Ltd v Deutsche Bank Guangzhou Branch* [2003] Jing Zhong Zi No 194 (Beijing High People's Court) discussed in Long Jiao (n 134) 35.

[152] *The Bank of East Asia Shanghai Branch v Sjanghai Jisheng Real Estate Co Ltd* [2001] Min Er Zhong Zi No 154 (Supreme People's Court) ('*Bank of East Asia*'), discussed in Long Jiao (n 134) 35; *Hin-pro International Logistics*

However, in a few cases, courts have disregarded the separability principle and interpreted the clause using the law applicable to the main contract.[153]

Although there is no express presumption of exclusivity of Choice-of-Forum clauses, some scholars argue that because judicial practice[154] shows a preference for interpretations favouring Chinese judicial sovereignty and protecting Chinese parties,[155] the result is to always enforce Choice-of-Forum clauses choosing Chinese courts even if they are non-exclusive.[156]

Since interpretation may be resolved by applying the Chinese Civil Code, Choice-of-Forum clauses may be interpreted 'according to the words used as well as considering the relevant clauses, nature and purpose of the act, customs, and the principle of good faith'.[157] If the clause is a standard contract term, article 498 of the Chinese Civil Code requires that it be interpreted based on its plain meaning. If multiple interpretations are possible, the clause is interpreted against the interest of the party who drafted it.[158]

In *Hin-pro International Logistics Limited v Compania Sud Americana De Vapore SA*, the relevant Choice-of-Forum clause stated:

> 23. Law and jurisdiction
>
> This Bill of Lading and any claim or dispute arising hereunder shall be subject to English law and the jurisdiction of the English High Court of Justice in London. If, notwithstanding the foregoing, any proceedings are commenced in another jurisdiction, such proceedings shall be referred to ordinary courts of law. In the case of Chile, arbitrators shall be competent to deal with any such disputes and proceedings shall be referred to the Chilean Ordinary Courts.

The Zhejiang High People's Court focused on the last two sentences and thus, interpreted this clause as not excluding the jurisdiction of Chinese courts[159] (ie, non-exclusive). This is in contrast with the English decisions, which interpreted the clause as exclusive.[160]

Chinese courts may also accept the characterisation of a dispute as tortious in order to bypass the Choice-of-Forum clauses, especially in bills of lading.[161] This approach has become common in maritime disputes, where parties characterise claims as torts, rather

Limited v Compania Sud Americana De Vapore SA (2013) Zhe Xia Zhong Zi No 144 (Zhejiang High People's Court) (CA) ('*Hin-Pro Logistics*').

[153] See eg, *Sumitomo Bank* (n 143); see Long Jiao (n 134) 35.

[154] See eg, Guangjian Tu and Zeyu Huang, 'People's Republic of China (PRC): Optional Choice of Court Agreements in the Vibrant Age' in Mary Keyes (ed), *Optional Choice of Court Agreements in Private International Law* (Spinger, 2020) 151, 159–60.

[155] See *Shandong Jufeng 2010* (n 138); *Hin-Pro Logistics* (n 152); see Liang Zhao (n 38) 560–61; Huanfang Du, 'Choice of Court Agreement with Foreign Elements in China: *Shandong Jufeng v. South Korea Mgame*' (2018) 13(2) *Frontiers of Law in China* 241, 253.

[156] CCPL (n 20) art 277.

[157] Chinese Civil Code (n 136) arts 142, 466.

[158] ibid art 498.

[159] *Hin-pro Logistics* (n 152).

[160] *Compania Sud Americana De Vapore SA v Hin-pro International Logistics Limited* [2014] EWHC 3632 (Comm), [32]–[34]; *Compania Sud Americana De Vapore SA v Hin-pro International Logistics Limited* [2015] EWCA Civ 401.

[161] See eg, *Jiangsu Guanyun International Economic and Trade Co Ltd v Compagnie Maritime D'Affretement and Burns Philp Agencies (HK)* [1999] GHFSZ No 41 (Guangzhou Maritime Court) discussed in Liang Zhao (n 38) 561 ('*Jiangsu Guanyun*'); also Provisions of the Supreme People's Court on Several Issues concerning the Application of Law during the Trial of Cases about Delivery of Goods without an Original Bill of Lading (最高人民法院关于审理无正本提单交付货物案件适用法律若干问题的规定) 2009 (adopted 26 February 2009) Supreme People's Court Interpretation No 1, art 3(1).

than contractual,[162] so as to fall outside the clause's scope and bring cases to Chinese courts. Interestingly, Chinese courts allow this even when the Choice-of-Forum clause explicitly covers torts or includes broad language like 'any dispute related to' or 'all disputes arising hereunder', which arguably include tort claims.[163]

C. Mandatory Rules, Public Policy, and International Interest

(i) Mandatory Rules

Article 279 of the CCPL grants Chinese courts exclusive jurisdiction over the following civil cases: (1) disputes concerning the establishment, dissolution or liquidation of legal organisations established in China, and the validity of resolutions made by such organisations; (2) disputes relating to the validity of intellectual property rights granted in China; and (3) contractual disputes involving Sino-foreign equity joint ventures, cooperative joint ventures, or contracts for the exploration and exploitation of natural resources within China.

The first and second grounds in article 279 are new, expanding Chinese courts' exclusive jurisdiction. The first covers organisations with their principal office or registration in China.[164] The second ground pertains only to the validity of intellectual property rights granted in China, excluding other disputes like infringements and royalty disputes.[165] The third ground, concerning Sino-foreign joint ventures, existed in the earlier CCPL versions. However, under the China Foreign Investment Law, these joint ventures must transition to structures under Chinese Company Law and the Chinese Partnership Enterprise Law by 2025, when they will be phased out.[166]

An action in China under article 279 will proceed, even if it breaches a Choice-of-Forum clause stipulating foreign courts.[167] Likewise, the *lis pendens* rule (article 281) and *forum non conveniens* principle (article 282) will not prevent a Chinese court from asserting jurisdiction over cases within its exclusive jurisdiction. Additionally, a foreign judgment breaching article 279 will not be enforced,[168] even if the originating foreign court had valid jurisdiction under a Choice-of-Forum clause.

The matters listed in article 34 of the CCPL, which fall under the exclusive jurisdiction of Chinese courts, should arguably also apply to any dispute. These matters include real estate disputes, which must be litigated where the property is located,[169] port operation disputes, which must be heard where the port is located,[170] and inheritance disputes, which should be heard by the court at the deceased's domicile at the time of death or where the main part of the inheritance estate is located.[171]

[162] Liang Zhao (n 38) 561.
[163] See ibid 562.
[164] Jie Huang, 'Developing Chinese PIL' (n 34) 226.
[165] ibid 211.
[166] ibid 226.
[167] CCPL (n 20) art 280.
[168] ibid art 301.
[169] ibid art 34(1).
[170] ibid art 34(2).
[171] ibid art 34(3).

(ii) Public Policy

Article 280 allows Chinese courts to dismiss cases involving Choice-of-Forum clauses stipulating foreign courts if they involve China's sovereignty, security, or public interests. A similar approach is allowed under article 280 (*forum non conveniens*) and article 300 on refusing recognition and enforcement of foreign judgments. Public policy now focuses on state interests, no longer covering those of organisations or individuals which was the case in the 2022 CCPL.[172] The public policy exception is also present in bilateral treaties, regional arrangements,[173] and in other Chinese laws,[174] including the Chinese Civil Code.[175] Issuances from the Communist Party,[176] judicial interpretations, and typical decisions (model cases) confirm its use to deny legal effects to acts,[177] including Choice-of-Forum clauses.

Public policy or 'public order' is not defined in the CCPL. Nonetheless, the SPC has clarified its meaning through judicial interpretations and model cases.[178] Public order includes: (1) fundamental policies of the Chinese Constitution, (2) China's national sovereignty and security, (3) international treaty obligations, (4) universally recognised principles of fairness and justice in international law, (5) fundamental legal principles of Chinese law, such as good faith, counter-terrorism, and the prohibition on gambling, (6) China's fundamental moral norms, and (7) China's fundamental and overall interests.[179]

Focusing on the 'socialist core values' of Chinese public policy, Meng argues that it serves to maintain national identity, social unity, and stability, and to protect individual rights, particularly in situations of power-imbalance like labour and consumer relations.[180] Public policy promotes specific values, with courts expected to enforce these when deciding cases. Meng further argues that the judicial implementation of public policy demonstrates the dominance of politics over law,[181] closely tied to the task of building a modern Chinese state.[182]

[172] See Jie Huang, 'Developing Chinese PIL' (n 34) 226.

[173] eg, China-UAE Treaty (n 84) art 12.

[174] eg, General Principles of Civil Law 1986 (China), art 150; Maritime Law (China), art 276.

[175] Chinese Civil Code (n 136) arts 143, 153.

[176] eg, Opinions on Cultivating and Practicing Socialist Social Values (People's Republic of China), General Office of the Central Committee of the Chinese Communist Party (December 2013), cited in Meng Rong, 'How Chinese courts implement public policies through judicial adjudication – taking cases in which courts implement "socialist core values" as the object of analysis' (2018) 3 *Legal Review* 184, 184.

[177] eg, Several Opinions of the Supreme People's Court on Cultivating and Practicing the Socialism Core Values (最高人民法院关于在人民法院工作中培育和践行社会主义核心价值观的若干意见) 2015 (adopted 12 October 2015) Supreme People's Court Fafa [2015] No 14; Interpretations of the Supreme People's Court on Several Issues Concerning Application of the Law of the People's Republic of China on Choice of Law for Foreign-Related Civil Relationships (I) (最高人民法院关于适用《中华人民共和国涉外民事关系法律适用法》若干问题的解释(一)) 2012 (adopted 28 December 2012) Supreme People's Court Interpretation No 24 ('Choice-of-Law Law Interpretation').

[178] eg, Third Group of Model Civil Cases Where People's Courts Vigorously Promoted the Core Socialist Values Published by the Supreme People's Court (最高人民法院发布第三批人民法院大力弘扬社会主义核心价值观典型民事案例) 2023 (adopted 1 March 2023); Second Group of Model Civil Cases Where the People's Courts Vigorously Promoted the Core Socialist Values Published by the Supreme People's Court [最高人民法院发布第二批人民法院大力弘扬社会主义核心价值观典型民事案例] 2022 (adopted 23 February 2022); Ten Model Civil Cases of Vigorously Carrying forward Core Socialist Values by the People's Courts Published by the Supreme People's Court (最高人民法院发布人民法院大力弘扬社会主义核心价值观十大典型民事案例) 2020 (adopted 13 May 2020).

[179] Choice-of-Law Law Interpretation (n 177).

[180] Meng Rong (n 176) 186–88.

[181] ibid 193.

[182] ibid 194.

Under article 143 of the Chinese Civil Code, to be valid, a juridical act must not violate public order.[183] Article 153 states that any act contrary to public order is void.[184] Thus, a Choice-of-Forum clause that violates Chinese public policy is considered void.

(iii) International and Foreign Interests

International and foreign interests are considered in enforcing Choice-of-Forum clauses under the CCPL. Article 281 allows suspension of Chinese proceedings based on the relative convenience of a foreign court (but not necessarily the court first seised of the matter), which is particularly relevant when foreign courts are non-exclusively chosen. Proceedings resume if the foreign court fails to hear or conclude the case within a reasonable time, requiring an evaluation of the foreign court's capacity, reasonableness, propriety, and efficiency. Similarly, article 282's *forum non conveniens* test evaluates the foreign court's convenience, with the same process applied if the Chinese court must resume hearing the case.

The principle of reciprocity under article 288 allows Chinese courts to consider international and foreign interests. Although the reciprocity required is now de jure, it still requires examination of the foreign court's laws and approach towards Chinese judgments. Under article 300, when refusing to recognise foreign judgments, Chinese courts assess whether the foreign jurisdiction meets Chinese legal standards. Although it is unclear which law determines whether reasonable notice and opportunity to be heard have been provided,[185] prior practice suggests Chinese law.[186] This also extends to fraud, which is also understood as part of the public law exception.[187] Hence, Chinese courts generally evaluate foreign actions against Chinese legal standards.

D. The Choice-of-Forum Clause and Protecting Weaker Parties

(i) Asymmetric Choice-of-Forum Clauses

Since the CCPL recognises both exclusive and non-exclusive clauses, choosing either Chinese or foreign courts, Chinese courts should also be able to recognise and enforce asymmetric clauses. However, their effect depends on (1) who brings the action, and (2) whether the party who brings the action has an exclusive or non-exclusive choice. If a Chinese court is chosen, whether in the exclusive or non-exclusive part, it can always assume jurisdiction.[188] Even the party with multiple jurisdiction options is unlikely to resist, as article 277 grants the chosen Chinese court jurisdiction, and this also serves as a basis to resist dismissal under article 282's *forum non conveniens* test.

[183] Chinese Civil Code (n 136) art 143.
[184] ibid art 153.
[185] Jie Huang, 'Developing Chinese PIL' (n 34) 230.
[186] See Yujun Guo, 'Country Report The People's Republic of China' in Adeline Chong, *Recognition and Enforcement of Foreign Judgments in Asia* (Asian Business Law Institute, 2017) 49, 66; Adeline Chong, 'Moving towards harmonisation in the recognition and enforcement of foreign judgment rules in Asia' (2020) 16(1) *Journal of Private International Law* 31, 50.
[187] Yujun Guo (n 186) 65; Chong (n 186) 51.
[188] CCPL (n 20) art 277.

Article 280 states that if a foreign court is exclusively chosen, Chinese courts can dismiss proceedings. Therefore, if the party litigating in China has an exclusive choice of a foreign court, the Chinese court will generally dismiss the case. However, if the party litigating in China has the option to file in multiple courts, even if the clause does not explicitly mention Chinese courts, the Chinese court may assume jurisdiction, subject to the *lis pendens* rule in article 281 and *forum non conveniens* in article 282.

In *Lai Jianping v ABN AMRO Bank*,[189] the Choice-of-Forum clauses stated that disputes should be resolved in Hong Kong, except that ABN AMRO Bank could litigate in other jurisdictions. Both the Shanghai Intermediate People's Court and Shanghai High People's Court upheld the asymmetric clause's validity. They interpreted it as being exclusive for the investor (Lai), and non-exclusive for the bank, confirming that the legal effect depends on who files the action, and the options available to that party.

(ii) Protecting Weaker Parties

Article 31 of the CCPL Interpretation requires businesses to adequately inform consumers of Choice-of-Forum clauses when used as standard contract terms. If not, consumers may file to nullify the clause in court.[190] This notice requirement is not in the CCPL itself but in the CCPL Interpretation. Judicial practice shows that reasonable notice is satisfied if the business draws the consumer's attention to the clause.[191] For online commercial contracts, the clause has to be written in noticeable form, such as in bold or in a different colour.[192] Furthermore, the length of the parties' relationship may also indicate sufficient notice.[193]

Article 26 of the Consumer Protection Law states that standard terms imposing unfair or unreasonable rules that restrict consumer rights can be declared void. Since Choice-of-Forum clauses are often standard-term clauses in consumer contracts, if they are deemed unfair – such as requiring litigation to be in a distant foreign court – they may be voided. Qin and Jing's study on wealth management product contracts in China found that terms limiting customers' dispute resolution options reflect power imbalances in favour of banks.[194] They also found that banks often require customers to advance fees, such as arbitration and attorneys' fees, to discourage litigation at the chosen forum.[195]

Article 42 of the Law on Choice of Law for Foreign-related Civil Relations ('Choice-of-Law Law') also limits applicable law options[196] in consumer contracts to either

[189] *Lai Jianping v ABN AMRO Bank NV* [2010] Hu Gao Min Wu (Shang) Zhong Zi No 49 (Shanghai High People's Court), discussed in Guangjian Tu and Zeyu Huang (n 154) 166.

[190] CCPL Interpretation (n 36), art 31.

[191] See Zheng Sophia Tang and Lu Xu, 'Choice-of-Court Agreements in Electronic Consumer Contracts in China' (2016) 23 *Pandora's Box* 21, 26.

[192] *Liao Yandong v Tencent* [2016] Case No 06646 (Foshan Intermediate People's Court of Guangdong, 24 May 2016), discussed in Zheng Sophia Tang and Lu Xu (n 191) 26.

[193] *Daizhibai v Hangzhou Leihuo Science & Technology Ltd* [2016] Case No 00129 (Lianyungang Intermediate People's Court of Jianggsu, 18 January 2016), discussed in Zheng Sophia Tang and Lu Xu (n 191) 26.

[194] Qin Zhou and Jing Feng, 'What We Do and Do Not Know About Standard Form Contracts? An Empirical Study of Wealth Management Product Contracts in China' (2021) 16 *Asian Journal of Comparative Law* 124, 141–42.

[195] ibid 142.

[196] ibid.

the law of the consumer's domicile or of the place of performance. While the law governing the main contract is independent from the law applicable to the Choice-of-Forum clause, the application of Chinese law to the main contract because of the consumer's domicile in China means that in consumer transactions, there is a high chance that both the main contract and aspects of the Choice-of-Forum clause (eg, validity and existence) are subject to Chinese law. A similar restriction applies to cross-border employment contracts under article 43.[197]

(iii) Contracts-of-Adhesion

Article 31 of the CCPL Interpretation requires businesses to adequately inform consumers of Choice-of-Forum clauses when included as standard contract terms. Similarly, the Chinese Civil Code mandates that the party responsible for the standard term must highlight any clauses that exempt or limit liability and explain them if requested.[198] The rules emphasise the importance of informing the other party or consumer about the Choice-of-Forum clause in standard-term contracts. Failure to comply with this notice requirement results in the term 'not becoming part of the contract'.[199]

Article 497 of the Chinese Civil Code states that a standard term is void if it deprives the other party of major rights. Arguably, a standard-term Choice-of-Forum clause that imposes an unreasonable burden on the other party (eg, a distant court location, waiving defences, or preconditions that practically discourage litigation) could be seen as severely limiting or depriving the other party's major rights, and thus invalid.

III. Indonesia

A. Enforcement of Choice-of-Forum Clauses

(i) Indonesia's Approach to Jurisdiction

Article 24 of the 1945 Indonesian Constitution[200] states that judicial power is exercised by the Supreme Court (*Mahkamah Agung*) and the other judicial bodies. The Supreme Court, Indonesia's highest court, hears appeals from the lower courts,[201] conducts judicial review of regulations lower than a statute (eg, *Peraturan Pemerintah* or implementing regulations issued by the president),[202] and supervises lower courts.[203] It also resolves jurisdictional

[197] Choice-of-Law Law (n 139) art 43.

[198] Chinese Civil Code (n 136) art 496(2).

[199] ibid.

[200] Constitution of the Republic of Indonesia 1945 (Indonesia) [tr Office of the Registrar and the Secretary General of the Constitutional Court of the Republic of Indonesia (Web Document): https://www.mkri.id/public/content/infoumum/regulation/pdf/uud45%20eng.pdf] ('Indonesian Constitution').

[201] ibid art 24A(1).

[202] ibid.

[203] Law on the Supreme Court (*Undang-Undang Tentang Mahkamah Agung*) Law No 14 of 1985 (Indonesia) art 38.

conflicts between courts[204] and has the power to reopen and reexamine cases involving enforceable verdicts (*Peninjauan Kembali*).[205]

Below the Supreme Court, the Indonesian judiciary has four branches: (1) general (*Pengadilan Umum*) and special courts (*Pengadilan Khusus*), (2) religious courts (*Pengadilan Agama*), (3) military courts (*Pengadilan Militer*), and (4) administrative courts (*Pengadilan Tata Usaha Negara*).[206] The Constitutional Court (*Mahkamah Konstitusi*), established under article 24C of the Indonesian Constitution, sits outside this hierarchy and is responsible for reviewing laws against the Constitution.[207]

First instance district courts (*Pengadilan Negeri*) hear most civil cases and have jurisdiction over matters not assigned to other courts. In some cities, special courts or chambers hear commercial matters,[208] while other special courts handle human rights, fisheries, labour, tax, anti-corruption, and children's cases.[209] High courts (*Pengadilan Tinggi*) in Indonesia's provinces hear appeals from the district courts,[210] with further appeals going to the Supreme Court.[211]

After gaining independence in 1945, Indonesia retained colonial laws and institutions. Three Dutch colonial civil procedure codes still define jurisdiction and procedure in general courts: (1) *Herziene Indonesisch Reglement* 1941 (Revised Indonesian Regulation or 'HIR'),[212] for indigenous populations in Java and Madura; (2) *Rechtsreglement Buitengewesten* 1927 (Civil Procedure Code for Legal Matters Outside Java and Madura or 'RBg');[213] and (3) *Reglement op de Burgerlijke Rechsvordering* 1857 (Civil Procedure Code or 'Rv')[214] for foreigners within Indonesia. Since the Japanese occupation during World War II, only the HIR and RBg apply, with the Rv as a supplementary code.[215]

Under article 118 HIR, article 142 RBg, and article 99 Rv, jurisdiction is determined by the principle of *actor sequitur forum rei* ('the plaintiff must sue in the proper forum'), which is guided by the principle of presence.[216] The primary rule states that the court with jurisdiction *in personam* is where the defendant resides or lives.[217] For multiple defendants,

[204] ibid art 28(1)(b).
[205] ibid art 28(1)(c).
[206] Indonesian Constitution (n 200) art 24(2).
[207] ibid art 24C(1).
[208] Law on General Courts (*Undang-Undang Tentang Peradilan Umum*) Law No 2 of 1986 (Indonesia), as amended by Law No 49 of 2009 art 8(2).
[209] See Tim Lindsey and Simon Butt, *Indonesian Law* (Oxford University Press, 2018) 85–86; Hikmahanto Juwana, 'Courts in Indonesia: a mix of Western and local character' in Jiunn-rong Yeng and Wen-Cheng Chang, *Asian Courts in Context* (Cambridge University Press, 2014) 307–11.
[210] See Lindsey and Butt (n 209) 90–91; Hikmahanto Juwana (n 209) 306.
[211] See Lindsey and Butt (n 209) 91–93; Hikmahanto Juwana (n 209) 306–7.
[212] Revised Indonesian Regulations 1941 (*Herziene Indonesisch Reglement* 1941) (Indonesia) art 118(1) ('HIR').
[213] Regulations on Legal Matters for the Outer Regions 1927 (*Rechtsreglement Buitengewesten* 1927) (Indonesia) ('RBg').
[214] Regulations on Civil Procedure 1857 (*Reglement op de Burgerlijke Rechsvordering* 1857) (Indonesia) ('Rv').
[215] See Afifah Kusumadara, 'Jurisdiction of courts chosen in the parties' choice of court agreements: an unsettled issue in Indonesian private international law and the way out' (2022) 18(3) *Journal of Private International Law* 424, 425 fn 1 ('Choice-of-Court Agreements').
[216] See Sudargo Gautama, 'International Civil Procedure in Indonesia' (1996) 6 *Asian Yearbook of International Law* 87, 91; Herliana Herliana and Sujayadi Sujayadi, 'Establishing Jurisdiction of Indonesian Courts in Transnational Contract Case: A Respond to Global Economic Changes' in Mirsa Umiyati, et al (eds), *Proceedings of the International Conference on 'Changing of Law: Business Law, Local Wisdom and Tourism Industry' (ICCLB 2023)* (Atlantis Press, 2023) 544, 549.
[217] HIR (n 212) art 118(1).

the plaintiff can choose any court in any of the defendants' domiciles.[218] If the defendant's domicile is unknown, the court of the plaintiff's residence has jurisdiction.[219] In cases involving immovable property, the lawsuit must be filed where the property is located.[220] These rules also apply to corporate entities, with the court at the company's legal seat having jurisdiction.[221]

All three procedural codes should apply only to matters occurring within Indonesia.[222] Nonetheless, for disputes involving foreign elements, courts still follow these rules.[223] Article 100 Rv allows an Indonesian party to sue a foreign party without a domicile in Indonesia in an Indonesian court. If the foreign defendant does not reside in Indonesia, the case should be filed where the plaintiff resides.[224] If the foreign defendant resides in Indonesia, the case should be filed at the district court of the defendant's domicile or residence.[225]

Indonesia recognises the principle of party autonomy, allowing parties to choose the court to hear their disputes (*Pilihan Forum*). Judicial practice and scholars base this freedom on article 1338 of the *Burgerlijk Wetboek* (Civil Code or 'BW'),[226] which states that a legally concluded agreement binds the parties insofar as the agreement is executed in good faith. Scholars agree that article 1338 allows both exclusive and non-exclusive Choice-of-Forum clauses, although their effect remains subject to the *actor sequitur forum rei* principle.[227] The procedural codes also permit a choice of domicile, which has the effect of granting the court in the chosen domicile exclusive jurisdiction,[228] albeit still subject to the *actor sequitur forum rei* principle. Scholars also argue that this capacity to choose a domicile is also a legal basis for the enforcement of exclusive Choice-of-Forum clauses.[229] Notably, article 99(16) Rv states that '[i]f there is a choice of court, a claim can be brought either to the court chosen by the parties', thus confirming the parties' autonomy to choose a forum. Furthermore, article 18(4) of the Electronic Information and Transaction Act 2008,[230] as amended, empowers parties to choose the courts, arbitration, or other means of dispute resolution.

As a civil law country, Indonesia's laws come from codes and statutes, with no formal recognition of judicial decisions as a legal source. However, under the principle of

[218] ibid art 118(2).
[219] ibid art 118(3).
[220] ibid.
[221] See Afifah Kusumadara, *Indonesian Private International Law* (Hart Publishing, 2021) 38–39 ('*Indonesian PIL*').
[222] See Kusumadara, 'Choice-of-Court Agreements' (n 215) 425.
[223] Kusumadara, 'Choice-of-Court Agreements' (n 215) 425.
[224] Rv (n 214) art 99.
[225] ibid.
[226] Civil Code (*Burgerlijk Wetboek*) (Indonesia); see *Societe Generale v Hari Raharja*, Supreme Court, Judgment No 3253K/PDT/1990, 30 November 1993; see also Alvansa Vickya and Tiurma M Pitta Allagan, 'Implications of Non-exclusive Choice of Forum Clauses in Determining the Competent Dispute Resolution Forum in Indonesia' (2022) 12(1) *Indonesia Law Review* 70, 71–72.
[227] HIR (n 212) art 118(4); Rv (n 214) art 99; See also Kusumadara, *Indonesian PIL* (n 221) 51–52; Vickya and Allagan (n 226) 71–72.
[228] HIR (n 212) art 118(4).
[229] See eg, Kusumadara, *Indonesian PIL* (n 221) 51; Vickya and Allagan (n 226) 72.
[230] Law on Electronic Information and Transactions (*Undang-Undang Tentang Informasi Dan Transaksi Elecktronik*) Law Number 11 of 2008 (Indonesia) as amended by Law No 9 of 2016 ('Electronic Information and Transaction Act 2008').

rechtsvinding,[231] judges must still decide cases even in the absence of specific laws. Judicial decisions act as gap fillers when statutes or codes lack rules, although they may sometimes contradict the textual interpretation.[232] Moreover, like other civil law systems, Indonesia's judicial decisions are complemented by a rich body of academic literature or 'doctrine' in academic texts.[233]

(ii) Prorogation and Derogation

Under article 118(4) HIR, parties may choose a domicile, which designates the court having jurisdiction, whether within Indonesia or overseas. In *Bernhard Josef Rifeel v PT Merck Indonesia*[234] ('*Rifeel*') the Supreme Court ruled that the Indonesian district court lacked jurisdiction, as the parties had chosen Swiss law and Switzerland as their domicile. Hence, the Swiss court was deemed the competent court to hear the dispute.[235]

A Choice-of-Forum clause, however, does not necessarily involve choosing a domicile. Parties may simply select a court under the freedom of contract (article 1338 BW) and confirmed under article 99(16) Rv. If the chosen court aligns with the *actor sequitur forum rei* principle, it excludes all other courts from hearing the dispute and gives the clause the classic effect of an exclusive jurisdiction clause by prorogating jurisdiction to the chosen court while excluding all other courts.

When the defendant's domicile is in another Indonesian territory, inconsistent with the *actor sequitur forum rei* principle, judicial practice shows that the *actor sequitur forum rei* may prevail.[236] Article 99(16) Rv addresses this, stating, '[i]f there is a choice of court, a claim can be brought either to the court chosen by the parties, or to the court in the district of the defendant's residence, depending on the plaintiff's choice'.[237]

Parties may also choose a foreign forum pursuant to article 1388 BW,[238] article 118(4) HIR or article 99(16) Rv. However, like domestic Choice-of-Forum clauses, even exclusive Choice-of-Forum clauses stipulating foreign courts remain subject to the *actor sequitur forum rei* principle. In *Bali Energi Ltd v Mitomo Shoji KK* ('*Bali Energi*'),[239] despite choosing the Tokyo district court, the plaintiff filed in the Central Jakarta District Court, where Bali Energi was based. Bali Energi objected, but the Court upheld its jurisdiction under article 118(2) HIR, thus confirming the *actor sequitur forum rei* principle. The Jakarta High Court affirmed this decision on appeal.

[231] Hikmahanto Juwana (n 209) 323.
[232] ibid.
[233] Lindsey and Butt (n 209) 77–78.
[234] *Bernhard Josef Rifeel v PT Merck Indonesia*, Supreme Court, Judgment No 1537K/Pdt/1989, 21 January 1991; see Priskila Penasthika, *Unravelling Choice of Law in International Commercial Contracts as an Illustrative Case Study* (Doctoral Thesis, Erasmus University Rotterdam, 29 September 2022) 87.
[235] Penasthika (n 234) 87.
[236] eg, *Bali Energi Ltd v Mitomo Shoji KK*, District Court of Central Jakarta, Judgment No 359/Pdt.G/2011/PN. Jkt Past, 31 July 2012 ('*Bali Energi*'); see Kusumadara, 'Choice-of-Court Agreements' (n 215) 427–28.
[237] Reglement op de Burgerlijke Rechsvordering 1857 (Indonesia), art 99(16).
[238] See Kusumadara, 'Choice-of-Court Agreements' (n 215) 424–25.
[239] *Bali Energi* (n 300); See Kusumadara, 'Choice-of-Court Agreements' (n 215) 428–29.

In *PT Pelayaran Manalagi v PT Asuransi Harta Aman Pratamana* ('*PT Pelayaran*'),[240] the Supreme Court ruled that Choice-of-Forum clauses choosing foreign courts can override the *actor sequitur forum rei* principle. Unfortunately, the decision was based on the applicable law, which was English law, not on the exclusive Choice-of-Forum clause.[241] Nonetheless, scholars argue this may suggest that foreign forum clauses could implicitly prevail over the *actor sequitur forum rei* principle.[242]

The choice of forum, whether within Indonesia or overseas, can also be non-exclusive, as allowed by article 1388 BW, article 118(4) HIR or article 99(16) Rv.[243] Since parties do not intend to derogate from Indonesian courts' jurisdiction, the principle of *actor sequitur forum rei* always applies to non-exclusive clauses. However, an Indonesian court's jurisdiction would still depend on the application of *forum non conveniens*, *lis pendens* and *res judicata* principles.

In *Morgan Stanley Company Inc v APP International Finance Company BV*[244] the parties had non-exclusive Choice-of-Forum clauses stipulating New York State and federal courts.[245] The Supreme Court ruled that APP was contractually bound by New York courts' jurisdiction, making New York courts the appropriate forum.[246] The choices of New York law and courts were key considerations.[247] The Kuala Tungkal District Court was considered 'Not the Appropriate Forum' due to fundamental differences in law,[248] challenges in applying New York law effectively,[249] the complexity of the financing transaction,[250] the minimal ties to Indonesia,[251] and the unlawful acts having occurred outside Indonesia.[252] Although not explicitly stated, this analysis aligns with the *forum non conveniens* principle.

(iii) Service of Process

A plaintiff commences an action by filing a request or petition (*Introductief Rekest*), usually at the court where the defendant resides.[253] As discussed, the district court at the defendant's domicile can always assume jurisdiction regardless of the Choice-of-Forum clause. While the case may be commenced in the chosen Indonesian court, this does not necessarily override the *actor sequitur forum rei* principle. Hence, as long as the court has jurisdiction *in personam*, which is either based on the Choice-of-Forum clause or the *actor sequitur forum rei* principle, service of process is allowed whether within or outside Indonesia.[254]

[240] *PT Pelayaran Manalagi v PT Asuransi Harta Aman Pratamana*, Supreme Court, Judgment No 1935 K/Pdt/2012, 14 January 2013 ('*PT Pelayaran*'); See Kusumadara, 'Choice-of-Court Agreements' (n 215) 429–30.
[241] *PT Pelayaran* (n 240) 59.
[242] Kusumadara, *Indonesian PIL* (n 221) 54.
[243] See, eg, Vickya and Allagan (n 226) 77–82.
[244] *Morgan Stanley Company Inc v APP International Finance Company BV*, Supreme Court, Judgment No 338PK/Pdt/2014, 7 January 2015.
[245] See ibid 83, 86, 100.
[246] See ibid 106.
[247] See ibid 103–106.
[248] See ibid 106–7.
[249] See ibid 107–8.
[250] See ibid 108–9.
[251] See ibid 109–12.
[252] See ibid 112–14.
[253] HIR (n 212) art 118(1).
[254] ibid art 121.

(iv) Dismissal and Stay of Actions

An exclusively chosen Indonesian court can assume jurisdiction under article 118(4) HIR and article 99(16) Rv, but the defendant may object to its jurisdiction at any stage.[255] If this chosen court does not align with the *actor sequitur forum rei* principle, the action may be dismissed.[256] Conversely, an action filed at an Indonesian court, despite contravening the exclusive Choice-of-Forum clause but consistent with the *actor sequitur forum rei* principle may not be dismissed,[257] as seen in *Bali Energi*. However, an action contravening both the exclusive Choice-of-Forum clause and the *actor sequitur forum rei* principle will be dismissed unless another jurisdictional basis exists.[258] Thus, a breach of the exclusive Choice-of-Forum clause, whether in favour of an Indonesian or foreign court, is not a conclusive ground for dismissal.

In *PT Rainbow Indah Karpet v PT TNT Skypak International Express* ('*PT Rainbow*'),[259] decided a year after *PT Pelarayan*, the Supreme Court upheld the dismissal, after applying *Rifeel* and ruling that the court whose law governs the contract (a Dutch court) should hear the dispute.[260] The Supreme Court emphasised the parties' agreement to an exclusive Choice-of-Forum clause stipulating Rotterdam courts and a Choice-of-Law clause choosing Dutch law.[261] While *PT Rainbow* correctly focused on the exclusive *Choice-of-Forum* clause, the reference to the *Choice-of-Law* clause obscures the court's reasoning. Notably, the Court did not clarify whether the *actor sequitur forum rei* principle can supersede foreign Choice-of-Forum clauses.

Similarly, breaching a non-exclusive Choice-of-Forum clause does not automatically warrant dismissal, as it does not derogate from Indonesian courts' jurisdiction. An Indonesian court with jurisdiction under the *actor sequitur forum rei* principle or another legal basis can still assume jurisdiction. Dismissal is possible if no jurisdictional grounds exist under Indonesian law. Furthermore, even if the court has jurisdiction, it may still dismiss the case based on *forum non conveniens*, *lis pendens* and *res judicata* principles.

Article 134 Rv contains both the *lis pendens* and *res judicata* principles, allowing Indonesian courts to dismiss cases previously litigated involving the same parties and subject matter.[262] If a related case is ongoing in another Indonesian court, proceedings may be stayed and consolidated.[263] However, Rv applies only to Indonesian proceedings, not foreign proceedings. Thus, parallel foreign proceedings, even under either an exclusive or non-exclusive Choice-of-Forum clause, do not automatically lead to a stay or dismissal of the Indonesian case,[264] raising the risk of inconsistent judgments especially since Indonesia does

[255] ibid arts 125, 133, 134.
[256] ibid art 134.
[257] ibid.
[258] ibid.
[259] *PT Rainbow Indah Karpet v PT TNT Skypak International Express*, Supreme Court, Judgment No 1238K/Pdt/2014, 27 November 2014; See Penasthika (n 234) 116–117.
[260] ibid 13–14.
[261] ibid.
[262] Rv (n 214) art 134.
[263] ibid.
[264] *PT Indah Kiat Pulp & Paper Tbk v Bank America National Trust Company*, Supreme Court, Judgment No. 445 PK/Pdt/2007, 19 August 2008 ('*PT Indah*'); See also Kusumadara, *Indonesian PIL* (n 221) 41–43.

not recognise and enforce foreign judgments, subject to certain exceptions.[265] Nonetheless, Kusumadara argues that a stay may be granted on the ground of *lis pendens* when recognition and enforcement of foreign judgment is possible.[266] Extending this argument further, if a foreign judgment has actually been recognised and enforced in Indonesia, the Indonesian court may also dismiss the domestic proceedings based on *res judicata*.

In *PT Indah Kiat Pulp & Paper Tbk v Bank America National Trust Company* ('*PT Indah*'),[267] the parties' indenture agreement included a Choice-of-Law clause choosing New York law and a non-exclusive Choice-of-Forum clause stipulating New York State or federal courts.[268] The bondholders argued that a case was already pending in New York and the plaintiff had participated in the proceedings.[269] However, the Bengkalis District Court exercised jurisdiction[270] and decided in favour of the plaintiff.[271] The Riau High Court[272] and Supreme Court upheld[273] this decision.[274] Upon extraordinary appeal, the Supreme Court annulled the prior decisions, ruling that the annulment of the financing agreements should have been filed in New York.[275] However, the Court confirmed the Bengkalis District Court's jurisdiction because the Choice-of-Forum clause was non-exclusive,[276] though its exercise was deemed inappropriate.

In some cases, Indonesian courts have refused to exercise jurisdiction despite a non-exclusive Choice-of-Forum clause choosing foreign courts. In *PT Abadi Adimulia v PT Unilever Indonesia*,[277] the parties chose Singapore courts as their non-exclusive forum. The Tangerang District Court ruled that it lacked jurisdiction because the parties have chosen Singapore courts.[278]

(v) *An Indonesian* Forum Non Conveniens

Indonesia has no statutory rule for *forum non conveniens*, but one of the early cases establishing the principle was *Richard Bruce Ness v Jane Perlez and the New York Times Company* ('*Ness*').[279] In *Ness*, the plaintiff commenced an action for defamation in the Central Jakarta District Court based on article 118(2) HIR and article 99(6) Rv, as one defendant resided in

[265] See Rv (n 214) art 436(1).
[266] Kusumadara, *Indonesian PIL* (n 221) 43.
[267] *PT Indah* (n 264).
[268] ibid 40–41.
[269] ibid 48.
[270] *PT Indah Kiat Pulp & Paper Tbk v Bank America National Trust Company*, District Court of Bengkalis, Judgment No 05/PDT.G/2003/PN-BKS, 21 September 2004 ('*PT Indah-Bengkalis*').
[271] *PT Indah* (n 264) 161, 192.
[272] *PT Indah Kiat Pulp & Paper Tbk v Bank America National Trust Company*, High Court of Riau, Judgment No 40/PDT/2005/PTR, 16 June 2005.
[273] *PT Indah Kiat Pulp & Paper Tbk v Bank America National Trust Company*, Supreme Court, Judgment No 381 K/Pdt/2006, 21 June 2006.
[274] *PT Indah* (n 264) 193.
[275] ibid 165–67.
[276] ibid 193.
[277] *PT Abadi Adimulia v PT Unilever Indonesia*, Tangerang District Court, Judgment No 269/Pdt.G/2018/PN.Tng, 29 May 2019.
[278] ibid 120–21.
[279] *Richard Bruce Ness v Jane Perlez and the New York Times Company*, District Court of Central Jakarta, Judgment No 181/PDT.G/2007/PN.JKT.PST, 8 October 2007; see Kusumadara, *Indonesian PIL* (n 221) 40–41.

central Jakarta.[280] The defendant argued *forum non conveniens*, noting that Perlez had moved to Islamabad,[281] and New York Times Company had no representative in Indonesia.[282] They also argued that any judgment might not be enforceable due to lack of treaties on recognition and enforcement of judgments between Indonesia and the defendants' home countries.[283] The Court agreed and dismissed the case based on *forum non conveniens*.[284]

In its reasoning, the Court cited Indonesian scholar M Yahya Harahap, who argued that the most appropriate forum is the one with the most real and substantial connection to the dispute.[285] Harahap identified factors such as convenience, costs, availability of witnesses and documents, the place where the parties reside or conduct business, and the governing law.[286] The Court applied these factors and concluded that Indonesia was not an appropriate forum, thus refusing to exercise jurisdiction.[287]

Subsequently, the same plaintiff filed a new case[288] against the same defendants but adding an Indonesian defendant residing in Central Jakarta. This time, the Central Jakarta District Court exercised jurisdiction,[289] reasoning that the allegedly defamatory *New York Times* article's subject was located at Buyat Bay, and thus the Court had jurisdiction.[290] The Court again referred to Harahap's list of connecting factors, which in turn was based on *Spiliada*.[291]

Although the *Ness* cases involved torts, they demonstrate the Indonesian courts' willingness to dismiss cases based on *forum non conveniens*. The Indonesian version, based on *Spiliada*, seeks the more appropriate forum. As in *Spiliada*, Indonesian courts may dismiss cases even if they have jurisdiction under the *actor sequitur forum rei* principle. Indonesian scholars widely acknowledge that the *forum non conveniens* principle is accepted in judicial practice.[292] Hence, *forum non conveniens* should apply to both non-exclusive and exclusive clauses.

In *Indah Kiat International Finance Company BV v Bank America National Trust Company*,[293] a case related to *PT Indah*, PT Indah's subsidiary filed a claim in the Bengkalis District Court.[294] Like in *PT Indah*, the financing agreements stipulated New York law and a non-exclusive choice of New York courts.[295] The Bengkalis court assumed jurisdiction because the choice of New York courts was non-exclusive, and ruled that the financing documents were null and void because the transactions were tortious under Indonesian

[280] Kusumadara, *Indonesian PIL* (n 221) 40.
[281] ibid.
[282] ibid.
[283] ibid.
[284] ibid.
[285] ibid 41.
[286] ibid.
[287] ibid.
[288] *Richard Bruce Ness v Jane Perlez*, District Court of Central Jakarta, Judgment No 408/Pdt.G/2007/PN.Jkt.Pst, 25 March 2009; Kusumadara, *Indonesian PIL* (n 221) 41.
[289] Kusumadara, *Indonesian PIL* (n 221) 41.
[290] ibid.
[291] ibid.
[292] ibid.
[293] *Indah Kiat International Finance Company BV v Bank America National Trust Company*, Supreme Court, Judgment No 1713K/Pdt/2007, 26 February 2008 ('*Indah Kiat*'); See Penasthika (n 234) 126–29.
[294] *Indah Kiat* (n 293) 3.
[295] ibid 17.

law.[296] The Riau High Court upheld this ruling.[297] On the appeal, the Supreme Court ruled that Indonesian law was irrelevant for assessing the agreement's validity.[298] It highlighted several factors favouring New York as the appropriate forum, including the choice of New York law as applicable law, the transaction's occurence outside Indonesia, and most parties being United States-based.[299] This reasoning reflects the *forum non conveniens* principle, with the Supreme Court concluding that the Bengkalis court was an inconvenient forum.[300] Nonetheless, the appeal was dismissed, recognising the Bengkalis court's jurisdiction since the Choice-of-Forum clause was non-exclusive and the choice of forum rested with the plaintiff.[301]

(vi) Anti-suit Injunctions and Other Relief

In *PT Indah*, the parties agreed to the non-exclusive jurisdiction of the New York courts. While the lawsuit in New York was ongoing, PT Indah filed an action in the Bengkalis District Court.[302] The Bengkalis court issued a provisional judgment restraining the defendants from pursuing legal action inside or outside Indonesia, with a US$100,000 per day penalty for non-compliance.[303] The Bengkalis court offered no clear reasoning for such measure other than its own jurisdiction. On extraordinary appeal,[304] the Supreme Court overturned both the final judgment and the provisional measure,[305] stating that the latter did not comply with Indonesian civil procedure.[306] Notably, the Supreme Court also made such reversals in other cases.[307] Hence, Indonesia still lacks statutory or judicial guidelines for issuing anti-suit injunctions, beyond protecting Indonesian parties' interests.[308] Hence, it remains unclear whether an anti-suit injunction may be issued, and whether Choice-of-Forum clauses have a role in their issuance.

(vii) Recognition and Enforcement of Foreign Judgments

As a general rule, foreign judgments are not recognised and enforced in Indonesia.[309] Indonesian scholars cite article 22a of *Algemene Bepalingen van Wetgeving voor Nedelandsch Indie* (General Provisions of Legislation for the Dutch East Indies or 'AB')[310] which requires

[296] ibid 185.
[297] ibid 185, 188.
[298] ibid 174–75.
[299] ibid 202–8.
[300] ibid 303.
[301] ibid 373–74.
[302] *PT Indah-Bengkalis* (n 270); see Kusumadara, Indonesian PIL (n 221) 43–44.
[303] Kusumadara, *Indonesian PIL* (n 221) 44.
[304] *PT Indah* (n 264).
[305] ibid 173; Kusumadara, *Indonesian PIL* (n 221) 44.
[306] Kusumadara, *Indonesian PIL* (n 221) 43–44.
[307] Eg, *Perusahaan Pertambangan Minyak dan Gas Bumi Negara v Karaha Bodas Company LLC*, Supreme Court, Judgment No 01/BANDING/WASIT.INT/2002, 8 March 2004; see Kusumadara, *Indonesian PIL* (n 221) 44–46.
[308] Kusumadara, *Indonesian PIL* (n 221) 46.
[309] ibid 176.
[310] General Provisions of Legislation for Dutch East Indies (Algemene Bepalingen van Wetgeving voor Nedelandsch Indie) (Indonesia) art 17 ('AB').

laws or treaties as the basis on which to execute foreign judgments in Indonesia.[311] At the moment, however, Indonesia is not a party to any bilateral or multilateral treaty for the reciprocal enforcement of foreign judgments.[312] Nonetheless, the International Convention on Civil Liability for Oil Pollution Damage, ratified by Indonesia in 1978,[313] requires recognition and enforcement of judgments related to oil pollution.[314] There is little discussion, however, on how Indonesian courts enforce this treaty. Another exception is article 724 in the Indonesian Commercial Code, which addresses maritime losses.[315] Outside of these exceptions, parties must re-litigate claims in Indonesia,[316] though foreign judgments can be used as evidence, albeit their evidentiary weight is unclear.[317] Furthermore, because recognition is distinguished from enforcement, as the former does not require an active action from the court unlike the latter, some legal scholars argue that declaratory or constitutive judgments, requiring only 'recognition' rather than 'execution', may be recognised in Indonesia.[318]

This approach means that foreign judgments involving Choice-of-Forum clauses, unless they fall under article 724 of the Indonesian Commercial Code, cannot be directly recognised or enforced in Indonesia. Parties may need to relitigate, even if doing so breaches an exclusive Choice-of-Forum clause, which may be unattractive as it exposes parties to uncertainty and possible damages because of breach. In turn, this may lead parties to simply choose an Indonesian forum or make their Choice-of-Forum clause non-exclusive – choices which may not be desirable. In addition, Indonesian parties may be asked to waive their right to pursue remedies for breach or be subject to contractual disadvantages like higher costs or fines. These situations raise the need for Indonesia to seriously revisit its rule on recognition or enforcement of foreign judgments, even if just in relation to Choice-of-Forum clauses. Becoming a party to the Choice-of-Court Convention may be a good solution.[319]

B. Existence, Validity, and Interpretation

(i) Issues of Existence and Validity

Indonesian courts address the issue of existence of contracts by applying article 1320 BW, which outlines the essential contractual elements: (1) a binding agreement, (2) legal capacity of the parties, (3) certainty of subject matter, and (4) a legal cause. While article 1320 concerns contract *validity*, Indonesian scholars argue that *existence* is inseparable from these conditions.[320] If any requirement is missing, the contract is void or voidable. Since

[311] Kusumadara, *Indonesian PIL* (n 221) 176.

[312] ibid; Sudargo Gautama (n 280) 98; Yu Un Oppusunggu, 'Country Report The Republic of Indonesia' in Adeline Chong (ed), *Recognition and Enforcement of Foreign Judgments in Asia* (Asian Business Law Institute, 2017) 91, 100.

[313] United Nations, 'International Convention on Civil Liability for Oil Pollution Damage' (webpage): https://treaties.un.org/Pages/showDetails.aspx?objid=08000002801083db (accessed 28 October 2024).

[314] International Convention on Civil Liability for Oil Pollution Damage, opened for signature 29 November 1969, 973 UNTS 3 (entered into force 19 June 1975) art 10 ('Oil Pollution Convention'); see Yujun Guo (n 186) 50.

[315] Kusumadara, *Indonesian PIL* (n 221) 176; Sudargo Gautama (n 312) 98.

[316] Kusumadara, *Indonesian PIL* (n 221) 177; Chong (n 186) 38.

[317] Chong (n 186) 38.

[318] Kusumadara, *Indonesian PIL* (n 221) 176; Priskila Pratita Penasthika, *Unravelling Choice of Law in International Commercial Contracts: Indonesia as an Illustrative Case Study* (Eleven, 2022) 183–84.

[319] See Kusumadara, 'Choice-of-Court Agreements' (n 215) 439–47.

[320] See eg, Suhadi Rizki Herdianto and Faisal Santiago, 'Legal Principles of Agreement: A Foundation in Contract Establishment' (Conference Paper, Proceedings of the International Conference on Law, Social Science, Economics, and Education, 16 April 2022).

Choice-of-Forum clauses stem from contractual freedom, their existence as contracts also depends on having all the requirements under article 1320 BW.

Article 24 BW allows parties to choose a residence other than their actual residence, provided it is in a deed. Applied to a choice of domicile, as allowed in article 118(4) HIR and article 99(16) Rv, this means that such choice should be in writing. Scholars have agreed that this requirement in writing extends to all forms of Choice-of-Forum clauses, even those not involving a choice of domicile.[321] Moreover, other formal requirements may also be required by the law of the place of performance under article 18(1) AB.

Kusumadara notes that Indonesian courts apply Indonesian law to determine the material or substantive validity of contracts with foreign elements when an Indonesian is a party.[322] Beyond this situation, it is unclear which law governs substantive validity. Should substantive validity of Choice-of-Forum clauses, then, still be determined by the law applicable to the contract or Indonesian law, just like China's approach? Indonesian law is also unclear on whether Choice-of-Forum clauses are separate from the main contract, such that a different law determines their validity.

Penasthika's study on Indonesian courts' handling of Choice-of-Forum and Choice-of-Law clauses revealed that the most common approach is to claim jurisdiction and apply Indonesian law, regardless of the Choice-of-Law and Choice-of-Forum clauses.[323] Most likely, Indonesian courts apply Indonesian law simply because they are more familiar with it.[324] The next most common approach is refusal of jurisdiction due to the choice of foreign law,[325] while the least common is refusal based on a foreign forum.[326] This unfamiliarity with foreign law may have also motivated the courts to dismiss the case despite their recognition of the Choice-of-Law clause. In any case, the top two approaches avoid applying foreign law to determine the Choice-of-Forum clause's validity.

(ii) Issues of Interpretation

Indonesian law is unclear on which law governs the interpretation of Choice-of-Forum clauses. As part of the main contract, these clauses may be subject to the contract's applicable law, which determines how the various contractual terms, including the Choice-of-Forum clause, are interpreted. Nonetheless, Indonesian courts have also emphasised the procedural nature of these clauses, suggesting that Indonesian law may apply as the forum law. However, similarly to China, the distinction between contractual and procedural may be irrelevant, and domestic law may apply to interpret Choice-of-Forum clauses regardless. Given Indonesian courts' approach to enforcing Choice-of-Forum clauses, it is likely that Indonesian law, as the forum law, applies to their interpretation. The strong preference for using Indonesian law in determining validity further supports this argument.

Article 36(1) of the Presidential Regulation No 63 of 2019 on the Use of Bahasa Indonesia (PR 63) which implements Law No 24 of 2009 on the National Flag, Language, Emblem and Anthem (Law 24) mandates the use of *Bahasa Indonesia* (Indonesian language) in contracts.

[321] See Kusumadara, *Indonesian PIL* (n 221) 52.
[322] ibid 105.
[323] Penasthika (n 234) 145.
[324] ibid.
[325] ibid.
[326] ibid.

In *Yani Haryanto v ED&F Man (Sugar) Ltd*, the Supreme Court ruled that this requirement is mandatory,[327] and non-compliance can lead to annulment of the contract.[328] The translation in the foreign party's national language and/or English may be used as equivalent or translation of the Indonesian text.[329] Nonetheless, under article 1338 BW, parties can specify that the English version prevails in case of inconsistency. Hence, to comply with PR 63, Choice-of-Forum clauses should be written both in the foreign language or English and in Indonesian, and any preference for the English version must be explicitly stated; otherwise, both versions are considered equivalent or the English text merely a translation.

The scope of the Choice-of-Forum clause – whether it covers only contractual claims or extends to non-contractual claims like torts – is unclear under Indonesian law. In *Bali Energi*, the defendants based their claim on torts to avoid the Choice-of-Forum clause stipulating Tokyo courts. However, the decision did not address this argument.

C. Mandatory Rules, Public Policy, and International Interest

(i) Mandatory Rules

In *Ir H Dadang Achmad* ('*Achmad*'), the Constitutional Court upheld the constitutionality of articles 55(2) and (3) of the Sharia Banking Act,[330] which allow Sharia banks and customers to choose their forum for dispute resolution, provided it is consistent with Sharia principles. The Court ruled that Indonesian religious courts have absolute jurisdiction over Sharia banking and the only alternative is through *Basyarnas* arbitration. Although *Achmad* did not declare the mandatory status of articles 55(2) and (3) of the Sharia Banking Act, the effect of the decision is to create a rule capable of superseding the parties' choice of jurisdiction and superimposing the Indonesian religious courts' jurisdiction.

(ii) Public Policy

Article 23 AB states that laws related to *ordre public* and morality cannot be waived by any action or agreement. Article 1336 BW reinforces this, stating that a contract's cause is invalid if it violates law, morality or public order. Also known as public policy, *openbare orde* or *ketertiban umum*, *ordre public*, according to Dutch and Indonesian scholars, should be understood as limiting the freedom of contract and relating to the promotion of order, peace, security and justice.[331] This approach is now reflected in various statutes[332] and in

[327] *Yani Haryanto v ED&F Man (Sugar) Ltd*, Supreme Court, Judgment No 1205K/Pdt/1990, 4 December 1991; see Kusumadara, *Indonesian PIL* (n 221) 29–30.

[328] Kusumadara, *Indonesian PIL* (n 221) 30.

[329] Regulation on the Use of Indonesian Language (Peraturan Tentang Penggunaan Bahasa Indonesia) Regulation of the President of the Republic of Indonesia No 63 of 2019 (Indonesia) art 36(3).

[330] Law on Islamic Banking (*Undang-Undang Tentang Perbankan Syariah*) Law No 21 of 2008 (Indonesia). *Ir H Dadang Achmad*, Constitutional Court Decision 93/PUU-X/2012, 29 August 2013.

[331] See Kusumadara, *Indonesian PIL* (n 221) 28; Huala Adolf, 'The Meaning of Public Policy under Indonesian Arbitration Law and Practice' (2021) 2(1) *Transnational Business Law Journal* 15, 26–27.

[332] eg, State Law on Administrative Courts (*Undang-Undang Tentang Peradilan Tata Usaha Negara*) Law No 5 of 1986 (Indonesia) as amended by Law No 9 of 2004; Law on Judicial Power (*Undang-Undang Tentang Kekuasaan Kehakiman*) Law No 48 of 2009 (Indonesia); Law on the Prohibition of Monopolistic Practices and Unfair Business Competition (*Undang-Undang Tentang Larangan Praktek Monopoli dan Persaingan Usaha Tidak Sehat*) Law No 5 of 1999 (Indonesia).

Supreme Court Regulation No 1 of 1990, which defines a breach of public policy as 'explicit violation of the fundamental principles of the Indonesian legal system and social system in Indonesia'.[333] Notably, this definition excludes certain economic matters and requires that it should affect the economy, security, and interest of society as a whole.[334] Notably, this definition has influenced arbitral decisions.[335] Moreover, such definition should also apply and limit the parties' intended effects of their Choice-of-Forum clauses. Hence, because foreign-issued anti-suit injunctions are considered to interfere with Indonesian sovereignty, and thus, violate Indonesian *ordre public*,[336] Indonesian courts may recognise anti-suit injunctions from chosen foreign courts as breaching public policy.

(iii) Foreign and International Interests

Indonesian courts may consider foreign and international interests under the *forum non conveniens* test, when they determine the relative convenience factors for the parties. However, foreign and international interests are not explicitly considered during the recognition and enforcement of foreign judgments, as Indonesia generally requires re-litigation. Curiously, the principle of comity is rarely discussed in Indonesian private international law, with Kusumadara even arguing that it has no role in this context.[337]

D. The Choice-of-Forum Clause and Protecting Weaker Parties

(i) Asymmetric Choice-of-Forum Clauses

Freedom of contract under article 1388 BW allows parties to agree on asymmetric clauses. No judicial decision deems this to be against Indonesian public policy. However, if the parties involved are considered 'weak parties', such as consumers and employees, or if the clause deprives parties of effective access to judicial remedy, these clauses may face strict scrutiny and not be enforced.

(ii) Protecting Weaker Parties

Indonesian law recognises consumers as 'weak parties' requiring special protection. Law No 8 of 1999 on consumer protection provides in article 23 that businesses refusing to respond to or compensate consumers may be sued at the Consumer Disputes Settlement Agency or in the court where the consumer resides,[338] thus overriding the *actor sequitur forum rei* principle.[339] This suggests that these venues remain available to consumers, even if

[333] Huala Adolf (n 331) 25.

[334] See eg, *PT Sumi Asih v Vinmar Overseas Ltd and AAA*, Central Jakarta District Court, Judgment No 271K/Pdt G/2010/PN.Jkt Pst, 31 May 2011.

[335] Huala Adolf (n 331) 24.

[336] *Astro Nusantara International BV v PT Ayunda Prima Mitra*, Supreme Court, Judgment No 877 K/PdtSus/2012, 26 March 2013.

[337] Kusumadara, *Indonesian PIL* (n 221) 177.

[338] Law on Consumer Protection (*Undang-Undang Tentang Perlindugan Konsumen*) Law No 8 of 1999 (Indonesia) art 23.

[339] See eg, *PT Garuda Indonesia (Persero) v Mahsin, SH*, Supreme Court, Judgment No 1317 K/Pdt.Sus-BPSK/2017, 19 December 2017.

an exclusive Choice-of-Forum clause designates another Indonesian or foreign court. Some scholars argue that attempts to bypass these venues would be null and void.[340]

Employees are also considered 'weaker parties' under Indonesian law. The Industrial Dispute Settlement Act 2004[341] vests industrial relations courts with jurisdiction over disputes involving employment rights, interests, termination, and labour unions,[342] including those involving foreign workers and Indonesian companies.[343] The principle of *actor sequitur forum rei* determines which court hears the dispute,[344] thus overriding any Choice-of-Forum clause when the dispute falls under the jurisdiction of the industrial relations court.

(iii) Contracts-of-Adhesion

Standard-form contracts are not prohibited under Indonesian law,[345] but may be void if they violate article 18 of Law No 8 of 1999 on consumer protection.[346] Prohibited clauses include terms unilaterally set by businesses or those which reduce consumer benefits or property.[347] While neither the BW nor Law No 8 of 1999 explicitly bans standard-form Choice-of-Forum clauses, they may be voided if they violate article 18, such as when added unilaterally or when the clause makes it too onerous for the consumer to challenge the business in the chosen court.

IV. Japan

A. Enforcement of Choice-of-Forum Clauses

(i) Japan's Approach to Jurisdiction

The Japanese Constitution vests judicial power in the Supreme Court, Japan's highest court, and the lower courts,[348] including (1) the summary courts, (2) the family courts, (3) the district courts, and (4) the high courts.[349] To administer judicial affairs, the Supreme Court

[340] See Kusumadara, *Indonesian PIL* (n 221) 61; Sujayadi Sujayadi, Tata Wijayanta and Herliana Herliana, 'Regulating Court Jurisdiction to Protect Weaker Parties: An Overview of the Indonesian Civil Justice System' (2023) 38(2) *Yuridika* 305, 312.

[341] Law on Settlement of Industrial Relations Disputes (*Undang-Undang Tentang Penyelesaian Perselisihan Hubingan Industrial*) Law No 2 of 2004 (Indonesia).

[342] ibid arts 2, 5, 56.

[343] ibid art 2.

[344] ibid arts 57, 81.

[345] See Jovita Irawati and Kevin Gorga Kennedy Hutagalung, 'Standard Clauses in Vehicle Purchase Credit Agreements in Indonesia: An Examination of Consumer Protection and Legal Enforcement' (2023) 25(2) *Journal of Judicial Review* 255, 259.

[346] ibid 260.

[347] ibid.

[348] The Constitution of Japan (日本国憲法) (Japan), art 76 [tr Ministry of Justice: https://www.japaneselawtranslation.go.jp/en/laws/view/174] ('Japanese Constitution').

[349] Supreme Court of Japan, 'Judicial System in Japan' (webpage): https://www.courts.go.jp/english/judicial_sys/index.html (accessed 28 October 2024).

is given rule-making powers.[350] Various laws define the courts' jurisdiction, with procedure governed mainly by the Japanese Code of Civil Procedure ('JCCP').[351] District courts serve as first instance courts, except in cases under the exclusive original jurisdiction of other courts. The defendant's domicile or the corporation's principal office in Japan,[352] along with several other connecting factors, generally determines jurisdiction.

In domestic actions, article 11 of the JCCP allows the parties to choose 'their court of jurisdiction by agreement, but only in the first instance'.[353] The requirements are: (1) the agreement must cover actions based on a specific legal relationship, and (2) it must be executed in a paper document or equivalent form.[354]

Prior to 2011, except where international treaties applied,[355] Japanese courts relied on *jori* (*naturalis ratio*), which is based on fairness between the parties and the sound and prompt administration of justice, when exercising international jurisdiction.[356] Courts also developed an approach of declining jurisdiction under 'exceptional circumstances', including where such exercise of jurisdiction would undermine fairness between parties and prompt and sound administration of justice.[357] In 2011, Act No 36[358] ('2011 Amendment') finally introduced rules involving the exercise of 'international jurisdiction' to the JCCP and the Civil Provisional Remedies Act[359] ('JCPRA').

The exercise of international jurisdiction involves two steps. First, the court must confirm a jurisdictional basis under Japanese law.[360] Under the JCCP, a court has general jurisdiction or 'all-purpose jurisdiction', regardless of the nature of the claim,[361] if it has jurisdiction over the defendant's domicile or residence,[362] or over a corporation which has its principal office in Japan.[363] Courts can also exercise specific jurisdiction in specific types of cases when a particular connecting factor is present.[364] The second step requires the court to determine whether it should *exercise* jurisdiction. The 'special circumstances test' under article 3-9 of

[350] Japanese Constitution (n 348) art 77.

[351] Code of Civil Procedure Act (民事訴訟法　平成八年六月二十六日法律第百九号) Act No 109 of 1996 (Japan) [tr Ministry of Justice: https://www.japaneselawtranslation.go.jp/en/laws/view/2053] ('JCCP').

[352] ibid art 3-2(3).

[353] ibid art 11.

[354] ibid.

[355] eg, Convention for the Unification of certain Rules relating to International Carriage by Air (with Additional Protocol), opened for signature 12 October 1929, 137 LNTS 11 (entered into force 13 February 1933) ('Warsaw Convention'); Convention on Limitation of Liability for Maritime Claims, opened for signature 19 November 1976, 1456 UNTS 221 (entered into force 1 December 1986); Convention on Supplementary Compensation for Nuclear Damage, opened for signature 12 September 1997, 36 ILM 1473 (entered into force 15 April 2015); Convention for the Unification of Certain Rules for International Carriage by Air, opened for signature 28 May 1999, 2242 UNTS 309 (entered into force 4 November 2003); Oil Pollution Convention (n 398).

[356] See eg, *Malaysian Airlines Bhd v Michiko Goto*, Supreme Court, Case No 130 (o) of 1980, 16 October 1981 [tr (1983) 26 *Japanese Annual of International Law* 122].

[357] *Family Co Ltd v Shin Miyahara*, Supreme Court, Case No HJ (1626) 74 [1998], HT (960) 102 [1998], 11 November 1997 [tr (1998) 41 *Japan Annual of International Law* 117] ('*Family Co*').

[358] Act No 36 of 2011 or Act on the Partial Revision of the Code of Civil Procedure and Civil Preservation Act (Japan) ('2011 Amendment').

[359] Civil Provisional Remedies Act (民事保全法　平成元年十二月二十二日法律第九十一号) Act No 91 of 1989 (Japan) [tr Ministry of Justice: https://www.japaneselawtranslation.go.jp/en/laws/view/3928] ('JCPRA').

[360] See Kazuaki Nishioka, 'Japan' in Anselmo Reyes and Wilson Liu (eds), *Direct Jurisdiction: Asian Perspectives* (Hart Publishing, 2021) 85, 86.

[361] JCCP (n 351) art 3-2.

[362] ibid art 3-2(1).

[363] ibid art 3-2(3).

[364] See eg, ibid art 3-3(viii), (iii).

the JCCP guides the court by considering factors or 'special circumstances', in determining whether to decline its exercise of jurisdiction.

Japan is not a party to the Choice-of-Court Convention or The Hague Judgments Convention. However, Choice-of-Forum clauses have been generally enforced since the 1975 *Chisadane*[365] decision, which remains as the Supreme Court's only ruling on these clauses. Nonetheless, the 2011 Amendment now provides an explicit statutory basis for Japanese courts to recognise and enforce Choice-of-Forum clauses.[366]

(ii) Prorogation and Derogation

Article 3-7(1) JCCP allows parties to select by agreement 'the country in which they are permitted to file an action with courts', enabling Japanese courts to enforce both exclusive and non-exclusive Choice-of-Forum clauses stipulating Japanese or foreign courts. Furthermore, if a Japanese court is exclusively chosen, jurisdiction can be exercised without applying the 'special circumstances test' under article 3-9 of the JCCP.[367] However, when the Choice-of-Forum clause is non-exclusive, even when Japanese courts are chosen, the 'special circumstances test' under article 3-9 must be applied.

When a foreign court is exclusively chosen, parties may 'invoke' the foreign court's jurisdiction, thus allowing the Japanese court to dismiss the claim in whole or in part.[368] When the choice of foreign court is non-exclusive, the Japanese court's jurisdiction remains, and the court may apply the 'special circumstances' test to decide whether to exercise its jurisdiction.[369] Nonetheless, this choice of foreign forum is given weight under this test or under other theories of international *lis pendens*.[370] Furthermore, derogation, either through exclusive or non-exclusive Choice-of-Forum clauses, is limited by exceptions, namely: (1) when Japanese courts have exclusive jurisdiction over the matter,[371] (2) provisions qualifying jurisdiction in consumer and employment matters,[372] (3) the chosen foreign court's inability to exercise jurisdiction by law or in fact,[373] and (4) public policy concerns.[374]

Articles 3-7 and 11(1) of the JCCP set different requirements for Choice-of-Forum clauses applicable to purely domestic and international transactions respectively. Under article 11(1), the agreement is only valid if it specifies a Japanese court of first instance. In contrast, it is sufficient for Choice-of-Forum clauses under article 3-7 to identify the forum or jurisdiction only, and not the specific court.[375] This is because, ultimately, it is up to the

[365] *Tokyo Kaijo Kasai Kabushi Kaisha v Koniglike Java China Daketvaat Litjein BV Amsterdam*, Supreme Court, Case (O) No 297 of 1973, 28 November 1975 [tr (1976) 20 *Japan Annual of International Law* 106] ('*Chisadane*').

[366] JCCP (n 351) art 3-7.

[367] ibid art 3-9.

[368] ibid art 3-7.

[369] ibid art 3-9.

[370] eg, Koji Takahashi, 'Japan: Quests for Equilibrium and Certainty' in Mary Keyes (ed), *Optional Choice of Court Agreements in Private International Law* (Springer Nature Switzerland, 2020) 261, 266 ('Quests for Equilibrium').

[371] JCCP (n 351) art 3-5.

[372] ibid art 3-7(5)–(6).

[373] ibid art 3-7(4).

[374] *Chisadane* (n 365).

[375] See Shunichiro Nakano, 'Agreement on Jurisdiction' (2011) 54 *Japanese Yearbook of International Law* 278, 287.

forum state to allocate domestic jurisdiction in accordance with its domestic procedural law. These differences raise the question of when a Choice-of-Forum clause is considered 'international', especially as the JCCP, unlike the Choice-of-Court Convention, does not define what 'international' is.[376] This lack of definition may create issues when Japanese courts are chosen but the foreign element is unclear, such as in disputes solely involving Japanese nationals.

(iii) Service of Process

Japanese civil litigation is based on fairness, prompt justice, and good faith.[377] Hence, service of process is required to initiate court proceedings,[378] along with service of all related documents on the defendant.[379] For defendants within Japan, service is made by the court clerk through special postal service or publication.[380] For defendants outside Japan, service follows The Hague Convention on Civil Procedure[381] and The Hague Service Convention[382] when applicable. If the recipient country is not a treaty member, service is conducted according to relevant national laws and the JCCP.[383]

When a civil complaint is filed under an exclusive clause stipulating Japanese courts, the Japanese court should allow service of process to the defendant, even if located outside Japan. However, if a foreign court is chosen in an exclusive clause and the Japanese court dismisses the complaint, no service occurs. If the Japanese court assumes jurisdiction due to exceptions or after applying the 'special circumstances test', service to the defendant will proceed.

For non-exclusive clauses, whether the chosen court is Japanese or foreign, service depends on whether exceptions apply and the outcome of the 'special circumstances test'. Service would proceed if the Japanese court chose or was required to exercise its jurisdiction.

(iv) Dismissal of Proceedings

When an exclusive Choice-of-Forum clause stipulates a Japanese court, the chosen Japanese court should not dismiss the action unless public policy concerns arise or the clause conflicts with articles 3-7(5) and 3-7(6) for consumer and employment disputes. Notably, because exclusive Choice-of-Forum clauses stipulating Japanese courts are exempt from the 'special circumstances test' (article 3-9), the threshold for a public policy exception should be high and the scope, strictly limited. Furthermore, the mandatory rules under article 3-5 do not apply because litigation occurs in Japan.

[376] See ibid 285.

[377] JCCP (n 351) art 2; see also Kazuaki Nishioka and Yuko Nishitani, *Japanese Private International Law* (Hart Publishing, 2021) 26–27.

[378] Nishioka and Nishitani (n 377) 30.

[379] ibid.

[380] JCCP (n 351) arts 98–107, 110.

[381] Convention Relating to Civil Procedure, opened for signature 1 March 1954, 286 UNTS 265 (entered into force 12 April 1957).

[382] The Hague Convention on the Service Abroad of Judicial and Extrajudicial Documents in Civil or Commercial Matters, opened for signature 15 November 1965, 658 UNTS 163 (entered into force 10 February 1969).

[383] JCCP (n 351) art 108; See also Nishioka and Nishitani (n 377) 30.

Similarly, when a Japanese court is chosen in a non-exclusive clause, the chosen Japanese court should not dismiss the complaint unless (i) 'special circumstances' exist under article 3-9, in which case, the dismissal may be in whole or in part and without prejudice, or (ii) such clause conflicts with articles 3-7(5) and 3-7(6) for consumer or employment disputes. Similarly, the mandatory jurisdiction rules under article 3-5 do not apply, although the public policy exception remains applicable.

A complaint should be dismissed when an exclusive Choice-of-Forum clause stipulates foreign courts. However, if 'special circumstances' exist under article 3-9, the Japanese court may exercise jurisdiction. The same result follows when article 3-7(5) (consumer disputes) 3-7(6) (employment disputes), or 3-7(4) (the foreign court's inability to exercise jurisdiction) or public policy require exercising jurisdiction. Moreover, the same limitations apply to non-exclusive clauses choosing foreign courts, thus when article 3-9, 3-7(5), 3-7(6) or 3-7(4) or public policy require jurisdiction to be exercised, the Japanese court may not dismiss the case. Nonetheless, when the clause is exclusive, the choice of a foreign forum should carry a greater weight.

Japan has yet to adopt an international *lis pendens* rule. Although proposed during the 2011 Amendment drafting, it was criticised due to the challenge of predicting whether a future foreign judgment would be recognised in Japan.[384] Hence, academic opinion remains divided.[385] One approach suggests a 'first-in-time' rule or applying article 142 of the JCCP (the domestic *lis pendens* rule) by analogy to international litigation.[386] Another approach is to apply the 'special circumstances test' under article 3-9,[387] which is also criticised for lack of clear criteria in determining which court should exercise jurisdiction.[388]

(v) Special Circumstances Test

Article 3-9, a major innovation introduced by the 2011 Amendment, traces its origins to the 1997 Supreme Court case, *Family Co Ltd v Shin Miyahara*.[389] It allows Japanese courts to dismiss a complaint, either in full or in part, without prejudice, when 'special circumstances' exist. The 'special circumstances test', while similar to *Spiliada*'s *forum non conveniens* analysis, has key differences. First, the test applies to both exclusive and non-exclusive clauses when a foreign court is chosen, unlike the *Spiliada* test, either in its original or modified version, which only applies to non-exclusive clauses. Second, dismissals under article 3-9 may be partial or complete and are without prejudice, whereas *forum non conveniens* in common law often dismisses the entire action. Third, the factors in article 3-9 are limited,[390] but broadly worded and include a catch-all phrase, 'and other circumstances', allowing courts to consider factors beyond those specified. Fourth, the focus is on whether Japan is an appropriate venue, not on the relative appropriateness of the foreign forum, which stands in contrast to the balancing required in the *Spiliada* and the Philippine versions of *forum*

[384] Nishioka and Nishitani (n 377) 41.
[385] ibid.
[386] ibid.
[387] ibid.
[388] ibid.
[389] *Family Co* (n 357).
[390] JCCP (n 351) art 3-9.

non conveniens. Fifth, while *forum non conveniens* dismissals are discretionary, debate exists in Japan on whether article 3-9 dismissals are mandatory or discretionary,[391] though the use of 'may' suggests they are discretionary.

Notably, article 3-9 does not provide a list of 'special circumstances' but only mentions their effect (ie, the trial and judicial decision by the Japanese court would be inequitable to the either party or prevent a fair and speedy trial). Hence, the court should look for 'special circumstances' which may adversely affect the trial and judicial decision (eg, inequity, unfairness, or delay). After identifying these 'special circumstances', the Japanese court should assess their impact, determining if they justify dismissing the action in whole or in part. In evaluating their effect, the court considers: (1) nature of the case, (2) the burden on the defendant, (3) the location of evidence, and (4) other circumstances.[392]

(vi) Anti-suit Injunction and Other Relief

In *Company X v Company Y1 and Company Y2*[393] ('*Company X*'), the Tokyo High Court examined granting injunctions for exclusive Choice-of-Forum clauses. The Court noted that while injunctions safeguard the public interest 'by way of restoring fair and equitable competition', they are civil remedies for damage or loss suffered from Antimonopoly Act breaches,[394] not for Choice-of-Forum clause violations. In short, an injunction depends on the claim's merits justifying an award of damages, not on the Choice-of-Forum clause's potential breach.

(vii) Recognition and Enforcement of Judgments

Except as covered by international treaties to which Japan is a party, domestic law, particularly article 118 of the JCCP, determines how foreign judgments are recognised in Japan. Under article 118, five requirements must be met: (1) a final and binding judgment, (2) the foreign court's indirect jurisdiction, (3) proper service of process, (4) conformity with Japan's public policy, and (5) reciprocity. If such requirements are present, recognition happens automatically.[395] As such, a foreign judgment rendered pursuant to a valid Choice-of-Forum clause could be recognised in Japan.

For foreign judgments involving Choice-of-Forum clauses, because the JCCP provides for certain formal and substantial validity requirements, these requirements should be complied with for purposes of recognition of the foreign judgment.[396] This 'mirror-image' approach, which Yokoyama observes,[397] means that foreign judgments must meet the same jurisdictional standards as Japanese courts. Hence, as regards foreign judgments involving Choice-of-Forum clauses, the relevant Choice-of-Forum clause (in order for Japanese courts to recognise the foreign court as validly vested with jurisdiction) should also comply

[391] See Nishioka and Nishitani (n 377) 39.
[392] JCCP (n 351) art 3-7.
[393] *Company X v Company Y1 and Y2*, Tokyo High Court, Case No 2017WLJPCA10256010, 25 October 2017 [tr Florence Cheung (2018) 61 *Japanese Yearbook of International Law* 416] ('*Company X*').
[394] ibid 418.
[395] Nishioka and Nishitani (n 377) 217.
[396] See Takahashi, 'Quests for Equilibrium' (n 370) 262.
[397] Jun Yokoyama, *Private International Law* (Kluwer Law International, 2nd edn, 2019) 162.

with the formal requirements under article 3-7(2)–(3), and the substantive requirements under article 3-5 (ie, those matters falling under the exclusive jurisdiction of Japanese courts), article 3-7(4) (ie, that the foreign court should be able to exercise jurisdiction as a matter of law and fact), and article 3-7(5)–(6) (ie, those matters relating to consumer and labour disputes).[398] Notably, in *Chisadane*, the Japanese Supreme Court clarified that reciprocity, which is a requirement for recognition and enforcement for foreign judgments, is not required in enforcing Choice-of-Forum clauses that derogate from Japanese jurisdiction.[399]

Enforcement of foreign judgments is governed by article 22(6) of the Civil Execution Act 1979.[400] Only judgments requiring the defendant to perform or refrain from a specific action are enforceable, and the court's review is limited to confirming compliance with article 118 of the JCCP and not revisiting the merits. Hence, a foreign judgment involving a valid Choice-of-Forum clause which complies with the article 118 requirements is enforceable in Japan. For monetary awards, the successful party must file an action for an enforcement judgment, or *exequatur (shikko hanketso)* before the court.

B. Existence, Validity and Interpretation

(i) Issues of Existence and Validity

Japanese law determines the validity of Choice-of-Forum clauses. Under article 3-7(2) of the JCCP, '[an agreement on jurisdiction] … is not valid unless it is made regarding actions that are based on a specific legal relationship, and executed by means of a paper document'. This includes electronic or magnetic records capable of recording the agreement's content.[401] Although article 3-7(2) outlines formal validity, the procedural characterisation of Choice-of-Forum clauses suggests these requirements also address existence.

JCCP's approach of using Japanese law to determine validity reflects pre-2011 Amendment cases. In *Sogo*, the Tokyo District Court said:

> Because such [jurisdiction] clause is an agreement in the nature of a procedural act, and because the question involved relates to the validity and effect of an agreement to exclude the jurisdiction of the courts of Japan, the law governing the validity and effect of the jurisdiction clause in question is not that of the law governing the contract. Instead, the international civil procedure law of Japan, the forum which is at issue, should apply.[402]

In *Sogo*, the Court noted that derogation is valid if the case does not fall under the Japanese courts' exclusive jurisdiction and if the chosen foreign court can hear the case.

The Japanese Supreme Court in *Chisadane* followed this approach, asserting that the formal validity of a Choice-of-Forum clause is governed by the principle of justice (*jori*)

[398] See also Takahashi, 'Quests for Equilibrium' (n 370) 262.
[399] *Chisadane* (n 365) 110.
[400] Civil Execution Act (民事執行法) Law No 4 of 1975 (Japan) [tr Ministry of Justice https://www.japaneselawtranslation.go.jp/en/laws/view/70/ja].
[401] JCCP (n 351) art 3-7(3).
[402] *Sogo Koeki Kabushiki Kaisha v Aktieselskabet Dampskibsselskabet Svenborg*, Tokyo District Court, Case No 6859 (wa), 17 October 1967 [tr (1969) 13 *Japanese Annual of International Law* 136, 143].

and the JCCP.[403] The Court explained that the formality requirement is met if a court in the chosen forum is designated 'and if the existence of such agreement between the parties and the contents thereof are explicit'.[404] Derogation is valid if (a) the case is not subject to Japan's exclusive jurisdiction, and (b) the designated foreign court has jurisdiction under its laws.[405] Significantly, the Court found no need to assess validity under the chosen forum's laws.[406]

Cases following *Chisadane* consistently reflect the same approach. Although decided in 2014, *X v Kabushiki Kaisha Nouvelle Vague Japon*[407] involved pre-2011 facts, with the Tokyo District Court applying Japanese law to determine the Choice-of-Forum clause's formal validity, despite French law governing the main contract.[408] The clause, designating the Commercial Court of Paris, was held to be valid because Japanese courts do not have exclusive jurisdiction over disputes relating to default on royalty payments, and 'it is possible to recognize the existence of jurisdiction of the court designated in the Jurisdiction Agreement'.[409] This approach was similarly applied in *X v MRI International, Incorporated* ('*MRI International*')[410] and *Vulcan International Services Ltd v Mukashiya Ltd*[411] ('*Vulcan*').

The JCCP 2011 Amendment requires that actions under a Choice-of-Forum clause be based on a specific legal relationship,[412] a requirement not expressly mentioned in the *Chisadane* case. Notably, article 2 of the Arbitration Act[413] contains the same requirement for arbitration agreements. The rationale is to 'ensure predictability for the parties and to prevent a situation where parties suffer from an unforeseen disadvantage'.[414] In *Shimano Manufacturing Co, Ltd v Apple Inc*[415] ('*Shimano*'), the Tokyo District Court applied this requirement for formal validity even though the Choice-of-Forum clause had been concluded before the 2011 Amendment.[416] Here, the Court referred to a similar requirement for domestic jurisdiction agreements, and then concluded that the requirement under the 2011 Amendment was for a 'similar underlying intention'.[417] In *Shimano*, the Court deemed the clause stipulating Californian courts – which stated '[i]f there is a dispute between the parties' and 'the terms of this Section apply whether or not the dispute arises out of or relates to the Agreement' – not to contain any limitation other than that there must

[403] *Chisadane* (n 365) 110.
[404] ibid.
[405] ibid 111.
[406] ibid.
[407] *X v Kabushiki Kaisha Nouvelle Vague Japon*, Tokyo District Court, Case No 2014WLJPCA03269011, 26 March 2014 [tr Tom Weiss (2016) 59 *Japanese Yearbook of International Law* 494].
[408] ibid 495.
[409] ibid.
[410] *X v MRI International, Incorporated*, Tokyo High Court, Case No HJ (2243) 28 [2015], 17 November 2014 [tr Florence Cheung (2017) 60 *Japanese Yearbook of International Law* 495, 497] ('*MRI International*').
[411] *Vulcan International Services Ltd v Mukashiya Ltd*, Tokyo District Court, Case No HT (1077) 282 [2002], 24 November 2000 [tr (2002) 45 *Japanese Yearbook of International Law* 168, 171] ('*Vulcan*').
[412] JCCP (n 351) art 3-7(2).
[413] Arbitration Act [仲裁法 平成十五年八月一日法律第百三十八号] Act No 138 of 2003 (Japan) [tr Ministry of Justice: https://www.japaneselawtranslation.go.jp/en/laws/view/4440] ('Arbitration Act').
[414] *Shimano Manufacturing Co Ltd v Apple Inc*, Tokyo District Court, Case No [2016WLJPCA02156001], 15 February 2016 [tr Kazuaki Nishioka (2017) 60 *Japanese Yearbook of International Law* 523, 525].
[415] ibid.
[416] ibid.
[417] ibid.

be a dispute between the parties.[418] Hence, the Choice-of-Forum clause did not relate to claims based on specific legal relationships,[419] and therefore, was invalid.

The JCCP mandates compliance with the substantive requirements in articles 3-5 (the exclusive jurisdiction of Japanese courts), 3-7(4) (the foreign court's ability to exercise jurisdiction), 3-7(5) (matters related to consumer disputes) 3-7(6) (matters related to employment disputes). However, they should be described more aptly as mandatory rules, although affecting the Choice-of-Forum clause's substantive validity. The JCCP, however, is silent as regards the law that determines other legal issues like legal capacity, fraud, or mistake. Some Japanese scholars[420] argue that the applicable law determined by the choice of law process under the Act on General Rules for Application of Laws ('JAGRAL')[421] governs these issues. Under JAGRAL's article 7, the formation and effect of a juridical act are governed by the law of the place chosen by the parties at the time of the act. This means that the chosen law should also determine the clause's substantial validity.[422] In the absence of choice, the law most closely connected applies.[423] In contrast, others[424] argue that the Japanese Civil Code determines issues related to contract formation and validity (eg, the legal effect of fraud, mistake and duress).[425] However, because this approach may undermine the parties' reasonable expectations, the view supporting the parties' capacity to designate foreign law to determine issues of formation and validity is gaining acceptance.[426]

Hence, one can see that in Japan, Choice-of-Forum clauses can be regarded as a 'contract of special character' – a '*soshô keiyaku*' or procedural contract.[427] While their effects are generally governed by Japanese procedural laws, aspects like substantive validity, where not covered by the JCCP, may fall under the law governing the contract or the Japanese Civil Code.

(ii) Issues of Interpretation

The JCCP does not specify which law governs the interpretation of Choice-of-Forum clauses, leaving it uncertain whether the law applicable to the contract or Japanese law should be used in interpreting Choice-of-Forum clauses. Notably, a review of cases show Japanese courts have used both. When Japanese law is cited, court often refer to *jori*, but their reasoning is ultimately based on one's own personal sense of reasonableness.[428]

[418] ibid.

[419] ibid.

[420] see eg Yokoyama (n 397) 154–55; Koji Takahashi, 'Damages for Breach of a Choice-of-Court Agreement' [2008] (10) *Yearbook of Private International Law* 57, 69 ('Damages for Breach'); Nishioka and Nishitani (n 377) 46.

[421] Act on General Rules for Application of Laws «法の適用に関する通則法 平成十八年六月二十一日法律第七十八号» Act No 78 of 2006 (Japan) [tr Ministry of Justice: https://www.japaneselawtranslation.go.jp/en/laws/view/3783] ('JAGRAL').

[422] ibid art 7.

[423] ibid art 8(1).

[424] See Nakano (n 375) 287–88.

[425] Civil Code (民法 明治二十九年四月二十七日法律第八十九号) Act No 89 of 1896 (Japan) [tr Ministry of Justice: https://www.japaneselawtranslation.go.jp/en/laws/view/4314] ('Japanese Civil Code').

[426] See Nakano (n 375) 288.

[427] Takahashi, 'Damages for Breach' (n 420) 69.

[428] See Takahashi, 'Quests for Equilibrium' (n 370) 268.

In *Nouvelle Japon*, the Tokyo District Court interpreted the clause 'any dispute … shall be submitted to the Commercial Courts of Paris, France',[429] as non-exclusive, noting the absence of 'exclusive' language as required by article 48 of the French Code of Civil Procedure.[430] This case is a rare instance where a Japanese court applied the contract's governing law to interpret the Choice-of-Forum clause.

The vast majority of cases, including *Chisadane*,[431] would refer to *jori* instead. In *Chisadane*, the Choice-of-Forum clause stated:

> Any and all suits under this transportation agreement shall be brought before the court of Amsterdam and no other courts shall have jurisdiction over any suit unless the carrier brings such suit before a court of other jurisdiction or voluntarily accepts the jurisdiction of such court.[432]

The Japanese Supreme Court interpreted this clause as exclusive without determining what law applied to the transportation agreement or the Choice-of-Forum clause. The Court reasoned that since the Amsterdam court had jurisdiction over the appellee's head office, and Japanese courts, over the appellee's branches, the Choice-of-Forum clause was intended to limit jurisdiction to the Amsterdam courts.[433] Although one can argue that the phrase 'no other courts shall have jurisdiction' points to exclusivity, the phrase following it makes such interpretation inconclusive.[434] In fact, the clause mentions other options; thus the reason given is arguably, incorrect. Therefore, Takahashi correctly argues that '[t]he tendency of the Japanese courts is to characterise a choice of court agreement as exclusive unless otherwise indicated'.[435]

In *Hiyoki*,[436] the Tokyo District Court considered whether the phrase 'dispute with respect to the supply and payment of goods' included torts, which was the cause of action under the claim.[437] The Court concluded that it did, as it still pertained to a 'dispute with respect to the supply and payment goods'.[438] This suggests that Japanese courts may allow causes of action outside contract law even if they are not explicitly stated. Notably, the Tokyo District Court did not refer to French law, the chosen law, in interpreting the Choice-of-Forum clauses, aligning instead with *Chisadane* by applying *jori* or natural reason.[439]

In *Vulcan*,[440] the Tokyo District Court examined whether the exclusive Choice-of-Forum clause stipulating English courts in clause 31 of the BIFA Conditions applied to the dispute. The plaintiffs argued that the BIFA Conditions were relevant only for freight forwarding businesses, not the financial services they provided to the defendant.[441] However, the Court found that the dispute encompassed both freight and credit obligations.[442] It observed that, since the credit component arose 'as a result of the plaintiff who deals in

[429] ibid.
[430] Code of Civil Procedure (France), art 48.
[431] *Chisadane* (n 365) 106.
[432] ibid 108–9.
[433] ibid 110.
[434] ibid 114.
[435] Takahashi, 'Quests for Equilibrium' (n 370) 268.
[436] *Hiyoki KK v Codif International SAS*, Tokyo District Court, Case No HT (1276) 332 [2008], 11 April 2008 [tr Michael Kuzma (2009) 52 *Japanese Yearbook of International Law* 688] ('*Hiyoki*').
[437] ibid 690.
[438] ibid.
[439] ibid.
[440] *Vulcan* (n 411) 168.
[441] ibid 169.
[442] ibid 170.

the present business lending an amount equivalent to the price of the merchandise to the defendant', it had a 'close and inseparable relationship with the freight business'.[443] Therefore, excluding BIFA Conditions from the loan would be 'contrary to the rational intention of the parties'.[444] This interpretation was followed even though the Court has recognised the 'exclusive jurisdiction of the courts of England in relation to disputes arising from obligations arising directly from the freight business'.[445] Hence, Japanese courts had no jurisdiction over the dispute.

Vulcan is an interesting demonstration of how Choice-of-Forum clauses are treated in Japanese law. First, the Court based its interpretation on *jori* without referencing any specific applicable law, thus highlighting that Japanese principles guide interpretation. Second, the Court did not strictly follow a contractual approach, which could limit the application and effect of the Choice-of-Forum clause. Notably, the exclusive Choice-of-Forum clause was contained in the BIFA Conditions and not in the trading contracts themselves, but somehow the Court extended their application to loan transactions when explicitly, the BIFA Conditions relate only to freight forwarding transactions. This approach reflects the clauses' status under Japanese law as not strictly 'contracts'. Finally, the Court emphasised the importance of the parties' intention, which was necessarily determined under Japanese law.

C. Mandatory Rules, Public Policy, and International Interest

(i) Mandatory Rules

Under article 3-5 of the JCCP, Japanese courts have exclusive jurisdiction over: (1) actions concerning companies and other legal persons established under Japanese law,[446] including those related to the company's registration, incorporation, dissolution, and internal affairs; (2) actions involving registration required to be made within Japan,[447] such as property or civil status registers; and (3) actions concerning the existence or validity of Japanese-registered intellectual property rights[448] (eg, patents, trademarks). Parties cannot override this jurisdiction, and foreign judgments arising from Choice-of-Forum clauses in breach of article 3-5 will not be recognised and enforced in Japan.

Japanese scholars note that copyright disputes are not covered by article 3-5,[449] as copyrights do not require registration for validity. Likewise, disputes unrelated to the *existence* or *validity* of intellectual property rights, such as infringement cases, are not exclusively under Japanese courts' jurisdiction.[450] Furthermore, foreign judgments or orders requiring registration or alteration to Japanese public registries may not be enforceable.[451] Likewise, a

[443] ibid.
[444] ibid.
[445] ibid.
[446] JCCP (n 351) art 3-5(1).
[447] ibid art 3-5(2).
[448] ibid art 3-5(3).
[449] See Yokoyama (n 397) 149.
[450] See ibid.
[451] See ibid.

Choice-of-Forum clause stipulating Japanese courts is unenforceable for disputes involving the registration of real property located abroad.[452]

Unless explicitly stated in article 3-5 of the JCCP, a substantive mandatory rule may not bar the enforcement of a Choice-of-Forum clause. In *Company X*,[453] the plaintiff argued that the exclusive clause choosing Michigan courts circumvented Japan's mandatory Antimonopoly Act[454] and public policy. However, the Tokyo High Court disagreed, noting that even if the Choice-of-Forum clause prevented the application of Japan's mandatory law, simply stating that the mandatory law (Antimonopoly Act) does not apply in the exclusive foreign jurisdiction would be insufficient to void the Choice-of-Forum clause.[455] In that sense, Nishioka correctly argues that '[t]he mere fact that a choice of court agreement could lead to a derogation from local competition law should not be regarded [as] insufficient to invalidate the agreement'.[456] He proposes instead that Japanese courts should confine themselves to 'considering whether, *as a matter of first impression* (that is, without looking into the merits), enforcement (1) would be unreasonable … and (2) would violate public policy in the sense of obviously undermining the domestic competition order'.[457]

(ii) Public Policy

Although not mentioned in the JCCP, public policy is recognised as an unwritten exception to the enforcement of Choice-of-Forum clauses.[458] Takahashi argues that no statutory basis for public policy is needed to 'safeguard the fundamental legal value of Japan'.[459] The public policy principle, as noted in *Chisadane*, often considers a clause unenforceable 'if it is excessively unreasonable and is against public policy'. Unreasonableness is key, and Nishioka identifies factors frequently assessed by courts: (1) Japan's connection to the dispute, (2) the connection of the designated court's location, (3) difficulties accessing the designated court, (4) the location of evidence, (5) circumstances related to the contract's formation, and (6) the necessity of protecting consumers.[460] Notably, many of these factors overlap with the 'special circumstances' test under article 3-9 and with the exceptions found in article 3-7 of the JCCP.

In *MRI International*,[461] the Tokyo High Court held that a valid Choice-of-Forum clause may not be enforced if it is extremely unreasonable and against public policy, especially in consumer-related cases. Hence, the Court denied the exclusive Choice-of-Forum clause stipulating Nevada courts, finding it 'extremely unreasonable' due to eight appellants

[452] See Takahashi, 'Quests for Equilibrium' (n 370) 264.
[453] *Company X* (n 393).
[454] Act on Prohibition of Private Monopolization and Maintenance of Fair Trade (私的独占の禁止及び公正取引の確保に関する法律　昭和二十二年四月十四日法律第五十四号) Act No 54 of 1947 (Japan) [tr Ministry of Justice: https://www.japaneselawtranslation.go.jp/en/laws/view/4256].
[455] *Company X* (n 393) 417.
[456] Kazuaki Nishioka, 'Choice of court agreements and derogation from competition law' (2020) 16(2) *Journal of Private International Law* 300, 313 ('Competition Law').
[457] ibid 314.
[458] eg, Takahashi, 'Quests for Equilibrium' (n 370) 264.
[459] eg, ibid.
[460] Nishioka, 'Competition Law' (n 456) 306.
[461] *MRI International* (n 410) 495.

residing in Japan, and one appellant not being bound by the clause.[462] The Court concluded that denying the eight appellants a legal avenue in Japan would contravene public policy.[463]

In *Yugen-Gaisha AR v APF Asset Management KK*,[464] ('*Yugen-Gaisha*') the court found an exclusive Choice-of-Forum clause stipulating Thai courts invalid as contrary to public policy. Given that all parties were Japanese, and the contract's formation and performance occurred in Japan, the court saw no reasonable grounds for designating Thai courts exclusively.[465] Furthermore, the court noted that requiring the Japanese appellants to litigate in Thailand would impose a 'great burden', making the choice of Thai courts 'egregiously unreasonable and against public policy, and thus invalid'.[466]

(iii) Foreign and International Interests

Under article 3-7(4), Japanese courts assess whether the chosen foreign court can exercise jurisdiction by law or in fact. If the foreign court lacks jurisdiction or is unable to exercise jurisdiction, the Choice-of-Forum clause choosing the foreign court will not be enforced. In *Yugen-Gaisha*, the Osaka High Court noted that since Thai courts could assume jurisdiction based on sufficient connecting factors under Thai procedural law, it was immaterial whether the exclusive Choice-of-Forum clause would actually be recognised in Thailand. In *Hiyoki*, the Tokyo District Court ruled that the presence of lay judges in Saint-Malo Commercial Court in France did not render the exclusive Choice-of-Forum clause unenforceable,[467] as there was no evidence to prove that the lay judges were unable to competently adjudicate on matters of fact and law.[468]

D. The Choice-of-Forum Clause and Protecting Weaker Parties

(i) Asymmetric Choice-of-Forum Clauses

Chisadane illustrates the treatment of asymmetric Choice-of-Forum clauses in Japan. The clause in question provided the carrier with an additional choice other than the clause in favour of Amsterdam – 'unless the carrier brings such suit before a court of other jurisdiction or voluntarily accepts the jurisdiction of such court'. The Japanese Supreme Court, however, interpreted the clause as exclusive, thereby missing the chance to address the legal status of asymmetric Choice-of-Forum clauses under Japanese law.

As discussed below, the JCCP restricts the forum options when the dispute involves consumers or employees. Outside of consumer and labour disputes, however, article 134 of the Japanese Civil Code offers guidance: '[a] juridical act subject to a condition precedent

[462] ibid 498.
[463] ibid.
[464] *Yugen-Gaisha AR v APF Asset Management KK*, Osaka High Court, Case No HJ (2225) 77 [2014], 20 February 2014 [tr Eriko Kadota (2015) 58 *Japanese Yearbook of International Law* 466].
[465] ibid 469.
[466] ibid.
[467] *Hiyoki* (n 436) 690.
[468] ibid 690.

is void if the condition is dependent only upon the intention of the obligor'. Hence, Nakano argues that a Choice-of-Forum clause is invalid if it provides no criterion for specifying the competent court, as this would permit one party unrestricted choice of forum.[469] Arguably, the second part of the Choice-of-Forum clause in *Chisadane* is an example of this.

(ii) Protecting Weaker Parties

The 2011 Amendment introduced statutory protections to consumers and employees concerning Choice-of-Forum clauses, drawing inspiration from European Union instruments such as the Brussels I Regulation.[470] Notably, the JCCP does not mention any nationality or domicile requirements for protection.[471]

Article 3-7(5) of the JCCP requires that Choice-of-Forum clauses in consumer contracts should not restrict the consumer's court options; otherwise, they are invalid under Japanese law. These clauses must permit actions in the consumer's domicile at the time of the contract formation.[472] Hence, when the Choice-of-Forum clause is exclusive, such clauses do not necessarily prevent litigation in other jurisdictions,[473] making them effectively non-exclusive in most circumstances. Exclusivity is upheld only if (1) the consumer files in the chosen forum, or (2) the business files in Japan or foreign court (both not chosen), and the consumer invokes the clause.[474] To illustrate, if a foreign court is exclusively chosen but the business files in Japan, and the consumer invokes the Choice-of-Forum clause, the Japanese court should dismiss the action. Similarly, if the business files in an unchosen foreign court and the consumer invokes the exclusive clause, Japanese law will again uphold such exclusivity.

Under article 3-7(6) of the JCCP, protections similar to those for consumers apply to employment disputes: Choice-of-Forum clauses should not limit the courts accessible to employees, or they will be invalid under Japanese law. A clause made at the end of a labour contract that allows for filing in the courts of the country where work was provided is valid.[475] However, if the clause mandates exclusivity, it does not bar filing in other courts,[476] making exclusivity generally not enforceable. Exclusivity is only recognised if the worker files in the chosen forum, or the business files in Japan or in another country (both not chosen), and the worker invokes the clause.[477]

In *Company X*,[478] the superior bargaining position of one contracting party was argued as a ground to avoid the exclusive choice of Michigan courts. The Tokyo High Court

[469] See Nakano (n 375) 286.
[470] Council Regulation (EC) No 44/2001 of 22 December 2000 on jurisdiction and the recognition and enforcement of judgments in civil and commercial matters [2001] OJ L 012/1; Takahashi, 'Quests for Equilibrium' (n 370) 265.
[471] See Takahashi, 'Quests for Equilibrium' (n 370) 267.
[472] JCCP (n 351) art 3-7(5)(i).
[473] ibid art 3-7(5)(i).
[474] ibid art 3-7(5)(ii).
[475] ibid art 3-7(6)(i).
[476] ibid.
[477] ibid art 3-7(6)(ii).
[478] *Company X* (n 393) 418.

dismissed this argument, stating that it pertained to the substance of the claim, and did not affect the validity of the jurisdiction clause.[479]

(iii) Contracts-of-Adhesion

When Japanese law is the applicable law, the use of a standard-form contract containing Choice-of-Forum clauses is circumscribed by good faith.[480] Absent good faith, the standard-form contract including the Choice-of-Forum clause would be considered not to have been consented to (ie, as if there was no contract to begin with).

[479] ibid.
[480] See Japanese Civil Code (n 425) arts 2(1), 548-2.

9

Conclusions

I. How do Courts Reason and Decide Choice-of-Forum Clause Issues?

This book explores, identifies, compares and explains the approaches of three common law jurisdictions (Singapore, Hong Kong, and Malaysia), a hybrid jurisdiction (the Philippines) and three civil law jurisdictions (China, Indonesia, and Japan) in Asia when Choice-of-Forum clauses in international commercial contracts are challenged in courts. It examines the characterisation of these clauses, the role of party autonomy, enforcement, how issues concerning the existence, validity and interpretation of such clauses are resolved, and the role of state and international interests.

- First Lesson: Characterisation determines the legal tools available.

The first lesson is that a court's reasoning depends on the legal tools available, which are determined by how Choice-of-Forum clauses are characterised. In Singapore, Hong Kong and Malaysia, courts view these clauses through both contract and procedural law lenses, while in the Philippines, they approach them mainly as procedural mechanisms with some contractual elements. China, Indonesia and Japan primarily treat these clauses as procedural. Furthermore, the balance between contract law and procedural law varies. Singapore and Hong Kong emphasise contractual consequences, while Malaysia and the Philippines focus more on the administration of justice aspect, thus highlighting court discretion and public law considerations. In China, Indonesia and Japan, while party consent remains the basis of jurisdiction, breaches of these clauses typically do not result in private law consequences. Across jurisdictions, however, procedural statutes and rules are not the sole sources of rules used in resolving Choice-of-Forum clause issues. In common law countries, courts draw from substantive (mainly contract law) and procedural laws. In the Philippines, China, Indonesia and Japan, while courts primarily resolve issues through procedural law, substantive law (eg, contract law, consumer law) is also used to resolve issues of existence, validity and interpretation of Choice-of-Forum clauses.

Even in common law jurisdictions, courts recognise that Choice-of-Forum clauses are not typical contracts. Firstly, unlike arbitration agreements, which derive their authority solely from party consent, Choice-of-Forum clauses rely also on state authority. Secondly, the doctrine of privity allows more exceptions, enabling courts to join non-parties more easily under their administration of justice function. Lastly, the doctrine of separability shields the Choice-of-Forum clause from defects in the underlying contract, distinguishing it from other contractual provisions.

- Second Lesson: Party autonomy guides courts' approaches.

This lesson emphasises party autonomy's crucial role in how courts across the seven jurisdictions approach Choice-of-Forum clause issues. Two aspects of party autonomy are relevant: the freedom to determine the contents of the Choice-of-Forum clause, and the freedom to control the flow of litigation. Both aspects are recognised in all jurisdictions and are fundamental in determining how courts resolve issues, provide remedies and exercise discretion.

The first aspect of party autonomy is common to common law, civil law and Choice-of-Court Convention regimes. In common law, this is understood as the freedom of contract, where parties freely negotiate and agree on lawful terms to serve their interests. In Singapore, Hong Kong and Malaysia, case law confirms that parties may include various promises, such as where to sue, and even what arguments cannot be raised. Despite this variety of promises, enforcing Choice-of-Forum clauses may be limited by their binary classification as either exclusive or non-exclusive. Starting with classification rather than interpreting the specific promises, however, may prevent courts from delivering outcomes intended by the parties. The Choice-of-Court Convention also recognises party autonomy by allowing parties to choose the court that will exclusively hear their dispute and exclude others. The other promises which parties can include depends on the law of the chosen court, given its role in determining validity. Civil law tradition also recognises this freedom, but its extent depends on the relevant jurisdiction's procedure. The Philippines follows the civil law approach, where party freedom depends on the rules of the venue, specifically rule 4, section 4(b) of the Rules of Court, which requires exclusive choice. Interestingly, while Indonesia anchors Choice-of-Forum clauses in the freedom of contract found in its Civil Code (*Burgerlijk Wetboek*), courts have not clarified what other promises may be included and how they may be enforced. The *actor sequitur forum rei* principle, the default jurisdictional principle in Indonesia, nonetheless may override Choice-of-Forum clauses, raising doubts about the possibility of including other effects in the clause.

The second aspect of party autonomy, namely the parties' ability to control their litigation, is recognised in both civil law and common law but is circumscribed by the forum's procedural rules and public law doctrines. In Singapore, Hong Kong and Malaysia, this includes making choices about the cause of action, defendants, court (even in breach of the Choice-of-Forum clause), specific defences, evidence, and strategies to expedite or delay the proceedings, including matters during enforcement. Parties may also waive their right to sue under the Choice-of-Forum clause, either expressly or impliedly. Following the adversarial system, the Philippines similarly recognises these freedoms. In China, Indonesia and Japan, courts have a greater control over proceedings due to the inquisitorial system. Procedural rules in these civil law jurisdictions are more explicit, often dictating how rules operate and what effects courts must follow in specific scenarios. As a result, courts may adopt a more formulaic approach, leaving less room for parties to influence the course of litigation or the issues they can raise. However, recent procedural changes, such as the introduction of the *forum non conveniens* and special circumstances tests, reflect the shift towards judicial discretion, thus bringing them closer to the common law approach. These developments may give parties more flexibility in developing litigation strategies.

- Third Lesson: Enforcement is determined by the forum court's procedure.

The enforcement of Choice-of-Forum clauses, even when they are considered contracts, depends on the forum court's procedural rules. Each jurisdiction has unique approaches, even between those sharing the common law heritage. These differences arise from factors such as history (eg, Hong Kong's reversion to China), economic ambitions (eg, Singapore's desire to establish itself as a premier dispute resolution centre), and the type of disputes and issues heard. The interplay between procedure, party autonomy, and court discretion also shapes these differences in enforcement. The Choice-of-Court Convention, by reducing court discretion, is a key factor driving changes in Asia.

Singapore has the most complex enforcement mechanism system. In addition to common law tests, Singapore courts apply the tests under the Choice-of-Court Convention and those unique to the SICC. When the Choice-of-Court Convention does not apply, the common law 'strong cause' test from *The Eleftheria* determines whether a Singapore court (other than the SICC) grants service out of the jurisdiction for a Singapore Choice-of-Forum clause or a stay in favour of a foreign exclusive Choice-of-Forum clause. The Singapore Court of Appeal in *Vinmar*[1] modified factor (d) of *The Eleftheria*, ruling that the absence of a genuine defence is irrelevant, thus limiting this factor to situations of abuse of process or denial of justice. The modified *Spiliada* test governs non-exclusive clauses. If parties intended the non-exclusive clause to function like an exclusive clause, or to give it greater weight against the other *forum non conveniens* factors, the 'strong cause' test also applies. In *Shanghai Turbo*,[2] the court held that when parties intend to give a non-exclusive clause greater weight (eg, by stating that they 'submit' to the named forum), the 'strong cause' factors apply. Foreseeable factors at the time of contracting carry little weight. Without this intention, the classic *Spiliada* analysis applies. For cases under the Choice-of-Court Convention, service out of Singapore and stay applications follow the tests in articles 5 and 6, with Choice-of-Forum clauses presumed exclusive. At the SICC, for exclusive Choice-of-Forum clauses not under the Choice-of-Court Convention and non-exclusive clauses, the test is whether exercising jurisdiction would contradict the SICC's international and commercial character or constitute an abuse of process.[3] Notably, the SICC does not require leave for service out of the jurisdiction either for exclusive or non-exclusive clauses. Anti-suit injunctions are available in all Singapore courts, applying common law tests. Meanwhile, recognition and enforcement of foreign judgments involving Choice-of-Forum clauses are allowed under common law and statutes. On the other hand, enforcement of foreign judgments under the Choice-of-Court Convention is governed by articles 8 to 15.

Except for judgments from Mainland China, Hong Kong courts apply common law tests. For exclusive clauses, relief is granted based on the test in *The Eleftheria*. The 'strong cause' test considers only extraordinary factors that are unforeseeable at the time of contract and in the interest of justice. Like Singapore, Hong Kong adopts the modified *Spiliada* test for non-exclusive clauses,[4] with relief depending on whether parties submitted to the named forum or the forum where the action has been commenced. Anti-suit injunctions are available for both exclusive and non-exclusive clauses after applying common law tests. Recognition and enforcement of foreign judgments are generally governed by common law and statutes. For Chinese judgments with exclusive Choice-of-Forum clauses, the Choice-of-Court Arrangement or the Judgments Arrangement applies. Notably, the provisions of the Choice-of-Court Arrangement are similar to the Choice-of-Court Convention.

[1] *Vinmar Overseas (Singapore) Pte Ltd v PTT International Trading Pte Ltd* [2018] 2 SLR 1271 (CA) ('*Vinmar*').
[2] *Shanghai Turbo Enterprises Ltd v Liu Ming* [2019] 1 SLR 779 (CA).
[3] Singapore International Commercial Court Rules of Court 2021 (Singapore), Ord 2 r 3(2).
[4] See *Noble Power Investments Ltd v Nissei Stomach Tokyo Co Ltd* [2008] HKCA 255.

Malaysia adheres to the 'strong cause' test from *The Eleftheria* for exclusive Choice-of-Forum clauses, though it considers convenience factors more readily than Singapore and Hong Kong. Recent cases like *United Overseas Bank*[5] and *Open Country Dairy*,[6] however, indicate a shift towards a more contractual approach. For non-exclusive clauses, Malaysia uses the traditional *forum non conveniens* test from *Spiliada*, where the Choice-of-Forum clause is one of many factors. The grant of an anti-suit injunction depends on common law tests. Likewise, enforcement and recognition of foreign judgments follow common law principles and statute.

Unlike common law jurisdictions, the Philippines does not grant a stay or anti-suit injunction, though similar forms of relief are available under its Rules of Court. Notably, Choice-of-Forum clauses do not affect extra-territorial service of summons, which solely depends on meeting the procedural requirements under the Rules of Court.[7] Hence, the Philippine approach aligns more closely with civil law jurisdictions. Breaches of Choice-of-Forum clauses can lead to a dismissal due to improper venue or non-compliance with conditions precedent. Choice-of-Forum clauses may also be relevant in motions to dismiss as part of *lis pendens* or *res judicata* arguments. *Forum non conveniens* may be argued during trial, in which case, Choice-of-Forum clauses may also be considered as a factor. Similarly, foreign judgments obtained in breach of Choice-of-Forum clauses may be refused recognition if the breach amounts to a 'want of jurisdiction' by the foreign court.

Procedural rules also determine the enforcement of Choice-of-Forum clauses in China, Indonesia and Japan. Relevant remedies include a stay, dismissal or revival of proceedings; dismissal or suspension due to *forum non conveniens*, *lis pendens* or *res judicata*; provisional measures acting as anti-suit injunctions, and recognition and enforcement of foreign judgments. Unlike in common law jurisdictions, procedural rules may determine issues beyond enforcement, such as existence, validity and interpretation of Choice-of-Forum clauses, though substantive forum law like the Civil Code may also be referred to.

- Fourth Lesson: Court discretion is an important element in the resolution of choice-of-forum clause issues.

Chapter five emphasised the key role of court discretion in the Choice-of-Forum clause analysis. Courts identify and characterise certain facts or elements to justify granting stays, service out of the jurisdiction, anti-suit injunctions, dismissals, preliminary injunctions, and other relief. In Singapore, Hong Kong and Malaysia, the Choice-of-Forum clause, viewed as contract, is the starting point for providing relief. This means that there is an important distinction between exclusive and non-exclusive clauses. For exclusive clauses, relief follows *The Eleftheria*. Courts in Singapore, Hong Kong and Malaysia consider *The Eleftheria* factors for service out of the jurisdiction and stays, except in Singapore, where factor '(d)' (ie, genuine desire for trial in the chosen court) is limited to situations where there is an abuse of process or denial of justice such that the prospect of a fair trial is undermined in the chosen forum. Relief for non-exclusive clauses still generally relies on the *forum non conveniens* test from *Spiliada*, except to the extent that in Singapore, the CCAA and the SICC Law have introduced new tests. When parties intend their non-exclusive Choice-of-Forum clause

[5] *United Overseas Bank Ltd v United Securities Sdn Bhd* [2021] 6 MLJ 897 (CA).
[6] *Open Country Dairy Ltd v Able Food Sdn* [2021] MLJU 969 (CA).
[7] *Dial Corp v Soriano* (1988) 161 SCRA 737, 742.

to have the same effect as exclusive clauses, modified *Spiliada* applies in Hong Kong and Singapore; thus 'strong cause' is required to allow breach of the clause. Malaysia still follows the classic *Spiliada* analysis for non-exclusive clauses.

Despite differences in treatment, the factors identified in *The Eleftheria* and *Spiliada* are similar, although their weight depends on the clause's classification. Factors like the location of evidence, convenience, and efficiency usually do not justify a stay under the 'strong cause' test. In contrast, convenience factors are key in the *forum non conveniens* test. Similarly, applicable law is less crucial in the context of exclusive clauses but vital for non-exclusive clauses. Factors with public policy implications, such as lack of genuine desire for trial, time-bars, loss of juridical advantage, foreign courts' competence, and multiplicity of proceedings, are important in both exclusive and non-exclusive Choice-of-Forum clause analysis.

In the Philippines, the absence of express contractual treatment of Choice-of-Forum clauses and the emphasis on the administration of justice function of the *forum non conveniens* principle have made the Philippine approach distinct. Even with an exclusive clause, the key factors are the competence and capability of local courts to deliver justice – their capacity for case-management, ability to decide effectively on law and facts, and power to enforce decisions. Additionally, relevance lies in whether the filing, in the Philippines or elsewhere, involves an abuse of court process. Furthermore, convenience factors are considered separately in the Philippine *forum non conveniens* analysis, regardless of the Choice-of-Forum clauses involved.

Court discretion is crucial in civil law jurisdictions when applying the newly-introduced tests similar to *forum non conveniens*. Even with these tests, however, formulaic approaches (eg, the tendency in China and Japan to treat clauses as exclusive despite lacking a presumption of exclusivity) may still shape judicial discretion. Discretion is also essential where no clear rules apply. While natural justice guides discretion, the lack of a doctrine of precedent can lead to inconsistent results and approaches. Hence, in Indonesia, it is unclear whether Choice-of-Forum clauses can override the default jurisdictional rules embodying the *actor sequitur forum rei* principle. To guide discretion, civil law jurisdictions need statutes, or in their absence, derivative instruments like model cases, judicial interpretations, and scholarly literature for consistency in judicial practice.

- Fifth Lesson: In common law jurisdictions, unlike the issue of existence, the applicable law closely determines issues of validity and interpretation. In the civil law jurisdictions and the Philippines, forum law generally determines all three.

In common law jurisdictions, the law that is selected by the choice of law process determines certain aspects of Choice-of-Forum clauses, particularly their validity and how they may be interpreted. Nonetheless, the specific effect of this applicable law depends on several factors, such as where the action was filed, the plaintiff's cause of action, the court's characterisation of Choice-of-Forum clauses, procedural rules, parties' control over the litigation, evidential rules, burden of proof, and legal reasoning.

The law applicable to Choice-of-Forum clauses may be different across jurisdictions, but a national law must apply. Notably, this law must be determinate, although different aspects of the clause may be governed by multiple legal systems. In common law jurisdictions, the law applicable to Choice-of-Forum clauses is the law applicable to the underlying contract, either expressly or impliedly intended by the parties. In the absence of choice, the law is determined by factors like the place of contracting, the parties' residence or business, the contract's nature and subject matter, and the place of performance. The law applicable to the underlying contract determines validity and interpretation. The law determining existence in common law is uncertain, with some decisions citing forum law while others the putative 'applicable law'. In Malaysia, Islamic law applies alongside the substantive law chosen in Islamic banking and finance contracts. However, Malaysian courts have yet to decide if *Shariah* principles could directly affect the validity of Choice-of-Forum clauses.

Under the Choice-of-Court Convention, the chosen court's law determines if the Choice-of-Forum clause is null and void, while other grounds for suspension and dismissal of actions are determined by forum law. In the Philippines, existence and validity are determined by the clause's compliance with the straightforward rule on venue under the Philippine Rules of Court: namely, that the 'parties have validly agreed in writing before the filing of the action on the exclusive venue thereof'.[8] Compliance with this rule renders the usual distinction between existence and validity irrelevant. Similarly, civilian courts generally apply forum law to substantive issues like existence, validity and interpretation, which stems from their procedural characterisation. Interestingly, the scope of forum law extends to local substantive laws like the Civil Code and consumer laws. The contract's applicable law generally plays a minor role, although courts, in some instances, have used this law to determine validity and interpretation. Due to the absence of a doctrine of precedent, the applicable law for resolving validity and interpretation remains uncertain until clarified by a statute or judicial interpretation.

- Sixth Lesson: Forum state and international interests can override party autonomy and applicable law.

The interests of the forum state, international community, and third-party states can limit the effects of Choice-of-Forum clauses, through mandatory rules, comity public policy or analogous concepts like public interest, public morals, and good customs.

Mandatory rules which embody important state interests affect Choice-of-Forum clauses in Singapore, Hong Kong and Malaysia at two levels: by specifying a forum for the dispute contemplated, or by overriding the applicable law. In both, the validity and interpretation of the Choice-of-Forum clause may be impacted. A rule's mandatory character may be explicit in the statute itself, but often, it is determined through statutory construction and confirmed by court decisions. The Philippines lacks an express doctrine of mandatory rules, but concepts like 'mandatory laws', 'prohibitive laws' or incontrovertible Constitutional provisions function similarly. 'Mandatory' laws affect Choice-of-Forum clauses by determining validity and interpretation, and at the enforcement and recognition of judgments stage,[9] as well as the *forum non conveniens* analysis by representing important state interests, thus justifying the Philippine proceedings, regardless of the chosen forum.

Mandatory rules in civil law countries can override or modify the legal effects of any act, including Choice-of-Forum clauses. In Japan, forum choice in consumer and employment contracts must comply with mandatory rules on where such suits may be filed, making exclusive Choice-of-Forum clauses 'non-exclusive' unless they align with these rules. In China and Japan, if a matter under a Choice-of-Forum clause falls within the exclusive jurisdiction of local courts, the clause choosing foreign forums will not be enforced. In Indonesia, for

[8] Rules of Court (Philippines), rule 4 s 4(b).
[9] See Civil Code (Philippines), art 17.

Islamic banking transactions governed by *Shariah*, religious courts have absolute jurisdiction, with *Basyarnas* arbitration as the only alternative. Outside these options, the chosen forum may not prevail. The content and impact of mandatory rules on Choice-of-Forum clauses vary. In China, rules for consumer and standard-term contracts require proper notice. Additionally, consumer laws on unconscionability may affect the enforcement when the chosen forum imposes an undue burden on consumers.

State interests are expressed through public policy, which includes analogous concepts like public order, natural justice, customs, morals and public interests. In Singapore, Hong Kong and Malaysia, public policy can affect Choice-of-Forum clauses by (1) rendering them illegal, void or unenforceable, (2) establishing 'strong cause' and influencing the *forum non conveniens* test, and (3) denying enforcement of foreign judgments. However, public policy is rarely used, as enforcing Choice-of-Forum clauses is also a matter of public policy. In the Philippines, public policy serves as an important counterweight to private interests of parties in the *forum non conveniens* test. In China, Indonesia and Japan, public policy also ensures that state interests and values are not overridden by Choice-of-Forum clauses. Although public policy remains wide and 'unruly', recent statutory developments have narrowed its scope to exclude purely private economic interests.

In all seven jurisdictions, 'weaker parties' like consumers and employees receive special protection. In the context of Choice-of-Forum clauses, this protection is expressed by not enforcing clauses which are against consumer protection laws, rendering certain 'unfair' or 'potestative' asymmetric clauses unenforceable or void, finding clauses which are unconscionable or unfair void because they deprive parties of access to justice, and subjecting standard-form clauses to greater scrutiny. This enhanced protection may alter the effects of Choice-of-Forum clauses, as seen in Japan.

Foreign state interests are considered when relevant treaties apply and when 'comity' is considered. They affect the analysis at the choice of law level, service out of jurisdiction, stay applications, anti-suit injunctions, recognition and enforcement of foreign judgments, and when the other forum is deemed 'unsuitable'. In China, Indonesia and Japan, foreign and international interests are considered when applying *forum non conveniens* and suspending or resuming proceedings due to *lis pendens*, reciprocity, and public policy.

- Bringing Everything Together

In sum, the following factors determine how courts in Singapore, Hong Kong, Malaysia, the Philippines, China, Indonesia and Japan decide Choice-of-Forum clause issues: (1) how courts characterise these clauses, (2) the exercise of party autonomy, (3) relevant procedural rules available for enforcing these clauses, (4) the discretion courts use in weighing factors for granting relief, (5) the choice of law process and its impact on existence, validity and interpretation of clauses, and (6) the overriding effect of state and international interests on party autonomy and the choice of law process.

Chapter two introduced a framework classifying Choice-of-Forum clause issues into three categories: (1) purely procedural (eg, issues on the enforcement aspect of the Choice-of-Forum clause or those concerning the court's administration of justice); (2) purely substantive (eg, issues of validity and existence); and (3) both substantive and procedural (eg, issues of interpretation). This framework reflects the dual relationship in Choice-of-Forum clause litigation – between the courts and parties, and between the parties themselves. As discussed in Chapters three and seven, the three interests previously identified by Keyes (party interests, forum state interests, and foreign and international community interests)[10] also affect the analysis of Choice-of-Forum clause issues. Hence, courts' approaches to Choice-of-Forum clause issues are defined by these three interests – party autonomy, state interests, and interests of the international community.

How courts approach the specific issues can therefore be illustrated thus:

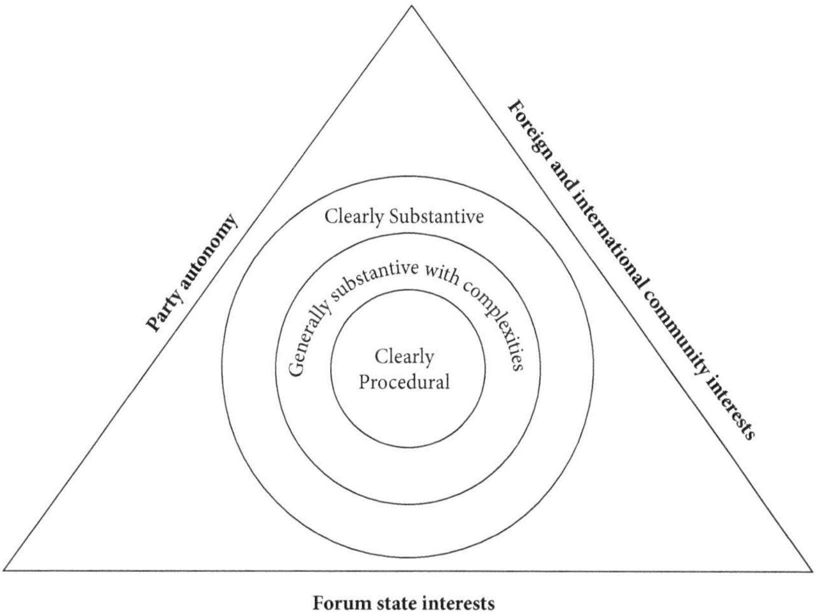

II. Implications for the Progressive Development of the Law in Asia

This book explores, identifies, compares and explains how courts in the seven featured Asian jurisdictions decide Choice-of-Forum clause issues in actual court disputes. The first section summarised how this is done across the seven jurisdictions. The final question this book addresses is the implications of these findings for the progressive development of the law of Choice-of-Forum clauses in Asia.

A. Implications for Parties

The key findings highlight the importance of careful drafting of Choice-of-Forum clauses. Parties should consider direct effects (eg, in relation to enforcement, validity, and recognition of judgments, and enforcement of other contractual promises such as waivers

[10] Mary Keyes, *Jurisdiction in International Litigation* (Federation Press, 2005) 178–225.

of jurisdictional objections), and indirect effects (eg, its role in determining the applicable law and the factors courts may consider). Given their impact on transaction risks, Choice-of-Forum clauses should be a key commercial consideration during negotiations. Even if private rights arising from Choice-of-Forum clauses are not recognised in civil law countries, these clauses should still be regarded as having significant legal and commercial effects, not merely boilerplate provisions. To develop best practices, parties, corporations, international organisations, and law firms can draft model Choice-of-Forum clauses for cross-border contracts. Regular use within industries can create customs and practices that courts may recognise.

The passive role of courts in adversarial systems, particularly in Singapore and Hong Kong, means that the development of the Choice-of-Forum law in Asia relies more on the litigation strategies and issues parties bring forward, thus highlighting the importance of party autonomy. Arguably, this greater role of party autonomy in Singapore and Hong Kong also explains why these jurisdictions have the most sophisticated and complex laws on Choice-of-Forum clauses.

Asian businesses should therefore increasingly embrace party autonomy, as it aligns well with their preference for flexibility.[11] In any case, surveys show strong regional support for party autonomy.[12] Further, the growing number of cases involving Choice-of-Forum clauses in Singapore and Hong Kong indicates readiness to enforce party autonomy, a position supported by the Asia Pacific Economic Cooperation (APEC) member states.[13] This also underscores the foundational role of consent, expressed through party autonomy, as the cornerstone of international dispute resolution.[14]

Given the higher transactional risks in Asia, there is more reason to recognise the importance of Choice-of-Forum clauses in mitigating risks. Notably, clauses choosing the Singapore and Hong Kong courts may be considered most effective in mitigating risks, as courts in both jurisdictions enforce these clauses with more consistency and reliability. However, the capacity of these clauses to manage risks may be less effective in Malaysia and the Philippines, where courts exercise greater discretion and focus more on administration of justice rather than private interests. In China and Japan, exclusive clauses are generally enforceable, but because they lack private law consequences, parties may find clauses stipulating Chinese and Japanese courts less effective, as damages or anti-suit injunctions are not available for breach. Indonesia may be considered the jurisdiction where these clauses are least effective; but even there, Choice-of-Forum clauses are still enforceable. On the other hand, non-exclusive clauses offer greater flexibility but may be less effective in managing risks. The Choice-of-Court Convention further strengthens the effectiveness of exclusive Choice-of-Forum clauses in mitigating risks by narrowing judicial discretion.

[11] See Veronica Taylor and Michael Pryles, 'The Cultures of Dispute Resolution in Asia' in Michael Pryles (ed), *Dispute Resolution in Asia* (3rd edn, Kluwer Law International, 2006) 5.

[12] See Singapore Academy of Law, *Study on Governing Law & Jurisdictional Choices in Cross-Border Transactions* (Survey, 11 January 2016).

[13] *Report on the APEC EC Workshop on Effective Enforcement of Business Contracts and Efficient Resolution of Business Disputes through the Hague Choice of Court Agreements Convention, Cebu, Philippines* (1 September 2015) https://www.hcch.net/upload/apec2015rpt.pdf (accessed 2 September 2024).

[14] See Linda Mullenix, 'Another Choice of Forum, Another Choice of Law: Consensual Adjudicatory Procedure in Federal Court' (1988) 57(3) *Fordham Law Review* 291, 314.

B. Implications for the Forum State

Forum states are crucial in developing the law on Choice-of-Forum clauses. This section first discusses the implications for the forum court, and then those for the forum state in general.

(i) Implications for the Forum Court

(a) Predictability, Reliability and Coherence

In Singapore, Hong Kong, Malaysia and the Philippines, courts rely on the doctrine of precedent by examining prior decisions and citing relevant statutes and procedural rules. This process involves identifying norms, applying them to the facts, and comparing similarities and differences between past cases. Courts frequently reference case law from England, the United States and other Commonwealth countries, thus engaging in comparative legal analysis. When case law offers no specific guidance, courts turn to scholarly writings.[15] Judicial reasoning also reflects an awareness of the complexities of commercial and cross-border transactions, considering both party interests and those of the international community. Even when emphasising discretion and public interests, courts' reasoning remains persuasive, never whimsical or based on non-legal considerations. In this way, judges in Singapore, Hong Kong, Malaysia and the Philippines in cases involving Choice-of-Forum clauses ensure that decisions involving Choice-of-Forum clauses are predictable, reliable and coherent.

In civil law jurisdictions, the absence of the doctrine of precedent diminishes the importance of court decisions as sources of law. Scholars in China[16] and Indonesia[17] note that this may affect the quality of writing, reasoning, and application of law. However, court decisions are important for establishing a predictable and coherent legal system. Hence to ensure predictability, reliability and coherence, the importance of instruments like judicial interpretations, model cases, and statutes is more pronounced in civil law jurisdictions. Scholarly writings, because of their significance in guiding courts,[18] should also be encouraged.

Nonetheless, in Asia, judicial institutions may not be strong and independent, may lack the necessary competence and resources to resolve complex cross-border issues, and

[15] See, eg, *PT Selecta Bestama v Sin Huat Huat Marine Transportation Pte Ltd* [2016] 1 SLR 729 (HC) [40] citing Adeline Chong; *Orchard Capital I Ltd v Ravindra Kumar Jhunjhunwala* [2012] 2 SLR 519 (CA) [3] citing Yeo Tiong Min; *Hong Kong and Shanghai Banking Corporation v Sherman* (1989) 176 SCRA 331, 336, citing Jovito Salonga, *Private International Law* (UP Law Center, 1981); *John Reginald Stott Kirkham v Trane US Inc* [2009] 4 SLR(R) 428, [34] (CA), citing Adrian Briggs; *Deltatre SPA v Hong Kong Sports Industrial Development Ltd* [2018] HKCFI 1942, [4] ('*Deltatre*') citing Adrian Briggs, *Agreements on Jurisdiction and Choice of Law* (Oxford University Press, 2008).

[16] See, eg, Wu Fan, 'Legal Reasoning in Chinese and Swiss Appellate Judgments – Exploring China's Path Towards Rule of Law' (2009) 2(1) *Tsinghua China Law Review* 19, 38–39; Leyton Nelson, 'Dispute Settlement with Chinese Characteristics: Assessing China's International Commercial Court' (Staff Research Report, US-China Economic Security Commission, 28 February 2023).

[17] See, eg, Priskila Penasthika, *Unravelling Choice of Law in International Commercial Contracts as an Illustrative Case Study* (Doctoral Thesis, Erasmus University Rotterdam, 29 September 2022) 129, 134, 143.

[18] eg, *Richard Bruce Ness v Jane Perlez and the New York Times Company* (District Court of Central Jakarta, Judgment No 181/PDT.G/2007/PN.JKT.PST, 8 October 2007), citing M Yahya Harahap, *Hukum Acara Perdata Tentang Gugatan, Persidangan, Penyitaan, Pembuktian, dn Putusan Pengadilan* (Sinar Grafika, 2016) 205; see Afifah Kusumadara, *Indonesian Private International Law* (Hart Publishing, 2021) 41.

may be vulnerable to corruption.[19] Court decisions have identified these problems when discussing comity or administration of justice factors. For example, lower court judges in the Philippines may lack the necessary skills to resolve private international law cases. Strengthening the rule of law, providing resources and training for judges, and making litigation outcomes predictable and transparent are therefore important. Furthermore, procedural rules should clearly allow exclusive Choice-of-Forum clauses choosing the forum court as among the grounds for allowing service outside jurisdiction, and with respect to exclusive Choice-of-Forum clauses choosing a foreign court, as the basis for a stay of local proceedings. In the Philippines, *forum non conveniens* should expressly be a ground for dismissal or affirmative defence.

However, purely legal solutions may be insufficient. Judicial reforms should address the very concerns mentioned in the cases – clogged dockets, lack of competence in deciding cross-border commercial issues, or even lack of translators. Heavy workloads hinder lower court judges from thoroughly examining evidence and conducting adequate research in complex commercial cases. This problem is exacerbated in cross-border disputes, underscoring the need for better resources and competence in Choice-of-Forum clause litigation. Addressing translation challenges is vital, especially with the rise in trade and investments between Asian countries, which increases the likelihood of courts dealing with non-English Choice-of-Forum clauses. Given the complexity and changes in this area of law, judges should be regularly updated on legal developments.

Asia similarly faces the challenges in private international law, as identified by Muir-Watt, who noted that its

> 'international' reach mirrored the representation carried by public international law of a world of multiple territorial states, so that it dealt exclusively with the consequences of contacts between state laws, ignoring forms of transnational normativity beyond the territorial community.[20]

Hence, traditional private international law rules, including those concerning party autonomy in Choice-of-Forum clauses, are challenged by globalisation and approaches towards territoriality. Again, these developments underscore the importance of consent as the basis of jurisdiction, emphasising the key role of Choice-of-Forum clauses in future civil procedures.

(b) Court Discretion

Party autonomy increasingly limits judicial discretion. In Singapore, the continued push favouring party autonomy has watered down factor '(d)' of the test in *The Eleftheria*. Under the Choice-of-Court Convention, judicial discretion is nearly absent. Hence, what the

[19] See, eg, Wei Cai and Andrew Godwin, 'Challenges and Opportunities for the China International Commercial Court' (2019) 68(4) *International and Comparative Law Quarterly* 869, 873–74; Penashthika (n 17) 190–94; Maria Ela L Atienza, *The Philippine Judiciary: Strengthening the Third Branch of Government* (Discussion Paper, University of the Philippines Center for Integrative and Development Studies, 2023) 21–29; Muhammad Nurul Houque, Muhammad Kaleem Zahir-ul-Hassan, Mohammad Arif Idrus and Tony van Zijl, 'Bribery and Corruption: Assessing the Fairness of the Malaysian Judicial System' (2020) 74 *Crime, Law and Social Change* 135.

[20] Horatia Muir-Watt, 'The Relevance of Private International Law to the Global Governance Debate' in Horatia Muir-Watt and Diego Fernandez-Arroyo (eds), *Private International Law and Global Governance* (Oxford University Press, 2015) 1, 2.

parties provide in the exclusive Choice-of-Forum clause dictates the relief which the court may grant. However, Chapter five highlights the continued importance of court discretion in the Choice-of-Forum clause analysis to ensure that justice is rendered. For example, none of the common law jurisdictions adopt a mechanistic approach to resolving the disputes. Furthermore, given the nature of legal reasoning in common law, there is always a need for court discretion in the analysis.

In Asia, court discretion is crucial in taking account of local customs and contexts, which inform interpretation, evidence, and the application of mandatory rules and public policy. While rules may be similar, courts may adapt them to local contexts. Court discretion is important when recognising the region's diversity and complexity. Discretion allows flexibility much needed in certain sectors, such as in considering differences in Islamic law opinions or *fatwās* which may be important in cross-border Islamic banking and finance disputes. Taylor and Pryles cautioned against expecting a uniform legal and commercial culture between 'Asia' and 'the West', noting that local cultures and economic conditions are too dynamic and diverse to be reduced to static components.[21] Hence, to expect a monolithic Asian approach to party autonomy is unrealistic.

Furthermore, there are pockets where forum interests of Asian countries may be more prominent than others. For instance, the idea of excluding consumer and employment contracts is expected, and their protection may continue to echo the rationale that parties with weak bargaining power require protection.[22] In the Philippines, the 'public interest' doctrine is frequently invoked to avoid Choice-of-Forum clauses in contracts involving overseas Filipino workers,[23] a practice likely to continue as long as the country remains a major labour-exporter. Consumer welfare concerns shape the approaches of advanced jurisdictions like Singapore, Hong Kong and Japan. Maintaining court discretion gives courts the space to give effect to these important state interests.

Even with court discretion, as seen in Chapter five, decisions are rarely arbitrary, inconsistent or incoherent. First, party autonomy significantly constrains judicial discretion, as courts can only consider factors raised by parties and proven in evidence. Second, legal reasoning in cases with foreign elements must take account of international community interests, a necessity for jurisdictions aiming to attract international trade and investments. Third, the common law's emphasis on precedent further limits court discretion. Hence, even when court discretion is maintained, its exercise is never unfettered.

(c) Judicial Cooperation

The cross-border character of Choice-of-Forum clause litigation and the procedural differences across Asian countries highlight the need for judicial cooperation. Pragmatic steps could include setting translation standards for contracts, court judgments and other documents used in other jurisdictions. Improving access to legal materials, such as through open access databases, and providing laws and cases in English, or simplifying the process of

[21] Taylor and Pryles (n 11) 18.

[22] Isabelle Veillard, 'The General and Commercial Character of the UNIDROIT Principles of International Commercial Contracts' (2007) 4 *International Business Law Journal* 479, 487–90.

[23] See, eg, *Saudi Arabian Airlines (Saudia) v Rebesencio* (2015) 746 SCRA 140; *Pakistan International Airlines Corp v Ople* (1990) 190 SCRA 90.

establishing foreign laws and documents, is essential.[24] Harmonising procedural rules based on international standards could reduce inconsistent legal treatment[25] and address issues like global forum-shopping or wasting judicial resources because of parallel proceedings. Judicial cooperation is also crucial for sharing knowledge of approaches, best practices and solutions in Choice-of-Forum clause litigation. This collaboration could extend to improving court competence and resources, such as through cross-jurisdictional training for court translators. Further, technological advancements, including translation tools, should be part of these discussions.

(ii) Implications for the Forum State

This book has highlighted issues which may require legislative attention. Chapter four describes how the SICC Law and CCAA have made Singapore a very complex jurisdiction when it comes to Choice-of-Forum clause analysis – 'four different tests for exclusive choice of court clauses, two different tests for non-exclusive choice of court cases, and five different tests for joining third parties'.[26] These complexities increase the risk of confusion for parties and courts, potentially undermining the predictability, reliability and coherence of the law. However, recent amendments to the Singaporean Rules of Court and the introduction of standalone SICC Rules are positive steps towards simplifying the treatment of Choice-of-Forum clauses in Singapore.

To further improve enforcement of Hong Kong judgments and given China's eventual accession, Hong Kong should reconsider joining (or adopting) the Choice-of-Court Convention regime. A wait-and-see approach could weaken its position as a premier dispute resolution centre. The positive experience under the Choice-of-Court Arrangement, which is similar to the Choice-of-Court Convention, further supports this move. Notably, Hong Kong courts have proven their ability to handle complex cases, as demonstrated by their adoption of the modified *Spiliada*, suggesting that they would adapt well to the Choice-of-Court Convention regime.

Malaysia should reconsider the role of the 'convenience' factors in the 'strong cause' test. Recent cases show a shift towards a more contract-oriented analysis,[27] yet *B Braun* still uses convenience factors as 'strong cause' even with exclusive Choice-of-Forum clauses.[28] To enhance predictability, the Malaysian Parliament could legislate for a definitive rule, fully adopting *The Eleftheria* and limiting the 'strong cause' to factors unforeseeable at the time of contracting or those 'so exceptional that [they go] to the interests of justice'.[29] This would align Malaysia with the other common law jurisdictions. Additionally, given Malaysia's

[24] See, eg, Lemuel Didulo Lopez, 'Philippines' in Kazuaki Nishioka (ed), *Treatment of Foreign Law in Asia* (Hart Publishing, 2023) 203, 218.

[25] See Alex Mills, *The Confluence of Public and Private International Law: Justice, Pluralism and Subsidiarity in the International Constitutional Ordering of Private Law* (Cambridge University Press, 2009) 288.

[26] Yeo Tiong Min, 'Staying Relevant: Exercise of Jurisdiction in the Age of SICC' (Yong Pung How Professorship of Law Lecture, Singapore Management University, 13 May 2015) 28.

[27] See *United Overseas Bank Ltd v United Securities Sdn Bhd* [2021] 6 MLJ 897 (CA); *Open Country Dairy Ltd v Able Food Sdn* [2021] MLJU 969 (CA).

[28] *B Braun Medical Industries Sdn Bhd v Pyramid Lines Singapore Pte Ltd* [2023] MLJU 2760, [8] (HC Kuala Lumpur).

[29] See *Deltatre* (n 15) [46].

leadership in Islamic banking and its proximity to Singapore, joining the Choice-of-Court Convention would improve the enforcement of Islamic banking-related judgments in other jurisdictions, especially in the European Union.

The Philippines lags in enforcing Choice-of-Forum clauses due to a lack of clear rules and limited awareness among many Filipino lawyers, judges and legislators about their importance and complexities. The approach in *The Bremen*, for example, remains absent in the Supreme Court decisions, despite the tendency of Philippine courts to refer to American decisions. This gap likely stems from the recent emphasis on party autonomy in dispute resolution. The law on international arbitration was only introduced in 2004,[30] and institutions like the Integrated Bar of the Philippines and Philippine Dispute Resolution Center are still working to raise public awareness about arbitration. As a result, it may take time for Filipino practitioners and businesses to fully grasp the significance of Choice-of-Forum clauses in international commercial contracts. However, it would be beneficial for Philippine Congress to pass legislation similar to the law on international arbitration, clarifying the nature, effects and remedies related to Choice-of-Forum clauses. The existing procedural rules on venue or the Civil Code are insufficient for addressing the complexities of these clauses in the Philippines.

Beyond the specific reforms in each jurisdiction, certain rules relevant to Choice-of-Forum clause analysis need clarification. For instance, the law governing the existence of Choice-of-Forum clauses should be clearly established. Given its fundamental nature and the public interests involved, it is advisable to have this issue determined by forum law. Furthermore, it would be beneficial for the legislatures to clarify whether a certain rule is mandatory or not (ie, whether it overrides the Choice-of-Forum clause, or the law chosen by the parties).

Recent legislative developments in China and Japan reflect positive attitudes towards enforcing Choice-of-Forum clauses. However, some key areas need clarification. In China, clear guidelines are needed on whether the actual connection requirement still applies to Choice-of-Forum clauses choosing foreign courts. In Japan, a clearer legislative distinction between international and domestic Choice-of-Forum clauses is needed. Indonesia should reconsider its adherence to the *actor sequitur forum rei* principle and confirm through legislation that Choice-of-Forum clauses prevail over rules reflecting the principle. Furthermore, all three jurisdictions would greatly benefit from joining the Choice-of-Court Convention.

C. Implications for Asian Countries and the International Community

(i) A Region Conducive to Party Autonomy

Colonialism and legislative reforms made in late nineteenth and early twentieth century have introduced party autonomy in Asia. As discussed in Chapters three and eight, all

[30] Alternative Dispute Resolution Act (Philippines).

jurisdictions have embraced and nurtured the principle, despite the 1990s political rhetoric advocating 'Asian' values over international (Western) norms.[31] Even with increased economic integration within Asia and with non-Asian partners, the default models for legal reform are largely the United States, England, and the European Union.[32] This influence is evident in recent legislative initiatives, such as Singapore's CCAA implementing the Choice-of-Court Convention, and Hong Kong and China's Judgments Arrangement, copying The Hague Judgments Convention. Similarly, procedural and substantive reforms in China, Indonesia and Japan have followed Western approaches. Court decisions, particularly in common law jurisdictions, including the Philippines, continue to refer to English, American and other Commonwealth cases.

Party autonomy supports the policy goals of many Asian states. As economic growth and modernisation are priorities, wealth creation has become essential to political legitimacy.[33] Attracting foreign investments is key to this goal, which necessitates laws that are familiar to Western investors. For example, Singapore's adoption of the Choice-of-Court Convention and the establishment of the SICC aim to attract foreign investments and to firmly position Singapore as a leading dispute resolution centre. Likewise, many Asian countries rely on foreign aid and loans for infrastructure development, with donors and foreign governments sometimes requiring legislation, including those promoting party autonomy.

The twenty-first-century landscape in Asia is therefore conducive to strengthening laws on party autonomy. Projects like the Choice-of-Court Convention and The Hague Judgments Convention are likely to be well-received by Asian countries.

(ii) A Case for the Choice-of-Court Convention and The Hague Judgments Convention

Though limited in scope, the Choice-of-Court Convention may serve as a catalyst for developments in the law of Choice-of-Forum clauses in Asia. This impact is evident in Singapore, and in the Hong Kong-China Choice-of-Court Arrangement. China's 2023 Amendment to the CCPL is likely a step towards eventual accession to the said convention.[34] Similarly, the work leading to The Hague Judgments Convention inspired the Judgments Arrangement,[35] highlighting the influence of international instruments on local and regional reforms. However, the complex effects of international treaties on domestic legal systems, as seen in Singapore, may have caused the hesitation among countries, including possibly why China has not yet acceded to the Choice-of-Court Convention.

There are strong reasons for Asian countries to adopt the Choice-of-Court Convention and The Hague Judgments Convention. A 2015 APEC Economic Committee report noted

[31] Taylor and Pryles (n 11) 7.

[32] ibid.

[33] ibid 9.

[34] See, eg, Jie Huang, 'Developing Chinese Private International Law for Transnational Civil and Commercial Litigation: The 2024 New Chinese Civil Procedure Law' (2023) 70 *Netherlands International Law Review* 205, 209.

[35] See Peggy Au Yeung, *Access to Justice and Sustainable Development: The Impact of the HCCH in an Inter-Connected World* (Conference Paper, HCCH Asia Pacific Week Hong Kong 2023, 12 September 2023) [14]–[17].

that some member economies are actively considering the Choice-of-Court Convention.[36] As more Asian countries consider accession, others are likely to follow. With competition for foreign investments increasing across Asia, a legal framework that ensures predictable outcomes for exclusive Choice-of-Forum clauses could provide a competitive advantage. Additionally, The Hague Judgments Convention offers a reliable global system for the recognition and enforcement of foreign judgments, regardless of whether a Choice-of-Forum clause is involved. Together, these treaties complement each other and strengthen the framework for cross-border litigation.

Currently, drafting an Asian treaty on Choice-of-Forum clauses is unrealistic due to the difficulty of achieving consensus. Asia's complexity, with its diverse legal systems, economic development, and politics, makes reaching an agreement challenging. The experiences at the Hague Conference during the Choice-of-Court Convention negotiations show the difficulties in bridging these differences.[37] Furthermore, the treaty record of Asian countries in addressing regional private law and procedural matters is not promising. Therefore, accession to the Choice-of-Court Convention and The Hague Judgments Convention offers a more feasible path for Asian countries to pursue reforms and foster a party autonomy-friendly environment in the region.

III. Towards an Asian Contribution to the Choice-of-Forum Clause Analysis

Asian jurisdictions have developed unique approaches to analysing Choice-of-Forum clause issues. China, Japan and the Philippines, for example, have created versions of the *forum non conveniens* test that differ from the common law approach. The modified *Spiliada* test used in Hong Kong and Singapore also differs from the English courts' version. Hong Kong and China have also incorporated the Choice-of-Court Convention and The Hague Judgments Convention – still being drafted at that time – into regional judicial arrangements tailored to local circumstances. Additionally, Islamic banking transactions have introduced new elements to the Choice-of-Forum clause analysis in Malaysia and Indonesia.

This book highlights that while Asian courts face legal issues common to many Choice-of-Forum clause disputes, they encounter unique challenges. A key area is the interpretation of Choice-of-Forum clauses written in local languages. In trying to understand the parties' intention, Asian courts can make a uniquely Asian contribution to the Choice-of-Forum clause analysis. By assigning legal significance to specific local words and phrases, courts enhance the legal vocabulary of local languages, promoting greater predictability and coherence in the interpretation of non-English language contracts. This is increasingly important, as Asian parties, who may not be using English language contracts, play a more active role in

[36] *Report on the APEC EC Workshop on Effective Enforcement of Business Contracts and Efficient Resolution of Business Disputes through the Hague Choice of Court Agreements Convention, Cebu, Philippines* (1 September 2015): https://www.hcch.net/upload/apec2015rpt.pdf (accessed 2 September 2024).

[37] See, eg, David Bennett, 'The Hague Convention on Recognition and Enforcement of Foreign Judgments – A Failure of Characterisation' in Talia Einvborn and Kurt Siehr (eds), *Intercontinental Cooperation Through Private International Law: Essays in Memory of Peter E. Nygh* (TMC Asser Press, 2004) 19.

international business. The rise in Choice-of-Forum disputes involving Chinese-language contracts in Hong Kong reflects this trend. Nonetheless, this process of interpretation may also have another dimension. For example, in their process of interpretation, courts may need to consider the Asian way of doing business, balancing the preference for flexibility with the need for legal certainty. How should Asian courts approach this query? This task, though challenging, will further advance the development of the law in Asia and allow a uniquely Asian contribution to the Choice-of-Forum clause analysis, thus securing the relevance of Choice-of-Forum clauses in this Asian century.

BIBLIOGRAPHY

Journal Articles

Abdullah A, 'The Doctrine of the Freedom of Contract *(Hurriyyat al-Taaqud)* in Islamic *Mu'amalat*: An exposition on the concepts and rules of the contract of *muqaqalah* in the construction industry' (2011) 50 *Islamic Studies* 365

Bae K-H, Purda L and Welker M, 'Credit rating initiation and accounting quality for emerging-market firms' (2013) 44(3) *Journal of International Business Studies* 216

Barrett PJ, 'Choice of Forum Provisions and the Intrastate Dilemma: Is Ouster Ousted? (1980) 48(4) *Fordham Law Review* 568

Black V and Pitel S, 'Forum-selection clauses: beyond the contracting parties' (2016) 12(1) *Journal of Private International Law* 26

Bodenheimer E 'The Public Policy Exception in Private International Law: A Reappraisal in the Light of Legal Philosophy' (1954) 12 *Seminar (Jurist)* 51

Borchers P, 'Forum Selection Agreements in the Federal Courts after Carnival Cruise: A Proposal for Congressional Reform' (1992) 67(1) *Washington Law Review* 55

Brekoulakis S, 'The Notion of the Superiority of Arbitration Agreements over Jurisdiction Agreements: Time to Abandon it?' (2007) 24(4) *Journal of International Arbitration* 341

Buang AH, 'Islamic Contracts in a Secular Court Setting? Lessons from Malaysia' (2007) 21(4) *Arab Law Quarterly* 317

Bufford K, 'Threshold or Procedural Issue: The Order of Interpretation Required by Contractual Choice-of-Law Provisions Versus the Law of the Forum Where the Suit is Commenced' (2016) 40(1) *American Journal of Trial Advocacy* 131

Buxbaum H, 'Forum Selection in International Contract Litigation: The Role of Judicial Discretion' (2004) 12(2) *Willamette Journal of International Law and Dispute Resolution* 185

Byrne C and Heneghan J, 'New Horizons? Trends Influencing Effective Projects and Construction Dispute Resolution in Ireland' (2011) 6(2) *Construction Law International* 9

Chandler, AT, 'Thailand: Something Special', *International Financial Law Review* (1 June 2011): http://www.iflr.com/Article/2855518/Thailand-Something-special.html

Chao Z, 'Research on the Contract of Civil Right of Action: The Influences of Judicial Experience on the Development of Legal Theory' [2017] (1) *The Jurist* 32

Chen CN, 'Recovery of Gambling Debts in Malaysia and Singapore' [2001] 1 *Malayan Law Journal* i

Chong A, 'Moving towards harmonisation in the recognition and enforcement of foreign judgment rules in Asia' (2020) 16(1) *Journal of Private International Law* 31

Clermont K, 'Governing Law on Forum-Selection Agreements' (2015) 66(3) *Hastings Law Journal* 643

Cowen Z and Mendes Da Costa D, 'The Contractual Forum: Situation in England and the British Commonwealth' (1964) 13(1) *American Journal of Comparative Law* 179

Drobnig U, 'Substantive Validity' (1992) 40(3) *American Journal of Comparative Law* 635

Farquharson I, 'Choice of Forum Clauses – A Brief Survey of Anglo-American Law' (1974) 8(1) *International Lawyer* 83

Fawcett JJ, 'Evasion of Law and Mandatory Rules in Private International Law' (1990) 49(1) *Cambridge Law Journal* 44

——, 'Forum Shopping – Some Questions Answered' (1984) 35(2) *Northern Ireland Legal Quarterly* 141

Ferri G and Liu L-G, 'How Do Global Credit-Rating Agencies Rate Firms from Developing Countries?' (2004) 2(3) *Asian Economic Papers* 30

Finder, S, 'More on People's Court Typical and Major Cases, or How Typical Cases are Tempered', *Supreme People's Court Monitor* (1 April 2022): https://supremepeoplescourtmonitor.com/2022/04/01/more-on-supreme-peoples-court-typical-and-major-cases-or-how-typical-cases-are-tempered/

Garnett R, 'Coexisting and Conflicting Jurisdiction and Arbitration Clauses' (2013) 9(3) *Journal of Private International Law* 361

——, 'The Hague Choice of Court Convention: Magnum Opus or Much Ado about Nothing' (2009) 5(1) *Journal of Private International Law* 161

Glasser C, 'Civil Procedure and the Lawyers: The Adversary System and the Decline of the Orality Principle' (1993) 56(3) *The Modern Law Review* 307

Godwin A, 'Obligations to Negotiate in Good Faith in Cross-Border Deals' (2013) 3 *Harvard Business Law Review Online* 92

Gonzalez E, 'The Hague Convention on Choice of Court Agreements of June 30, 2005: A Mexican View' (2006) 13(1) *Southwestern Journal of Law and Trade in the Americas* 37

Grossi S, 'Forum Non Conveniens as a Jurisdictional Doctrine' (2013) 75(1) *University of Pittsburgh Law Review* 31

Guan ST, 'Choice of Law in *Forum Non Conveniens* Analysis' (2010) 22(2) *Singapore Academy of Law Journal* 440

Guodong Du and Meng Yu, 'Forum Non Conveniens in China: The Most Stringent Standards Ever?' *China Justice Observer* (13 February 2019): https://www.chinajusticeobserver.com/a/forum-non-conveniens-in-china-the-most-stringent-standards-ever

Helveston M and Jacobs M, 'The Incoherent Role of Bargaining Power in Contract Law' (2014) 49(4) *Wake Forest Law Review* 1017

Hillman R and Rachlinski J, 'Standard-Form Contracting in the Electronic Age' (2002) 77(2) *New York University Law Review* 429

Ho LC, 'Anti-Suit Injunctions in Cross-Border Insolvency: A Restatement' (2003) 52(3) *International and Comparative Law Quarterly* 697

Hook M, 'The Choice of Law Agreement as a Reason for Exercising Jurisdiction' (2014) 63(4) *International and Comparative Law Quarterly* 963

Huala A, 'The Meaning of Public Policy under Indonesian Arbitration Law and Practice' (2021) 2(1) *Transnational Business Law Journal* 15

Huanfang D, 'Choice of Court Agreement with Foreign Elements in China: *Shandong Jufeng v. South Korea Mgame*' (2018) 13(2) *Frontiers of Law in China* 241

Huang J, 'Developing Chinese Private International Law for Transnational Civil and Commercial Litigation: The 2024 New Chinese Civil Procedure Law' (2023) 70 *Netherlands International Law Review* 205

Huang Z, 'International Jurisdiction under the 2005 Hague Convention on Choice of Court Agreements: Implications for China' (2017) 47(2) *Hong Kong Law Journal* 555

Hu H, 'Damages for Breach of Choice of Court Agreements: Foreign Experience and Domestic Approach' (2022) 3(3) *Foundation for Law and International Affairs Review* 97

Houque, MN, Zahir-ul-Hassan MK, Idrus MA and van Zijl T, 'Bribery and corruption: assessing the fairness of the Malaysian judicial system' (2020) 74 *Crime, Law and Social Change* 135

Jovita I and Hutagalung KGK, 'Standard Clauses in Vehicle Purchase Credit Agreements in Indonesia: An Examination of Consumer Protection and Legal Enforcement' (2023) 25(2) *Journal of Judicial Review* 255

Kamba WJ, 'Comparative Law – A Theoretical Framework (1974) 23(3) *International and Comparative Law Quarterly* 485

Kasi A, 'Anti-suit Injunction in Enforcement of Arbitration Agreement and Exclusive Jurisdiction Agreement' [2013] (6) *Malayan Law Journal* i

Kennett W, '*Forum Non Conveniens* in Europe' (1995) 54(3) *Cambridge Law Journal* 552

Kessler F, 'Contracts of Adhesion – Some Thoughts about Freedom of Contract' (1943) 43(5) *Columbia Law Review* 629

Keyes M, 'Party Autonomy in Dispute Resolution: Implied Choices and Waiver in the Context of Jurisdiction' (2015) 58 *Japanese Yearbook of International Law* 223

Keyes M and Marshall BA, 'Jurisdiction agreements: exclusive, optional and asymmetrical' (2015) 11(3) *Journal of Private International Law* 345

King FT, 'Chinese Bilateral Judgment Enforcement Treaties' (2017) 40(1) *Loyola of Los Angeles International and Comparative Law Review* 1

Knight CJS, 'The Damage of Damages: *Agreements on Jurisdiction and Choice of Law*' (2008) 4(3) *Journal of Private International Law* 501

Kusumadara A, 'Jurisdiction of courts chosen in the parties' choice of court agreements: an unsettled issue in Indonesian private international law and the way out' (2022) 18(3) *Journal of Private International Law* 424

Lee J, 'Non-exclusive Jurisdiction Clauses-Changing Approaches?' [2003] (2) *Singapore Journal of Legal Studies* 593

Lenhoff A, 'The Parties' Choice of a Forum: "Prorogation Agreements"' (1961) 15(3) *Rutgers Law Review* 414
Liang Z, 'Party autonomy in choice of court and jurisdiction over foreign-related commercial and maritime disputes in China' (2019) 15(3) *Journal of Private International Law* 541
Lorenzen E, 'Huber's De Conflictu Legum' (1919) 13(2) *Illinois Law Review* 375
Marcus D, 'The Perils of Contractual Procedure: A Revised History of Forum Selection Clauses in the Federal Courts' (2008) 82(3) *Tulane Law Review* 973
Marshall BA and Keyes M, 'Australia's Accession to the Hague Convention on Choice of Court Agreements' (2017) 41(1) *Melbourne University Law Review* 246
Mason L, 'Inadequacy and Ineffectuality: Hong Kong's Consumer Protection Regime Against Unfair Terms in Standard Form Contracts' (2014) 44 *Hong Kong Law Journal* 83
McConnaughay P, 'Rethinking the Role of Law and Contracts in East-West Commercial Relationships' (2001) 41(2) *Virginia Journal of International Law* 427
Meng R, 'How Chinese courts implement public policies through judicial adjudication – taking cases in which courts implement "socialist core values" as the object of analysis' (2018) 3 *Legal Review* 184
Merrett L, 'Interpreting non-exclusive jurisdiction agreements' (2018) 14(1) *Journal of Private International Law* 38
Mills A, 'The Hague Choice of Court Convention and Cross-Border Commercial Dispute Resolution in Australia and the Asia-Pacific' (2017) 18(1) *Melbourne Journal of International Law* 1
Mullenix L, 'Another Choice of Forum, Another Choice of Law: Consensual Adjudicatory Procedure in Federal Court' (1988) 57(3) *Fordham Law Review* 291
Nakano S, 'Agreement on Jurisdiction' (2011) 54 *Japanese Yearbook of International Law* 278
Nelson L, 'Choice of court agreements and derogation from competition law' (2020) 16(2) *Journal of Private International Law* 300
Nie Y, 'Overview of the 2023 Amendments to Chinese Procedure Law' in *Conflict of Laws* (22 September 2023): https://conflictoflaws.net/2023/overview-of-the-2023-amendments-to-chinese-civil-procedure-law/
Noyes H, 'If you (Re)build It, They Will Come: Contracts to Remake the Rules of Litigation in Arbitration's Image' (2006) 30(2) *Harvard Journal of Law and Policy* 579
Örücü E, 'Methodological Aspects of Comparative Law' (2006) 8(1) *European Journal of Law Reform* 29
Oseni U, 'The Legal Implications of "*Fatwā* Shopping" in the Islamic Finance Industry: Problems, Perceptions and Prospects' (2016) 30(2) *Arab Law Quarterly* 107
Ozaeta H and Bautista MC, 'Security over Collateral Philippines', *Lex Mundi* (webpage): http://www.lexmundi.com/images/lexmundi/practicegroups/bankfinance/ socsurvey/philippines.pdf
Perillo J, 'Selected Forum Agreements in Western Europe,' (1964) 13(1) *American Journal of Comparative Law* 162
Philomin, L, 'Singapore to remake itself as Asia's legal hub with new commercial court', *Reuters* (12 February 2014): http://in.reuters.com/article/2014/02/11/singapore-law-idINDEEA1A0JC20140211
Qin Z and Feng J, 'What We Do and Do Not Know About Standard Form Contracts? An Empirical Study of Wealth Management Product Contracts in China' (2021) 16 *Asian Journal of Comparative Law* 124
Rasyid A, 'Relevance of Islamic Disputes Resolution Processes in Islamic Banking and Finance' (2013) 27(4) *Arab Law Quarterly* 343
Reus A, 'Judicial Discretion: A Comparative View of the Doctrine of Forum Non Conveniens in the United States, the United Kingdom, and Germany' (1994) 16(2) *Loyala of Los Angeles International and Comparative Law Review* 455
Robertson D, 'Forum non conveniens in America and England: "a rather fantastic fiction"' (1987) 103(3) *Law Quarterly Review* 398
Rosenne S, 'The Forum Prorogatum in the International Court of Justice' (1953) 6(1) *Revue Hellenique de Droit International* 1
Sanchez G, 'The Future of the Hague Convention on Choice of Court Agreements' (2008) 17(2) *International Law Students Association Quarterly* 12
Sanchez Fernandez S, 'Choice-of-Court Agreements: Breach and Damages Within the Brussels I Regime' [2010] (12) *Yearbook of Private International Law* 377
Sancho Villa D, 'Jurisdiction over Jurisdiction and Choice of Court Agreements: Views on the Hague Convention of 2005 and Implications for the European Regime' [2010] (12) *Yearbook of Private International Law* 399
Schuaib F, 'The Islamic Legal System in Malaysia' (2012) 21(1) *Pacific Rim Law & Policy Journal* 85
Schulz A, 'The Hague Convention of 30 June 2005 on Choice of Court Agreements' [2005] (7) *Yearbook of Private International Law* 1
Sudargo G, 'International Civil Procedure in Indonesia' (1996) 6 *Asian Yearbook of International Law* 87

Sujayadi S, Wijayanta T and Herliana H, 'Regulating Court Jurisdiction to Protect Weaker Parties: An Overview of the Indonesian Civil Justice System' (2023) 38(2) *Yuridika* 305

Takahashi K, 'Damages for Breach of Choice-of-Court Agreement' [2008] (10) *Yearbook of Private International Law* 57

Tan D and Yeo N, 'Breaking Promises to Litigate in a Particular Forum: Are Damages an Appropriate Remedy?' [2003] (4) *Lloyd's Maritime and Commercial Law Quarterly* 435

Tan SH, 'A New-Found Significance for Non-Exclusive Jurisdiction Agreements' [2000] (1) *Singapore Journal of Legal Studies* 298

Taylor D, 'The Forum Selection Clause: A Tale of Two Concepts' (1993) 66(3) *Temple Law Review* 785

Tham CH, 'Damages for breach of English jurisdiction clauses: more than meets the eye' [2004] (1) *Lloyd's Maritime and Commercial Law Quarterly* 46

Trakic A, 'Statutory protection of Malaysian consumers against unfair contract terms: Has enough been done?' (2015) 44(3) *Common Law World Review* 203

Tu G, 'Recognition and Enforcement of Mainland China's Civil and Commercial Judgments in Hong Kong – an update' (2017) 25(2) *Asia Pacific Law Review* 190

——, 'Arrangement on Mutual Recognition and Enforcement of Judgments in Civil and Commercial Matters between China and Macau: Inherent Problems, Six Years' Experience and the Way Forward' (2013) 43(1) *Hong Kong Law Journal* 349

Veillard I, 'The General and Commercial Character of the UNIDROIT Principles of International Commercial Contracts' [2007] (4) *International Business Law Journal* 479

Vickya A and Allagan TMP, 'Implications of Non-exclusive Choice of Forum Clauses in Determining the Competent Dispute Resolution Forum in Indonesia' (2022) 12(1) *Indonesia Law Review* 70

von Mehren AT, 'Adjudicatory Jurisdiction: General Theories Compared and Evaluated' (1983) 63(2) *Boston University Law Review* 279

Wei C and Godwin A, 'Challenges and Opportunities for the China International Commercial Court' (2019) 68(4) *International and Comparative Law Quarterly* 869

Woodward Jr W, 'Saving the Hague Choice of Court Convention' (2008) 29(3) *University of Pennsylvania Journal of International Law* 657

Wu F, 'Legal Reasoning in Chinese and Swiss Appellate Judgments – Exploring China's Path Towards Rule of Law' (2009) 2(1) *Tsinghua China Law Review* 19

Yeo TM, 'Statute and Public Policy in Private International Law: Gambling Contracts and Foreign Judgments' (2005) 9 *Singapore Yearbook of International Law* 133

——, 'The Contractual Basis of the Enforcement of Exclusive and Non-Exclusive Choice of Court Agreements' (2005) 17(1) *Singapore Academy of Law Journal* 306

Yip M, 'The Resolution of Disputes Before the Singapore International Commercial Court' (2016) 65(2) *International and Comparative Law Quarterly* 439

Yntema H, 'The Historic Bases of Private International Law' (1953) 2(3) *American Journal of Comparative Law* 297

Zhang X and Smart P, 'Development of Regional Conflict of Laws on the Arrangement of Mutual Recognition and Enforcement of Judgments in Civil and Commercial Matters between Mainland China and Hong Kong SAR' (2006) 36(3) *Hong Kong Law Journal* 553

Zheng ST, 'Declining Jurisdiction by *Forum Non Conveniens* in Chinese Courts' (2015) 45(1) *Hong Kong Law Journal* 351

Zheng ST and Xu L, 'Choice-of-Court Agreements in Electronic Consumer Contracts in China' (2016) 23 *Pandora's Box* 21

Chapters in Books

Adams M, 'Doing What Doesn't Come Naturally. On the Distinctiveness of Comparative Law' in Mark Van Hoecke (ed), *Methodologies of Legal Research Which Kind of Method for What Kind of Discipline?* (Hart Publishing, 2011)

Aguiling-Pangalangan E, 'Philippines' in Alejandro Carballo Leyda (ed), *Asian Conflict of Laws* (Kluwer Law International, 2015)

Bennett D, 'The Hague Convention on Recognition and Enforcement of Foreign Judgments – A failure of characterisation' in Talia Einvborn and Kurt Siehr (eds), *Intercontinental Cooperation Through Private International Law: Essays in Memory of Peter E Nygh* (TMC Asser Press, 2004) 19

Chong A, 'Choice of Law for Void Contracts and Their Restitutionary Aftermath: The Putative Governing Law of the Contract' in Paula Giliker (ed), *Re-examining Contract and Unjust Enrichment* (Koninklijke Brill, NV, 2007) 155

Dawar N and Bagga C, 'Is Your Business Model Ready to Drill into the Core of the Diamond?' in Anil Gupta, Toshiro Wakayama, and U Srinivasa Rangan (eds), *Global Strategies for Emerging Asia* (Jossey-Bass, 2012)

Echenberg D, 'Negotiating international contracts: Does the process invite a review of standard contracts from the point of view of national legal requirements?' in Giuditta Cordero-Moss (ed), *Boilerplate Clauses, International Commercial Contracts and the Applicable Law* (Cambridge University Press, 2011)

Fawcett JJ, 'General Report' in JJ Fawcett (ed), *Declining Jurisdiction in Private International Law: Reports to the XIVth Congress of the International Academy of Comparative Law Athens, August 1994* (Clarendon Press, 1995) 1

Furmston M, Tolhurst GJ and Mik E, 'Formation and the Concept of Agreement' in Michael Formston and GJ Tolhurst (eds), *Contract Formation: Law and Practice* (Oxford University Press, 2nd edn, 2015) 1

Gupta A and Wang H, 'Building the Next-Generation Global Enterprise' in Anil Gupta, Toshiro Wakayama, and U Srinivasa Rangan (eds), *Global Strategies for Emerging Asia* (Jossey-Bass, 2012)

Hartley T, 'Mandatory rules in international contracts: the common law approach' in Hague Academy of International Law (ed), *Collected Courses of the Hague Academy of International Law* (Brill Nijhoff, 1997) vol 266

Herliana H and Sujayadi S, 'Establishing Jurisdiction of Indonesian Courts in Transnational Contract Case: A Respond to Global Economic Changes' in Mirsa Umiyati, et al (eds), *Proceedings of the International Conference on 'Changing of Law: Business Law, Local Wisdom and Tourism Industry' (ICCLB 2023)* (Atlantis Press, 2023) 544

Hikmahanto J, 'Courts in Indonesia: a mix of Western and local character' in Jiunn-rong Yeng and Wen-Cheng Chang, *Asian Courts in Context* (Cambridge University Press, 2014)

Iguchi N and Kamimura N, 'Japan' in Alejandro Carballo Leyda (ed), *Asian Conflict of Laws* (Kluwer Law International, 2015) 67

Lee YS, Kin SY and Kim SN, 'Republic of Korea' in Alejandro Carballo Leyda (ed), *Asian Conflict of Laws* (Kluwer Law International, 2015) 85

Lopez LD, 'The Curious Case of International Commercial Contracts in Asia' in Muruga Perumal Ramaswamy (ed), *Harmonising Trade Law to Enable Private Sector Regional Development* (Victoria University of Wellington, Hors Serie Volume XX, 2016) 253

——, 'Philippines' in Kazuaki Nishioka (ed), *Treatment of Foreign Law in Asia* (Hart Publishing, 2023) 203

Mabbett I, 'Buddhism and Freedom' in David Kelly and Anthony Reid (eds), *Asian Freedoms: The Idea of Freedom in East and Southeast Asia* (Cambridge University Press, 1998)

Muir-Watt H, 'The Relevance of Private International Law to the Global Governance Debate' in Horatia Muir-Watt and Diego Fernandez-Arroyo (eds), *Private International Law and Global Governance* (Oxford University Press, 2015) 1

Nishioka K, 'Japan' in Anselmo Reyes and Wilson Liu (eds), *Direct Jurisdiction: Asian Perspectives* (Hart Publishing, 2021) 85

Oberhammer P, 'Party Autonomy and Procedural Law: A Few Comments from an Austrian Perspective' in Mattias Dahlberg (ed), *Party Autonomy – Civil Procedural Views on Party Autonomy, Franz Klein, EU Law and More* (Iustus Förlag, 2011) 51

Oberhammer P and Domej T, 'Germany, Switzerland, Austria (circa. 1800-2005)' in CH van Rhee (ed), *European Traditions in Civil Procedure* (Intersentia, 2005) 103

Oppusunggu YU, 'Country Report: The Republic of Indonesia' in Adeline Chong (ed), *Recognition and Enforcement of Foreign Judgments in Asia* (Asian Business Law Institute, 2017) 91

Purevdorjiin M, 'Mongolia' in Alejandro Carballo Leyda (ed), *Asian Conflict of Laws* (Kluwer Law International, 2015) 145

Takahashi, K, 'Japan: Quests for Equilibrium and Certainty' in Mary Keyes (ed), *Optional Choice of Court Agreements in Private International Law* (Springer Nature Switzerland, 2020) 261

Taylor V and Pryles M, 'The Cultures of Dispute Resolution in Asia' in Michael Pryles (ed), *Dispute Resolution in Asia* (Kluwer Law International, 3rd edn, 2006)

Thongpackdee C and Sucharitkul V, 'Thailand' in Alejandro Carballo Leyda (ed), *Asian Conflict of Laws* (Kluwer Law International, 2015) 233

Tu G and Huang Z, 'People's Republic of China (PRC): Optional Choice of Court Agreements in the Vibrant Age' in Mary Keyes (ed), *Optional Choice of Court Agreements in Private International Law* (Spinger, 2020) 151

van Caenegem RC, 'History of European Civil Procedure' in Mauro Cappelletti (ed), *Civil Procedure, International Encyclopedia of Comparative law Vol XVI* (Mohr Siebeck & Martinus Nijhoff Publishers, 2014) 14

van Rhee CH, 'Introduction' in CH van Rhee (ed), *European Traditions in Civil Procedure* (Intersentia, 2005) 3
——, 'English Civil Procedure until the Civil Procedure Rules (1998)' in CH van Rhee (ed), *European Traditions in Civil Procedure* (Intersentia, 2005) 129
——, 'Harmonisation of Civil Procedure: An Historic and Comparative Perspective' in XE Kramer and CH van Rhee (eds), *Civil Litigation in a Globalising World* (Asser Press, 2012) 39
Wang JY and Li D, 'China: Litigation & Dispute Resolution Laws and Regulations 2023' in Justin Michaelson (ed), *Global Legal Insights: Litigation & Dispute Resolution* (Global Legal Group Ltd, 12th edn, 2023) 32.
Weixia G, 'China' in Anselmo Reyes (ed) *Recognition and Enforcement of Judgments in Civil and Commercial Matters* (Hart Publishing, 2019) 31
Xiao Y and Liang W, 'Mainland China' in Alejandro Carballo Leyda (ed), *Asian Conflict of Laws* (Kluwer Law International, 2015) 1
Xin C, 'History of Private International Law' in Xiaohong Liu and Zhengyi Zhang, *Chinese Private International Law* (Hart Publishing, 2021) 15
Yee S, 'Article 40' in Andreas Zimmermann, Christian Tomuschat, Karin Oellers-Frahm and Christian Tams (eds), *The Statute of the International Court of Justice: A Commentary* (Oxford University Press, 2nd edn, 2012) 920
Yujun G, 'Country Report: The People's Republic of China' in Adeline Chong, *Recognition and Enforcement of Foreign Judgments in Asia* (Asian Business Law Institute, 2017) 49

Books

Agabin P, *Mestizo: The Story of the Philippine Legal System* (University of the Philippines College of Law, 2011)
Ahmed M, *The Nature and Enforcement of Choice of Court Agreements* (Hart Publishing, 2017)
Allens, Linklaters, Widyawan & Partners, *Legal Guide to Investment in Indonesia* (Allens, Linklaters, Widyawan & Partners 2014)
Baker & McKenzie, *Asia Pacific Guide to Mergers & Acquisitions* (Baker & McKenzie, 2013)
Brand R *Transaction Planning Using Rules on Jurisdiction and the Recognition and Enforcement of Judgments* (Hague Academy of International Law, 2014)
Brand R and Herrup P, *The 2005 Hague Convention on Choice of Court Agreements: Commentary and Documents* (Cambridge University Press, 2009)
Brand R and Jablonski S, *Forum Non Conveniens: History, Global Practice, and Future Under the Hague Convention on Choice of Court Agreements* (Oxford University Press, 2007)
Briggs A, *Agreements on Jurisdiction and Choice of Law* (Oxford University Press, 2008)
——, *Civil Jurisdiction and Judgments* (Informa Law, 6th edn, 2015)
——, *Private International Law* (Oxford University Press, 2014)
——, *The Principle of Comity in Private International Law* (Brill Nijhoff, 2012)
Chenyang Z, *Win in Chinese Courts* (Springer, 2023)
Chong A and Yip M, *Singapore Private International Law* (Oxford University Press, 2023)
Collier JG, *Conflict of Laws* (Cambridge University Press, 2nd edn, 1994)
Cordero-Moss G, *International Commercial Contracts: Applicable Sources and Enforceability* (Cambridge University Press, 2014)
DiMatteo LA, *International Contracting: Law and Practice* (Kluwer Law International, 2013)
Engelmann A, *A History of Continental Civil Procedure* (Robert Wyness Millar trans, Little Brown & Co, 1927)
Ervo L and Nylund A (eds) *Current Trends in Preparatory Proceedings: A Comparative Study of Nordic and Former Communist Parties* (Springer, 2016)
Fawcett JJ, *Declining Jurisdiction in Private International Law: Reports to the XIV Congress of the International Academy of Comparative Law Athens, August 1994* (Clarendon Press, 1995)
Fentiman R, *International Commercial Litigation* (Oxford University Press, 2nd edn, 2015)
Francisco VJ, *Revised Rules of Court in the Philippines* (2nd edn, 1973) 366
Garnett R, *Substance and Procedure in Private International Law* (Oxford University Press, 2012)
Gribbs S and North P, *International Civil Procedure* (Kluwer Law, 2003) 183
Hartley T, *Choice-of-Court Agreements under the European and International Instruments* (Oxford University Press, 2013)

——, *International Commercial Litigation: Text, Cases and Materials on Private International Law* (Cambridge University Press, 2009)
——, *The Modern Approach to Private International Law: International Litigation and Transactions from a Common-Law Perspective* (Brill Nijhoff, 2006)
Huang J, *Interregional Recognition and Enforcement of Civil and Commercial Judgments: Lessons for China from US and EU Law* (Bloomsbury Publishing Plc, 2014)
Huang Z, *Party Autonomy in Choice of Court under Chinese Inter-Regional Conflict of Laws* (Doctoral Dissertation, University of Macau, 2022)
Johnston G and Harris P, *The Conflict of Laws in Hong Kong* (Thomson Reuters, 3rd edn, 2017)
Keyes M, *Jurisdiction in International Litigation* (Federation Press, 2005)
Kusumadara A, *Indonesian Private International Law* (Hart Publishing, 2021)
LexisNexis, *Halsbury's Laws of Malaysia* (online at 29 March 2019) 190 Civil Procedure
——, *Halsbury's Laws of Malaysia* (online at 29 March 2019) 90 Conflict of Laws
LexisNexis Singapore, *Halsbury's Laws of Singapore*, vol 6(2) (at 1 November 2009)
Lindsey T and Butt S, *Indonesian Law* (Oxford University Press, 2018)
Lipman F and Qiu LD, *International Strategic Alliances Joint Ventures Between Asian and US Companies* (World Scientific, 2nd edn, 2014)
Mills A, *Party Autonomy in Private International Law* (Cambridge University Press, 2018)
——, *The Confluence of Public and Private International Law: Justice, Pluralism and Subsidiarity in the International Constitutional Ordering of Private Law* (Cambridge University Press, 2009)
Mortensen R, Garnett R and Keyes M, *Private International Law in Australia* (LexisNexis Butterworths, 3rd edn, 2015)
Nishioka K and Nishitani Y, *Japanese Private International Law* (Hart Publishing, 2021)
Nygh P, *Autonomy in International Contracts* (Clarendon Press, 1999)
Penasthika P, *Unravelling Choice of Law in International Commercial Contracts: Indonesia as an Illustrative Case Study* (Eleven, 2022)
Rosenne S, (ed) Malcolm Shaw, *Rosenne's Law and Practice of the International Court, 1920-2015* (Brill Nijhoff, 5th edn, 2016) vol 2
Salonga J, *Private International Law* (Regina Publishing Co, 1995)
——, *Private International Law* (Central Lawbook Publishing Co, 1979)
Scheela W, *Venture Capital in Asia: Investing in Emerging Countries* (Business Expert Press, 2014)
Symeonides S, *Private International Law: Idealism, Pragmatism, Eclecticism. General Course on Private International Law* (Brill Nijhoff, 2017)
Tolentino A, *Commentaries and Jurisprudence on the Civil Code of the Philippines* (Central Professional Books, Inc, 1990) vol 1, 4
Tomasic R and Wolff L (eds), *Commercial Law in East Asia* (Ashgate, 2014)
von Mehren, AT, *Adjudicatory Authority in Private International Law: A Comparative Study* (Brill Academic Publishers, 2006)
Yahya Harahap, M, *Hukum Acara Perdata Tentang Gugatan, Persidangan, Penyitaan, Pembuktian, dn Putusan Pengadilan* (Sinar Grafika, 2016)
Yee S, *Towards an International Law of Co-progressiveness* (Martinus Nijhoff Publishers, 2004)
Yeo TM (ed), *Articles on Singapore Law (2005)* (Singapore Academy of Law, 2005)
Yokoyama J, *Private International Law* (Kluwer Law International, 2nd edn, 2019)
Zhang M, *Chinese Contract Law: Theory and Practice* (Martinus Nijhoff Publishers, 2006)

Reports, Conference Papers, Government Documents, Theses

American Bar Association, *Recommendation Adopted by the House of Delegates August 7-8, 2006* (Survey 2006)
Atienza ME, *The Philippine Judiciary: Strengthening the Third Branch of Government* (Discussion Paper, University of the Philippines Center for Integrative and Development Studies 2023)
Getman-Pavlova I, 'The Concept of "Comity" in Ulrich Huber's Conflict Doctrine' (*Working Paper No BRP 13/Law/2013*, National Research University Higher School of Economics, 2013)

Giuliano, M and Lagarde P, Report on the Convention on the law applicable to contractual obligations, OJ C 1982, 21/10/1980
Gleeson J, 'An Australian Perspective on International Commercial Litigation: The Challenges and Opportunities' (Conference Paper, International Litigation in the Asia Pacific, Wuhan University, China, 23–24 September 2013)
Goh S, 'Chapter 24. Insurance Law', Singapore Academy of Law: Laws of Singapore (25 January 2019) para 24.4.1: https://www.singaporelawwatch.sg/Results/ch-24-insurance-law
Hartley T and Dogauchi M, *Explanatory Report on the Convention of 30 June 2005 on Choice of Courts Agreements*, ed Permanent Bureau (Hague Conference on Private International Law, 2013)
Judiciary of the United Kingdom, 'History' (webpage): https://www.judiciary.gov.uk/you-and-the-judiciary/going-to-court/high-court/queens-bench-division/courts-of-the-queens-bench-division/commercial-court/58005-2/
——, 'Shorter and Flexible Trial Procedures Pilot Schemes' (webpage, October 2015): https://www.judiciary.gov.uk/wp-content/uploads/2015/09/Shorter-and-Flexible-Trial-Schemes-Announcement.pdf
Long J, *Choice of court agreements in international civil and commercial law: a comparative study of Chinese law, the 2005 Hague Choice of Court Convention and the Brussels I Recast Regulation* (LLM Thesis, University of Glasgow, 2020)
Lopez LD, *When Choice of Forum Clauses in International Commercial Contracts are Challenged: Key Lessons from Asian Jurisdictions* (DPhil Thesis, University of Melbourne, 2019)
Ministry of Justice, 'Legislative History, Act Governing Relations between the People of the Taiwan Area and the Mainland Area in Laws & Regulations Database of The Republic of China (Taiwan)' (webpage): https://law.moj.gov.tw/ENG/LawClass/LawHistory.aspx?pcode=Q0010001
National People's Congress of the People's Republic of China, 'State Structure of the People's Republic of China – The Supreme People's Court' (webpage): http://www.npc.gov.cn/zgrdw/englishnpc/stateStructure/2007-12/06/content_1382076.htm
Nelson L, 'Dispute Settlement with Chinese Characteristics: Assessing China's International Commercial Court' (Staff Research Report, US-China Economic Security Commission, 28 February 2023)
Peel E, 'Forum Shopping in the European Judicial Area – Introductory Report' (*Oxford Legal Studies Research Paper No 39/2006*, University of Oxford Faculty of Law, September 2006)
Penasthika P, *Unravelling Choice of Law in International Commercial Contracts as an Illustrative Case Study* (Doctoral Thesis, Erasmus University Rotterdam, 29 September 2022)
Report on the APEC EC Workshop on effective enforcement of business contracts and efficient resolution of business disputes through the Hague Choice of Court Agreements Convention, Cebu, Philippines (1 September 2015): https://www.hcch.net/upload/apec2015rpt.pdf
Singapore Academy of Law, 'Report of the Law Reform Committee on the Hague Convention on Choice of Court Agreements 2005' (Report, Singapore Academy of Law, March 2013)
——, *Study on Governing Law & Jurisdictional Choices in Cross-Border Transactions* (Survey, 11 January 2016)
Suhadi RH and Santiago F, 'Legal Principles of Agreement: A Foundation in Contract Establishment' (Conference Paper, Proceedings of the International Conference on Law, Social Science, Economics, and Education, 16 April 2022)
Supreme Court of Japan 'Judicial System in Japan' (webpage): https://www.courts.go.jp/english/judicial_sys/index.html
——, 'Questions and Answers on Civil Procedure' (website): https://www.courts.go.jp/english/judicial_sys/qa_on_Civil_Procedure/index.html
Supreme Court Singapore, 'Role and structure of the Supreme Court' (webpage, 22 June 2024): https://www.judiciary.gov.sg/who-we-are/role-structure-supreme-court
——, 'Singapore Judicial System', (webpage, 3 September 2018): https://www.supremecourt.gov.sg/about-us/the-supreme-court/singapore-judicial-system
Tang, ZS, 'Choice of Court Convention and the People's Republic of China' (Presented at HCCH 2005 Choice of Court Convention: Fostering Access to Justice for Cross-Border Commerce in the Asia Pacific Region, 22 March 2024)
UK Government, 'Commercial Court' (webpage): https://www.gov.uk/courts-tribunals/commercial-court
Yeo TM, 'Staying Relevant: Exercise of Jurisdiction in the Age of SICC' (Yong Pung How Professorship of Law Lecture, Singapore Management University, 13 May 2015)
——, 'International Litigation in Asia: Will the Hague Choice of Court Convention Make Any Difference' (Conference Paper, Japanese Society of International Law Annual Meeting, Shizuoka, 12–14 October 2013)
Yeung PA, 'Access to Justice and Sustainable Development: The Impact of the HCCH in an Inter-Connected World' (Conference Paper, HCCH Asia Pacific Week Hong Kong 2023, 12 September 2023)

INDEX

www.ingramcontent.com/pod-product-compliance
Ingram Content Group UK Ltd.
Pitfield, Milton Keynes, MK11 3LW, UK
UKHW050944290926
15470UKWH00005B/1618

9 781509 967513